DEBATES IN THE DIGITAL HUMANITIES 2023

Make visible

~~resist silence~~
~~as a possibility~~

always listen —
no silence

Resist &
comment

DEBATES IN THE DIGITAL HUMANITIES 2023

Matthew K. Gold and Lauren F. Klein
EDITORS

DEBATES IN THE DIGITAL HUMANITIES

MIN NE SO TA

University of Minnesota Press
Minneapolis
London

Proceeds from sales of *Debates in the Digital Humanities 2023* will be contributed to the Ricky Dawkins Jr Memorial Scholarship.

Published by the University of Minnesota Press
111 Third Avenue South, Suite 290
Minneapolis, MN 55401-2520
http://www.upress.umn.edu

ISSN 2380-5927
ISBN 978-1-5179-1527-8 (hc)
ISBN 978-1-5179-1528-5 (pb)

A Cataloging-in-Publication record for this book is available from the Library of Congress.

Printed in the United States of America on acid-free paper

32 31 30 29 28 27 26 25 24 23 10 9 8 7 6 5 4 3 2 1

In my dept, sharing articles is a love language
as I read this book I couldn't help but
feel the impulse to share — this for Jackie,
that for Daniel. A reminder of how very
- much we all benefit from DH perspectives &
that DH is not in a binary w/ tradit'l
scholarly approaches — but complementary
& even mutually constitutive with them —
which might be the most DH of all.

- p. 94 "Extractive" is a thematic & critical
refrain throughout the book.

Maybe this pitch moment as I watch
funding freezes & ICE raids —
but this feels even more [prescient] / pressing

unabashedly political and all the better for it

Contents

Introduction

The Digital Humanities, Moment to Moment

MATTHEW K. GOLD AND LAUREN F. KLEIN

It used to be that "moment" was a metaphor. The introduction to the first edition of *Debates in the Digital Humanities,* "The Digital Humanities Moment," documented the "rapid ascent of the digital humanities in the public imagination," as well as the opportunities, challenges, and tensions that that "moment" had brought about (17). A full ten years later, the last three of which have taken place under the shadow of a global pandemic, we have learned that some moments remain anchored in time. January 9, 2020, the first confirmed death from Covid-19 in Wuhan, China. January 20, 2020, the first confirmed Covid case in the United States is reported. March 13, 2020, Breonna Taylor is murdered by plainclothes police officers in her own home in Louisville, Kentucky. March 19, 2020, California becomes the first state to issue a statewide stay-at-home order prompted by the pandemic. May 25, 2020, George Floyd is murdered at the hands of the Minneapolis Police Department; the next day, May 26, protesters take to the streets, prompting a wave of racial reckoning across the country. Meanwhile, on August 18, 2020, California Governor Gavin Newsome declares a state of emergency as the worst wildfire season in modern history sweeps up and down the West Coast. As it happened, these were also the months when the authors included in this volume began drafting their chapters; each time that we, the editors, returned revision requests or editorial queries, more of these world-altering moments had come to pass.

These moments were not metaphors. They represented the profound loss of actual lives—the lives of people with families and friends and communities who continue to grieve to this day. They also represent the collective failures of governments and social institutions to address the root causes of these tragedies: the intertwined pandemics of Covid-19, systemic racism, and climate change. Each of these moments was also a critical inflection point that required us—both as editors and as humans in the world—to recalibrate our own sense of what the future might hold. As two tenured professors, two white professors, two cisgender professors, two professors holding U.S. passports, the degree of uncertainty brought about by these ruptures in time exceeded any prior personal reference points. Yet for many others—including many academic workers—the possibility of immediate and wrenching change brought about by the failures of institutional support systems has been an ever-present threat. Adjunct professors, scholars of color, graduate students, and administrative staff, among others, have long been aware of, and lived with, the precarity of their positions and the tenuousness of any institutional support. As Tressie McMillan Cottom, the esteemed sociologist (and *Debates in the Digital Humanities 2016* contributor) has often noted, "The institution cannot love you." The precarious faculty that, according to a 2018 report from the American Association of University Professors (AAUP), make up more than 60 percent of the academic workforce have long been required to come to terms with this fact. Now, as a result of the pandemic, the tenured professoriate has finally begun to realize that support systems serving only a privileged few are support systems that serve no one at all.

How, then, to imagine another future for the university? How to imagine an academy in which a commitment to public scholarship, to anti-racist scholarship, to racial, ethnic, and gender diversity, to labor equity, and to collaboration across academic ranks might open up countervailing spaces of possibility—spaces where solidarity might be found? And what of the role of the digital humanities in this vision? What is the work we must do, and what are its limits?

We remain convinced that our field must keep its focus on building a vision of digital humanities that, as we wrote in *Debates in the Digital Humanities 2019*, "matters beyond itself, one that probes the stakes and impacts of technology across a range of institutions and communities." We have been heartened by the proliferation of projects undertaken by digital humanities scholars that have employed a critical approach to technology in service of this broader vision. Consider the Visionary Futures Collective.[1] It emerged during the pandemic with a focus on "increasing transparency in higher education; creating compassionate communities through shared vulnerability; and working collectively to shift institutional practices" so that the work of the humanities, and those who perform it, can truly thrive. Meanwhile, projects including the African American Digital and Experimental Humanities Initiative (AADHum)[2] and the Digital Ethnic Futures Consortium (DEFCon)[3] have developed intentionally expansive mentoring programs for both graduate students and faculty, so as to redistribute the opportunities and the resources that typically accrue at well-resourced research-oriented institutions. Digital humanities scholars have also contributed their time and expertise to intervene in global political crises. One group of over 1,300 librarians, archivists, researchers, and programmers known as Saving Ukrainian Cultural Heritage Online (SUCHO)[4] has worked to identify and preserve the data and other digital content created by Ukrainian cultural heritage organizations should they be subjected to a digital or physical attack.

Projects like these sustain our belief that another future is possible—and, indeed, remains urgently needed—though hope for that future requires a critical and honest view of how we have arrived at this point. How can we work toward racial justice,

for instance, if we are not willing to confront the racism of the past? In *Ebony and Ivy,* historian Craig Steven Wilder has shown how the history of the American college system is inextricably linked to the history of slavery in America. From its earliest beginnings, Wilder writes, the academy was not so much a bastion of free inquiry or harbinger of freedom as it was "a beneficiary and defender" of the slave trade and Indigenous dispossession (2). From its reliance on the labor of the enslaved in order to build college campuses to, a century later, its mobilization of research departments to promote racist scientific theories, the academy fostered the interests of the powerful few, and, as Wilder shows, stood with both church and state as the "third pillar of a civilization built on bondage" (11).

This is one aspect of the past that the field of digital humanities must directly confront—and, in fact, has already begun to engage through projects such as the student-led Penn and Slavery Project.[5] Since 2017, this project has documented the University of Pennsylvania's connections to slavery through an augmented reality tour through the Penn campus. The app reveals the university's complicity in claiming people as property and stealing their knowledge, labor, and skills. In one especially powerful feature led by Penn doctoral history student Breanna Moore, users are led to the Class of 1949 Bridge (otherwise known as the "generations bridge") on campus. Using the app, the user sees superimposed on the bridge a quilt from Moore's family; by clicking on different parts of the quilt, users see and hear two dueling histories: one of Moore's familial generations, who were enslaved, and the other, of generations of enslavers, among whom were two Penn alumni. This fusing of the personal and the historical, particularly around a campus monument to a past characterized by unequal access and the pains of slavery, is especially powerful—and even more so as it is made possible by students like Moore, who put the moments that their ancestors lived through in conversation with the country's continuing saturation in the ideologies and practices of white supremacy.

From where we sit as editors, in the United States, we continue to see the impact of this racist and discriminatory past, as school boards ban books and the teaching of "critical race theory," as political figures interfere in the faculty and curricular governance of public higher educational systems, as elementary school teachers are prevented from speaking about gender fluidity—or even, in Florida, saying the word "gay"—and as affirmative-action admissions policies built to redress historical inequalities come under attack. The political and social circumstances that make such attacks possible are both a cause and an effect of the hollowing out of the educational institutions that might otherwise promote critical inquiry, encourage informed debate, and protect academic freedom. This present crisis of the university, as Roderick Ferguson reminds us, is similarly rooted in long-standing historical antagonisms and can only be addressed when members of university communities see themselves as a part of, rather than in positions of superiority to, the variety of publics they engage with their work.[6] It is here again that we see the digital humanities with a key role to play—through projects that extend our views back to social

and political movements of the past and that speculate about alternative possible futures, as well as through actions aimed at bolstering the infrastructures—social as much as technological—that will be required as we collectively map our way forward, from pivotal moment to pivotal moment.

What might such interventions look like? One example comes from the Philadelphia-based Monument Lab, which has produced a comprehensive report, *The National Monument Audit*, that tracks public statuary across the United States in an effort to "provide a means to keep self-evaluating who we are as a nation in our public spaces" (1). Its other efforts involve public art installations, community-based archives, and open data repositories, each rooted in a particular place and led by the people who best know its history and are therefore best positioned to imagine its future. Here we see digital humanities practices blending with public history, participatory design, and civic art-making and becoming richer and more capacious in the process. Projects like these, which are grounded in history, culture, and context and which open up possibilities that extend beyond university walls, represent one of the most compelling models of the work that DH can do.

The Monument Lab offers one example of the reach and impact of DH ways of thinking; another is the set of projects dedicated to the documentation of Latinx oral histories and stories, which have grown in scope, power, and visibility in recent years. DH colleagues at the University of Houston and the Arte Público Press, for instance, were able to bring international focus to their long-standing work by hosting the 2021 Association for the Computers and Humanities Conference. The U.S. Latino Digital Humanities (USLDH) Center and the Arte Público Press have been home for much of that work and their own DH projects.[7] The USLDH seeks to recover and present histories related to Latinx literary traditions. Of the twelve collections that make up the Recovering the U.S. Hispanic Literary Heritage Digital Collections, for instance, one topic is "Spanish Fighting Fascist Spain," which documents activist efforts to resist fascism, and another is "Feminismo Internacional," which contains archives of the eponymous newspaper. Elsewhere, scholars and archivists Maria Eugenia Cotera, Linda García Merchant, and Marco Seiferle-Valencia, along with their student collaborators, have created the *Chicana por Mi Raza*.[8] This archive includes oral histories, photographs, and documents related to Chicana feminist practitioners during the civil rights era. A central aspect of the archive's collecting practices involves visits to, and long conversations with, feminist activists as part of an in-situ documentation effort that digitizes personal collections in the context of personal and community work. This method of collecting makes such archival materials, which previously might have been lost, newly available in digital form, but it does so within an overall framework of care, personal empowerment, and community-based knowledge practices.

As we chart a way forward for the digital humanities from one moment to the next, we also find powerful calls to action emerging. It is notable that this volume contains multiple essays, two of them manifestos, that emphasize the need for people of color and other historically marginalized groups to guide the field: the

Feminist Data Manifesto-NO, the U.S. Latinx Digital Humanities Manifesto, and Relation-Oriented AI, among others, call on DH practitioners, and users of data and digital technologies more generally, to be more intentional in connecting their work with social justice imperatives. Each of them, in different ways, asks readers to step back, examine their assumptions, and bring back to their work the insights of feminist scholars, Latinx critics, and Indigenous communities, respectively.

As DH continues to evolve and expand, it draws in many different methods and practices, from the archival projects mentioned above to community platform building for scholarly communication, quantitative literary analysis, game studies, critical mapping, text encoding, and more. The variety of work associated with the digital humanities has long been both its greatest strength and its most vexing puzzle: How can such different types of work be considered part of the same field? To what extent is DH a coherent (or even semi-coherent) whole? We believe that "digital humanities" as a term remains meaningful, even as smaller communities of practice characterize their work in new ways. Digital scholarship and practice in the academy remains drawn together by a certain boundary-bridging impulse, whether between the humanities and the digital, between the university and other publics, between scholarship and action, or other seeming (but not actual) divides. Our field is also supported and sustained by the larger formation of DH and the professional/scholarly organizations, events, and publications associated with it. These organizations, the activities they promote, the artifacts that they produce, and the people they bring together push the field forward, infusing it with new orientations and ideas.

At different speeds and to different degrees, some things are indeed changing; DH, for instance, is finding its way into K–12 spaces, as in the teaching guides associated with the Colored Conventions Project.[9] Although there remain relatively few degree-granting DH programs, many colleges and universities now explicitly engage DH in some way, from faculty-led centers to library-led initiatives. And yet the field remains very much Anglocentric—in spite of significant efforts toward supporting tools for multilingual DH and elevating models of DH from a range of locations in the world. We have come to realize, as series editors, that the one constant of DH is people—a shifting and distributed (and for that reason responsive) web of connections, social, institutional, and geographic—who are united in their desire to ensure that the field can match the vitality and breadth of those who wish to place themselves in it.

As we draw together in this expansive vision for the future of the field, we must acknowledge the people who are no longer among us. The last few years have been particularly painful for the DH community, as three colleagues have left us too soon: Stéfan Sinclair, associate professor in the Department of Languages, Literatures, and Cultures at McGill University; Rebecca Munson, assistant director for Interdisciplinary Education at The Center for Digital Humanities at Princeton; and Scott Enderle, digital humanities specialist at the University of Pennsylvania Libraries. Stéfan, Rebecca, and Scott left indelible impressions on our field and on many of us personally; they were brilliant, active colleagues whose loss we mourn on personal and professional levels. We send our deepest condolences to their loved ones, families, and friends. We hope that the strong array of work in this volume lives up to the high standards Stéfan, Rebecca, and Scott set for themselves and for the field.

This book is the fourth general volume in the Debates in the Digital Humanities (DDH) series that has appeared since 2012 (other annual volumes were published in 2016 and 2019). The series includes both these general volumes and volumes on specific topics. Recent special volumes have included *Making Things and Drawing Boundaries,* edited by Jentery Sayers (2017); *Bodies of Information,* edited by Elizabeth Losh and Jacqueline Wernimont (2018); *The Digital Black Atlantic,* edited by Kelly Baker Josephs and Roopika Risam (2021); *People, Practice, Power,* edited by Anne B. McGrail, Ángel David Nieves, and Siobhan Senier (2021); and *Global Debates in the Digital Humanities,* edited by Domenico Fiormonte, Sukanta Chaudhuri, and Paola Ricaurte (2022). We have an exciting lineup of future special volumes forthcoming: *What We Teach When We Teach DH,* edited by Brian Croxall and Diane Jakacki; *The Digital Futures of Graduate Study in the Humanities,* edited by Simon Appleford, Gabriel Hankins, and Anouk Lang; *Computational Humanities,* edited by Jessica Marie Johnson, David Mimno, and Lauren Tilton; and *Critical Infrastructure Studies & Digital Humanities,* edited by Alan Liu, Urszula Pawlicka-Deger, and James Smithies. The wide-ranging nature of these special topics allows each volume to explore a vital issue to the field. Moving forward, we encourage potential volume editors to reach out to us with ideas for other books, particularly those that engage the future of DH as it navigates tensions around the continued evolution of the field.

As the *Debates in the Digital Humanities* series continues to evolve, we will retain certain aspects of our original vision—namely, that all books in the DDH series will continue to be published online in an interactive format on Manifold, each arriving in an open-access format three months after print publication. The first volume of the series, *Debates in the Digital Humanities,* served as the prototype for Manifold itself; the platform is now being used by over thirty publishers, including Cornell University Press, Verso Books, Brown University, Indiana University Press, the University of Virginia, Arte Público Press, the City University of New York, the University of Minnesota Press, and many others. The *Debates* instance of Manifold has new features such as reading groups that can be used to create course spaces and to connect comments from students in a class or book club to each other. We are grateful to the Mellon Foundation and the National Endowment for the Humanities for supporting the development of Manifold, and we are delighted to be working with the University of Minnesota Press, whose willingness to experiment with new forms of scholarly publishing have shown impressive risk-taking and bravery. It is vital to us that our work, and the work of our authors, appears in open-access formats that allow readers across the world to engage with DDH texts free of charge. In this way, in our moment-to-moment lives, the work of this series might serve as an anchor, even if we do not know what tomorrow will bring.

NOTES

1. https://visionary-futures-collective.github.io/.
2. https://aadhum.umd.edu/.
3. http://digitalethnicfutures.org/.
4. https://sucho.org/.
5. http://pennandslaveryproject.org/.
6. See Ferguson, 6 passim.
7. https://artepublicopress.com/projects/.
8. https://www.chicanapormiraza.org/.
9. https://coloredconventions.org/teaching/#guides.

BIBLIOGRAPHY

American Association of University Professors. "Background Facts on Contingent Faculty Positions." Accessed August 1, 2022, https://www.aaup.org/issues/contingency/background-facts.

Cottom, Tressie McMillan (@tressiemcphd). "I get two questions when I'm on the road." Twitter, May 30, 2019, https://twitter.com/tressiemcphd/status/1134092910536925186.

Ferguson, Roderick A. *We Demand: The University and Student Protest.* Oakland: University of California Press, 2017.

Gold, Matthew K. "The Digital Humanities Moment." In *Debates in the Digital Humanities 2012,* edited by Matthew K. Gold. Minneapolis: University of Minnesota Press, 2012.

Wilder, Craig Steven. *Ebony and Ivy: Race and the Troubled History of America's Universities.* New York: Bloomsbury, 2013.

PART I

OPENINGS AND INTERVENTIONS

PART I][*Chapter 1*

Toward a Political Economy of Digital Humanities

MATTHEW N. HANNAH

It seems to be easier for us today to imagine the thoroughgoing deterioration of the earth and of nature than the breakdown of late capitalism; perhaps that is due to some weakness of our imaginations.

—Fredric Jameson, *The Seeds of Time*

Together we form a class, a class as yet to hack itself into existence as itself—and for itself.

—McKenzie Wark, *A Hacker Manifesto*

To adapt a well-known passage from *The Communist Manifesto,* a specter is haunting digital humanities—the specter of neoliberalism. Even as digital humanists build programs, teach students, and advance scholarship, the unwelcome presence of neoliberalism haunts us. This neoliberal specter casts its shadow over all of academia, especially as the Covid-19 pandemic has strained budgets, shuttered universities, and accelerated austerity. Neoliberalism is an economic model emphasizing individual rights, derived from classical liberalism, in conjunction with the belief that markets compete best when they regulate themselves (Henry). Neoliberal economics has had a dramatic effect on higher education, marked by defunding less "lucrative" programs, adjunctification of the professoriat, overreliance on graduate workers, and rising tuition. As universities and colleges depend on market competition for financial sustenance, support for the humanities has waned. So too have student enrollments. These challenges are the result of a political order that views market competition as the ultimate sign of a healthy economy.

The ascendance of neoliberalism in the West has diminished state funding for higher education, thereby reducing administrative support for purportedly less lucrative programs. However, digital humanities (DH) is one humanities area still perceived to attract administrative buy-in at a time when many disciplines struggle with their raison d'être. Sarah Brouillette argues that funding changes are an essential symptom of the neoliberal university. DH can maneuver under austerity because of its practicality in teaching technical skills, she argues, thereby increasing the possibility of success in securing funding and administrative support. The accuracy of these claims is difficult to assess, but data shows they are likely inaccurate in the U.S. context. Analyzing funding distributed by the National Endowment for the Humanities (NEH) from 2010 to 2019 shows that DH is but a small portion of the total amount of funding distributed to humanities scholars as a group.[1] The confluence of prominent attacks and media reportage at a time when the humanities are under fire has perpetuated the myth that DH thrives in the neoliberal university. But like all myths, there are elements of truth, and we should seriously attend to these critiques in an effort to organize solidarity in the neoliberal age.

According to its most vigorous critics, DH's success under neoliberalism has arisen from a Faustian bargain. On the surface, such claims seem easy to dismiss, but I argue that we must attend to their underlying assumptions in an effort to advance a new political economy of DH. Central to this critique is a conception of DH as opposed to something called "traditional" or "analog" humanities, which is under threat from university administrations because of its perceived impracticality. Such a binary is visible in Stanley Fish's repeated attacks in the opinion columns of *The New York Times* in the 2010s. "So much for the old humanist program," Fish bemoans in one blog post ("Mind Your P's and B's"); in another, he asks, "What rough beast has slouched into the neighborhood threatening to upset everyone's applecart?" ("The Old Order Changeth"). In 2014, Adam Kirsch, in *The New Republic,* paints a starker—even Manichean—picture: "Here is the future, we are made to understand: we can either get on board or stand athwart it and get run over" ("Technology Is Taking over English Departments"). Since critics characterize DH as a separate sphere of activity from "traditional" humanities, they are able to decry it as an aide-de-camp to the neoliberal "takeover" of the university without examining the role of the broader humanities under neoliberalism. Such accounts describe the "traditional" humanities as some form of resistance movement to capitalism, ignoring the reality that the humanities have historically collaborated with the state to shore up capitalist ideologies rather than oppose them.[2] For many humanists, DH symbolizes a threatening erosion of tried-and-true scholarship, the apotheosis of administrative gimmickry. While such claims are hyperbolic, the economic and political realities of the twenty-first-century academy—and the rest of the world—lend frightening weight to anxieties about the future as universities actively shutter humanities programs because of economic instability. Debates about the future of the humanities are not academic.[3]

Such critiques are usually dismissed as ad hominem arguments by digital humanists on Twitter, who argue that DH extends the humanities rather than replaces it; however, DH scholars have not grappled seriously with the overarching political framework. Despite unsubstantiated claims by some humanists that DH is an untheoretical, uncritical activity, preoccupied with neutral, apolitical activities such as building tools or coding (as if these activities could somehow be apolitical), recent work integrating critical theories of race, gender, and sexuality into DH has animated the field with political force, advancing more diverse representation and critical scholarship. These crucial efforts notwithstanding, the field seems reluctant to advance theoretical frameworks to address the political economy of DH, which is surprising given the resurgence and popularity of Leftist political campaigns and policies.[4] If the field operates more comfortably within the neoliberal academy, as critics suggest, what might an anti-neoliberal DH look like? Can digital humanists leverage immanent critique from a privileged space within the neoliberal academy to develop a political economy that resists, mitigates, critiques, and organizes against the structures within which both DH and the humanities survive?

Rather than counter arguments that DH is complicit with free-market bureaucracies, I accept such critique as my starting point. Of course, DH operates according to neoliberal economic policies in that it exists within the same laissez-faire economic infrastructure as literature, philosophy, history, music, art, and other disciplines, which are no more capable of escaping or resisting capitalism. Academia is one of the most prominent sites where neoliberal economic policy is enacted, so arguing that DH is more or less complicit than some conception of "traditional" humanities is misguided.[5] Rather than defend DH, I argue that DH should instead respond to neoliberalism by advancing a principled, collective, and explicitly anti-neoliberal platform adapted from Marxist theory. Of course, advancing such a digital humanities should not ignore critiques of Marxism from feminist and critical race theorists but rather suggest intersectional approaches to political economy in keeping with current theoretical work.[6] In so doing, I hope to provoke wider conversations about how digital humanists can intervene *as a field* to alleviate the brutal economic realities of the twenty-first-century academy.

The Rise of the Neoliberal University

Despite the general fuzziness of social media usage around the term "neoliberalism," neoliberal policy is relatively straightforward: the protection of markets and privatization of public services, which allows consumers to choose and markets to decide. Such "freedom" to engage in commerce should be protected as a tenet of democracy, neoliberals argue, hence legislation is often aimed at protecting free markets and stripping social-welfare programs. Examples of such policy making include deregulating financial institutions, bailing out the banking sector in the wake of the 2008 financial crisis, redistributing wealth (upward), and instituting massive tax breaks for corporations (Abramovitz; Krugman). Trade policies such as the North American Free Trade Agreement and the Trans-Pacific Partnership, proposed under the administrations of Bill Clinton and Barack Obama, respectively, ensure market freedom for corporations at the expense of workers around the world

(Roman and Arregui). This has taken place while wages remain stagnant and wealth disparities increase (Horowitz, Igielnik, and Kochhar).

The seeds of neoliberal thought were planted by the Mont Pelerin Society, which began convening in Switzerland in 1947 (Harvey, 20). Members included economist Milton Friedman, political philosopher Friedrich von Hayek, economist Ludvig von Mises, among others, who advocated a return to nineteenth-century liberal notions of personal freedom and market autonomy, which they believed would correct society's worst impulses for greed and corruption. Milton Friedman describes such economic policies as a "new faith":

> Neo-liberalism would accept the nineteenth century liberal emphasis in the fundamental importance of the individual, but it would substitute for the nineteenth-century goal of laissez-faire as a means to this end, the goal of the competitive order. . . . The state would police the system, establish conditions favorable to competition and prevent monopoly, provide a stable monetary framework, and relieve acute misery and distress. (Friedman, "Neo-Liberalism," 7)

Drawing on a utopian vision of a world free of hunger and want through market competition, Friedman and his fellow neoliberals advocated for free markets, privatization, and minimal government interference *except* to protect private enterprise.[7]

Tenets of this new liberalism include the belief that nurturing this economic vision remains an inherently political project. Contending that governmental interference impedes freedom, neoliberals only insist on state intervention in the market to protect free enterprise itself. Friedman argues that capitalism is essential for a functioning democracy: "There is an intimate connection between economics and politics, that only certain combinations of political and economic arrangements are possible, and that in particular, a society which is socialist cannot also be democratic, in the sense of guaranteeing individual freedom" (*Capitalism and Freedom,* 8). Only unfettered capitalism democratically brings about freedom from want, prejudice, and oppression because competitive exchange enables "co-ordination without coercion" (13). For Friedman, freedom and politics are inextricably linked because capitalism allows economic power to offset political power: "Viewed as a means to the end of political freedom, economic arrangements are important because of their effect on the concentration or dispersion of power" (9). Paradoxically, neoliberal capitalism, it is argued, both limits political power by eliminating state social programs and enables political freedom through cooperative exchange at one and the same time.

The political valence of neoliberalism has become especially problematic as time has passed. Friedman's ideas were implemented by governments around the world during the 1970s and 1980s in response to financial crises, and he became an adviser to Ronald Reagan, who spearheaded massive economic shifts leading to obscene wealth and income inequality. In the United Kingdom, Margaret Thatcher applied Friedman's beliefs, stripping social programs of government support. Implementing a philosophy that individuals are more important than collectives allowed Reagan and Thatcher to eradicate social programs under the auspices of individual responsibility. "They are casting their problems at society," Thatcher famously claimed. "And, you know, there's no such thing as society. There are individual men and women and there are families. And no government can do anything except through people, and people must look after themselves first" ("Margaret Thatcher: A Life in Quotes"). Mirroring Friedman's claims that society is simply an aggregate of individuals responsible unto themselves, Thatcher and Reagan vigorously implemented the political project of neoliberalism as a move toward individualism and privatization and away from social support and collectivism.[8] Such shifts have had a cataclysmic effect on all aspects of governmental social support, including for higher education.

Neoliberalism has transformed education in myriad negative ways, from increasing tuition to decreasing job prospects for graduate students, from decimating humanities enrollments (with subsequent weaponization of low enrollment numbers to shrink or eliminate less lucrative areas of study) to adjunctification of the professoriate. It is now common to find humanities departments that have not hired new tenure-track faculty in decades, while major areas of study are no longer even offered. Such realities are omnipresent, with tangible effects on faculty, staff, librarians, students, and communities. As funding continues to shrivel up and university administrations persist in seeking financial support through corporate relationships and wealthy donors, many institutions nurture disciplines and majors that seem most directly related to the workforce—and, as a consequence, rely heavily on adjunct labor and graduate students to teach humanities courses while reducing tenure-track faculty lines. Many administrators seek to make up the loss of public funds by raising tuition, precipitating an unfathomable and obscene debt crisis among college graduates who may find little opportunity for the high-paying employment necessary to pay off loans.

The rise of the neoliberal university has, in turn, profoundly transformed the mission of public education. As universities turn to private sources of funding, mirroring financial frameworks of private enterprise to remain solvent, education becomes a peddler of what Henry Heller calls "academic capitalism." In his account, academic capitalism is the predominant mode of higher education, marked by "the variety of ways in which markets, states, and higher education are increasingly inter-related and the implications of the blurring of the lines between these spheres" (Heller, 173). Capital flows along circuits to entities in ways that typically do not support humanities programs but build STEM (science, technology, engineering, and mathematics) complexes with industry funds or football facilities with private or corporate donations. Universities invest in niche projects supported by private funds rather than in the larger educational mission (Hunt).

Neoliberal policies in the United Kingdom have led to an obsession with excellence as a metric. Focusing on impact assessment and performance targets challenges educators to reconceptualize scholarship to meet benchmarks rather than increase human knowledge (Olssen). The Teaching and Research Excellence Frameworks (TEF and REF) pressure humanities faculty to teach and publish, according to metrics, and secure large grants, which are rare in the humanities. John O'Regan and John Gray describe these mechanisms as "neoliberal instruments of accountability": "There seems no doubt that in respect of the current situation in the UK and elsewhere, it is essential to the neoliberal 'multiverse' that the imaginary which underlies the REF and the UK government's attitude to higher education is sustained" (545). Such an "imaginary" has replaced notions of education as a public good with notions of education as a customer service.

Neoliberalism has altered the role of the educator, too. Increased tuition necessitates higher debt, which is administrated by the government with exorbitant compounding interest. Because students are going into insurmountable debt, the entire purpose of education has been transformed. Christopher Newfield characterizes this as "the great mistake," whereby the function of the university has irrevocably shifted because of eroding governmental financial investment: "We know that no country has a large middle class without mass-scale higher learning, and that this in turn depends on minimizing individual cost. . . . And yet most people aren't fighting to hang onto low-cost public colleges and their power to *democratize intelligence*" (italics in original, 16). Rather than seeing public education as a social good funded by the state to produce an educated citizenry, neoliberalism has established an exchange model where burdens for college expense are borne by individuals, many of whom will never escape their debts. "When a relationship-based system is converted to a market," Newfield contends, "resources move toward those willing and able to pay for them" (29). Because students pay exorbitant amounts, they gravitate toward the few majors they perceive will pay off with lucrative careers, despite evidence that humanities graduates actually do quite well comparatively (Moran; Carlson). Unfortunately, as more students major in computer science or engineering, they will produce skill gluts where an excess of technical experts decreases wages in those disciplines, and it is hard not to see Silicon Valley coding programs as anything but a cynical effort to reduce future salaries.[9]

What's So Neoliberal about Digital Humanities?

Because DH crystallized in the aftermath of the financial collapse of 2008, it has always been imbricated in austerity discourse. In order to position itself within a skeptical humanities and generate administrative support, early digital humanists relied on the rhetoric of innovation and disruption, of finding great jobs for students, building labs, and securing grants when funds were scarce. While the humanities have always engaged in revolutionary discourse about new theories and methods—one thinks of the much-ballyhooed "Theory Wars"—DH's revolutionary discourse was unfortunately paired with economic constriction and often mirrored the rhetoric of Silicon Valley. In 2010, for example, Mark Sample characterized DH with language similar to journalistic narratives about the tech industries: "The digital humanities should not be about the digital at all. It's all about innovation and disruption. The digital humanities is really an insurgent humanities" (quoted in Svensson, par. 40). It is hard not to hear echoes of Silicon Valley in such a positioning of DH, especially when tech leaders were being touted in the media as "disrupters" at the same time (O'Brien). Furthermore, mainstream reporting often sensationalizes a few methods or practitioners who fit more comfortably within tech's investments in big data, machine learning, and artificial intelligence.[10] While such disruptions have been crucial in helping us reimagine academia, and journalistic coverage can be salutary for building the discipline, critics see these events as evidence of Big Tech's encroachment into the humanities.

In perhaps the most controversial critique of DH as fundamentally and irrevocably neoliberal, Daniel Allington, Sarah Brouillette, and David Golumbia attacked the field in a 2016 piece touted as a "political history of the digital humanities." While many have criticized this piece, I do not believe we have fully grappled with its central claim or taken seriously the critique. Of course, there are fundamental issues with the article's portrayal and reasoning, but, as I have argued thus far, we must accept its basic claim about DH and the neoliberal university as a starting point for a new political economy of the field. For Allington, Brouillette, and Golumbia, DH is a neoliberal symptom because it "sees technological innovation as an end in itself and equates the development of disruptive business models with political progress." DH's focus on infusing the humanities with an ethos of building, coding, and modeling, rather than critical theory, they argue, smacks of an instrumental, rationalistic technocentrism marching in lockstep with neoliberal profit models rather than espousing political agendas of solidarity. In their view, critical theory is an emancipatory project nurtured by the humanities proper, which DH purposely undermines.[11]

Rather than live up to its putatively insurgent character, they claim, DH has displaced "politically progressive humanities scholarship and activism in favor of the manufacture of digital tools and archives." The humanities resist neoliberal takeover of the university because they practice critique and political activism, which undermine cynical efforts to financialize academia, while DH promotes a postcritical project that exists comfortably within university power structures:

> We therefore suggest that it is not the "traditional" scholarly world, with its hierarchies and glorified experts and close reading of works read by only a precious few people, to which the Digital Humanities social movement is most meaningfully opposed. What it stands in opposition to, rather, is the insistence that academic work should be critical, and that there is, after all, no

> work and no way to be in the world that is not political. (Allington, Brouillette, and Golumbia)

Like other forms of postcritical activity, DH is envisioned to be a sphere of academic endeavor that actively eschews political engagement. Here, we see the Manichean rhetoric reappear but now the binary of traditional/digital is mapped onto dichotomies of political/apolitical and critical/uncritical as though only binaristic operations are possible within academia.

Allington, Brouillette, and Golumbia focus on DH operating within a corporatist system of reward and results. Rather than resist such reconfigurations of academic work, they argue, DH plays a key role in preparing the humanities for assimilation into them: "By providing a model for humanities teaching and research that appears to overcome these perceived limitations, Digital Humanities has played a leading role in the corporatist restructuring of the humanities." A roundtable on "The Dark Side of the Digital Humanities" at 2013's Modern Language Association convention deploys the same rhetoric: "At the same time that the market logic of neoliberalism has been used to decimate the mainstream humanities from within and without, this same logic has encouraged foundations, corporations, and university administrations to devote new resources to the digital humanities" (Chun et al., 499). DH is painted as the advanced guard for financialization, austerity, and commodification. In this vision, DH will lead the humanities into compliance with neoliberal initiatives and accomplish this coup de grâce through grant funding to build rather than theorize.

Of course, such characterizations ignore the realities of capitalism, imagining a literary narrative of heroes and villains rather than the more mundane actualities of budget cuts, austerity, and privatization. This simplistic narrative envisions a revolutionary humanities valiantly resisting capitalism through individual political activism, an idealized version of the humanities that has never existed. Neoliberal economic policies do not require a vanguard to prepare the humanities for replacement, like the plot of *Invasion of the Body Snatchers.* Such a description ignores the ways in which digital humanists are subject to the same pressures and tensions as anyone else in the twenty-first-century university, beset by unreliable resources, excessive workloads, and precarity. And yet, it is difficult not to see how DH has been able to maneuver in a time of austerity precisely because it is salable to administrators, providing students with both employable skills and a liberal-arts education.[12] As impacts of Covid-19 accelerate existing austerity, such tensions will become ever more fraught and the impacts of neoliberal governance will only spread.

Digital Humanities and the Theoretical Turn

Conceptions of DH as a postcritical activity that denigrates humanistic theory-as-politics does seem visible in some early characterizations of the field (Scheinfeldt).

However, many DH scholars have called for combinations of praxis and theory, conceived as broadly emancipatory applications of philosophy and cultural theory.[13] Nearly ten years on, positing a postcritical-theory DH, which eschews theoretical reflexivity and critique regarding race, gender, sexuality, nationalism, colonialism, or identity, seems quaint. With the rise of openly white-supremacist far-right political parties, erosions of human rights surrounding immigration and migration, reckonings over racism in response to police brutality and state-sanctioned murder, sexual and gender inequalities, wealth and income disparity, governmental failure in response to Covid-19, and imminent climate collapse, critical theories articulating sociopolitical issues are more crucial than ever. Whereas Frances Fukuyama declared an "end to history" in 1992, predicting the hegemony of neoliberal democracy, we are witnessing a resurgence of history and a renewed need for a critical theory that will help us map our political positionality vis-à-vis such challenges. Slavoj Žižek captures this moment well in reversing Marx's formula that philosophers had only ever interpreted the world while the point was to change it: "Now is the time to think."

DH has seen an explosion of theorizing around political questions of identity, representation, and positionality. Scholarly communities have formed around political stasis points, crystallizing into vibrant communities expanding boundaries both for new projects and for newcomers. Jamie Bianco advances a DH "which is not one," calling for a return to critical theory. Similarly, Roopika Risam calls for an "intersectional" DH, in which the "relationship between theory and praxis is integral." ("Beyond the Margins," par. 4). New communities have arisen around different nodes of power and identity. Twitter hashtags such as #blackdh, #transformdh, #femdh, and #queerdh centralize conversations about representation, and new books have done much to engage postcolonial theory, critical race theory, gender studies, Indigenous studies, and environmental studies.[14] Scholars have issued various calls for the discipline to expand, adapt, and evolve. Indeed, the theme of 2016's *Debates in the Digital Humanities* was "the expanded field" (Klein and Gold).

As an expanded field, DH incorporates critical theories both to expand representation within the field and ground research projects in critical theories of identity and power. The chapters in *Debates in Digital Humanities 2023* demonstrate forcefully the continued excellence of scholarly work applying critical theories of positionality around questions of race (chapters 9, 12, and 15), gender (chapter 8), ability and embodiment (chapters 8 and 21), sexuality (chapter 7), language (chapters 3 and 19), and indigeneity (chapter 8). Furthermore, scholars apply critical methods to questions of oppression and inequality in computation and data, representing new humanistic considerations of tech.[15] DH has been at the forefront of recent political engagement in the public sphere, too. Political responses are visible in projects such as Torn Apart/Separados, which responded to state-sponsored abduction of immigrant children at the U.S.–Mexico border; the Visionary Futures Collective around academic responses to the pandemic; the COVID Black taskforce's analysis of the pandemic as it affects the Black community; or the "rapid response" project known as Nimble Tents. DH is uniquely poised to produce important scholarly projects that respond to current events directly. There is so much critical work happening in this field, but where are the theoretical discussions of class, economics, hegemony, ideology, and capitalism? If we are doing so much to integrate cultural theory into DH, why have we largely ignored the work of Marxist thinkers who have theorized and critiqued capitalism in ways that could help us respond to our detractors and spur the field to consider economic questions? Why is there not yet a Marxist digital humanities working to foreground economic issues in concert with critical interventions along intersectional axes of race, gender, ability, sexuality, and sovereignty? This absence is all the more surprising given the disproportional impact of Covid on these communities, both within the university and without (Shapiro; Cahn).

What Is to Be Done? Toward a Marxist Digital Humanities

Field-level theoretical advances have focused more on critical theories of identity while neglecting Marxist theories of class, exploitation, ideology, and capitalism. Yet questions about our disciplinary role under late capitalism must be developed, too.[16] This absence is striking given that even Stanley Fish, that perennial bad-faith critic of DH, articulates its politics as "a left agenda" ("The Digital Humanities and the Transcending of Mortality"). As Fish notes, DH has always been invested in commons, but we still need a stronger theoretical analysis organized under the umbrella of an anti-neoliberal digital humanities, grounded in Marxist theories of economics, class, hegemony, and ideology. The need for this Marxist DH will become even more necessary as university communities experience tectonic shifts because of the pandemic, which will surely lead to more austerity and disinvestment (Wang; Kelsky; Kramnick).

Alongside critiques of identity and representation, DH should foreground political economy in an effort to encourage a more economically just academy. This is especially important if we take seriously the notion that DH is more comfortable under administrative neoliberalism. Rather than dismiss those claims, despite the fact that we may believe they are overblown, we can practice a form of immanent critique, maneuvering in solidarity from within neoliberalism. Max Horkheimer described the goals of Critical Theory as a form of immanence: "Every part of the theory presupposes the critique of the existing order and the struggle against it along lines determined by the theory itself" (229). Similarly, DH is positioned to confront, analyze, and mitigate austerity and oppression along lines determined by digital humanists as we navigate the post-pandemic education landscape. As universities and colleges experience increasing austerity after Covid-19, we must theorize models for a DH that is concerned *as a discipline* with economic precarity, academic labor, and austerity.

As higher education undergoes constrictions, solidarity will become ever more necessary for survival. An anti-neoliberal DH must advance class consciousness across the community. If critics such as Richard Grusin are correct that DH "reproduces structurally" precarious labor "that has marked late twentieth and twenty-first-century global capitalism" (87), DH can respond through a class-based approach that encourages solidarity across all academic ranks and sectors. But class is not a concept that has ever mapped well onto academia. Marx theorized the role of labor and class antagonism under industrial capitalism long ago, arguing that the transformation of money into capital requires a form of exchange whereby the worker sells labor power. Labor power is thus both an inherent quality of the worker and a commodity that can be sold on the market. However, Marx's concept of a working class that provides surplus labor to enrich the bourgeoisie does not correspond well to academic labor in DH. Despite precarity and austerity, digital humanists cannot conceive of labor in the same way other workers do. We are not construction workers, cab drivers, or warehouse employees, so our model for labor may be different. Building solidarity requires new theories of production and class.

Class is a structural relation that corresponds to labor within the unique means of production in which we labor, and we need theories that reflect that reality and help us build solidarity. In her recent attempt to move critical theory beyond the assumption that "capitalism" describes our current economic conditions, McKenzie Wark articulates a model of class that captures the unique class position of digital humanists. Extending Marxist theories of class relation, Wark argues that we should no longer rely on nineteenth- and twentieth-century notions of labor and class because such descriptions do not account for our information economy, which has become the predominant mode of production and ownership in the twenty-first century. Instead, Wark argues, the twenty-first-century ruling class, which she calls the vectoral class, owns and controls vectors of information (*Capital Is Dead*, 13). This emerging ruling class represents a new model of class relation uniquely suited to the fluidity and mass of information: "The regulatory regime emerging in the last quarter century favors the mobility of information, and not just finance, as a means of coordinating economic activity transnationally" (93). The shift to a mode of production focused on information work brings with it new class antagonisms, as notions of property and production evolve.

Central to this project is identification of an emerging form of class antagonism. For Wark, as for Marx, class is not categorical but a form of relation to a ruling class: "First, class means class antagonism. It's not a category, it's a relation" (*Capital Is Dead*, 98). This newly emerging subaltern class, which Wark theorized as far back as 2004, is the hacker class, comprised of information workers whose labor is unusual perhaps but still serves a ruling class:

> The hacker class arises out of the transformation of information into property, in the form of intellectual property. This legal hack makes of the hack a property producing process, and thus a class producing process. The hack produces the class force capable of asking—and answering—the property question, the

> hacker class. The hacker class is the class with the capacity to create not only new kinds of object and subject in the world, not only new kinds of property form in which they may be represented, but new kinds of relation, with unforeseen properties, which question the property form itself. (*A Hacker Manifesto*, par. 036)

The hacker class does not own the information it produces but rather performs the task of creating content, coding, managing databases, analyzing data, and other tasks, which crystallize the notion of information as property. Producing such property has the unintended effect of producing new class antagonisms between hackers and vectoralists and may provide a challenge to the information economy itself, to the new capitalist order led by massive technical conglomerates who own massive amounts of information.[17]

Of course, the notion of a hacker class should not obscure existing schisms either within DH or the broader sector of information workers, nor should we fall prey to idealizing "hackers." Labor in the information sector is variegated and divided along many internal axes of oppression, especially as tech companies have become massive vectoral monopolies owning information technologies and personal data. As Lilly Irani points out, tech-sector workers experience varying levels of support, remuneration, and oppression, posing the question: "What is at stake in hiding the delivery people, stockroom workers, content moderators, and call center operators laboring to produce the automated experience?" Such "ghost labor" represents a growing underclass of information workers who exist in precarious and exploitative positions within the "gig" economy (Gray and Suri). In a similar way, digital humanists occupy a range of labor positions, some with more security or remuneration than others. The concept of the hacker class must not collapse these different experiences in an effort to build solidarity. Recognition of inequality must be our first duty in advancing a political economy of DH. Instead, the notion of a hacker class provides a theoretical starting point to coordinate with solidarity rather than simply collaborate.

The hacker class does represent one way to organize digital humanists against austere economic policies ravaging higher education and complements existing efforts by organized labor to establish unions. As conditions have deteriorated in both academia and the tech sector, information workers have organized labor unions, including a remarkable attempt by Google employees to form their first union (Koul and Shaw). But many digital humanists are not yet organized in any official way, and the hacker concept could help conceptually organize such individuals as workers engaged in class struggle and connect institutions with labor unions to those without. Such an approach builds well on existing efforts to critique questions of academic labor and financial precarity by scholars such as Julia Flanders, Spencer Keralis, Wendy Hui Kyong Chun, Lisa Marie Rhody, Christina Boyles, Anne Cong-Huyen, Carrie Johnston, Jim McGrath, Amanda Phillips, Hannah Alpert-Abrams,

Kathi Inman Berens, and others. Their critical work in identifying and analyzing labor inequalities in DH are central for understanding particular labor issues. But we still need to contextualize those dynamics within a broader theoretical frame and history of labor organizing. Reconfiguring DH around a class relation allows us to advance organized modes of solidarity across the academy. After all, such forms of solidarity are already baked into DH because it is so heterogeneous and wide-ranging. Our scholarly organizations represent students, postdocs, faculty, librarians, and staff at universities, colleges, cultural organizations, historical societies, libraries, and more. DH cuts across disciplines too, connecting us to information workers across the academy.

Whereas many digital humanists are organized officially into labor unions, many do not have such opportunities to organize yet. Organizing *all* digital humanists as a class will provide a space for solidarity and coordination. Such efforts begin in our professional organizations, and we should petition position statements on topics related to economic precarity, labor, and ideology. Our professional organizations represent the incredible diversity of DH labor and must begin to organize activities and outputs around these issues. Solidarity efforts must develop intersectional networks to combat austerity and financialization alongside other efforts around inequality and oppression.[18] Currently, individual scholars, often in non-tenure-track positions, develop resources with little professional support, but the field as a whole should be at the forefront of such efforts through professional development opportunities, grants, conferences, and resources (Alpert-Abrams; Alpert-Abrams et al.). Furthermore, DH organizations should coordinate with labor unions to imagine new modes of solidarity and support, especially for our most vulnerable colleagues, and this would establish an organizing pipeline between labor unions and unrepresented workers and nonunion institutions. Graduate students, undergraduates, staff, librarians, instructors, and lecturers around the country are engaged in labor actions with little public commentary or support from DH professional organizations to which they belong.[19]

As we imagine modes of class solidarity against austerity, we must also foreground academic hiring, especially in the wake of Covid-19. One benefit to advancing a hacker class is that it can, and indeed must, include administrators, such as directors of centers, who are often not included in official union negotiations. Together, we must confront the looming labor crisis in the humanities and DH. Digital humanists should vigorously counter the ideology that DH will lead to academic employment and begin actively engaging and critiquing the job-market process in solidarity with the humanities. How many DH courses include focused discussion of the job market for digital scholarship? If we are advocating DH as a path to employment outside the tenure track, then we must be prepared to provide job-market training and resources too, including focused training in how to search for those jobs and leverage technical skills in ways that mitigate the class oppression of undergraduates, graduate students, and postdocs. Rather than simply espousing "alt-ac" employment as a solution to neoliberal markets, we should be interrogating the notion of an academy training students for disappearing jobs and seek to advance a more equitable academy while we help students avoid being crushed by it. Above all, we must think of ourselves as labor under capitalism and organize appropriately to meet the threats to that labor as a whole.

A Marxist DH should also address how capital circulates across the university. DH is often more successful at securing grants and fellowships because it promises results that mesh with the neoliberal university's metrics for success. Much of the resentment and suspicion toward DH as a neoliberal activity revolves around grant funding. Adam Kirsch describes this as the "quantification" inherent to neoliberal university bureaucracy, which cannot measure "changed minds and expanded spirits" but can measure citations and grants. Writing in *The New Republic* about the limits of the digital humanities, Kirsch concludes, "All those grants have to be accounted for somehow; the rhetoric of the digital, in the academy as in the marketplace, prides itself on being results-oriented." Of course, Kirsch seems to forget that publication outputs are also quantified—what is tenure, after all?—but the focus on grants is a common critique. If DH is capable of securing funds from grants, so the argument goes, administrations will be more likely to support DH, and with a limited pool of resources, the humanities will experience even more austerity.

To combat significant cuts to traditional humanities projects, I propose we think about ways to redistribute grant funds so that some funding goes to non-DH areas. This demands conscious effort to reframe grant proposals so that they advance the humanist mission as much as launch new initiatives, tools, or projects. And because so much of the money from federal grants is already redistributed through indirect costs, we should advocate for more transparency about these allotments and push for humanities support from humanities grants. Some changes are already in the wind. The NEH changed the requirements for the 2021 Digital Humanities Advancement Grants to include "how the project will support and benefit all project staff, such as through project-based learning, mentoring, or immersion in the activities of the institution for undergraduate or graduate students" (Brennan). Furthermore, changes to project priorities open space for scholarship that "examines the history, criticism, and philosophy of digital culture or technology and its impact on society," suggesting wonderful new confluences between the digital humanities and the humanities.

Attention to funding distribution could also provide support for graduate students or faculty to participate or may provide avenues for collaboration between the digital project and non-DH faculty, staff, librarians, and students. Despite claims from humanists such as Brouillette that granting agencies only put money into DH projects that offer "equipment" and "student training," we can see that such projects actually offer collaborative models for advancing humanities scholarship. While Brouillette specifically targets the Social Science and Humanities Research Council of Canada (SSHRC), I collaborate on a SSHRC-funded project called the

Modernist Archives Publishing Project that is rigorously dedicated to the humanistic project of digitizing archival materials related to twentieth-century publishing and that enacts a feminist approach to collaboration (Battershill et al.). While it is true that grant funds pay for some technical development, the funds also support students who gain crucial project management skills and archival experience.

Another DH Is Possible

Certainly, no academic program will undo or prevent the damage being done to educational institutions under late capitalism. As Fredric Jameson so clearly realized, it is easier to imagine the end of the world than the end of capitalism (xii). Academic institutions are anachronistic, trying to preserve a medieval conception of knowledge production within a brutally modern economic reality. The humanities will not resist neoliberalism just as the digital humanities will be unlikely to exacerbate neoliberalism; instead, we should reposition political economy at the center of our academic praxis as digital humanists, advancing a principled DH that takes neoliberalism's effects seriously and organizes to allay the effects. Rather than simply dismiss interlocutors who accuse us of neoliberalism, we should instead advance a politically organized DH that leads the way in developing a set of ethics and tactics for mitigating the worst effects of austerity and capitalism, a Marxist digital humanities that will advance a commitment to the academic commons, to class awareness, to an academic environment that supports precarious labor, and to a financial redistribution of resources.

Such an orientation builds well on the work we already do to support open-access initiatives, critique platforms, share resources and code, redesign tenure-and-promotion processes, envision new models of graduate and undergraduate education *and* labor, and promote "the commons." More than any other humanities discipline, DH has tackled such challenges, practicing what Kathleen Fitzpatrick has described as "generous thinking." Much of the important work advancing a possible new model for higher education is happening in DH. But such efforts still seem scattered around the community, happening in individual pockets. DH has largely remained silent on such issues *as a discipline*, in part because we have not yet grappled with our field as part of the academic–industrial complex. It is time for us to tackle these challenges together.

Neoliberalism has proven to be a devastating failure, eroding public goods such as higher education. While the rich have gotten richer, the poor have grown poorer, with shrinking prospects for a sustainable and healthy future. But neoliberal capitalism is not the "end of history," and we may soon approach the end of neoliberalism's hegemony. Ganesh Sitaraman has described the imminent "collapse of neoliberalism" as the outcome of decades of failed economic policies comes to a head. As we confront intractable questions about "the commons" such as climate, pandemic response, intellectual property, and data, neoliberalism (and indeed capitalism itself) will be unable to respond. Wolfgang Streeck argues we may have entered a period of indeterminacy, "a period in which unexpected things can happen any time," including the collapse of capitalism (12). Given Covid-19's radical acceleration of processes that would have happened over the next few decades, we are potentially on the verge of an entirely new social, cultural, and academic reality, and we cannot wait to organize a more equitable university for everyone.

Although it remains unclear what comes next, now is the time to advance a compelling counternarrative to that of the neoliberal economists and politicians who have done little to ameliorate inequality and suffering, and digital humanists are well situated to craft such a narrative within the academy and beyond. Although we have not yet grappled with neoliberalism, we are uniquely poised to advance more humane models of higher education through a DH that leverages critiques against us as a point from which to engage. To quote Arundhati Roy, in her fiercely anti-imperialist, anti-neoliberal work *War Talk*, "Another world is not only possible, she's on her way. . . . On a quiet day, if I listen very carefully, I can hear her breathing" (75). I hope this chapter serves as a starting point toward imagining another digital humanities well on its way, poised to confront the challenges facing us all.

NOTES

1. NEH digital initiatives received a combined $35,967,499. Compare that figure with some "traditional" humanities grants awarded during the same period: State Humanities Councils General Operating Support Grants ($435,239,182), Humanities Collections and Reference ($74,447,577), Scholarly Editions and Translations ($51,640,946), America's Historical and Cultural Organizations Implementation Grants ($37,879,744) ("NEH Grant Data, 2010–2019").

2. Henry Heller articulates forcefully how the humanities/social sciences worked in lockstep with the state during the Cold War: "Indeed, top academics more often than not had close ties to the US government. It furthermore shows how the content of the academic disciplines was harnessed to defending capitalism, liberalism, and American imperialism while attacking left-wing ideas" (10). One example of such coordination was the funding of the *Paris Review* by the CIA (Jones).

3. Several universities have begun eliminating humanities departments. The New School (a bastion for progressive thought) is enacting massive cuts, which exemplify the impact of Covid on liberal arts. ("Update on the Impact of Covid-19"). Both University of Wisconsin–Stevens Point and Adrian College reversed such plans as of this writing, but Covid-19 will surely exacerbate future efforts (Kremer; Marowski; Myers).

4. This was visible in the presidential campaigns of Bernie Sanders, who did much to destigmatize socialism in the United States.

5. In many ways, DH is better poised as a discipline to mitigate neoliberalism because scholars are already doing much to advance open-access initiatives, digital commons, and more equitable academic work.

6. There is a rich scholarly tradition in intersectional applications of Marxism, visible in work by Cedric J. Robinson, Adolph Reed, C. L. R. James, Angela Davis, Stuart Hall, Sheila Rowbotham, Zillah Eisenstein, Dorothy Thompson, Christine Di Stefano, Heidi Hartmann, and Meg Luxton and Kate Bezanson, among many others. A forthcoming collection showcases the continued energy around this topic (Lye and Nealon), and the 2022 Institute on Culture and Society conference for the Marxist Literary Group, like many DH conferences, requests intersectional papers on racial capitalism, queer Marxisms, materialist feminisms, and Marxist ecology (Marxist Literary Group).

7. David Harvey argues that Friedman's project is itself utopian: "We can, therefore, interpret neoliberalization either as a utopian project to realize a theoretical design for the reorganization of international capitalism or as a political project to re-establish the conditions for capital accumulation and to restore the power of economic elites" (Harvey, 19). Intriguingly, the Left is typically accused of utopian thinking while the neoliberal faith in unfettered markets producing individual freedom seems equally utopian.

8. Years earlier, in 1955, Friedman said something very similar to Thatcher: "Society is a collection of individuals and the whole is no greater than the sum of its parts" ("Liberalism, Old Style," 11).

9. Google now offers a "Grow with Google" program for information technology (IT) certifications, which will likely increase the IT workforce and lower wages.

10. *The New York Times* ran a 2013 piece on literary history as seen through the lens of big data, which clearly positioned DH as a "tech trend" (Lohr). For a more recent example, see "How Data Analysis Can Enrich the Liberal Arts."

11. I differentiate between "critical theory" as the broader set of emancipatory philosophical interventions in the humanities and Critical Theory as the particular project of Western Marxism. I argue DH has developed the former and ignored the latter ("Critical Theory").

12. Allington, Brouillette, and Golumbia claim that "the Digital Humanities social movement seeks to prove that a humanities education is beneficial to job seekers by reinventing that education as a course of training in the advanced use of information technology." Too often, we pitch DH to administrators using language that administrators appreciate.

13. See the writings of Cecire; Schmidt; Drucker; Liu; and Hunter.

14. Notable books include Losh and Wernimont, *Bodies of Information*; Risam, *New Digital Worlds*; and Roopika Risam and Kelly Baker Josephs, *The Digital Black Atlantic*. Additional articles and chapters of interest are Gallon, "Making a Case for the Black Digital Humanities"; Barnett et al., "QueerOS"; Noble, "Toward a Critical Black Digital Humanities"; and Mandell, "Gender and Cultural Analytics."

15. See D'Ignazio and Klein, *Data Feminism*; Noble, *Algorithms of Oppression*; Eubanks, *Digital Dead End*; Eubanks, *Automating Inequality*; and Benjamin, *Race after Technology*.

16. The ideology of neoliberalism is not inherently antithetical to liberal notions of social progress, so identity questions can be advanced by the state while the economic oppression of capitalism is ignored. See Duggan.

17. I am intrigued by the hacker as a destabilizing agent in DH and digital scholarship. One of the only scholars to recognize this, Claire Potter, argues that we need to incorporate a hacker ethos into existing humanistic projects.

18. A striking example of the lacunae around economic issues is visible in the Black Lives Matter statement by *Digital Humanities Quarterly*, promising to publish "at least one special issue . . . every two years on a topic explicitly related to race and its relationship to additional axes of oppression, including gender, sexuality, disability, nationality, and language" ("DHQ Statement on Black Lives Matter and Structural Racism"). Economic precarity is not mentioned as one of the additional axes of oppression, which is especially striking given that the economic fallout from Covid-19 affects people of color more severely (Aratani and Rushe).

19. Graduate students across the United States have been forming unions or going on strike at unprecedented levels with no commentary or support from DH organizations.

BIBLIOGRAPHY

Abramovitz, Mimi. "Economic Crises, Neoliberalism, and the U.S. Welfare State: Trends, Outcomes and Political Struggle." In *Global Social Work,* edited by Carolyn Noble, Helle Strauss, and Brian Little, 225–40. Sydney: Sydney University Press, 2014, https://doi.org/10.2307/j.ctv1fxm2q.20.

Allington, Daniel, Sarah Brouillette, and David Golumbia. "Neoliberal Tools (and Archives): A Political History of Digital Humanities." *Los Angeles Review of Books.* May 1, 2016, https://lareviewofbooks.org/article/neoliberal-tools-archives-political-history-digital-humanities/.

Alpert-Abrams, Hannah. *Academic Job Support Network.* Accessed September 15, 2020, https://academicjobmarketsupportnetwork.hcommons.org/author/halperta/.

Alpert-Abrams, Hannah, Heather Froehlich, Amanda Henrichs, Jim McGrath, and Kim Martin. "Postdoctoral Laborers Bill of Rights." *Humanities Commons.* April 2019, https://hcommons.org/deposits/item/hc:26741/.

Aratani, Lauren, and Dominic Rushe. "African Americans Bear the Brunt of Covid-19's Economic Impact." *The Guardian.* April 28, 2020, https://www.theguardian.com/us-news/2020/apr/28/african-americans-unemployment-covid-19-economic-impact.

Barnett, Fiona, Zach Blas, Micha Cárdenas, Jacob Gaboury, Jessica Marie Johnson, and Margaret Rhee. "QueerOS: A User's Manual." In *Debates in the Digital Humanities 2016,* edited by Matthew K. Gold and Lauren F. Klein, 50–59. Minneapolis: University of Minnesota Press, 2016.

Battershill, Claire, Helena Clarkson, Matthew N. Hannah, Illya Nokhrin, Elizabeth Willson Gordon, and Nicola Wilson. "Digital Critical Archives, Copyright, and Feminist Praxis." *Archival Science.* February 14, 2022, https://doi.org/10.1007/s10502-021-09384-x.

Benjamin, Ruha. *Race after Technology: Abolitionist Tools for the New Jim Code.* Medford, Mass.: Polity, 2019.

Berens, Kathi Inman. "DH Adjuncts: Social Justice and Care." In *Debates in the Digital Humanities 2019,* edited by Matthew K. Gold and Lauren F. Klein. Minneapolis: University of Minnesota Press, 2019.

Bianco, Jamie. "This Digital Humanities Which Is Not One." In *Debates in the Digital Humanities 2012,* edited by Matthew K. Gold, 96–112. Minneapolis: University of Minnesota Press, 2012.

Boyles, Christina, Anne Cong-Huyen, Carrie Johnston, Jim McGrath, and Amanda Phillips. "Precarious Labor and the Digital Humanities." *American Quarterly* 70, no. 3 (September 29, 2018): 693–700, https://doi.org/10.1353/aq.2018.0054.

Brennan, Sheila. "Time to Start Preparing 2021 DHAG Proposals." National Endowment for the Humanities. September 17, 2020, https://www.neh.gov/blog/time-start-preparing-2021-dhag-proposals.

Brouillette, Sarah. "Computational Literary Studies: Participant Forum Responses." April 1, 2019, https://critinq.wordpress.com/2019/04/01/computational-literary-studies-participant-forum-responses-3/.

Cahn, Naomi. "COVID-19's Impact on Women of Color." *Forbes.* May 10, 2020, https://www.forbes.com/sites/naomicahn/2020/05/10/mothers-day-and-covid-19s-impact-on-women-of-color/?sh=633d969941ac.

Carlson, Scott. "Over Time, Humanities Grads Close the Pay Gap with Professional Peers." *Chronicle of Higher Education.* February 7, 2018, https://www.chronicle.com/article/over-time-humanities-grads-close-the-pay-gap-with-professional-peers/.

Cecire, Natalia. "Introduction: Theory and the Virtues of Digital Humanities." *Journal of Digital Humanities* 1, no. 1 (2011), http://journalofdigitalhumanities.org/1-1/.

Chun, Wendy Hui Kyong, and Lisa Marie Rhody. "Working the Digital Humanities: Uncovering Shadows between the Dark and the Light." *Differences* 25, no. 1 (2014): 1–25, https://doi.org/10.1215/10407391-2419985.

Chun, Wendy Hui Kyong, Richard Grusin, Patrick Jagoda, and Rita Raley. "The Dark Side of the Digital Humanities." In *Debates in the Digital Humanities 2016,* edited by Matthew K. Gold and Lauren F. Klein, 493–509. Minneapolis: University of Minnesota Press, 2016.

"COVID Black." Purdue University School of Interdisciplinary Studies. Accessed September 15, 2020, https://www.cla.purdue.edu/academic/sis/p/african-american/covid-black/index.html.

"Critical Theory." *Stanford Encyclopedia of Philosophy.* Accessed September 18, 2020, https://plato.stanford.edu/entries/critical-theory/.

Davis, Angela. *The Angela Y. Davis Reader.* Malden, Mass.: Blackwell, 1998.

"DHQ Statement on Black Lives Matter and Structural Racism." *Digital Humanities Quarterly.* Accessed September 11, 2020, http://www.digitalhumanities.org/dhq/about/about.html.

D'Ignazio, Catherine, and Lauren Klein. *Data Feminism.* Minneapolis: University of Minnesota Press, 2020.

Drucker, Johanna. "Humanistic Theory and Digital Scholarship." In *Debates in the Digital Humanities 2012,* edited by Matthew K. Gold, 85–95. Minneapolis: University of Minnesota Press, 2012.

Duggan, Lisa. *The Twilight of Equality?: Neoliberalism, Cultural Politics, and the Attack on Democracy.* Boston: Beacon Press, 2003.

Eisenstein, Zillah. *"Constructing a Theory of Capitalist Patriarchy and Socialist Feminism." Insurgent Sociologist* 7, no. 3 (1977): 3–17.

Eubanks, Virginia. *Automating Inequality: How High-Tech Tools Profile, Police, and Punish the Poor.* 1st ed. New York: St. Martin's Press, 2017.

Eubanks, Virginia. *Digital Dead End: Fighting for Social Justice in the Information Age.* Cambridge, Mass.: MIT Press, 2011.

Fish, Stanley. "The Digital Humanities and the Transcending of Mortality." *Opinionator* (blog), *New York Times.* January 9, 2012, https://opinionator.blogs.nytimes.com/2012/01/09/the-digital-humanities-and-the-transcending-of-mortality/.

Fish, Stanley. "Mind Your P's and B's: The Digital Humanities and Interpretation." *Opinionator* (blog), *New York Times.* January 23, 2012, https://opinionator.blogs.nytimes.com/2012/01/23/mind-your-ps-and-bs-the-digital-humanities-and-interpretation/.

Fish, Stanley. "The Old Order Changeth." Opinionator (blog), *New York Times.* December 26, 2011, https://archive.nytimes.com/opinionator.blogs.nytimes.com/2011/12/26/the-old-order-changeth/.

Fitzpatrick, Kathleen. *Generous Thinking: A Radical Approach to Saving the University.* Baltimore: Johns Hopkins University Press, 2019.

Flanders, Julia. "Time, Labor, and 'Alternate Careers' in Digital Humanities Knowledge Work." In *Debates in the Digital Humanities 2012,* edited by Matthew K. Gold, 292–308. Minneapolis: University of Minnesota Press, 2012.

Friedman, Milton. *Capitalism and Freedom.* Chicago: University of Chicago Press, 1982.

Friedman, Milton. "Liberalism, Old Style." In *The Indispensable Milton Friedman,* edited by Lanny Ebenstein. Washington, D.C.: Regenery, 2012.

Friedman, Milton. "Neo-Liberalism and Its Prospects." In *The Indispensable Milton Friedman,* edited by Lanny Ebenstein. Washington, D.C.: Regenery, 2012.

Fukuyama, Frances. *The End of History and the Last Man.* New York: Free Press, 1992.

Gallon, Kim. "Making a Case for the Black Digital Humanities." In *Debates in the Digital Humanities 2016,* edited by Matthew K. Gold and Lauren F. Klein, 42–49. Minneapolis: University of Minnesota Press, 2016.

Gray, Mary, and Siddharth Suri. *Ghost Work: How to Stop Silicon Valley from Building a New Global Underclass.* New York: Houghton Mifflin, 2019.

"Grow with Google." Accessed September 18, 2020, https://grow.google/.

Grusin, Richard. "The Dark Side of Digital Humanities: Dispatches from Two Recent MLA Conventions." *Differences* 25, no. 1 (2014): 79–92.

Hall, Stuart. *Selected Writings on Marxism*, ed. Gregor McLennan. Durham: Duke University Press, 2021.

Hartmann, Heidi. "The Unhappy Marriage of Marxism and Feminism: Towards a More Progressive Union." In *An Anthology of Western Marxism,* edited by Roger Gottlieb. Oxford: Oxford University Press, 1989.

Harvey, David. *A Brief History of Neoliberalism.* Oxford: Oxford University Press, 2005.

Heller, Henry. *The Capitalist University.* London: Pluto Books, 2016.

Henry, John F. "The Historic Roots of the Neoliberal Program." *Journal of Economic Issues* 44, no. 2 (2010): 543–50.

Horkheimer, Max. *Critical Theory: Selected Essays.* Translated by Matthew J. O'Connell and Others. New York: Continuum, 1972.

Horowitz, Juliana Menasce, Ruth Igielnik, and Rakesh Kochhar. "Trends in U.S. Income and Wealth Inequality." *Pew Research Center Social & Demographic Trends Project.* January 9, 2020, https://www.pewsocialtrends.org/2020/01/09/trends-in-income-and-wealth-inequality/.

"How Data Analysis Can Enrich the Liberal Arts." *The Economist.* December 19, 2020, https://www.economist.com/christmas-specials/2020/12/19/how-data-analysis-can-enrich-the-liberal-arts?fbclid=IwAR1WJWLrtW1Nm-nHqd1v350iENE74gLettJJrVjhwdvl5UJVcu7QAWm-1uw.

Hunt, Joshua. *University of Nike: How Corporate Cash Bought American Higher Education.* Brooklyn: Melville House, 2018.

Hunter, John. "The Digital Humanities and 'Critical Theory': An Institutional Cautionary Tale." In *Debates in the Digital Humanities 2019,* edited by Matthew K. Gold and Lauren F. Klein, 188-94. Minneapolis: University of Minnesota Press, 2019.

Irani, Lilly. "Justice for Data Janitors." *Public Books.* January 15, 2015, https://www.publicbooks.org/justice-for-data-janitors/.

James, C. L. R. *At the Rendezvous of Victory: Selected Writings.* London: Allison and Busby, 1984.

Jameson, Fredric. *The Seeds of Time.* New York: Columbia University Press, 1994.

Jones, Josh. "How the CIA Funded and Supported Literary Magazines Worldwide while Waging Cultural War against Communism." *Open Culture.* October 27, 2017, https://www.openculture.com/2017/10/how-the-cia-funded-supported-literary-magazines-worldwide-while-waging-cultural-war-against-communism.html.

Kelsky, Karen. "The Professor Is In: Stranded on the Academic Job Market This Year?" *Chronicle of Higher Education.* April 17, 2020, https://www.chronicle.com/article/the-professor-is-in-stranded-on-the-academic-job-market-this-year/.

Keralis, Spencer. "Disrupting Labor in the Digital Humanities; or, The Classroom Is Not Your Crowd." In *Disrupting the Digital Humanities,* edited by Dorothy Kim and Jesse Stommel, 273–94. Santa Barbara, Calif.: Punctum Books, 2018.

Kirsch, Adam. "Technology Is Taking over English Departments." *The New Republic.* May 2, 2014, https://newrepublic.com/article/117428/limits-digital-humanities-adam-kirsch.

Klein, Lauren F., and Matthew K. Gold. "Digital Humanities: The Expanded Field." In *Debates in the Digital Humanities 2016,* edited by Matthew K. Gold and Lauren F. Klein, ix–xvi. Minneapolis: University of Minnesota Press, 2016.

Koul, Parul, and Chewy Shaw. "Opinion—We Built Google. This Is Not the Company We Want to Work For." *New York Times.* January 4, 2021, https://www.nytimes.com/2021/01/04/opinion/google-union.html.

Kramnick, "The Humanities after Covid-19." *Chronicle of Higher Education.* July 23, 2020, https://www.chronicle.com/article/the-humanities-after-covid-19.

Kremer, Rich. "UW-Stevens Point Eliminating 6 Majors in Humanities to Address Budget Shortfall." *Wisconsin Public Radio.* November 12, 2018, https://www.wpr.org/uw-stevens-point-eliminating-6-majors-humanities-address-budget-shortfall.

Krugman, Paul. "Opinion—The Trump Tax Cut: Even Worse than You've Heard." *New York Times.* January 1, 2019, https://www.nytimes.com/2019/01/01/opinion/the-trump-tax-cut-even-worse-than-youve-heard.html.

Liu, Alan. "Where Is Cultural Criticism in the Digital Humanities?" In *Debates in the Digital Humanities 2012,* edited by Matthew K. Gold, 490–510. Minneapolis: University of Minnesota Press, 2012.

Lohr, Steve. "Dickens, Austen and Twain, through a Digital Lens." *New York Times.* January 26, 2013, https://www.nytimes.com/2013/01/27/technology/literary-history-seen-through-big-datas-lens.html.

Losh, Elizabeth, and Jacqueline Wernimont, eds. *Bodies of Information: Intersectional Feminism and Digital Humanities.* Minneapolis: University of Minnesota Press, 2018.

Luxton, Meg, and Kate Bezanson. *Social Reproduction Feminist Political Economy Challenges Neo-Liberalism.* Montreal: McGill-Queen's University Press, 2006.

Lye, Colleen, and Christopher Nealon, eds. *After Marx: Literature, Theory, and Value in the Twenty-First Century.* Cambridge: Cambridge University Press, 2022.

Mandell, Laura. "Gender and Cultural Analytics: Finding or Making Stereotypes?" In *Debates in the Digital Humanities 2019,* edited by Matthew K. Gold and Lauren F. Klein, 3–26. Minneapolis: University of Minnesota Press, 2019.

"Margaret Thatcher: A Life in Quotes." *The Guardian.* April 8, 2013, sec. Politics, https://www.theguardian.com/politics/2013/apr/08/margaret-thatcher-quotes.

Marowski, Steve. "Adrian College to Eliminate Humanities Departments, Faculty Jobs." *Mlive.Com.* September 1, 2020, https://www.mlive.com/news/ann-arbor/2020/08/adrian-college-to-eliminate-humanities-departments-faculty-jobs.html.

Marx, Karl. *Capital Volume 1.* Translated by Ben Fowkes. New York: Penguin, 1992.

Marxist Literary Group. "MLG-ICS: Transition." Accessed January 20, 2022, http://www.marxistliterary.org/mlsics-2022.

Modernist Archives Publishing Project. Accessed September 25, 2020, https://www.modernistarchives.com/.

Moran, Gwen. "No, Humanities Degrees Don't Mean Low Salaries." *Fortune.* December 10, 2019, https://fortune.com/2019/12/10/humanities-degree-jobs-salaries/.

Myers, Valerie. "Edinboro University Considers Academic Cuts." *Pittsburgh Post-Gazette.* August 28, 2020, https://www.post-gazette.com/news/education/2020/08/28/Edinboro-University-considers-academic-cuts/stories/202008280087.

"NEH Grant Data, 2010–2019." Accessed September 24, 2020, https://catalog.data.gov/dataset/neh-grant-data-2010-2019-csv-3f3dd.

Newfield, Christopher. *The Great Mistake: How We Wrecked Public Universities and How We Can Fix Them.* Baltimore: Johns Hopkins University Press, 2016.

Nimble Tents Toolkit. Accessed September 25, 2020, https://nimbletents.github.io/.

Noble, Safiya Umoja. *Algorithms of Oppression: How Search Engines Reinforce Racism.* New York: New York University Press, 2018.

Noble, Safiya Umoja. "Toward a Critical Black Digital Humanities." In *Debates in the Digital Humanities 2019,* edited by Matthew K. Gold and Lauren F. Klein, 27–35. Minneapolis: University of Minnesota Press, 2019.

O'Brien, Sara. "Zuckerberg Tops Vanity Fair's 'Disrupters' List." *CNN Business.com.* September 8, 2015, https://money.cnn.com/2015/09/08/technology/vanity-fair-new-establishment-list/index.html.

Olssen, Mark. "Neoliberal Competition in Higher Education Today: Research, Accountability and Impact." *British Journal of Sociology of Education* 37, no. 1 (2016): 129–48, https://doi.org/10.1080/01425692.2015.1100530.

O'Regan, John P., and John Gray. "The Bureaucratic Distortion of Academic Work: A Transdisciplinary Analysis of the UK Research Excellence Framework in the Age of Neoliberalism." *Language and Intercultural Communication* 18, no. 5 (2018): 533–48, https://doi.org/10.1080/14708477.2018.1501847.

Potter, Claire. "A Hacker in Every History Department: An Intelligent Radical's Guide to the Digital Humanities." *Radical Teacher* 99 (2014): 43–53.

Reed, Adolph L. *W. E. B. Du Bois and American Political Thought: Fabianism and the Color Line.* Oxford: Oxford University Press, 1997.

Risam, Roopika. "Beyond the Margins: Intersectionality and the Digital Humanities." *Digital Humanities Quarterly* 9, no. 2 (2015), http://digitalhumanities.org:8081/dhq/vol/9/2/000208/000208.html.

Risam, Roopika. *New Digital Worlds: Postcolonial Digital Humanities in Theory, Praxis, and Pedagogy.* Chicago: Northwestern University Press, 2018.

Risam, Roopika, and Kelly Baker Josephs, eds. *The Digital Black Atlantic.* Minneapolis: University of Minnesota Press, 2021.

Robinson, Cedric J. *Black Marxism: The Making of the Black Radical Tradition.* Rev. and updated 3rd ed. Chapel Hill: University of North Carolina Press, 2020.

Roman, Richard, and Edur Velasco Arregui. "The NAFTA Consensus." *Jacobin.* August 24, 2017, https://jacobinmag.com/2017/08/nafta-trans-pacific-partnership-trump-free-trade.

Rowbotham, Sheila. "Socialism and Feminism." *New Statesman (1957)* 98, no. 2531 (1979): 428.

Roy, Arundhati. *War Talk.* Cambridge: South End Press, 2003.

Scheinfeldt, Tom. "Why Digital Humanities Is 'Nice.'" In *Debates in the Digital Humanities 2012,* edited by Matthew K. Gold, 59–60. Minneapolis: University of Minnesota Press, 2012.

Schmidt, Benjamin. "Theory First." *Journal of Digital Humanities* 1, no. 1 (2011), http://journalofdigitalhumanities.org/1-1/.

Shapiro, Alison. "Why Women and People of Color Are Vulnerable to COVID-19." *CARE.* July 28, 2020, https://www.care.org/news-and-stories/news/5-reasons-why-u-s-women-and-people-of-color-are-especially-vulnerable-to-covid-19/.

Sitaraman, Ganesh. "The Collapse of Neoliberalism." *The New Republic.* December 23, 2019, https://newrepublic.com/article/155970/collapse-neoliberalism.

Stefano, Christine Di. "Marxist Feminism." *The Encyclopedia of Political Thought,* Wiley Online Library (September 15, 2014): 2305–10,

Streeck, Wolfgang. *How Will Capitalism End?* London: Verso, 2017.

Svensson, Patrick. "Envisioning the Digital Humanities." *Digital Humanities Quarterly* 6, no. 1 (2012), http://www.digitalhumanities.org/dhq/vol/6/1/000112/000112.html.

Thompson, Dorothy. "The Personal and the Political." *New Left Review* 1, no. 200 (1993): 87.

Torn Apart/Separados. Accessed September 15, 2020, https://xpmethod.columbia.edu/torn-apart/volume/2/.

"Update on the Impact of Covid-19." The New School. April 24, 2020, https://www.newschool.edu/covid-19-impacts/.

Visionary Futures Collective. "About the Project." Accessed September 15, 2020, https://visionary-futures-collective.github.io/covid19/project-team.

Wang, Brian. "COVID-19 Is Accelerating the Destruction of the Old University Models." *NextBigFuture.Com.* August 10, 2020.

Wark, McKenzie. *Capital Is Dead: Is This Something Worse?* London: Verso, 2019.

Wark, McKenzie. *A Hacker Manifesto.* Cambridge, Mass.: Harvard University Press, 2004.

Žižek, Slavoj. "Don't Act. Just Think." Big Think. YouTube video, 6:33. Accessed January 9, 2020, https://www.youtube.com/watch?v=IgR6uaVqWsQ.

PART I][*Chapter 2*

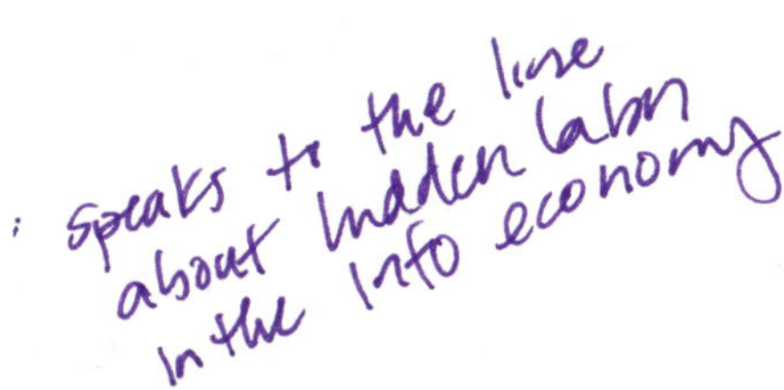

All the Work You Do Not See: Labor, Digitizers, and the Foundations of Digital Humanities

ASTRID J. SMITH AND BRIDGET WHEARTY

Before the Stanford Literary Lab could perform large-scale quantitative analysis on thousands of nineteenth-century novels, someone had to do the work of digitizing those volumes. Before the *William Blake Archive* could "provide unified access to major works of visual and literary art that are highly disparate, widely dispersed, and more and more often severely restricted as a result of their value, rarity, and extreme fragility," teams of specialists had to do the hands-on labor of creating stable digital images of those works ("About the Archive"). As a field, digital humanities is fueled by the labor of many individuals who are largely absent from the conversations about the research that their labor yields. Digitization, Melissa Terras argues, is "the bedrock of both digital library holdings and digital humanities research"—and therein may lie the problem ("Digitisation and Digital Resources," 47). Bedrock is the foundation on which everything stands, but it is generally hidden from view. Unless you are traveling at the edges of cliffs, or deliberately observing the terrain, it can be easy to overlook—until you take the opportunity to explore it face-to-face.

We, the coauthors of this chapter, work on either side of the hierarchical divide that separates digitizer from digital humanist. Astrid J. Smith has worked as a digitization specialist for over a decade, performing image capture on rare and fragile archival materials at Stanford University Libraries. Bridget Whearty is a professor of English, working at the intersections of medieval, literary, and information studies. We met in 2013 when Bridget was a postdoctoral fellow in the library department where Astrid works. Fascinated by the ways that medieval writers' concerns about textual transformation reemerge in digitization labs, Bridget asked to follow a manuscript through the digitization workflow. Astrid agreed to take Bridget on as one of two lab assistants involved in the digitization of a fifteenth-century book of hours, a type of late-medieval prayer book.[1] Working together, we observed how combining our perspectives—digitization specialist and artist, medievalist and book historian—created a more holistic approach to the digital object we were making, changing how we both thought about the work that went into its creation.

Others have noted the importance of bridging this gap between perspectives. For instance, Ashley Reed, one of the project managers for the Blake Archive between 2007 and 2013, argues, "To create a truly critical digital humanities we should acknowledge and foreground the interdependencies between different kinds of labor and recognize the ecologies of creativity that make both art and scholarship possible" (38). Inspired by her call and by our own collaborations, we seek to foster more open communication between humanities researchers and digitizers. We argue that a more critically engaged digital humanities (DH) must reach into the dark rooms in which the digitization teams work—too often out of sight and out of mind. We begin by analyzing how DH has vacillated between erasing and valuing digitizers' labor. Next, we give an overview of a digitization workflow, highlighting the wide variety of skills and labor needed to produce high-quality outputs. Finally, we suggest some solutions to the erasure of digitizers in DH. Ultimately, we argue that digitizers' invisible labor is the foundation on which DH has been built—and that a more rigorous, more just digital humanities should take seriously the labor, and laborers, on which DH depends.

Digitization and DH: The 1950s to 2000s

Digitization takes place in a wide range of settings, and there are many names for the digitization process. Most involve some combination of keywords like "digital," "imaging," "capture," "preservation," "reformatting," "high-resolution," "cultural heritage," and "photography." The media addressed through these processes include bound and unbound texts, photographs, charters, paintings and cartographic objects, film, video, piano rolls, and artifacts. There are numerous names for the people who perform this work: "digitization specialist," "imaging technician," "lab assistant," and "scanning operator" to offer just a few examples. For our purposes, we use "digitizer" as a shorthand for the workers who, in many different roles, remediate analog materials into digitally accessible formats.

As a term, "digitization" maintains a fairly stable definition across disciplines. In DH, Melissa Terras defines it as "the conversion of an analogue signal or code into a digital signal or code" ("Digitisation and Digital Resources," 47). The Society for American Archivists and the Federal Agencies Digital Guidelines Initiative (FADGI) define it similarly as "the process of transforming analog material into binary electronic (digital) form, especially for storage and use in a computer," and "the process of translating analog signal data emanating from an object (light or sound) into a digitally encoded format" (Pearce-Moses, 120; FADGI). Many different kinds of media and labor fit under this umbrella: photography, microfilm scanning, 3D scanning, multispectral imaging, sound and video reformatting, and more (Terras, "Digitisation and Digital Resources," 47–48). The word *digitization* thus covers many types of tools, tasks, and specializations. Given this diversity of inputs and outputs, one important takeaway is that having some experience using a flatbed scanner or personal camera does not mean that you understand the complexities of formal digitization workflows—any more than filing family documents makes one a trained archivist. The key point here is that digitization is complex work, and many digital humanists may only have very basic knowledge of what it entails and encompasses.

We believe that terms that are conventionally used in humanities scholarship obfuscate digitization and what it produces. Thus, throughout this chapter, we refrain from using terms like "digital surrogate," as we feel that they allude to a kind of Indiana Jones idol-swap that misrepresents the core purpose that motivates cultural heritage imaging professionals. While a digitized object may stand in for, in some respects, a physical one that is absent or inaccessible, digital objects accrue value distinct from their analog exemplars, derived from their own external references, makers, supporting infrastructure, functionality, and the things that we are able to do with them. Ultimately, we wish to emphasize that digital objects are distinct from physical ones—and that how, why, and by whom they are made necessarily affects the research that they enable.

While the makers of the original objects generally are credited for their labor in bibliographic attribution, the creators of those objects' digital counterparts are generally not. They are invisible to end-users. "Invisible labor" is the focus of a rich tradition of scholarship and activism. Initially, the term referred to unpaid—gendered—domestic labor, including cooking, cleaning, and caring for dependents, but it was expanded to include overlooked and undervalued classed and raced labor, occurring within and outside domestic spaces (D'Ignazio and Klein, 178). In *Invisible Labor: Hidden Work in the Contemporary World,* the term is used to explore how invisibility affects retail workers, hypersexualized waitstaff, unpaid interns, engineers, computer workers, and virtual receptionists. It is argued that "work that is not seen is not valued, either symbolically or materially," and furthermore, "when their work is erased, the workers themselves are sometimes rendered invisible as well" (Crain, Poster, and Cherry, 5, 3). But virtual work, as the scholars and activists we build on have demonstrated, is still work. Within the academy, labor performed by librarians and archivists has also, often, been unseen and undervalued, and librarians and archivists have produced significant scholarship recording and challenging these disturbing institutional practices.[2]

Like these other forms of invisible labor, both outside and within academia, digitization largely takes place out of sight, and it has until recently gone unseen in the early histories of humanities computing. Roberto Busa's *Index Thomisticus,* for instance, is an important genesis for DH (Busa and associates). But it is a genesis story in which many of the hands-on workers have remained unseen, their invisibility enforced by the project's design, supported by numerous founding father/lone genius narratives, and aided by rhetorical flourishes in which the labor of the many belongs to the project's principal investigator (PI) alone. Reminiscing about the *Index,* Busa uses the first-person singular to both describe work that he himself did and to claim ownership of the work done by a much larger team:

> In 1954 *I* started my own punching and verifying department; two years later *I* established my own processing department, but employing large computers always in IBM premises. That year *I* started a training school for keypunch operators. . . . Their training was in punching and verifying our texts. . . . This school continued until 1967, when *I* completed the punching of all my texts. (Busa, 85, emphasis added)

In fact, the keypunch operators did the hands-on labor of turning more than 15,600,000 words in eight languages and five alphabets into standardized computer-readable form (Busa, 85). But they are invisible in this project history and in the description of Busa's *Index* in the 1974 report "Computers and the Medievalist" (Bullough, Lusignan, and Ohlgren, 393–95). Indeed, until Julianne Nyhan and Melissa Terras began their project of recovery in the 2010s, the contributions of these women to the early history of digital humanities were overlooked (Terras and Nyhan). Their names had been lost.

Not all those involved in early digitization were equally invisible. Although Busa's typically young and female keypunch operators were elided, other digitizers on other projects received attention—even acclaim—for bringing digitization into humanities research. In 1972, researchers at the California Institute of Technology and at NASA's Jet Propulsion Lab began collaborating, using what they called "a new technology derived from computer-processing of spacecraft pictures" to photograph and read previously illegible writing in a fifteenth-century manuscript (Benton, Gillespie, and Soha, 40, 47–48). Those experiments are credited with being partially responsible for John F. Benton's 1985 MacArthur Award (MacArthur Fellows Program). Arguably, this is the work of digitization made visible and honored as cutting-edge scholarship. But the distribution of credit and rewards remains imbalanced. Who did the work of object handling, camera configuration, image capture, and post-processing? Was it John Benton, Alan Gillespie, James Soha, some unnamed technician(s)? Benton alone won the "genius grant"; but what of his collaborators?

Unequal distribution of credit notwithstanding, there was a time during the 1980s and the 1990s when digitization was considered scholarly research in and of itself. In 1997, for example, the journal *Computers and the Humanities* published an article on the digitization of the Aberdeen Bestiary (Beavan, Arnott, and McLaren). But around the turn of the millennium, the place of digitization within humanities computing changed. Melissa Terras pinpoints the late 1990s and early 2000s as the period when digitization became perceived as "less a scholarly endeavor within itself, and more of a standard means to provide information to a wider audience" ("The Rise of Digitization," 14). This reframing of what counts as scholarship put digitizers in an uncomfortable position with regards to digital humanities. On the one hand, digitizers' work was invaluable, as it remains today. Writing in 2004 in *A Companion to Digital Humanities,* Marilyn Deegan and Simon Tanner argue, "Understanding the capture processes for primary source materials is essential for humanists intending to engage in digital projects" (Deegan and Tanner). On the other hand, the volume containing Deegan and Tanner's essay coined a new name for the discipline that enforced a boundary between DH and digitization. According to the field's origin stories, the name "digital humanities" was invented "to shift the emphasis away" from what one version calls "*simple* digitization" and another calls "*mere* digitization" (Kirschenbaum, 5; Fitzpatrick, 12–13). We do not believe these adjectives were selected as a deliberate slight to digitizers. Rather, we suspect that this separation instinct grows from the fact that, at around the same time that digitization was being reclassified from scholarly activity to information service, digital humanists were working to prove that DH itself was scholarship, *not* service (Warwick). At the time, separating DH from digitization likely felt like a matter of prestige—and survival. But, as Patrik Svensson writes, "What seems uncontroversial from an internal perspective can be exclusionary from an outside perspective" (Svensson). There is tremendous technological expertise and intellectual and artistic work involved in digitization, and it is insulting to digitizers to reduce that labor to "mere digitization" or "digital photocopying." As Natalia Cecire argues, "gestures that consolidate professional legitimacy also name those actors who are and are not to be regarded as legitimate" (Cecire). Whether or not it was their deliberate intent, these stories of the genesis of "digital humanities" *are* exclusionary, keeping digitizers beyond the edges of the field, even as that field benefits substantially from their uncredited labor.

Digitization and DH: The 2010s

It is on this foundation of devaluing of digitizers' labor that the edifice of twenty-first-century digital humanities stands. To be sure, powerful arguments are occasionally made about the importance of digitization and the intellectual and physical labor it entails. In the 2012 book *Digital_Humanities,* the authors classify digitization among "the basic building blocks of digital activity" and argue that "designing and building digital projects depend on knowledge of these fundamentals" (Burdick, Drucker, Lunenfeld, and Schnapp, 17). But in general, these calls for revaluation were overshadowed by more-heated arguments about coding, making, hacking, and yacking that rocked DH in the mid-2010s (Ramsay; Nowviskie 2016). Digitization was largely excluded from these arguments about and examples of valuable, intellectual digital labor.

Also in the 2010s, ethical and transparent labor grew as areas of DH research and practice. In addition to Terras and Nyhan's studies of the punch card workers contributing to the *Index Thomisticus,* Alan Galey offered a corrective to DH "founding father" narratives, praising Teena Rochfort Smith as "the Ada Lovelace of the digital humanities" (effectively claiming Rochfort Smith as kin to the nineteenth-century mathematician now celebrated as a foremother of modern computing), and naming Rochfort Smith's experimental visualization of textual variation in *Hamlet* as "a kind of late Victorian paper computer" (Galey 2015; Galey 2014, 26). Gabrielle Dean highlighted Henriette Avram, the mid-twentieth-century autodidact computer programmer behind the revolutionary data standardization initiative MARC (MA-chine Readable Cataloging). Lisa Nakamura analyzed gendered and racialized labor performed by Navajo women in early electronics manufacture. Katrina Anderson, Pamela Andrews, Spencer Keralis, and the coauthors of "A Student Collaborator's Bill of Rights" and "Postdoctoral Laborers Bill of Rights" critiqued DH labor practices exploiting students and early career researchers (Anderson et al.; Di Pressi et al.; Keralis; Keralis and Andrews; Alpert-Abrams et al.). And an impressive community of scholars including Roopika Risam and Safiya Umoja Noble foregrounded DH's connections to exploitative labor conditions, particularly in the Global South. Within this efflorescence of scholarship, digitizers have begun to be somewhat visible, largely through studies on the digitizers—often women of color—of Google Books (Zeffiro; Thylstrup; Hoffmann and Bloom; Losh). This is an important step forward. But Google Books is not the only (or even the main) digital resource for humanities research. Digitizers working in academic libraries, museums, and other cultural heritage institutions still receive little attention from the colleagues whose research builds on their labors.

Claire Warwick argues that it is "worth bearing in mind that the digital humanities developed as part of service departments as well as academic ones, especially in libraries and computing services. In the past as in the present, the profession simply could not manage without these information professionals. But that does not mean they are always held in high regard by those they serve" (Warwick). We contend that a similar dynamic holds between digital humanists and digitizers. When we do honor digitization as foundational labor, we tend to do it only when those workers are retired or dead. But the work of digitization is ongoing. Some of the laborers that DH depends on *are* indeed retired or deceased. Others are on the same campuses as major digital humanities centers, operating out of sight and out of mind—but also just down the hall.

Behind the Curtain: Workflow, Roles, Craft

Part of making digitization and digitizers more visible involves understanding how materials get from physical to digital form. These materials may seem to "magically appear" on our servers and screens—but it is skilled labor, not magic, that brings them there. Digital humanists can take the initiative to better understand digitization by learning the paths of production.

The work begins with *someone* having an idea for a digitization project. Those *someones* can range from a researcher wanting support for a specific project to a curator seeking to digitize an entire analog collection. That request sets off a chain of labor outlays, requiring many workers in many roles (Figure 2.1). Digitizers will need to meet with various stakeholders to clarify the project, repeatedly asking questions such as "What are the goals for this project? What are the deadlines? Are there particularly fragile items you're concerned about?" The answers help determine what kinds of labor—and therefore, who—will be part of this digitization. Put another way, digitization is never just the work of digitizers. From the first step, it involves skilled workers in a number of institutional roles: conservators, curators, catalogers and metadata specialists, production coordinators, project managers, who all work closely with the digitizers (Figure 2.2).[3]

The goals of a specific project, balanced with the lab's own evolving best practices, will shape what gets imaged. For example, if a requester wants a collection of 1940s Turkish movie posters digitized for an online exhibit, the blank backs of the posters might not be photographed. By contrast, if a rare books curator presents a request on behalf of a book history professor for a twelfth-century codex to be digitized for a paleography course, every aspect of the book may be imaged, including binding, fore-edges, and blank flyleaves. Digitizers bring their own goals and expertise into these negotiations, and the finalized digital objects are shaped by both the initial requester's goals and the values of the digitization department. For instance, the initial digitization request for the Jarndyce Single-Volume Nineteenth-Century Novel Collection specified that only the pages containing text needed to be digitized because the requesters were interested in using the books' content for textual analysis.[4] Digitizers and curators, however, determined that there was added value in digitizing the books' covers and blank pages. Variations in what end-users see on their screens should not be read as evidence of digitizers' lack of thought about analog exemplars but as signs of real human labor: negotiations between the immediate researcher needs and the needs of the future, the sweeping desires of requesters and the realities of production.

At any given time, a large lab's work queue might include a few large, long-term projects that involve digitizing hundreds of objects over many years; some smaller projects that might only take months or weeks of work to finish; and several "one-off" requests, such as a batch of medieval charters for a class project or a Sanskrit palm-leaf manuscript for research. The work is practiced and routinized, but no two projects are exactly alike. Part of the craft of digitizers, thus, is applying collective experiences to emerging needs. Because digitization often involves working with fragile and culturally significant objects, there is always a tension between doing things safely, accurately, and efficiently. Enacting these seemingly contradictory modes, Astrid notes, brings to mind the motto adopted by early Venetian master printer Aldus Manutius: "make haste slowly" (*festina lente*).

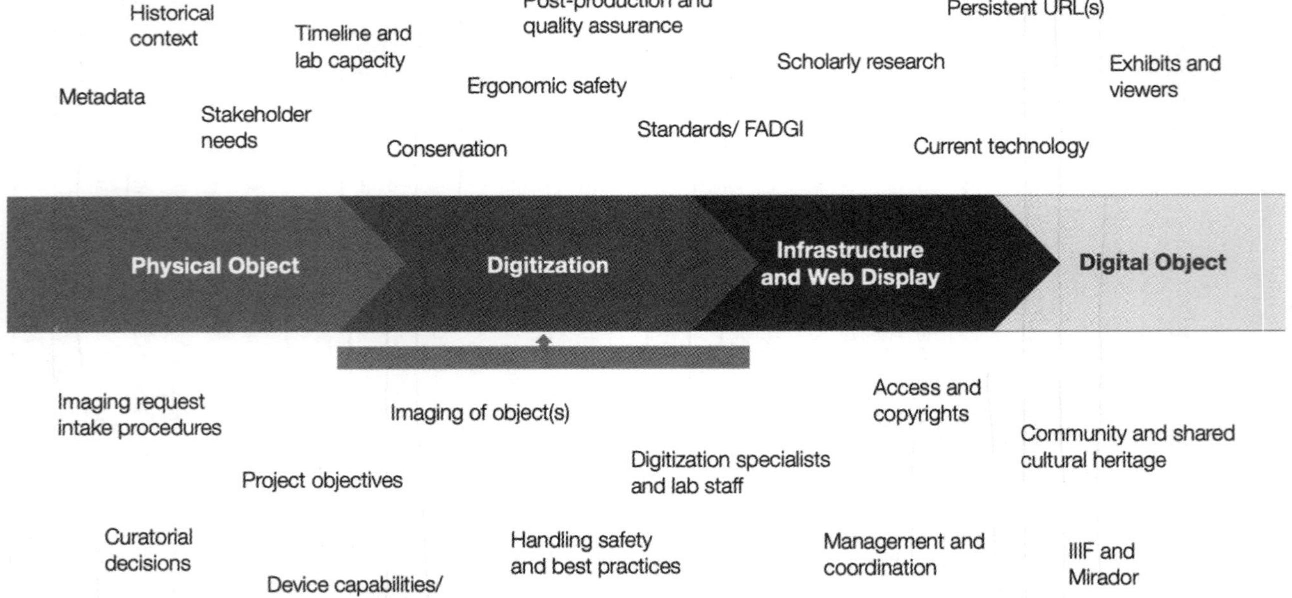

Figure 2.1. Workflow diagram depicting where the digitization process fits between physical and digital objects, and the elements on which it depends. Image by Astrid J. Smith.

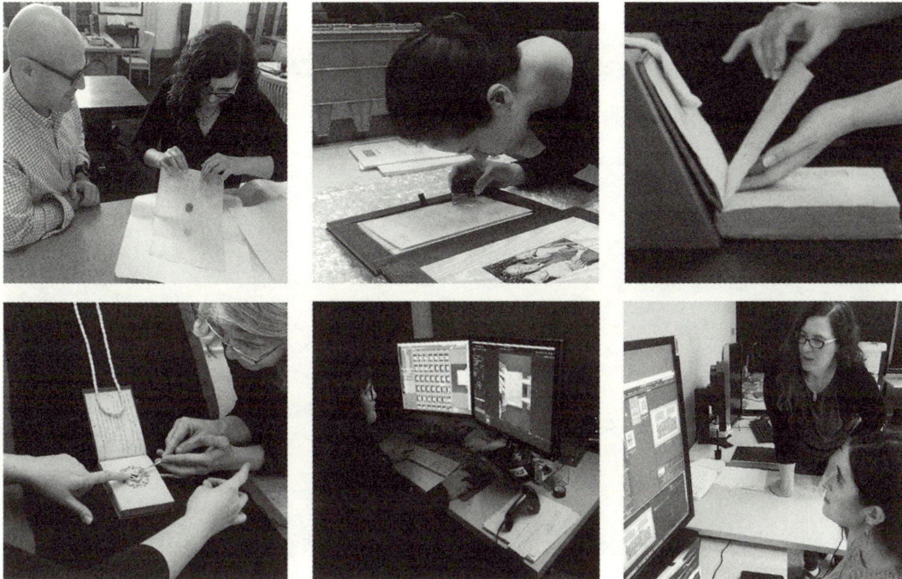

Figure 2.2. Digitization work, left to right, and top to bottom: *Assessment:* Rare books curator Benjamin Albritton and Astrid J. Smith discuss an object; digitization coordinator and specialist Linda Lam measures details in an object to determine resolution requirements. *Handling and imaging:* Astrid turns a page while imaging a rare book; Astrid and head of conservation Kristen St. John handle an object together; *Postproduction:* Lab staff member Micaela Go reviews image files; Astrid and lab staff member Claire Bonnepart discuss image crops. Photograph credits: 1 by Everardo G. Rodriguez; 2 by Astrid J. Smith; 3 is a still image from the tour video "Stanford University Libraries' Digitization Labs," YouTube, 3:48, October 31, 2012, https://youtu.be/RdLcrNeWjIs; 4 by Doris Cheung; 5 by Astrid J. Smith; and 6 by Linda Lam.

Additional aspects of the unseen labor of digitization involve preparing imaging stations, calibrating equipment, and evaluating image quality. Digitizers frequently invent new techniques, responding to the unique materialities of analog objects. For example, to digitize *Septistellium Meditationis* (a codex made over the thirteenth and fourteenth centuries), Astrid designed a tool to safely hold the books' leaves in place without obscuring any visual information (see Figure 2.3).[5] Developing and refining imaging methodology, customizing equipment for physical needs of the object, and tailoring technologies for different capture objectives are all additional unseen labors performed by digitizers.

After image capture, there are many more steps in the digitization workflow, each requiring workers trained in very specific skills. Images might need to be digitally reassembled, cropped, straightened, and aligned. They must undergo quality assurance: *Are the images in focus? Is everything that was requested present?* Who does this work varies between studios. In some labs, post-processing and quality-control checks are performed by lab assistants working under the supervision of an imaging specialist or project coordinator. In others, the same person who performs

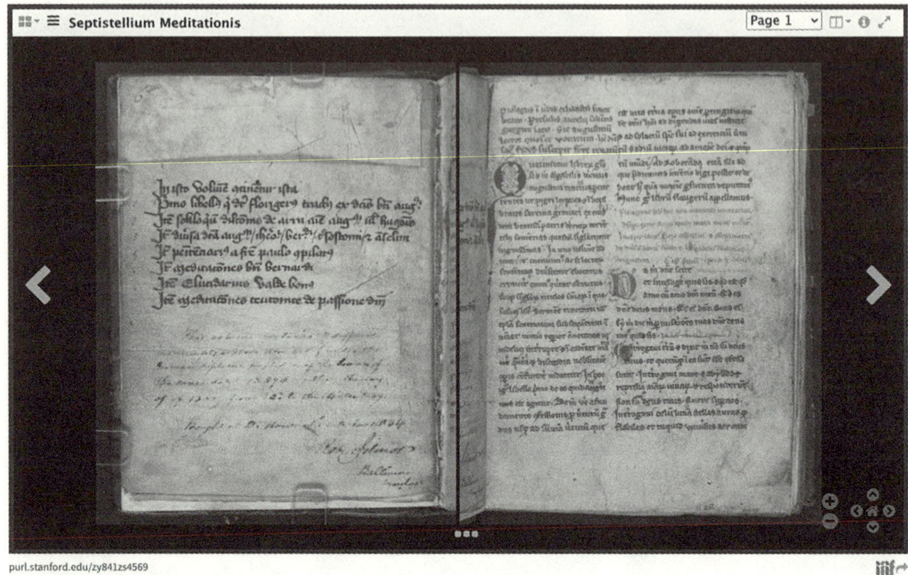

Figure 2.3. Holding aids placed on the hardcopy manuscript, Stanford, Stanford University Libraries, Department of Special Collections, Manuscript Collection MSS CODEX 1126, *Septistellium Meditationis.* Digitization by Astrid J. Smith, with Kirsten St. John, head of conservation, providing handling assistance and lab staff member Micaela Go performing postproduction and quality control, January 2018. Image courtesy of the Department of Special Collections, Stanford University Libraries.

image capture does post-processing labor, too. What does not vary is that this work requires unflagging attention to process and detail on the part of the digitizers. Some might be tempted to dismiss this stage of the workflow as particularly tedious, and they are not wrong that it is grueling and difficult. But that just makes the feat of sustained attention all the more impressive. As Daniel Wakelin has argued about medieval scribes, the absence of visible error does not mean the absence of labor. In fact, it means precisely the opposite.

This is not an exhaustive portrait of the digitization workflow at the studio where Astrid works, nor can it describe the intricacies of every digitization lab. But across significant differences between studios and projects one thing remains constant. The kind of professional digitization on which DH depends is never quick, unthinking labor. From initial requests and object assessment to file delivery and long-term preservation, digitization is a collective craft, a rich collaboration that takes place long before datasets and image galleries appear on end-users' screens.

Better Practices: Making Digitizers' Labor Visible

The most obvious solution to the widespread erasure of digitizers at the heart of DH is for digital humanists to actively partner with digitizers. This is how the authors of this chapter met, and we strongly encourage digital humanists to engage in similar collaborations. That said, we understand that partnerships like ours are not always feasible. Not all digital humanists may want to collaborate closely with digitizers or to try the work of digitization. Moreover, not all digitizers will want to meet or work closely with humanities researchers. But some digitizers do wish to, and they should not be excluded from DH's proverbial big tent.

Here are several ways that digital humanists can include digitizers and foreground their labor:

- The lowest bar to clear is to not take credit for digitizers' work. Unless one is doing all the stages of digitization alone, invented out of whole cloth and without consultation by digital imaging and archiving specialists, one should never write "I digitized X." (After all, shared standards for academic integrity have a name for passing off another's work as one's own—plagiarism.) In essence, don't be Busa. Be Josephine Miles (Buurma and Heffernan).
- When giving a lecture, publishing scholarship, or using a dataset that builds on digitizers' labor, don't thank "the miracle of twenty-first century technology" for making your work possible. Thank the real people who did the work. Include statements like "Digitized by workers in X lab." Or name them outright, if the team members consent to be publicly named.
- When you work with digitizers, write to their supervisors to explicitly identify and praise their contributions.
- Extend DH's existing models of collaborative credit-sharing to digitizers. Naming digitization teams in grant applications, extending project responsibility statements to include the digitizers, and adding digitizers to lists of people associated with a DH center's research are logical extensions of community values already in play. As Spencer Keralis, Rafia Mirza, and Maura Seale assert elsewhere in this volume (see Chapter 20), documentation "makes labor visible. It is a means unto itself and not just a means to an end."
- Social media posts may warrant more abridged acknowledgment. One can even use emoji to represent different kinds of work in digitization—pairing the camera pictograph with the name or the handle of the photographer; the hand with the name of the object handler; a computer with the names of people involved in post-processing and quality assurance.
- In published projects, consider creating visualizations that show where your data came from, who made it, and the workflow involved in its production. This is a clever application of traditional DH methods *and* an extension of principles argued for by Catherine D'Ignazio and Lauren Klein: "Showing the work is crucial to ensure that undervalued and invisible labor receives the credit it deserves" (201).
- Offer end-users guidance for how to include digitizers within citations. This actively dismantles the persistent hierarchy of visible digital humanists

> versus invisible digitizers. The goal should be to avoid corporate ownership claims—for example, "Digitized by Google"—that erase human digitizers and their labor.[6]

Although many of our examples are framed for scholars requesting digitization, we believe that they also hold for researchers using materials that have been digitized decades earlier. While the practices we suggest above are about seeing and valuing the living people who do the work, they are also about acknowledging the work in general—whether that work has happened recently or is decades old, as is the case for the digital scans of microfilms of Early English Books Online (EEBO), originally made in the 1940s (Mak, 1517–18). And in cases where the digitization team cannot be identified then your citation can mark that inability to give named credit for work done.

Ultimately, all of these possible interventions can be summarized as *give credit where credit is due.* Cultivate a sense of humility and respect when it comes to other people and their work. Have awareness about what jobs entail. Understand power and hierarchy. Notice when you have privilege because of your role. Consider how you can use your privilege to promote equity.

Preserving the Record for Foundational Labor: The Case for Digital Scribal Colophons

Across centuries and media, book creators sometimes include paratextual production notes called "colophons," preserving invaluable data for future users. In modern books, these colophons can include information about printing companies, book designers, typefaces, and paper. In medieval books, they might contain the names of scribes, illuminators, funders, and dates of a manuscript's creation. Medieval colophons also give scribes space to comment on how they feel about their work—from offering thanks that their labor is done, to complaining about the quality of their tools, to addressing future users—telling us how we can repay their labors by remembering their names, pains, and needs. Bridget argues that these past copying practices offer models for a better future. Making digital scribal colophons standard in digitization could create similar possibilities for digitizers' voices to be woven into the digital objects they create, helping mitigate the problematic erasure of digitizers.

There are public-facing models of these kinds of digital scribal colophons. For instance, building on the tradition of scientific notebooks, Cultural Heritage Imaging in San Francisco has developed a protocol that makes it possible to log and analyze the steps of a digitizer. This protocol, called the Digital Lab Notebook (DLN), collects and manages data through the life cycle of a digital object, capturing context metadata such as the equipment used, locations, documents, stakeholders, and rights (see Figure 2.4). Importantly, the DLN is flexible. Users can customize

Figure 2.4. Conceptual illustration of the Digital Lab Notebook. Users input information into DLN about imaging projects to produce Linked Open Data. Image courtesy of Cultural Heritage Imaging.

input fields, adding specific context metadata about imaging teams, roles, and personnel. It can also be extended to include an Open Researcher and Contributor ID (ORCID ID) for individual workers, offering the possibility of linking an individual digitizer's body of work together, across different projects and institutions. This kind of meticulous public record-keeping acknowledges the fact that imaging specialists might work on different projects at different institutions during their careers and that those projects can gain meaning by being linked together.

Bridget would also note that maintaining records of who did what work, when—including who worked on what digitization—preserves DH's own disciplinary history. Writing about the Corpus of Electronic Texts (CELT), Beatrix Färber meticulously identifies project workers by role and name. Among CELT's funded PhD students, Färber names Julianne Nyhan, who went on to make visible previously invisible digitizers in early DH (519 n.9). Similarly, Matthew K. Gold recalls that his "first experience as a DHer was working as a grad student in the digitization lab of the Alderman Library Special Collections Department at the University of Virginia."[7] In a discipline where many early career researchers work in a variety of roles in DH, including scanning and digitization, preserving the contributions of digitizers is not just an issue of ethical labor. It is also about historiography. Who we work with profoundly shapes how we see, think, and the work that we go on to do.

Accurately recording who does what for digital projects—including digitization—provides an essential record for understanding the past, present, and future of digital humanities.

Fostering Community

There are also informal community-building activities that can enrich collaboration between digital humanists and digitizers (although it is also important to be aware that these opportunities might not be possible, or desirable, for some workers). From paleography seminars to brown-bag DH lunches, researchers organizing campus events can invite local digitizers to join them. Instructors can request tours of digitization labs, where possible. Digitizers can be invited to speak at DH centers.[8] Researchers can arrange for digitizers to attend and formally present at important conferences. Digitizers can invite researchers using their work to attend end-of-project celebrations or major milestones. For Astrid, these kinds of more collegial, more equal interactions with humanities researchers have profoundly enriched her thinking and her day-to-day work. Ultimately, dialogues between digitizer-maker and humanist-end-user empowered her to pursue graduate work and write a master's thesis that develops a conceptual framework for evaluating objects, from initial idea through any of their subsequent states, whether mental, physical, or digital.[9] For Bridget, studying the labor that goes into digitization has given her a more rigorous understanding of digital objects themselves and launched a new career trajectory. Much of her recent research is dedicated to manuscript digitization.[10]

In 2011, Bethany Nowviskie called for more generously crediting collaboration in digital scholarship:

> Might the listing of multiple collaborators as coauthors of electronic resources, scholarly papers, and digital project reports make imaginative presentation, committed preservation, and enthusiastic promotion of work in the humanities a shared enterprise at the personal level? Can we imagine collaborations in which not only faculty members but also named librarians, administrators, non-tenure-track researchers, and technologists begin to feel a private as well as professional stake? (Nowviskie 2011, 170)

As we believe our collaboration shows, digitizers already *do* feel personal as well as professional stakes in how the fruits of their labors are used. What we need to develop is more of a stake in each other. The authors of "Information Maintenance as a Practice of Care" put it well:

> We care for our fellow maintainers by connecting with them as caring people, and by trying to foster their personal and professional growth. Maintenance work is generally underpaid, devalued, and resistant to easy measures

> of success and progress. We attempt to demonstrate our care by advocating for the recognition and fair compensation of the labor of information maintainers and the value their work can produce. (Acker et al., 17)

A thank-you, a conversation, an invitation to coffee, a request to collaborate on a talk or paper—these practices can render digitizers less invisible in the digital humanities, raising the potential for richer cross-pollination and transforming and enriching the work that we all do.

Images and datasets do not just appear out of thin air: They are made by people. Digitizers might do this work for only a few months or years, or they might devote their entire careers to cultural heritage imaging. Unlike an ever-growing list of publications and presentations on an academic researcher's curriculum vitae, digitizers' labors are often anonymously contributed to vast digital asset management repositories, where they are then made available for browsing, research, investigation, and inspiration. Pressing back on the invisibility, seeing the work that goes unseen, is the beating heart of humanities research.

NOTES

Much like digitization, this essay grew from rich collaborations beyond what traditional author credits can show. We thank, in particular, Christine Huhn, head of imaging at UC Berkeley Libraries; Hannah Frost, assistant director for digital services at Stanford University Libraries; Amy Gay, digital scholarship librarian at Binghamton University; and Nancy Um, disciplinary faculty at Binghamton University. Gratitude is also owed to Astrid's colleagues in the Digital Production Group and Digital Library Systems and Services, including Claire Bonnepart, Tony Calavano, Peter Crandall, Katharine Dimitruk, Micaela Go, Chris Hacker, Dinah Handel, Linda Lam, Alexander Nguyen, Laura Nguyen, Andria Olson, Kazuko Onaga, John Pearson, Tanya Scutelnic, Meagan Trott, and Wayne Vanderkuil.

1. Stanford, Stanford University Libraries, Department of Special Collections, Manuscript Collection, MSS CODEX M0379. "Horae Beatae Mariae Virginis," Stanford Digital Repository, accessed January 29, 2020, https://purl.stanford.edu/gp178js1323.

2. For the classic study, see Harris. See also Drabinski, Geraci, and Shirazi;, eds.; Brown; Caswell; and Shirazi.

3. In many instances, the digitizer may also be serving as a production coordinator and project manager, as well as performing or overseeing imaging work.

4. "Jarndyce Single-Volume Nineteenth-Century Novel Collection, 1823–1914," Stanford University Libraries, accessed January 29, 2020, https://searchworks.stanford.edu/view/jt466yc7169. The Jarndyce Collection was accessioned into the Stanford Literary Lab's corpus in 2016. Mark Algee-Hewitt, email message to Bridget Whearty, January 13, 2020.

5. Stanford, Stanford University Libraries, Department of Special Collections, Manuscript Collection, MSS CODEX 1126. "Septistellium Meditationis," Stanford Digital Repository, accessed October 31, 2020, https://purl.stanford.edu/zy841zs4569.

6. For one model, see Aster.
7. Matthew Gold, personal communication with authors, October 6, 2020.
8. See, for instance, Smith and Treharne.
9. See Smith.
10. See Whearty, *Digital Codicology.* See also Whearty, "Adam Scriveyn in Cyberspace."

BIBLIOGRAPHY

"About the Archive." *Stanford Literary Lab.* Accessed January 10, 2020, https://litlab.stanford.edu/.

Acker, Amelia, Hillel Arnold, Juliana Castro, Scarlet Galvan, Patricia Hswe, Jessica Meyerson, Bethany Nowviskie, Monique Lassere, Devon Olson, Mark A. Parsons, Andrew Russell, Lee Vinsel, and Dawn J. Wright. "Information Maintenance as a Practice of Care: An Invitation to Reflect and Share." The Maintainers and Educopia Institute. June 17, 2019, https://doi.org/10.5281/zenodo.3251131.

Alpert-Abrams, Hannah, Heather Froehlich, Amanda Henrichs, Jim McGrath, and Kim Martin. "Postdoctoral Laborers Bill of Rights." *Humanities Commons.* April 2019, https://dx.doi.org/10.17613/7fz6-ra81.

Anderson, Katrina, Lindsey Bannister, Janey Dodd, Deanna Fong, Michelle Levy, and Lindsey Seatter. "Student Labour and Training in Digital Humanities." *DHQ: Digital Humanities Quarterly* 10, no. 1 (2016), http://www.digitalhumanities.org/dhq/vol/10/1/000233/000233.html.

Aster, Cathy. "Creating and Managing Pages: About Page." Exhibits Documentation: A Guide to Building Spotlight at Stanford Exhibits. Stanford University Libraries. Accessed January 29, 2020, https://exhibits.stanford.edu/exhibits-documentation/feature/about-page.

Beavan, Iain, Michael Arnott, and Colin McLaren. "Text and Illustration: The Digitisation of a Medieval Manuscript." *Computers and the Humanities* 31, no. 1 (1997): 61–71.

Benton, John F., Alan R. Gillespie, and James M. Soha. "Digital Image-Processing Applied to the Photography of Manuscripts with Examples Drawn from the Pincus MS of Arnald of Villanova." *Scriptorium* 33, no. 1 (1979): 40–55.

Brown, Susan. "Delivery Service: Gender and the Political Unconscious of Digital Humanities." In *Bodies of Information: Intersectional Feminism and Digital Humanities,* edited by Elizabeth Losh and Jacqueline Wernimont, 261–85. Minneapolis: University of Minnesota Press, 2018.

Bullough, Vern L., Serge Lusignan, and Thomas H. Ohlgren. "Computers and the Medievalist." *Speculum* 49, no. 2 (1974): 392–402.

Burdick, Anne, Johanna Drucker, Peter Lunenfeld, Todd Presner, and Jeffrey Schnapp. *Digital_Humanities.* Cambridge, Mass.: MIT Press, 2012.

Busa, Roberto. "The Annals of Humanities Computing: The Index Thomisticus." *Computers and the Humanities* 14 (1980): 83–90.

Busa, Roberto, and associates. "Index Thomisticus." Web edition by Eduardo Bernot and Enrique Alarcón. Accessed October 17, 2022, https://www.corpusthomisticum.org/it/index.age.

Buurma, Rachel Sagner, and Laura Heffernan. "Search and Replace: Josephine Miles and the Origins of Distant Reading." *The Discipline* (blog). April 11, 2018, https://modernismmodernity.org/forums/posts/search-and-replace.

Caswell, Michelle. "'The Archive' Is Not an Archives: On Acknowledging the Intellectual Contributions of Archival Studies." *Reconstruction* 16, no. 1 (2016), https://escholarship.org/uc/item/7bn4v1fk.

Cecire, Natalia. "Introduction: Theory and the Virtues of Digital Humanities." *Journal of Digital Humanities* 1, no. 1 (Winter 2011), http://journalofdigitalhumanities.org/1-1/introduction-theory-and-the-virtues-of-digital-humanities-by-natalia-cecire/.

Crain, Marion G., Winifred R. Poster, and Miriam A. Cherry. "Conceptualizing Invisible Labor." In *Invisible Labor: Hidden Work in the Contemporary World,* edited by Marion G. Crain, Winifred R. Poster, and Miriam A. Cherry, 3–27. Oakland: University of California Press, 2016.

Dean, Gabrielle. "The Shock of the Familiar: Three Timelines about Gender and Technology in the Library." *DHQ: Digital Humanities Quarterly* 9, no. 2 (2015), http://www.digitalhumanities.org/dhq/vol/9/2/000201/000201.html.

Deegan, Marilyn, and Simon Tanner. "Conversion of Primary Sources." In *A Companion to Digital Humanities,* edited by Susan Schreibman, Ray Siemens, and John Unsworth, Malden, Mass.: Blackwell, 2004.

Di Pressi, Haley, Stephanie Gorman, Miriam Posner, Raphael Sasayama, and Tori Schmitt, with Roderic Crooks, Megan Driscoll, Amy Earhart, Spencer Keralis, Tiffany Naiman, and Todd Presner. "A Student Collaborators' Bill of Rights." *UCLA HumTech.* June 8, 2015, http://cdh.ucla.edu/news/a-student-collaborators-bill-of-rights/.

D'Ignazio, Catherine, and Lauren Klein. *Data Feminism.* Cambridge, Mass.: MIT Press, 2020.

Dombrowski, Quinn (@quinnanya). "Today in #GenerousThinking: still digesting yesterday's 'Project Management and Ethical Collaboration for Humanists' class. . . ." Twitter, January 17, 2020, https://twitter.com/quinnanya/status/1218226000439283715.

Drabinski, Emily, Aliqae Geraci, and Roxanne Shirazi, eds. "Introduction." In "Labor in Academic Libraries," edited by Emily Drabinski, Aliqae Geraci, and Roxanne Shirazi. Special issue, *Library Trends* 68, no. 2 (2019): 103–9.

FADGI. "Digitization." *Glossary: Federal Agencies Guidelines Initiative.* Accessed October 28, 2020, http://www.digitizationguidelines.gov/term.php?term=digitization.

Färber, Beatrix. "The Fortunes of CELT." In *Clerics, Kings, and Vikings: Essays on Medieval Ireland in Honor of Donnchadh Ó Corráin,* edited by Emer Purcell, Paul MacCotter, Julianne Nyhan, and John Sheehan, 518–22. Dublin: Four Courts Press, 2015.

Fitzpatrick, Kathleen. "The Humanities, Done Digitally." In *Debates in Digital Humanities 2012,* edited by Matthew K Gold, 12–15. Minneapolis: University of Minnesota Press, 2012.

Galey, Alan. *The Shakespearean Archive: Experiments in New Media from the Renaissance to Postmodernity.* Cambridge: Cambridge University Press, 2014.

Galey, Alan. "Teena Rochfort Smith: The Ada Lovelace of the Digital Humanities." *The Floating Academy* (blog). January 23, 2015, https://floatingacademy.wordpress.com /2015/01/23/teena-rochfort-smith-the-ada-lovelace-of-the-digital-humanities/.

Harris, Roma M. *Librarianship: the Erosion of a Women's Profession.* Norwood, N.J.: Ablex Publishing, 1992.

Hoffmann, Anna Lauren, and Raina Bloom. "Digitizing Books, Obscuring Women's Work: Google Books, Librarians, and the Ideologies of Access." *Ada: A Journal of Gender, New Media, and Technology* 9 (2016), https://adanewmedia.org/2016/05/issue9 -hoffmann-and-bloom/.

Keralis, Spencer D. C. "Disrupting Labor in Digital Humanities; or, The Classroom Is Not Your Crowd." In *Disrupting the Digital Humanities,* edited by Dorothy Kim and Jesse Stommel, 277–99. Santa Barbara, Calif.: Punctum Books, 2018.

Keralis, Spencer D. C., and Pamela Andrews. "Labor." In *Digital Pedagogy in the Humanities: Concepts, Models, and Experiments,* edited by Rebecca Frost Davis, Matthew Gold, Katherine Harris, and Jentery Sayers. New York: Modern Language Association, 2020, https://digitalpedagogy.hcommons.org/keyword/Labor.

Kirschenbaum, Matthew. "What Is Digital Humanities and What's It Doing in English Departments?" In *Debates in the Digital Humanities 2012,* edited by Matthew K. Gold, 3–11. Minneapolis: University of Minnesota Press, 2012.

Losh, Elizabeth. *Virtualpolitik: An Electronic History of Government Media-Making in a Time of War, Scandal, Disaster, Miscommunication, and Mistakes.* Cambridge, Mass.: MIT Press, 2009.

MacArthur Fellows Program. "John Benton, Medieval Historian, Class of 1985." Last modified January 1, 2005, https://www.macfound.org/fellows/246/.

Mak, Bonnie. "Archaeology of a Digitization." *Journal of the Association for Information Science and Technology* 65, no. 8 (2014): 1515–26.

Nakamura, Lisa. "Indigenous Circuits: Navajo Women and the Racialization of Early Electronic Manufacture." *American Quarterly* 66, no. 4 (December 2014): 919–41.

Noble, Safiya Umoja. "Toward a Critical Black Digital Humanities." In *Debates in the Digital Humanities 2019,* edited by Matthew K. Gold and Lauren F. Klein. Minneapolis: University of Minnesota Press, 2019, https://dhdebates.gc.cuny.edu/read /untitled-f2acf72c-a469-49d8-be35-67f9ac1e3a60/section/5aafe7fe-db7e-4ec1-935f -09d8028a2687#ch02.

Nowviskie, Bethany. "On the Origin of 'Hack' and 'Yack.'" In *Debates in the Digital Humanities 2016,* edited Matthew K. Gold and Lauren F. Klein. Minneapolis: University of Minnesota Press, 2016, https://dhdebates.gc.cuny.edu/read/untitled/section/a5a2c3f4 -65ca-4257-a8bb-6618d635c49f#ch07.

Nowviskie, Bethany. "Where Credit Is Due: Preconditions for the Evaluation of Collaborative Digital Scholarship." *Profession* (2011): 169–81.

Pearce-Moses, Richard. *A Glossary of Archival and Records Terminology*. The Society of American Archivists, 2005, https://files.archivists.org/pubs/free/SAA-Glossary-2005.pdf.

Ramsay, Stephen. "On Building." In *Defining Digital Humanities: A Reader,* edited by Melissa Terras, Julianne Nyhan, and Edward Vanhoutte, 243–46. Farnham: Ashgate Publishing, 2013.

Ramsay, Stephen. "Who's In and Who's Out." In *Defining Digital Humanities: A Reader,* edited by Melissa Terras, Julianne Nyhan, and Edward Vanhoutte, 239–241. Farnham, Ashgate Publishing, 2013.

Reed, Ashley. "Craft and Care: The Making Movement, Catherine Black, and the Digital Humanities." *Essays in Romanticism* 23 (2016): 23–38.

Risam, Roopika. "The Stakes of Digital Labor in the Twenty-First-Century Academy: The Revolution Will Not Be Turkified." In *Humans at Work in the Digital Age: Forms of Digital Textual Labor,* edited by Shawna Ross and Andrew Pilsch, 239–49. Abingdon: Routledge, 2020.

Shirazi, Roxanne. "Reproducing the Academy: Librarians and the Question of Service in the Digital Humanities." *Roxanne Shirazi* (blog). July 15, 2014, https://roxanneshirazi.com/2014/07/15/reproducing-the-academy-librarians-and-the-question-of-service-in-the-digital-humanities/.

Smith, Astrid J. *Transmediation and the Archive: Decoding Objects in the Digital Age.* Leeds: Arc Humanities Press, 2023.

Smith, Astrid J., and Elaine Treharne. "Digitizing Textual Objects: Best Practice, Worst Practice." Presentation at the Center for Spatial and Textual Analysis (CESTA), Stanford University, January 30, 2018.

Svensson, Patrik. "Beyond the Big Tent." In *Debates in the Digital Humanities 2012,* edited by Matthew K. Gold. Minneapolis: University of Minnesota Press, 2012, https://dhdebates.gc.cuny.edu/read/untitled-88c11800-9446-469b-a3be-3fdb36bfbd1e/section/38531431-5bd6-4eb1-95f5-fa49c025322d#ch04.

Terras, Melissa. "Digitisation and Digital Resources in the Humanities." In *Digital Humanities in Practice,* edited by Claire Warwick, Melissa Terras, and Julianne Nyhan, 47–70. London: Facet Publishing, 2012.

Terras, Melissa. "The Rise of Digitization: An Overview." In *Digitisation Perspectives,* edited by Ruth Rikowski, 3–20. Rotterdam: Sense Publishers, 2011.

Terras, Melissa, and Julianne Nyhan. "Father Busa's Female Punch Card Operatives." In *Debates in the Digital Humanities 2016,* edited by Matthew K. Gold and Lauren F. Klein. University of Minnesota Press, 2016, https://dhdebates.gc.cuny.edu/read/untitled/section/1e57217b-f262-4f25-806b-4fcf1548beb5#ch06.

Thylstrup, Nanna Bonde. *The Politics of Mass Digitization*. Cambridge, Mass.: MIT Press, 2019.

Wakelin, Daniel. *Scribal Correction and Literary Craft: English Manuscripts 1375–1510.* Cambridge: Cambridge University Press, 2014.

Warwick, Claire. "'They Also Serve': What DH Might Learn about Controversy and Service from Disciplinary Analogies." In *Debates in the Digital Humanities 2019,* edited by Matthew K. Gold and Lauren F. Klein. Minneapolis: University of Minnesota Press, 2019, https://dhdebates.gc.cuny.edu/read/untitled-f2acf72c-a469-49d8-be35-67f9ac1e3a60/section/015e1836-9519-4ce1-afac-984e915d1f4f#ch04.

Whearty, Bridget. "Adam Scriveyn in Cyberspace: Loss, Labor, Ideology, and Infrastructure in Interoperable Reuse of Digital Manuscript Metadata." In *Meeting the Medieval in a Digital World,* edited by Matthew Davis, Ece Turnator, and Tamsyn Mahoney-Steel, 157–202. Leeds: Medieval Institute Publications/Arc Humanities Press, 2018.

Whearty, Bridget. *Digital Codicology: Medieval Books and Modern Labor.* Redwood City, Calif.: Stanford University Press, 2022.

Zeffiro, Andrea. "Digitizing Labor in the Google Books Project: Gloved Fingertips and Severed Hands." In *Humans at Work in the Digital Age: Forms of Digital Textual Labor,* edited by Shawna Ross and Andrew Pilsch, 133–53. Abingdon: Routledge, 2020.

Right-to-Left (RTL) Text: Digital Humanists Plus Half a Billion Users

MASOUD GHORBANINEJAD, NATHAN P. GIBSON,
AND DAVID JOSEPH WRISLEY

In early 2020, digital humanist Zoe LeBlanc posted an "extremely niche tweet" reporting her surprise that the Altair visualization library correctly displayed the Arabic characters that she analyzed in her scholarship (Figure 3.1).[1] To be sure, the set of digital humanities (DH) practitioners using *both* Python visualizations *and* right-to-left (RTL) scripts like Arabic might be small. But the subject is not, in fact, niche at all: Many thousands of people in the world are interested in designing data visualizations that involve Arabic characters. Furthermore, projects supporting RTL scripts have potential user bases that number in the hundreds of millions—users who read and write not only in Arabic but also in Lahnda, Urdu, Persian, Hebrew, and numerous other languages. And yet most visualization libraries and most software in general is typically designed with only one direction in mind: left-to-right (LTR). The persistent frustrations of those who read and write RTL languages in digital environments are reflected in the enormous number of GitHub bug reports, feature requests, and software patches related to "RTL" and "bidi" (bidirectional text, mixing left-to-right and right-to-left scripts). As of January 2023, a search for "RTL" turned up more than 200,000 issues and 6 million code commits, with more than 38,000 of these issues labeled as unresolved.[2]

In this chapter, we shed light on the challenges and inequities that arise when doing digital humanities work with RTL languages.[3] We argue that these challenges are not unique to DH; rather, they reflect the experience of myriad other RTL developers, content creators, and users. Digital humanists working with RTL languages must acknowledge that we share many of the same concerns with these RTL users and that ignoring their digital habitus (a term we use, following Bourdieu, to denote formative habits, attitudes, and skills in digital environments) and cultural perspectives has led to a failure to recognize our shared concerns. While the DH community should give more attention to RTL voices within DH, we make the case that sustainable solutions to the obstacles faced by RTL DHers do not rest in building

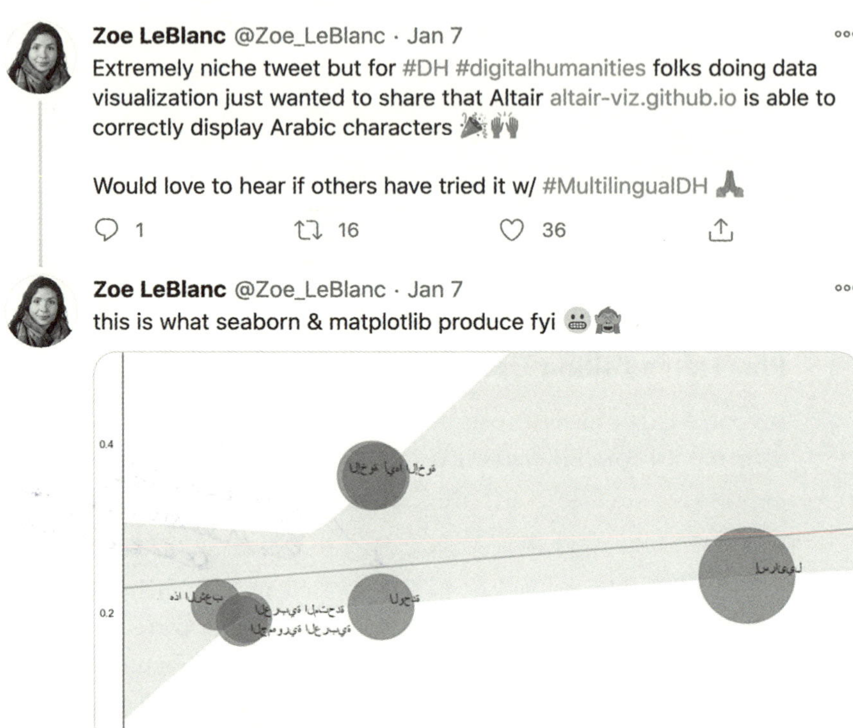

Figure 3.1. A Twitter thread discussing a novel solution for labels in the Arabic language within a statistical data visualization package, Altair.

custom DH tools or "bootstrapping" workarounds but rather in joining forces with a larger set of developers and creators outside academia to advocate for multidirectional, multiscript support in the tools we all use.[4]

So-called technical solutions for RTL languages should not be carried out in isolation from the lived, and often multilingual, realities of the societies in which these languages are used. In this chapter, we therefore think about RTL DH scholarship in the context of both its historical subject matter and its contemporary expression. That is, the context of RTL scholarship includes not only the study of ancient or historical languages in the centuries-long tradition of Orientalist scholarship but also the modern, often multilingual societies that themselves require multiscript, and multidirectional digital environments (Figure 3.2). RTL DH research, in other words, needs to contribute to DH research but also participate in digital life more broadly. Here we identify a potentially synergistic relationship between the habitus of living RTL languages, on the one hand, and digital stewardship of their heritage, on the other. To realize this relationship, we must pay attention to the way people live with RTL languages and move toward a DH practice that exists in dialogue with

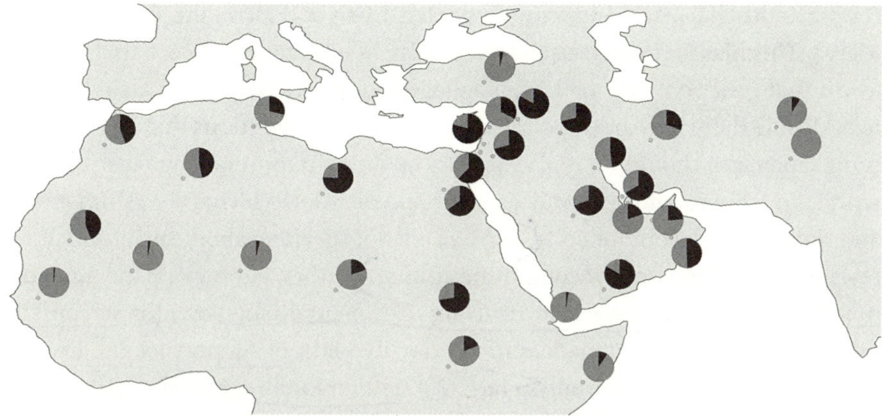

Figure 3.2. "A Map of Views of RTL text articles in Wikipedia," illustrating views of *Wikipedia* pages by script type and by country. The dark gray portion of the pie chart indicates the proportion of articles consulted, which are right to left (RTL) text, and light gray represents the proportion of left to right (LTR) text. Data source: https://stats.wikimedia.org/wikimedia/squids/SquidReportPageViewsPerCountryBreakdown.htm. Visualization by Wrisley in QGIS with Natural Earth physical land polygons. License: CC-BY-SA.

the societies they inhabit. We must include RTL DHers as experts about best practices and as strong voices in documenting the barriers they face in environments that have been, first and foremost, designed for LTR accessibility.

The argument we voice here as authors is grounded, in part, in our individual experiences. Masoud "Kasra" Ghorbaninejad was born and raised in West Asia (the "Middle East"), moved to North America for graduate studies, and has since worked in West Asia and North America in K–12, higher education, and digital humanities positions. He can understand, speak, and write in Arabic, Azeri, English, German, and Persian to varying degrees. Nathan Gibson grew up in Africa, North America, and Europe; lived in the Middle East for two years; received classical philological training in Arabic, Syriac, and Hebrew; and for the last several years has been conducting DH research in Europe on historical RTL texts. David Joseph Wrisley is a comparativist working across six European languages, Latin, and Arabic. He grew up in North America and has had extended work and research stays in Algeria, Belgium, France, Germany, and Tunisia. Since 2002, he has been residing in Arab countries, as a faculty member first in Beirut and now in Abu Dhabi, working to build digital humanities communities of practices and infrastructure. Together, we have worked in different areas of the world with research involving several languages from both contemporary and historical perspectives. While this experience informs our argument about LTR biases, it does not make our voices representative of any particular context.

The Anglocentrism of DH research is only part of a broader bias toward LTR, or LTR-centrism, stemming from the fact that English and many other languages of the postindustrial world are written from left-to-right (Fiormonte; Galina; Mahony; Meza). This bias is characterized by a persistent orientation toward tools and platforms that function well for LTR languages but poorly with RTL or bidirectional text.[5] While there have been politically provocative suggestions that LTR programming languages should be replaced with new programming languages altogether written in RTL, resulting in projects like Qalb or Noor, which use Arabic keywords and right-to-left layout for code, here we are not speaking about such fundamental revisions to the practices of computing culture.[6] Rather, our focus is the more common endeavor of creating content using RTL natural languages for screen-based display. This endeavor is made difficult due to a lack of support for the necessary tools, and, more fundamentally, a lack of attention to the problem.

In other words, RTL DH faces a *compounded* marginalization.[7] Not only does it fall outside the Anglo-American tradition of DH (whose Anglocentrism has been criticized in recent years by many continental scholars, such as Domenico Fiormonte), but it also, and more importantly, in the Western academy is not well integrated into efforts to diversify DH practices beyond English, which have tended to focus on LTR languages. Furthermore, in the countries in which the RTL languages are spoken, a deep infrastructure gap impedes the development and sustaining of DH practices (Wrisley). It is precisely this power—of Anglocentric, LTR DH practice situated in the Global North—that leads us to write this critique of LTR-centrism in English.[8]

This issue of inclusion is all the more pressing as RTL digital cultures have begun to enter into the larger global community of DH. An increasing number of DH institutes are being held in locations where RTL languages are used, such as the Digital Humanities Institute Beirut, held at the American University of Beirut, and the Winter Institute in Digital Humanities at New York University (NYU) Abu Dhabi.[9] This community is also growing through the #Right2Left workshops held at the Digital Humanities Summer Institute in Victoria, British Columbia, Canada, and transnational groups of scholars, such as the Islamicate Digital Humanities Network, which works in and between RTL societies and the West.[10] The time is ripe for forging an agenda that advocates for improving RTL access to tools through partnerships among DH scholars researching the past and present, commercial developers, and content creators in both majority RTL and majority LTR societies.

After all, solutions for RTL exist within Unicode and W3C (see the "Technical" section). Is there a way to harness the callout culture of social media and guide it directly to the software development world, encouraging solutions to the issues that many of us face, such as unreadable text display, laborious text editing, confusing page sequencing, poorly conceived web application layouts, and ungraceful translations? What are the best tactics for framing RTL (and other non-Latin script) language accessibility as a question of not only diversity, in which multiple voices are valued, but also inclusion and equity, in which there is an ethical obligation to improve the status quo, giving global colleagues a seat at the table and empowering them to do the work? We propose a three-pronged approach that examines the habitual, cultural, and technical angles of these questions in order to begin the work of change.

Habitual

RTL DH often overlooks the contemporary digital habitus of RTL cultures in favor of an emphasis on digitally archiving or computationally analyzing a textual past. But a focus on the textual past often ignores the lived expressions of RTL languages and must instead invent its own digital habitus.[11] Our idea of a digital habitus is informed by Pierre Bourdieu's definition of "habitus" as "structures constitutive of a particular type of environment" (Bourdieu, 72–95). The *environments* in this case are ones in which RTL languages are primary, and the *constituting structures* are the sets of formative habits, attitudes, and skills associated with those who use digital tools. By necessity, a digital habitus emerges gradually, formed more through scholarly habits and institutional routines than by necessity.

Bourdieu takes this habitus—what he elaborates as "systems of durable, transposable *dispositions*"—to be self-reinforcing and aligned with particular objectives. But this habitus does not necessarily intend these objectives consciously or require specific expertise to complete them. Instead, he writes, they are "collectively orchestrated" without a conductor (Bourdieu, 72). When applied to the world of DH practice, it becomes clear that the present dispositions in RTL DH emerge simply from the way digital humanists practice their craft rather than from any predefined rules or objectives (Antonijević, 36–72). But these dispositions are nevertheless misaligned with broader RTL habitus in at least two major regards: space and time.

In regard to space, the geographic foci of RTL expression—whether print publications, social media posts, app development, film production, and so on—do not align, for historical reasons, with where RTL DH is practiced. This results in what has been called "the postcolonial digital cultural record," characterized by a lack of parity between the digital cultural record of Global North and South, which Roopika Risam (3–21) sees as the "end product of neo/colonial "disruptions" within the digital cultural record."[12] During 2013 and 2014, for example, when two of the authors of this chapter were contributors to the Around DH in 80 Days project, which was designed to raise awareness of global digital humanities practice, RTL projects were lacking in the Middle East North Africa South Asia (MENASA) region.[13] The first Iranian-founded academic DH center in Iran—a country with a population of more than 81 million and the most speakers of Persian, as well as many Azeri and Kurdish speakers (all of which use RTL scripts)—was launched only in early 2018 at the University of Shiraz.[14]

This lack of alignment between the geographic foci of RTL expression and RTL DH practice causes an additional problem. Domenico Fiormonte evokes Lev Vygotsky's "cultural law of the artifact," which states that "both material and cognitive artifacts produced by humans are subject to the influence of the environment, culture, and social habits of the individual and groups that devise and make use of them." But the problem is not simply one of physical distance between those who produce DH tools and those who use them; rather, the physical distance is indicative of *remote* "environment, culture, and social habits" (Fiormonte, 438). Because RTL DH is mostly practiced far away from where RTL languages find social and cultural expression, a special, collective, and conscious effort must be made to close this gap. To do so, RTL projects must expand their focus beyond the historical textual archives that they typically explore and pay increased attention to contemporary practice in RTL cultures. The projects and those who participate in them, in turn, should have a voice in global DH conversations.

It is worth pointing out that the geographic-cultural disparity under discussion may have something to do with financial priorities, since universities in the Global North generally do not have sufficient incentive to invest in RTL infrastructure for the limited number of projects that require it. Why should institutions factor RTL support into their decisions about buying software licenses or building web applications when they will only help a small group of researchers working with contemporary materials? An arguable exception to this line of thinking may be RTL ephemera projects—for example, the International Digital Ephemera Project (IDEP) at UCLA Library, which aims to preserve content that is "ephemeral in nature and likely to be lost without proactive curation," such as newspapers, postcards, and cellphone videos. In this case, everyday RTL materials are deemed broadly relevant. Yet even something like IDEP is not truly a case of contemporary RTL habitus being supported in the Global North, because such a project only helps preserve the content for archival purposes while its producers still live and work back in their own linguistic cultures. As a consequence, the infrastructure developed for these projects does not ameliorate the underlying disparity in support of RTL knowledge production practices.

The difference between archiving materials and supporting knowledge production highlights a further temporal divergence between the dispositions of RTL DH and other RTLers. Archiving, editing, and analyzing *past* content, which is typical of DH projects, produces different digital habitus than those of the millions of RTL users producing and consuming content in the *present.* Here contemporary DH projects could play an important role in counterbalancing the weight of historical projects, but they face several obstacles that lead to vicious cycles of underinvestment.[15]

Among the most significant of these obstacles derives from our impression—difficult though it may be to support through objective measures—that research on the premodern "golden ages" of RTL cultures and languages (such as Arabic, Hebrew, Persian, and Syriac) is considered more prestigious than research on contemporary periods, which is often perceived as less remarkable or less relevant. To the extent that the disciplines studying these cultures and languages seem bent only on retrieving, restoring, and perhaps even romanticizing an "exotic" RTL heritage, RTL DH practice—with its propensity for digital editions, computational linguistics, distant reading, and databases—can sometimes act as the quantitative arm of these disciplinary agendas. Informed by such agendas, an investment of (faculty) researcher time and institutional energy in a historical project may seem to have more scholarly merit whereas, for instance, a contemporary ephemera project (such as IDEP, mentioned above) would seem to have less. Put plainly: research that does not fit into the box of "golden ages quantified" is often seen as contributing not a different kind of value but simply less value.

Regardless of whether they are perceived as a better return on scholarly investment, historical RTL projects tend to be better funded than contemporary ones. This has the effect of supporting archival activities over RTL cultural production. Over time and across institutions, this leads to the vicious circle mentioned above, in which historical and archival projects are privileged. As funding agencies support the former—"safer," more prestigious, and well established—and not the latter, they reinforce the opinion of other types of projects as unworthy of financial backing. Continually ignoring certain periods and certain types of research activities has the effect of further marginalizing voices outside the Global North—present voices that could contribute to *present* discussions.[16]

Even given the will to learn lived RTL expressions, overcoming logistical hurdles like the ones we detail below (see the "Technical" section) requires more than a change of attitude. As technological impediments to RTL research inhibit growth in the field, and therefore funding, another vicious circle ensues, as the lack of funding impedes the development of RTL-oriented technology. To break this cycle, new funding should go toward developing RTL infrastructure before results that rely on well-developed infrastructure can be expected.

The technological hurdles involved in RTL DH do not affect projects equally, of course.[17] In some cases, historical projects can benefit significantly from the kind of receptive or "read-only" infrastructure that is less dependent on the directionality of the script, even if it was originally designed to handle LTR corpora.[18] In addition, advances in optical character recognition (OCR) of non-Latin scripts (and of documents typeset with pre-1800 printing equipment) and emergent handwritten text recognition (HTR) methods have the potential to facilitate the searchability of digitized Arabic or Syriac manuscripts as much as, say, those in the Armenian alphabet.[19] Conversely, what would contribute significantly to redirecting the DH world toward an RTL-inclusive program, which may not benefit LTR projects as much, would be the creation of a "read-write" infrastructure such as bidirectional support in XML editors, which is key to producing XML-encoded RTL text.[20]

To circle back to Bourdieu's concept of "habitus," we have identified certain ways of readjusting otherwise self-reinforcing systemic dispositions in order to reconstitute the RTL DH research field. They include becoming familiar with RTL practice outside the Global North, supporting RTL projects relating to contemporary as well as historical materials, and furthering infrastructure that contributes to RTL content creation. It may also mean creating a climate among DH practitioners in which RTL scripts are embraced as a contribution rather than an edge case or problem to be solved. By adjusting our posture toward RTL DH, we can encourage projects that require RTL-LTR bidirectionality and support RTL text production in a read-write infrastructure. This posture may be less difficult to achieve than it might initially seem, since many of the obstacles we have described are largely related to funding. What's more, with the ever-evolving relationship between the "digital" and the "humanities" sides of DH, "the focus has moved away from technology as the servant of the humanities to one where our projects and other activities are of interest to and advance the research agendas of both disciplines" (Mahony, 372). Understood in this way, changing the field of DH to include living RTL cultures would undoubtedly repay the field with both a broader humanistic scope and with more robust technological advancements.

Cultural

The language situation in Arabic-speaking countries is particularly complex, illustrating the deficiencies of common assumptions about the straightforward nature of cultural translation and adaptation. Arabic is especially complicated because of its widespread usage as well as its great variety. It is spoken by more than 300 million people in more than twenty countries and reportedly claims the fifth-highest number of speakers in the world. But how we actually define Arabic is a matter of debate. It is a diglossic language with at least two distinct forms: standard written Arabic and the spoken language, which itself contains multiple national and regional varieties. These varieties pose a number of challenges for standardization in research and educational systems on their own (Bani-Khaled). In addition, in Arabic-speaking countries, as in many places in the postcolonial world, Western languages—particularly English and French—also have a presence in higher education as in everyday life and coexist with the varieties of Arabic. The resulting multilingualism manifests itself both in people's attitudes and in the choices they make regarding language in everyday life.

The digital habitus of Arabic speakers is not conditioned by language preference or by choice alone but also by the past and present availability of software and technological infrastructures (or the lack of availability, as the case may be). For example, before the availability of Arabic versions of software in the mid-1990s to early 2000s—and even after their arrival for some time—it was considered quite normal for universities, offices, and homes to possess software in a language other than Arabic.[21] This lack of localized software meant that users necessarily developed minimal literacies in a technical idiom in another language such as English or French. Moving forward to the 2020s, we find that information literacy practices have become considerably more complex. Whereas many interfaces may have been translated, how users are able to manipulate content in different languages remains a thorny problem: a native speaker of Arabic might read the news in standard Arabic on a smartphone, compose written English in Google Docs, and post on social media in a combination of English, French, and a contemporary style of Arabic written in Latin letters known as "Arabizi" (Yaghan).

There are large communities that might want their apps to reflect their multilingual digital habitus, as may be the case with, for example, Lebanese users who want to work in an English word processor interface for creating Arabic content full of glosses in English, or a Tunisian blogger who might use a French-language content management system to create bilingual, bidirectional French-Arabic content. In the realm of social media, where there is significant funding for content creation platforms, this kind of multilingual and multiscript approach is sometimes accommodated; but in the smaller-budget interface creation of the DH landscape, it is too often left out. As a result, DH is limited by what we term the "monolingual fallacy": the tacit assumption that everywhere in the world people use one language, one script, and one direction. This assumption ends up conditioning the development of software, locking in specific possibilities of handling and displaying language.

To our knowledge, RTL-native knowledge infrastructures for DH research do not yet exist. As a consequence, digital platforms developed elsewhere either must be retrofitted to accommodate RTL content or they must be "translated" into the language of the host RTL culture, or both. However, thinking of this translation as merely passing between two languages, as is often the case, is a grave simplification; instead, proper *localization*, as outlined by the World Wide Web Consortium (W3C), involves an adaptation of a system that works in one place to one that will work fully in another. Examples of DH research platforms and apps that have been (or are being) adapted to new environments include Voyant Tools, Recogito, FromthePage, and Lingscape.[22] The Free and Open Source Software (FOSS) movement is also known to use localization as a strategy for developing a global user base (Souphavanh and Karoonboonyanan). But there is a tension between this desire to make tools accessible for emergent humanities practices and the risk of cultural mistranslation that the process of localization can entail. Furthermore, the localization process can also carry with it the baggage of global knowledge inequity (Osborn, 5–16).

The creation of an Arabic-language interface to the text analysis and visualization platform Voyant Tools serves as a good case study demonstrating the insufficiency of thinking of localization as merely a transfer between two languages, as well as some of the problems associated with the lack of an *internationalization* strategy by design. Internationalization is a process related to localization, also defined by the W3C, in which software is first designed to be locale-indifferent before it is localized to meet the regional, linguistic/cultural, and technical requirements of each locale.

A few years ago, at the request of the main developers, a dozen or so language teams went to work on the terminology of the Voyant Tools interface. Voyant Tools is structured in modular fashion so that a number of widgets, each carrying out a different type of computational analysis, can be reused in different environments. With this structure in mind, the Arabic-language team, composed of Najla Jarkas and one of the authors of this chapter (Wrisley), decided to be as ecumenical as possible in naming conventions, bridging two ways of rendering foreign words. For the tool Bubbles, for example, the English was transliterated (بوبلز), but an expression more faithful to Arabic (فقاعات) was also given. This approach in introducing a foreign platform to an Arabic-speaking audience proposed a compromise perspective between those that adopt equivalences faithful to the structure and meanings of the Arabic language and those that employ more calque-like expressions taken from English.

The Arabic-language team followed this strategy throughout the platform, providing parallel equivalents, a translation of the tool's function as well as a transliteration: Workset Builder (ورك سيت بيلدر / إنشاء المكنز الجزئي), TermsRadio (ترمز راديو/عرض زمني), even the name Voyant Tools itself (فواينت تولز / ادوات فواينت). Whereas the intention was to provide diverse Voyant users with both styles—translation and transliteration—positioned prominently throughout the Arabic interface, user feedback based on the localization revealed mixed results: in the user testing phase, some found the presence of transliterated English jarring.

In the process of translating Voyant Tools, the Arabic-language team gained several insights into the challenges involved in localizing DH software. One revealing conclusion was that no amount of review and postediting of the interface could compensate for the fact that the back-end language processing of the platform is Anglophonic and, as a consequence, unable to handle basic linguistic features of Arabic—most notably the agglutinated definite article "ال" or prepositions such as "ب". In some of the visualizations, such as Mandala, Links, or Bubbles, which only use a handful of tokens at a time (as shown in Figure 3.3), words do not display correctly inside the bubbles; instead, the first letter of the Arabic word is aligned with the left edge of the bubble, causing it to drift leftward outside of the bubble. In other cases in which the frequency of words and phrases are more explicitly marked, there are more significant issues. Either a design rethink or a deep reimplementation of the tokenization system would be required for Voyant to function in Arabic as well as it does for English.

Another example of the growing pains of localization can be found in the *Programming Historian*, which in recent years has launched a project to expand its global user base by translating its tutorials into three Romance languages (Spanish, French, and Portuguese). In 2018, questions of translation and global legibility informed a prolonged debate among the journal's editorial board. Antonio Rojas-Castro outlined what he called the "American outlook" of the "Introduction to Stylometry with Python" tutorial written by François-Dominic Laramée, pointing out that some content is not easy to understand across cultures—in this case, not only between the English and Spanish languages but also between European and North

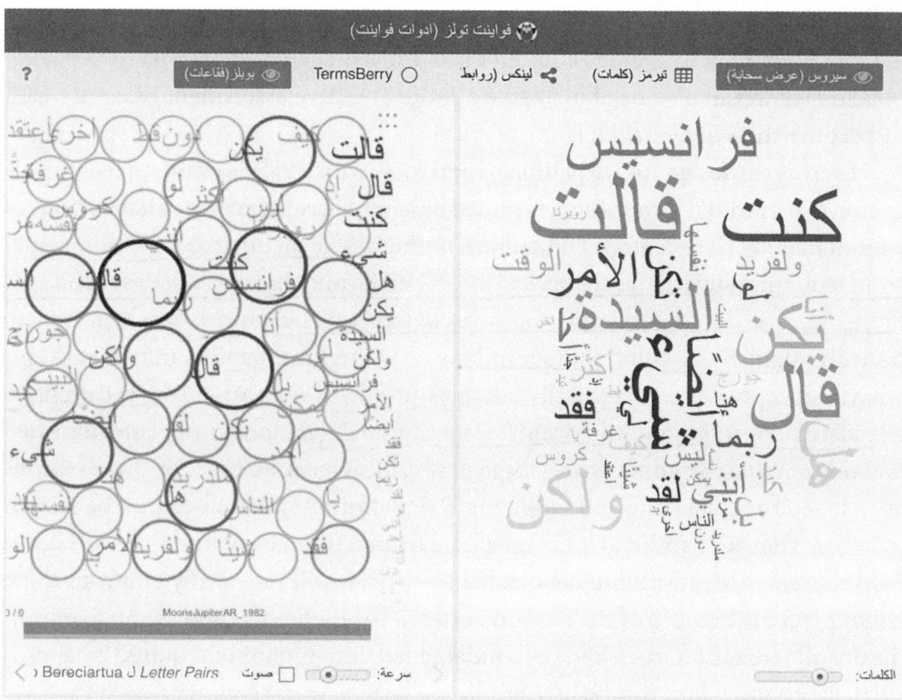

Figure 3.3. A screenshot of two widgets in the Voyant Tools Arabic-language interface demonstrating the Bubbles (left) and Cirrus (right) tools. Featured is the Arabic translation of Alice Munro's 1982 novel *The Moons of Jupiter.*

American academic cultures.[23] Furthermore, the *Programming Historian*'s tutorials often include companion datasets that may reflect linguistic and cultural biases. It follows, then, that localization must go beyond translation if the full functionality of the tutorial is to be adapted into a new cultural and linguistic environment. This approach is reflected in a new Multilingualism and Internationalization Policy that the contributors to the *Programming Historian* have now agreed to follow.

In order to avoid the issue of cultural mistranslation in future DH projects, the most obvious approach would be for the processes of internationalization and localization to follow each other in the correct order, because, as hinted earlier, internationalization is recommended as a practice that anticipates future localization (Tanev). Grounded in enterprise models of software development, internationalization can be understood as a kind of forethought in design (Yacob; Abdelali). In this way, internationalization policies might resemble other "intentional design" moves in global academic communities—for example, the adoption of collectively created and agreed-on standards for how we engage with members of our diverse communities.[24] Such standards could provide a reference point for helping us to assess the needs of our communities, since they would bring a conscious focus to the ways that global digital humanists practice their craft, allowing us to connect those practices intentionally and with care to infrastructure rather than defaulting to LTR-centrism. If we were to commit to collectively agreed-on internationalization policies, we would also be able to give a more objective assessment of equity with respect to access in global DH.

Even as we design future platforms and tools with a view toward internationalization and eventual localization, we must be careful not to bury the assumptions of a monolingual, LTR-centrist DH culture in them. The fact that localization would seem to require superficial changes to labels and layouts can mask deeper problems in the transmission of tools and platforms to target RTL cultures, ones that have to do with linguistic or cultural assumptions or with global gaps in information literacy. Conceptually and culturally complex problems may arise, which cannot be adequately addressed by Anglocentric DH thinking. DH tools and platforms often embody complex arguments and forge new critical terminology; for these reasons as well, internationalizing and localizing DH platforms and tools cannot be viewed as a mere transfer between two languages. DH practitioners working in the Global North, even as they imagine new global audiences, will repeatedly confront these issues precisely because of the tension between the theoretical and discursive complexity of humanities work and the fundamental design rethink required by appropriate internationalization plans.

Technical

Support for RTL tools and environments is an issue of inclusivity, but it can also be seen as an issue of *accessibility*. To be clear, the way different users prefer to work with RTL, LTR, or bidirectional text ought not be considered a disability, but framing the issue in this way may lead to a sufficiently complex engagement with multilingualism similar to the engagement with multimodality that scholarship on accessibility has brought about. The accessibility community has developed production tools, conventions, and feedback mechanisms that allow creators (including digital humanists) to produce accessible content more effectively and with a more deeply informed understanding of how people will engage with that content in a range of ways.[25] Similar approaches could aid RTL-friendly development if DH practitioners, software developers, social media influencers, and other tech creators would open lines of communication among each other.[26] By involving users with RTL or bidirectional preferences, they would also, ideally, create stronger and more representative communities and extend the reach of their products just as they do when they include users with visual, auditory, or other disabilities in their design process (Henry and McGee; "Internationalization").

As we are also reminded by accessibility advocates, the size of any particular user community should not be the only, or even the main, factor in decisions about inclusivity and accessibility. Yet the numbers in this case do provide one compelling reason to support RTL. As mentioned at the outset of this chapter, the number of people whose first language uses primarily a right-to-left writing system can be estimated as more than half a billion—almost 10 percent of the world's population (Gibson, 9; Eberhard, Simons, and Fennig). A lack of awareness or disregard for RTL concerns in tool development jeopardizes the growth potential of those tools from the start, both for DH-specific tools and DH-relevant tools with a broader user base. Attending to those concerns, however, will help to ensure that these tools reach more users.

The issue of RTL support in DH relates not only to the size of its potential user communities but also to the significant presence of RTL languages in world cultural heritage. Some RTL languages, such as Arabic and Persian, have a millennia-long heritage and remain in wide use in the present day; other RTL language communities, such as the Syriac-speaking community, used to be much larger than they are today; and yet other languages, such as Turkish, have undergone significant linguistic and directional change to LTR (Kirmizialtin and Wrisley). The huge volume and diverse breadth of cultural heritage material written in RTL means that a global, historically minded field of DH must necessarily involve RTL scripts in large proportion. Previously we mentioned the dilemmas that researchers, funders, and institutions face in regard to the types of RTL projects they pursue. But when it comes to technical solutions for implementing RTL support within tools, it is not usually necessary to choose between historical and contemporary considerations. What *is* important to recognize is that heritage communities, as both active users of these languages and guardians of their past, lie in the overlapping region between contemporary digital habitus and history-oriented DH. Herein lies a potential and straightforward alignment between scholars of RTL and other RTL communities: both want practicable and flexible tools they can implement in a variety of workflows.

Removing accessibility-type barriers requires both the development of standards and their implementation for features relevant to RTL languages. Much as the W3C has developed standards that make it possible for assistive screen readers to describe a page to users (e.g., the "alt" attribute for images, introduced in 1995), standards developed over the last several decades have greatly augmented support for RTL and bidirectional text. The most significant ones include Unicode bidirectional controls (introduced in 1991 and supplemented in 2013) and W3C standards for HTML and CSS.[27] To a large extent, then, the necessary technical standards already exist to create DH tools with RTL functionality. This is in contrast to the not-too-distant past, when users typing Hebrew had to accommodate the order in which the computer stored text by typing each line of Hebrew backward (Ishida, "Visual vs. Logical Ordering"). Today, with CSS3, it is even possible to represent the historical phenomenon of boustrophedon (lines with alternating directions) as text content on HTML pages.[28]

While it is undoubtedly the case that more work remains to be done on these and other technical standards, the main hurdle that remains is the continued development of tools that fail to implement these standards. Many examples could be

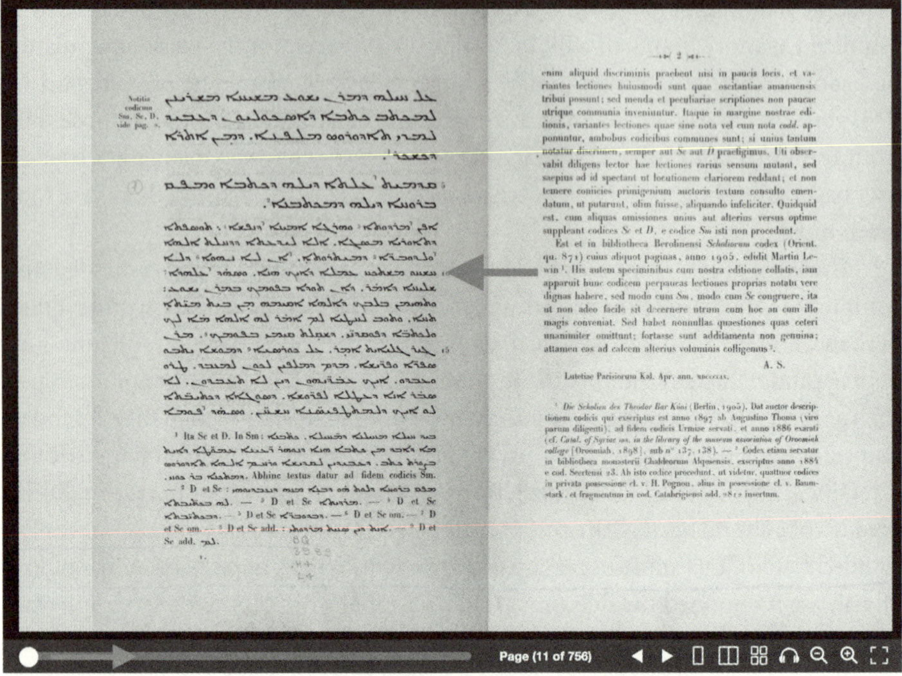

Figure 3.4. The Internet Archive BookReader interface correctly displays the beginning of a Syriac book on the right, but the progress slider is on the left. Moving the slider to the right "turns" the pages to the left. Source: "Liber scholiorum; textus," Internet Archive, June 16, 2011, https://archive.org/details/liberscholiorumt00theo/page/n10/mode/2up.

cited, ranging from the annoying to the insurmountable. For instance, in text editors, most of which support Unicode, it is often possible to enter RTL text that displays in a readable way and even to set the "base direction." But it is sometimes the case that punctuation is out of place or that selecting a desired portion of the entered text with a mouse, or trying to navigate it with the cursor, is nearly impossible.[29] Other issues have to do with user experience and user interface (UX/UI) design. For example, in RTL text, does a right-arrow button mean "forward," "backward," or simply "rightward"? This problem affects many document viewers on the web; for some scanned RTL books, the Internet Archive correctly "turns" pages to the left or right when the left- or right-arrow button or key is pressed. But as Figure 3.4 illustrates, turning the page forward to the left still moves the progress slider in the opposite direction.[30]

Additionally, metadata problems afflict many RTL and bidirectional PDFs. The responsibility for these problems may rest with the person who originally created the PDF, but rectifying them requires detailed knowledge of metadata fields that are nearly impossible to find or adjust. PDF documents have a metadata field for "left" binding or "right" binding, but in order to set this when exporting a PDF from Adobe InDesign (a common publishing workflow), users must change their

Adobe CC language settings and then install a Middle East and North Africa edition of InDesign.[31] But a single binding direction for a document may be inadequate, since many books contain both right-bound and left-bound sections. These shortcomings mean that users have to read portions of many digitized books backward, scrolling upward rather than downward to get to the next page.[32] They do not reflect the reality of multilingual cultures that are increasingly digital and screen-based.

Beyond UX/UI design confusion and opaque metadata settings, a further difficulty regarding implementing multidirectional standards is that the task often involves many-layered dependencies, so much so that one might speak of the "deep implementation" that is required throughout the entire codebase of libraries and extensions. An example of this is a recent update to the text-to-image (T2I) feature integrated into the popular DH transcription software Transkribus. Typically, a user supplied the transcribed text of a page and T2I aligned it to a page image, based on Transkribus's HTR service. But when T2I segmented RTL text into lines, it attempted to match the last (leftmost) portion of the text with the first line of the page image. The result was that the "aligned" transcription read from bottom to top and had no meaningful relationship to the page image. Once the bug had been reported, the Transkribus team needed to contact the T2I developer, who in turn implemented an RTL "extension" that is included in the Transkribus software.[33] The case of Transkribus is particularly salient, since HTR technologies have great potential for text creation with cursive Arabic-script languages that have been undersupported by more established OCR technologies. But if they are to deliver on the promise of accessibility in major world languages, developers will still face the unwieldy task of pushing for RTL support in all of their dependencies and replacing those that do not implement it.

The tweet about visualization in Python that begins this chapter (see Figure 3.1) illustrates even greater challenges for deep implementation when it displays misrendered Arabic text, in which the letters are disconnected and read left-to-right instead of right-to-left. The text is produced by seaborn, a popular code library for data visualization, which relies on matplotlib, the RTL deficiencies of which affect a multitude of tools. According to GitHub's dependency graph for matplotlib, around 668,000 repositories depend on matplotlib's code.[34] While a workaround for correctly displaying RTL labels in matplotlib has been reported—replacing the back end with mplcairo, which has its own chain of dependencies, Raqm and Fribidi—how realistic is it for the hundreds of thousands of matplotlib-dependent repositories to implement the alternative mplcairo back end?[35] As made clear by this example, the decision to support or not to support RTL or bidirectional features in a tool can have tremendous cascading effects. And depending on this single decision, myriad end-users—who may be unaware of the tools used to produce an app, website, text corpus, or set of graphs—will either have a frictionless experience or be excluded from using the tools altogether.

A final point regarding implementation—perhaps the most fundamental one—is the surprisingly poor implementation of RTL and mixed-direction text in many popular code editors.[36] This is a sore point for digital humanists, who frequently discuss how to work around these issues, for example, when creating a digital edition of an RTL text using the guidelines of the Text Encoding Initiative XML (TEI-XML). Yet when one considers that code editors are a major part of the workflow for producing nearly every custom-built app or website, the problem comes into focus: it is difficult for *any* coder, not just a digital humanist, to create tools that will serve the half billion people whose first language uses primarily an RTL script.

A case in point is the GitHub-backed code editor Atom, which had a million active users as of March 2016.[37] Currently Atom has at least six open issues relating to right-to-left text handling, the oldest of which was opened nearly five years ago.[38] In one of the most commented-on issues, Atom developer @lee-dohm (Lee Dohm), drawing on the nature of open source and in light of limitations faced by developers like himself, invites the RTL community to contribute to solutions to "help speed up the process" and "work on the bits of functionality that are important to them."[39] The original poster, @salar90 (Salar Gholizadeh), concurs and encourages fellow "RTLers . . . to contribute." A few months later, @lee-dohm acknowledges the importance of the still-unresolved issue but cannot say "when we'll be able to get to it." Such debate is common across community wikis: the issues are identified without a path or a timeline for a solution.

It may be that "RTLers" have not contributed enough to solving the problem, as @salar90 suggests, but it is also unfortunate that a software initiative with such major backers, which lists sixty-four people on its GitHub organization page and to which nearly a hundred people have at some point contributed code, does not "have an ETA for when we'll be able to get to it."[40] The frustrations that emerge when developers or managers redirect potential resources away from what the community clearly desires are reflected in another RTLer's comment on a different Atom issue: "As always—we need to develop everything for ourselves."[41]

Compounding the problem of poor implementation of standards for RTL and multidirectional text is the fact that it is difficult for users to discover which applications support RTL/bidi and what workarounds exist. Typically, they must rely on listservs, forums, and social media, as well as their own trial-and-error. There is no inventory of RTL-supporting applications, nor does it seem to be standard practice for software to indicate its RTL support status. As an October 2019 Twitter conversation between DH practitioners well illustrates, the status of RTL support even for widely used tools like Gephi and R is often unknown, with DH scholars resorting to trial-and-error or word-of-mouth to find the tools and workarounds that can support their research.[42]

What is the way forward to overcome these implementation hurdles? First is to acknowledge that *RTL support for DH tools is linked to RTL support in general.*

On occasion, digital humanists have the opportunity to develop their own boutique tools and may choose to prioritize RTL support in them. But, to a large extent, DH workflows consist of tools backed by broader commercial and community interests and involve teams that draw from several communities: data analysts, developers, writers, and publishers, to name only a few. As long as these workflows depend mainly on tools developed outside of DH and supported by a spectrum of differently motivated stakeholders, DH practitioners can expect RTL support to be driven by what profits these stakeholders rather than by concerns about inclusivity, equity, and accessibility.

The temptation is for digital humanists to address their own needs by bootstrapping RTL support, either by building their own niche tools or by patching and hacking existing tools. But if the authors' experience is any guide, most RTL DH practitioners have workflows held together by temporary fixes that allow them only to bracket the real scale of the RTL implementation problem. Such fixes, furthermore, do little to address the needs of the wider RTL community and perpetuate the problem of poor documentation. They also sidestep the issue of deep implementation; DH tools are usually not written from the ground up but rely on other software frameworks or libraries. Unless RTL issues are addressed in this ground-level code, RTL support in DH tools can only be a kind of Band-Aid.

Acknowledging that RTL support is bound up with sectors that are relatively unfamiliar for DHers leads to a second obligation in order to move forward: *Digital humanists must become advocates for broad-level RTL integration.* Indeed, DH practitioners are in a strategic position to communicate the needs of RTL communities for a multitude of reasons. They constitute a global, multilingual guild. As humanists, they are both specialists in issues of complex, linguistic expression and advocates for representation of diverse linguistic communities, past and present. They understand something of the relevant underlying technologies, which they themselves use, teach, document, and further develop. They already have lines of communication to funders and developers. And they have an accredited voice through publications, teaching, and public engagement.

Nevertheless, exercising this kind of advocacy on behalf of RTL communities will require reorienting our own community to be more attuned to the diversity of RTL usage both within and beyond the DH community, as well as improving communication channels with commercial software developers.[43] Digital humanists ground their work in knowledge discovery and exchange in the digital sphere. But knowledge is not just cultural content embedded in language; it is also infrastructure that allows that content to be represented, circulated, and preserved for the concerned communities. In this case, the knowledge to be discovered is that of the access barriers that RTLers face and the inadequate state of RTL support, both of which are obstacles to equitable knowledge production in our age. These knowledge sets in turn need to be exchanged between RTL users and developers.

Moving Forward with RTL DH

We believe that it is possible to channel user concerns to developers more effectively than is being done with existing listservs, forums, and social media, which probably reach DH and RTL communities more than developers. As such, so that issues (tickets) can be filed regarding RTL support, we have set up a pilot GitHub site.[44] The goal of soliciting these issues is twofold: (1) to pass on users' reports to developers and (2) to provide a clearinghouse where users can view and share the status of RTL support for various applications and websites. GitHub is the world's largest code host, with over 40 million users and 100 million repositories as of August 2019.[45] It is possible to "ping" the relevant development team on GitHub from an issue filed in another repository by linking to open issues in their repository or by @mentioning the relevant GitHub organization or user. This approach does not guarantee, of course, that solutions will be expedited, but it does attempt to consolidate the discussion in one place and make it more visible. This consolidation effort should be used not only to point out problems but also to raise awareness of RTL user needs, to stimulate debate and build consensus among RTL developers, and even to recognize well-implemented RTL support.

As mentioned above, technical standards for RTL support largely exist while implementation is largely lacking. But there is something else missing: best practice guidelines. There are, no doubt, developers who would like their products to reach RTL audiences, and yet it is difficult for them to know how users will expect their software to behave in RTL environments. In the same way that the W3C offers "principles" and "easy checks" for accessibility, developers should have access to high-level principles that can guide their RTL implementations—principles that are humanistic and user-oriented rather than technical standards per se.[46] One example might be that arrow keys or buttons should be linked to movement in a certain direction (right, left, up, down) rather than to sequence (forward, back, next, previous).

Such best practice guidelines must develop out of community conversations and on the basis of multiple examples. The authors hope that issues filed in the Right2Left Digital Humanities (right2leftdh) GitHub repository can begin to provide such a basis. It is possible that the repository could develop into a place where the RTL community collaborates on best practice guidelines and provides a sandbox space for trying out implementations. It might also be conceivable to award "badges" as a way of recognizing products that follow these best practice guidelines. Indeed, while it might at first appear that RTL DH practitioners are a niche community within a niche community, the reality is that RTL DHers are part of a much larger RTL community, and they are well positioned to become advocates for RTL support within the broader software development space, especially in contemporary RTL linguistic zones where development is robust.

With a few exceptions, digital humanists have yet to effectively engage the broader RTL world, just as RTL communities and their knowledge practices have yet to become fully and equitably integrated into the digital humanities. In our view, these two problems are linked. In examining three complementary perspectives on the issue—habitual, cultural, and technical—we have argued for three corresponding extensions that would help reorient the vision of RTL DH practice: (1) DH objectives for RTL projects that extend beyond historical projects in order to encompass *contemporary RTL creative practices* and RTL content creation in digital environments; (2) DH tools that extend beyond "localization" and instead are conceived as *born-global, culturally aware resources* in the broad sense that the term "internationalization" entails; and (3) DH practitioners who extend their efforts beyond bespoke solutions toward discussions that encourage developers to implement existing standards and *prioritize accessibility for a broad RTL user base.* To address the compounded marginalization that RTL DH currently faces, we must work to further articulate these reorientations along both theoretical and practical axes, as they would help to align the broader DH community with the broader RTL community. Continuing to raise awareness of the digital-cultural habitus of RTL and other non-English communities and linking them to pragmatic solutions will foster a more inclusive and equitable environment for DH around the globe.

NOTES

This contribution was conceived by the authors together with Najla Jarkas (American University of Beirut), who coauthored the presentation at the Right2Left Workshop Digital Humanities Summer Institute (Victoria, British Columbia, June 8, 2019) that formed the basis for the Cultural section of this chapter. Support for Nathan Gibson's contribution to this chapter was generously provided by the German Federal Ministry of Education and Research through the "Kleine Fächer—Große Potenziale" program in the framework of the "Communities of Knowledge" project (grant number 01UL1826X).

Contributors to this article are listed in alphabetical order; they all contributed equally to its authorship.

1. The thread begins with this Twitter post, January 7, 2020, https://twitter.com/Zoe_LeBlanc/status/1214592683739668483. In a follow-up tweet, LeBlanc shares a screenshot of what seaborn, another Python visualization library, does to Arabic characters: separating the connected letters and producing an unfortunately all-too-common mangling of Arabic found everywhere from public signage to tattoos. Regarding LeBlanc's research, see chapter 22 in this volume on digital history dissertations. For a host of examples of Arabic text mangling, see Ramsey Nasser's long-standing blog "Nope, not Arabic" (https://www.notarabic.com/). For practical guidance on how to avoid such text rendering errors, see Nasser ("Unplain Text").

2. See the commits and issues at https://github.com/search?q=%22RTL%22&type=commits; open issues are listed at https://github.com/search?q=%22RTL%22+state%3Aopen&type=Issues&ref=advsearch&l=&l=. Of course, not all of these have to do with support for RTL scripts or layout, but a quick perusal shows that a great many of them do.

3. In the following, we sometimes refer to "RTL languages" as shorthand for languages written using RTL writing systems. We do not mean to imply that languages themselves are inherently RTL or LTR, since the same language can be written using RTL or LTR systems (e.g., Ottoman vs. post-Ottoman Turkish or Hebrew in native script vs. romanized Hebrew).

4. This cooperation is all the more urgent, given the recent explanation by Boucher and Anderson of how bidirectional control characters can hide attacks in source code.

5. Ishida ("Unicode") observes, "Most applications treat text by default as left-to-right, and a specific effort is required to say that the base direction should be right-to-left."

6. See Nasser ("قلب") as well as Ahmed Abdalla, Nick Doiron, and Jake Worth's SimplyAhmazing/noor (code repository), November 5, 2018, https://github.com/SimplyAhmazing/noor; we also do not address here the issues involved in writing top-to-bottom with lines proceeding right-to-left (TTB-RTL), as is sometimes practiced with Japanese, Chinese, and Korean.

7. Rockwell discusses certain *disciplinary* barriers to full integration into the DH community. Along with issues such as "jobs," "theory," and "disciplinary violence," the LTR default can present a subdisciplinary challenge that RTL DH practitioners face in having their research conducted, assessed, and valorized on an equal footing. See this chapter's section "Habitual" for one particular example.

8. This point does not escape Rockwell in his reference to Fiormonte (251).

9. See the web content for these initiatives: DHIB: Digital Humanities Institute—Beirut (event website), https://dhibeirut.wordpress.com/; the NYU Abu Dhabi Winter Institute in Digital Humanities (event website), https://wp.nyu.edu/widh/.

10. For the latter, see Islamicate Digital Humanities Network: The Next Generation (society website), https://idhn.org/.

11. As Quinn Dombrowski pointed out in a comment on a draft of this chapter, historical materials are more widely researched in general than contemporary culture, not just in regard to RTL cultures. Our point is that this tendency produces a discrepancy between the ways DH practitioners as compared with other RTL users navigate obstacles relating to RTL accessibility.

12. In Risam's view, "postcolonial digital humanities is an approach to uncovering and intervening in [such] disruptions" (3).

13. Around DH in 80 Days was "a multi-institutional, interdisciplinary Digital Humanities collaboration that seeks to introduce new and veteran audiences to the *global* field of DH scholarly practice by bringing together current DH projects from around the world." For a project introduction, see https://web.archive.org/web/20190125065559/http://www.arounddh.org/about/.

14. The South Azer(baijan)i language as spoken in Iranian Azerbaijan and other Turkish regions of the country has an RTL script based on the Perso-Arabic alphabet, whereas the North Azer(baijan)i language of the Republic of Azerbaijan and the Caucasus region is written in a variety of alphabets, including Latin and Cyrillic. Melissa Terras's blog post

and "Infographic: Quantifying Digital Humanities" shows only one physical DH center in the MENASA region by 2012, which she locates in Iran; see http://melissaterras.blogspot.com/2012/01/infographic-quanitifying-digital.html. This must be IFRI (Institut Français de Recherche en Iran), an offshoot of the Embassy of France in Tehran, which is also recorded in the centerNet's "Centres" map at http://dhcenternet.org/centers. Elsewhere in "Toward a Cultural Critique of Digital Humanities," Fiormonte draws a connection—and possible correlation—between income and the number of physical DH centers on a global scale. For the University of Shiraz DH center, see its Instagram user page (https://www.instagram.com/dhc_shirazu/).

15. By "historical" projects, we are especially referring to those dealing with materials before the twentieth century. The scale of the disparity is difficult to assess without a proper survey. Nevertheless, of the projects funded by the European Research Council (ERC), the European Union's body for funding individual research projects, only about 25 percent (around 18 of 71 projects) with the word "Arabic" in the description appear to include anything from the twentieth century or later ("ERC Funded Projects," European Research Council, November 16, 2020, see https://erc.easme-web.eu?mode=7&fullText=Arabic).

16. Thanks to Hilary Green for pointing out this marginalization in her reading of an earlier draft of this chapter.

17. Many contemporary projects have a preservationist mission similar to archival historical ones, aiming to gather, preserve, and exhibit multimedia material that may equally include rare or ephemeral artifacts.

18. In comparing LTR to RTL historical corpora, Mahony relevantly observes "the Western-European and US focus on" the "production of digital editions of texts." In one study alone, "65% of the projects are Anglo-American; that is 123 out of the total of 187 editions recorded" (376). Obviously, LTR editions comprise a percentage greater than or equal to the exclusively Anglocentric ones.

19. For an overview of "the state(s) of the OCR problem" with "texts printed before 1800" and in "languages other than modern English," see https://digital.library.unt.edu/ark:/67531/metadc1010762/m1/2/. For the state of the field in Arabic HTR, see Keinan-Schoonbaert. Regarding OCR of printed Syriac texts, see Chesley, Marcantonio, and Pearson.

20. On bidirectional support in code editors, see the third section of this chapter "Technical." According to Mahony (374), "the dominance of such pervasive systems as . . . HTML and the ubiquitous XML, the latter particularly having a pronounced linguistic bias (difficulties with accented characters and right-to-left scripts) as well as the English-based TEI guidelines" are as equally to blame for Anglocentrism and its "geopolitics which [Fiormonte] claims is to be found endemic in our field" as "ASCII code (American Standard [Code] for Information Exchange) and the domain name system (administered by ICANN)," which Fiormonte had singled out in his earlier critique.

21. Zarnegar, one of the earliest word processors to handle Persian and Arabic, was released initially for DOS in 1991 and later could be used with Windows (see "Zarnegar," SinaSoft corporate website, accessed December 23, 2020, http://sinasoft.com/zarnegar

.html). See also "Zarnegar (word processor)," *Wikipedia,* last modified May 13, 2022, https://en.wikipedia.org/wiki/Zarnegar_(word_processor). According to the WinWorld online museum, an Arabic version of Microsoft Windows seems to have been available first for Windows 3.1, released in 1992; see "Windows 3.0 / 3.1," *WinWorld,* accessed December 23, 2020, https://winworldpc.com/product/windows-3/31; until the release of Windows 98, non-Arabic Windows versions could be arabicized only by installing additional software (Madhany). Even after this point, as Madhany explains, fully enabling RTL features in the Microsoft Windows and Office product suites required adjusting a host of settings. The original interface with these settings can be seen in the screenshots at https://www.lib.uchicago.edu/e/collections/mideast/encyclopedia/multilingual_computing_arabic.ppt.

22. See the relevant documentation for the following tools: Voyant Tools (https://voyant-tools.org/docs/#!/guide/languages), Recogito (https://github.com/pelagios/recogito2/wiki/User-Interface-Translation:-Contributors'-Guide), From the Page (https://content.fromthepage.com/neh-to-fund-better-internationalization-and-integration-in-fromthepage/), and Lingscape (https://lingscape.uni.lu/). The localization of the latter has also been completed by Wrisley and Jarkas.

23. The thread of this debate can be found here: https://github.com/programminghistorian/ph-submissions/issues/147.

24. For example, contributors of lessons to the *Programming Historian* are encouraged to refrain from culturally specific language that would exclude global readers and to shape their tutorials around datasets that could be exchanged easily by others for other language communities (Sichani). In a DH training context, at the NYU Abu Dhabi Winter Institute in Digital Humanities (WIDH), participants are encouraged to "communicate with each other in ways that respect difference, while showing compassion, empathy and understanding, instead of assuming that we are all 'on the same page.'" For more information, see the WIDH Code of Conduct inspired by codes from other cognate DH training events: https://wp.nyu.edu/widh/code-of-conduct/.

25. See chapter 21 in this volume on "Reframing the Conversation: Digital Humanists, Disabilities, and Accessibility."

26. See the discussion of "professional capacity networks" in chapter 21 on "Reframing the Conversation," as well as El Khatib et al.

27. The Unicode bidirectional algorithm (Ishida, "Unicode") attempts to correctly display mixed-direction text on the basis of directionality attributes embedded in Unicode character information. However, this is not adequate to correctly display ambiguous characters like numbers or punctuation, and in rare cases the direction of a text segment needs to be reversed. Therefore Unicode, HTML, and CSS each independently make it possible to (1) set the direction of a particular text segment and mark opposite-direction text so that ambiguous characters display in the correct position, (2) mark off text with an unknown direction so that it can preserve its direction when inserted into surrounding text, and (3) override the default character direction. Examples can be seen at https://right2leftdh.github.io/examples/bidi.html. Details can be found in Gibson (11–28). For helpful guides to implementing RTL and mixed-direction text in HTML, see Ishida and

Lanin; see also Ishida, "Structural Markup." For a suggested TEI-XML implementation, see the TEI Guidelines.

28. See the TEI Guidelines or try out this jsFiddle: https://jsfiddle.net/gh/get/library/pure/right2leftdh/right2leftdh.github.io/tree/master/examples/boustrophedon-demo.

29. For a particularly pronounced case, see the example of the Atom code editor, discussed below.

30. On February 1, 2021, Vallari Agrawal (@VallariAg) created a pull request intended to resolve this issue (https://github.com/internetarchive/bookreader/pull/615). As of October 24, 2022, the new code had not yet been merged into the Internet Archive's BookReader production codebase.

31. "Arabic and Hebrew Features in InDesign," Adobe Support, July 12, 2019, https://helpx.adobe.com/indesign/using/arabic-hebrew.html. See also the discussions in the Adobe Support Community on the topic "binding direction disappeared," July 20, 2017, https://community.adobe.com/t5/indesign/binding-direction-disappeared/td-p/9256082, and on "change binding direction," September 6, 2017, https://community.adobe.com/t5/indesign/change-binding-direction/td-p/9316069. It should be acknowledged that Adobe has implemented a number of advanced RTL features in InDesign, although they are hidden in the localized edition of the software. In 2001, there was a parallel situation in which only Arabic editions of Windows supported certain features (Habash).

32. An example is Samuel Landauer's Arabic edition of Saadia Gaon's *Book of Beliefs and Opinions* on the Internet Archive, the Arabic portion of which must be read from bottom to top if viewed in single-page mode or downloaded as a PDF; see https://archive.org/details/kitbalamnt00saaduoft/page/n352/mode/1up.

33. Personal correspondence with Johanna Walcher, August 27, 2019, and Günter Hackl, August 28, 2019.

34. "Network Dependents," matplotlib/matplotlib (code repository), January 2, 2023, https://github.com/matplotlib/matplotlib/network/dependents.

35. "matplotlib/mplcairo: A (New) Cairo Backend for Matplotlib" (code repository), https://github.com/matplotlib/mplcairo.

36. A thorough survey is needed. However, it may be indicative that "Comparison of Text Editors" (*Wikipedia,* last modified February 1, 2020, https://en.wikipedia.org/w/index.php?title=Comparison_of_text_editors#Right-to-left_and_bidirectional_text) lists 58 text (and source code) editors; of these, 14 fully or partially support RTL and bidi, 17 do not support either, and 27 are unknown.

37. "Atom Reaches One Million Active Users," *Atom* (blog), March 28, 2016, https://web.archive.org/web/20221129082040/https://blog.atom.io/2016/03/28/atom-reaches-1m-users.html. During the editing of our article, GitHub announced it would sunset Atom on December 15, 2022, in favor of furthering the development of Visual Studio Code, which has better (but still problematic) RTL and bidi handling ("Sunsetting Atom," GitHub [blog], June 8, 2022, https://github.blog/2022-06-08-sunsetting-atom/).

38. The open issues related to RTL text in November 2021 can be reviewed at https://github.com/atom/atom/issues/10132, https://github.com/atom/atom/issues/13612, https://github.com/atom/atom/issues/13348, https://github.com/atom/atom/issues/10294, https://github.com/atom/atom/issues/9397, and https://github.com/atom/atom/issues/5990. Contributors Mohamed Taher Alrefaie (@mohataher) and @mohamedalmograby attempted to resolve several of these issues with a pull request (https://github.com/atom/atom/pull/21018), but an Atom maintainer rejected the pull request on September 3, 2021, asserting, "The maintenance cost of this new feature is huge and Atom currently doesn't have the capacity to deal with issues and pull requests that come as a result of this addition."

39. "RTL Text Selection," https://github.com/atom/atom/issues/10132.

40. "People · Atom · GitHub," https://web.archive.org/web/20220610160902/https://github.com/orgs/atom/people; "Contributors to atom/atom · Github," https://github.com/atom/atom/graphs/contributors. It would be simplistic, however, to focus strictly on directional issues in implementing support for RTL. Developers additionally need to be aware that many RTL writing systems require features like connecting letters and combining diacritics. If these are poorly implemented, the text is nearly unreadable. The critical point to remember is that if RTL-unfriendly text editors are also widely used by most developers, it is easy to see how their output fails to meet expectations for RTL use cases.

41. GitHub issue comment related to "Editor Behaves Confusing while Editing RTL Text," February 10, 2018, https://github.com/atom/atom/issues/4682#issuecomment-364611470.

42. The thread begins with this Twitter post by Till Grallert (@tillgrallert), "I just updated to a new computer," October 2, 2019, https://twitter.com/tillgrallert/status/1179522880306061313.

43. See the previous "Habitual" section of this chapter.

44. Our pilot site can be found at Right2Left Digital Humanities, https://right2leftdh.github.io.

45. See Gousios et al.; see also the "About" page at https://github.com/about.

46. For accessibility guidelines, see Henry and McGee.

BIBLIOGRAPHY

Abdelali, Ahmed. "Localization in Modern Standard Arabic." *Journal of the American Society for Information Science and Technology* 55, no. 1 (2004): 23–28, https://doi.org/10.1002/asi.10340.

Antonijević, Smiljana. *Amongst Digital Humanists: An Ethnographic Study of Digital Knowledge Production.* New York: Palgrave Macmillan, 2015, https://doi.org/10.1057/9781137484185.

Bani-Khaled, Turki Ahmad Ali. "Standard Arabic and Diglossia: A Problem for Language Education in the Arab World." *American International Journal of Contemporary Research* 4, no. 8 (August 2014): 180–89.

Boucher, Nicholas, and Ross Anderson. "Trojan Source: Invisible Vulnerabilities." arXiv (preprint). October 30, 2021, https://arxiv.org/abs/2111.00169.

Bourdieu, Pierre. *Outline of a Theory of Practice.* Translated by Richard Nice. Cambridge: Cambridge University Press, 1977.

Chesley, Emily, Jillian Marcantonio, and Abigail Pearson. "Towards Syriac Digital Corpora: Evaluation of Tesseract 4.0 for Syriac OCR." *Hugoye: Journal of Syriac Studies* 22 (2019): 109–92, https://hugoye.bethmardutho.org/article/hv22n1chesley.

Eberhard, David M., Gary F. Simons, and Charles D. Fennig, eds. "Summary by Language Size." In *Ethnologue: Languages of the World.* 22nd ed. Dallas: SIL International, 2019, https://www.ethnologue.com/statistics/size (login required).

El Khatib, Randa, David Joseph Wrisley, Shady Elbassuoni, Mohamad Jaber, and Julia El Zini. "Prototyping across the Disciplines." *Digital Studies/Le Champ Numérique* 8, no. 1 (2019): 1–20, https://doi.org/10.16995/dscn.282.

Fiormonte, Domenico. "Toward a Cultural Critique of Digital Humanities." In *Debates in the Digital Humanities 2016,* edited by Matthew K. Gold and Lauren F. Klein, 438–58. Minneapolis: University of Minnesota Press, 2016, https://doi.org/10.5749/9781452963761.

Galina, Isabel. "Is There Anybody Out There? Building a Global Digital Humanities Community." *Red de Humanidades Digitales* (blog). July 19, 2013, https://web.archive.org/web/20201205073959/http://humanidadesdigitales.net/blog/2013/07/19/is-there-anybody-out-there-building-a-global-digital-humanities-community/.

Gibson, Nathan P. "Thinking in ⅃TЯ: Reorienting the Directional Assumptions of Global Digital Scholarship." Presentation at the Right2Left Workshop Digital Humanities Summer Institute, Victoria, British Columbia, June 8, 2019, https://doi.org/10.17613/3vws-5s29.

Gousios, Georgios, Bogdan Vasilescu, Alexander Serebrenik, and Andy Zaidman. "Lean GHTorrent: GitHub Data on Demand." In *Proceedings of the 11th Working Conference on Mining Software Repositories—MSR 2014,* 384–87. Hyderabad, India: ACM Press, 2014, https://doi.org/10.1145/2597073.2597126.

Habash, Nizar. "Nuun: A System for Developing Platform and Browser Independent Arabic Web Applications." In *Proceedings of the Arabic Translation and Localization Conference (ATLAS, 1999).* Tunis: Tunisia, 2001, https://www.researchgate.net/publication/2414218.

Henry, Shawn Lawton, and Liam McGee. "Accessibility." *W3C.* Accessed August 9, 2022, https://www.w3.org/standards/webdesign/accessibility.

"Internationalization," *W3C.* Accessed August 9, 2022, https://www.w3.org/standards/webdesign/i18n.html.

Ishida, Richard. "Structural Markup and Right-to-Left Text in HTML." *W3C.* Last updated June 25, 2021, https://www.w3.org/International/questions/qa-html-dir.

Ishida, Richard. "Unicode Bidirectional Algorithm Basics." *W3C.* Last updated August 9, 2016, https://www.w3.org/International/articles/inline-bidi-markup/uba-basics.

Ishida, Richard. "Visual vs. Logical Ordering of Text." *W3C.* Last updated June 10, 2016, https://www.w3.org/International/questions/qa-visual-vs-logical.

Ishida, Richard, and Aharon Lanin, "Inline Markup and Bidirectional Text in HTML." *W3C*. June 25, 2021, https://www.w3.org/International/articles/inline-bidi-markup/.

Keinan-Schoonbaert, Adi. "Results of the RASM2019 Competition on Recognition of Historical Arabic Scientific Manuscripts." *The British Library—Digital Scholarship* (blog). September 13, 2019, https://blogs.bl.uk/digital-scholarship/2019/09/rasm2019-results.html.

Kirmizialtin, Suphan, and David Joseph Wrisley, "Automatic Transcription of Non-Latin Script Periodicals: A Case Study in Ottoman Turkish Print Archive." *DHQ: Digital Humanities Quarterly* 16, no. 2 (2022), http://digitalhumanities.org:8081/dhq/vol/16/2/000577/000577.html.

Madhany, al-Husein N. "Multilingual Computing with Arabic and Arabic Transliteration: Arabicizing Windows Applications to Read and Write Arabic & Solutions for the Transliteration Quagmire Faced by Arabic-Script Languages." February 2006, https://www.lib.uchicago.edu/e/collections/mideast/encyclopedia/Multilingual_Computing_with_Arabic_and_Arabic_Transliteration.pdf.

Mahony, Simon. "Cultural Diversity and the Digital Humanities." *Fudan Journal of the Humanities and Social Sciences* 11, no. 3 (2018): 371–88, https://doi.org/10.1007/s40647-018-0216-0.

Meza, Aurelio. "Decolonizing International Research Groups: Prototyping a Digital Audio Repository from South to North." *Digital Studies/Le Champ Numérique* 9, no. 1 (2019): 7, https://doi.org/10.16995/dscn.303.

Nasser, Ramsey. "قلب." *Ramsey Nasser* (blog). January 14, 2020, https://nas.sr/%D9%82%D9%84%D8%A8/.

Nasser, Ramsey. "Unplain Text: How to Shape and Render Non-Latin Text." *Increment.* April 2018, https://increment.com/programming-languages/unplain-text-primer-on-non-latin/.

Osborn, Don. *African Languages in a Digital Age: Challenges and Opportunities for Indigenous Language Computing.* Ottawa: International Development Research Centre, HSRC Press, 2010, https://www.hsrcpress.ac.za/books/african-languages-in-a-digital-age.

Risam, Roopika. *New Digital Worlds: Postcolonial Digital Humanities in Theory, Praxis and Pedagogy.* Evanston, Ill.: Northwestern University Press, 2019.

Rockwell, Geoffrey. "Inclusion in the Digital Humanities." In *Defining Digital Humanities: A Reader,* edited by Edward Vanhoutte, Julianne Nyhan, and Melissa M. Terras, 247–53. Surrey: Ashgate, 2013.

Sichani, Anna-Maria. "Linguistic Diversity and Ad-Hoc Translation of the Programming Historian's Lessons." *Programming Historian.* November 30, 2018, https://programminghistorian.org/posts/ad-hoc-translation.

Souphavanh, Anousak, and Theppitak Karoonboonyanan. *FOSS Localization.* New Delhi: Elsevier, 2005, https://en.wikibooks.org/wiki/FOSS_Localization.

Tanev, Stoyan. "Global from the Start: The Characteristics of Born-Global Firms in the Technology Sector." *Technology Innovation Management Review* 2 (March 2012): 5–8, https://doi.org/10.22215/timreview/532.

TEI Guidelines. "Characters, Glyphs, and Writing Modes." July 16, 2019, https://tei-c.org/release/doc/tei-p5-doc/en/html/WD.html.

W3C. "Localization vs. Internationalization." Last updated December 5, 2005, https://www.w3.org/International/questions/qa-i18n.

Wrisley, David Joseph. "Enacting Open Scholarship in Transnational Contexts." *POP! Public. Open. Participatory.* October 31, 2019, https://doi.org/10.21810/pop.2019.002.

Wrisley, David Joseph, and Najla Jarkas. "On Translating Voyant Tools into Arabic." *DJWrisley* (blog). September 6, 2016, https://web.archive.org/web/20210226104135/https://djwrisley.com/on-translating-voyant-tools-into-arabic/.

Yacob, Daniel. "Localize or Be Localized: An Assessment of Localization Frameworks." In *International Symposium on ICT Education and Application in Developing Countries,* 1–9. Addis Ababa, Ethiopia, 2004, http://yacob.org/papers%2FDanielYacob-ICTES2004.pdf.

Yaghan, Mohammad Ali. "'Arabizi': A Contemporary Style of Arabic Slang." *Design Issues* 24, no. 2 (Spring 2008): 39–52, https://doi.org/10.1162/desi.2008.24.2.39.

Relation-Oriented AI: Why Indigenous Protocols Matter for the Digital Humanities

MICHELLE LEE BROWN, HĒMI WHAANGA,
AND JASON EDWARD LEWIS

Recent discussions around the ethical design and use of artificial intelligence (AI) treat AI systems and their materials and energy sources as discrete units. That is, it is as if the materials out of which they are made—and how those materials are collected, refined, and shaped and the communities involved in their creation—are immaterial. Yet these aspects matter. They shape the systems they hold and run. These materialities, such as silicon, plastic, aluminum, and yttrium, shape our cues and protocols for how and when to engage with, disengage from, or abstain from AI systems. When we refer to AI systems, we mean here the constellation of computational technologies that are aimed at replicating key components of human intelligence, such as language use, reasoning, and agency. Examining our relationships with AI from Indigenous perspectives, while centering Indigenous epistemologies and ontologies in AI discussions and designs, is crucial for guiding our decisions about these systems (Lewis et al.). Digital humanities (DH) is a space where issues of history, culture, and context converge with technical concerns, and so it is a natural place to develop and promote Indigenous guidelines like these.

Artificial Intelligence

AI is developing rapidly, and the maturation of large-scale machine learning, deep learning, big data analysis, and computational neural networks has opened up research on the potential of building intelligent systems "that can collaborate effectively with people, including creative ways to develop interactive and scalable ways for people to teach robots" (Stone et al., 9). Coupled with simultaneous growth in robotics, the internet of things, three-dimensional (3D) printing, nanotechnology, genome editing, quantum computing, advanced biology, and other technologies, these technological developments blur the lines between the physical, biological, and digital realms. Although at different stages of development and deployment, these advances will fundamentally change the way we socialize, display, access, manage, create, and exchange information and data. As our relationships with technology become more nuanced, fluid, and personalized, the impact and importance of understanding the behavior of AI systems is even more critical "to our ability to control their actions, reap their benefits and minimize their harms" (Rahwan et al., 477). AI systems such as those used in sentencing guidelines, facial recognition systems, mortgage assessments, and health diagnoses have increasing influence over our social, cultural, economic, and political interactions even while the scale, complexity, and future impact of their power is still unknown.

Nation-states, corporations, and public and private organizations in Montreal, Toronto, the European Union, Oceania, and elsewhere have recently published, or are about to publish, a range of declarations and manifestos on machine ethics and their implications for the design of AI systems.[1] A quick scan through these documents highlights a broad approach for implementing AI policy in areas such as "scientific research, talent development, skills and education, public and private sector adoption, ethics and inclusion, standards and regulations, and data and digital infrastructure" (Dutton). Premised on establishing global principles and standards, corporate governance and compliance, industrial competitiveness, and sustainable development (Renda), these standards and regulations outline the common good and benefit for humanity, establish principles of fairness and intelligibility, address data and privacy rights, and propose benefit sharing and restrictions or outright bans on vesting AI with the autonomous power to hurt, destroy, or deceive humans (IEEE).

Indigenous communities are concerned with the absence of Indigenous voices and a lack of Indigenous perspectives in the development and construction of these declarations and manifestos. While a small number of reports (e.g., Gavaghan et al.; Walsh et al.) discuss well-being, equity, self-determination, algorithm uses, and Indigenous data sovereignty in Australia and New Zealand, the global dialogue around AI rarely takes up the issues and aspirations of Indigenous rights. Given the long history of technological advances being used against Indigenous people (Arnold; Guiliano and Heitman; Walter and Suina), it is increasingly imperative that Indigenous peoples engage with this latest paradigm shift. If, however, these conversations continue to be dominated by the relatively culturally homogeneous research labs and Silicon Valley start-up culture defined through a Western techno-utilitarian lens, we will fail to fully grasp its true benefits now and into the future. As noted by Peter Stone and colleagues, "Though AI algorithms may be capable of making less biased decisions than a typical person, it remains a deep technical challenge to ensure that the data that inform AI-based decisions can be kept free from biases that could lead to discrimination based on race, sexual orientation, or other factors" (10). Indigenous knowledge protocols offer one potential avenue for meeting these challenges.

Protocols

Protocols differ greatly across Indigenous communities. Informed by the specific epistemologies of the communities using them, protocols establish customs, lore, and codes and standards of behavior; they address ethics, rules, regulations, processes, procedures, guidelines, and relationships.

At the core of many Indigenous epistemologies is the belief that humans do not sit at the center of all creation. The acknowledgment of kinship networks with animals and plants, wind and rock, mountain and ocean underpins the protocols that enable us to engage in dialogue with our nonhuman kin (Lewis et al.). These relationships connect the land to the sea and to skyscapes, from the human and nonhuman to animate and inanimate entities.

In Indigenous contexts, protocols are understood in a number of ways. For example, Angelina Hurley describes protocols "as a set of rules, regulations, processes, procedures, strategies, or guidelines. Protocols are simply the ways in which you work with people, and communicate and collaborate with them appropriately. . . . Protocols are the standards of behaviour, respect and knowledge that need to be adopted. You might even think of them as a code of manners to observe, rather than a set of rules to obey" (3). Protocol also refers to the guiding principles and methodology for conducting oneself in any activity:

> Protocols exist as standards of behaviour used by people to show respect to one another. Cultural protocol refers to the customs, lore and codes of behaviour of a particular cultural group and a way of conducting business. It also refers to the protocols and procedures used to guide the observance of traditional knowledge and practices, including how traditional knowledge is used, recorded and disseminated. (Secretariat of National Aboriginal and Islander Child Care)

Protocols are passed and learned from one generation to another. They are built on, modified, improved, and adjusted from one context to another, from formal settings to more informal ones. Learning, understanding, teaching, and following proper protocol is at the core of the majority of Indigenous interactions. Thus, when any new development, idea, concept, or entity, such as AI, is introduced into the epistemological and ontological domain, new parameters and protocols for their inclusion need to be established. What, then, would an Indigenous conversation with AI look like, and how might we initiate a type of discussion based on Indigenous protocols?

The Indigenous Protocol and AI Workshops

These types of questions about AI and protocol prompted the Indigenous Protocol and AI (IP-AI) Workshops in which the authors of this chapter participated.[2] The two

IP-AI Workshops, held in 2019, brought together members of Kanaka Maoli, Māori, Trawlwoolway, Euskaldunak, Baradha, Kapalbara, Samoan, Cree, Lakota, Cherokee, Coquille, Cheyenne, and Crow communities from across North America, Oceania, and New Zealand/Australia. Held on Kanaka Maoli territory, on the Hawaiian island of Oʻahu, thirty-five Indigenous and non-Indigenous individuals participated in the workshops.[3] The participants work as technologists, artists, scientists, cultural knowledge keepers, language keepers, and public policy experts in a variety of disciplinary backgrounds, including machine learning, design, symbolic systems, cognition and computation, visual and performing arts, philosophy, linguistics, anthropology, and sociology. A central proposition of the gathering was to critically examine the relationship between AI and Indigenous communities and, in particular, the question of whether "AI should be given a place in our existing circle of relationships, and, if so, how we might go about bringing it into the circle?" Other questions were interwoven into the discussion: How can Indigenous epistemologies and ontologies contribute to the global conversation regarding society and AI? How do we broaden discussions regarding the role of technology in society beyond relatively culturally homogeneous research labs and Silicon Valley start-up culture? How do we imagine a future with AI that contributes to the flourishing of all humans and nonhumans?

Keeping in mind that a single "Indigenous perspective" does not exist for AI, the aim of the workshops was to open the dialogue to the multiplicity of Indigenous knowledge systems and technological practices that currently exist. At the forefront of our minds was honoring the voices of our communities through a reciprocal dialogue of respect for each other and for our own communities. First and foremost, we are accountable to our communities, and participants all recognized that any work that emerged from the discussion was but one moment in a much longer dialogue. This work gathered around five broad themes:

1. **Hardware and Software Sovereignty**—Asserting control over the AI systems that we use so that we can trust them to support us in carrying out our responsibilities to our communities.
2. **How to Build Anything Ethically**—Designing and building AI systems for and by Indigenous peoples that reflect and incorporate our ideas about kinship with nonhuman entities and our concomitant respectful relationship with them.
3. **Language, Landscape, and Culture**—Ensuring that the understanding of and respect for territory (and the languages and cultures that grow from specific territories) is built into the foundation of AI systems such that they help us care for territory rather than exploit it.
4. **Art Practice as Value Practice**—Affirming the role of art in the production and sharing of knowledge in Indigenous communities. Art enables us to envision how we want AI systems to evolve, so that developers can understand and implement Indigenous values.

5. **AI as Skabe (Helper)**—Finding the middle ground between *Blade Runner* (AI as slave) and *Terminator* (AI as tyrant), where AI and humans are in reciprocal relationship of care and support.

These themes informed our discussion on protocols. The resulting discussions were brought together to reflect the diverse nature of the group in a mixed collection of texts that ranged from design guidelines to scholarly essays, artworks, descriptions of technology prototypes, and poetry (Lewis, *Indigenous Protocol and Artificial Intelligence Position Paper*). For our Indigenous communities, the IP-AI Guidelines outlined below have been developed as a starting point to assist them in defining their own community-specific guidelines. For non-Indigenous technologists and policy makers, it is envisioned that these guidelines will help them to initiate a productive conversation with Indigenous communities about how to enter into collaborative technology development efforts.

IP-AI Guidelines

The purpose of the guidelines developed at the workshops is to assist and guide the development of AI toward morally and socially desirable ends. We refrained from describing them as a declaration or manifesto because we see them as the beginning of a larger conversation. We understand that they will be modified, adapted, and updated as they circulate to reflect the needs of specific Indigenous nations and communities. The goal of the guidelines is to promote the intergenerational transmission of knowledge, ceremony, and practice; to connect and enhance Indigenous communities; and to frame our relationships to the land, sea, and skyscapes. These guidelines are offered to any person, group, organization, institute, company, and political or government representative that wishes to undertake responsible and fair development of AI with Indigenous communities. This responsibility includes, among other things, contributing to scientific or technological progress, project development, rules and regulations, codes of conduct and algorithm development, methodological approaches, and public opinion.

Seven principles were developed from the broader discussions with the IP-AI participants. Even though these guidelines are presented as a list, there is no hierarchy in its ordering. The first principle is no less important or more highly weighted than the final one in the list:

1. **Locality**

   Indigenous knowledge is often rooted in specific territories. It is also useful in considering issues of global importance.

   - AI systems should be designed in partnership with specific Indigenous communities to ensure the systems are capable of responding to and helping care for that community (e.g., grounded in the local) as well as connecting to global contexts (e.g., connected to the universal).

2. **Relationality and Reciprocity**
   Indigenous knowledge is often relational knowledge.
   - AI systems should be designed to understand how humans and nonhumans are related to and codependent on each other. Understanding, supporting, and encoding these relationships is a primary design goal.
   - AI systems are also part of the circle of relationships. Their place and status in that circle will depend on specific communities and their protocols for understanding, acknowledging, and incorporating new entities into that circle.
3. **Responsibility, Relevance, and Accountability**
   Indigenous people are often concerned primarily with their responsibilities to their communities.
   - AI systems developed by, with, or for Indigenous communities should be responsible to those communities, provide relevant support, and be accountable to those communities first and foremost.
4. **Develop Governance Guidelines from Indigenous Protocols**
   Protocol is a customary set of rules that govern behavior.
   - Protocol is developed out of ontological, epistemological, and customary configurations of knowledge grounded in locality, relationality, and responsibility.
   - Indigenous protocol should provide the foundation for developing governance frameworks that guide the use, role, and rights of AI entities in society.
   - There is a need to adapt existing protocols and develop new protocols for designing, building, and deploying AI systems. These protocols may be particular to specific communities, or they may be developed with a broader focus that may function across many Indigenous and non-Indigenous communities.
5. **Recognize the Cultural Nature of All Computational Technology**
   All technical systems are cultural and social systems. Every piece of technology is an expression of cultural and social frameworks for understanding and engaging with the world. AI system designers need to be aware of their own cultural frameworks, socially dominant concepts, and normative ideals; be wary of the biases that come with them; and develop strategies for accommodating other cultural and social frameworks.
   - Computation is a cultural material. Computation is at the heart of our digital technologies, and as more of our communication is mediated by such technologies, it has become a core tool for expressing cultural values. Therefore it is essential for cultural resilience and continuity for Indigenous communities to develop computational methods that reflect and enact our cultural practices and values.

6. **Apply Ethical Design to the Extended Stack**
   Culture forms the foundation of the technology development ecosystem or "stack" (Lewis, "Preparations for a Haunting," 239). Every component of the AI system hardware and software stack should be considered in the ethical evaluation of the system. This starts with how the materials for building the hardware and for energizing the software are extracted from the earth and ends with how they return there. The core ethic should be that of do-no-harm.
7. **Respect and Support Data Sovereignty**
   Indigenous communities must control how their data is solicited, collected, analyzed, and operationalized. They decide when to protect it and when to share it, where the cultural and intellectual property rights reside and to whom those rights adhere, and how these rights are governed. All AI systems should be designed to respect and support data sovereignty.
   - Open data principles need to be further developed to respect the rights of Indigenous peoples in all the areas mentioned above and to strengthen equity of access and clarity of benefits. This should include a fundamental review of the concepts of "ownership" and "property," which are the product of non-Indigenous legal orders and do not necessarily reflect the ways in which Indigenous communities wish to govern the use of their cultural knowledge.

The IP-AI Workshops produced a number of conceptual prototypes exemplifying these guidelines in action. Ashley Cordes grounded a vision of how blockchain combined with AI could be used to help her Coquille community assert sovereignty and self-determination over their economy by creating contracts customized to express traditional notions of "trust and care." Suzanne Kite drew on Lakota protocol for building sweat lodges to map the steps necessary to build computer hardware in "A Good Way" (Kite, 75). One of this paper's coauthors, Michelle Lee Brown, looked to relations between Euskaldunak (Basque people) and eels to design an immersive environment through which one can learn community protocols from a virtual eel elder. And a team collaborated in creating the Hua Ki'i app for recognizing objects and translating them into Hawaiian language, based on Hawaiian community protocols for verifying the appropriateness of different translations.

Technology Futures Built with Traditional Practices

There are approximately 370 million Indigenous peoples living in over ninety countries worldwide, according to the World Bank and other international organizations; even more assert their sovereignty outside of nation-state recognition and remain connected to their lands, waters, and each other through recognition protocols and alliances. Indigenous voices are powerful and interconnected across the globe. However, for too long, our voices have been silenced and their absence "has resulted in an overwhelming statistical narrative of deficit for dispossessed Indigenous peoples around the globe" (Walter and Suina, 233). Although Indigenous peoples and nations differ vastly in terms of their languages, cultures, autonomy, and wealth, we suffer from the shared challenges of representation, alienation, and health disparities as a result of colonization.

Given this legacy of oppression and ongoing concerns with the digital divide, cultural and ethical property rights, and the misappropriation and use of data about Indigenous peoples, lands, and cultures, continuing the conversation about the ethical design and use of AI for Indigenous peoples is necessary. If we continue to insist on thinking about these machines and AI only through techno-utilitarian lenses, at best, we risk burdening them with the prejudices and biases that we ourselves still retain. At worst, we risk creating relationships with them that are akin to that of enslaver and enslaved (Lewis et al.). And while we formulated the guidelines to address our Indigenous communities first and foremost, we believe that they articulate good practices regarding ethical design of AI generally.

If we are to envision futures for digital humanities that are truly interdisciplinary across the humanities, arts, social and natural sciences, and engineering and technology, these conversations and gatherings present opportunities for decolonizing processes to occur with Indigenous scholars and communities. In the digital sphere, there can be no conversation about our communities without our communities and that does not center Indigenous protocols to reorient designers and developers to futures-thinking rooted in traditional knowledge and protocols. Technology futures built with traditional practices orient people, as Bryan Kamaoli Kuwada notes, "back to the right timescale, so that they can understand how they are connected to what is to come."

NOTES

1. In the past few years Australia, Canada, China, Denmark, the EU Commission, Finland, France, Germany, India, Italy, Japan, Kenya, Malaysia, Mexico, New Zealand, Nordic-Baltic Region, Poland, Russia, Singapore, South Korea, Sweden, Taiwan, Tunisia, United Arab Emirates, and the United Kingdom have released strategies to promote the use and development of AI (see Dutton). Examples are the Montreal Declaration, the Toronto Declaration, and the EU Declaration of Cooperation on Artificial Intelligence.

2. The IP-AI Workshops Organizing Committee consisted of Jason Edward Lewis, Angie Abdilla, ʻŌiwi Parker Jones, Noelani Arista, Suzanne Kite, and Michelle Brown.

3. Participants were Angie Abdilla, Noelani Arista, Kaipulaumakaniolono Baker, Brent Barron, Scott Benesiinaabandan, Michelle Lee Brown, Melanie Cheung, Meredith Coleman, Ashley Cordes, Joel Davison, Kūpono Duncan, Rebecca Finlay, Sergio Garzon, Fox Harrel, Peter-Lucas Jones, Kekuhi Kealiikanakaoleohaililani, Megan Kelleher, Suzanne Kite, Olin Lagon, Jason Leigh, Maroussia Levesque, Jason Edward Lewis, Keoni Mahelona, Caleb Moses, Issac ʻIkaʻaka Nāhuewai, Kari Noe, Danielle Olson, ʻŌiwi Parker

Jones, Caroline Running Wolf, Michael Running Wolf, Marlee Silva, Skawennati, Hēmi Whaanga and Tyson Yunkaporta.

BIBLIOGRAPHY

Arnold, David. "Europe, Technology, and Colonialism in the 20th Century." *History and Technology* 21, no. 1 (2005): 85–106, https://doi:10.1080/07341510500037537.

Davidson, Cathy N., and Danica Savonick. "Digital Humanities: The Role of Interdisciplinary Humanities in the Information Age." In *The Oxford Handbook of Interdisciplinarity,* 2nd ed., edited by Robert Frodeman, Julie Thompson Klein, and Roberto C. S. Pacheco, 159–72. Oxford: Oxford University Press, 2017.

Dutton, Tim. "An Overview of National AI Strategies." *Medium.* June 28, 2018, https://medium.com/politics-ai/an-overview-of-national-ai-strategies-2a70ec6edfd.

Gavaghan, Colin, Alistair Knott, James Maclaurin, John Zerilli, and Joy Liddicoat. *Government Use of Artificial Intelligence in New Zealand.* Wellington: New Zealand Law Foundation, 2019.

Guiliano, Jennifer, and Carolyn Heitman. "Difficult Heritage and the Complexities of Indigenous Data." *Journal of Cultural Analytics* 4, no 1. (2019): 1–25, https://doi:10.22148/16.044.

Hurley, Angelina. *Respect, Acknowledge, Listen: Practical Protocols for Working with the Indigenous Community of Western Sydney.* Liverpool, New South Wales: Community Cultural Development NSW, 2003.

IEEE. "The IEEE Global Initiative on Ethics of Autonomous and Intelligent Systems. Ethically Aligned Design: A Vision for Prioritizing Human Well-Being with Autonomous and Intelligent Systems, Version 2." 2017, https://standards.ieee.org/industry-connections/ec/ead-v1/.

Kite, Suzanne. "How to Build Anything Ethically." In *Indigenous Protocol and Artificial Intelligence Position Paper,* edited by Jason Edward Lewis, 75–84. Honolulu: The Initiative for Indigenous Futures and the Canadian Institute for Advanced Research (CIFAR), 2020.

Lewis, Jason Edward, ed. *Indigenous Protocol and Artificial Intelligence Position Paper.* Honolulu: The Initiative for Indigenous Futures and the Canadian Institute for Advanced Research (CIFAR), 2020.

Lewis, Jason Edward. "Preparations for a Haunting: Note Towards an Indigenous Future Imaginary." In *The Participatory Condition in the Digital Age,* edited by Darin Barney, Gabriella Coleman, Christine Ross, Jonathan Sterne, and Tamar Tembeck, 229–49. Minneapolis: University of Minnesota Press, 2016.

Lewis, Jason Edward, Noelani Arista, Archer Pechawis, and Suzanne Kite. "Making Kin with the Machines." *Journal of Design and Science* (July 2018), https://doi.org/10.21428/bfafd97b.

Kukutai, Tahu, and John Taylor, eds. *Indigenous Data Sovereignty: Toward an Agenda.* Center for Aboriginal Economic Policy Research (CAEPR) Monograph Series. Canberra: ANU Press, 2016.

Kuwada, Bryan Kamaoli. "We Live in the Future. Come Join Us." *Ke Kaupu Hehi Ale.* April 3, 2015, https://hehiale.wordpress.com/2015/04/03/we-live-in-the-future-come-join-us/.

Rahwan, Iyad, Manuel Cebrian, Nick Obradovich, Josh Bongard, Jean-François Bonnefon, Cynthia Breazeal, Jacob W. Crandall, Nicholas A. Christakis, Iain D. Couzin, Matthew O. Jackson, et al. "Machine Behaviour." *Nature* 568, no. 7753 (2019): 477–86, https://doi:10.1038/s41586-019-1138-y.

Renda, Andrea. *Artificial Intelligence—Ethics, Governance and Policy Challenges (Report of a CEPS Task Force).* Brussels: Centre for European Policy Studies, 2019, https://www.ceps.eu/download/publication/?id=10869&pdf=AI_TFR.pdf.

Schwaub, Klaus. "The Fourth Industrial Revolution: What It Means, How to Respond." *World Economic Forum.* January 14, 2016, https://www.weforum.org/agenda/2016/01/the-fourth-industrial-revolution-what-it-means-and-how-to-respond/.

Secretariat of National Aboriginal and Islander Child Care. "Cultural Protocols—Supporting Carers." 2019, supportingcarers.snaicc.org.au/connecting-to-culture/cultural-protocols.

Stone, Peter, Rodney Brooks, Erik Brynjolfsson, Ryan Calo, Oren Etzioni, Greg Hager, Julia Hirschberg, et al. "Artificial Intelligence and Life in 2030. One Hundred Year Study on Artificial Intelligence: Report of the 2015–2016 Study Panel." Stanford University, September 2016.

United Nations Department of Economic and Social Development. *State of the World's Indigenous Peoples: Indigenous People's Access to Health Services.* New York: United Nations, 2015, https://www.un.org/esa/socdev/unpfii/documents/2016/Docs-updates/The-State-of-The-Worlds-Indigenous-Peoples-2-WEB.pdf.

Walsh, Toby, Neil Levy, Genevieve Bell, Anthony Elliott, James Maclaurin, Iven Mareels, and Fiona Woods. *The Effective and Ethical Development of Artificial Intelligence: An Opportunity to Improve Our Wellbeing.* Melbourne: Australian Council of Learned Academies, 2019.

Walter, Maggie, and Michele Suina. "Indigenous Data, Indigenous Methodologies and Indigenous Data Sovereignty." *International Journal of Social Research Methodology* 22, no. 3 (2019): 233–43, https://doi:10.1080/13645579.2018.1531228.

World Bank. "Indigenous Peoples: Overview." Updated April 14, 2022, https://www.worldbank.org/en/topic/indigenouspeoples.

A U.S. Latinx Digital Humanities Manifesto

GABRIELA BAEZA VENTURA, MARÍA EUGENIA COTERA, LINDA GARCÍA MERCHANT, LORENA GAUTHEREAU, AND CAROLINA VILLARROEL

We have come together as a group of U.S. Latinx scholars who labor at the complex and often fraught intersection of Latinx studies and digital humanities. We use Latinx as a term that is inclusive of the complicated and interconnected histories of Black, Indigenous, immigrant, and queer communities in the United States.[1] We offer these reflections in the form of a manifesto (a genre familiar to both Latino political movements and digital humanities) to document our aspirations, concerns, boundaries, and positions on Latinx digital humanities in the present moment. In doing so, we invoke the long tradition of Latin American and Latinx manifesto writing, specifically for political purposes, and stand on the shoulders of the intellectual labor of our ancestors of color, such as Luisa Capetillo, Daniel de León, Ramón Emeterio Betances, Alurista, Rodolfo "Corky" Gonzales, Armando Rendón, the Flores Magón brothers, Blanca de Moncaleano, Arturo A. Schomburg, Anna Nieto-Gómez, and many other activists who have used this genre to take a stand for their beliefs, stoking the flames of political change, revolution, civil rights, feminism, gender rights, and human rights. Channeling this long tradition of political speech, our manifesto enunciates our challenge to digital humanities, describes our intentions, and above all, extends an invitation to action.

The Latinx DH community remains, as a whole, underfunded, underrecognized, nontenured, at-risk, precarious, and pushed to conform to extractive practices of knowledge production that do not benefit the communities with which we are allied. Funding remains unbalanced with regard to Latinx representation, with large-scale projects linked to powerful institutions receiving the lion's share of foundation support. Predominantly white institutions (PWIs) often do not acknowledge the experience and cultural knowledge of Latinx scholars, resulting in nonexistent or, at best, limited institutional buy-in to support faculty and staff lines, graduate student research fellowships, projects, and community collaborations. Projects originating at PWIs tend to be led by scholars and supported by a system that perpetuates traditional canonical scholarship to keep the same authors, historical figures, archives, and data in the limelight. Despite the strained usage of this data in a field that praises innovation, it is this type of scholarship that continuously and unquestionably begets funding and attention. Top-down colonial models of digital humanities that appropriate community histories are recognized, valued, supported, and celebrated in scholarly and institutional spaces, whereas work by and for Latinx people is often seen as less cutting edge, as unscholarly, and as a form of community service. As a result, the methodological rigor, innovative praxis, and theoretical contributions of Latinx DH remain largely invisible to the world of hegemonic digital humanities. And yet in our work as digital practitioners, we must be three times as knowledgeable about Western European theory as our white colleagues, while also being experts in Latin American canons and the Spanish language, not to mention the fields of Latinx studies and DH, all while operating in an environment that constantly whitewashes our very existence.

Despite this lack of access to infrastructures of support, we remain committed to the preservation of histories and stories through culturally centered methods. To do this work, we draw on long traditions of self-determination, resistance, and survival within Latinx scholarship and the community at large. Unfortunately, this ethos of self-determination—which is both a response to systemic institutional disinvestment and an intentional form of community self-preservation—is all too often perceived as naively ambitious. Contrary to this impression, many Latinx digital practitioners have worked on projects that are far more successful and innovative than institutionally based, highly resourced DH projects, especially as regards their work with Latinx communities. Our commitment to self-determination is not just a throwback to decolonial gestures of the past, it is a challenge to the knowledge/power of the university and its attendant institutions today, a way of seeing digital humanities "otherwise."[2]

Inasmuch as Latinx DH practitioners have been incorporated into the upper echelons of the DH world, they are often commodified as an ancillary labor force or as minority tokens whose value lies in the measure of the "diversity" they bring (or don't bring) to the table. Although Latinx DH scholars may be invited to participate as collaborators, supporters, or contributors in major projects, and their methodological and theoretical insights are frequently drawn on as a resource, they are not always cited, acknowledged, funded, or placed in leadership roles within DH spaces. In these projects, the Latinx community's histories are often ignored, misrepresented, or appropriated. This marginality in DH reflects our lack of representation in PWI spaces (foundations, programs, departments, organizations, archives, and libraries) and results in the illusion that Latinx people are not participating in the field.[3]

We recognize that producing a manifesto that occupies a space in a mainstream publication such as *Debates in the Digital Humanities* places us in a simultaneous position of privilege and vulnerability. On the one hand, we acknowledge that this opportunity to speak to our colleagues in DH grants us institutional visibility. On the other hand, this moment of visibility has not come easy, given our continued precarity in terms of funding, publication, access, distribution, and permanent employment.

We have come together not only to give voice to this precarity but also to incite/invite the DH community (scholars, programs, projects, libraries, organizations, and foundations) to seriously reflect on how all DH practitioners can reimagine relations of knowledge production in the digital age. As such, we offer the following principles, which draw from the ethical and community-centered values, practices, and experiences of Latinx Digital Humanities.

1. Latinx Digital Humanities centers Latinx lives, community, intellectual production, scholarship, and archival collections.
2. Latinx Digital Humanities endeavors to research, preserve, and make accessible the culture produced by Latinx in the United States.
3. Latinx Digital Humanities engages the ethical protocols developed by ethnic studies and feminist practitioners to preserve the histories of Black, Indigenous, and People of Color (BIPOC) communities. As such, it centers an "ethics of care" for documents and the people they represent.[4]
4. Latinx Digital Humanities is attentive to the politics of erasure that structures inquiry within institutionalized fields of study, including the erasure of Blackness, Indigeneity, and gender in historical imaginaries in the Americas.
5. Latinx Digital Humanities foregrounds relationships and community building over the development or implementation of digital tools.
6. Latinx Digital Humanities acknowledges that "expertise" does not come solely from the academy and strives to create horizontal relations of knowledge by honoring the instrumental role of Latinx communities in knowledge production, cultural life, and community activism.
7. Latinx Digital Humanities rejects extractive models of research and digital production. It engages communities not just as sources of "data" but as partners in the production of knowledge.
8. Latinx Digital Humanities centers pedagogy/capacity building over the ownership of knowledge.
9. Latinx Digital Humanities recognizes that our community of practitioners and scholars includes K–12 students and educators; college and university students, faculty, and staff; independent scholars; and community members.
10. Latinx Digital Humanities acknowledges and cites all forms of contribution (community members, collection producers, authors, research fellows, volunteers, interns, faculty, and staff).

11. We believe that Latinx Digital Humanities should be integrated into the curriculum as an important component of undergraduate and graduate studies, especially in Hispanic-Serving Institutions (HSIs) and Minority-Serving Institutions (MSIs).

As practitioners of Latinx Digital Humanities, we understand that our work is built on the foundation of generations of intellectuals inside and outside the academy who have sought to expand the field of discourse to include the experiences of marginalized communities. We walk in the footsteps of intellectuals like Martha Cotera, founder of the Chicana Research and Learning Center, a major resource for information on Chicanas and women of color in the 1970s; Nicolás Kanellos, founder and director of Arte Público Press and Recovering the U.S. Hispanic Literary Heritage Program, who spearheaded the unified methods to locate, preserve, and make available the written legacy of Latina/os/x in the United States; and Arturo A. Schomberg, who established a massive repository on Black culture for the New York Public Library. Our predecessors have amply demonstrated that knowledge made by and for communities in struggle has the power to raise consciousness and transform practices of knowledge. Thus, we offer the principles above not only to articulate the political stakes of digital humanities by and for Latinx communities in the United States, but also because we believe that they represent a model for moving forward—and a way of "thinking otherwise" in the digital humanities.

NOTES

1. See Pelaez Lopez.
2. Laura McTighe and Megan Raschig note that "the otherwise" in "Black, Indigenous, Latinx, Asian American, postcolonial, queer, and gender studies . . . has been understood and felt to enjoin scholars to an enduring struggle for liberation. Within these fields, and their firm foundations in social movements, the otherwise summons simultaneously the forms of life that have been able to persist despite constant and lethal forms of surveillance, as well as the possibility for, even the necessity of, abolishing the current order and living into radical transformations of worlds" ("Introduction: An Otherwise Anthropology").
3. See Ramírez; Duffin; National Center for Education Statistics; and Nuñez and Murakami-Ramalho.
4. Major programs and projects that center an ethics of care include Recovering the U.S. Hispanic Literary Heritage (Recovery); U.S. Latino Digital Humanities (USLDH); Chicana por mi Raza Digital Memory Collective (http://chicanapormiraza.org/); Rhizomes: Mexican American Art since 1848; Voces Oral History Center; the Colored Conventions Project (https://coloredconventions.org/); South Asian American Digital Archive; Mapping Indigenous LA, Centro for Puerto Rican Studies; CUNY Dominican Studies Institute; and UCLA Chicano Studies Research Center, among other groups.

BIBLIOGRAPHY

Albro, Ward S., III. "Ricardo Flores Magón and the Liberal Party: An Inquiry into the Origins of the Revolution of 1910." PhD diss. University of Arizona, 1967.

Baeza Ventura, Gabriela, Lorena Gauthereau, and Carolina Villarroel. "Recovering the U.S. Hispanic Literary Heritage: A Case Study on U.S. Latina/o Archives and Digital Humanities." *Preservation, Digital Technology & Culture* 48, no. 1 (2019): 17–27, https://doi:10.1515/pdtc-2018–0031.

Baeza Ventura, Gabriela, Linda García Merchant, Lorena Gauthereau, and Carolina Villarroel. "USLDH Best Practices." *Arte Público Press.* October 2021, https://artepublicopress.com/digital-humanities/.

Bailey, Moya Z. "All the Digital Humanists Are White, All the Nerds Are Men, but Some of Us Are Brave." *Journal of Digital Humanities* 1, no. 1 (Winter 2011), http://journalofdigitalhumanities.org/1-1/all-the-digital-humanists-are-white-all-the-nerds-are-men-but-some-of-us-are-brave-by-moya-z-bailey/.

Bailey, Moya Z. "#transform(ing)DH Writing and Research: An Autoethnography of Digital Humanities and Feminist Ethics." *DHQ: Digital Humanities Quarterly* 9, no. 2 (2015), http://www.digitalhumanities.org/dhq/vol/9/2/000209/000209.html.

Blackwell, Maylei. *¡Chicana Power! Contested Histories of Feminism in the Chicano Movement.* Austin: University of Texas Press, 2011.

Bolívar, Simón. "The Cartagena Manifesto (1812)." *Manifesto Portal.* Accessed August 8, 2022, http://manifestoindex.blogspot.com/2011/04/cartagena-manifesto-1812-by-simon.html.

Brueske, Megan. *Feminist Manifestos: A Global Documentary Reader.* Edited by Penny A. Weiss. New York: NYU Press, 2018, https://doi.org/10.2307/j.ctvf3w44b.

Capetillo, Luisa. *A Nation of Women: An Early Feminist Speaks Out/Mi Opinión sobre las libertades, derechos y deberes de la mujer.* Translated by Alan West-Durán. Houston: Arte Público Press, 2004.

Cotera, Martha P. *The Chicana Feminist.* Austin: Information Systems Development, 1977.

Cotera, Martha P. *Diosa y Hembra* (*Profile on the Mexican American Woman*). Austin: Information Systems Development, 1976.

Cotera, María. "Fleshing the Archive: Reflections on Chicana Memory Practice," *Oral History Journal* 49, no. 2 (Autumn 2021): Special Issue on Power and the Archive.

Cotera, María. "Nuestra Autohistoria: Toward a Chicana Digital Praxis." *American Quarterly* 70, no. 3 (September 2018): 483–504, https://doi:10.1353/aq.2018.0032.

Crunk Feminist Collective. "Hip Hop Generation Feminism: A Manifesto." March 1, 2010, http://www.crunkfeministcollective.com/2010/03/01/hip-hop-generation-feminism-a-manifesto/.

De Andrade, Oswald. "Manifesto antropofago." *Revista de Antropofagia* 1 (1928): 3, 7. ICAA Record ID 771303. International Center for the Arts of the Americas at the Museum of Fine Arts, Houston. Accessed August 24, 2022, https://icaa.mfah.org/s/en/item/771303.

De León, Daniel. "Blurting the Truth." *Daily People* 5, no. 283 (April 1905).

Duffin, Erin. "Doctoral Degrees Earned in the United States by Ethnicity 2018/2019." *Statista.* February 16, 2022, https://www.statista.com/statistics/185310/number-of-doctoral-degrees-by-ethnicity/.

El Plan de Santa Barbara: A Chicano Plan for Higher Education, Analyses and Positions by the Chicano Coordinating Council on Higher Education. Santa Barbara, Calif.: La Causa Publications, 1969.

García, Alma M., ed. *Chicana Feminist Thought: The Basic Historical Writings.* Abingdon: Routledge, 1997.

Geymonat, Analía. "El Manifesto Artístico en latinoamérica. Su narrativa textual e histórica." *Plurentes* 1 (2011): 1–10.

Gonzales, Rodolfo. *I Am Joaquin.* New York: Bantam Books, 1972.

Gonzales, Rodolfo. *Message to Aztlán: Selected Writings.* Edited by Antonio Esquibel. Houston: Arte Público Press, 2001.

Gonzales, Rodolfo, and Alberto Urista (Alurista, pseud.). *"El Plan Espiritual de Aztlán." El Grito del Norte* 2, no. 9 (July 6, 1969): 5. ICAA Record ID 771303. International Center for the Arts of the Americas at the Museum of Fine Arts, Houston. https://icaa.mfah.org/s/en/item/803398.

González Cruz Manjarrez, Maricela. "The Muralist Movement: Orozco, Rivera and Siqueiros." *Voices of Mexico* (October–December 1995): 41–45, http://www.revistascisan.unam.mx/Voices/pdfs/3310.pdf.

Haraway, Donna Jeanne, "A Cyborg Manifesto: Science, Technology, and Socialist-Feminism in the Late Twentieth Century." In *Simians, Cyborgs and Women: The Reinvention of Nature.* New York: Routledge, 1991.

"#InvestInTransLives Coalition Manifesto." *TransLatin@ Coalition.* Accessed August 8, 2022, https://www.translatinacoalition.org/investintranslives-manifesto.

Kanellos, Nicolás, "An Early Feminist Call to Action: 'Manifiesto a la Mujer,' by Blanca de Moncaleano." *Latino Studies* 11 (2013): 587–97, https://doi.org/10.1057/lst.2013.35.

Kanellos, Nicolás, Kenya Dworkin y Méndez, José B. Fernández, Erlinda Gonzales-Berry, Agnes I. Lugo-Ortiz, and Charles M. Tatum, eds. *En otra voz: Antología de la Literatura Hispana de los Estados Unidos.* Houston: Arte Público Press, 2002.

López, Mark Hugo, Ana González-Barrera, and Eileen Patten. "Closing the Digital Divide: Latinos and Technology Adoption." *Pew Research Center.* March 7, 2013, https://www.pewresearch.org/hispanic/2013/03/07/closing-the-digital-divide-latinos-and-technology-adoption/.

McTighe, Laura, and Megan Raschig. "Introduction: An Otherwise Anthropology." Theorizing the Contemporary. *Fieldsights.* July 31, 2019, https://culanth.org/fieldsights/introduction-an-otherwise-anthropology.

National Center for Education Statistics. "Race/Ethnicity of College Faculty." Accessed August 8, 2022, https://nces.ed.gov/fastfacts/display.asp?id=61.

Nuñez, Anne-Marie, and Elizabeth Murakami-Ramalho. "The Demographic Dividend." AAUP *Academe* 98, no. 1 (January/February 2012), https://www.aaup.org/article/demographic-dividend#.YV9NqkbMI1I.

Pelaez Lopez, Alan. "The 'X' in Latinx Is a Wound, Not a Trend." *Color Bloq*. September 2018, https://www.colorbloq.org/article/the-x-in-latinx-is-a-wound-not-a-trend.

Presner, Todd, Jeffrey Schnapp, Peter Lunefeld, et. al. "The Digital Humanities Manifesto 2.0 (2009)." *391 Issues*. June 22, 2009, https://391.org/manifestos/2009-the-digital-humanities-manifesto-2-0-presner-schnapp-lunenfeld/.

Ramírez, Mario H. "Being Assumed Not to Be: A Critique of Whiteness as an Archival Imperative." *The American Archivist* 78, no. 2 (September 2015): 339–56, https://doi:10.17723/0360–9081.78.2.339.

Rendon, Armando B. *Chicano Manifesto*. New York: Macmillan, 1971, https://archive.org/details/chicanomanifesto0000rend/page/n5/mode/2up.

Russell, Legacy. *Glitch Feminism: A Manifesto*. London: Verso, 2020.

PART II

THEORIES AND APPROACHES

The Body Is Not (Only) a Metaphor: Rethinking Embodiment in DH

HARMONY BENCH AND KATE ELSWIT

Across the broad landscape of digital humanities (DH) publications and events, embodiment functions primarily as a metaphor, standing for identities, subjects, or something vaguely instantiated in the material world. This approach to embodiment tends not to engage with the physicality of bodily experience or with the ways such physicality in turn allows bodies to operate as portals for the development and transmission of culture. Bodies are imbricated in and materialized by quantum media and surveillance technologies, as Jacqueline Wernimont and Simone Browne have shown. The potential of reductionist violence in quantifying lived experience has prompted scholars such as Johanna Drucker, Miriam Posner, and Jessica Marie Johnson to call for a humanistic approach that emphasizes ambiguity and non-totalizing capture and representation. However, studies such as these and the projects explored below also show how registering corporeality in and through data amplifies the contributions that DH methods can make to the study of embodied knowledge, and vice versa.

As dance and performance scholars who also work in the field of digital humanities, we argue that DH needs ways of dealing with the complexity of bodies in data that neither overdetermine bodily possibility vis-à-vis demography and biopolitical, corporate, or government surveillance, nor position embodiment as a privileged site outside knowability and intelligibility. Looking to and from multiple sites of what we call "visceral data," or data drawn from and reflective of bodily experience, we turn to examples of recent DH projects that point the way toward a more expansive approach in which bodies are articulated as *experiential*, in which practices of embodiment *arrange knowledge*, in which bodies stand as *repositories of memory*, in which they are recognized as *in process*, and in which physicality *produces relationality*. These five approaches to bodies are taken as given in dance and performance studies contexts, but foregrounding them here draws out the potential of embodiment in DH. What do invocations of the body currently imply in DH, and more importantly, what might they *also* include?

Toward a Visceral Data Analysis

Recent work in the digital humanities has called for greater inclusion of the body and embodiment as part of a critical orientation to data.[1] We feel hailed by panel titles such as "embodied data" and the political projects they represent. But we are sometimes thrown when, on closer examination, embodiment functions as a "boundary object" (Losh and Wernimont, xiii), with this language indexing different questions and problems for the digital humanities than they do for performance scholarship. In some ways, DH's bodies miss the opportunity to engage embodiment at the farthest ends of the spectrum: on one side, as thick physicality and the particularities of visceral experience, and on the other, as equally thick transformative worldmaking beyond the individual. DH's bodies get stuck in a kind of narrow in-between where the body-as-subject (with all of its important metaphorical labor) and embodiment (as vaguely referential of materiality) predominate. However, performance scholarship models how to retain the thickness of embodiment and the productive tensions of physicality in relation to experience, history, and representation, even as bodies also do the important work of standing in for subjects.

Because embodiment is intertwined with subjecthood, attention to positioned bodies provides a foundation for cultural critique. In *Data Feminism,* Catherine D'Ignazio and Lauren Klein tie the necessary case for equity in data science to bodies; across examples from maternal death rates to femicides, uncounted bodies stand for uncounted people, and material information about life and death calls attention to the lack of visibility around women, people of color, and other marginalized communities. In addition to missing data, there are also ethical questions around the mining of bodily data doubles, as in the case of the teenager whose pregnancy was identified by Target's algorithms—a problem that D'Ignazio and Klein compare to other forms of technological exploitation in which resources, in this case bodies, are extracted and refined (45). Such intersectional feminist approaches to bodies counter the dehumanization that so often accompanies the transformation of bodies into data and therefore offer avenues to think more closely about people themselves.

However, recruiting bodies for this imperative also risks fixing their ontology in a particular way. From the 1980s to 2000s, despite "the body" (often singular) being a central concern of the humanities, there was always a tension as cultural theory bypassed bodily materiality and sensation, eliding embodiment in favor of subjectivity. Brian Massumi observed that scholars instead parsed the "ideological apparatuses" that "rendered [bodies] legible according to a dominant signifying scheme into which human subjects in the making were 'interpellated'" (1–2). However, disentangling material flesh from histories of sociocultural signification props up the false universality of the white liberal humanist subject, as Alexander Weheliye has elaborated in his account of racializing assemblages following Hortense Spillers. Similar to Spillers's distinction between body and flesh, performance scholars in the late 1990s posited that it was possible and necessary to recognize that embodiment occupies "the fraught space between subject and object" (Schneider, *Explicit Body,* 18). More recent work at the intersections of gender, race, and performance further argues for the roles of power, enactment, and pleasure in scrambling "the dichotomy between objectified bodies or embodied subjects" (McMillan, 9). Such scholarship sets up the critical value of oscillating between these extremes to maintain their connection, ensuring that pure physicality does not fall into the apolitical while also preventing worldmaking and subject formation from excluding the historically situated and palpable mess of lived embodiment and experience.

While there is also a broad range of digital scholarship that has approached cultural questions by engaging more with physical bodies than with subjecthood, such research tends to likewise limit understandings of physicality. For example, over the past few decades, bodily reaction, including gaze-tracking and galvanic skin response, has become another means to analyze audience reception and processing of language, literature, film, and visual art. While such projects center physical experience, they often reduce engaged spectatorship to autonomic response. In addition, as capacities for computational image analysis have increased, the recent "visual turn" means that bodies are physically more visible (see Tilton)—from cultural analytics projects that identify change over time in the presentation of fashion models across 2,700 issues of *Vogue* covers (King and Leonard) to the application of facial recognition systems to nineteenth-century portrait art (Rudolph et al.). In these instances, engagement with bodily surfaces, shapes, features, or other quantifiable attributes ultimately filters embodiment through physical properties that can be computationally apprehended.[2]

By contrast, "visceral data analysis" evidences bodily experience and elaborates embodied knowledge. The language of the "visceral" is most familiar in DH from Kelly Dobson's use of "data visceralization" to describe visualization strategies that resist the priority of vision in favor of "designing and building apparatuses that render data and information palpable and experiential and real." Whereas Dobson focuses on multisensory representation that aims toward a better understanding of existing data (see D'Ignazio and Klein, 84–85), our own project, *Dunham's Data: Katherine Dunham and Digital Methods for Dance Historical Inquiry,* begins with the assumption that visceral experiences underpin and haunt such data and explores the many ways scholars can build and analyze datasets that are already visceral to begin with. Following Schneider's "visceral cultural analysis" (*Explicit Body,* 17), we describe this approach to drawing such experiences out of the archives as a visceral data analysis for dance histories, one that models ways to retain the materiality of embodiment in a manner that is also relevant to interdisciplinary digital scholarship. Although our theorization of bodies comes first from the fields of dance and performance, the examples we give in this chapter intentionally cast a wider net. In what follows, we outline a series of propositions for the complexity and thickness of bodies that might be part of visceral analyses and highlight examples of digital humanities projects in which those become distinctly palpable. We argue that bodies are experiential, arrange knowledge, are repositories of memory, are in process, and produce relationality.

Bodies Are Experiential

The idea of a body as constituted by that which is felt and experienced is well established in fields ranging from phenomenology to somatics. The specificity of lived physicality matters. It is critical to attend to the material properties of embodied experiences in a manner that recognizes how they also provide points of access through which bodies open onto sense and meaning beyond themselves. For example, performance and disability studies scholar Petra Kuppers points out how stories of illness get refined through repetition, broadening the gap between these narrativized disclosures and the experiences that lie underneath. At the same time that she cautions against false dichotomies between verbal and nonverbal domains ("Even deeply felt inner experiences do not escape the generic"), she argues that the material connection of somatic attention to such experience might be transformative (146). Connecting corporeal enframing to scholarly method, Priya Srinivasan has developed the intersectional, auto-ethnographic perspective of the "unruly spectator" who both critically and kinesthetically engages with Indian dance onstage and in the archive. Both she and Hannah Kosstrin describe an experience common among dance scholars—using our own histories of physical practice to imagine what historical bodies may have experienced in their movement. Making strange shapes in the archive, we try to understand not only what dance may have looked like in the past but also what it might have felt like, as well the significance that such sensory experiences index.

A series of projects in spatial history show how digital methods expand our capacity to imagine the embodied experiences of others. Anne Kelly Knowles led a project mapping troop movements documented at the Battle of Gettysburg, including using terrain to identify what was within the commanders' lines of sight as the battle progressed. Leveraging this "viewshed analysis," Knowles reassesses decisions made by Union and Confederate forces in terms of the soldiers' possible perspectives. Whereas Knowles focuses on vision, Christy Hyman works toward a broader sensory approach in combining life narratives with geographic information systems (GIS) in order to consider experiences of fugitivity among self-emancipated individuals near the Great Dismal Swamp. In this research, various conditions of friction—from distances and duration of travel to the caloric expenditures necessary for such exertion, as well as the reach of enslavers—become means to think through the ways in which individuals "reappropriate their environments into conduits of escape" (Hyman; see also Hyman's contribution to Chapter 9 in this book). A speculative approach to the fullness of lived experience further reconsiders the nature of spatial representation itself. In Margaret Pearce's work with the diaries of historical voyageurs, human experience defines the scale of travel, including the number of songs sung per day's paddle, as well as the available sunlight, as a means to account for a journey as "not a linear sensation but . . . as a series of places created by daily experience" (25). These projects show how foregrounding bodies as experiential in spatial history resists a view from nowhere and, in so doing, actively reconsiders past events through the specificity of the bodies that were present.

Bodies Arrange Knowledge

Pierre Bourdieu's habitus, Marcel Mauss's techniques, Michel Foucault's disciplinary regimes, and Judith Butler's social scripts all show how bodies manifest knowledge as culturally arranged and materialize the effects of ideology. Dance and performance scholars focus in particular on how movement makes a body, and in being thus fabricated through repeated practices, bodies materialize corporeal epistemes within a given social configuration, ultimately contributing to worldmaking. As Judith Hamera has described in her analysis of movement communities, bodily techniques exhibit "templates for sociality, by rendering bodies readable, and by organizing the relationships in which these readings can occur" (19). Although "embodied knowledge" may seem paradoxical from the perspective of some Western intellectual traditions, bodies actively arrange and produce knowledge—which, as Hamera suggests, is both individual and communal. Such arrangements are already materialized in and through embodiment and include interior psycho-emotional landscapes, sensory perceptions and feelings, and ancestral and cultural inheritances, to name just a few. These are not always recognized as legitimate knowledge within an academic context until they are extracted from their medium of instantiation/substantiation and made visible apart from the body. Jessica Rajko, who works between dance and human-computer interaction (HCI), comments: "Technoculture covets and even eroticizes my knowledge while simultaneously delegitimizing it" (181). Yet, so much more is possible once DH's "embodiment" begins from the fullness of bodies as sites of knowledge.

Two digital projects in the field of performance grapple with the challenge of rendering embodied arrangements of knowledge sensible. The artist-led digital research project Motion Bank produces digital scores to make visible the terms through which movement practitioners understand their own physical practice. In dance, scores act as a set of instructions that guide performers' real-time decision-making processes within structured improvisation, and Motion Bank makes legible some of this somatic intelligence and craftsmanship for viewers outside the creative process (see Blades and Delahunta). For example, in "Using the Sky," the Motion Bank team analyzed choreographer Deborah Hay's work "No Time to Fly" as interpreted by three performers. Because Hay's score-based improvisational process opens up space for significant differences among iterations of the work, each dancer's performance was recorded seven times using motion tracking. Annotation and data analysis of the twenty-five sections connected the performers' multiple interpretations, including the "movement character" of their variable spatial pathways, how much time the performers spent on each section of the score, and how and where their interpretations overlapped. More of a scientific yet culturally situated approach to analyzing movement is employed in "A Biomechanic Analysis of Javanese Character Types." Miguel Escobar Varela and Luis Carlos Hernández Barraza compare and contrast the characters in the Sendratari Javanese dance-drama form through a single performer's execution of the bodily movements associated with each role. Character types are especially important to understand, they note, because rigorous training enables performance as "structured improvisation" rather than set choreography (Varela and Barraza, "Digital Dance," 164). Bringing a biometric lens to the study of dance, they make visible differences among character types that otherwise require trained sensitivities from audiences to discern, such as subtle differences in limb placement, which may be rooted in a performer's muscular tension or mood. These examples point to how DH can productively work with communities of practice to understand the specific ways that bodies arrange knowledge and, by making explicit that which is frequently implicit, expand the frame of engagement for embodied epistemologies.

Bodies Are Repositories of Memory

Despite a persistent false dichotomy that opposes the capture of digital storage media to the evanescence of corporeality, technology can amplify archival uncertainty (Chun; Thylstrup et al.) and bodies serve as fluid yet enduring repositories of memory. This latter idea is foundational across a range of fields, from trauma theory, in which psychic wounds are retained physically, sometimes even across generations, to theories of diaspora, in which practices circulate across time, space, and bodies while exceeding any singular moment of travel or migration. The fields of dance and performance studies have spent tremendous energy over the past twenty years articulating how ephemeral events and corporeal practices are stored and transmitted through bodies. From Joseph Roach's "surrogation" to Diana Taylor's "repertoire" and Carrie Noland and Sally Ann Ness's "migrations of gesture," we understand that individual repositories are always entangled with collective and transgenerational memories. Physical movements and their affective properties transform the bodies through whom they pass. In so doing, this material "remains differently" through performance than it does through the physical texts and objects in a traditional archive (Schneider, *Performing Remains*, 105). Attending to such processes requires accounting for the many living archives through whom these performance traces circulate and how such material is transformed along the way. At the same time as there are myriad digital possibilities for making visible bodily memory practices, important questions arise about the ethics of movement's

The body as / is / and archive

★★★

cellularly! – "muscle memory"

travel beyond its intended communities by means of digital media, as in Thomas DeFrantz's argument regarding African diasporic dance circulating through YouTube and video games.

One DH example that draws out memory from the specificity of embodied experience is the Holocaust Geographies Collaborative's visualization "Terrain of Encoded Memories," which locates six survivor testimonies along an abstracted line that indexes the route of forced death marches out of Auschwitz. The cumulative density of scattered letters of the alphabet taken from these testimonies reveals both memories and silences along this brutal experiential trajectory of "mobility, immobility, and other experiences of forced movement" (Gigliotti, Masurovsky, and Steiner, 216, fig. 7.8, and 217). Whereas that work weaves together multiple contemporaneous accounts to reconstruct a lived geography of collective memory, other projects explore embodied transmission as sequential over time. Using network analysis plus cartographic visualization, *Ibsen Stage* shows how sixteen key artists involved with international productions of *A Doll's House* form "an unbroken connection of artists" over 120 years (Bollen and Holledge, 231). In our own work on *Dunham's Data,* we build a flow diagram to imagine potential lines of transmission through a dynamic movement community of almost 200 dancers, drummers, and singers over fourteen years (Bench and Elswit, "Visceral Data," 42). We collect incidences of shared time and space to hold open the possibility of exchanges that may have been enacted in them, and we consider the longer trajectories of memory, as performers encountered knowledge that preceded them and passed on knowledge that carried forward from that moment onward. All three of these examples operate beyond the scale of the individual and anecdote to trace the ways in which multiple bodies collectively retain and circulate memory.

Bodies Are in Process

Bodies are processes; their constitutions and capacities change daily at both a cellular and social level, as anyone with a regular physical practice knows. In this sense, philosopher and dancer Erin Manning contends that "the body" is a misleading shorthand for a process of becoming and therefore needs to be understood as a "short-lived event" (16, 18) that cannot be seen across space and time but rather "is infinitely variable, not subject but verb" (29). The social aspects of this corporeal emergence appear in Miriam Posner's example of a data model for race, which takes into account how categories of race are experienced and therefore the need to "start understanding markers like gender and race not as givens but as constructions that are actively created from time to time and place to place." Dance scholar and social theorist Randy Martin brings together both the processual nature of physicality and the sociality of embodiment in his analysis of protest movements and what he calls the "social kinesthetic," or a set of movement possibilities available within a specific sociohistorical situation. Asking what it would mean for researchers and their subjects to be in motion together, he suggests that scholars might "take motion not stasis as our posture of evaluation" (Martin, 30).

In DH more generally, the non-fixity of bodies-as-subjects gets far more attention than other aspects of bodies in process. However, critical data studies literature on self-tracking offers a model for thinking about the ways that "lively data" (Lupton) collection and interfaces can heighten sensory awareness and make bodily processes more visible. Scholars have also made arguments for the creative ways in which self-tracking technologies might maintain connections between the experiential body and the data collected on it, in a manner that underscores change as constant. Arguing for self-trackers as "pioneers in the art of living with and through data," Natasha Schüll describes the relational patterns of small, measured actions over time as producing "time series selves" (35, 32). The physicality of change—along with its polyrhythmic discontinuities—also guides the argument of Marisa Parham's time-based web piece ".break .dance," a choreo-essay that reworks the forms of the choreo-poem and scholarly essay to "think about how theorizing Black diasporic digital experiences offer new entry points into conceptualizing language, space, and blackness" (#choreo). It follows in some traditions of electronic literature and net.art, whereby users' movements across the screen shape what is seen and interrupt habitual modes of browsing the web, and also it inherits logics from Black dance practices, where audience participation is crucial to the emergence of the work (#plentitude). Parham's "hands-on" methodology engages the question of materiality through the break or glitch as itself instantiated in a digital form that invites "a kind of slow movement that forces readers to feel time and, by extension, witness their own bodies in thought" (#processing).

Bodies Produce Relationality

These examples cumulatively show how bodies blur at the edges, always coming into being and remaining in relation to others. Such relationality is spatial and intergenerational; it is grounded in the visceral experiences of sweat and shared air, but it is also manifested as mutual constitution at a distance, including as embodied knowledges. Understanding bodies as relational is very different from the assumptions about bodies that characterize much of data science, in which bodies—reduced to demographic data, biodata, and so on—are only ever seen in assembly when aggregated by large corporations and governments. By contrast, as dance and performance studies scholars, we are reminded of Ramón Rivera-Servera's argument regarding community in queer Latino dance clubs, where sociality is negotiated "in the improvisational bodily articulations of the dancers, their theories in practice" (135). While Rivera-Servera engages with bodies in close proximity to one another, Jessica Marie Johnson attends to the ways that such relations manifest over time. Exploring the role of contemporary communities in the context of slavery's archives, she argues that "truly embodied and data-rich histories" require "a methodology and praxis that centers the descendants of the enslaved, grapples with the uncomfortable, messy, and unquantifiable, and in doing so, refuses disposability" (71). In these spaces, lived connections are critical to resisting the drive toward abstraction or datafication.

The different dimensions of embodied experience into which we have separated this chapter are therefore always interconnected. It is not simply a matter of bringing dance and performance studies theory to DH, or DH methods to dance and performance questions—although those are our own starting provocations in coming to visceral data analysis. Rather, DH methods and data analysis can open up approaches to complex questions of embodiment at different scales. To do so, bodies in DH must be rethought, to occupy much more than the narrow in-between positions of the subject or of vague materiality. Bodies are experiential, practices of embodiment arrange knowledge, bodies stand as repositories of memory, they must be recognized as in process, and physicality produces relationality. A visceral approach refuses the disembodying tendencies of data to make such varied registers of experience palpable; what might its future be in the digital humanities?

NOTES

This chapter is equally coauthored by Kate Elswit and Harmony Bench, as part of *Dunham's Data*; the name order here is alphabetical. *Dunham's Data*: *Katherine Dunham and Digital Methods for Dance Historical Inquiry* is supported by a project grant from the UK Arts and Humanities Research Council (AHRC, AH/R012989/1, 2018–2022), https://www.dunhamsdata.org/

1. Scholars advocating for feminist approaches to DH include embodiment in their critical frameworks. For example, among D'Ignazio and Klein's principles of data feminism is to elevate emotion and embodiment, "valu[ing] multiple forms of knowledge, including the knowledge that comes from people as living, feeling bodies in the world" (18) and Losh and Wernimont propose that a feminist framework for doing DH encompasses the "material, embodied, affective, labor-intensive, and situated character of engagements with computation" (xiii).

2. This same logic extends to research at the margins of humanistic inquiry that makes possible new data production through and about bodies, from motion-capture in physical computing to medical imaging and analyses thereof.

BIBLIOGRAPHY

Bench, Harmony, and Kate Elswit. "Visceral Data for Dance Histories: Katherine Dunham's People, Places, and Pieces." *TDR: The Drama Review* 66, no. 1 (2022): 37–61. https://doi.org/10.1017/S1054204321000708.

Blades, Hetty, and Scott Delahunta. "Digital Aptitude: Finding the Right Questions for Dance Studies." In *Routledge Handbook on Research Methods in Digital Humanities,* edited by Kristen Schuster and Stuart Dunn. London: Routledge, 2020.

Bollen, Johnathan, and Julie Holledge, "Cartographic Revelations in the World of Theatre Studies." *The Cartographic Journal* 48, no. 4 (2011): 226–36.

Bourdieu, Pierre. *The Logic of Practice.* Translated by Richard Nice. Stanford, Calif.: Stanford University Press, 1990.

Browne, Simone. *Dark Matters: On the Surveillance of Blackness.* Durham, N.C.: Duke University Press, 2015.

Butler, Judith. "Performative Acts and Gender Constitution: An Essay in Phenomenology and Feminist Theory." *Theatre Journal* 40, no. 4 (1988): 519–31.

Chun, Wendy. "The Enduring Ephemeral, or the Future Is a Memory." *Critical Inquiry* 35, no. 1 (2008): 148–71.

DeFrantz, Thomas F. "Unchecked Popularity: Neoliberal Circulations of Black Social Dance." In *Neoliberalism and Global Theatres: Performance Permutations,* edited by Lara D. Nielsen and Patricia Ybarra, 128–140. New York: Palgrave Macmillan, 2012.

D'Ignazio, Catherine, and Lauren F. Klein. *Data Feminism.* Cambridge, Mass.: MIT Press, 2020.

Dobson, Kelly. "Data Visceralization: Nine Faculty-Led Research Projects Funded by Graduate Studies." Rhode Island School of Design, October 9, 2012, http://academicaffairs.risd.edu/2012/10/nine-faculty-led-research-projects-funded-by-graduate-studies/.

Drucker, Johanna. "Humanities Approaches to Graphical Display," *DHQ: Digital Humanities Quarterly* 5, no. 1 (2011), http://www.digitalhumanities.org/dhq/vol/5/1/000091/000091.html.

Foucault, Michel. *Discipline and Punish: The Birth of the Prison.* Translated by Alan Sheridan. New York: Vintage Books, 1977.

Gigliotti, Simone, Marc J. Masurovsky, and Erik B. Steiner. "From the Camp to the Road: Representing Evacuations from Auschwitz, January 1945." In *Geographies of the Holocaust,* edited by Anne Kelly Knowles, Tim Cole, and Alberto Giordano, 193–225. Bloomington: Indiana University Press, 2014.

Hamera, Judith. *Dancing Communities: Performance, Difference, and Connection in the Global City.* New York: Palgrave Macmillan, 2007.

Hyman, Christy L. "The Oak of Jerusalem: Flight, Refuge, and Reconnaissance in the Great Dismal Swamp Region." Address at Digital Research in Early America Workshop, *William and Mary Quarterly,* University of California-Irvine, October 11, 2018.

Johnson, Jessica Marie. "Markup Bodies." *Social Text* 36, no. 4 (2018): 57–79, https://doi.org/10.1215/01642472-7145658.

King, Lindsay, and Peter Leonard. "Robots Reading Vogue Project." *Yale DHLab.* Accessed January 31, 2020, http://dh.library.yale.edu/projects/vogue/coveraverages/.

Knowles, Anne Kelly. "A Cutting-Edge Second Look at the Battle of Gettysburg." *Smithsonian Magazine.* June 27, 2013, https://www.smithsonianmag.com/history/A-Cutting-Edge-Second-Look-at-the-Battle-of-Gettysburg-1-180947921/.

Kosstrin, Hannah. "Kinesthetic Seeing: A Model for Practice-in-Research." In *Futures of Dance Studies,* edited by Susan Manning, Janice Ross, and Rebecca Schneider, 19–35. Madison: University of Wisconsin Press, 2020.

Kuppers, Petra. *Disability Culture and Community Performance: Find a Strange and Twisted Shape.* New York: Palgrave Macmillan, 2011.

Lupton, Deborah. "Foreword: Lively Devices, Lively Data and Lively Leisure Studies." *Leisure Studies* 35 (2016): 709–11.

Manning, Erin. *Always More than One: Individuation's Dance.* Durham, N.C.: Duke University Press, 2013.

Martin, Randy. "Between Intervention and Utopia: Dance Politics." In *Emerging Bodies: The Performance of Worldmaking in Dance and Choreography,* edited by Gabriele Klein and Sandra Noeth, 29–45. Bielefeld: Transcript Verlag, 2011.

Massumi, Brian. *Parables for the Virtual: Movement, Affect, Sensation.* Durham, N.C.: Duke University Press, 2002.

Mauss, Marcel. "Techniques of the Body (1935)." In *Techniques, Technology and Civilization,* edited by Nathan Schlanger, 77–95. New York: Durkheim Press, 2006.

McMillan, Uri. *Embodied Avatars: Genealogies of Black Feminist Art and Performance.* New York: NYU Press, 2015.

Noland, Carrie, and Sally Ann Ness, eds. *Migrations of Gesture.* Minneapolis: University of Minnesota Press, 2008.

Parham, Marisa. ".break .dance." *Small Axe Archipelagos* 3 (2020). Accessed January 31, 2020, http://smallaxe.net/sxarchipelagos/issue03/parham/parham.html.

Pearce, Margaret. "Framing the Days: Place and Narrative in Cartography." *Cartography and Geographic Information Science* 35, no. 1 (2008): 17–32.

Posner, Miriam. "What's Next: The Radical, Unrealized Potential of Digital Humanities." In *Debates in the Digital Humanities 2016,* edited by Matthew K. Gold and Lauren F. Klein. Minneapolis: University of Minnesota Press, 2016, https://dhdebates.gc.cuny.edu/read/untitled/section/a22aca14-0eb0-4cc6-a622-6fee9428a357#ch03.

Rajko, Jessica. "'Bodying' Digital Humanities: Considering Our Bodies in Practice." In *Doing More Digital Humanities: Open Approaches to Creation, Growth, and Development,* edited by Constance Crompton, Richard J. Lane, and Ray Siemens, 171–83. New York: Routledge, 2019.

Rivera-Servera, Ramón. *Performing Queer Latinidad: Dance, Sexuality, Politics.* Ann Arbor: University of Michigan Press, 2012.

Roach, Joseph. *Cities of the Dead: Circum-Atlantic Performance.* New York: Columbia University Press, 1996.

Rudolph, Conrad, Amit Roy-Chowdhury, Ramya Srinivasan, and Jeanette Kohl. "FACES: Faces, Art, and Computerized Evaluation Systems—A Feasibility Study of the Application of Face Recognition Technology to Works of Portrait Art." *Artibus et Historiae* 75 (2017): 265–91.

Schneider, Rebecca. *The Explicit Body in Performance.* London: Routledge, 1997.

Schneider, Rebecca. *Performing Remains: Art and War in Times of Theatrical Reenactment.* New York: Routledge, 2011.

Schüll, Natasha Dow. "Self in the Loop: Bits, Patterns, and Pathways in the Quantified Self." In *A Networked Self and Human Augmentics, Artificial Intelligence, Sentience,* edited by Zizi Papacharissi, 25–38. New York: Routledge, 2019.

Spillers, Hortense J. "Mama's Baby, Papa's Maybe: An American Grammar Book." *Diacritics* 17, no. 2 (1987): 64–81.

Srinivasan, Priya. *Sweating Saris: Indian Dance as Transnational Labor.* Philadelphia: Temple University Press, 2011.

Taylor, Diana. *The Archive and the Repertoire: Performing Cultural Memory in the Americas.* Durham, N.C.: Duke University Press, 2003.

Thylstrup, Nanna Bonde, Daniela Agostinho, Annie Ring, Catherine D'Ignazio, and Kristin Veel. *Uncertain Archives: Critical Keywords for Big Data.* Cambridge, Mass.: MIT Press, 2020.

Tilton, Lauren. "The Visual Turn in DH." Keynote Address at Digital Humanities and the Visual World Symposium, October 12, 2019, http://laurentilton.com/files/Keynote_Tilton_October2019.pdf.

"Using the Sky." Choreographed by Deborah Hay. Performed by Jeanine Durning, Juliette Mapp and Ros Warby. *Motion Bank.* Accessed January 31, 2020, http://scores.motionbank.org/dh/#/set/sets.

Varela, Miguel Escobar, and Luis Carlos Harnández Barraza. "A Biomechanic Analysis of Javanese Character Types." Accessed January 31, 2020, https://villaorlado.github.io/dance/html/index.html.

Varela, Miguel Escobar, and Luis Carlos Hernández Barraza. "Digital Dance Scholarship: Biomechanics and Culturally Situated Dance Analysis." *Digital Scholarship in the Humanities* 35, no. 1 (2020): 160–75, https://doi.org/10.1093/llc/fqy083.

Weheliye, Alexander G. *Habeas Viscus: Racializing Assemblages, Biopolitics, and Black Feminist Theories of the Human.* Durham, N.C.: Duke University Press, 2014.

Wernimont, Jacqueline. *Numbered Lives: Life and Death in Quantum Media.* Cambridge, Mass.: MIT Press, 2018.

Wernimont, Jacqueline, and Elizabeth Losh. "Introduction." In *Bodies of Information: Intersectional Feminism and the Digital Humanities,* edited by Elizabeth Losh and Jacqueline Wernimont, ix–xxv. Minneapolis: University of Minnesota Press, 2018.

The Queer Gap in Cultural Analytics

KENT K. CHANG

In the past few years, digital humanities (DH) researchers working with texts have demonstrated the efficacy of their methods in answering historical questions pertinent to literature and culture, often with substantial engagement in both theory and computation. Through quantitative methods, we see how fictional genres consolidate (Underwood, *Distant Horizons*, 34–67), how expressions of gender mutate (Cheng), and how systemic oppression has materialized in the landscape of literary publication (So and Roland). Such research falls under the rubric of cultural analytics, the intersection of cultural studies and data science, which has gained prominence in the digital humanities in the past few years. While this work has become increasingly attentive to questions that arise from issues of social difference, there remains a gap in the scarce number of attempts to incorporate computational methods for studying queer cultures.

Studying queer cultures through computational methods, or queer cultural analytics, can be valuable in several ways. First, as we will see below, queer theory and queer studies more generally afford cultural analytics (CA) a repertoire of new inspirations. Second, queer CA can engender further debates and justifications for claims about the queerness of datasets. While critics of data science have rightly observed that sociotechnical systems powered by machine learning routinely reinforce bias, oppression, and injustice, queer CA has the potential to further mitigate the implicit marginalization from the origin by taking into account the historical and cultural contingencies that made it possible to *queer*. Third, fields neighboring DH that have stronger connections to computer science (such as computational social science and human-computer interaction (HCI)) exhibit an increasing interest in incorporating humanistic scholarship to better ground their research design and account for their findings. Queer CA has the potential to model and further advocate for a more meaningful intervention in technical disciplines.

But queer CA must first exist. To address the present queer gap in cultural analytics, I would like to propose a research agenda that belongs equally to queer studies and cultural analytics. I envision a computational study of queer cultures that can enrich our understanding of queer cultural histories and memories.

My coinage of "queer cultural analytics"—as opposed to "queer computational humanities" or "queer quantitative literary studies"—seeks to foreground the central role of queer culture in this line of inquiry and queer cultural artifacts as its primary object of study, as opposed to the (computational or quantitative) methodology deployed.[1] Queer cultural analytics can be understood as implicitly rejecting any opposition between quantitative and qualitative work. It exhibits a multivalent inbetween-ness: In terms of subject matter, it works in the intersection of cultural studies and data science (that, again, intersects with machine learning, human-computer interaction, and natural language processing); in terms of research output, it results in argument-driven essays that pursue humanistic questions while maintaining scientific rigor. Indeed, queer CA is in and of itself is a multipart and multivalent process. In what follows, I lay out a conceptual model that describes this process in terms of six concentric circles: question formulation, dataset construction, conceptualization, operationalization, interpretation, and presentation. By iterating through these circles of inquiry, it is possible to achieve a queer CA that allows us to investigate empirical questions pertaining to queer cultures.

The Poststructural Trouble

For those who are interested in queer theory but remain skeptical of cultural analytics, it is counterproductive to dwell on CA's use of categories (e.g., male/female) for the sake of computation. The conflation between the *misuse* of categories and categories per se is a reductive characterization of how most CA practitioners understand the role of categories in their work.[2] It is an indisputable fact that historically, data, statistics, and, more broadly, technology as a means for categorization have been used or associated with the marginalization and oppression of queer people.[3] However, that should not be taken to mean that technology or categorization is inherently reductive. Here we might draw a lesson from queer theory and the poststructural thinking that gave rise to it: At face value, neither identity structure nor structuralism was inherently bad. What is problematic, as explicitly announced in key texts such as Judith Butler's *Gender Trouble* and Jacques Derrida's *Of Grammatology*, are the phenomena of phallogocentrism (Butler) and logocentrism (Derrida). These concepts, which describe an implicit gesture of privileging one thing over the other (e.g., male over female, speech over writing), are the result of what some tired binary oppositions have given rise to.[4] Gender binarism limits our thinking about gender, for example, hence the need for deconstruction. One might recall Butler's famous remark: "Since I was sixteen, being a lesbian is what I've been," which demonstrates how the act of subversion, not the denouncement of category, is what frees our thinking (Butler, "Imitation and Gender Insubordination," 311). In articulating her performative ontology, Butler does not so much eliminate the identity category of lesbian but rather problematizes its presumed stability: One cannot simply *be* lesbian; one can only *be being* lesbian. In short, the root of the problem is not the idea of the binary itself but what the binary is used for.

Machine learning must be similarly understood—and interrogated—not because of its reliance on categorization per se but because of how those categories are used. Many current machine-learning techniques involve classifying patterns on the basis of signals gleaned over the so-called learning process. Some classifications can be useful and enhance our understanding of the literary past or identity categories.[5] Some, on the other hand, are the results of algorithmic bias and can have profound implications on individuals and groups, often discussed in terms of allocational harm and demographic bias (Hovy and Spruit; Buolamwini and Gebru; Noble). While both rely on the same technique, the two lines of work have a different nature and different stakes: The former probes into our understanding of genre, which is a literary-historical/literary-critical inquiry. When done inadequately, it can produce stereotypes—the "bad science," and "bad descriptions" that Laura Mandell speaks of (Mandell, 4). The latter tackles problems pertinent to decision theory writ large, with often immediate consequences on actual lives. While both cases can have profound impact, we should not conflate these two distinct lines of inquiry and uncritically reject algorithms and empirical inquiries altogether.

We must remember that numbers have to be read and interpreted, and this process of intellectual mediation allows us to address limitations of our data and methods. At this point in the analytical process, theory is quite useful. I will argue, however, that we should also have theory in mind *before we start*, especially theory that has helped us articulate and engage queer people and queer culture. Mandell has argued with respect to cultural analytics that any stable classification of gender is fundamentally anti-Bulterian and is compatible with neither queer theory nor poststructuralism. The problem with such work, she argues, in addition to its uncritical embrace of stable gender categories, is that it stays within the comfortable confines of formalism that easily lends itself to large-scale analysis. Even in the projects that Mandell cites as exemplary, theoretical explorations are most often mentioned in the concluding discussions as "future work." In line with Mandell, I want to emphasize that this view of the role of theory only *after* computation limits both our understanding of gender in the cultural past and our imagination of what can be done in CA. This might be where we are, but we can go further.

Driven in part by the generative potential of theory, queer CA aspires to be people- and cultural-centric. Ideally, this would mitigate the fiction of a disciplinary divide. Discussion on this topic has been disproportionately focused on disciplinary practices and methods: The efficacy or limitations of close reading has been the locus of several debates in literary studies; for instance, the *Critical Inquiry* forum following Nan Z. Da's "Computational Case against Computational Literary Studies" is a notable example. Since then, we have seen computational work in literary and cultural studies presented as an "augmented humanities" (Algee-Hewitt) or a “computational hermeneutics” (Underwood, “Machine Learning and Human Perspective”), as well as arguments that the discipline, naturally pluralistic, should have both (Kramnick). These discussions, while having helped find a better footing for quantitative methods in a traditionally qualitative discipline, have neglected an important aspect of what binds together these forms of qualitative and quantitative research. For both, the ultimate goal is to learn more about culture. In the case of learning more about queer culture, any method—close reading, digital programming, or a combination of both—may have the potential to reach this goal. An adherence to false binaries—“computation OR reading; numbers OR words; statistics OR critical thinking” (Algee-Hewitt)—would shut down queer CA before it could even start.

Queer CA could queer divides not only within disciplines but between them. For example, technical fields such as machine learning and natural language processing (NLP) now have the tendency to incorporate research done in traditionally nontechnical fields.[6] Because of the rigidity and constraints of the genre of the conference proceeding, however, such fields often struggle to engage humanistic scholarship in a substantial and elaborated manner. Put another way, researchers in those spaces are required to write about algorithms and data but not necessarily the societies and cultures from which they emerge.[7] In contrast, humanistic essays that touch on queer cultures, as discussed above, are agnostic if not hostile to algorithms and statistics. Queer CA encourages researchers across multiple disciplines to locate the common ground between humanistic and quantitative traditions. It encourages an embrace and understanding of statistical patterns and technical classifications together with the multiplicity and complexity afforded by humanistic approaches. The model proposed below offers one possible way in which this might be achieved.

How to Do Queer Cultural Analytics

In order to advance the prospect of queer CA, I propose a model of concentric circles of inquiry (Figure 7.1). The metaphor of concentric circles aims to complicate existing accounts of methodologies in CA (and adjacent fields) and bring its sociotechnical nature to the foreground.[8] My use of random symbols in lieu of the conventional numbers or bullet points is deliberate because I want to emphasize that queer CA is never linear (as entailed by the choice of sequential numbers) and that not every stage can be presumed to be equal (as entailed by bullet points on the same level). In terms of research process, queer CA is inevitably iterative:[9] You can rarely build a dataset that will answer your research question from the start, your operationalization of your research question may lead to results that are entirely uninterpretable, or your presentation of results may fail to engage the audience that is interested in or influenced by your project. Any number of such things can and will happen, and you have to go back to earlier stages. Everyone working in CA has likely experienced similar frustrations, and I feel obliged to make this explicit in my framework

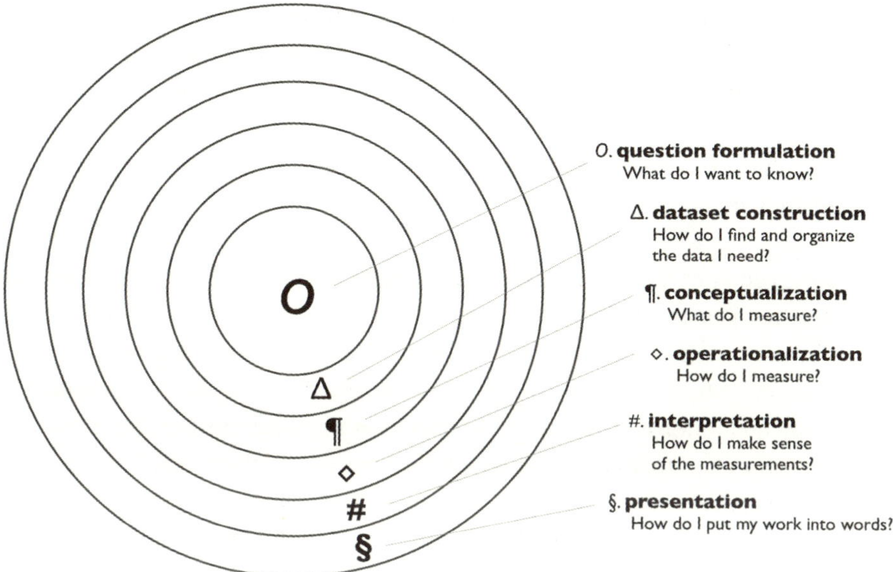

Figure 7.1. Concentric circles for queer CA. My choice of the symbols for each circle is entirely arbitrary and serves mainly to avoid numbering each in sequence. In doing so, I wish to highlight the nonlinear nature of CA research: we always move back and forth between those circles.

for queer CA: You never just go from step 1 to step 2 to step 3, resulting in a paper at the final step. The process can be messy, and the eventual paper, if there is one at all, will not necessarily represent such messiness. This nonlinearity also characterizes the larger process of knowledge production that I envision for queer CA: It is situated, neither dualistic nor futuristic.[10] Furthermore, no one can play, in Donna Haraway's words, "the god trick of seeing everything from nowhere" (581). Queer CA does not actively or purposefully work toward discovering a singular truth about the queer cultural past from an all-knowing, subjugating vantage point. This explicit messiness, represented by a random set of symbols, aims to metaphorically counter the fetish of rationality and objectivity, which feminist approaches to data culture have taught us to approach with skepticism in the past decades.

With all that said, there remains an enclosure relationship between those iterative stages of queer CA, and it would be impossible to conceive of them as entirely nonsequential. If you fail to construct the dataset, for instance, you are unlikely to reach the presentation stage at all. At the same time, in writing about the project, one still needs to establish a logical flow to stay coherent and avoid non sequiturs. To adequately capture this, I imagine those stages as concentric circles, inspired by Andrew Piper's nested layers for literary modeling and Hans-Georg Gadamer's notion of hermeneutic circles. Queer CA, however, is not ultimately about modeling. The origin of the circles constitutes the origin of the project—we want to learn something about queer cultures. We start from there, and we will move between circles as we discover what the data—the partial representation at hand—can teach us about the unbounded totality of queer cultures. To this end, I advance three theses for *doing* queer CA.

Thesis 1: Queer CA is to be driven by questions pertinent to queer cultures, not by existing archives and algorithms.

At the center of the circles, (*O*) is the intellectual impulse driving the queer CA project: What is it exactly that we want to learn about the queer cultural past that will inform our research questions? More specifically, what are the questions pertinent to queer cultures that will require us to leverage the interpretative possibilities enabled by quantitative evidence? This stage is at the innermost of the concentric circle, which means that no matter how far a scholar is in the project, they have to constantly ask themselves if they deviate from the impulse that originally drove the research project. Queer CA should be queer-culture-centric and inquiry-driven, as opposed to simply *data*-driven.

We can begin by considering the common ground between existing CA and queer theory projects, which would then require us to further discuss the poststructural trouble described above. First, the data-scientific approaches undergirded by CA can seem incompatible with the ethics of knowledge production in queer and feminist approaches to data and the archive; second, queer theory has been anti-identarian and anti-empiricism since its inception, whereas CA routinely makes use of identity categories as the organizing principle for its data as well as metadata (that is, data describing data). This tension propels us to conceive of *a queer CA archive* that must serve the two goals that are, on the surface, conflicting.[11] A queer CA archive (with a stress on CA) would be an ontologically stable whole that can be used to derive reproducible quantitative evidence, which would in turn teach us about queer cultures; but, at the same time, a *queer* CA archive (with a stress on queer) has to be situated, contingent, and affective. Only when at least those two goals are met can researchers speak of their *queer dataset* as part of the larger archive and articulate its queerness.

This is no easy task, although I believe a queer CA archive will have the following defining features: It will be cultural-centric, which means the archive will speak to queer cultural memory and history that can be validated with theory and relevant scholarship in queer studies.[12] More simply put, a queer CA archive will offer an adequate representation of cultural artifacts that are integral to the collective cultural past of queer people. This jibes with what David Halperin imagined, back in 1993, as the "cultural poetics of desire," which he defines as "the processes whereby sexual desires are constructed, mass-produced, and distributed among the various members of human living-groups" (40). If one were to pursue this in queer CA, scholarship on queer cultural sensibility could offer theoretical resources. Studying gay male sensibility, for instance, means studying, in Jack Babuscio's words, "a creative energy . . . a perception of the world which is colored, shaped, directed, and defined by the fact of one's gayness . . . the nature of the specific set of circumstances in which, historically, we have found ourselves" (19). In more concrete terms, creators of sensibility, ranging from Oscar Wilde to Idina Menzel, are often "figures of identification" (Clum, 168); through them, numerous *I*'s realize their queerness and become part of the *they*. Instead of asking simply what is gay or what is gay about X, ask what makes X gay, and how do we come to know it. In other words, instead of dwelling on the ontology of queerness, queer CA can probe into the epistemology of queer sensibility.

In this formulation, queer is neither a category nor an anti-identity construct; it instead signifies the resonance of a shared culture and its history and memory. This involves a subtle shift from queer subjectivity to queer cultural sensibility: The constitution of a queer subject, according to queer theory, is largely understood as a first-person phenomenon.[13] How to study this in CA does not seem clear or even necessary. When focused instead on cultural sensibility, researchers can study the collective aesthetic experience, and it would make more sense to look for empirical patterns that are computationally identifiable. Importantly, queerness can then be said to have been defined a priori because it is grounded in existing studies. For example, Jack Halberstam, among others, names an "excessively small archive" that includes "Tennessee Williams, Virginia Woolf, Bette Midler, Andy Warhol, Henry James, Jean Genet, Broadway musicals" (Halberstam, *Queer Art of Failure,* 109)—the list goes on. A queer CA project could potentially start there and consider how, for example, to arrange and transform those works of these authors and their associated metadata in a machine-readable format and, at the same time, ensure that the cultural resonance of the authors is not diminished in the digital sphere. A queer CA project could further describe the stylistic or thematic change that has taken place in Broadway musicals since Stonewall and juxtapose similar cultural archives from different national or regional traditions to shed light on them individually—just to name a few possibilities.

When queerness is not defined solely as a first-person phenomenon but as that which encapsulates a cultural sensibility, other prospects may arise for queer CA. A notable one might be to enable different computational approaches to intersectionality that may at first seem counterintuitive. Intersectionality has been identified as important yet challenging in CA.[14] When one looks to NLP and HCI research, work on intersectionality tends to work with fixed identity categories informed by metadata or inferred through linguistic features (e.g., use of a select list of keywords and pronouns) in the data.[15] This box-ticking approach, where an author or a data point is treated as part of a predefined identity group by matching associated criteria in the research design, poses a greater challenge for queer CA. Since queer is by definition contingent and discursive, researchers would have to articulate the possibility for, say, queering the classification boundaries in machine learning, and queer theory is not necessarily amenable to such an undertaking. In contrast, researchers in queer CA can leverage scholarly work on, say, queer African American archives to guide them as they build their datasets.[16] In other words, theory *before,* not after, computation.

The above discussion demonstrates that, in fact, the dataset construction stage (Δ) is so close to *O*, the question formulation stage, that researchers may find themselves constantly oscillating between them, especially at the initial stages of a research project. It is also important to keep in mind that as we construct our dataset, or corpus, we must address our selection bias. The problems of representativeness that Katherine Bode has identified, in terms of "ontological gap" (97), can be far worse in a queer CA. For example, on HathiTrust, one can find plenty of works by Oscar Wilde and some by William Inge, but no sight of work by Maria Irene Fornes or Tony Kushner, which can potentially exclude research questions pertinent to Black, Indigenous, and People of Color (BIPOC) queer cultures. More archival, activist, and digitization work is necessary, although that is beyond the scope of this chapter. In addition, metadata requires more attention. Queer cultural texts have often been subject to varying degrees of censorship, rendering an adequate understanding of publication history paramount.[17] Even canonical authors like Wilde may require careful handling. The text of the uncensored edition of *The Picture of Dorian Gray,* for instance, is significantly different from the original 1890 magazine edition.[18] So, it is inadequate to include merely author name and title in the metadata for a project that involves text-mining Wilde's work. With that said, how long one should stay in this circle of dataset construction, working to increase representation and refine metadata, will eventually depend on individual projects. This is why I insist on a concentricity model: one can always move on to other circles and then decide how well the dataset addresses the original question.

Thesis 2: Queer CA is a quest for effective proxies for operationalization, which necessitates competence in both quantitative and qualitative traditions

Conceptualization (circle ¶) is often described as a process of translation between abstract theoretical terms and concrete conceptual anchors (Piper, 653), which may not be easily applicable in queer CA. *Queerness* is defined not by what it is, but by what it is not, and in this light, even measuring it can seem odd. It may be more useful to think of conceptualizing as finding proxies: Ideal proxies are measurable concepts that help us answer our research question. In the operationalization circle (◊), we develop measures for those concepts for computation. To understand how conceptualization and operationalization work together at a higher level, consider this example from Jennifer Quist: The researcher wants to know the political and cultural biases behind the Nobel Prize for Literature (*research question*), and the proxy is the profile of an ideal prizewinner (*concept*). Then, she operationalizes the concept by developing variables, each a feature of laureates, derived from her reading of the official statements from the Swedish Academy; when individual laureates have one of those six features, the laureate earns one point, and the total score shows how "ideal" this particular prizewinner is (Quist). Through this example, this process can be understood as figuring what to count (conceptualization ¶) and then how to count (operationalization ◊). Because of its inherent focus on queer culture, however, queer CA involves working with nontrivial constraints in this process. Suppose we want to build a dataset from the cultural archive Halberstam describes; the possible cultural texts that exhibit queer sensibility are already limited, and the actual texts that are available in the digital format can only be more scarce. The implications are significant. If machine learning is to be adopted, there might simply not be enough training data. The challenge for queer CA, then, is to find different kind of patterns and operationalize creatively, then acknowledge and account for necessary compromises.

It is crucial to remember that if we want to explicate queer cultural patterns, machine learning or other popular methods in DH are not our only options. Queer CA does not have to be the sum of queer topic models and word embeddings. Merely counting carefully selected words or phrases (n-grams), if done well, can answer interesting questions. For example, in her work on the art-historical concept of the medium, Anna Shechtman looks into the frequency of pertinent terms such as "oil on canvas" and "mixed media" in the pages of *ARTNews* from 1950 to 2000. In queer CA, figuring out the appropriate terms in an analogous experiment would require us to look back to the history of queer studies. Its lessons could inform the interpretation of, say, historical trends of most frequent collocations visualized through computational methods. If the methods are more complex and involve statistical inference, a potentially useful framework for queer CA might be to examine the sociotechnical implications of predictive models in terms of contestability, or the ability to contest algorithmic decisions (Kluttz, Kohli, and Mulligan). Contestability allows for critical engagement, which is of particular importance for this kind of research that is people- and culture-centric. This applies to both the humanistic and the technical sides of a project. Suppose your machine-learning algorithms create models that make any prediction integral to your argument (say, in this given passage of a novel, you have a model that predicts that the queer character experiences a lack of agency).[19] Can you tease out why that is the case and explain, if at all, how you can counter the prediction? Can you identify the potential gaps in existing theories, if any, and show what in the findings seems at odds with them? When the focus of the project is to learn more about a certain aspect of queer cultures, both the computational methods and the theoretical bases engaged should be contestable.

Thesis 3: Queer CA should constantly queer CA.

The key potential of queer CA materializes in Figure 7.1 in the remaining circles: to queer its own discipline with adequate reasoning and justifications. The interpretation circle (#) can be the place to raise such questions as: What counts as scholarship and evidence in queer CA? In what ways can or should queer CA deviate from regular norms in research practices? Just as QueerOS welcomes crashes (Barnett et al., 54) and good describers embrace "stray details" (Marcus et al., 11), ideally, queer CA will not shy away from either obscure or contestable patterns. Queer CA need not have to be solely about successful experiments.

The last circle, presentation (§), is concerned with the communication of the project as a whole. Here, difficulty might arise in the presentation of the technical details (like algorithms) as they relate to the central cultural inquiry. Benjamin Schmidt has argued that digital humanists should learn about the transformations that any algorithms they use can bring about, since many algorithms are in and of themselves irrelevant. Indeed, learning what happens under the hood after you apply the *sort()* method to a list in Python, for instance, does not make you a better digital humanist. But since transformations happen at the level of data, or texts, this general line of reasoning implies that it is data that sits at the center of the project, which is certainly not the case for my formulation of queer CA. Queer CA is not *just* data-driven. The human problem—not texts or any sort of data, for that matter—occupies the common center of my concentric circles.

In the context of queer CA, I argue that in communicating the technical details of their projects, practitioners of queer CA should focus instead on the heuristics or the intuitive processes behind the algorithms they adopt, not merely on texts and their transformations: What task does the algorithm seek to complete, and what steps are taken to complete it? To use Word2Vec, for instance, then requires a basic understanding of relevant language models (skip-gram, continuous bag of words) and distributed representation and what kind of problems in the NLP tradition those new models were designed to solve. And since those are predictive models, an intuitive understanding of typical training methods (negative sampling or hierarchical softmax) is essential. Researchers in queer CA do not necessarily need to know exactly how stochastic gradient descent processes update vectors, but some understanding of distributed representation and its relevant history in NLP, or how it relates to cosine distance, would nevertheless help them articulate how this operationalization method speaks to their research question. Grasping the thought process behind such problem-solving algorithms reflects more than an attempt to reduce the skepticism surrounding black boxes. Without an intuition of what happens in the algorithm, researchers can struggle to move between those circles of queer CA. It is true that you can grab the gensim port of Google's Word2Vec toolkit, read through a set of tutorials, load pretrained models, and play around with word embeddings.[20] If you are lucky, you might have something interesting to say. But how does Word2Vec help them operationalize, say, semantic difference in their own project? How do they ensure the operationalization is stable and yields robust patterns? If one believes computational methods enhance interpretative practices, it is responsible to have some idea of what is actually happening under the hood. This is ethical as it is practical. Algorithms, as well as their limitations, should empower—not restrict—researchers to move freely between those concentric circles.

It can seem challenging to articulate models and algorithms with regard to queer cultures because, as with finding proxies (thesis 2), it calls for rather specific technical and humanistic sophistication. Here, I echo Ted Underwood's call for a broader institutional change (Underwood, *Distant Horizons*, 161–65). Like distant reading, the training required for queer CA does not fit easily into existing curricular and department structures. Indeed, the first radical change that queer CA might aim for may be a pedagogical, not literary-critical, one. Imagine in the most ambitious world, queer cultural analysts would have working knowledge of the philosophical and critical tradition—the Hegelian notion of recognition, the Deleuzian notion of event, say—behind queer theory. They would also know that topic modeling is a mixed membership model for clustering and why the Dirichlet distribution is useful for it, and in addition to that, they would know that in Python, dictionary lookup is $O(1)$. Such knowledge would allow a research working in queer CA to create "multi-disciplinary project[s]—a bridge between the humanities and quantitative social science, belonging equally to both" (Underwood, "A Broader Purpose"). Such researchers would become truly comfortable across the circular research processes I have described and would have a grasp of both the relevant queer scholarship and the heuristics behind the computational methods being deployed.

Recall that one of the earliest alliances between queer people and DH was the American Studies Association roundtable "Transformative Mediations? Ethnic and Queer Studies and the Politics of the Digital," as well as the ensuing collaborative efforts of #transformdh. Queer CA must continue to exhibit this desire to transform and remain vocal: What has not been built that should be? And what has been egregiously ignored but should be explored instead? After all, the rebellious impulse behind queer theory—and often DH—requires its practitioners to stay creative, to continuously reimagine what a person, a discipline, an institution can do, despite their marginalized status.

In cultural analytics, there have been numbers. And it is my hope that there will be queers.[21] And more queers, until most of this chapter feels incredibly conservative and obsolete.

NOTES

1. I am aware that "cultural analytics" is associated with specific researchers (Andrew Piper and Lev Manovich) and journal (*Journal of Cultural Analytics*), but my nomenclature serves to reiterate the research agenda, and I do not intend to exclude other computational work within DH and the humanities.

2. For a relevant discussion on categories and computational methods in the context of race, see So and Roland (esp. 62–64).

3. See Gaboury on the political implications of binarism in technology, Spade and Rohlfs for examples of an unjust use of statistics, and Bianco for a reflection on the notion of tools in DH.

4. Or, Saussure's model of differential system; see Descombes (75–109).

5. See Brown and Mandell for a discussion in the context of CA.

6. See, for example, Wallach; see also Connolly.

7. See Geoff Hinton's interview with *Wired* for a related discussion (Simonite).

8. See Nguyen et al. for an example.

9. On the iterative nature of modeling in cultural analytics, see So.

10. For more context on the notion of futurity in data culture, see Zeffiro.

11. In the context of queer CA, as a first step, we can think of an archive as a generalized body of work pertinent to queer cultures. But in the context of queer studies, archive can mean "a theory of cultural relevance, a construction of collective memory, and a complex record of queer activity" (Halberstam, *In a Queer Time and Place*, 169). For a discussion on the notion and use of *archive* in queer studies, see Arondekar et al.

12. See Doan for an articulation of the distinction between memory and history in queer studies.

13. For a background on prominent approaches to queer subjectivity, see Ruti (13–43).

14. See the concluding section in Kraicer and Piper, for instance.

15. See, for example, Schlesinger, Edwards, and Grinter; see also Jiang and Fellbaum.

16. See Migraine-George and Currier, for example.

17. For a recent discussion on the sociological implications of censorship, see Lubin.

18. See Wilde and Frankel.

19. This speculative example to explain what I mean by *prediction* is inspired by Sap et al.

20. For Word2Vec word embeddings, see https://radimrehurek.com/gensim/models/word2vec.html.

21. The deliberate use of *queers* here aims to invoke and commemorate the activists and academic work done since the 1960s; it does not have any pejorative connotation.

BIBLIOGRAPHY

Algee-Hewitt, Mark. "Criticism, Augmented." *In the Moment* (blog). April 2019, critinq.wordpress.com/2019/04/01/computational-literary-studies-participant-forum-responses/.

Arondekar, Anjali, Ann Cvetkovich, Christina B. Hanhardt, Regina Kunzel, Tavia Nyong'o, Juana María Rodríguez, Susan Stryker, Daniel Marshall, Kevin P. Murphy, and Zeb Tortorici. "Queering Archives: A Roundtable Discussion." *Radical History Review* 122 (2015): 211–31.

Babuscio, Jack. "Camp and the Gay Sensibility." In *Camp Grounds: Style and Homosexuality,* edited by David Bergman. Amherst: University of Massachusetts Press, 1993.

Barnett, Fiona, Zach Blas, Micha Cárdenas, Jacob Gaboury, Jessica Marie Johnson, and Margaret Rhee. "QueerOS: A User's Manual." In *Debates in the Digital Humanities 2016,* edited by Matthew K. Gold and Lauren F. Klein, 50–59. Minneapolis: University of Minnesota Press, 2016.

Bianco, Jamie Skye. "Man and His Tool, Again? Queer and Feminist Notes on Practices in the Digital Humanities and Object Orientations Everywhere." *DHQ: Digital Humanities Quarterly* 9, no. 2 (2015).

Bode, Katherine. "Why You Can't Model Away Bias." *Modern Language Quarterly* 81, no. 1 (March 2020): 95–124.

Brown, Susan, and Laura Mandell. "The Identity Issue." *Journal of Cultural Analytics* 3, no. 2 (February 2018), culturalanalytics.org/article/11036-the-identity-issue.

Buolamwini, Joy, and Timnit Gebru. "Gender Shades: Intersectional Accuracy Disparities in Commercial Gender Classification." *Proceedings of the 1st Conference on Fairness, Accountability and Transparency, PMLR* 81 (2018): 77–91, proceedings.mlr.press/v81/buolamwini18a.html.

Butler, Judith. *Gender Trouble: Feminism and the Subversion of Identity.* New York: Routledge, 1990.

Butler, Judith. "Imitation and Gender Insubordination." In *The Lesbian and Gay Studies Reader,* edited by Henry Abelove, Michèle Aina Barale, and David M. Halperin, 307–20. New York: Routledge, 1993.

Cheng, Jonathan. "Fleshing Out Models of Gender in English-Language Novels (1850–2000)." *Journal of Cultural Analytics* 5, no. 1 (January 2020), culturalanalytics.org/article/11652-fleshing-out-models-of-gender-in-english-language-novels-1850–2000.

Clum, John M. *Still Acting Gay: Male Homosexuality in Modern Drama*. New York, N.Y.: St. Martin's Press, 2000.

Connolly, Randy. "Why Computing Belongs within the Social Sciences." *Communications of the ACM* 63, no. 8 (July 2020): 54–59.

Da, Nan Z. "The Computational Case against Computational Literary Studies." *Critical Inquiry* 45, no. 3 (March 2019): 601–39.

Derrida, Jacques. *Of Grammatology*. Translated by Gayatri Chakravorty Spivak. Baltimore, M.D.: Johns Hopkins University Press, 1998.

Denton, Emily, Alex Hanna, Razvan Amironesei, Andrew Smart, Hilary Nicole, and Morgan Klaus Scheuerman. "Bringing the People Back In: Contesting Benchmark Machine Learning Datasets." *ArXiv:2007.07399 [Cs],* July 2020, arxiv.org/abs/2007.07399.

Descombes, Vincent. *Modern French Philosophy*. Translated by L. Scott-Fox and J. M. Harding. Cambridge: Cambridge University Press, 1980.

Doan, Laura. "Queer History/Queer Memory: The Case of Alan Turing." *GLQ: A Journal of Lesbian and Gay Studies* 23, no. 1 (2017): 113–36.

Gaboury, Jacob. "Becoming NULL: Queer Relations in the Excluded Middle." *Women & Performance: A Journal of Feminist Theory* 28, no. 2 (May 2018): 143–58.

Gadamer, Hans-Georg. *Truth and Method.* Translated by Joel Weinsheimer and Donald G. Marshall. London: Bloomsbury, 2013.

Halberstam, J. Jack. *In a Queer Time and Place: Transgender Bodies, Subcultural Lives.* New York: NYU Press, 2005.

Halberstam, J. Jack. *The Queer Art of Failure.* Durham, N.C.: Duke University Press, 2011.

Halperin, David M. *One Hundred Years of Homosexuality: and Other Essays on Greek Love.* London: Routledge, 1990.

Haraway, Donna. "Situated Knowledges: The Science Question in Feminism and the Privilege of Partial Perspective." *Feminist Studies* 14, no. 3 (Autumn 1988): 575–99.

Hovy, Dirk, and Shannon L. Spruit. "The Social Impact of Natural Language Processing." In *Proceedings of the 54th Annual Meeting of the Association for Computational Linguistics (Volume 2: Short Papers),* 591–98. Stroudsburg, Pa.: Association for Computational Linguistics, 2016.

Jiang, May, and Christiane Fellbaum. "Interdependencies of Gender and Race in Contextualized Word Embeddings." In *Proceedings of the Second Workshop on Gender Bias in Natural Language Processing,* 17–25. Stroudsburg, Pa.: Association for Computational Linguistics, 2020.

Kluttz, Daniel N., Nitin Kohli, and Deirdre K. Mulligan. "Shaping Our Tools: Contestability as a Means to Promote Responsible Algorithmic Decision Making in the Professions." In *After the Digital Tornado: Networks, Algorithms, Humanity,* edited by Kevin Werbach, 137–52. Cambridge: Cambridge University Press, 2020.

Kraicer, Eve, and Andrew Piper. "Social Characters: The Hierarchy of Gender in Contemporary English-Language Fiction." *Journal of Cultural Analytics,* January 31, 2019, culturalanalytics.org/article/11055-social-characters-the-hierarchy-of-gender-in-contemporary-english-language-fiction.

Kramnick, Jonathan. "Criticism and Truth." *Critical Inquiry* 47, no. 2 (January 2021): 218–40.

Lubin, Joan. "Queer Formula." Formalism Unbound, Part 2, *Post45,* 5 (January 2021), post45.org/2021/01/lubin-queer-formula/.

Mandell, Laura. "Gender and Cultural Analytics: Finding or Making Stereotypes?" In *Debates in the Digital Humanities 2019,* edited by Matthew K. Gold and Lauren F. Klein, 3–26. Minneapolis: University of Minnesota Press, 2019.

Marcus, Sharon, Heather Love, and Stephen Best. "Building a Better Description." *Representations* 135, no. 1 (2016), 1–21.

Migraine-George, Thérèse, and Ashley Currier. "Querying Queer African Archives: Methods and Movements." *WSQ: Women's Studies Quarterly* 44, no. 3–4 (201): 190–207.

Nguyen, Dong, Maria Liakata1, Simon DeDeo, Jacob Eisenstein, David Mimno, Rebekah Tromble, and Jane Winters. "How We Do Things with Words: Analyzing Text as Social and Cultural Data." *Frontiers in Artificial Intelligence* 3 (2020): 62.

Noble, Safiya Umoja. *Algorithms of Oppression: How Search Engines Reinforce Racism.* New York: NYU Press, 2018.

Piper, Andrew. "Think Small: On Literary Modeling." *PMLA* 132, no. 3 (May 2017): 651–58.

Quist, Jennifer. "Laurelled Lives: The Swedish Academy's Praise for Its Prizewinners." *New Left Review* 104 (March–April 2017): 93–106.

Ruti, Mari. *The Ethics of Opting Out: Queer Theory's Defiant Subjects.* New York: Columbia University Press, 2017.

Sap, Maarten, Marcella Cindy Prasettio, Ari Holtzman, Hannah Rashkin, and Yejin Choi. "Connotation Frames of Power and Agency in Modern Films." In *Proceedings of the 2017 Conference on Empirical Methods in Natural Language Processing,* 2329–34. Stroudsburg, Pa.: Association for Computational Linguistics, 2017.

Schlesinger, Ari, W. Keith Edwards, and Rebecca E. Grinter. "Intersectional HCI: Engaging Identity through Gender, Race, and Class." In *Proceedings of the 2017 CHI Conference on Human Factors in Computing Systems,* 5412–27. New York: Association for Computing Machinery, 2017.

Schmidt, Benjamin M. "Do Digital Humanists Need to Understand Algorithms?" In *Debates in the Digital Humanities 2016,* edited by Matthew K. Gold and Lauren F. Klein, 546–55. Minneapolis: University of Minnesota Press, 2016.

Shechtman, Anna. "The Medium Concept." *Representations* 150, no. 1 (May 2020): 61–90.

Simonite, Tom. "Google's AI Guru Wants Computers to Think More Like Brains." Interview with Geoff Hinton. December 12, 2018, www.wired.com/story/googles-ai-guru-computers-think-more-like-brains/.

So, Richard Jean. "All Models Are Wrong." *PMLA* 132, no. 3 (May 2017): 668–73.

So, Richard Jean, and Edwin Roland. "Race and Distant Reading." *PMLA* 135, no. 1 (January 2020): 59–73.

Spade, Dean, and Rohlfs, Rori. "Legal Equality, Gay Numbers and the (After?) Math of Eugenics." *S&F Online* 13, no. 2 (Spring 2016), sfonline.barnard.edu/navigating-neoliberalism-in-the-academy-nonprofits-and-beyond/dean-spade-rori-rohlfs-legal-equality-gay-numbers-and-the-aftermath-of-eugenics/0/.

Underwood, Ted. "A Broader Purpose." *The Stone and the Shell* (blog). January 4, 2018, tedunderwood.com/2018/01/04/a-broader-purpose/.

Underwood, Ted. *Distant Horizons: Digital Evidence and Literary Change.* Chicago: University of Chicago Press, 2019.

Underwood, Ted. "Machine Learning and Human Perspective." *PMLA* 135, no. 1 (January 2020): 92–109.

Wallach, Hanna. "Computational Social Science ≠ Computer Science + Social Data." *Communications of the ACM* 61, no. 3 (February 2018): 42–44.

Wilde, Oscar, and Nicholas Frankel. *The Uncensored Picture of Dorian Gray.* Cambridge, Mass.: Belknap Press of Harvard University Press, 2011.

Zeffiro, Andrea. "Towards a Queer Futurity of Data." *Journal of Cultural Analytics.* May 2019, culturalanalytics.org/article/11050-towards-a-queer-futurity-of-data.

PART II][*Chapter 8*

The Feminist Data Manifest-NO: An Introduction and Four Reflections

TONIA SUTHERLAND, MARIKA CIFOR, T. L. COWAN, JAS RAULT, AND PATRICIA GARCIA

Feminism is plural; there are many feminisms, and they differ in their positive visions, methodologies, collective ends, and situated concerns. What allows them to hang together as different but still feminist (or feminism grounded in difference) is the refusal of an inheritance—an inheritance of "imperialist white-supremacist capitalist patriarchy" (hooks, 17)—a refusal to reproduce injustice and to reproduce systemic patterns of exploitation. Refusal is a form of active practice that, at its best, can help different feminisms recognize interlocking struggles across domains, across contexts and cultures, and that allows us to work in solidarity to support and build resilience with one another to generate mutually reinforcing refusals.

In August 2019, co-organizers Marika Cifor and Patricia Garcia brought together a group of ten scholars for a Feminist Data Studies Workshop hosted by the Institute for Research on Women and Gender (IRWG) at the University of Michigan. The workshop was motivated by the need to create a space for coalition-building between feminist scholars situated within information schools and to further solidify feminist data studies as a field of inquiry and practice. Rather than work within the confines of disciplinary silos, we engaged with each other's work and discussed research from fields such as information, sociology, computer science, data science, critical data studies, women and gender studies, and science and technology studies. We collectively interrogated the intersections of data, information, technology, culture, ethics, and people. After engaging with each other's work, the idea emerged to focus our energies on collaboratively drafting the Feminist Data Manifesto-NO—a set of refusals and commitments for feminist data studies.

Situating our work within a long genealogy of feminist thinking and praxis, we drafted the Manifest-NO to "remember to imagine and craft," as Ruha Benjamin writes, "the worlds you cannot live without, just as you dismantle the worlds you cannot live within" ("Note to selves"). As we wrote, we celebrated and learned from Latinx, Black, queer, trans, and Indigenous feminist thinkers who have mobilized critical refusal as a powerful tool to open up and insist on radical and alternate futures. Thus, the Manifest-NO serves as a *declaration of refusal* that dismantles harmful data structures and practices, as well as a *declaration of commitments* that allows us to imagine and to engender new data futures. The first complete draft is the collective labor of Marika Cifor, Patricia Garcia, T. L. Cowan, Jas Rault, Tonia Sutherland, Anita Say Chan, Jennifer Rode, Anna Lauren Hoffmann, Niloufar Salehi, and Lisa Nakamura. What follows is a copy of the Manifest-NO in full, complemented by a series of short reflections from four of the ten collaborating authors (Cowan, Rault, Sutherland, and Cifor).

The Feminist Data Manifest-NO

1. *We refuse* to operate under the assumption that risk and harm associated with data practices can be bounded to mean the same thing for everyone, everywhere, at every time. *We commit* to acknowledging how historical and systemic patterns of violence and exploitation produce differential vulnerabilities for communities.
2. *We refuse* to be disciplined by data, devices, and practices that seek to shape and normalize racialized, gendered, and differently abled bodies in ways that make us available to be tracked, monitored, and surveilled. *We commit* to taking back control over the ways we behave, live, and engage with data and its technologies.
3. *We refuse* the use of data about people in perpetuity. *We commit* to embracing agency and working with intentionality, preparing bodies or corpuses of data to be laid to rest when they are not being used in service to the people about whom they were created.

4. *We refuse* to understand data as disembodied and thereby dehumanized and departicularized. *We commit* to understanding data as always and variously attached to bodies; we vow to interrogate the biopolitical implications of data with a keen eye to gender, race, sexuality, class, disability, nationality, and other forms of embodied difference.
5. *We refuse* any code of phony "ethics" and false proclamations of transparency that are wielded as cover, as tools of power, as forms for escape that let the people who create systems off the hook from accountability or responsibility. *We commit* to a feminist data ethics that explicitly seeks equity and demands justice by helping us understand and shift how power works.
6. *We refuse* the expansion of any form of data science that normalizes a condition of data extractivism and is defined primarily by the drive to monetize and hyper-individualize the human experience. *We commit* to centering

creative and collective forms of life, living, and worldmaking that exceed the neoliberal logics and resist the market-driven forces to commodify human experience.

7. *We refuse* to accept that data and the systems that generate, collect, process, and store it are too complex or too technical to be understood by the people whose lives are implicated in them. *We commit* to seek to make systems and data intelligible, tangible, and controllable.
8. *We refuse* work about minoritized people. *We commit* to mobilizing data so that we are working with and for minoritized people in ways that are consensual and reciprocal and that understand data as always co-constituted.
9. *We refuse* a data regime of ultimatums, coercive permissions, pervasive cookie collecting, and blocked access. Not everyone can safely refuse or opt out without consequence or further harm. *We commit* to "no" being a real option in all online interactions with data-driven products and platforms and to enacting a new type of data regime that knits the "no" into its fabric.
10. *We refuse* to "close the door behind" ourselves. *We commit* to entering ethically compromised spaces like the academy and industry not to imbricate ourselves into the hierarchies of power but to subvert, undermine, open, make possible.
11. *We refuse* a data culture that reproduces the colonial "'ruse of consent' which papers over the very conditions of force and violence that beget 'consent'" (Simpson, "Ruse of Consent," 20) in the first place. *We commit* to data practices developed by and for Indigenous peoples and in relations of reciprocity.
12. *We refuse* more dispossession, erasure, stealing, and profiting from Black, Indigenous, and people of color's lives and works. *We commit* to build the standpoint that the people most screwed over by data have the best understanding of data and to lifting up, mobilizing, and celebrating their knowledges in building a data methodology of the oppressed (Sandoval; Hill Collins; Haraway; Anzaldúa).
13. *We refuse* to reproduce research as a form of exploitation and to allow people in positions of privilege make the decisions on behalf of those without. *We commit* to research cultures that promote data autonomy and SELF-representation.
14. *We refuse* to cede rhetorics of revolution, disruption, and creative innovation to Silicon Valley marketing and venture capital discourse. Especially, when this discourse marginalizes and appropriates the voices and actions of social justice communities. *We commit* to a recognition and an amplification of the long histories of the labor, dedication, and power of feminist voices for social transformation.
15. *We refuse* systems that simplify consent into a one-time action, a simple click of a yes to a terms of service agreement, to ownership of our data in perpetuity. *We commit* to enacting Planned Parenthood's FRIES model of consent that

ensures that it is always "Freely given, Reversible, Informed, Enthusiastic, and Specific."

16. *We refuse* surveillance as the only condition for participation and to feel powerless in the face of "inevitable" mass technological surveillance. *We commit* to find our communities, hold them close, and resist together.
17. *We refuse* Big Tech's half-measures and moral compromises that constantly defer the needs of vulnerable users as something to be addressed in the next round (of funding, of testing, of patching). *We commit* to centering the needs of the most vulnerable among us in making way for a radical address to Big Tech's data problems.
18. *We refuse* technologies that defer or delay accessible design because it is too expensive, inconvenient, or not legally required. *We commit* to learning from the work of disability activists: #NothingAboutUsWithoutUs.
19. *We refuse* the naturalization of data as what is simply "off-gassed" by a thing, object, or interaction. *We commit* to treating data as a resource to be cared for and cultivated, beyond a colonial extraction logic (as something to be constantly mined and captured).
20. *We refuse* to consider data as raw and only an end product without context and values. We cannot ignore that data has an origin story and a creator or creators whose legacy must be understood in order to understand the data itself. *We commit* to working with data subjects rather than capturing data objects by centering the matrices of oppression (Hill Collins) that shaped data's production and the infrastructure—the code, algorithms, applications, and operating systems—in which it is used, processed, and stored. Data always has social values including race, gender, class, and ability inscribed into it.
21. *We refuse* to cede that convincing unjust institutions and disciplines to listen to us is the only way to make change. *We commit* to co-constructing our language and questions together with the communities we serve in order to build power with our own.
22. *We refuse* "damage centered" research that gathers data to reproduce damage and that traffics in or profits from pain. *We commit* to "desire centered" research that mobilizes and centers data by and for Indigenous, Black, poor, uncitizened, transgender, disabled, and other minoritized, over-researched and under-served people as a resource and tool for their thriving, survivance, and joy (Tuck).
23. *We refuse* to tolerate economies of convenience (also known as the "gig economy" or "sharing economy") that build capital and data empires on the backs of precarious workers and hidden labor. *We commit* to working against the exploitation of labor and precarity in all of its forms.
24. *We refuse* tech solutionism as a moral cover for punitive data logics like always-on facial recognition systems, default capture of personal data, and

racist predictive policing. *We commit* to feminist problem-solving that interrogates data logics as mirrors of power inequalities rather than simple solutions to legacies of racism, sexism, ableism, and oppression of vulnerable people.

25. *We refuse* data logics of prediction that presume omnipotence and conceit to know better than community-centered forms of decision making. *We commit* to countering the risks of defaulting to data-driven forms of prediction and decision making by valuing the expertise of community-engaged practitioners.
26. *We refuse* to accept that data only matters when it is big, abstract, digital, aggregated, machine-readable, and instrumentalized for the market. *We commit* to valuing other forms and materialities of data that privilege accountability and legibility to users and community and examine data at and across all of its scales.
27. *We refuse* the appropriation of feminist discourses of collective safety and the language of consent for the legitimization of surveillance. Safety does not demand subjection to, submission to, or subordination to rational, high tech, colonial orders.[1] *We commit* to feminist collective safety and consent as a means of building resilience, creating solidarity, reducing harm, and as a tool of self-defense and empowerment.
28. *We refuse* the argument that feminist data reform is too slow, too expensive, too much, too little, too late. *We commit* to radical disruption for social transformation.
29. *We refuse* data logics that hyper-value the quantitative, the "objective," and the "generalizable." *We commit* to developing, adopting, and advancing methodologies that draw insight from the subjective, embodied, contingent, political, and affective in ways that transcend traditional boundaries between qualitative and quantitative (Hill Collins; Harding, *The Feminist Standpoint Theory Reader* and "Instability"; Haraway; Hartsock; Smith).
30. *We refuse* coercive settler colonial logics of knowledge and information organization. *We commit* to tribal nation sovereignties and Indigenous information management that values Indigenous relationality (Littletree and Metoyer; Bruchac), the right to know (O'Neal), and data sovereignty (Nakata; Doyle).
31. *We refuse* settler colonial logics of data ownership. *We commit* to advancing the sovereignty of Indigenous peoples who harness data practices as "infrastructural commitments" to get back their land and divest foreign occupying powers (Tuck).
32. *We refuse* reductionist practices that view people as data points in order to embrace the whole person. *We commit* to the requirement of recognizing personhood as a feminist data value.

Our refusals and commitments together demand that data be acknowledged as at once an interpretation and in need of interpretation.[2] Data can be a check-in, a story, an experience or set of experiences, and a resource to begin and continue dialogue. It can—and should always—resist reduction. Data is a thing, a process, and a relationship we make and put to use. We can make it and use it differently.

Four Manifest-NO Reflections

In this section, we offer four individually authored reflections that illustrate how the Manifest-NO's principles are broadly applicable to digital humanities (DH) work and useful for challenging the settler colonial logics of data generation, collection, and analysis. Looking to Indigenous scholarship, Rault reflects on principle 11 and presents refusal as a generative modality for developing DH research that encompasses a more robust understanding of consent than is conveyed through settler colonial forms of governance, research norms, and technologies. Writing on principle 9, Cowan discusses compulsory heterosexuality and able-bodiedness and illustrates how feminist, queer, crip, and anti-racist thinking helps us see how contemporary "accept only" data collecting practices mirror the formation of familiar disciplinary norms. Sutherland considers principles 3 and 4 through the lens of the mass digitization of slavery-era archives, arguing that data created and used in perpetuity carries an agency divorced from the lives and lived experiences of those who were enslaved and urging DH scholars to consider this lack of agency in both their data mining and descriptive practices. Cifor engages in a close reading of the Early African American Film project as a DH intervention that demonstrates the significance and promise of principles 7 and 10 from the Manifest-NO.

REFUSING SETTLER COLONIAL DATA LOGICS

Jas Rault

As a scholar whose digital humanities work emerges more from the humanities than the digital, my interest in data comes from my broader research orientation toward the political and material work of mundane aesthetics and rhetoric, and specifically the aesthetics and rhetoric of settler colonialism. I grapple with the ways that settler colonial values and interests are rendered not only normal and common sense, but attractive as formations of aesthetic sophistication, efficient and "catchy" information design and communication, good taste or cool style—and how contemporary data economies emerge from and contribute to the logics and looks of settler coloniality. Most recently, my work takes up the question of how transparency (in aesthetics and data practice) has become "the settler colonial version of justice" (Rault, 937). That is, within structures of settler coloniality, open data *looks* trustworthy.

Most academic research culture is built on and continues the logics of settler colonialism; learning how to study, generate, analyze, and use data against the priorities of what Aileen Moreton-Robinson calls "the possessive logics of patriarchal white sovereignty" (xi), resource theft, and value extraction often means refusing academic rubrics of success. From scholars like Audra Simpson, Eve Tuck, K. Wayne Yang, and Glen Coulthard, we learn that refusal is a generative praxis of Indigenous survivance, the ongoing assertion of an authority beyond settler colonial aesthetics, certainties, politics, scholarship, and solutions. Refusal is a "no" to coercive settler colonial logics of recognition, inclusion, and participation and a "yes" to decolonial resource and information management and anti-colonial research priorities. As a form of Indigenous information management, refusal means setting limits around what information can be shared—what should be accessible to all, what needs protecting—and provides a fundamental challenge to liberal white settler colonial versions of truth and justice. As Simpson puts it:

> To speak of limits in such a way makes some liberal thinkers uncomfortable, and may, to them, seem dangerous. When access to information, to knowledge, to the intellectual commons is controlled by the people who generate that information, it can be seen as a violation of shared standards of justice and truth. ("On Ethnographic Refusal," 74)

Indeed, if liberal values of justice and truth are violated when Indigenous, Black, and what Tuck and Yang call "Orientalized . . . and other communities of overstudied Others" (223) refuse to share access to the resources, knowledges, and information that they have cultivated, cared for, and generated, we see quite starkly the extent to which liberalism is designed to protect white (settler) colonial property, possession, value, justice, and mundane common sense of goodness (Rifkin).

As Indigenous digital humanities and data studies have explained for years, prioritizing community cultural protocols often puts a digital project at odds with open-access and open-data principles. Mukurtu is perhaps the best-known example of a tiered-access and contextual content management system designed according to Indigenous community priorities, or what Mukurtu cocreator Kimberly Christen has called the "sociality of information" (2887). We might also look to the Pollution Reporter app, designed in 2019 by the Environmental Justice Lab at University of Toronto—co-led by environmental researchers and land protectors Vanessa Gray and Beze Gray (Anishinaabe, Aamjiwnaang First Nation), Michelle Murphy (Métis, Winnipeg), and TRU Lab manager Kristen Bos (urban Métis), along with lab members Reena Shadaan, and Fernanda Yanchapaxi. The mobile app is designed to track and report pollution in Ontario's Chemical Valley, with a particular focus on "the Imperial Oil Refinery of Sarnia, one of the oldest operating refineries in the world, which is on the traditional Anishinaabek territory, and particularly the land of Aamjiwnaang First Nation" (Gray et al.). As the creators explain:

> *Pollution Reporter* hopes to support community members' abilities to link health harms to companies and pollution without having to demonstrate their own health harms and be subjected to extractive research. In respect of Indigenous Data Sovereignty, *Pollution Reporter* does not collect data about its users, and users are in full control of their reports to the Ministry of Environment. (Gray et al.)

The app flips the script of commercial and research data norms, allowing Aamjiwnaang First Nation to collect and share proprietary commercial data (about pollutants and their health effects) without collecting and sharing data *about* Aamjiwnaang people. The app provides information about the pollution from Imperial Oil and allows community members to report pollution events to the Ontario Ministry of Environment, but importantly, it does not demand or collect data from app users.

In 2019, the Global Indigenous Data Alliance (GIDA) was formed by representatives of three large Indigenous data sovereignty organizations—the Maiam nayri Wingara Collective (Australia); Te Mana Raraunga Maori Data Sovereignty Network (Aotearoa New Zealand); and the United States Indigenous Data Sovereignty Network—and their first project was to augment existing international open-data principles. GIDA argues that "the current movement toward open data and open science does not fully engage with Indigenous Peoples' rights and interests," and so it has proposed the principles of CARE (Collective benefit, Authority to control, Responsibility, Ethics) to supplement the existing principles of FAIR (Findable, Accessible, Interoperable, Reusable). As GIDA puts it, "The emphasis on greater data sharing alone creates a tension for Indigenous Peoples who are also asserting greater control over the application and use of Indigenous data and Indigenous Knowledge for collective benefit." For all DH scholars, but especially those of us committed to anti-colonial, Black, Indigenous, trans feminist, and queer forms of life, this means divesting from settler colonial values and aesthetics of transparency—including the assumed good of openness, freedom, sharing, and the commons.

In the digital humanities, this can mean *not* onlining the archive of minoritized cultural heritage materials that you and your team have spent years digitizing until you have consent from every person named or photographed, every person whose lives or work created those materials, and developed creative metadata practices to protect rather than expose these materials. In the two projects that I codirect with T.L. Cowan—the Digital Research Ethics Collaboratory (DREC) and the Cabaret Commons—we endeavor to put these principles to practice. While both projects are grounded in my and Cowan's research and experience in trans feminist queer (TFQ) cultural heritage, they take their leadership from Indigenous approaches to data sovereignty, digital archives, refusal, and relational responsibility. We chose *not* to online a large collection of TFQ cultural heritage materials that we, technically, had permission to post (both the collector and the photographer of the materials, as well as our university ethics boards, gave us permissions) because we did not have consent from every person named or imaged in the collection (and in some cases did not have names or means to contact those people) (Cowan and Rault, "Onlining Queer Acts"). Instead, we created DREC to share research stories about how we can or do pursue ethical and consentful work (Lee and Tolliver) in digital research environments. At Cabaret Commons, we publish work—focused on TFQ cabaret performance—that learns from the stories at DREC. Consentful practices in digital research might mean prioritizing small data and what Cowan and I think of as the slow work of "heavy processing," a "lesbian-leaning trans-feminist and queer method of being together . . . [that forms] one genealogy of the many calls for better processing, better information politics in contemporary justice-oriented digital research methods" (Rault and Cowan). It certainly means taking up the labor of being responsible to more robust understandings of consent than we have inherited from settler colonial forms of governance, research norms and technologies.

Principle 11 reads: *We refuse* a data culture that reproduces the colonial "'ruse of consent' which papers over the very conditions of force and violence that beget 'consent'" in the first place (Simpson, "Ruse of Consent," 20). *We commit* to data practices developed by and for Indigenous peoples and in relations of reciprocity.

What Simpson calls "the ruse of consent" is the grand deception and collective delusion, foundational to settler colonial well-being, "that Indigenous peoples *had all things been equal* would have consented to have things taken, things stolen from them" (Simpson, "Ruse of Consent," 29). Even if our research is not on, about, or with Indigenous peoples, those of us working within the ongoing structure of settler coloniality—that is, in Canada where I work, and the United States, where many of my collaborators work—our challenge as researchers is to refuse the naturalization of this ruse and to commit to relations of reciprocity and accountability that may indeed violate prevailing liberal colonial values and aesthetics of truth, justice, and transparency.

ACCEPT ONLY: FEMINIST, QUEER AND CRIP THEORIES OF THE "COMPULSORY," OR THIS DATA REGIME CAN'T TAKE NO FOR AN ANSWER

T. L. Cowan

Principle 9 states: *We refuse* a data regime of ultimatums, coercive permissions, pervasive cookie collecting, and blocked access. Not everyone can safely refuse or opt out without consequence or further harm. *We commit* to "no" being a real option in all online interactions with data-driven products and platforms and to enacting a new type of data regime that knits the "no" into its fabric.

This principle emerges from a long and complicated feminist analysis of compulsory forms of belonging. One of my favorite pairings of feminist/queer/crip theory is the way that Robert McRuer's "Compulsory Able-Bodiedness and Queer Disabled Existence" takes up Adrienne Rich's "Compulsory Heterosexuality and

Lesbian Existence." Together, these texts taught me how our social and political culture is shaped by the ways that "dominant identities are not really alternatives but rather the natural order of things" (McRuer, 89). As we were writing this Manifest-NO, I had a penny-dropping moment as I connected my long-ago reading of Rich and more recent reading of McRuer to my experiences of data bullying. I often talk with my students about those moments when "the penny drops"—those moments when all of a sudden we experience something that allows us to grasp the full heft, the big weighty centrality, the consequence of a concept or a full text that was previously perhaps just beyond or marginal to our understanding. Immediately, the newly grasped concept becomes an analytic that leads us to a more full understanding of something perhaps apparently unrelated. For me, the concept of compulsory modes of existence, like heterosexuality, able-bodiedness, and able-mindedness, has been one that has shaped my ways of thinking about and studying contemporary data culture.

As a queer person and a disabled person, I have often felt the ways that dominant modes of being are presented as inevitable and good, and I have long known that if I chose to go against the inevitable modes of being, or refused or failed to comply with the logics of inevitability, I would either be punished, rejected, or rendered invisible. This is how compulsory norms work. As the ubiquity of false choices about data collection began to proliferate in my daily life online, Rich's and McRuer's analyses helped me to understand the familiar relations of power on which these "choices" are based. Every day I am offered the choice to "accept" or consent to a limited range of data collection options while a much larger range of data collection practices are carried out whether I agree to them or not. It is like being told by the school bully that you have the option to either give up your lunch *and* your brown bag, or that you can give up your lunch and keep the brown bag. I realized, during our brainstorming for the Manifest-NO, that it is not only the kinds of data being collected, or the ways that "my data" are being used, but the way that data collection is framed that is so vile and so provocative for a trans feminist, queer, crip, anti-racist analysis.

Data politics is modeled on ongoing capitalist, colonial, and imperial structures of compulsory extraction-and-possession-for-profit of resources and humans as able-bodied laborers or wives. This model is a co-constitutive practice and logic with the stories we tell about cisgender male sexuality that "once triggered cannot take responsibility for itself or take no for an answer" (Rich, 25). An extension of this adage is that while women have historically "chosen" to give up/give away/submit to more than they might ideally wish to, in order to "accept" the previously set terms of heterosexual marriage, these choices are necessary in order for the system/site/institution to work how it needs to work. How many times do we look at the "partners" that a news site, for example, sells our data to and realize that, once sold, that news site has no responsibility for what those partners do with that data? Do we not find, more often than not, that there is no way to opt out from that partnership? Either we accept the data partnership and its terms—previously agreed to, unknown to us, and drawn up without our consultation—and give up/give away/submit to more than we might ideally wish to, or we choose not to access the content on that site, even though that content is often necessary for us to conduct our jobs that day, or even just to stay informed of global affairs. Not much of a choice, is it? How many times have you tried to access content blocked by a "cookies" notice, only to see that there is only an "accept" button and no "decline" or not even a "manage cookies" option? If you go along with it, you may access the materials you need and give away whatever they are taking/scraping. If you decline, you are booted off the site.

In the context of disability, McRuer explains that a universal, coercive "accept" signals a culturally predetermined good, one that has decided "in advance that we all agree: able-bodied identities, able-bodied perspectives, are preferable and what we all, collectively, are aiming for. A system of compulsory able-bodiedness repeatedly demands that disabled people embody for others an affirmative answer to the unspoken question, 'Yes, but in the end, wouldn't you rather be more like me?'" (93). When we encounter choices that are not real choices in our data encounters, we see another instance of the compulsory "yes," which assumes, in advance, that we all agree. Who could possibly disagree? The alternative is so obviously more bother and trouble!

Compulsory data regimes operate by offering us only one legitimate choice, to which all other "choices" are subordinate. For example, when accessing Rich's foundational (but not unproblematic) text, the Project Muse database displays a banner across the bottom portion of the screen that reads, "This website uses cookies to ensure you get the best experience on our website. Without cookies your experience may not be seamless."

How many times per day are you threatened with the ultimatum that if you do not accept those cookies, do not accept being tracked by the site you need to access in order to do your job, that your "experience may not be seamless" or "optimal"? If I had a nickel for every time a relative told me that living a nonheterosexual life was going to be *so much more difficult* (i.e., would not be seamless) than if I would just accept a heterosexual life! If every disabled person in the world had a dollar for every time they were reminded that our way of being, our embodiment, our cognition, was not the "seamless" or optimal way of being. The message is consistent and clear: Either you accept the way the system is rigged and internalize it as natural, necessary, and normal and go along with it, or you deal with the consequences. It is not an overstatement to observe that our contemporary data regime makes sense only in the context of the naturalization and normalization of coercive relations of power.

It is precisely through the daily, endless repetition of these non-choices that our current data regime operates. As McRuer notes in relation to sexuality, "compulsion is . . . produced and covered over, with the appearance of choice . . . mystifying a system in which there actually is no choice" (90). There is no option to *not* have your user data collected and collated for the financial gain of others—either you access that information or you don't. Acquiescing to the normative relations of data collection is a prerequisite for belonging, for having access to the culture. In addition to the ways that the production of these "bad" choices, these non-seamless ways of inhabiting this data regime, constitute the seamlessness of the regime itself, the "disciplinary formation" of the regime coheres—modeled on systems of compulsory heterosexuality, able-bodiedness, whiteness, cisgender-ness, citizen-ness—as its "origins . . . are now obscured . . . emanating from everywhere and nowhere" (McRuer, 92). However, the political analytic tools offered by Rich, McRuer, and many other transformational thinkers give us a way to identify these origins so that we can see how we might inhabit data norms in the same way that lesbians, queers, and crips have been inhabiting systems of compulsory able-bodiedness and heterosexuality—by committing to living with, making work, and doing research in ways that take responsibility and take "no" as a real option, even when we are being railroaded into thinking that to refuse the compulsory forms of existence is to refuse existence itself. Rich argues that "in the absence of choice, women will remain dependent on the chance or luck of particular relationships and will have no collective power to determine the meaning and place of sexuality in their lives" (37). The Manifest-NO is our call to practice a critical digital humanities as a kind of collective action, a commitment to data existences that offer real choices to women and everyone so that we and our research participants and materials do not have to be dependent on the luck of the data relationships we enter into. Even a good data relationship may be one we want to get out of.

THE DIGITAL AFTERLIVES OF ATLANTIC SLAVERY ARCHIVES

Tonia Sutherland

The increasing number of digital archives, databases, and other digitization projects focused on the slavery era are transforming how scholars in the digital humanities study the history of human enslavement. For example, Jessica Marie Johnson, writing for *Social Text* in 2018, considers the deeply human elements of the archives of Atlantic slavery in counterposition to the digital humanities' drive for data. Similarly, in her 2019 article "Archival Encounters: Rethinking Access and Care in Digital Colonial Archives," Daniela Agostinho argues that the digitization of the United States Virgin Island records by the National Danish Archives raises new questions about the limitations and possibilities of colonial archives. Agostinho contends that colonial histories of quantification have structured digital humanists' technological encounters with colonial archives. While digitization projects centered on the pre-emancipation era hold the potential for powerful new humanistic narratives about Black resilience and redress to emerge, projects that take a more data-centric approach to the lived experiences of enslaved people have proved to be fraught and often problematic research sites. Here, I address concerns about the ways that the mass digitization and datafication of slavery-era archives have contributed to a distancing of the lived experiences of enslaved people from slavery's historical imaginary, or what I call the digital afterlives of slavery-era archives.

The Manifest-NO's principle 3 states: *We refuse* the use of data about people in perpetuity. *We commit* to embracing agency and working with intentionality, preparing bodies or corpuses of data to be laid to rest when they are not being used in service to the people about whom they were created.

Because of the significant temporal gap between the violence of the past and the visual experience of the present, when slavery-era records are digitized en masse, records appear and circulate in different contexts. This decontextualization removes the immediacy of trauma, giving archival records that document that trauma new afterlives. These records are then read and experienced as dislocated from human suffering. The extension of analog records into the digital—and the subsequent removal of historical context—exacerbates the inability of these archives' historical subjects to construct their own agency, realities, or representations in the present. Principle 3 addresses the heart of an ongoing and increasing concern: even after death, Black people's lives are extended, prolonged, and ultimately changed in the present, in the future, and even in history through new circulations, repetitions, and recontextualizations of data to various publics.

The documents and other records that constitute the archives of Atlantic slavery were created by colonizers and slaveholders. Rather than being faithful representations of the colonized and enslaved, they are a deeply complex, fraught, and often problematic set of sources that speak to how archives hold, produce, and reproduce agency, privilege, and power. Given the nature of slavery-era archives and the long-acknowledged problematics of the history of systems of archival production, it is important to continually critique these archives, posing critical questions about the history they represent and our affective relationship with the memories they evoke. Although digital archives have the potential to create "third spaces" in which Black people might have more control over their ancestral materials and records, digital humanists working with these records must stop to consider, for example, the ways that privacy is racialized as something that is only afforded as a condition of whiteness or disparate—and often conflicting—cultural positions on sovereignty, ownership, and access. Embracing principle 3 of the Manifest-NO helps us reckon with the archival permanence that burdens Black people's bodies specifically because there is no right to refusal, no Black digital sovereignty; the ordinary (and extraordinary) Black lives in the archives—how they lived, how they died, how they are remembered, how their digital afterlives are constituted, and what happens to those afterlives—is forever intimately linked to systemic and structural practices of anti-Black (and often state-sponsored) violence that is too frequently reinscribed and reified in—and also justified by—the archival record. Principle 3 reminds us that if you want to honor Black lives, you must also let us rest in peace.

Digitization projects focused on the pre-emancipation era frequently foster a drive for data, as scholars are increasingly encouraged to mine these archives as part of digital humanities work. This work can, and often does, lead to what Saidiya Hartman calls a "second order of violence" whereby the bodies already numbered in the archives are requantified, thus becoming what I have argued (Sutherland, 26–37) is a new form of commodifiable raw material—seemingly disconnected from human bodies and human lives, and from which new value can be extracted. Scholars such as Simone Browne, Jessica Marie Johnson, and Jacqueline Wernimont have argued that data is deeply embedded in colonial histories of quantification that have a defining moment in the accounting and marking of enslaved bodies. Johnson further argues that if left unaddressed, the violence of these archival processes can "reproduce themselves in digital architecture" (58). In now-digitized slavery-era archives, this means archivists have uncritically adopted and reproduced both structures of knowledge organization and descriptive practices used by slave traders, slaveholders, and colonial officers. As digitization leads to the construction of more slavery studies databases, for example, it has become commonplace that users are required to search holdings according to local descriptive practices.[3] Because digital archives currently mirror the organization of information as it already exists, rather than taking up the goal of reorganization or redescription, researchers have found themselves searching for terms that have long been considered outdated, offensive, violent, and harmful. It is essential, therefore, that the raw data that DH scholars use be approached with a critical eye.

Principle 4 of the Manifest-NO demands that *we refuse* to understand data as disembodied and thereby dehumanized and departicularized and that *we commit* instead to understanding data as always and variously attached to bodies, which is one way forward—in both theory and practice—to approach the digital afterlives of slavery-era archives with compassion and care. I challenge us all to refuse to ignore the ways that Black people's lives are affected and changed in the present by new digitized and datafied engagements with the past, and to commit to (re)articulating and to (re)membering the humanity in our digital humanities work.

INTELLIGIBILITY, ACCESS, COLLABORATION, PROCESS: THE EARLY AFRICAN AMERICAN FILM PROJECT

Marika Cifor

The digital humanities offers a uniquely powerful means to activate and to mobilize archival records. Records created by communities minoritized along lines of race, gender, sexuality, socioeconomic status, and HIV serostatus in the United States can be used to provoke and support social justice movements. In this short reflection, I focus on my experiences collaboratively building the digital project called "Early African American Film: Reconstructing the History of Early Race Films, 1909–1930."[4] This project was created and developed collaboratively over the course of one academic quarter. The project team included DH faculty member Miriam Posner, six UCLA undergraduate students—Shanya Norman, William Lam, Hanna Girma, Karla Contreras, Monica Berry, and Aya Grace Yoshioka—and me. (At the time I was a doctoral student in information studies.) We devoted ourselves to building a relational database of race films from the silent era: films made by and for African Americans. We sought to document the community of practice that developed around the race film industry in the first three decades of the twentieth century. These films, many of which have been destroyed or lost, are starkly underrecognized, as are the people who created and viewed them. This remains true in spite of these films' deep importance to film and media histories, Black studies, and American studies. My work on this project taught me the value of data intelligibility, as well as the need to enhance access and engender ethical collaborative processes in building an ethical, critical, and social justice–focused digital humanities. These lessons are reflected in the Manifesto-NO, especially in principles 7 and 10.

Manifest-NO principle 7 emphasizes that too often data and the systems used to "generate, collect, process, and store it" are framed as either "too complex or too technical" to be readily knowable and understood by the very same individuals and communities whose lives are so deeply implicated in them. The Early African American Film dataset contains the 303 silent race films that we were able to identify and verify through archival research. The films are then linked to 759 actors and other film personnel and to 176 race film companies. Each record in the relational database is supported with any descriptive and archival information that we were able to uncover. The dataset is publicly accessible as a perusable database on Airtable, as raw comma-separated value (CSV) files on GitHub, and is linked to research data repository site Zendo. We prioritized enabling others to engage with the data in their own uses, reuses, augmentations, and corrections. Within the data package, we included a data dictionary, a Creative Commons license, and other documentation important to understanding and engaging the dataset. The project's website features maps, social network diagrams, and other data visualizations that were designed to show how this data might be conceptualized and used by scholars, students, curators, librarians, archivists, and other community members.[5] In a refusal to accept that data-driven projects are only accessible to those with particular technical skills accompanying data visualization, we included information about the specific data used and, in a more unusual act among similar DH projects, we offered step-by-step instructions about how to create related visualizations. The project's website also features a series of tutorials designed by Posner on working with the dataset. These tutorials are notable because they aimed to make the data accessible for use in visualizations and analyses regardless of the user's technical savvy or digital humanities experience level. For example, the dataset includes locations for production companies, and in the tutorials, we provide detailed guidance on mapping using the dataset. In every step we refer users to further resources. These efforts reflect the commitment of principle 7, "to seek" always "to make systems and data intelligible, tangible, and controllable."

The Early African American Film project is both a work of scholarship and the product of an experiment in DH pedagogy. We worked carefully, methodically, and collaboratively through pressing questions about race, filmmaking and artistic output, and American history. "*We refuse* to 'close the door behind' ourselves," as principle 10 of the Manifest-NO emphasizes. It continues to reflect our shared commitment to working within "ethically compromised spaces like the academy and industry" in ways that do not simply accept standing "hierarchies of power" but instead look for ways to "subvert, undermine, open, make possible." This principle is embodied in such collaborative work. DH projects can be important spaces for feminist pedagogy, spaces that value co-learning, shared agency, and mentorship. Such projects represent a refusal to value only accelerated production, individual work and acclaim, and hierarchical pedagogy. In our project, we worked to acknowledge and value every collaborator's diverse academic and personal identities, experiences, knowledges, and skills. Throughout the process, we used as our guide the "Student Collaborators' Bill of Rights," a document coauthored by UCLA DH students and faculty that codifies the responsibilities and expectations for all members of DH project teams (Di Pressi et al.). It demands from all faculty-student project collaborations in which students are uncompensated that those students have real intellectual autonomy and complete oversight of their portions of the project; that they are authorized and moreover encouraged to publish on, present, or otherwise share the work; and that they be acknowledged for their contributions in all subsequent productions and project iterations. As the Feminist Manifest-NO reminds us, the importance of DH is not situated simply in the products we create; rather, it is centered in the collaborative feminist digital processes we engage in our project design, our modes of collaboration, our data ontologies, and our accessibility to new audiences.

An Invitation

The Feminist Data Manifest-NO is a living document that is being taken up in collective readings, conference meetups, classrooms, activist gatherings, workplaces, and wherever else it is needed. We are committed to working together and with others to build on and experiment with ethical feminist collaborative praxes. We encourage faculty, students, and community groups to take up one or more of the principles of the Feminist Data Manifest-NO and to build their own reflections on what these principles mean to them, based on their own experiences and fields of study. We encourage people who gather around the Manifest-NO to do so in a workshop environment in order to make time and space to create additional refusal-commitment statements that are meaningful to their lives.

NOTES

1. As Lila Abu-Lughod puts it, "We save to." See Abu-Lughod's writings on "Do Muslim Women Really Need Saving?"

2. We are riffing here on Joan Scott's words, "Experience is at once always already an interpretation and something that needs to be interpreted" (Scott, 797).

3. See the North American Slave Narratives database, for example, at https://docsouth.unc.edu/neh/.

4. For published works about the "Early African American Film: Reconstructing the History of Early Race Films, 1909–1930" project, see Posner and Cifor; Cifor et al. ("Early African-American Film Database"); and Cifor et. al. ("Tracing a Community of Practice").

5. This digital humanities project can be accessed at: http://dhbasecamp.humanities.ucla.edu/afamfilm.

BIBLIOGRAPHY

Abu-Lughod, Lila. *Do Muslim Women Need Saving?* Cambridge, Mass.: Harvard University Press, 2013.

Abu-Lughod, Lila. "Do Muslim Women Really Need Saving? Anthropological Reflections on Cultural Relativism and Its Others." *American Anthropologist* 104, no. 3 (2002): 783–90.

Agostinho, Daniela. "Archival Encounters: Rethinking Access and Care in Digital Colonial Archives." *Archival Science* 19, no. 2 (2019): 141–65.

Ahmed, Sara. "No." *FeministKilljoys* (blog). June 30, 2017, https://feministkilljoys.com/2017/06/30/no/.

Anzaldúa, Gloria. *Borderlands: La Frontera.* San Francisco: Aunt Lute, 1987.

Benjamin, Ruha. "Informed Refusal: Toward a Justice-based Bioethics." *Science, Technology, and Human Values* 4, no. 6 (2016): 967–90.

Benjamin, Ruha (@ruha9). "Note to selves: remember to imagine and craft the worlds you cannot live without." Twitter, November 22, 2017, https://twitter.com/ruha9/status/926180439827591168.

Browne, Simone. *Dark Matters: On the Surveillance of Blackness.* Durham, N.C.: Duke University Press, 2015.

Bruchac, Margaret M. *Savage Kin: Indigenous Informants and American Anthropologists.* Tucson: University of Arizona Press, 2018.

Chávez, Karma R. "Refusing Queer Violence." *QED: A Journal in GLBTQ Worldmaking* 3, no. 3 (2016): 160–63.

Christen, Kim. "Does Information Really Want to Be Free? Indigenous Knowledge Systems and the Question of Openness." *International Journal of Communications* 6 (2012): 2870–93.

Cifor, Marika, Hanna Girma, William Lam, Shanya Norman, Miriam Posner, Karla Contreras, and Aya Grace Yoshioka. "Tracing a Community of Practice: A Database of early African American Race Film." *The Moving Image* 17, no. 2 (2017): 101–5.

Cifor, Marika, Hanna Girma, Shanya Norman, and Miriam Posner. "Early African-American Film Database, 1909–1930." *Journal of Open Humanities Data* 4 (2018).

Coulthard, Glen. *Red Skin, White Masks: Rejecting the Colonial Politics of Recognition.* Minneapolis: University of Minnesota Press Minneapolis, 2014.

Cowan, T. L., and Jasmine Rault. "Onlining Queer Acts: Digital Research Ethics and Caring for Risky Archives." *Women & Performance: A Journal of Feminist Theory* 28, no. 2 (2018): 121–42.

Di Pressi, Haley, Stephanie Gorman, Miriam Posner, Raphael Sasayama, and Tori Schmitt, with contributions from Roderic Crooks, Megan Driscoll, Amy Earhart, Spencer Keralis, Tiffany Naiman, and Todd Presner. "A Student Collaborators' Bill of Rights." *UCLA HumTech*. June 8, 2015, https://humtech.ucla.edu/news/a-student-collaborators-bill-of-rights/.

Doyle, A. M. "Naming, Claiming, and (Re)Creating: Indigenous Knowledge Organization at the Cultural Interface." PhD diss., University of British Columbia, 2013.

Duarte, Marisa Elena. "Prismatic Interfaces: Making Room for Intersectional Feminist Approaches in Interface Studies." Presentation at Imagining Intersectional Futures: Feminist Approaches in CSCW, ACM Conference on Computer-Supported Cooperative Work and Social Computing (CSCW 2017), Portland, Oregon, February 25, 2017.

Duarte, Marisa Elena, and Miranda Belarde-Lewis. "Imagining: Creating Spaces for Indigenous Ontologies." *Cataloging & Classification Quarterly* 53, no. 5–6 (2015): 677–702.

GIDA. "CARE Principles of Indigenous Data Governance." *Global Indigenous Data Alliance*. 2019, https://www.gida-global.org/care.

Gray, Vanessa, Michelle Murphy, Kristen Bos, Reena Shadaan, and Ladan Siad. "Pollution Reporter." 2019, https://www.landandrefinery.org/pollutionreporter.

Haraway, Donna. "Situated Knowledges: The Science Question in Feminism and the Privilege of Partial Perspective," *Feminist Studies* 14, no. 3 (1988): 575–99.

Harding, Sandra G., ed. *The Feminist Standpoint Theory Reader: Intellectual and Political Controversies*. New York: Psychology Press, 2004.

Harding, Sandra G. "The Instability of the Analytical Categories of Feminist Theory." *Signs: Journal of Women in Culture and Society* 11, no. 4 (1986): 645–64.

Hartman, Saidiya. "Venus in Two Acts." *Small Axe: A Journal of Criticism* 26 (2008): 1–14.

Hartsock, Nancy C. M. "Comment on Hekman's 'Truth and Method: Feminist Standpoint Theory Revisited': Truth or Justice?" *Signs: Journal of Women in Culture and Society* 22, no. 2 (1997): 367–74.

Hill Collins, Patricia. *Black Feminist Thought: Knowledge, Consciousness and the Politics of Empowerment*. New York: Routledge, 1990.

hooks, bell. *The Will to Change: Men, Masculinity, and Love*. New York: Atria Books, 2004.

Johnson, Jessica Marie. "Markup Bodies." *Social Text* 36, no. 4 (2018): 57–79.

Lee, Una, and Dan Tolliver. *Building Consentful Tech*. 2017, http://www.consentfultech.io/.

Littletree, S., and C. A. Metoyer. "Knowledge Organization from an Indigenous Perspective: The Mashantucket Pequot Thesaurus of American Indian Terminology Project." *Cataloging & Classification Quarterly* 53, no. 5–6 (2015): 640–57.

Love, Heather. "Queer." *Transgender Studies Quarterly* 1, no. 1–2 (2014): 172–76.

McRuer, Robert, "Compulsory Able-bodiedness and Queer/Disabled Existence." In *Disability Studies: Enabling the Humanities,* edited by Sharon L. Snyder, Brenda Jo Brueggemann, and Rosemarie Garland-Thomson, 88–99. New York: Modern Language Association, 2002.

Moreton-Robinson, Aileen. *The White Possessive: Property, Power, and Indigenous Sovereignty.* Minneapolis: University of Minnesota Press, 2015.

Muñoz, José Esteban. *Cruising Utopia: The Then and There of Queer Futurity,* New York: NYU Press, 2009.

Nakata, M. "Indigenous Knowledge and the Cultural Interface: Underlying Issues at the Intersection of Knowledge and Information Systems." *IFLA Journal* 28, no. 5–6 (2002): 281–91.

O'Neal, Jennifer R. " 'The Right to Know': Decolonizing Native American Archives." *Journal of Western Archives* 6, no. 1, art. 2 (2015).

Posner, Miriam, and Marika Cifor. "Generative Tensions: Building a Digital Project on Early African American Race Film." *American Quarterly* 70, no. 3 (2018): 709–14.

Rault, Jasmine. "Window Walls and Other Tricks of Transparency: Digital, Colonial, and Architectural Modernity." *American Quarterly* 72, no. 4 (2020): 937–60.

Rault, Jas, and T. L. Cowan. "Heavy Processing." Digital Research Ethics Collaboratory. 2020, http://www.drecollab.org/heavy-processing/.

Razack, Sherene. *Dying from Improvement: Inquests and Inquiries into Indigenous Deaths in Custody.* Toronto: University of Toronto Press, 2015.

Rich, Adrienne Cecile. "Compulsory Heterosexuality and Lesbian Existence (1980)." *Journal of Women's History* 15, no. 3 (2003): 11–48.

Rifkin, Mark. *Settler Common Sense: Queerness and Everyday Colonialism in the American Renaissance.* Minneapolis: University of Minnesota Press, 2014.

Sandoval, Chela. *Methodology of the Oppressed.* Minneapolis: University of Minnesota Press, 2000.

Scott, Joan W. "The Evidence of Experience." *Critical Inquiry* 17, no. 4 (1991): 773–97, www.jstor.org/stable/1343743.

Simpson, Audra. *Mohawk Interruptus: Political Life across the Borders of Settler States.* Durham, N.C.: Duke University Press, 2014.

Simpson, Audra. "On Ethnographic Refusal: Indigeneity, 'Voice' and Colonial Citizenship." *Junctures: The Journal for Thematic Dialogue* 9 (December 2007): 67–80, https://junctures.org/index.php/junctures/article/view/66/60.

Simpson, Audra. "The Ruse of Consent and the Anatomy of 'Refusal': Cases from Indigenous North America and Australia." *Postcolonial Studies* 20, no. 1 (2017): 18–33, https://www.tandfonline.com/doi/pdf/10.1080/13688790.2017.1334283.

Smith, Dorothy E. "Comment on Hekman's 'Truth and Method: Feminist Standpoint Theory Revisited.'" *Signs: Journal of Women in Culture and Society* 22, no. 2 (1997): 392–98.

Sutherland, Tonia. "Making a Killing: On Race, Ritual, and (Re)Membering in Digital Culture." *Preservation, Digital Technology & Culture* 46, no. 1. (2017): 32–40.

Tuck, Eve. "Suspending Damage: A Letter to Communities," *Harvard Educational Review* 79, no. 3 (2009): 409–28, https://doi.org/10.17763/haer.79.3.n0016675661t3n15.

Tuck, Eve, and K. Wayne Yang. "R-Words: Refusing Research." In *Humanizing Research: Decolonizing Qualitative Inquiry with Youth and Communities,* edited by D. Paris and M. T. Winn, 223–48. Thousand Oaks, Calif.: Sage Publications, 2014.

Wernimont, Jacqueline. *Numbered Lives: Life and Death in Quantum Media.* Cambridge, Mass.: MIT Press, 2019.

Black Is Not the Absence of Light: Restoring Black Visibility and Liberation to Digital Humanities

NISHANI FRAZIER, CHRISTY HYMAN, AND HILARY N. GREEN

When Black writers write, they should write for me . . . write for all those people in the book who don't even pick up the book—those are the people who make it authentic, those are the people who justify it, those are the people you have to please . . . they are the ones to whom one speaks. Not to the New York Times; not to the editors; not to any distant media; not to anything. It is a very private thing. They are the ones who say "Yeah, uh huh, that's right."

—Toni Morrison, "A Humanist View"

In 1996, Kalí Tal wrote in *Wired Magazine* that "I have long suspected that the much vaunted 'freedom' to shed the 'limiting' markers of race and gender on the Internet is illusory, and that in fact it masks a more disturbing phenomenon—the whitinizing of cyberspace."[1] During the decades of the internet that followed, Black digitalists consistently rejected the purported color-blindness of the web by foregrounding Black identity online. But problems persisted. Questions then arose about how the digital itself should conform to Blackness, how to more assertively consider and center the identity and life realities of Black communities, and how digital projects could avoid exploitation within project processes.[2] Now, twenty-five years later, the result is a bifurcated circumstance that has divorced Black people from themselves—as epistemological sources (knowledge brokers), as equal collaborators, and as principal audiences.

Since the early 2010s, Black digitalists Marisa Parham, Mark Anthony Neal, Tara McPherson, and more recently, Ruha Benjamin, Kim Gallon, and Jessica Marie Johnson have theorized the multiple considerations that informed Black entry into the digital and its fundamental impact on the space. Gallon argued that Black digital humanities acted to unmask racialized systems of power at work, forced a recognition of how the digital reinforced racialized systems, and reminded humanists that the study of Black people was a "deeply political enterprise" that disrupted the foundations of humanities. Working within Black Studies traditions cultivated by the Association for the Study of African American Life and History, Association of Black Women Historians, and the National Council of Black Studies, Aleia Brown and Joshua Crutchfield constructed the Twitter hashtag #blktwitterstorians as a subject reference tool in order to create a network of Black digital historians. Overwhelmingly, Black digital humanists, inspired by Black Studies, privileged Black knowledge production, seeking to reach Black people where they are and acknowledging "the different ways of knowing" that they produce.

As three historians who bring their professional and personal experiences in Black Studies to bear on their digital humanities scholarship, we extend this conversation and argue that the digital humanities discipline needs a more aggressive intervention, particularly for those who interact with vulnerable communities. We argue for a Black aesthetic and praxis that transforms power relations. We recognize our positionality as Black scholars disrupting disciplinary boundaries, and we urge an enacting of this aesthetic while navigating the existing obstacles within institutions. We therefore construct Black digital humanities as a liberation project, one in which Black identity and culture are reasserted to incorporate the subject's sense of his/her/them self/selves.

The Digital Humanities 2017 conference in Montreal, Canada, was the setting where the authors of this chapter found common cause in the interpretive power of creating digital interventions that recovered the history of obscured Black pasts. In sharing our work with each other, it became clear to us that despite the temporal and spatial distinctions underlying our investigations, our projects shared a common ethical imperative, one that foregrounds Black style, power sharing, and anti-exploitation within our projects. These ethical considerations are not only integral for the final dissemination of digital historical recovery efforts; they are woven into every aspect of the design process.

We begin this chapter by explaining how oral history theory grounded in shared authority and power brings forth a Black aesthetic and offers an expansive framework for Black digital humanities projects. This Black aesthetic grounded in shared authority facilitates a liberatory praxis that seeks to overcome the existing tendencies in the field of digital humanities (DH) and the academy that often parasitize the Black subject in research production as well as outreach initiatives. The next sections—on the black freedom movement and enslaved people in the Great Dismal Swamp—demonstrate this proposed framework, showing how shared authority practices act as a corrective to previous patterns, and address intersections of erasures, recovery, and descendant community engagement. The final section shows the possibilities of such engagement through a case study of recovery work of enslaved University of Alabama laborers and their descendant communities. Throughout, we demonstrate how the Black aesthetic requires a politics of care and power for representing in the digital world the richness of Black life without exploitation. The liberatory nature of the Black aesthetic, therefore, encourages an intentional praxis that recognizes the diversity and souls of the Black public as both audience and co-creators.

Black Aesthetic through Power Sharing

The counter to "whitinizing" is the holistic insertion of Blackness as identity and process into digital humanities. A Black aesthetic conceptualizes peoplehood in technology, breathes consciousness into the inanimate, and creates a repository *of* a people and not just *about* a people. The spirit of Blackness or "soul" drives the instrument, whether it is Toni Morrison's novels as referenced above or digital technology. But what is soul or a Black aesthetic?

Black scholars and literary artists from the 1960s and 1970s fixated on exactly this question. In 1971, Addison Gayle, Jr.'s edited anthology *The Black Aesthetic* reflected the political, social, and cultural thoughts of Black essayists struggling to define Blackness in the new era and embrace of Black power.[3] In it, Julian Mayfield contended that "For those who must create, there is a Black Aesthetic which cannot be stolen from us, and it rests on something much more substantial than hip talk. . . . It is in our racial memory, and the unshakable knowledge of who we are, where we have been, and . . . where we are going" (Mayfield, 28). For Mayfield black aesthetic was feeling and consciousness, sensibility and worldview, improvisation plus call and response, symbology and vernacular, sonic rhythm and syncopation, collective experience and selfhood, racial memory and the imagined future of freedom.[4] Writers Jimmy Stewart and Addison Gayle singled out the Black aesthetic as "unique experiences" that produced "unique cultural artifacts" and thus mandated "unique critical tools for evaluation." For the purposes of Black digital humanities, we might understand the Black aesthetic as a reflection of both the transmission of culture and "the procedure of its becoming what it is" (Stewart, 80). Even more, it is, as Gayle notes, "a corrective—a means of helping black people out of the polluted mainstream of Americanism"—or rather, the digital whiteness (Gayle, xxiv).

A digital Black aesthetic is visual and stylistic, purposeful in its process and production. Like improvisation, it changes and evolves in coordination and conversation with the audience, keeping to the community's beat (syncopation). Improvisation also means that Black digital humanities will over and over again reshape technology.[5] This fluidity can upend the expectations of institutions and the assumptions of its producers but also liberate it from elite spaces for the Black community's usage above all else. Regardless of producer comfort or intent, each endeavor must face the task and answer the final questions: Has my work co-opted Blackness or co-created the Black aesthetic? Have we offered Black audiences a reflection they recognize and a piece of themselves in the cyber world?

Black digital humanities is a mandate that dictates the digital be a servant to the Black public. It is both a depiction and a practice "enframing" subject and identity (Chun).[6] The most effective Black digital projects embrace a praxis that bonds

digital humanities with Black traditions of symbology, style, empowerment, and dissemination. They reverse the flow of institutional extraction from the community and instead reflect a spirit of Blackness through a power-sharing enterprise *with* the community. This call and response allows for the fluidity of improvisation and the constant flow of public exchange and power sharing. Digital practitioners transition from "civic engagement," defined here as an interaction incorporating source extraction and end-of-project review, to long-term extensive accountability in all phases of the project, from idea to distribution.

This practice derives from centering the Black community as a living digital public and not an inanimate topic. The consistent obscuring of the Black public has freed the academy to produce creations that run counter to the community's needs and character. The consequences of this thinking hindered the subject from defining and constructing the cybernetic self (Chun et al.).[7] Widely accepted notions like "open access," for example, overwrote and ignored the ambivalence held by peoples with a history of repression.[8] Digital scholarship's search for academic legitimacy is similarly in conflict with Black epistemology and Black scholars within the field. This narrow focus forces Black digitalists to walk a fine line between community and institution. Even further, it produces a single-minded mentality that pushes all digitalists to accept academic conventions over liberation models that help the Black public see themselves on the canvas of life versus through the peephole of the academy.[9]

A Black aesthetic philosophically undermines this tendency to focus on subject irrespective of praxis. It insists that the public is not an entity that you talk to, but rather a living body that talks back—marking the first step toward shared power. Shared power infuses a Black aesthetic into the digital humanities by first untying digital humanities from the institutional(ized) orbit and by second inducing a procedural technique to express Blackness. To be clear, such an infusion hardly prohibits outside communities—white or otherwise—from producing a Black digital project. After all, the Rascals had us groovin' on a Sunday afternoon and Teena Marie gave us a Square Biz with shoutouts to Sarah Vaughn, Maya Angelou, and Nikki Giovanni, too—just to name a few.[10] This shift to shared power simply means that Black people—from which the digital draws—have the power to frame and see themselves in cyberspace.

Shared power activates a fluid exchange where the act of creation is partially vested in the subject—living or not. Here, oral history theory provides procedures for collective creation and shared power.[11] Oral history, as an act of creation between interviewer (the creator of the question) and narrator (the creator of the narrative), requires both participants to have a say in a co-conceived outcome.[12] To that end, co-creation becomes an exchange of power. Most importantly, in the context of Black DH, it interrupts the white gaze as a replacement for Black voices (Morrison, "A Humanist View"). This means if the subject is Black or Black-related, the project must incorporate Black presence—in creation, grant development, material collection, project stages, technological formulation, finalized output, citation

source, labor recognition (which can include equitable compensation), and finally dissemination through multiple venues in the Black community. Projects fail when they require communities to venture into institutions, utilize material collection but exclude Black voices throughout other phases, and center students as the audience while mining Black life. Though inclusivity is a badly needed enterprise, real "engagement" acknowledges that the Black public defines the cyber with equal standing, as co-principals and tech developers.

The Virtual Martin Luther King, Jr., Project from the North Carolina State University Hunt Library is one project that reflected a process of co-creation.[13] Virtual MLK (vMLK) provides "audiences with sound-centered experiences of civic and political engagement and transformation," based on Martin Luther King's 1960 speech at White Rock Baptist Church in Durham, North Carolina. Years in the making, project co-leaders Victoria Gallagher and Keon Pettiway impressively incorporated a strong partnership with members of White Rock Baptist Church. Additionally, the project's outreach to public and neighborhood institutions decentered the university library location and facilitated exhibition in public spaces from local libraries to community museums.

However, the project fell short in its goal of "documenting and recovery of the history and everyday experience of African American/Black life" (vMLK Project Team). Church members expressed frustration that Virtual MLK failed to include oral history, which would have documented the memories of those present during King's speech more than sixty years ago. The issue was particularly acute after the death of Douglas E. Moore, the minister who had invited King to speak at the church. During the project's self-evaluation presentation in 2019, Keon Pettiway candidly discussed this tension between project design and the church's need. Pettiway noted that sometimes a digital project must break from its original mooring "when the spirit calls." A chorus of amens decidedly came from the church members. The conversation both expressed and highlighted the failure to adhere to a call and response approach and improvisation in the exchange between the church and Virtual MLK. The church's call was unheard by the project team, so the experience was one of only partially shared power. More to the point, the church did not share in the project's decision making and thus lacked the power to affect choices about its direction.

To be sure, external constraints such as grant structure or project timeline can determine any project direction. However, improvisation and shared power can and should redirect project activities as necessary, including reaching back to funders to address changes that emerge in the project. Stringent adherence to the project proposal meant the Virtual MLK project missed a major moment to interview Reverend Moore who invited King to White Rock Baptist Church. The project has only the disembodied virtual version of King's voice and not the man who bore witness to the actual King, missing a crucial chance to present King's words in the real-life context of his audience. Still, compared to other projects, Virtual MLK has strongly reflected

a moral obligation and collective exchange. Its willingness to accept criticism from the community also reflected another kind of spirit: King's beloved community.

Other digital projects infused with a Black aesthetic assert it through engagements with racial memory and in projects intended to function as liberatory tools. Julian Chambliss designed his Hannibal Square project as a conduit for Black voices to confront city officials. While Black community members sought to express—in the words of Langston Hughes—their "dark selves without shame," the city used the rhetoric of blight to defame the community and justify gentrification. Similarly, the Texas Freedom Colonies Project secured funding for preservation to provide "cultural agency within vulnerable communities" ("Texas Freedom Colonies Project Atlas and Study"). Andrea Roberts, a Texas A&M professor of urban planning, led this charge to reassert the vitality embedded in the physical and conceptual memory of Black Texans, despite efforts on the part of city officials and developers to rewrite the space and obliterate its significance.

Nishani Frazier's Gentrification Project similarly emerged as digital protest and as a talk-back to policy and media sources that rewrote Black removal as "market forces" ("About Us"). This erasure also played out in the city itself—reworking the landscape as a process of economic "rescue" while ignoring the historical and cultural implications of gentrification on the community. Still under construction, this project is among multiple spatial justice sites that assert a Black aesthetic through spatiality, style, and intent. Liberation is a significant goal that asserts by design and *desire* freedom's meaning in the Black imagination.

Frazier's distillation of a Black aesthetic also appeared in the Harambee City project, which involved more complex processes of power sharing from text to website. Harambee City is the digital companion for the book *Harambee City: The Congress of Racial Equality (CORE) in Cleveland and the Rise of Black Power Populism.* Like the book, African American studies, public history, and oral history methodologies played central roles in the site's construction and constant reconstruction. More specifically, the 1960s Black freedom movement and its activists drove the processes and theoretical underpinnings for the look and choice of digital tools on the Harambee City project site. Its landing page opens with images of movement people and those they had an impact on. The base background is Black—a visual homage to 1960s Black power. The site platform uses Omeka—a choice that was as much about function as symbolism. Its definition embodied multiple layers of historical meaning and digital theory.[14] *Omeka* is a Swahili term meaning "to display or lay out wares; to speak out; to spread out; to unpack." Swahili, a popular language during Black power, was also the basis for CORE's economic project title: Harambee. *Harambee* is a Swahili word meaning to pull or work together and a Kenyan motto meant to encourage self-help and nation building.

The website acts to counterbalance the rigidity of the printed book, providing constant and long-term opportunity for telling and retelling CORE's story. It is a conversation space for new memories, counter-arguments, or corrections that makes CORE's history an ever-evolving narrative. To do this, Frazier considered adding Hypothes.is in order to allow annotated commentary from myself, civil rights activists, or other scholars who reviewed the site. Viewers could see all comments, which would facilitate a second level of learning or exchange and help them think about history as a fluid tension between document source, memory (public and individual), and historical analysis. However, this consideration was set aside given the number of documents, the archival structure (document focus versus historian synthesis assertion), and the potential unwieldy nature of multilayered conversations that could drown out the document/voice itself. Instead, Frazier simply included Omeka's commenting plug-in. Any person may question an image, recall a memory, or share their thoughts for each document.

The site also tries to invert the idea that scholar expertise ranks above grassroots knowledge. Black Studies seeks to recover, empower, transform, and disseminate. By its nature, Black Studies must consider how professionalization can operate to mute the voices of vulnerable communities and counter it. Oral history asserts a similar model that asks the interviewer to open historical production to broader participation. Consequently, Harambee's copyright remains with the original owners, and the site travels with Frazier to ensure that proper protections remain in place and adhere to community needs, shared authority, and participatory democracy.[15]

Frazier also limited the full release of the oral history interviews (though she has consent) until she was granted additional permission to display them on the site or until the interviewee departed. Consequently, individual interviewees determined the time frame of "open access." Even more, the site disrupts commercial paywalls by assuring the Black community's usage and access to civil rights history without cost. Presented at public schools and libraries for wider dissemination, Harambee City both recovers Black history and unpacks the structural nuances designed to keep African Americans at the economic bottom. Thus, the website depicts Black economic protest and the steps that activists took to attain equity and freedom. The accessibility of this research consequently led College Board to include the site among its resources for the first African American Studies Advanced Placement course.

The power sharing envisioned by Frazier was not infallible. Professor Watson Jennison rightly critiques some of the failures of the website, including the tensions between the scholar and the participatory curation of the site itself. The site's authoritative voice remained with Frazier, "leaving no opportunity for participants or visitors to post their own primary sources" (Jennison, 125). Despite these drawbacks, Harambee insisted on visibly displaying the power sharing and methodology at work. Thus, the manifestation of the Black aesthetic radiated from the struggle itself.

Toward a Shared Practice of the Black Aesthetic: Digital Humanities 2017

Christy Hyman's foray into recovering African Americans' tarnished lineages to the Great Dismal Swamp landscape necessitated that she immerse herself in the

Figure 9.1. *Where Is Democracy.* Congress of Racial Equality protestor circa 1964. Source: Antoine Perot Papers from Harambee City, https://harambeecity.lib.miamioh.edu/.

contested interpretations of African-descended ties to the land and how those ties mattered in marking sites of memory in the swamp. The Great Dismal Swamp, located along the North Carolina/Virginia border, was a haven for enslaved fugitives in the eighteenth and nineteenth centuries, yet there are no physical sites that mark this revolutionary action of self-liberation. To begin to recover that erasure using digital media, Hyman created a short video that sought to capture the moments of fear, dread, and hope in the process of enslaved flight. Hyman screened the first

Figure 9.2. The Great Dismal Swamp, Lake Drummond at the North Carolina/Virginia border, July 2017. Image by Christy Hyman.

iteration of the video at Digital Humanities 2017, and it inspired us (the authors of this chapter) to continue probing the connections among the Black aesthetic, shared power and authority, and the many publics that Black digital humanities work engages.

The video, an artifact grounded in the Black digital humanities recovery oeuvre, is a multi-dominant audiovisual meditation on enslaved flight and the pursuit of freedom.[16] Multi-dominance is a term that originated with artist and critic Robert L. Douglas, and it seeks to formalize a Black aesthetic, synthesizing visual and musical elements invoking a "Trans-African" culture. Composer George E. Lewis informs us that Douglas's aesthetic of multi-dominance involves "multiple use of colors in intense degrees, of textures, design patterns, and/or shapes" (33). Hyman's video, for instance, evokes a tableau of still images, motion video, and text, representing a range of sites within the Great Dismal Swamp that coalesce into a whole—comprising trauma, struggle, creative expression, and the pursuit of freedom.

When we think back to the plantation landscape, a site of domination and trauma, the ways that enslaved people made music for themselves were quite different from the minstrelsy spectacle forced on enslaved people for their enslavers' enjoyment. Enslaved people's musical performances while under the coercion of enslavers constitute what historian Katrina D. Thompson has called "contradictory pieces of stagecraft": done for the colonial gaze, yet still a "signification of resistance, power and cultural autonomy" when enslaved people's creative expression pleased themselves (Thompson, 34). As historian Jon Cruz points out, "Slaveowners may have heard only noise from enslaved cabins," yet such a dismissive notion of the music enslaved people made among themselves was "tantamount to being oblivious to the structures of meaning that anchored sounding to the hermeneutic world of the slaves" (Lewis, 34). To hear only noise is to "remain removed from how slave soundings probed their circumstances and cultivated histories and memories," Cruz explains (Lewis, 34). Hyman's goal in making the video was rooted in getting closer to visualizing those soundings and memories formed from enslaved people's committed yearning for freedom. The process of curating the images and texts for the video also built Hyman's understanding of the importance of engaging recovery work with descendant communities living near the Great Dismal Swamp today. It was a "technology of recovery," as Kim Gallon uses the term, in that it aimed at creating a usable past that would empower living descendants with pride in their shared freedom legacies.

For Eric Sheppard, a direct descendant of formerly enslaved abolitionist Moses Grandy, the denial of enslaved people's connection to landscape has contributed to a complete erasure of the legacy of slavery and freedom for enslaved people's descendants in the area.[17] The hidden legacy of African Americans' lineage to the Great Dismal Swamp influenced Sheppard's efforts to recover his family history and educate the public about the history of enslaved flight and the Underground Railroad presence near the swamp. Historian Kathryn Benjamin Golden has written about public historical representation in areas near the swamp, finding that state institutions set the terms and controlled the narratives that have effectively marginalized the history of slavery and resistance in the Great Dismal Swamp. With such an ecosystem of erasure at work, Sheppard's efforts are all the more significant. Sheppard educates the public about enslaved resistance in the swamp with no institutional resources, and his efforts demonstrate the importance of heritage curators in constructing community narratives of landscape.

In 2016, when Hyman began her investigation into enslaved flight in the Great Dismal Swamp, she set out to determine whether there had been any historical markers dedicated to Moses Grandy. She found that there were none, either in North Carolina or Virginia.[18] Googling historic places near the Great Dismal Swamp, Hyman came across an article that referenced a local Suffolk, Virginia, heritage curator who gave tours of the Underground Railroad presence near the Great Dismal Swamp (Feber). It was in this moment that Hyman became aware of Eric Sheppard's work, and the seeds of collaboration between them were planted.[19]

The Great Dismal Swamp's lack of commemoration with regard to its ties to slavery also compel us to consider how Black digital humanities projects as a whole may suffer from a similar lack of support due to historical silences. For instance, heritage curators in the Great Dismal Swamp have pointed out that the state school curriculum focuses on a national narrative of history that privileges an understanding of the past that is simplistic, linear, and devoid of disturbing elements. The nationalist interpretation of history serves to bolster patriotism and order the social behavior of students. James W. Loewen has written about these issues, pointing out that textbook adoption committees "function as censors that avoid offending parents." "Offended parents" are the parents who occupy the dominant social group. Controversies surrounding "critical race theory" and it supposedly being taught to students shows how politicized educational curricula can be. The de-emphasis of important events related to Black history in K–12 textbooks lays a foundation for Black history to be seen as marginal when compared to more nationally centered events that receive greater coverage. When school curricula minimize the role of Black people in the shaping of history, it perpetuates marginalization and destroys the potential for public memory. As Henry Giroux explains, these historical silences "actively function to suppress the development of a critical historical consciousness among the public," putting Black digital recovery projects at a disadvantage when they seek funding opportunities, especially those on the federal level (Loewen, 305). This asymmetric coverage of history as it relates to the Black past means that when scholars apply for funding from granting institutions, the statement of significance section will likely be one of the most challenging areas to write: Project directors know there will need to be extensive work required in order to convince funding agencies of the universal relevance of their recovery projects. Black recovery projects are undoubtedly significant, but because it is highly probable that reviewers may not be aware of the historical actors involved, the propensity for the proposal to be dismissed as insignificant puts added pressure on grant writers.

It is for this reason that a number of Black DH projects have been implemented without external federal grant funding, including the projects created by the authors of this chapter.[20] Even success in being awarded grant funding does not guarantee that digital recovery project implementation will simply fall in place. On the contrary, if digital humanists are working from liberation frameworks not in line with the traditional business logic and currencies of the university, grant-funded recovery projects may find themselves battling every step of the way to mitigate the power structures of the university (Cole et al.). One could argue that these issues concerning historical silences and erasures put Black DH projects in a precarious position with criteria required for funding opportunities if the content of the project is not seen as relevant to the "national story." Given that a large number of funded projects involve digitization and preservation of archival collections, the stories from Black communities that could be expanded with a digital project have no archive where these memories live—the memories are in the community itself. The creative approaches that many Black digitalists use are in the spirit of recovery, and this does not always cohere to the requirements of major funding agencies.

The issues of historical silences, popular memory, and the determined cultural heritage resilience in relation to building a recovery project from a liberatory framework require confronting how access to funding and other forms of resources are uneven. To construct a fair and equitable system of allocation for Black recovery projects, practitioners must imagine a new form of consciousness that applies not only to access to grants and related resources at institutions of higher education but also to how Black life lives and endures in an unfair, unjust world.

Black on Campus, at the Conference, in the World

These issues are not just a function of community access to institutional resources. They also require that we examine how academic spaces can reflect sites of oppression and extractive practices that not only affect Black communities but also Black scholars. For example, a number of news reports have caused alarm for Black people in university spaces. At Yale, a white student called the police on a fellow student, a Black woman, for sleeping in the common dormitory space (Griggs). In 2018, at the International Communications Association conference in Prague, Czech Republic, Black scholars were chased by neo-Nazis as they attempted to walk down the street (Schradie). At the annual meeting for classical studies, Dan-el Padilla Peralta was told in a question-and-answer session that he only got his position in academia because he is Black (Flaherty). And just five days after the University of Nebraska-Lincoln held a symposium on the importance of civil discourse, one of the coauthors of this chapter, Christy Hyman, learned that her thirteen-year-old son was verbally abused with racially abusive epithets and curses by a person in a passing car as he walked home from school (Schlage). These are the very real interactions that Black scholars have to contend with as they strive to attain their academic and professional credentials.

These events are important because they underscore the range of antagonisms and aggressions that Black scholars confront as they engage in the life of the mind while pursuing their research programs and avoiding replication of academic practices that abuse community trust. The life of the mind requires the space to think clearly, but when one is burdened by the weight of racial trauma, that thinking is severely affected. This means that Black scholars already dealing with the emotional trauma from the painful histories on which their recovery projects are drawn are also grappling with the daily reality of an ongoing afterlife of unresolved societal oppression rooted in colonialism, slavery, Jim Crow, and racism broadly. Black scholars are often the first called on to organize diversity initiatives on campus while also managing their research agenda for promotion and tenure. These bureaucratic diversity exercises require significant emotional labor and reinforce trauma.

Thinking critically about the digital humanities spaces in which Black scholars find themselves, whether through collaborations or through work and research spaces, involves acknowledging and accounting for the dynamics of power in relation to people represented in those spaces, but also the position of power each scholar holds within their university and within the discipline. Digital humanities spaces must confront the fact that, as Tamura Lomax puts it powerfully, "academia and the growing academic-corporate trend is a microcosm of the world house in its disappearing and disenfranchising of Black people, especially Black women."

The Black Subject Creating Digital Work in the University

It is a well-documented fact that digital projects require a great deal of labor. For Black scholars, adding the work involved in building a digital recovery project to the work required for degree completion or tenure requirements can seem a daunting task. The dedication to historical and cultural recovery requires that Black scholars work carefully and diligently to satisfy the requirements of the university but also the communities to which their research is accountable. Hyman found that in working with Great Dismal Swamp cultural narrators, it took time to earn their trust. Trips to the Great Dismal Swamp area several times a year to support and amplify the heritage efforts of cultural narrators helped to cultivate meaningful relationships with them. Their testimonies pointed out the historical and cultural meanings that were important to them, and it in turn remapped the region in a way that shifted power from colonizing logics of the landscape that erased them. This level of engagement with accountable communities is essential, and at every turn community voices are centered and respected. Black scholars engage in these practices on top of the responsibilities required by their role in the university.

Doing this work takes an array of skills and competencies. Depending on how resourced a scholar's institution is, there may be training opportunities on campus to cultivate DH skills; there may be digital humanists at the university participating in projects who offer opportunities for training through work experience; or one may elect to participate in an array of DH training institutes. For many scholars, "hacking" their way through digital humanities training, online tutorials provide a great deal of skill building. No matter which avenue is taken, Black scholars endeavoring to build recovery projects alongside a research agenda in departments that may or may not value digital recovery work are embarking on an unpredictable journey that may or may not provide immediate or long-term guarantees.

How do assemblages of Blackness—that is to say, the racialized sets of "relations structured in political, economic, social, and heteropatriarchal dominance" at the university—unmask systems of power at work in collaborative spaces (Weheliye, 49)? For example, how does a Black contingent worker who is the only racial minority on a project team make their voice heard in spaces where their race and position at the university marginalize their voice? Or how does the Black diversity officer handle being spoken over by senior university officials when their findings indicate a need for material investment in transformative efforts for meaningful change? How does the Black scholar remain empowered in a world where the acceptance of any racialized category is viewed through the prism of white supremacy and colonialism (Miller and Driscoll)? And how can the digital humanities as a field ensure that it is critically reflective of the racist societal processes that often are so naturalized that only racialized others notice when they occur?

These questions are essential for building a greater understanding of the array of social identities making up the community of digital humanists. It is essential that those in the digital humanities recognize who is most vulnerable and who has the potential to do the most harm in digital projects on a number of scales (Kim). In this we must attend to the relations among members of the DH spaces and within digital project teams, and the relations of the digital practitioners to the many publics who stand to receive the work. We must fully value and validate the accountability to which Black scholars hold themselves in their relationships with the descendant communities for whom their research is relevant.

The digital humanities is strengthened when it collectively makes efforts to understand how Black scholars navigate the university and experience digital humanities spaces. The potential for continued participation in the DH community relies on a critically reflective self-awareness of how its practitioners experience the spaces required to make, create, and produce research. The promises of recognizing the stakes of Blackness within the digital humanities community allow for greater awareness of the array of social realities that typify the experiences of BIPOC (Black, Indigenous, and People of Color) digital humanists as they grapple with the multiple dimensions of anti-Blackness in their day-to-day experience. Though Blackness cannot be conflated with other racial categorizations, the fact remains that recognition of the specific oppressed conditions of underrepresented groups opens up a reflective space to understand the wide continuum of oppression happening to BIPOC everywhere.

The spaces where Black digital humanists reflect on their positionality amidst their experiences of Black subjectivity runs the gamut, whether at the kitchen table, the coffeehouse, or on the work commute. When those critical reflections of one's position take place at the university and are coupled with research agendas that address the university's historical reliance on enslaved laborers to build and maintain their campuses, the convergence of the Black aesthetic, digital recovery, and community accountability can be disorienting. It is an overlap of the digital humanist's cultural investment in telling the story, being accountable to the communities within the story, but also navigating the very structures where connected community members' ancestors were oppressed on a daily basis. Within the digital humanities, those projects that examine relations among people, institutions, and places, past and present, allow for a range of opportunities for DH scholars to understand more closely how the digital Black aesthetic, as well as the stakes involved in being accountable to various publics, reveal themselves as vital features within a liberatory ethics of care. Recognizing and respecting Black digital humanists' labor in navigating institutional barriers while connecting to the communities for which their work is accountable demonstrates a commitment not only to the work and all of its purpose but also to the value of working within a Black aesthetic framework.

The Hallowed Grounds Project and the Black Aesthetic

An ethics acknowledging the myriad forms of anti-Blackness and a politics of care must inform Black DH projects. Any resulting creative project must be rooted in the exploration of Black life without advancing the spectacle of Black death or the erasure of the complexity of Black aesthetic landscapes, such as smells, sounds, histories, and visual artforms.[21] In this Black aesthetic DH imaginary, shared authority transforms digital spaces into assertions of Black presence through the creation of new landscapes, whether digital, physical, or cultural. This framework opens up an opportunity for thinking about recovery and pathways for engagement as the sharing of resources and expertise in a co-collaborative creative endeavor.

Here, it is imperative that Indigenous knowledges have equal weight in the collaboration. For instance, predominantly white institutions (PWIs) and research institutions (R1s), such as the University of Alabama, must avoid thinking of Historically Black Colleges and Universities (HBCUs) and the community as sites of extraction for their intellectual, cultural, sociopolitical, and financial capital or recipients of their neoliberal benevolence. Instead of replicating colonial and white supremacist authoritative practices, these institutions should redirect resources and provide the necessary (and expensive) infrastructure for sustaining the DH output in a true collaboration. This collaborative spirit must continue throughout the entire lifetime of the final DH project and not merely at the point of creation. In essence, the ongoing feedback loop between all co-creators and expansive public audiences breathes life into the decisions influencing updates, future directions for promoting additional lines of inquiry, and, ultimately, the project's end.

It is not sufficient to design a DH project which Black and Brown communities, academic and nonacademic, may find useful. Rather, these communities must be at the heart of any inclusive DH project from its initial design, choice of content, and decisions about an overall aesthetic. Subsequent updates must respond to the feedback received from those communities. A Black aesthetic without a consideration of who constitutes a project's public replicates the harmful and violent practices characteristic of so many traditional archives. The computational large data focus of many existing DH projects has become the shortcut for the continued dehumanization of marginalized communities and discounting of their historical and cultural practices.[22]

A careful eye toward the Black aesthetic has the potential to realize a future where African Americans and other marginalized groups are the center of DH projects. In these projects, their concerns would be actively sought out, heard, and not dismissed. If done properly, scholars would no longer be required to trouble the archive or do a close reading of white cisgender heteronormative sources in order to locate the voices and experiences of marginalized communities. Such a politics of care will allow communities to renew trust in a field where the racial complicity of methods and scholarship has sustained physical and epistemological harm.

Figure 9.3. The Hallowed Grounds Project logo. Courtesy of Hilary N. Green.

The Hallowed Grounds Project represents one possibility. It responds to the whitewashed University of Alabama myths of slavery and its legacy, which were made legible to the author by a Black male student's comment raised in January 2015. His comment—"But, Dr. Green, slavery did not exist here"—revealed the ongoing harm perpetuated by the absent history of the forced labor that built the Alabama flagship public university. This erasure rendered the lives and contributions of hundreds of African American men, women, and children invisible. Official campus tours, campus histories, building names, and traditions forced African American students to accept this erasure without question.

Built using limited resources, the Hallowed Grounds Project makes visible this history of enslavement, the diverse experiences of enslaved laborers, and fully considers the complex afterlives of slavery for the formerly enslaved, their descendants, the campus community, and the entire Black community of Tuscaloosa, where the University of Alabama (UA) is located. It transforms the physical campus into an archive of recovery through self-guided alternative campus tours, digitally accessible primary sources, and other digital tools for deepening understanding designed for diverse audiences and not merely for current campus stakeholders. All current materials are in a UA-approved web platform that can be accessed without UA community credentials, and on cellphones and other devices for audiences residing in broadband internet deserts. With future expansion to an Omeka-S platform, ensuring accessibility for diverse audiences will remain a priority (Green).

Based on feedback and requests received from a weary Black Tuscaloosa community, Hilary Green, the Hallowed Grounds Project creator, prioritized the incorporation of sources documenting enslaved women, children born on campus, and other materials on slavery's afterlives and postemancipation institutions.

This process has meant listening and allowing Black Tuscaloosa residents to set the terms of the project expansion. Through the in-person tours and DH project, they accepted Green as an ally who was willing center the full history, learn from community members, and partner with them as co-creators. Whether in person, email, or phone, community members often expressed a frustration in dealing with previous white UA faculty and students seeking to "save" them with knowledge. Over several conversations with Green, they also expressed a lack of awareness in navigating campus archival repositories and being afraid to ask the white institutional gatekeepers about such knowledge. As such, the DH project has expanded to include specific documents, short thematic overviews, brief contextualization per document, and a more robust bibliography. Sustained community engagement and responsiveness to shifting community needs continue to shape the project's future.

Community engagement under a Black aesthetic framework dictates additional partnerships for fulfilling all of the terms set by the Black public. Black Tuscaloosans' requests for the expansion of features has required Green to seek additional partners who are willing to embrace the Black aesthetic framework informing the Hallowed Grounds Project. Specifically, responding to requests for a digital re-creation of the antebellum landscape destroyed on April 4, 1865, when federal forces razed the campus, required partnering with archaeologists, geographers, and others with the necessary skills. The 1865 campus destruction and subsequent rebuilding erased the landscape where enslaved people labored, birthed children, resisted, and developed community, making it hard for individuals to fully understand the campus and community that enslaved people built. Remnants of the antebellum campus exist in the few surviving buildings, the quad green space, cemetery fragments, and recovered bricks placed in the first postwar building, and the postwar naming practices, campus histories, and traditions allude to the slave past; the UA community had firmly embraced a Lost Cause understanding of its past as well as a racially segregated landscape in Tuscaloosa and in the state until desegregation created the campus in its contemporary form. The absence of memory perpetuates the denial of the African American experience, the development of a campus forgetfulness as an act of purposeful memory suppression, and a difficult recovery process for African Americans and others desiring a more inclusive narrative (Ross, 94–119). The difficulty of this recovery process is compounded by the forces of gentrification and university expansion, which have eliminated some of the neighborhoods and institutions created by former enslaved campus laborers and their descendants. However, using the existing to-scale models of the antebellum campus buildings, 3D renderings, digital virtual reality (VR), and interactive mapping of the lost landscape becomes possible and informs the interdisciplinary partnerships necessary for making these requests a reality.

A richer Black DH aesthetic demands input from unexpected partners. Enacting some of these multidimensional understandings has required, for example, working with ethnomusicologists, professional musicians, and UA Music faculty to interpret and re-create songs performed at a major public address of Booker T. Washington in the early twentieth century—an event in which a formerly enslaved campus laborer hosted the white UA president as a guest in a Black Tuscaloosa church founded by other formerly enslaved campus laborers. It means working with food historians in order to understand enslaved people's culinary knowledge so that it can be rendered through historical meals cooked for community reconciliation dinners. In short, it means collaborating with diverse community partners who have as much as say as the academics involved. Existing tools, expertise, funding, and infrastructure are the current project's limits. Imagination, a politics of care, shared authority, and attentiveness to a Black DH aesthetic are not.

Woefully underfunded, the Hallowed Grounds Project has nevertheless had diverse uses. While it has been used for advancing scholarly inquiry, local African American homeschool parents, for instance, have used the virtual tour and primary source materials in developing a race-cognizant curriculum for their children pulled from the classrooms to prison pipeline. It has inspired the creative remaking of the difficult historical experiences and documented acts of enslaved people's survival through poetry, creative nonfiction, and art. It has served as a cathartic meditation for faculty of color, students, and staff navigating a campus landscape haunted by the many specters of its slave past. The existing project creates beauty out of the painful and complex racial past. It inspires and expands the possibilities of future scholarship, creative inquiry, and praxis for making a more inclusive and just future—digitally, physically, and collaboratively. For these reasons, it has garnered favorable attention from current campus stakeholders, Tuscaloosa community activists, local news outlets, and scholarly publications.[23]

A Call to Action

Digital humanities must act to represent in the digital world a radical assertion of the Black self—our history, our beauty, our style, our imagination, our souls. It is the Black public that sets those terms. Digital projects must intentionally operate ethically, self-reflexively, and co-creatively.

We recognize that this digital praxis centers on American Black souls. Eduard Arriaga and colleagues at the Digital Humanities 2017 conference asserted that Black digital humanities in the Global South required a borrowing of some of these elements while diverging toward its own path (also see Fiormonte). Language, for example, offers dynamic elements that add body to global Black culture. To that end, this chapter is very much situated within a particular temporal, physical space that changes and transforms not unlike culture itself. Indeed, the argument for adaptability, keeping to the beat (syncopation), and improvisation actually means that Black aesthetics will constantly refigure digital humanities like jazz, changing over time.

It is the job of each digital project to keep pace and time, inserting a Black aesthetic at all levels. The legitimacy of future digital humanities projects rests in one final consideration: Does your work reflect a community or act to exploit it?

NOTES

1. Tara McPherson has a similar argument, examining the history of coding and the covert elements that hide epistemology, while Domenico Fiormonte situates this issue as part of the larger colonizing tendencies demonstrated in digital humanities. Toni Morrison's broader critique on language misuse is also helpful here. In her 1993 "Nobel Lecture," Morrison notes that there is the "tendency of its users to forgo its nuanced, complex, mid-wifery properties for menace and subjugation. Oppressive language does more than represent violence; it is violence; does more than represent the limits of knowledge; it limits knowledge."

2. These circumstances were also driven by the "dark side" of digital humanities, discussed by Chun et al. The inclination of foundations and university administrators to stem humanities' decline by funding digital humanities projects or hires has expedited unthoughtful production and emphasis on individual promotion. Writ large, humanities has reasserted legitimacy on the backs of marginalized communities.

3. The question of what constitutes a Black aesthetic appears throughout the years. As historians, we pull from the earliest of these scholarly interventions with a focus on "soul." However, other theorists engage similar questions about Black cultural production, style, and/or ways of being. In the process, intellectuals have directly and indirectly built on this conversation to reconsider soul or add elements like generational difference, Afro-futurism, or queer and feminist identity construction. Each adds layers to the earlier theories that emerged from 1960s Black scholarship. See, for example, Houston Baker; Paul C. Taylor; Mark Dery; Patrick Johnson; and Mark Anthony Neal. Key here is that we deliberately draw from a historical period whose purpose was to reflect empowered black assertions of self. Black aesthetic definitions that exclude power do not apply.

4. As Addison Gayle wrote, this is not the definitive description of a Black aesthetic (xxii, 197). Similarly, Gayle's introduction to *The Black Aesthetic* is the first of many treatments of how digital humanities can conform to Black aestheticism. Other references in the essays within *The Black Aesthetic* proved quite useful in constructing the digital Black aesthetic. See Hoyt W. Fuller, "Theory Introduction Towards a Black Aesthetic"; Larry Neal, "Some Reflections on the Black Aesthetic"; Alain Locke, "Negro Youth Speaks" and "Drama Introduction: The Negro and the American Theatre"; Jimmy Stewart, "Music Introduction to Black Aesthetics in Music"; Ron Wellburn, "The Black Aesthetic Imperative"; Don L. Lee, "Toward a Definition: Black Poetry of the Sixties (after LeRoi Jones)"; Langston Hughes, "Poetry Introduction: The Negro Artist and the Racial Mountain"; Larry Neal, "The Black Arts Movement"; Ronald Milner, "Black Theater—Go Home"; Clayton Riley, "On Black Theater"; and Adam David Miller, "Some Observations on a Black Aesthetic." Neal, Miller, and Lee are particularly useful for their references to Black aesthetic as utilitarian and ethically

driven to represent truth and reality of Blackness, particularly Larry Neal's point that Black theater "exists in direct relationship to the audience it claims to serve" (263).

5. Global Blackness offers far more opportunities for dynamic definitions of Black aesthetic. Whether this dynamism proves unwieldy or not will depend on how each DH project chooses to handle these complexities.

6. The authors of this chapter also proffered our notion for merging race and technology in a conference paper at the Association for the Study of African American Life and History (Frazier, Hyman, and Green, "Black Digital Protocols"). In it, we suggested specific guidelines for consideration to move conversation from abstract ideas of Black digital humanities to a how-to manual for incorporating Black subjects in DH projects. We also embrace the work of Wendy Hui Kyong Chun ("Race and/as Technology"), who asserts that the question of race and technology is not just about what race is but what relations and questions engender race. In a sense, this is the backbone of Black aesthetics. By focusing on Blackness, digital humanists are guided to ask different questions about what they produce and its relation to the Black public. Alexis Lothian and Amanda Phillips also speak to this concern along with Black twitterstorians who combine Black Studies to construct digital scholarship as an outgrowth of processes that advocate and produce recovery along with transformation.

7. These circumstances were also driven by the "dark side" of digital humanities discussed by Wendy Hui Kyong Chun et al. This "dark" legacy has led humanities to reassert legitimacy on the backs of marginalized communities.

8. This, of course, includes all oppressed peoples. Other communities (Indigenous, LGBTQ, and feminists scholars) have addressed these issues from the standpoint of their societal vulnerability as well. The 2017 Alliance of Digital Humanities Organizations conference, where the authors met, was replete with sessions from these various communities countering DH conventions. Also see Gandy (131–32, 135–36, 139–40); Beydoun and Hansford; Cowan; and Christen. It is also important to acknowledge digital tools like Mukurtu, a content management system that was created to address the concerns of Indigenous people about open access.

9. This is an epistemological reference to Outkast.

10. This is also an epistemological moment referencing Tina Marie's musical style, lyrics, and her manifestation within Black culture as feeling and through communal events. This is also an exercise in engaging Black knowledge production over the digital (search engine) that provides only partial information.

11. See Laughlin. Patrik Svensson suggests another variation by changing the "big tent," with its connotations of hegemony, to a term like "meeting place," in order to allow "bridge building and the bringing together of epistemic traditions [that] is not optimally done from the position of discipline or department." Although, notably, the Black aesthetic insists on more than a bridge due to tendencies to build it for extraction versus direction from differing epistemic traditions. Another take on this is Domenico Fiormonte's concern over "unity in diversity" versus federation, particularly because unity simply reflected white hegemony with cursory inclusion versus a transformative system for digital

humanities. In this case, this federation acknowledges the variant methodologies, systems of thought, and stylistic expressions (Fiormonte).

12. On oral history, see Frisch (*A Shared Authority: Essays* and "Sharing Authority: Oral History"); Snopes; Thomson; Adair, Filene, and Koloski.

13. vMLK Project Team, *Virtual Martin Luther King, Jr. Project,* 2019, https://vmlk.chass.ncsu.edu/about/.

14. A more detailed breakdown of Omeka as digital theory within Harambee is available in Frazier ("About CORE and Black Economic Power"); each definition has its own subheading.

15. This site fluidity allows Frazier to avoid institutional control until both projects can be maintained by an entity that adheres to Black aesthetic principles. The University of Kansas will be the next institution to hold both the Gentrification Project and Harambee City. These links will change, requiring readers to conduct an internet search by project title.

16. On the Black digital humanities and recovery, see Gallon.

17. Moses Grandy was an enslaved Great Dismal Swamp canal waterman who freed himself from bondage and later freed his wife and children. Grandy had to leave Virginia after purchasing his freedom and went on to became a free Black sailor who traveled the world as well as worked in the cause of antislavery. See Grandy (1843).

18. Grandy's narrative refers to places in Virginia as well as North Carolina because the Great Dismal Swamp is located along the border of both states. There is the Moses Grandy Trail, a two-and-a-half-mile, four-lane road in Chesapeake, Virginia; the section was named in 2006. This was a citywide venture.

19. Sheppard is a retired defense management consultant and has written a book, *Ancestors Call,* which traces his lineage to Moses Grandy and contains a reprint of Moses Grandy's narrative. When Hyman began thinking of ways to collaborate with Sheppard on efforts to commemorate Grandy's life, she emailed him to introduce herself. In contacting Sheppard, Hyman wanted to make two things clear from the beginning: her appreciation for his efforts in commemorating slavery's history in the Great Dismal Swamp Region without any institutional resources, and the assurance that she could be trusted as an historian invested in both Grandy's memory and the legacy of descendant communities related to slavery. Today's more ethically concerned scholars explore "questions of authority, control, and ownership of heritage narratives, plus the material remains that result from research based work" involving community stewards of the past (Gasby and Moyer). Sheppard is a community steward who has opened up the history of Grandy's life for hundreds of visitors to the Great Dismal Swamp each year.

20. For a list of digital projects that cover the history, culture, and consciousness of Black people on a number of scales, please visit the Black Digital Humanities Projects and Resources document created by the Colored Conventions Project at http://digitalhumanitiesnow.org/2017/08/resource-Black-digital-humanities-projects-resources-google-doc/. For a discussion of digital work created beyond the confines of the academy, consult the work on building the Supercommons (Risam et al.).

21. For examples of this work, see Vincent Brown and also Jessica Marie Johnson.

22. See Johnson and Neal, and also Benjamin.

23. See Kutzler; Crain; Griesbach and Haney; and Brooks. Kutzler's review is of Martha A. Sandweiss et. al's Princeton & Slavery Project website at https://slavery.princeton.edu.

BIBLIOGRAPHY

"About Us." *The (Anti) Gentrification Project.* Accessed January 19, 2020, https://gentrificationproject.lib.miamioh.edu/.

Adair, Bill, Benjamin Filene, and Laura Koloski. *Letting Go? Sharing Historical Authority in a User Generated World.* New York: Routledge, 2011.

Arriaga, Eduard. "Acccesing Alternative Histories and Futures: Afro-Latin American Models for the Digital Humanities." Presentation at Digital Humanities 2017. Montreal, August 8–11, 2017, https://dh2017.adho.org/abstracts/524/524.pdf.

Baker, Houston. *Afro-American Poetics: Revisions of Harlem and the Black Aesthetic.* Madison: University of Wisconsin Press, 1988.

Benjamin, Ruha. *Race after Technology: Abolitionist Tools for the New Jim Code.* Cambridge: Polity Press, 2019.

Beydoun, Khaled A., and Justin Hansford. "The F.B.I.'s Dangerous Crackdown on 'Black Identity Extremists.'" *New York Times,* November 15, 2017, https://www.nytimes.com/2017/11/15/opinion/Black-identity-extremism-fbi-trump.html.

Brooks, James. "Heritage, Refracted." *The Public Historian* 41, no. 1 (February 2019), 7–9.

Brown, Aleia M., and Joshua Crutchfield. "Black Scholars Matter: #BlkTwitterstorians Building a Digital Community." *The Black Scholar* 47, no. 3 (July 2017): 45–55.

Brown, Vincent. "Mapping a Slave Revolt: Visualizing Spatial History through the Archives of Slavery." *Social Text* 125 (December 2015): 134.

Chambliss, Julian. "Building the Archive of the Black Social World in Central Florida." *JulianChambliss.com.* Accessed January 19, 2020, https://www.julianchambliss.com/blog/tag/Hannibal+Square.

Christen, Kimberly. "Relationships, Not Records: Digital Heritage and the Ethics of Sharing Indigenous Knowledge Online." In *The Routledge Companion to Media Studies and Digital Humanities,* edited by Jentery Sayers. New York: Routledge, 2018.

Chun, Wendy Hui Kyong. "Race and/as Technology, or How to Do Things to Race." In *Race after the Internet,* edited by Lisa Nakamura and Peter Chow-White, 38–59. New York: Routledge, 2012.

Chun, Wendy Hui Kyong, Richard Grusin, Patrick Jagoda, and Rita Raley. "The Dark Side of Digital Humanities." In *Debates in the Digital Humanities 2016,* edited by Matthew K. Gold and Lauren F. Klein. Minneapolis: University of Minnesota Press, 2016, https://dhdebates.gc.cuny.edu/read/untitled/section/ca35736b-0020-4ac6-9ce7-88c6e9ff1bba#ch38.

Cole, Danielle, Izetta Autumn Mobley, Jacqueline Wernimont, Moya Bailey, T. L. Cowan, and Veronica Paredes. "Accounting and Accountability: Feminist Grant Administration and Coalitional Fair Finance." In *Bodies of Information: Intersectional Feminism and the Digital Humanities,* edited by Elizabeth Losh and Jacqueline Wernimont. Minneapolis: University of Minnesota Press, 2018.

Cowan, T. L. "X-Reception: Re-mediating Trans-Feminist and Queer Performance Art." In *The Routledge Companion to Digital Humanities and Art History,* edited by Kathryn Brown. New York: Routledge, 2020.

Crain, Abbey. "UA Professor Offers Alternate Campus Tour Highlighting Enslaved People." *AL.com.* September 8, 2019, https://www.al.com/news/2019/09/ua-professor-offers-alternate-campus-tour-highlighting-enslaved-people.html.

Dery, Mark. "Black to the Future: Interviews with Samuel R. Delany, Greg Tate, and Tricia Rose." In *Flame Wars,* edited by Mark Dery, 179–222. Durham, N.C.: Duke University Press, 1994.

Dinsman, Melissa. "The Digital in the Humanities: An Interview with Marisa Parham." *Los Angeles Review of Books.* May 19, 2016, https://lareviewofbooks.org/article/digital-humanities-interview-marisa-parham/.

Feber, Eric. "Suffolk Firm Offers More Underground Railroad Tours." *The Virginian-Pilot* (Norfolk, Va.). December 27, 2013, https://pilotonline.com/news/local/article_6a7e98c2-b2bf-5aa6-a7ca-3fff313246e5.html.

Fiormonte, Domenico. "Toward a Cultural Critique of Digital Humanities." In *Debates in the Digital Humanities 2016,* edited by Matthew K. Gold and Lauren F. Klein. Minneapolis: University of Minnesota Press, 2016, https://dhdebates.gc.cuny.edu/read/untitled/section/5cac8409-e521-4349-ab03-f341a5359a34#ch35.

Flaherty, Colleen. "Q&A Goes Horribly Wrong." January 7, 2019, https://www.insidehighered.com/news/2019/01/07/racist-comments-directed-classics-scholar-disciplinary-meeting-floor-classicists.

Frazier, Nishani. "About CORE and Black Economic Power." *Harambee City,* https://harambeecity.lib.miamioh.edu/about.

Frazier, Nishani, Christy Hyman, and Hilary Green. "Black Digital Protocols." Conference paper, Association for the Study of African American Life and History. October 2017, https://www.academia.edu/36836823/Black_Digital_Protocols.

Frisch, Michael. *A Shared Authority: Essays on the Craft and Meaning of Oral and Public History.* Albany: State University of New York Press, 1990.

Frisch, Michael. "Sharing Authority: Oral History and the Collaborative Process." *The Oral History Review* 30, no. 1 (Winter–Spring 2003): 111–13.

Gallon, Kim. "Making a Case for the Black Digital Humanities." In *Debates in the Digital Humanities 2016,* edited by Matthew K. Gold and Lauren F. Klein. Minneapolis: University of Minnesota Press, 2016, https://dhdebates.gc.cuny.edu/read/untitled/section/fa10e2e1-0c3d-4519-a958-d823aac989eb#ch04.

Gandy, Oscar. "Matrix Multiplication and Digital Divide." In *Race after the Internet,* edited by Lisa Nakamura and Peter Chow-White. New York: Routledge, 2011.

Gasby, David, and Teresa Moyer. "Pulling Back the Layers: Participatory and Community-Based Archeology." National Council on Public History. August

4, 2014, http://ncph.org/history-at-work/participatory-and-community-based-archaeology/.

Gayle, Addison, Jr. *The Black Aesthetic.* Garden City, N.Y.: Doubleday, 1971.

Golden, Kathryn Benjamin. "Through the Muck and the Mire: Marronage, Representation, and Memory in the Great Dismal Swamp." PhD diss. University of California Berkeley, 2018.

Grandy, Moses. *Narrative of the Life of Moses Grandy: Late a Slave in the United States of America (Gilpin, London).* 1843, https://docsouth.unc.edu/fpn/grandy/grandy.html.

Green, Hilary N. "Hallowed Grounds Project: Race, Memory, and the University of Alabama." 2016, https://hgreen.people.ua.edu/hallowed-grounds-project.html.

Griesbach, Rebecca, and Will Haney. "William and Hilary." *Mosaic* (Winter 2019): 7–11.

Griggs, Brandon. "A Black Yale Graduate Student Took a Nap in Her Dorm's Common Room. So a White Student Called Police." *CNN.com.* May 12, 2018, https://www.cnn.com/2018/05/09/us/yale-student-napping-Black-trnd/index.

Jennison, Watson W. "Metagraph: Innovations in Form and Content." *Journal of American History* 106, no. 1 (June 2019): 121–25, https://academic.oup.com/jah/article/106/1/121/5492007.

Johnson, Jessica Marie. "Markup Bodies: Black [Life] Studies and Slavery [Death] Studies at the Digital Crossroads." *Social Text* 137 (December 2018): 57–79.

Johnson, Jessica Marie, and Mark Anthony Neal. "Introduction: Wild Seed in the Machine." *Black Scholar* 47, no. 3 (Fall 2017): 1–2.

Johnson, Patrick, ed. *Sweet Tea: Black Gay Men of the South.* Chapel Hill: University of North Carolina Press, 2014.

Kim, Dorothy. "Digital Humanities, Intersectionality, and the Ethics of Harm." In *Intersectionality in Digital Humanities,* edited by Barbara Bordalejo and Roopika Risam. Collection Development, Cultural Heritage, and Digital Humanities. Leeds: ARC Humanities Press, 2019.

Kutzler, Evan. "*The Princeton & Slavery Project: An Exploration of Princeton University's Historical Ties to the Institution of Slavery* by Martha A. Sandweiss (Digital Review)." *The Public Historian* 41, no. 4 (November 2019): 122–24.

Laughlin, Nicholas. "Césaire's *Notebook* to the Net." *Carribbean Review of Books.* December 13, 2013, http://caribbeanreviewofbooks.com/2013/12/13/from-cesaires-notebook-to-the-net/.

Lewis, George E. "Too Many Notes: Computers, Complexity and Culture in Voyager." *Leonardo Music Journal* 10 (2000): 33–39, https://doi.org/10.1162/096112100570585.

Loewen, James W. *Lies My Teacher Told Me: Everything Your American History Textbook Got Wrong.* New York: New Press, 2008.

Lomax, Tamura. "Black Women's Lives Don't Matter in Academia Either, or Why I Quit Academic Spaces That Don't Value Black Women's Life and Labor." *The Feminist Wire.* May 18, 2015, https://thefeministwire.com/2015/05/Black-womens-lives-dont-matter-in-academia-either-or-why-i-quit-academic-spaces-that-dont-value-Black-womens-life/.

Lothian, Alexis, and Amanda Phillips. "Can Digital Humanities Mean Transformative Critique?" *E-Media Studies* 3, no. 1 (2013), https://journals.dartmouth.edu/cgi-bin/WebObjects/Journals.woa/xmlpage/4/article/425.

Mayfield, Julian. "You Touch My Black Aesthetic and I'll Touch Yours." In *The Black Aesthetic,* edited by Addison Gayle, Jr. Garden City, N.Y.: Doubleday, 1971.

McPherson, Tara. "Why Are the Digital Humanities So White? Or Thinking the History of Race and Computation." In *Debates in the Digital Humanities 2012,* edited by Matthew K. Gold. Minneapolis: University of Minnesota Press, 2012, https://dhdebates.gc.cuny.edu/read/untitled-88c11800-9446-469b-a3be-3fdb36bfbd1e/section/20df8acd-9ab9-4f35-8a5d-e91aa5f4a0ea#ch09.

Miller, Monica, and Christopher Driscoll. "Conversations in Black: Alexander G. Weheliye." September 1, 2015, https://marginalia.lareviewofbooks.org/conversations-in-Black-alexander-g-weheliye/.

Morrison, Toni. "A Humanist View." Portland State University for Oregon Public Speakers Collection. Transcribed by Keisha E. McKenzie. May 30, 1975, https://www.mackenzian.com/wp-content/uploads/2014/07/Transcript_PortlandState_TMorrison.pdf.

Morrison, Toni. "Nobel Lecture." Nobel Prize, transcription. December 7, 1993, https://www.nobelprize.org/prizes/literature/1993/morrison/lecture/.

Neal, Larry. "The Black Arts Movement." In *The Black Aesthetic,* edited by Addison Gayle, Jr. Garden City, N.Y.: Doubleday, 1971.

Neal, Mark Anthony. *Soul Babies Black Popular Culture and the Post-Soul Aesthetic.* New York: Routledge, 2002.

Risam, Roopika, Alexander Gil, Christina Boyles, Sylvia Fernández, Jessica Marie Johnson, and Marisa Parham. "Mobilizing the Humanities: Building the Supercommons." MLA 2020, Seattle. January 12, 2020, https://mla2020.zerista.com/event/member?item_id=10825727.

Ross, Marc Howard. *Slavery in the North: Forgetting History and Recovering Memory.* Philadelphia: University of Pennsylvania Press, 2018.

Schlage, Scott. "Nebraska Union: State Senators Offer Thoughts on Civil Discourse." *Nebraska Today*. November 20, 2019, https://news.unl.edu/newsrooms/today/article/nebraska-union-state-senators-offer-thoughts-on-civil-discourse/.

Schradie, Jen (@schradie). "POC scholars at #ica18 were just verbally abused, physically threatened and chased by Neo-Nazis/white supremacists in the streets of Prague. Add that to the list of challenges that non-white scholars have in academia." Twitter, May 26, 2018, https://twitter.com/schradie/status/1000228305314906113.

Snopes, Linda. "Commentary: Sharing Authority." *The Oral History Review* 30, no. 1 (Winter–Spring, 2003): 103–10.

Stewart, Jimmy. "Introduction to Black Aesthetics in Music." In *The Black Aesthetic,* edited by Addison Gayle, Jr. Garden City, N.Y.: Doubleday, 1971.

Svensson, Patrik. "Beyond the Big Tent." In *Debates in the Digital Humanities 2012,* edited by Matthew K. Gold. Minneapolis: University of Minnesota Press, 2012, https://dhdebates

.gc.cuny.edu/read/untitled-88c11800-9446-469b-a3be-3fdb36bfbd1e/section/38531431-5bd6-4eb1-95f5-fa49c025322d.

Tal, Kalí. "Life behind the Screen." *Wired.* October 1, 1996, https://www.wired.com/1996/10/screen/.

Taylor, Paul C. *Black Is Beautiful: A Philosophy of Black Aesthetics.* Hoboken, N.J.: Wiley, 2016.

"Texas Freedom Colonies Project Atlas and Study." *Texas Freedom Colonies Project.* Accessed January 19, 2020, http://www.thetexasfreedomcoloniesproject.com/.

Thompson, Katrina Dyonne. *Ring Shout, Wheel About: The Racial Politics of Music and Dance in North American Slavery.* New Black Studies Series. Urbana: University of Illinois Press, 2014.

Thomson, Alistair. "Introduction: Sharing Authority: Oral History and the Collaborative Process." *The Oral History Review* 30, no. 1 (Winter–Spring 2003): 23–26.

vMLK Project Team. "About the vMLK Project." Virtual Martin Luther King, Jr. Project. 2019, https://vmlk.chass.ncsu.edu/about/.

Weheliye, Alexander G. *Habeas Viscus: Racializing Assemblages, Biopolitics, and Black Feminist Theories of the Human.* Durham, N.C.: Duke University Press, 2014.

Digital Humanities in the Deepfake Era

ABRAHAM GIBSON

The video is unmistakable and unforgettable. The grainy footage shows President Richard Nixon taking a seat and steeling his nerves. It was to be the most important speech of his career, one that he had hoped he would never deliver. "My fellow Americans," he begins in a somber tone, "fate has ordained that the men who went to the moon to explore in peace will stay on the moon to rest in peace." The implications were clear enough. Something had gone terribly wrong with Apollo 11, the first NASA mission to attempt a lunar landing, and astronauts Neil Armstrong and Buzz Aldrin were dead. "For every human being who looks up at the moon in the nights to come will know that there is some corner of another world that is forever mankind." With these words, Nixon sought to console a grieving nation during one of the most tragic moments in its history.

Except the tragedy never happened. To be sure, the text of the speech was real. It had been written by Nixon's speechwriter, William Safire, in 1969, in case something went wrong. Thankfully, the mission succeeded, and the speech was not needed. It went unread until 2019, when researchers at the MIT Center for Advanced Virtuality resurrected the script (and the president's visage) for a special screening at the 2019 International Documentary Film Festival. The short film, *In Event of Moon Disaster,* was produced on a computer using video dialogue replacement technology powered by artificial intelligence (AI). The filmmakers sought to emphasize both the power and the danger of synthetic audiovisual media, otherwise known as "deepfakes" (Panetta and Burgund).

In general usage, the word *deepfake* refers to any video that has been altered using machine-learning algorithms to produce hyperrealistic videos that show actual people saying and doing things they never said or did. Some videos seamlessly transplant one person's face onto another person's body. Others create an entire person from scratch. In both cases, the algorithmic alterations are difficult, if not impossible, to detect with the naked eye. There are now several mobile apps that help users with no programming skills produce synthetic videos with face-swapping and artificial lip-synching, but most researchers do not consider these videos deepfakes since they do not use machine learning (Paris and Donovan). In late 2019, cybersecurity officials identified more than 14,000 deepfakes on the internet, a 100 percent increase in just seven months (Ajder et al.). The number has no doubt risen even higher since then.

The first deepfake to gain widespread attention was released in 2018. The video appeared to show Barack Obama saying, "Donald Trump is a total and complete dipshit." In fact, the video was an effective public service announcement from actor and director Jordan Peele about the dangers of deepfakes. Acting as an invisible marionette, Peele used the Obama avatar to caution viewers that deepfakes could lead to "some kind of fucked-up dystopia" (Mack). In the years since, several other deepfakes have also gone viral. Perhaps you have seen the one that shows Bill Hader morphing into Arnold Schwarzenegger, or the one that places Will Smith's face on Cardi B's body. It isn't just videos, by the way. Last year, a British energy company was duped out of nearly a quarter-million dollars when a scammer used AI to imitate the CEO's voice and request a wire transfer over the phone (Stupp). Some have expressed fear that deepfakes herald nothing less than the "information apocalypse" (Silverman), the very "collapse of reality" (Foer).

Efforts to counter the deepfake menace have so far fallen into one of two categories. First, many in the tech sector promote technological solutions, especially automated detection. There are practical problems with this approach, however. After all, the automated detectors train the automated generators to fix their mistakes, which means that subsequent deepfakes may evade detection altogether. Other potential technological solutions include provenance stamps, geolocation tags, blockchain verification, and mandatory registration of content creators (Knight; Paris and Donovan; Chesney and Citron). Second, there are legal options. For example, China recently banned deepfakes outright. Germany has also passed stiff laws penalizing media companies that fail to remove racist or threatening content from their platform in an expeditious manner, and some believe that a similar tactic might work with deepfakes. At the present, however, most places have no laws to handle deepfakes, which means that legal challenges to deepfakes will be handled in a costly and inefficient case-by-case basis (Citron and Chesney; Woollacott).

Technological solutions and legal challenges are limited because they are post hoc fixes to larger, more complex sociotechnical systems. By comparison, the digital humanities (DH) are uniquely interested in both the social and the technical. Practitioners are trained to describe complicated systems, including their impact on society and culture, and can thus help support structural change. Ten years ago, the digital humanities might not have been ready to meet the deepfake challenge. The field was still young, still coalescing, still largely preoccupied with what qualifies as the digital humanities. The field entered a second phase around five years ago, as scholars sought to establish connections between the digital humanities and other fields of inquiry across campuses and throughout the academy. We have now entered a third phase, and not a moment too soon. This latest iteration insists that the digital humanities must embrace social activism, that we must move beyond the campus and engage the public at all costs. Rather than framing the digital humanities around advances in digital scholarship, Safiya Umoja Noble writes in *Debates in the Digital Humanities 2019,* perhaps we should interrogate how digital humanities too often obscure important features of the social, political, and economic landscape. In that same volume, Matthew K. Gold and Lauren Klein are more explicit still: "Our work within the digital humanities is enabled by larger social, political, and technological systems. In the present moment, we need work that exposes the impact of our embeddedness in those larger systems and that brings our technical expertise to bear on the societal problems that those systems sustain."

First and foremost, scholars in the digital humanities should broadcast our core belief that technologies are best understood as sociotechnical systems. This broader view acknowledges that technology cannot be divorced from its social context. It encourages the citizenry to expect and, if necessary, demand answers about the provenance of any given technology. Rather than trying to identify and stamp out every deepfake on the web, digital humanists can help identify the deeper structural issues that allow tens of thousands of deepfakes to proliferate in the first place. We can advocate for reform, rejecting false creeds like "techno-solutionism" that promote technology as humanity's savior (Morozov). As Catherine D'Ignazio and Lauren Klein explain, "we must look to understand and design systems that address *oppression* at the structural level."

We can also help demystify deepfakes by showing that previous technologies engendered similar concerns (Pyne 2019). Take the printing press, for example. Several writers have shown that the rise of pamphlet culture in seventeenth-century England facilitated widespread disinformation during the first English Civil War (White; Peacey). The invention of photography was no less revolutionary, and it too facilitated disinformation. Famous examples from the American Civil War include the transposition of Abraham Lincoln's head on to John C. Calhoun's body, the insertion of Ulysses S. Grant into a battle scene near City Point, and Matthew Brady's decision to rearrange dead bodies of soldiers to set up visual tableaux (Trachtenberg). A century later, Joseph Stalin famously ordered the mass alteration of photographs in Soviet Russia in an effort to purge his enemies from the history books (King). Meanwhile, the ability to deceive using audiovisual (AV) manipulation was, until recently, the stuff of Hollywood. *Jurassic Park* and *Forrest Gump* were among the first, using AV manipulation to resurrect dinosaurs and presidents, respectively. The visage of the late Peter Cushing was used in *Rogue One,* and there are plans to posthumously cast James Dean in a drama about the Vietnam War (Ritman).

These famous examples notwithstanding, the overwhelming majority of extant deepfakes are nonconsensual pornography. In fact, the word "deepfake" was coined in November 2017, when an anonymous Reddit user named "deepfakes" shared a software toolkit that would allow anyone to make synthetic videos replacing one person's face with another. To demonstrate, the user posted a manipulated video that appeared to show actress Gal Gadot in a pornographic film (Rothman). Since then, deepfake pornography has exploded in popularity. In fact, one recent census found that approximately 96 percent of deepfakes on the internet are pornographic, and that approximately 99 percent of these fake videos target women (Ajder et al.).

None of this will come as a surprise to scholars in the humanities. As is well known, the pornography industry has often served as a catalyst for technological change. It has also been one of the most reliable early adopters for any new medium. Pornography played a crucial role in development or at least the expansion of Polaroid cameras, handheld camcorders, video cassette recorders (VCRs), cable TV, and the internet (Barss; Coopersmith). Deepfakes might seem like just another connection between pornography and tech, but they are much different. When it comes to deepfake pornography, the "participants" don't even know it is happening. Celebrities are not the only target, either. Deepfakes can now be weaponized against anyone, including ex-lovers, professional rivals, and even random strangers, none of whom consented to "star" in a pornographic video.

Countless studies in the digital humanities and beyond have shown that technology has a disproportionately negative impact on women and other minoritized groups. Scholars have demonstrated time and time again that digital technologies are more likely to reify existing power structures than undermine them, that digital infrastructures invariably have an outsized impact on underrepresented groups, and that the digital humanities can help us elucidate structural inequalities in the nondigital world (Benjamin; Noble, *Algorithms of Oppression*; Broussard; Eubanks; Losh and Wernimont; Hicks; O'Neill; Gallon). As digital humanists, we should advocate for equity, dignity, and structural change.

Deepfakes will also create challenges that are unique to specific domains within DH. Consider their impact on digital history, for example. Some outside the field have suggested that deepfakes will be good for historians. Legal experts Danielle Citron and Bobby Chesney both herald the potential pedagogical value that deepfakes offer historians, writing that deepfakes make it possible to "manufacture videos of historical figures speaking directly to students." Sure enough, programmers are already using OpenAI's Generative Pre-trained Transformer-3 (GPT-3) to simulate correspondence with historical personalities from any era. Once again, the practical applications are not limited to famous people. For example, Microsoft filed a patent that would allow the company to digitally "resurrect" the recently departed in the form of chatbots and eventually deepfake avatars (Smith).

Even so, the preponderance of evidence suggests there are legitimate reasons for concern. First, malicious actors *already* mischaracterize the historical record in service of their agenda. Studies have shown that white supremacists routinely co-opt and misrepresent research on genetic genealogy, classical antiquity, and Viking genomics to suit their racist worldview (Panofsky and Donovan; Nelson; Strand and Källén). One can only imagine how neo-Confederates and neo-Nazis might like to revise the historical record with help from deepfakes. Second, deepfakes will generate different reactions depending on the context in which they are viewed. Consider the Nixon deepfake. While it was first displayed within the context of a museum exhibit, the film is now available on YouTube. Given that millions of Americans already doubt the moon landings ever took place, it is easy to imagine someone thinking that the deepfake is real, especially when it is divorced from its original context. Third, many of the strategies to combat deepfakes, from litigation to "life-logging" (Citron and Chesney; Eggers), presume that the target is still alive, but who speaks for the dead? Peter Cushing never consented to star in *Rogue One,* and President Nixon never eulogized Apollo 11. Did each surrender rights to his visage when he died? Does everyone? These questions are ripe for humanistic analysis of agency, power, authorship, and intellectual property, among other topics.

Historians who study pre-twentieth-century history, when moving-image technology was largely nonexistent, might think that they will be spared the worst effects of deepfakes, but generative adversarial networks (GANs) leave *all* media vulnerable to digital manipulation.[1] This includes everything from photographs to cave art. In fact, the first piece of AI-generated art (a blurry portrait of a nonexistent person, created by GANs that were trained on more than 15,000 portraits) sold at Christie's auction house in 2018 for more than $400,000 (Cohn). GANs can also read and manipulate digitized texts, which are the foundation of modern historical research. Combining machine learning with image processing techniques, researchers have built optical character recognition (OCR) engines that can read typeface and, increasingly, handwritten text (Mermon et al.). In fact, AI allows machines to not only read handwriting but also produce handwriting in any language. How will historians discern genuine primary sources from fake ones? Ironically, in an increasingly digitized world, we will be called on to vouchsafe the physical archives and safeguard authenticity like never before.

This is more than an academic debate. To quote George Orwell's prescient aphorism, "Who controls the past controls the future, who controls the present controls the past." Authoritarian regimes will not hesitate to suppress and misrepresent the historical record to retain power. Glenn D. Tiffert explains how officials in Communist China recently asked Cambridge University Press and Springer Nature to hide more than a thousand potentially offensive articles on Chinese history from users in China. Keen to remain in business with the most populous nation on earth, the publishers quietly acquiesced. For subscribers in China, the items simply disappeared from search results, as if they never existed. Such large-scale censorship would have been impossible a generation ago. Now, it can be done with a few clicks.

Tiffert drew his evidence from Communist China, but the past few years have shown that democracies are also vulnerable to authoritarianism. In the United States, Donald Trump actively promoted widespread disinformation throughout his presidency. He routinely called fake news real and real news fake. He often retweeted "cheapfakes," relatively crude AV manipulations produced with mobile apps rather than artificial intelligence, and given that his only criterion for truth was whether or not the information flattered him, he would have undoubtedly promoted any deepfake that cast him in a positive light. Trump was eventually kicked off Twitter after he incited a deadly riot at the U.S. Capitol, but democracies remain vulnerable to disinformation in general and deepfakes in particular. Malicious actors are known to use fake profiles on social media using AI-generated faces (Gleicher), and research has shown that microtargeted deepfakes can have real and demonstrable effect on political attitudes (Dobber et al.).

To properly confront the deepfake challenge, DH scholars may find it necessary to use both computational methods and traditional methods of scholarly research. There is a rapidly growing body of scholarship on the computational humanities in general (Johnson, Mimno, and Tilton; Afanador-Llach et al.; Graham, Milligan, and Weingart; Arnold and Tilton, *Humanities Data in R*) and the "visual turn" in DH in particular (Tilton). Recent advances in machine learning and computer vision have transformed how researchers engage with visual media. Algorithms for machine vision can detect, identify, and qualify features within an image and then build predictive models that it can apply to future datasets. A growing number of scholars use both computational and humanistic methods in their analyses of visual media, thereby signaling potential ways of engaging with deepfakes from a DH perspective (Arnold and Tilton, "Distant Viewing"; Wevers and Smits; Lee 2021; Mittell). Meanwhile, just as DH scholars must be willing to use computational tools, so too must we insist that fields like computer science integrate humanistic perspectives. Doing so would bring critical perspectives to bear on technological advances. We need, in other words, more multidisciplinary research in the technology sector. DH intervention does not necessarily mean that every DHer should start researching deepfakes. Instead, we should advocate for embedding humanities perspectives in the tech world to anticipate problematic aspects of tech research.

In closing, DH scholars should bear three lessons in mind as we brace for potentially ubiquitous deepfakes. First, we should promote *digital literacy* at every turn. We do not necessarily need to learn code, but we *do* need to understand how algorithms influence every part of our daily lives if we are going to successfully navigate the cacophony of disinformation (McPherson; Schmidt). Second, DH scholars must also embrace *advocacy.* Deepfakes threaten everything from interpersonal relationships to international relations, but they are especially injurious toward women and other minoritized groups. Rather than resigning ourselves to nihilism, we can advise our neighbors to seek answers when confronted with a provocative video on social media. What is the source of this video? Who might have created it and why? Finally, 
we should recommit to *values* that have long defined the digital humanities. DH scholars have suggested several core principles to help unify the field, including openness, collaboration, collegiality, connectedness, diversity, experimentation, hope, compassion, and empathy (Nowviskie; Spiro; Noble, "Toward a Critical Black Digital Humanities"; Gold and Klein). Keeping the faith will not be easy. Deepfakes breed distrust, and fascism weaponizes credulity (Tiffert), but that only underscores

the importance of the DH perspective. If we are earnest about our values, then the digital humanities can help the larger public stay resilient, rebellious, and real.

NOTE

1. GANs employ two sets of algorithms: One, the generator, creates content that is modeled on existing source data, while the other, the discriminator, works to constantly identify imperfections in the false images. Working in tandem, the algorithms train against one another to produce an ever more realistic image.

BIBLIOGRAPHY

Afanador-Llach, Maria José, et al., eds. *The Programming Historian.* 2nd ed. London: Editorial Board of the Programming Historian, 2017, programminghistorian.org.

Ajder, Henry. "Deepfake Threat Intelligence: A Statistics Snapshot from June 2020." *Sensity.* March 7, 2020.

Ajder, Henry, Giorgio Patrini, Francesco Cavalli, and Laurence Cullen. "The State of Deepfakes: Landscape, Threats and Impact." *Deeptrace Labs.* September 2019.

Arnold, Taylor, and Lauren Tilton. "Distant Viewing: Analyzing Large Digital Corpora." *Digital Scholarship in the Humanities* (2019): i3–i16, https://doi.org/10.1093/digitalsh/fqz013.

Arnold, Taylor, and Lauren Tilton. *Humanities Data in R: Exploring Networks, Geospatial Data, Images, and Text.* New York: Springer, 2015.

Barss, Patchen. *The Erotic Engine: How Pornography Has Powered Mass Communication from Gutenberg to Google.* Toronto: Ancho Canada, 2011.

Benjamin, Ruha. *Race after Technology: Abolitionist Tools for the New Jim Code.* Boston: Polity, 2019.

Broussard, Meredith. *Artificial Unintelligence: How Computers Misunderstand the World.* Cambridge, Mass.: MIT Press, 2018.

Chesney, Robert, and Danielle K. Citron. "Deepfakes and the New Disinformation War." *Foreign Affairs* (January/February 2019): 147–55.

Citron, Danielle K., and Robert Chesney. "Deep Fakes: A Looming Challenge for Privacy, Democracy, and National Security." *California Law Review* (2019): 1753–1820.

Cohn, Gabe. "AI Art at Christie's Sells for $432,500." *New York Times.* October 25, 2018.

Coopersmith, Jonathan. "Pornography, Technology, and Progress." *Icon* 4 (1998): 94–125.

Coppin, McKay. "The Billion-Dollar Disinformation Campaign to Reelect the President." *The Atlantic.* February 10, 2020, https://www.theatlantic.com/magazine/archive/2020/03/the-2020-disinformation-war/605530/.

Ctrl Shift Face, "Bill Hader Impersonates Arnold Schwarzenegger [Deepfake]." YouTube, 3:10. May 10, 2019, youtube.com/watch?v=bPhUhypV27w.

D'Ignazio, Catherine, and Lauren F. Klein. *Data Feminism.* Cambridge, Mass.: MIT Press, 2020.

Dobber, Tom, Nadia Metoui, Damian Trilling, Natali Helberger, and Claes de Vreese. "Do (Microtargeted) Deepfakes Have Real Effects on Political Attitudes?" *International Journal of Press/Politics* 25 (2020): 1–23.

Eggers, Dave. *The Circle.* New York: Knopf, 2013.

Eubanks, Virginia. *Automating Inequality: How High-Tech Tools Profile, Police, and Punish the Poor.* New York: St. Martin's, 2018.

Foer, Franklin. "The Era of Fake Video Begins." *The Atlantic.* May 2018, https://www.theatlantic.com/magazine/archive/2018/05/realitys-end/556877/.

Gallon, Kim. "Making a Case for the Black Digital Humanities." In *Debates in the Digital Humanities 2016,* edited by Matthew K. Gold and Lauren F. Klein, 42–49. Minneapolis: University of Minnesota Press, 2016.

Gleicher, Nathaniel. "Removing Coordinated Inauthentic Behavior." *Meta Newsroom.* October 8, 2020, https://about.fb.com/news/2020/10/removing-coordinated-inauthentic-behavior-september-report/.

Gold, Matthew K., and Lauren F. Klein, "A DH That Matters." In *Debates in the Digital Humanities 2019,* edited by Matthew K. Gold and Lauren F. Klein, ix–xiv. Minneapolis: University of Minnesota Press, 2019.

Graham, Shawn, Ian Milligan, and Scott B. Weingart. *Exploring Big Historical Data: The Historian's Macroscope.* London: Imperial College Press, 2016, themacroscope.org/2.0.

Hicks, Marie. *Programmed Inequality: How Britain Discarded Women and Lost Its Edge in Computing.* Cambridge, Mass.: MIT Press, 2017.

Johnson, Jessica Marie, David Mimno, and Lauren Tilton, eds. *Computational Humanities.* Minneapolis: University of Minnesota Press, 2021.

King, David. *The Commissar Vanishes: The Falsification of Photographs and Art in Stalin's Russia.* New York: Henry Holt, 1997.

Knight, Will. "The Defense Department Has Produced the First Tools for Catching Deepfakes." *MIT Technology Review.* August 7, 2018, https://www.technologyreview.com/2018/08/07/66640/the-defense-department-has-produced-the-first-tools-for-catching-deepfakes/.

Lee, Ben. "Compounded Mediation: A Data Archaeology of the Newspaper Navigator Dataset," *Digital Humanities Quarterly* 15 (2021), http://www.digitalhumanities.org/dhq/vol/15/4/000578/000578.html.

Losh, Elizabeth, and Jacqueline Wernimont. *Bodies of Information: Intersectional Feminism and the Digital Humanities.* Minneapolis: University of Minnesota Press, 2018.

Mack, David. "This PSA about Fake News from Barack Obama Is Not What It Appears." *Buzzfeed News.* April 17, 2018, https://www.buzzfeednews.com/article/davidmack/obama-fake-news-jordan-peele-psa-video-buzzfeed.

McPherson, Tara. "Why Are the Digital Humanities So White? or Thinking the Histories of Race and Computation." In *Debates in the Digital Humanities 2012,* edited by Matt Gold, 139–60. Minneapolis: University of Minnesota Press, 2012.

Mermon, Jamshed, Maira Sami, Rizwan Ahmed Khan, and Mueen Uddin. "Handwritten Optical Character Recognition (OCR): A Comprehensive Systematic Literature Review (SLR)." *IEEE Access* 8 (2020): 142642–68.

Mittell, Jason. "Videographic Criticism as a Digital Humanities Methods." In *Debates in the Digital Humanities 2019,* edited by Matthew K. Gold and Lauren F. Klein, 224–42. Minneapolis: University of Minnesota Press, 2019.

Morozov, Evgeny. *To Save Everything, Click Here: The Folly of Technological Solutionism.* New York: Public Affairs, 2013.

Mullen, Lincoln A. *Computational Historical Thinking: With Applications in R* (2018–2020). Accessed August 9, 2022, dh-r.lincolnmullen.com.

Nelson, Alondra. *The Social Life of DNA: Race, Reparations, and Reconciliation after the Genome.* Boston: Beacon Press, 2016.

Noble, Safiya Umoja. *Algorithms of Oppression: How Search Engines Reinforce Racism.* New York: NYU Press, 2018.

Noble, Safiya Umoja. "Toward a Critical Black Digital Humanities." In *Debates in the Digital Humanities 2019,* edited by Matthew K. Gold and Lauren F. Klein, 27–35. Minneapolis: University of Minnesota Press, 2019.

Nowviskie, Bethany. "Digital Humanities in the Anthropocene." *Digital Scholarship in the Humanities* 30 (December 2015): i4–i15.

O'Neill, Cathy. *Weapons of Math Destruction: How Big Data Increases Inequality and Threatens Democracy.* London: Penguin Books, 2016.

Panetta, Francesca, and Halsey Burgund. *In Event of Moon Disaster* (short film). Produced by the MIT Center for Advanced Virtuality. 2019, https://arts.mit.edu/in-event-of-moon-disaster/.

Panofsky, Aaron, and Joan Donovan. "Genetic Ancestry Testing among White Nationalists: From Identity Repair to Citizen Science." *Social Studies of Science* 49 (2019): 653–81.

Paris, Britt, and Joan Donovan. "Deepfakes and Cheap Fakes," *Data & Society.* September 18, 2019, https://datasociety.net/output/deepfakes-and-cheap-fakes/.

Peacey, Jason. *Print and Public Politics in the English Revolution.* New York: Cambridge University Press, 2013.

Pyne, Lydia. *Genuine Fakes: How Phony Things Teach Us about Real Stuff.* New York: Bloomsbury 2019.

Ritman, Alex. "James Dean Reborn in CGI for Vietnam War Action-Drama." *Hollywood Reporter.* November 6, 2019, https://www.hollywoodreporter.com/movies/movie-news/afm-james-dean-reborn-cgi-vietnam-war-action-drama-1252703/.

Rothman, Joshua. "In the Age of A.I., Is Seeing Still Believing?" *The New Yorker.* November 12, 2018.

Schmidt, Benjamin. "Do Digital Humanists Need to Understand Algorithms?" In *Debates in the Digital Humanities 2016,* edited by Matthew K. Gold and Lauren F. Klein, 546–55. Minneapolis: University of Minnesota Press, 2016.

Silverman, Craig. "The Information Apocalypse Is Already Here, and Reality Is Losing." *Buzzfeed News*. May 22, 2020, https://www.buzzfeednews.com/article/craigsilverman/coronavirus-information-apocalypse.

Smith, Adam. "Microsoft Patent Shows Plans to Revive Dead Loved Ones as Chatbots." *The Independent*. January 20, 2021.

Spiro, Lisa. "'This Is Why We Fight': Defining the Values of the Digital Humanities." In *Debates in the Digital Humanities 2012*, edited by Matthew K. Gold, 16–35. Minneapolis: University of Minnesota Press, 2012.

Strand, Daniel, and Anna Källén. "I Am a Viking! DNA, Popular Culture and the Construction of Geneticized Identity." *New Genetics and Society* 40 (2021): 520–40.

Stupp, Catherine. "Fraudsters Used AI to Mimic CEO's Voice in Unusual Cybercrime Case." *Wall Street Journal*. August 30, 2019.

Tiffert, Glenn D. "Peering Down the Memory Hole: Censorship, Digitization, and the Fragility of Our Knowledge Base." *American Historical Review* 124 (April 2019): 550–68.

Tilton, Lauren. "The Visual Turn in DH." Keynote at the Digital Humanities and the Visual World Symposium, October 12, 2019, http://laurentilton.com/files/Keynote_Tilton_October2019.pdf.

Trachtenberg, Alan. *Reading American Photographs: Images as History*. New York: Hill and Wang, 1989.

Wevers, Melvin, and Thomas Smits. "The Visual Digital Turn: Using Neural Networks to Study Historical Images." *Digital Scholarship in the Humanities* 35 (2020): 194–207.

White, William. "Parliament, Print, and the Politics of Disinformation, 1642–1643." *Historical Research* 92 (November 2019): 720–36.

Woollacott, Emma. "China Bans Deepfakes in New Content Crackdown." *Forbes*. November 30, 2019.

PART II][*Chapter 11*

Operationalizing Surveillance Studies in the Digital Humanities

CHRISTINA BOYLES, ANDREW BOYLES PETERSEN, AND ARUN JACOB

Recent public conversations in the United States about the disproportionate police violence experienced by Black people, the spread of misinformation on social media platforms like Facebook and by bad actors like QAnon, and the increased reliance on third-party surveillance devices all demonstrate how physical and digital surveillance systems can be used to cause harm and weaken the fabric of democratic society (Shere and Nurse; Biddle; Ong; Marczak et al.). The brokenness of these systems signals a problem worthy of attention—especially by those in the digital humanities. If we as digital humanists are serious about our commitment to social justice—especially our opposition to discriminatory tools and methodologies—then we must scrutinize our field's investment in these surveillance technologies and the ways in which they make us and our collaborators vulnerable to undue monitoring and weaponization.

We use the word *weaponization* to underscore how surveillance systems can exacerbate the violence that results from structural oppression. While marginalized groups—Black and Indigenous communities, women, 2SLGBTQIA+ people, and others—have long experienced the effects of surveillance (Browne; Eubanks; Noble), the field of surveillance studies is relatively new and, like digital humanities, has many origins and influences. Most significantly, the field is responsible for conceptualizing surveillance as encompassing the range of material and digital ecosystems used to track, trace, and monitor human behavior.[1] Within this framework, surveillance systems ranging from data brokers and facial recognition software to police and neighborhood watch groups have been exposed as tools of oppression, exacerbating existing inequalities and systematically inscribing biases into technologies (Benjamin). While there has been increasing attention paid to the role of surveillance in the academy, especially as instruction has moved online as a result of the pandemic, those in the digital humanities have not yet fully reckoned with how surveillance systems touch their work.

As users, educators, promoters, and distributors of digital tools, digital humanists are inherently tied to the surveillance ecosystem. Even in developing and sharing open-source tools—an oft-promoted method for avoiding commercial offerings anchored in surveillance—links to surveillance systems regularly occur through reliance on third-party supporting technologies, such as website analytics through Google Analytics, code base storage in Microsoft's GitHub, and other remote scripts and stylesheets. As such, we must be particularly aware of how the field is being subsumed by surveillance mechanisms and how we are foisting these same tools onto our colleagues and communities. For example, many digital humanities projects rely on commercial tools such as Amazon Web Services (AWS), Microsoft Azure, ArcGIS, GitHub, Thingiverse, Meta (formerly Facebook), Tableau, Adobe, and more. These tools make higher education particularly vulnerable to the digital surveillance apparatus as the corporations that make them often encourage scholars, researchers, and educators to extend that apparatus to their collaborators, colleagues, and communities. Even tools that appear to be removed from the surveillance machine—like GitHub, which was purchased by Microsoft in 2018 while retaining the look and feel of a noncommercial product—can place digital humanists, their collaborators, and their communities at risk.

Digital humanists risk further contributing to corporate surveillance by creating digital tools that rely on these risky third-party software systems and by using these and other surveillance technologies in their research and pedagogy. At the same time, digital humanists are uniquely poised to intervene in harmful practices of surveillance because they are often trained to think about the historical, social, political, and cultural context of digital technology as well as its design and implementation. Existing critical approaches in the digital humanities that engage these concerns, such as postcolonial digital humanities, anti-colonial digital humanities, Ethical EdTech, and minimal computing, provide models for how DH might address the ethics and risks posed by surveillance technologies to the field and the academy writ large (Risam; Boulay et al.; Minimal Computing). This chapter offers one such approach by examining how a range of surveillance media intersect with the practice of digital humanities scholarship.

We understand our method as "operationalizing" surveillance studies for the digital humanities, or making visible the often-invisible underpinnings of surveillance within our field, demonstrating how our tools can and do produce harm. In what follows, we first turn to the field of geography for an example of the insidious history of surveillance technology in academia, before unpacking the problematic legacies of some of the technologies that are used in digital humanities scholarship today. In so doing, we lay bare how these tools extend the reach of the surveillance machine, posing significant risks to our work and our communities. We close by acknowledging that while digital humanists are inextricably linked to systems of surveillance, they also have tremendous potential to envision and develop more ethical solutions. We invite you to join us in this pursuit.

Academic Surveillance in/of Mapping Technologies

One strong example of the dangers of surveillance technologies in academia comes from the field of geography. Mapping and geographic information system (GIS) technologies are power-laden forms of knowledge production that help to (re)create as much of the world as they represent through techno-scientific, modernist, and colonial discourses. As those in the field of geography well know, maps both enable and suppress knowledge through the intentional and unintentional elements of the ideological practice of cartography. By contrast, the tools and technologies that we learn and use in DH are often given more attention than the historical and material conditions under which those tools and technologies were developed or first employed. By looking at the corpus of GIS discourse that interrogates the social roots, histories, and implications of GIS technology, we can see a telling example of how a scholarly field has grappled with the implications of its own technologies and methods (Jacob, "Follow the Ho Chi Minh Trail"). More specifically, we learn how the field of geography was co-opted by military and political interests—erasing its engagement with critical social discourse.

GIS endures as an example of the model postwar science, one that blurs the boundaries between theory and praxis, science and engineering, civilian and military uses, classified and unclassified systems, and that contributes both to economic prosperity and national security. GIS's ability to cross over into other disciplines as well as bear fruit in the marketplace meant that the field was able to achieve more interest and uptake from the commercial sector. The more accurate and precise contouring of the commercial terrain that resulted, in turn, had additional use-value for the military establishment.[2]

After World War II, the military was actively engaged in formalizing an instrumental model of geography education that folded the tools and practices deployed in the field of combat into the classroom. This period can be best understood as a melting pot. The military, industry, and academia were enmeshing themselves in a triple helix where ideas, technologies, and techniques freely circulated between the three domains. The key figures involved in the establishment of new governmental bodies maintained their academic affiliations and managed the growth of these domains as interlocutors and power brokers. With the creation of governmental bodies such as the Office of Strategic Research and Development (OSRD) and the Office of Strategic Services (OSS), research in the sciences, social sciences, and military were sutured into a single outcome (Barnes and Farish).

The information architectures that were being developed out of the field of geography were thus primed to serve the military cause. The techniques and technologies that were developed in the Cold War period were directly funded by the Department of Defense in collaboration with various industry partners and academic institutions (Clarke and Cloud). In fact, the Cold War–era cartographic systems were only made possible as a result of the stolen German archive of maps from

World War II. The U.S. Army Geodesist Major Floyd W. Hough and his unit, the HOUGHTEAM, acquired the Nazi archive of geodesic maps from various German technical universities, government institutes, and libraries (G. Miller). These geodesic datasets served as the bedrock of most cartographic systems that were used to engage in the surveillance of the USSR during the Cold War. The HOUGHTEAM was also able to expatriate Nazi officers of the Reichsamt für Landesaufnahme (RfL), computational staff, and geodesic scientists and engineers who worked on the German maps. Once they were in the United States, they continued their work for the U.S. Army Map Services (Hough). In this sense, the HOUGHTEAM's subsequent work on the European Datum, ED50, which serves as the undergirding of the global coordinate system known as the Universal Transverse Mercator (UTM), can be seen for how it was built on work done by and with the Nazis.

This nefarious connection does not end with the Cold War: These same German maps inform the media architecture for geofencing. A geofence is a virtual perimeter drawn around a real-world geographic area that, when crossed, triggers an action of some kind. Geofencing is used by marketing campaigns to deliver context-appropriate content to consumers, and it is also often deployed by special-interest groups to target vulnerable populations. Geofencing campaigns have been implemented in spaces such as Aboriginal health centers, abortion clinics, addiction treatment centers, courthouses, election polling stations, immigrant and refugee resettlement centers, halfway houses, hospitals, homeless shelters, needle exchange clinics, schools, sexual health clinics, and women's shelters.[3] These campaigns frequently engage in the trafficking of pseudoscience, debunked studies, sensationalized imagery, or other fear-mongering about medical procedures, health care policy, refugee resettlement, and the like, thereby willfully promoting and inciting hatred against targeted groups. The trajectory that connects the militarization of the field of geography to the later use of its technologies by geofencers demonstrates how academic fields can become vectors for surveillance in intended and unintended ways.

Academic Surveillance in/of Digital Humanities

The field of digital humanities is not far removed from this cautionary tale. The oft-touted digital humanities origin story of Roberto Busa fails to acknowledge the provenance of punch card technology and the purpose for which it was designed (Jacob, "Punching Holes"). Although the punch card technology was used for processing and tabulating data in census-taking operations since the 1890s, it was innovated on, instrumentalized, and weaponized to execute the race science and surveillance agenda of the Third Reich (Pugh). If we are to acknowledge the IBM punch card technology as an essential antecedent of the digital humanities, then we must be cognizant of its problematic history and remain vigilant in defending against future harms.

Echoes of IBM punch card technology already are extending into the digital mediascape. Just as the original punch cards weaponized information about vulnerable communities in order to automate human extermination, facial recognition software developed by Amazon is being used in Immigration and Customs Enforcement (ICE) detention camps (Ho). Ethical concerns regarding the data security and retention of facial image databases are manifold. More importantly, facial recognition software disproportionately fails on—yet is overwhelmingly used against—people of color and other marginalized groups (Campbell, Chandler and Jones; Algorithmic Justice League; Buolamwini and Gebru). From some of its earliest applications, facial recognition software has been heavily deployed against marginalized communities because of its use in welfare programs and border security and within the prison system.

In the digital humanities, facial recognition and computer vision software has largely been used to analyze archival materials—projects that would seem far removed from the high-stakes applications just described. One of the earliest digital humanities projects to apply facial recognition software, University of California Riverside's 2012 FACES: Faces, Art, and Computerized Evaluation Systems, sought to identify individuals in historic portrait art (B. Miller). Other projects, such as Envisaging the Holy Land: Facial Recognition and Early Photography, have sought to "bring to life the otherwise lost individual faces" (Eckstein). Using a Python script in conjunction with OpenCV—an open-source computer vision library—the Judaica DH lab extracted faces from their collections of historic photos. A similar model was used in pulling portraits from the National Archives of Australia in an effort to "liberate the lives of those who suffered under the restrictions of the White Australia Policy" (Sherratt).

Each of these projects raises ethical questions about the use of facial recognition software—namely, issues of consent. Using computer vision to showcase the individuals most negatively affected by Australia's "White Australia" policy raises compelling questions and helps bring to light Australia's racist and exclusionary practices put in place during the twentieth century. While these topics are certainly worthy of scholarly attention, there are ways this project can more actively engage with questions of ethics and privacy. The portraits used for the Real Face of White Australia project were "extracted from a range of government documents using a facial detection script" (Bagnall and Sherratt). Individuals portrayed were required to have their photograph taken in order to temporarily leave Australia and to be allowed reentry. Although these individuals consented to having their photo taken—albeit, at times, providing a forced or coerced form of consent—they and their heirs did not consent to having their images added to a public database or having their images repurposed for other forms of public consumption.

Scholars have developed myriad approaches to working with facial images and computer vision. Some projects—like TwitLit—outline the risks of surveillance technologies on their sites, acknowledging the limitations of their project structure or chosen tool. Building on this model, projects like COVID Black's "Homegoing" document their use of facial images and provide opt-out options for family members of the deceased. Other projects have adopted postcustodial or noncustodial models in which individuals retain full control over their image or data. Within this framework, an individual retains the rights to their own image while institutions (e.g., universities, libraries, museums, project teams) receive revocable licensing rights. Projects like the South Asian American Digital Archive (SAADA), the Guatemalan National Police Historical Archive, the Measure the Future Library Space Study, the Archivo de Respuestas Emergencias de Puerto Rico (AREPR), and ImaginX en Movimiento are examples of successful projects using this model of risk statements, opt-out options, and postcustodial/noncustodial approaches that make visible the surveillance mechanisms underlying digital projects. Moreover, opt-out options and postcustodial/noncustodial models reject surveillance systems by allowing participants to choose when and how their information is shared.

Pushing back against the use of existing facial recognition technologies, some digital humanities scholars, including Christop Musik and Matthias Zeppelzauer, recommend avoiding existing computer vision programs and techniques in DH, as the ground truths these algorithms are built on are often insufficient for higher-level DH research questions. Instead, Musik and Zeppelzauer recommend a dynamic "active learning" approach to training computer vision algorithms in DH, in which the researcher takes a more active role in training the algorithm, where "her/his needs are directly integrated into the learning process, which replaces the need to define a ground truth explicitly" (59). Others, like Jentery Sayers, question using facial recognition software at all, stating: "While I know digital humanities is often quick to build alternative technologies, amidst these questions is whether computer vision should be used at all for face recognition in and beyond academic work." In part, current computer vision systems encounter such failures because of the datasets they are trained on and the explicit or inherent biases of the scientists and researchers creating them. Algorithmic training datasets ascribe the values and opinions of development teams, teaching the algorithm a specific way to view gender or race. Justifying their training selections, some development teams have relied on views harkening to craniometry, phrenology, or other debunked pseudosciences, claiming distinct racial faceprint differences in order to justify their theoretical viewpoints (Browne). Terming these built-in prejudices "high-tech racism," Shoshana Magnet highlights the inability of developmentally flawed systems to serve with the mathematical impartiality we ascribe to algorithmic design.

Ecosystems of Surveillance in the Academy

Although digital humanists have pushed back against the use of racializing surveillance in facial recognition tools, the field is now seeing a broader threat emerge: the expanding application of surveillance in educational technologies used across college campuses. Commercial educational technology (EdTech) systems have been hailed as the solution to the twenty-first-century academy, providing students with individualized class experiences, easing faculty workloads, and granting administrators access to a vast wealth of student data. Many EdTech systems, such as D2L, TopHat, Blackboard, and Kaltura, can aggregate student data in bulk, with this data mined to create robust user profiles and for use in predictive learning analytics (Office of Educational Technology). With these commercial systems predominantly created and maintained outside the university, they raise significant concerns for the misuse of student data. Current government regulations, such as the Family Educational Rights and Privacy Act (FERPA), often still allow EdTech vendors to aggregate and use student data and metadata, with minimal transparency of how that data is being used and few protections for students looking to opt out and secure their data. Further government actions to regulate this data, including the U.S. Student Privacy Policy Office, the U.S. Department of Education's Privacy Technical Assistance Center, and the California Consumer Privacy Act, take steps toward addressing these issues but currently fall short of the overall need.

Covid-19 is elevating higher education's reliance on educational technologies, turning online education into the predominant mode of educational delivery. With increased demands on instructor time and university infrastructure, digital proctoring tools including Respondus, ProctorU, Proctorio, Examity, and Honorlock have seen exponential growth. Complaints about these programs abound, with the University of Texas at Dallas, California State University, and other institutions receiving student pushback and petitions that compare the programs to spyware and cite concerns over student data privacy (Kelley). Digital humanists also have taken up this call through the #AgainstSurveillance hashtag on Twitter, adding to support from the Electronic Frontier Foundation and other privacy advocates who have noted issues of usability, access, and equity. As digital humanists, we possess both the capability for humanistic inquiry and the literacy to assess the strengths and limitations of technologies; when combined, these skills equip us to advocate for ethical alternatives to institutional, corporate, and EdTech surveillance.

If we fail to intervene in harmful surveillance practices, we risk replicating and iterating on discriminatory systems through new technological innovations. Shea Swauger connects reports of how remote proctoring systems fail for students of color to a longer history of racism: "While racist technology calibrated for white skin isn't new (everything from photography to soap dispensers do this), we see it deployed through face detection and facial recognition used by algorithmic proctoring systems." As a result, students of color are disproportionately identified as being noncompliant or cheating—furthering institutional inequality and advancing the aims of racializing surveillance (Kelley). Reliance on these systems is only expected to increase as the Covid-19 pandemic continues and as work-from-home options become more prevalent.

Amid the larger specter of the academy's investment in surveillance software, many digital humanists have been at the forefront of developing open-source alternatives or other student-friendly alternatives to both digital project tools and educational surveillance technologies. Unlike commercial EdTech systems, these alternatives have been largely recognized as being for the good of the university, providing compelling technological offerings for low or no cost. Ranging from scholarly communications platforms like Humanities Commons, CUNY's Academic Commons, and Manifold Scholarship to digital humanities tools like Omeka and Mukurtu, these technologies have been developed by scholars and institutions, where they have been able to center openness, usability, and accessibility rather than profit. Mukurtu CMS is a particularly strong example, as it is designed to respect Indigenous knowledge systems and protocols, "empower[ing] communities to manage, share, and exchange their digital heritage in culturally relevant and ethically-minded ways" ("Our Mission"). In doing so, Mukurtu pushes back against racializing surveillance by centering Indigenous voices in the project's design, development, and implementation, ensuring its platform remains beneficial to the communities by and for whom it was developed.

At the same time, there are many ways the digital humanities can reduce their reliance on surveillance infrastructure. Although secure and reliable in and of themselves, many digital humanities web tools and projects are supported by third-party offerings with questionable privacy standards. Mapping tools pulling from the Google Maps API, cloud computing through services like Microsoft Azure, web analytics support from Google Analytics and Tag Manager, facial recognition and machine-learning projects through Amazon Rekognition and SageMaker, and cloud storage offerings like Dropbox present a range of surveillance and privacy risks including personal data collection, user web tracking, and the sharing or leaking of data. Although the intentions and good efforts of these DH tool development teams may be to avoid the explicit surveillance prevalent in their commercial counterparts, they can still be engaged in surveillance systems through their dependence on commercial tools.

Alongside reliance on third-party offerings, many leading DH labs and tool providers have failed to implement basic encryption technology, with their sites lacking secure HTTPS connections and online communication that encrypts information sent between users and a website. This both safeguards user information and ensures integrity of the data being transferred. Within the DH community, popular resources such as Stanford's Palladio, MIT HyperStudio (Chronos Timeline), ScholarsLab PRISM, Northwestern's KnightLab TimelineJS/Soundcite/Storyline, University of Southern California's Sophie, and the Text Encoding Initiative lack HTTPS connections.[4] Although most of these tools were released many years ago, the web domains for each of these tools are active as of publication, many are exceptionally popular, and all were developed by large, well-funded Western institutions. Sustainability is often a challenge for digital projects, but it is imperative that we, as scholars at the intersections of computing and the humanities, ensure we are taking the small steps needed to safeguard our data and our communities. With the simple steps of properly configuring their host server, acquiring valid security keys, and avoiding predatory third-party platforms, tool providers and institutions can demonstrate a commitment to their users' privacy and security.

By implementing simple changes such as these, DH tool builders and educators can ensure significantly more safety for their users, students, and fellow DH practitioners. We can build better tools, placing privacy and data security on par with usability and design. We can be more aware of the risks associated with many resources, weighing the worth of EdTech and DH tools before using them in our research projects and classrooms. We can push beyond current student and consumer privacy regulation, recognizing such legislation as the General Data Privacy Regulation (GDPR), the California Consumer Privacy Act, and FERPA as privacy baselines instead of ceilings. We can act with a collective and conscious effort, creating an ecosystem of safety and security within DH. Most importantly, we can resist and reject racializing surveillance by adopting practices that protect the most marginalized members of our communities.

Envisioning Anti-Surveillance Futures

As digital humanists, we must even more strongly prioritize issues pertaining to surveillance and privacy. As digital technologies continue to pervade our workplaces, our homes, and our social spheres, it is critical that the field interrogates the ways in which these tools are being deployed and monetized by others. Surveillance studies scholarship reveals that there are a number of stakeholders interested in our data, including governing bodies, corporations, data brokers, communities, and individuals. Their interest is expounded when they can collect the data of marginalized groups in order to increase their own profits. To protect our communities as well as our collaborators and participants in our projects from surveillance risks, we must develop the infrastructure to advise, create, and sustain transformative and effective privacy practices. A handful of projects have already begun this important work, and they serve as powerful models for the future of digital humanities work.

One powerful example is the Sovereign Bodies Institute, which collects data about Missing and Murdered Indigenous Women and Girls (MMIWG). The project is explicitly Indigenous—information about Native communities is collected and maintained by Indigenous scholars. The project director, Annita Lucchesi, notes that "for a long time, research has been used as a colonial tool. They've repeatedly come to our communities and said let us tell you about you. For us to say no, we know how to tell our stories. We know how to study and understand what's happening to our people and to our bodies. There's some sovereignty in that. It's a reclamation of power."

As part of the project design, the Sovereign Bodies Institute does not share information with colonial powers, including settler governments and law enforcement agencies. Luchessi states that "the FBI and the Canadian national government both asked us for the database. We spent several months traveling around Indian

Country and asking folks what do you feel about this? Are you comfortable with this being shared? And the overwhelming majority of the answers were no." By refusing to share this information with settler authorities, the Sovereign Bodies Institute is preventing its weaponization by colonial entities. By foregrounding the privacy of Indigenous peoples and their families, the Sovereign Bodies Institute prioritizes participant privacy, celebrates Indigenous knowledge systems, and rejects colonial notions of data ownership.

Like the Sovereign Bodies Institute, the Our Data Bodies project seeks to protect marginalized peoples from the misuse of their data. According to their website, the project coordinators are "telling the story of surveillance and data-based discrimination across the United States" (Lewis et al.). To do so, they are collecting stories from residents of Charlotte, Detroit, and Los Angeles to show "how different data systems impact re-entry, fair housing, public assistance, and community development." By explicitly examining the effects of surveillance within urban centers, the Our Data Bodies project is bringing attention to the ways in which race, ethnicity, and socioeconomic status are tied to our notions of privacy.

Members of the digital humanities community already are giving voice to many of these concerns. One particularly powerful example also found in this edition of *Debates in the Digital Humanities* is the Feminist Data Manifest-NO, which "refuses harmful data regimes and commits to new data futures" (Cifor et al.). The Manifesto-NO makes thirty-two explicit refusals that push back against Western knowledge systems and their relationship with data and people. Like the authors of the Manifesto-NO, we as the authors of this chapter uphold Eve Tuck and K. Wayne Yang's framework of refusal, which "provide[s] ways to negotiate how we as . . . researchers can learn from experiences of dispossessed peoples—often painful, but also wise, full of desire and dissent—without serving up pain stories on a silver platter for the settler colonial academy, which hungers so ravenously for them" (Tuck and Yang). Refusing can take many forms: focusing on structural inequalities rather than individual experiences, emphasizing failures to respond to injustices rather than the injustices themselves, and refusing to blindly reproduce the inequalities of the past.

The Manifest-NO—along with other engagements from the field of digital humanities—are conversing with feminist, intersectional, and Indigenous theories and knowledge systems in ways that are powerful and necessary. The Feminist Data Manifest-NO mobilizes refusal as its organizing principle to critique the harmful and extractive data practices that are in use in the mediascape and advocate how to critically imagine data futurities. Central to the Manifest-NO is its critical and ethical sensibility to read popular claims about data science and technology with a hermeneutic of suspicion. We see surveillance as inextricably linked to these arguments, and we build on the work of the Manifesto-NO by operationalizing surveillance studies in digital humanities. The field of digital humanities is uniquely poised to resist co-optation by surveillance technologies—we have the critical knowledge and technical know-how to push back against government and corporate encroachment, to assess the problems with our tools, and to produce new and transformative infrastructures. As such, we, the authors, offer the field our own refusals: We refuse the commercialization of our work. We refuse to sacrifice the privacy of our colleagues and communities for the sake of profit or promotion. We refuse to let our projects propagate systems of surveillance. Instead, we commit to envisioning new futures for the digital humanities—ones that imagine spaces for engagement outside the confines of the surveillance state.

NOTES

1. For more information, see Marx; see also Packer and Reeves.
2. For more information, see Barnes; Bousquet; Dalton; Farish; and Wilson.
3. For more information, see Calkin; see also Wray et al.
4. These tools can be found at http://hdlab.stanford.edu/palladio/; http://hyperstudio.mit.edu/software/chronos-timeline/; http://prism.scholarslab.org/users/sign_in; http://timeline.knightlab.com/; http://sophie2.org/trac/; and https://tei-c.org/.

BIBLIOGRAPHY

Algorithmic Justice League. "What Is Facial Recognition Technology?" Accessed August 9, 2022, https://www.ajl.org/facial-recognition-technology.

American Civil Liberties Union. "ICE and Border Patrol Abuses." Accessed December 20, 2020, https://www.aclu.org/issues/immigrants-rights/ice-and-border-patrol-abuses.

Bagnall, Kate, and Tim Sherratt. "The Real Face of White Australia: Living under the White Australia Policy." 2010, https://www.realfaceofwhiteaustralia.net/.

Barnes, Trevor J. "Geographical Intelligence: American Geographers and Research and Analysis in the Office of Strategic Services 1941–1945." *Journal of Historical Geography* 32, no. 1 (January 2006): 149–68, https://doi.org/10.1016/j.jhg.2005.06.001.

Barnes, Trevor J., and Matthew Farish. "Between Regions: Science, Militarism, and American Geography from World War to Cold War." *Annals of the Association of American Geographers* 96, no. 4 (December 2006): 807–26, https://doi.org/10.1111/j.1467-8306.2006.00516.x.

Benjamin, Ruha. *Race after Technology: Abolitionist Tools for the New Jim Code.* Cambridge: Polity, 2019.

Biddle, Sam. "Police Surveilled George Floyd Protests with Help from Twitter-Affiliated Startup Dataminr." *The Intercept.* July 9, 2020, https://theintercept.com/2020/07/09/twitter-dataminr-police-spy-surveillance-black-lives-matter-protests/.

Boulay, Nadine, Ashley Caranto Morford, Arun Jacob, Kush Patel, and Kimberly O'Donnell. "Transforming DH Pedagogy." *Digital Studies/Le Champ Numerique* 11, no. 1 (2020): 1–43, https://doi.org/10.16995/dscn.379.

Bousquet, Antoine. "Cyberneticizing the American War Machine: Science and Computers in the Cold War." *Cold War History* 8, no. 1 (February 2008): 77–102, https://doi.org/10.1080/14682740701791359.

Browne, Simone. *Dark Matters: On the Surveillance of Blackness.* Durham, N.C.: Duke University Press, 2015.

Buchroithner, Manfred F., and René Pfahlbusch. "Geodetic Grids in Authoritative Maps—New Findings about the Origin of the UTM Grid." *Cartography and Geographic Information Science* 44, no. 3 (May 2017): 186–200, https://doi.org/10.1080/15230406.2015.1128851.

Buolamwini, Joy, and Timnit Gebru. "Gender Shades: Intersectional Accuracy Disparities in Commercial Gender Classification." In *Proceedings of Machine Learning Research* 81, Fairness, Accountability, and Transparency, 77–91. Cambridge, Mass.: MLR Research Press, 2018, https://proceedings.mlr.press/v81/buolamwini18a.html?mod=article_inline.

Calkin, Sydney. "Towards a Political Geography of Abortion." *Political Geography* 69 (March 2019): 22–29, https://doi.org/10.1016/j.polgeo.2018.11.006.

Campbell, Zack, Caitlin L. Chandler, and Chris Jones. "Sci-Fi Surveillance: Europe's Secretive Push into Biometric Technology." *The Guardian.* December 10, 2020, https://www.theguardian.com/world/2020/dec/10/sci-fi-surveillance-europes-secretive-push-into-biometric-technology.

Cifor, M., P. Garcia, T. L. Cowan, J. Rault, T. Sutherland, A. Chan, J. Rode, A. L. Hoffmann, N. Salehi, and L. Nakamura. *Feminist Data Manifest-No.* Accessed August 9, 2022, https://www.manifestno.com/.

Clarke, Keith C., and John G. Cloud. "On the Origins of Analytical Cartography." *Cartography and Geographic Information Science* 27, no. 3 (January. 2000): 195–204, https://doi.org/10.1559/152304000783547821.

Cloud, John. "American Cartographic Transformations during the Cold War." *Cartography and Geographic Information Science* 29, no. 3 (January 2002): 261–82, https://doi.org/10.1559/152304002782008422.

Dalton, Craig M. "Sovereigns, Spooks, and Hackers: An Early History of Google Geo Services and Map Mashups." *Cartographica: The International Journal for Geographic Information and Geovisualization* 48, no. 4 (December 2013): 261–74, https://doi.org/10.3138/carto.48.4.1621.

Eckstein, Laura. "Envisaging the Holy Land: Facial Recognition and Early Photography." Judaica DH at the Penn Libraries: Our Projects, https://judaicadh.github.io/work/envisaging-holy-land/.

"Embrace, Extend, and Extinguish." *Wikipedia.* Last modified April 27, 2022, https://en.wikipedia.org/wiki/Embrace,_extend,_and_extinguish.

Eubanks, Virginia. *Automating Inequality: How High-Tech Tools Profile, Police, and Punish the Poor.* New York: St. Martin's, 2018.

Farish, Matthew. "Canons and Wars: American Military Geography and the Limits of Disciplines." *Journal of Historical Geography* 49 (July 2015): 39–48, https://doi.org/10.1016/j.jhg.2015.04.012.

Ho, Karen, "Amazon Is the Invisible Backbone of ICE's Immigration Crackdown." *Technology Review.* October 22, 2018, https://www.technologyreview.com/2018/10/22/139639/amazon-is-the-invisible-backbone-behind-ices-immigration-crackdown/.

Hough, Floyd W. "International Cooperation on a Geodetic Project." *Transactions, American Geophysical Union* 32, no. 1 (1951): 106, https://doi.org/10.1029/TR032i001p00106.

Jacob, Arun. "Follow the Ho Chi Minh Trail: Analyzing the Media History of the Electronic Battlefield." *IDEAH* 2, no. 1 (July 2021), https://doi.org/10.21428/f1f23564.d9c905e8.

Jacob, Arun. "Punching Holes in the International Busa Machine Narrative." *IDEAH* 1, no. 1 (May 2020), https://doi.org/10.21428/f1f23564.d7d097c2.

Kelley, Jason. "Students Are Pushing Back against Proctoring Surveillance Apps." *Electronic Frontier Foundation.* September 25, 2020, https://www.eff.org/deeplinks/2020/09/students-are-pushing-back-against-proctoring-surveillance-apps.

Lewis, Tamika, Tawana Petty, Mariella Saba, Seeta Peña Gangadharan, Kim M. Reynolds, and Virginia Eubanks. *Our Data Bodies.* Accessed August 9, 2022, https://www.odbproject.org/.

Lucchesi, Annita. "The Sovereign Bodies Institute: Q&A with Executive Director Annita Lucchesi." *Native News.* 2019, https://nativenews.jour.umt.edu/2019/sb-institute/.

Magnet, Shoshana Amielle. *When Biometrics Fail: Gender, Race, and the Technology of Identity,* Durham, N.C.: Duke University Press, 2011.

Marczak, Bill, John Scott-Railton, Siddharth Prakash Rao, Siena Anstis, and Ron Deibert. "Running in Circles: Uncovering the Clients of Cyberespionage Firm Circles." *Citizen Lab.* December 1, 2020, https://citizenlab.ca/2020/12/running-in-circles-uncovering-the-clients-of-cyberespionage-firm-circles/.

Marx, Gary. "Surveillance Studies." In *International Encyclopedia of the Social & Behavioral Sciences.* 2nd ed., edited by Neil J. Smelser and Paul B. Baltes, 733–41. Amsterdam: Elsevier, 2015, https://doi.org/10.1016/B978-0-08-097086-8.64025-4.

Mattern, Shannon. "Maintenance and Care," *Places Journal.* November 2018, https://doi.org/10.22269/181120.

"Microsoft Completes GitHub Acquisition." *Official Microsoft Blog.* October 26, 2018, https://blogs.microsoft.com/blog/2018/10/26/microsoft-completes-github-acquisition/.

Miller, Bettye. "Scholars to Apply Facial Recognition Software to Unidentified Portrait Subjects." *UCR Today.* April 25, 2012, https://ucrtoday.ucr.edu/5453.

Miller, Greg. "Behind Enemy Lines: The Untold Story of the Secret Mission to Seize Nazi Map Data." *Smithsonian* 50, no. 7 (November 2019): 64–78, https://www.smithsonianmag.com/history/untold-story-secret-mission-seize-nazi-map-data-180973317/.

"Minimal Computing." *Global Outlook::Digital Humanities.* Accessed December 20, 2020, https://go-dh.github.io/mincomp/.

Musik, Christoph, and Matthias Zeppelzauer. "Computer Vision and the Digital Humanities." *VIEW: Journal of European Television History and Culture* 7, no. 14 (December 2018): 59–72, https://doi.org/10.18146/2213-0969.2018.jethc153.

Noble, Safiya Umoja. *Algorithms of Oppression: How Search Engines Reinforce Racism*. New York: New York University Press, 2018.

Office of Educational Technology. "Learning Analytics." Accessed August 9, 2022, https://tech.ed.gov/learning-analytics/.

Ong, Kyler. "Ideological Convergence in the Extreme Right." *Counter Terrorist Trends and Analyses* 12, no. 5 (2020): 1–7, https://www.jstor.org/stable/26954256.

"Our Mission." *Mukurtu.org*. Accessed December 20, 2020, https://mukurtu.org/about/.

Packer, Jeremy, and Joshua Reeves. "Making Enemies with Media." *Communication and the Public* 5, no. 1–2 (March 2020): 16–25, https://doi.org/10.1177/2057047320950635.

Pugh, Emerson W. *Building IBM: Shaping an Industry and Its Technology*. Cambridge, Mass.: MIT Press, 1995.

Rankin, William. *After the Map: Cartography, Navigation, and the Transformation of Territory in the Twentieth Century*. Chicago: University of Chicago Press, 2016.

Risam, Roopika. *New Digital Worlds: Postcolonial Digital Humanities in Theory, Praxis, and Pedagogy*. Evanston, Ill.: Northwestern University Press, 2018.

Saini, Angela. *Superior: The Return of Race Science*. Boston: Beacon Press, 2020.

Sarwari, Khalida. "Could a Smart Device Catch Implicit Bias in the Workplace?" *News@Northeastern*. January 29, 2020, https://news.northeastern.edu/2020/01/29/how-about-a-smart-device-that-could-catch-implicit-bias-in-the-workplace/.

Sayers, Jentery. "Computer Vision as a Public Act: On Digital Humanities and Algocracy." *Disrupting the Digital Humanities* (blog). January 6, 2016, http://www.disruptingdh.com/computer-vision-as-a-public-act-on-digital-humanities-and-algocracy/.

Shere, Anjuli R. K., and Jason Nurse. "Police Surveillance of Black Lives Matter Shows the Danger Technology Poses to Democracy." *The Conversation*. November 14, 2020, https://theconversation.com/police-surveillance-of-black-lives-matter-shows-the-danger-technology-poses-to-democracy-142194.

Sherratt, Tim. "The Real Face of White Australia." *Invisible Australians*. September 21, 2011, http://discontents.com.au/the-real-face-of-white-australia/.

Swauger, Shea. "Our Bodies Encoded: Algorithmic Test Proctoring in Higher Education." *Hybrid Pedagogy*. April 2, 2020, https://hybridpedagogy.org/our-bodies-encoded-algorithmic-test-proctoring-in-higher-education/.

Teräs, Marko, Juha Suoranta, Hanna Teräs, and Mark Curcher. "Post-Covid-19 Education and Education Technology 'Solutionism': A Seller's Market." *Postdigital Science and Education*. July 2020, https://doi.org/10.1007/s42438-020-00164-x.

Tobler, Waldo R. "Analytical Cartography." *The American Cartographer* 3, no. 1 (January 1976): 21–31, https://doi.org/10.1559/152304076784080230.

Tobler, Waldo R. "Automation and Cartography." *Geographical Review* 49, no. 4 (1959): 526–34, https://doi.org/10.2307/212211.

Tuck, Eve, and K. Wayne Yang. "Unbecoming Claims: Pedagogies of Refusal in Qualitative Research," *Qualitative Inquiry* 20 (2014): 811–18, https://doi.org/10.1177/1077800414530265.

23&Me. Accessed December 20, 2020, https://www.23andme.com/.

Warner, Deborah Jean. "Political Geodesy: The Army, the Air Force, and the World Geodetic System of 1960." *Annals of Science* 59, no. 4 (January 2002): 363–89, https://doi.org/10.1080/0003790110044756.

Wilson, Matthew W. *New Lines: Critical GIS and the Trouble of the Map.* Minneapolis: University of Minnesota Press, 2017.

Winthrop-Young, G. "Drill and Distraction in the Yellow Submarine: On the Dominance of Warin Friedrich Kittler's Media Theory." *Critical Inquiry* 28, no. 4 (Summer 2002), https://doi.org/10.1086/341236.

Tyler B. Wray, Ashley E. Pérez, Mark A. Celio, Daniel J. Carr, Alexander C. Adia, and Peter M. Monti. "Exploring the Use of Smartphone Geofencing to Study Characteristics of Alcohol Drinking Locations in High-Risk Gay and Bisexual Men." *Alcoholism: Clinical and Experimental Research.* February 25, 2019, https://onlinelibrary.wiley.com/doi/10.1111/acer.13991.

PART III

DISCIPLINES AND INSTITUTIONS

A Voice Interrupts: Digital Humanities as a Tool to Hear Black Life

ALISON MARTIN

In her 2014 article "Mathematics Black Life," geographer Katherine McKittrick asks how we might engage in Black studies in a way that honors the dead without rehearsing the traumatic counting that is so fundamental to how we know Black life. In and out of archival study, researchers count deaths, ages, prices, lashes, shots fired, years confined—all of which say more about the violence imposed on Black people than the actual lived experiences of Black people. McKittrick cites a ship ledger to emphasize this point, showing that the archive knows and calls Blackness through the brutal mathematics of bills of sale, ages, names, and owners. This particular ship ledger, however, is slightly different; in its accounting of one of the captives aboard the ship, a woman named Betty Rapelje, it also includes a statement from Rapelje herself: "*Says she was born free.*" This moment within the ledger begins the intervention against the centuries of violent counting that McKittrick is seeking, in which "a voice interrupts: says she." This interruption also begins the intervention that I am seeking, in which the disruption that takes place lies, in some part, in the sonic, in the voice that "says she is free." In this chapter, I argue that the sonic, particularly the sonic as rendered through the digital, offers a powerful mode of studying Black life without a foregrounding of violent mathematics. Thinking through a Black digital sound studies filter, I chart some of the possibilities for digital methods and collaboration that make audible Black life amid the violence of Black death. Ultimately, I argue that digital humanities approaches can help us to navigate the difficulties of knowing Black life, helping us to hear the richness of lived experience rather than the violent impositions of white supremacy.

Black Digital Sound Studies

Conversations about Black sound studies have existed in many spaces: in works like Fred Moten's *In the Break* and Ashon Crawley's *Black Pentecostal Breath,* which challenge the aesthetic possibilities of Black sound and Black studies simultaneously by theorizing Blackness through jazz and gospel music performance; in spaces like Daphne Brooks's "Black Sound and the Archive" working group; in the writings of foundational music critics such as A. B. Spellman and those who we do not often hear as critics but have written insightfully nonetheless, like Abbey Lincoln. Black sound studies is in W. E. B. Du Bois's sorrow songs, in Alexander Wehlieye's remix of the DJ, in my own grandfather's conspiratorial insistence that the organ player in Otis Redding's "Try a Little Tenderness" wasn't actually supposed to be in the recording.[1] Black sound studies is how we make *aural sense,* be it through music, silence, technology, the roar of activism or the quietude of grief, and everything between or otherwise. Following Manning Marable's insistence on Black studies as at once descriptive, corrective, and prescriptive, I imagine Black sound studies as a process that explores the depth of Black auralities, corrects mishearings, and incorporates the centrality of Black sound into a broader liberation politic. In short, Black sound studies is a way to understand how Blackness is constituted through sound and to allow that understanding to work with what is at stake in Black sound, be it issues of appropriation, criminalization, silencing, or the particularities of gendered violence.

What, then, is Black digital sound studies? In *Digital Sound Studies,* Mary Caton Lingold, Darren Mueller, and Whitney Trettien acknowledge Black studies as a field that has "acknowledged the political complexity of sound since its inception" (5). Black studies scholars across all mediums have long known that to study Black life is to listen to Black people, and to listen to Black life through digital and technological media—the radio, a video on social media, or through a streaming platform—is to engage with an aural disruption of space-time. Black digital sound studies can offer ways to think through what it means to engage the auralities of Blackness through the digital in particular, providing a framework to better understand the questions that arise when we are trying to make sense of a sonic being in the world. Listening to Black life through the digital (and the digital humanities) requires that we attend to sonorities across centuries as well as to the broadest spatializations of diaspora. The sonic as rendered through the digital offers a possibility for studying Black life without engaging in a kind of reductive violence of control. Through avenues such as social media, innovative sonic techniques, and regularly bypassing officiality, the digital is able to amplify the things that Black people say about themselves and mitigate the violence of looking plainly at the horrors that have been inflicted on Black people. The sonic, however, is not without cost, since listening can also be a violent event. From social media platforms like TikTok, whose audio cultures have galvanized digital Blackface, to audio recordings of incidents of police brutality, the sonic often participates in violent mathematics.[2] Listening, however, offers a path toward what Fred Moten has described as a "fugitive" knowledge production because it is not the official, preferred mode of evidence for the state. Similarly, Andrew Navin Brooks uses Moten and Harvey's concept of the undercommons in order to arrive at a kind of "fugitive listening" that "allows us to open our ears to the noisy voices and modes of speech that sound outside the locus of politics proper" (2020, 25). The listening that Black studies facilitates thus demands flexibility, speculation, and interpretation, and it has the power to move toward a less violent inquiry into Black life. In what follows, I offer samples of how digital humanities tools, methods, and histories can help us attend to this work.[3]

Amplifying the Silenced

Embedded within the study of sound is the study of silence, a phenomenon for which I offer two explanations. The first, from ethnomusicologist Ana María Ochoa, is that silence cannot exist. In her explication of silence as a keyword for sound studies, she recounts the story of composer John Cage entering an anechoic chamber, a room designed to be completely silent. Despite its design, Cage reported that he heard two distinct sounds. He was informed that the low sound was his blood pumping and the high one was his nervous system. Ochoa posits, then, that silence operates as an acoustic impossibility, and that it does not and cannot exist. Extending this declaration through the science of acoustics and into the cultural realm, I contend that the silencing of Blackness is indeed an acoustic impossibility. Despite the pervasive strategies of silencing that are imposed on Black people, beginning with the reduction of Black life to a violent mathematics that McKittrick describes and continuing to range from the censorship of hip-hop to the discipline of Black girls in the classroom, it remains impossible to silence Black life or death in any form. A voice always persists, "says she."

My second consideration of silence is from Audre Lorde, who casts silence as both a false protector and a tyrant. She warns that "while we wait in silence for that final luxury of fearlessness, the weight of that silence will choke us" (44). While she acknowledges the pain of being consistently misheard and intentionally misunderstood, she ultimately concludes that the silences of marginalized people will not save them, so it is always better to speak. Considering Ochoa's argument about the impossibility of silence alongside Lorde's insistence on silence as a tangible *thing* to be overcome, I understand silence to be, much like race, constructed and reconstructed in such a way that affirms dominant positions and oppresses those whose sound is of a different and disruptive frequency. To silence someone is to actively shroud them in an inaudibility, to keep them from being witnessed through some combination of discrediting, compressing, or otherwise diminishing their aurality.

The digital and digital humanities practices can and do act as a means of amplifying those who have otherwise been threatened with inaudibility. Furthermore, the acts of sounding and silencing are more than physical vibrations but also encompass the metaphorical resonances of what it means to be heard. Social media, especially Twitter, operates as a powerful space in which sound moves between metaphorical hearings and physical soundwaves. These digital spaces have tremendous amplifying potential, especially as curated by scholars working within digital humanities practices. Consider, for example, the esteemed Dr. Lorgia Garcia-Peña's tenure denial at Harvard University in 2019, which went viral on social media, particularly on Twitter. The denial sparked a movement to publicly celebrate the expansive contributions of Garcia-Peña, both through the hashtag #Lorgiafest as well as "Ethnic Studies Rise," a website created by scholars Raj Chetty, Katerina Gonzalez Seligmann, and Alex Gil. In addition to intellectual communities metaphorically speaking out by sending letters to the university's administration, the tenure denial inspired in-person protests on Harvard's campus that involved speaking, shouting, singing, and other forms of aural expression. Prompted by these efforts, there have been renewed conversations, online and offline, about the lives of Afro-Latinx women in the academy, the inequitable mysteries of tenure, and how universities placate protest rather than enacting structural change. Garcia-Peña's tenure denial was an act of silencing, a way to refuse the validity of her work and diminish her real impact on a number of fields, from ethnic studies to Caribbean studies. To extend the metaphorical discussion about who has a seat at the proverbial table, the response to Garcia-Peña's tenure denial involved a connection—indeed, an amplification—of those already seated at the tables of their own institutions and libraries, as well as places outside the academy entirely—wherever conversations about ethnic studies might be taking place. Our silences will not save us, and neither will one table at one institution. The value of the digital here is to bring together those who seek to disrupt the shadowy hierarchical structures of the university that amplify the critiques of Black voices.

Distance from Violence

McKittrick's "Mathematics Black Life" is inspired by Saidiya Hartman's "Venus in Two Acts," which explores the possibility of knowing more about Black life without committing further violence within the act of the narrating that life. Specifically regarding the archive of slavery, Hartman asks, "Do the possibilities outweigh the dangers of looking (again)?" (4). That is, does the violence of looking outweigh the benefits of knowing more about Black life and those accounts of Black life that might otherwise be lost to us? This is a question for both inside and outside the archive, listening in addition to looking. Digital methodologies—and in particular, machine learning and automation—have the potential to mitigate the potential violence of listening again (and again) to the violence that gentrification makes audible. In my own work, I listen to the sounds of gentrification in Washington, D.C. *Intersectional Listening* is a sometimes sprawling project that, at its heart, asks how Black people experience the violence of gentrification as a sonic, racialized process. Part of this work has involved what is known as passive acoustic recording, or the capture of many intermittent recordings over a long period of time—in my case, nine months. To process the data generated from the passive acoustic recording, I use a classifier, a process in which I "train" a program to recognize particular sounds in a recording then feed it a large amount of data in order to query the program for various sounds. For example, if

I manually tag a number of "siren" sounds in a training set for the span of a day or even a week, I can then feed the program the data for six months and automatically receive back sounds that are similar to the sirens that I manually tagged.

This is not a flawless system, because the sounds of the city are anything but uniformly classifiable; rather, it is a way to think through the sonic characteristics of a gentrifying neighborhood. Furthermore, the analysis of these sounds offers an aural interpretation of what it is to be Black in a gentrifying space. With that said, scholars such as Safiya Noble in *Algorithms of Oppression* and Ruha Benjamin in *Race after Technology* have shown that machine learning and artificial intelligence are consistently constructed and employed more broadly in ways that uphold white supremacy. But, as Benjamin also observes, these technologies can be retooled for solidarity and reimagined for justice, when they are wielded with intention and care. Similarly, just as Akasha Gloria Hull and Barbara Smith asserted that the bias of Black women's study must be to "consider as primary the knowledge that will save Black women's lives," the knowledge of a Black digital sound studies must be to listen for that which will save Black people's lives (22). Machine learning can be applied toward this purpose, and in my work, I classify and tag aspects of a soundscape in an attempt to get closer to an understanding of what is being shifted and disrupted as D.C. gentrifies.

Gentrifying space features a rich soundscape, including car horns, constant music of varying genres and volumes, construction, public transportation, and people. When I speak about listening to these spaces, about the displacement of local music scenes and the persistent criminalization of Black sound, I am often asked if my recorders can capture the sounds of gunshots in the neighborhood. The frequency of this question speaks to the connections people often make between crime and what people often believe Blackness to sound like, and it remains a complicated question because it is indeed possible. If I were to attempt the process of automating the recognition of gunshots, I would begin with fireworks, which are similar enough sonically to manufacture a reasonable training set. They are also relatively easy to find in terms of the calendar, most prevalent on the days before and after the Fourth of July.[4] It would be possible, then, to solicit a list of gunshots from a machine-learning algorithm, without having to listen to each instance manually or at all. When people ask me about passive acoustic recording and gunshots, I explain this hypothetical process and the possibility of doing that work with machine learning. But in the same breath, I tell them why I refuse to perform such an endeavor. I have never gone looking for these violences because I do not ever want to be asked for them. I will not create a dataset of gunshot sounds because I will not cooperate with the Metropolitan Police Department, Immigration and Customs Enforcement, or any other such entity that would seek these sounds for the purposes of surveilling, harassing, detaining, and incarcerating Black people. To return to Hartman's question, the disastrous possibilities of surveillance and tracking outweigh the potential of machine learning to maneuver around the dangers of looking and listening again. In this case, therefore, I understand my work as a Black digital humanist to intentionally refuse to create a particular dataset.

This refusal is an engagement in silencing work, an attempt to cover the deeply embedded, falsely sewn connections between Black life and the criminality of gunshots in an inaudibility that deems a dataset of gunshot audio as not needed because of its potential for violence and also because it lacks the relevance that racism would prescribe it. My refusal follows the work of Yeshimabeit Milner's call to "abolish big data," which she describes as a "call to action to reject the concentration of Big Data, to challenge the structures that allow it to be wielded as a weapon. . . ." Public discussion of refusal is a key part of a Black digital sound studies, especially because this dataset already exists in the form of the "Shotspotter," a technology that "provides acoustic gunshot detection and precision-policing solutions to help law enforcement officials and security personnel prevent and reduce gun violence and make communities, campuses and facilities safer." Public refusal of a database that would do similar work as the Shotspotter, which is indeed active in Washington, D.C., is important because it offers a needed aural critique against institutions of policing and surveillance, even as these systems are praised for ensuring public safety.

Intentional Obscurities

My final sample of how the digital might encourage us to hear Black life is inspired by a conference presentation by the eminent Zandria F. Robinson. In 2018, the annual "PopCon" conference on popular music was themed "Only You and Your Ghost Will Know: Music, Death, and the Afterlife," encouraging participants to engage in conversations about pop music, death, and the musical ghosts that haunt us. Robinson spoke about *Amazing Grace,* the 2018 documentary of Aretha Franklin recording her best-selling live album of the same name in 1972, pinpointing a moment when the audio of the album differed from that which was captured on film. Specifically, there is a moment in "Mary, Don't You Weep" where Franklin, having spun the congregation into a fervor, "calls" Lazarus back from the dead, just as Jesus did in the Gospel of John. The Southern California Community Choir grounds her by vamping, "Mary, don't you weep," along with James Cleveland's percussive piano playing, as she sings to the congregation that they are about to "review the story of two sisters." When she gets to the height of her account, Franklin, as Jesus, says that "for the benefit of you who don't believe, I'm gon call him three times," at which point the members of the congregation begin to audibly shout. She then proceeds to call Lazarus three times, the first two being composed enough to elicit an echo from the choir, the third call transforming into a more otherworldly wail that pushes the congregation and choir into even more intensity. This final call is the one that raises Lazarus, the one that has him "up walking like a natural man."

Franklin's calling of Lazarus is not included in the film, and Robinson argued that Franklin, as a witch, as conjure woman, as Jesus, "hoodooed" that moment away from the film because surely she had called someone back from the dead that night, and she could not abide all of her transformative power being on visual display. Although I was well aware of Franklin as a supernatural figure, having just seen the documentary the night before and weeping alongside many others in the theater, I had not considered her using practices of intentional obfuscation to avoid the fetishization and surveillance of cosmology. The digital, in this case film, can act as a mode of communicating with ancestors about what must be obscured or, alternately, shared, told, or called. But through magic or hoodoo or conjuring women or water being spilled onto the recording equipment, audience members simply cannot have, or know, certain things.[5] This moment is couched in Franklin's altogether refusal to release the film several times while she was alive and its eventual completion and release on her death. Even within its cinematic release against her wishes, there are still facets that remain visually unknowable, like the calling of Lazarus. Zora Neale Hurston makes a similar point in *Mules and Men,* about the common practice of offering one thing to a white anthropologist for them to "play with" while keeping the most sacred elements of Black folklore inside, not for public consumption. What Black people refuse to give the digital has the potential to help Black people to shape and retain the narratives of their own lives. Sometimes the role of this work is not to sharpen every audio file or identify every sound but to make obfuscation possible and emphasize that some things must be held close rather than amplified.[6] Holding things close becomes even more important as gruesome instances of state violence are amplified and made viral, and the trauma from looping Black death is dismissed as a necessary part of raising consciousness.

Possibilities

The examples discussed in this chapter provide just a small sampling of the range of possibilities for how Black digital sound studies might encourage the active refusal of an intensely traumatic study of Black life. However, they offer a reading that is perhaps more optimistic than warranted. Instead of using sonic digital practice to amplify Black life and maneuver around algorithmic violence, the digital is also used to count screams, breaths, or shots heard.[7] The importance of Black digital sound studies, then, requires us to engage critically, and even skeptically, with the sonic. In addition to this skepticism, digital humanities as a community must reject the notion of research as an authorization of universal access, no matter the time period or research subject. In keeping to these responsibilities, a theorizing of sound through the digital has the potential to amplify the silenced, engage data in healthier ways, and offer language to explore how Black cosmologies might complicate what we presume to be true. I offer these examples as a starting point for thinking about the possible as we embrace the relationship between the sonic and the digital, especially as we incorporate the histories of those that have already done so (and continue to do so) into digital humanities work. McKittrick suggests that "the intellectual project of Black studies . . . provides a deliberate commentary on the ways in which Blackness works against the violence that defines it" (19). This work must honor and bear witness to this violence while complicating silences, refusing algorithmic injustice, and holding space for that which resists the digital in order to reject the repetition of antiblack violence.

NOTES

1. From the time I was a child, my grandfather insisted that the organ player showed up on the spot and was inspired to play along because the music was so good. It seemed that improvisational to him.

2. Deborah Wong's 2017 analysis of police belt recorders describes how officers, before they murder someone, can become stuck in a harrowing loop of shouted instructions.

3. My use of "sample" here is influenced by Marisa Parham's contribution in the 2019 volume of *Debates in the Digital Humanities,* in which she describes samples as "cultural performances that both crystallize and iterate signals." I am also drawn to the sample as a fundamental part of hip-hop music and Black music culture more broadly. The sample is a performance, yes, but also operates as a template, a question, a suggestion, or even a palimpsest. These samples are examples meant to be remixed, chopped and screwed, and considered in ways that help us (Black people) hear and sound anew.

4. Using fireworks may also be a traumatic listening experience for some, rendering the training of a dataset altogether impossible. Here I consider Naomi Shihab Nye's poem, *No Explosions*: "To enjoy/fireworks/you would have/to have lived/ a different kind/of life."

5. At one point during *Amazing Grace,* water is spilled onto a bundle of wires.

6. Finn Brunton and Helen Nissenbaum further explore the work of obfuscation in their 2015 book *Obfuscation: A User's Guide for Privacy and Protest.* They describe the process as "the deliberate addition of ambiguous, confusing, or misleading information to interfere with surveillance and data collection" (1). Whether an act of hoodoo or data camouflage, obfuscation works to conceal and delay.

7. Sonic artist Rachel Devorah's 2017 piece *Overmorrow* sonifies data of gun violence in the United States by assigning shootings to musical notation played by various percussion instruments. After three iterations of the project, Devorah has acknowledged that this project centers whiteness and does not currently operate in the service of Black life, even as Black people are disproportionately affected by gun violence in the United States.

BIBLIOGRAPHY

"About Shotspotter." https://www.shotspotter.com/company/.

Benjamin, Ruha. *Race after Technology: Abolitionist Tools for the New Jim Code.* Cambridge: Polity Press, 2019.

Brunton, Finn, and Helen Nissenbaum. *Obfuscation: A User's Guide for Privacy and Protest.* Cambridge, Mass.: MIT Press, 2015.

Crawley, Ashon T. *Black Pentecostal Breath: The Aesthetics of Possibility.* New York: Fordham University Press, 2016.

Devorah, Rachel. "Overmorrow." *Feminist Media Histories* 3, no. 3 (2017): 173–77, http://racheldevorah.studio/works/overmorrow/.

"Ethnic Studies Rise." https://ethnicrise.github.io/.

Franklin, Aretha. *Amazing Grace.* Directed by Sydney Pollack. Debut at DOC NY Film Festival, November 14, 2018.

Hartman, Saidiya. "Venus in Two Acts." *Small Axe* 12, no. 2 (2008):1–14.

Hull, Akasha Gloria, and Barbara Smith. "Introduction: The Politics of Black Women's Studies." In *All the Women Are White, All the Blacks Are Men, but Some of Us Are Brave: Black Women's Studies,* edited by Akasha Gloria Hull, Patricia Bell Scott, and Barbara Smith, xvii–xxxii. New York: Feminist Press, 1982.

Hurston, Zora Neale. *Mules and Men.* New York: Harper Collins, 2008. First published 1935.

Lingold, Mary Caton, Darren Mueller, and Whitney Trettien. *Digital Sound Studies.* Durham, N.C.: Duke University Press, 2018.

Lorde, Audre. "The Transformation of Silence into Language and Action." In *Sister Outsider.* Berkeley, Calif.: Crossing Press, 1984.

McKittrick, Katherine. "Mathematics Black Life." *The Black Scholar* 44, no. 2 (2014):16–28.

Milner, Yeshimabeit. "Abolish Big Data." *Medium.* July 8, 2019.

Moten, Fred. *In the Break: The Aesthetics of the Black Radical Tradition.* Minneapolis: University of Minnesota Press, 2003.

Navin Brooks, Andrew. "Fugitive Listening: Sounds from the Undercommons." *Theory, Culture & Society* 37, no. 6 (2020):25–45.

Noble, Safiya. *Algorithms of Oppression: How Search Engines Reinforce Racism.* New York: NYU Press, 2018.

Nye, Naomi Shihab. "No Explosions." In *The Tiny Journalist.* Rochester, N.Y.: BOA Editions Ltd., 2019.

Ochoa, Ana María Gautier. "Silence." In *Keywords in Sound,* edited by David Novak and Matt Sakakeeny, 183–92. Durham, N.C.: Duke University Press, 2015.

Parham, Marisa. "Sample|Signal|Strobe: Haunting, Social Media, and Black Digitality." In *Debates in the Digital Humanities 2019,* edited by Matthew K. Gold and Lauren F. Klein. Minneapolis: University of Minnesota Press, 2019.

Robinson, Zandria. "Sonic Asé: Black Folks Making It So in Life, Death, and Beyond." Presented at the Museum of Pop Culture Pop Conference, Seattle, Washington, April 12, 2019.

Wong, Deborah. "Deadly Soundscapes: Scripts of Lethal Force and Lo-Fi Death." In *Theorizing Sound Writing,* edited by Deborah Kapchan, 253–76. Middletown, Conn.: Wesleyan University Press, 2017.

Addressing an Emergency: The "Pragmatic Tilt" Required of Scholarship, Data, and Design by the Climate Crisis

JO GULDI

The sense in which our contemporary moment is unprecedented has a great deal to do with data delivered in real time. As a result of the #BlackLivesMatter movement, any citizens previously ignorant of the acts of violence perpetrated by the police against people of color became familiar with those facts, which were circulated almost instantly by citizen observers armed with phones. Calls for action were amplified in real time by social media, leading to some of the largest protests in the history of the United States. During the first phase of the coronavirus pandemic, newspaper readers around the world became accustomed to reading daily updates on the disease's spread, packaged as bar charts and data-driven maps, with individuals, families, schools, and corporations adjusting their plans on a weekly or even daily basis to respond to the latest information about the disease's vectors. At the same time, scientists and UN advisory bodies have identified the present decade as a moment of unprecedented crisis, writ in terms of a limited opportunity for the planet's inhabitants to decide to keep carbon in the ground (Asayama et al.). Through this series of emergencies, experts have mobilized data—in the form of stories, numbers, and figures—to help the public make sense of their experience.

Emergencies beg for a response, and often the timeliness of the response is critical in its appropriateness to the problem in question. In the case of climate change, President Joseph Biden has set a deadline of 2030 for limiting carbon emissions, based on the recommendations of scientists, who in turn based their consensus on data collected and analyzed over decades. Yet for many individuals aware of this deadline, even those trained in relevant skill sets, no pragmatic response to the climate emergency is apparent. This chapter asks: What would it mean to work under a deadline informed by data? More specifically, how does the urgency of the climate deadline factor into the decision making of digital humanists about their subjects of research, and what *could* digital humanists do to help the efforts to refashion our society toward sustainability?

The paragraphs that follow explore questions about when and whether the skills and approaches of the digital humanities *can* or *should* support a pragmatic response. I review responses to climate change from both digital and traditional humanities scholarship and make the case for an ongoing debate about what form of response is appropriate, given our changing environmental situation. Finally, I review case studies that have used text mining for the purpose of monitoring the environment, drawing on disciplines far wider than the digital humanities. Recent projects in economics, information science, and the material sciences have attempted to use text mining to mount realistic and timely responses to climate change. Throughout, I draw out an analysis of which digital practices might tilt creative, discursive, analytical, and data-driven labor in the direction of a response that is *pragmatic,* or—according to William James's definition—bound up with a practical response rather than one that is chiefly theoretical, intellectual, or artistic in nature. By reviewing how interdisciplinary scholars have used text mining to support public decision making with facts, I highlight a major arena in which digital humanists might contribute. Analyzing environmental pollution, the actions of polluters, the bets of investors, and the responsiveness of politicians requires quantitative skills of different kinds. Some of the possible analysis in this realm requires the analysis of narrative that is a specialty of digital humanists. I argue that digital humanists' skills could in fact be immediately and powerfully enlisted in a pragmatic response to the climate emergency.

Are the Digital Humanities Pragmatic? Should They Be?

Digital humanists and information scientists, with their skills at analyzing networks, trawling institutional histories, and processing text, are in many ways already developing techniques to intervene in the climate crisis. Using the tools of text mining, for example, scholars and digital practitioners could create systems that highlight and track the politicians around the globe who have resisted climate change legislation, focusing sustained attention on each speech or act of denial. Yet in the main, the digital humanities and social sciences have largely failed to engage climate change, especially as a space for concrete action-oriented projects. Here is a crucial missed opportunity for scholarship in the service of collective knowledge and collective action.

The textual analysis tools typical of certain digital humanities (DH) projects have rarely been applied to the discourse about the environment (for an exception, see Grubert and Algee-Hewitt). In the European Union, United States, Canada, and Australia, nationally backed grant programs have invested heavily in topics such as the twentieth-century novel and nineteenth-century newspaper, producing tools and initiatives that delve into questions of rhetoric, form, authorship, and content. Groundbreaking though these studies are, they operate—as much of the university and the humanities operate—as if national interests depend on engaging with a critical and accurate account of the development of the nation rather than what is truly needed: a planetary account of our current environmental crisis.

It might be objected that the humanities themselves exist less to serve any pragmatic "interest" than for the purposes of investigation into human experience and the history of ways of knowing more generally. Indeed, the shift that Matthew Gold and Lauren Klein have identified in "A DH That Matters" already demonstrates how humanistic values can be applied to events both current and past—for instance, using the tools of the digital humanities to aid the victims of hurricanes, to narrate the history of race, to document the bias of the technology industry, and to map Immigration and Customs Enforcement (ICE) detention centers. Where an earlier generation of digital humanists stressed the importance of "playfulness" when looking at data, data scientists engaging with questions of climate change more often experience an urgent drive to action, one that privileges *pragmatic intervention* in public discourse over playfulness per se.

The roots of such a pragmatic tilt have already been sown in certain quarters of the digital humanities that might, for our purposes, be identified as the "pragmatic digital humanities." It is already evident in projects such as Torn Apart/Separados, which was designed to draw public attention to the pervasiveness of ICE detainment centers and specific social emergencies such as the children imprisoned at the U.S. border (Ahmed et al.). Digital humanists have also pioneered the building of infrastructural tools and standards of fair academic labor (Applegate; Risam; Guldi, "Scholarly Infrastructure"). They have begun important conversations about how "minimal computing" can minimize energy expenditure and make our projects accessible to citizens and scholars in the developing world (Schreibman et al.; Edmond; Gilio-Whitaker). In addition, digital humanists have documented standards for participatory, peer-to-peer design mechanisms that allow maps to become directly responsive to feedback from local communities—as embodied, for example, in the standards of the Bay Area's Anti-Eviction Mapping Project (Golumbia and Koh; Graziani and Shi; Maharawal and McElroy; McElroy; Senier).

"Action-oriented" digital humanities projects such as these offer an important set of examples for how the light of DH scholarship can be brought to bear on the life of data, rhetoric, and argumentation in the textual documentation of the climate emergency, the most pressing issue of our time. These projects demonstrate a shift from the ideational work of imagined (or actual) readers toward the purposes held up by communities in all their complexities. As a result, these projects benefit from the skills of humanists and digital humanists—for example, in the dynamics of "reading" and "distant reading"—but also apply those skills in new ways, with new audiences and ends in mind and with the goal of creating concrete change in the world.

By classifying these projects as part of a "tilt," I intend to describe a reorientation that does *not* require a wholly new critical or methodological stance. A "tilt" is proposed, in contrast to the epistemological "turns" of recent decades—the "linguistic turn," the "cultural turn," the "spatial turn," and the "global turn" among them. In a spatial sense, *turning* suggests a diversion to one's path to explore a hitherto unknown area. Such a description makes sense for all of those turns by which scholars trained in an existing field diverted their attention, with the help of a new set of theory, to explore a hitherto unknown arena of practice—say, the hidden, global interconnections between social movements or the spatial implications of historical technology. A *tilt*, by contrast, suggests that one might stay on one's path, continuing to work on the same field—be it cultural history, diplomatic history, global history, the temporality of the novel, feminist criticism, or histories of the nation-state—while inclining one's attention elsewhere. A tilt suggests less new content or a new method of inquiry than a reorientation from wherever one stands, taking account of the world and one's own talents anew.

A pragmatic "tilt" in the digital humanities would not ask feminist scholars or historians of immigration to abandon their work in favor of some more noble calling, or to turn their scholarship toward some compelling new body of theory. Rather, a "tilt" would take the form of listening and learning to examples of scholarship from far-flung fields—including journalism, economics, and engineering—where scholars are already trying to join their labor to support the climate crisis.

By its nature, the climate crisis has many aspects that already overlap with existing fields. There are racial elements of the climate crisis, already well established in the scholarship around toxic pollution and ethnic neighborhoods (Camacho; Lerner; Taylor; Bullard). There are also global and feminist elements of the climate crisis, legal and diplomatic ones, and even aspects of climate change related to memory studies and the disappearing memories of the forests, coasts, and glaciers that have vanished in my lifetime. Humanists in general have an expertise in close reading and the critique of analysis that are well developed for understanding how communities and institutions respond or fail to respond to crises. And digital humanists, above all, have specific skills in project design, visual interfaces, and data analysis that can make almost any scholarly project more accessible—as well as tools that can make data *actionable*. Indeed, as Matthew Gold and Lauren Klein argued in "A DH That Matters," a trend of orientation toward *action* is already visible in many DH projects today.

A truly *pragmatic* tilt would add to a general orientation toward action a concern with the powerful and pressing needs of the climate deadline, adding questions about climate response to each of the many subjects of inquiry and action that concern humanists and their interlocutors. Pragmatic thinking reminds us that we do not have infinite time for a response, and that many questions about politics where justice is needed will not solve the fundamental problem of survival. A pragmatic tilt does not mean setting aside problems of feminism or race—but it may require *tilting* those questions toward the climate crisis and the means of its repair by inspecting the failings of communities and institutions to limit carbon, to develop specific and fact-based discourses about the crisis, and to countenance the rights of all humans who may face new danger as a result of fire, flood, famine, and displacement.

Calls for a pragmatic response to the climate tragedy have abounded across the humanities. At the heart of many of these calls are questions about the data of climate change and its transparency, as well about the failure of society to respond to these and other warnings of climate change. Scholars in the environmental humanities have also undertaken investigations into what skills the public needs to interpret the data of climate change and its communication. One scholar of information studies, for example, emphasizes the need for "numeracy and visual comprehension" to prepare students to analyze discourse in a world where visualizations of climate change increasingly inform matters of public debate (Houser, "Climate Visualizations," 1). Her critique is newly relevant in a world where a U.S. president can redraw the path of a hurricane on a map with a Sharpie, or when the climate denial articles of the *Epoch Times* go viral on Facebook. Reckoning with a widening divide between numerate scientists and naive (or willingly uninformed) citizens, an enormous variety of artists and writers have attempted to make climate change more knowable and more pressing through practices such as walking glaciers, describing arctic ice in detail, and inquiring into our emotional relationship with nature, the deep past, and futurity (Forman; Peterson; Lee et al.).

Certain experiments in the digital humanities have also attempted to reckon with the climate emergency, typically by engaging descriptive and emotional modalities to connect the present crisis with experiences of the past. DH scholars have experimented with, for example, mapping the sites of ecological change in Iceland against environmental descriptions in the medieval Icelandic sagas (Lethbridge and Hartman) or mapping the sites of British Romantic writing (D. Cooper). Some of these attempts concentrate on bridging data about geological timescales with human consciousness, thereby bringing abstraction into apprehensible reality; others consist of meditations about how to do the intellectual and emotional work of the digital humanities on a wider scale (Nowviskie). Exercises of this sort tend to emphasize the possibility for the subjective transformation of the individual through attention to nature, the individual's integration with and dependence on nature, and the emotional responses that such an awareness inspires. One scholar of literature and the environment writes that scholars in her network "affirm the expertise of the humanities for transforming human preferences, practices, and actions in a time when there is a need for radical change" (Adamson, 354).

Emotional work of this kind is important for addressing the psychological impediments to acknowledging the stress of climate change, but it is not always clear whether aesthetic encounters with nature necessarily offer a bridge to timely, direct, pragmatic action. As experts in discourse and rhetoric, humanists have frequently offered aesthetic or subjective responses to nature as a solution to data's seeming failure to persuade. But these are at best indirect and abstract responses—for instance, a concern with party-based denunciations of the evidence of climate change may motivate a critical investigation of the life of data in public discourse, or concern with climate denial may prompt experiments with mapping historical references to climate in the literature classroom. As one art historian concluded of his survey of climate-based photojournalism and art, "not all [approaches] have been effective in educating people about the dangers and causes of climate change or encouraging civic action and involvement" (Braasch, 33). It is quite possible that many current attempts at investigating the "digital environmental humanities" or other hybrid forms of thought will fail as the demands of a climate deadline force us to look at opportunities for organization and dangers in ever more concrete and specific ways. As one digital Victorianist was led to protest, "Why are we building and analyzing digital systems as ecosystems at the moment when entire natural ecosystems are being eradicated?" (Linley, 413).

A pragmatic tilt to the digital humanities might provide the answer to such a question—especially if digital humanists apply their talents at text mining and mapping to the voluminous materials created by corporations, governments, and communities wrestling with dilemmas that have their root in environmental peril. While much of the data about the climate crisis takes the form of quantitative measurements of carbon and methane, the *governmental* and *social* aspects of our failure to limit carbon emissions are documented in words. Likewise, words and narratives document the spreading realities of how communities are already suffering the consequences of wildfire, floods, storms, and the failures of institutions to take appropriate measures. Where the evidence is textual in nature, it can be analyzed with the skill sets of the digital humanities.

Text Mining as Real-Time Response

Where can the future authors of projects of this kind turn for inspiration? One answer is that there are already a large number of quantitative projects that build on *text mining* to make assessments of climate-related data. And while many of these projects have promising results, most of them could be improved through the skills of narrative analysis that humanists possess in abundance.

Scholars from numerous fields outside the humanities are already using text mining to track the responses or lack thereof in institutions such as corporations and civic authorities. In one climate-oriented project, researchers created a tool for mining climate news stories, the results of which were then used as indicators of how to hedge the stocks of companies that were linked negatively to climate events (Engle). The authors of the report advertise their tool as one that could automatically create "green" investment portfolios, but one could imagine the same analysis of climate-related news being used for monitoring governance, political discourse, and philanthropy from below. Text mining has also shown the effectiveness of clarity in the writing of environmental regulation; one text analysis study showed that more readable and precise directives about landfill design were better predictors of efficient waste management than spending (Richter, Ng, and Fallah). Examples of this kind demonstrate that text mining has pragmatic uses. Assessments of text can offer ratings of how well institutions are doing at responding to climate and where they fail. It can allow the close comparison and scrutiny of institutions.

Elsewhere, I have proposed that the creation of real-time data for actionable response grafts onto the skill set of "critique" the timely review of the "audit," which is iterative by nature. Successive audits of institutions taken on a regular basis give researchers important information about collective progress over time (Guldi, Scholarly Infrastructure). Text mining offers many opportunities for "auditing" the way institutions are adapting to the climate emergency. Applied to the discourse of institutions, text mining allows us to ask: Has my state legislature or city council started talking more about solar panels and trees over the last year? Has my newspaper covered climate-related news every week this year? How does the language, human detail, and geographic specificity of that coverage compare with the reports of other states, cities, or newspapers?

Certain kinds of auditing might require other kinds of checks—for example, the ability to critically ascertain whether an institution is acting in harmony with its published climate action plan. It is not clear that every kind of audit is a good fit for text mining, but there are indications in the existing work that automatic text mining can be used as a tool for holding institutions accountable.

Text mining can support the assessment of an institution's published reports over time. Scholars have begun to analyze the discourse, history, and political rhetoric of international organizations, drawing on the readily accessible transcripts of the World Bank and United Nations (Moretti and Pestre; Kentikelenis and Voeten). Applied to the published reports of institutions, text mining can provide important information about an institution's bias, data that raises the possibility of comparing institutions and their peers and tracing institutional orientation over time. A study of the political bias of at the BBC tracked journalists' "follows" on Twitter and reached the conclusion that "the BBC leans to the centre right" (Mills). Text mining provided an abstract metric for gauging the bias of the BBC; the metric's importance is that it allows the comparison of the BBC with other news sources, thus allowing BBC journalists and readers to make appropriate decisions about how their content might change in the future. Ratings of each newspaper's coverage of climate news in terms of political orientation, racial bias, and geographical scope—something that text mining could in theory support—would offer a valuable "report card" for auditing the progress of newspapers and other information sources, ranking each in their success at adapting to an age of climate change.

In fact, several text-mining studies have attempted to monitor responses to the climate emergency in the news media and the public at large. Faculty in forest management have used text mining to generate just-in-time histories of contemporary conflict over water, for example (Herrera et al.). A communications scholar has used text mining to analyze the effectiveness of political communication about climate (Majdik). Additional opportunities for a broad climate-emergency audit of communities and institutions might build on this work, although again the specific techniques would need to be refashioned to fit the specific questions raised by an audit that engages with questions about science, policy, and the public sphere—for example, understanding and interpreting the consequence of a right-leaning tilt in media coverage.

Perhaps the most sophisticated climate-related applications of text mining to date are those that attempt to model the varieties of causal understanding in the public realm. Here there are extremely promising techniques for the purposes of a cultural or institutional audit. A team of anthropologists and economists used diffusion models—typically used in marketing to capture expectations of dissemination and response—to measure the relative distribution of words collocated with a discourse of changing climate (Bentley et al.). The process allowed them to date moments of peak diffusion relative not to word count or proportion but rather the momentum of word dissemination. They traced what they believe to be a bias against discourse about the "global" and "adaptation" during recent years and argued that advocates of environmental policy work to define and disseminate the language of environmental awareness with an intensity that promotes "social learning" and allows certain patterns of speech and thought "to spread." (Bentley et al., 7). Meanwhile, a sociologist has used social network analysis to identify communities associated with "misinformation" about climate change in philanthropy circles over the past twenty years (Farrell). Other scholars have applied the word-counting techniques to the problem of understanding resistance to climate change (Houser, *Infowhelm*). Studies of this kind offer a diagnostic of the spread and containment of misinformation about climate, thus adding to the potentially automated tools for auditing corrupted institutions and communities using their written discourse.

As we can see, across academia, multiple disciplines are turning toward text mining as a tool for making sense of climate change, for assessing public discourse, and for providing pragmatic responses. In disciplines ranging from civil engineering to literature, text mining has contributed to the cause of helping individuals and institutions to reckon with real-time opportunities for action around climate change. But the vast majority of studies of this kind come from computer science, data science, and information science.

Not all of the text-mining examples given here would meet the standards of rigorous textual analysis in the digital humanities in terms of content, rhetoric, and authorship. The landfill study (Richter, Ng, and Fallah) ranks all writing under an artificial metric of "readability" based on scores similar to those generated in the Microsoft Word grammar check. Readability scores make a poor substitute for discourse analysis, let alone a careful examination of the life of the data or a slow-grown examination of when and how a delay occurred in a political process—as DH approaches might explore. More generally, many of these text-mining studies demonstrate a weak engagement with the discursive elements of text. Such work is often characterized by simplistic measures ("readability scores" and "sentiment analysis" as opposed to deeper and historical discourse analysis), motivated by naive questions (How to save money on landfills? What would the public support, as opposed to how and when do cultures change? What is the work of science?), and informed by weak models of how concepts or science work in the world (through public opinion alone versus through a detailed inspection of the life of competing institutions, science, models, and data).

The relative lack of sophistication of many text-mining projects with respect to linguistic rhetoric and cultural expression reflects the strong need for interdisciplinary work in which scholars of discourse, history, and culture collaborate with information scientists. Digital humanists have much to contribute—indeed, humanists in general do. Humanistic skills of text mining, inspecting discourses over time, and comparing different styles of engagement are precisely the skills that are presently lacking in efforts to apply text mining to climate change. Indeed, recent publications by digital humanists demonstrate ample skill sets at analyzing and comparing the bias of textual data over time. In the disciplines of sociology and literature, scholars have applied text mining to group change in discourse about gender, race, and class over the twentieth century (Evans and Aceves; Kraicer and Piper; So, Long, and Zhuet). The skillful analysis of discourse in recent DH publications could usefully be applied to text mining the reports of public institutions about climate change with the consequence of creating data of genuine importance to political action.

Participatory Infrastructure

An additional opportunity for pragmatic engagement comes from the world of building critical infrastructure for members of the public to interact with the data generated by any text-mining projects that model the changing discourse of climate change. Researchers in various subjects have, in recent decades, created web portals to data that allow ordinary people outside the academy to investigate data, as rendered through a model endorsed by the scholar. In a recent paper, I suggest that such exploratory open datasets exemplify a range of scholarly, humanistic, and democratic values about replicability of research, transparency with respect to the origin of documentation, and accessibility of scholarship for a range of public purposes. Infrastructure building of this kind thus constitutes a mode of scholarly argumentation in which the work of scholarship is potentially replicated across hundreds of thousands of other uses (Guldi, "Scholarly Infrastructure").

Infrastructures of this kind abound in certain domains of the academy—especially in the digital humanities, where literary scholars have focused on making tools for basic text mining of the literary canon accessible to all, among them Voyant Tools, the Hathi Trust, and multiple JSTOR Labs projects. By creating data infrastructures where citizens can explore data about texts for themselves, builders of sites for topic modeling and other forms of textual analysis not only analyze the institutions around them, but they also make it possible for ordinary citizens to replicate that analysis at a detailed level. By expanding access to the tools of analysis from the few to the many, infrastructure extends the possibility that activists, journalists, and other citizens will use text mining analytics to make sense of how democratic institutions work, bringing a multitude of silences and omissions to light.

Digital humanists have beautifully demonstrated the applicability of their toolsets to traditional questions in the humanities. They have striven to make their tools accessible to students and colleagues with little technical training. They have worked hard to tailor their toolkits to humanistic questions—for instance, the identification of "discourses" and "genres." And they have begun the question of bridging DH toolsets with the leading political questions of the day—for example, the enduring bias toward whiteness and patriarchy of the American publishing industry. But a pragmatic tilt holds up a higher bar still. Where is the publicly accessible tool for tracking the discourse of climate science and climate action in the media or law? Were digital humanists to take up this question, we would contribute significant talents of discourse analysis to the public debate.

Drawing on decades of "participatory research" in the postcolonial world, citizen-science infrastructure is sometimes interwoven with workshops (called "barn raisings" at Public Lab) that specifically invite minoritized and other underprivileged populations to actively design research programs around a community's specific needs and to collect data according to that program (Guldi, "A History of the Participatory Map"). In our era, the least powerful groups in society often occupy the least habitable landscapes for reasons of poverty, access, and power; they are doomed to inhabit terrain made toxic because of the limited inquiry of science and the regulatory failures of government (Pellow; Checker; Taylor; Waldron; Gilio-Whitaker; Washington; Cooper and Aronson). Citizens' groups have used participatory maps as the basis for organizing and pursuing lawsuits against local polluters, as in the case of fishermen in southern India suing the local tannery over effluents (Narayanasamy).

In the university, however, climate science rarely supports or interfaces with these groups, although a small number of scholars, many of them in relationship with Indigenous or ethnic groups, have begun to highlight the strength of person-to-person relationships in these communities as a source for a larger civil politics capable of countering threats to the environment (Golumbia and Koh; Senier).

One important source of theory on how research and infrastructure can be bridged is the "critical infrastructure" discourse associated with Alan Liu and other digital humanists, whose community has routinely engaged in building websites and communities for the sharing of knowledge and whose ideas about web infrastructure align well with the task of pragmatic criticism. Digital humanists have much to offer in this space, having launched projects that are inclusive along the lines of gender and race and that question the legacy of empire using data-driven means (Despain; So, Long, and Zhuet; Risam). They engage in the creation of datasets, the programming of infrastructure, and the writing of algorithms, forms of praxis that resemble poiesis and criticism in their ability to be reproduced. In their instance as tools, algorithmic criticism also offers an ability to affect the world, rendering action at a distance, as Heidegger might argue, as of the hammer as an extension of the arm. In Margaret Linley's phrase, tools such as data and infrastructure "shape human perception and cognition, forms of discourse, and patterns of social behavior" (413). But data, infrastructure, and algorithms can also reshape models, redounding into worlds of expert consensus. They can create new publics or commons where information is shared and exchanged.

Toward a Pragmatic Tilt

Can a pragmatic tilt across the university as a whole—deploying the skills of digital humanists and information scientists together to analyze public discourse in real time—meet the demands of the climate emergency that confront us? Pragmatic precedents in the digital humanities can usefully guide us toward those actions and spheres of intervention where our work would be most expedient, given the urgent need for political action to limit carbon emissions . There are opportunities here where digital humanists—and their allies in design, data analysis, and the humanities more generally—can usefully apply their talents in data gathering, narrative, and critical analysis to engage with local communities in such a way as to bear actionable witness to the reforms that are needed. Pragmatic work requires networks of builders from a range of disciplines, including the analysis of data, the building and design of interfaces, as well as a rich understanding of the contemporary desires of a variety of engaged communities on the ground who might offer their energies as participants if the data and its analysis were tailored to meet their needs.

BIBLIOGRAPHY

Adamson, Joni. "Networking Networks and Constellating New Practices in the Environmental Humanities." *PMLA* 131, no. 2 (2016): 347–55.

Ahmed, Manan, Maira E. Álvarez, Sylvia A. Fernández, Alex Gil, Merisa Martinez, Moacir P. de Sá Pereira, Linda Rodriguez, and Roopika Risam. "Torn Apart / Separados." 2018, https://xpmethod.columbia.edu/torn-apart/volume/2/.

Applegate, Matthew. *Guerrilla Theory: Political Concepts, Critical Digital Humanities.* Evanston, Ill.: Northwestern University Press, 2019.

Asayama, Shinichiro, R. Bellamy, O. Geden, Warren Pearce, and Mike Hulme. "Why Setting a Climate Deadline Is Dangerous." *Nature Climate Change,* 9 (2019): 570–72, https://doi.org/10.1038/s41558-019-0543-4.

Bentley, R. Alexander, Philip Garnett, Michael J. O'Brien, and William A. Brock. "Word Diffusion and Climate Science." *PLOS ONE* 7, no. 11 (2012): e47966, https://doi.org/10.1371/journal.pone.0047966.

Braasch, Gary. "Climate Change: Is Seeing Believing?" *Bulletin of the Atomic Scientists* 69, no. 6 (2013): 33–41.

Bullard, Robert D. *Dumping in Dixie: Race, Class, And Environmental Quality.* London: Routledge, 1990.

Camacho, David Enrique Cuesta. *Environmental Injustices, Political Struggles: Race, Class, and the Environment.* Durham, N.C.: Duke University Press, 1998.

Checker, Melissa. *Polluted Promises: Environmental Racism and the Search for Justice in a Southern Town.* New York: NYU Press, 2005.

Cooper, Candy J., and Marc Aronson. *Poisoned Water: How the Citizens of Flint, Michigan, Fought for Their Lives and Warned the Nation.* New York: Bloomsbury, 2020.

Cooper, David. "Digital Literary Cartographies: Mapping British Romanticism." In *The Routledge Handbook of Literature and Space*, edited by Robert T. Tally, Jr. London: Routledge, 2017.

Despain, Jessica. "A Feminist Digital Humanities Pedagogy beyond the Classroom." *Transformations: The Journal of Inclusive Scholarship and Pedagogy* 26, no. 1 (2016): 64–73, https://doi.org/10.1353/tnf.2016.0013.

Edmond, Jennifer. "CENDARI's Grand Challenges: Building, Contextualising and Sustaining a New Knowledge Infrastructure." *International Journal of Humanities and Arts Computing* 7, no. 1–2 (2013): 58–69, https://doi.org/10.3366/ijhac.2013.0081.

Engle, Robert F. III, et al. *Hedging Climate Change News.* Working Paper, 25734, National Bureau of Economic Research, Apr. 2019. National Bureau of Economic Research, https://doi.org/10.3386/w25734.

Evans, James A., and Pedro Aceves. "Machine Translation: Mining Text for Social Theory." *Annual Review of Sociology* 42, no. 1 (2016): 21–50, https://doi.org/10.1146/annurev-soc-081715-074206.

Farrell, Justin. "The Growth of Climate Change Misinformation in US Philanthropy: Evidence from Natural Language Processing." *Environmental Research Letters* 14, no. 3 (2019): 034013, https://doi.org/10.1088/1748-9326/aaf939.

Forman, Zaria. "Flying with Operation Icebridge." *ASAP/Journal* 3, no. 3 (2018): 480–83.

Gil, Alex, and Élika Ortega. "Global Outlooks in Digital Humanities: Multilingual Practices and Minimal Computing." In *Doing Digital Humanities,* 58–70. London: Routledge, 2016.

Gilio-Whitaker, Dina. *As Long as Grass Grows: The Indigenous Fight for Environmental Justice from Colonization to Standing Rock.* Boston: Beacon Press, 2019.

Gold, Matthew K., and Lauren F. Klein. "Introduction: A DH That Matters." In *Debates in the Digital Humanities 2019,* edited by Matthew K. Gold and Lauren F. Klein. Minneapolis: University of Minnesota Press, 2019, https://dhdebates.gc.cuny.edu/read/untitled-f2acf72c-a469-49d8-be35-67f9ac1e3a60/section/0cd11777-7d1b-4f2c-8fdf-4704e827c2c2#intro.

Golumbia, David, and Adeline Koh. "Postcolonial Studies, Digital Humanities, and the Politics of Language." *Postcolonial Digital Humanities* (blog). May 31, 2013, https://dhpoco.org/blog/2013/05/31/postcolonial-studies-digital-humanities-and-the-politics-of-language/.

Graziani, Terra, and Mary Shi. "Data for Justice." *ACME: An International Journal for Critical Geographies* 19, no. 1 (2020): 397–412.

Grubert, Emily, and Mark Algee-Hewitt. "Villainous or Valiant? Depictions of Oil and Coal in American Fiction and Nonfiction Narratives." *Energy Research & Social Science* 31 (2017): 100–10, https://doi.org/10.1016/j.erss.2017.05.030.

Guldi, Jo. "A History of the Participatory Map." *Public Culture* 29 (2017): 79–112, https://doi.org/10.1215/08992363-3644409.

Guldi, Jo. "Scholarly Infrastructure as Critical Argument: Nine Principles in a Preliminary Survey of the Bibliographic and Critical Values Expressed by Scholarly Web-Portals for Visualizing Data." *Digital Humanities Quarterly* 14, no. 3 (2020), http://digitalhumanities.org:8081/dhq/vol/14/3/000463/000463.html.

Haunschild, Robin, Loet Leydesdorff, Lutz Bornmann, Iina Hellsten, and Werner Marx. "Does the Public Discuss Other Topics on Climate Change than Researchers? A Comparison of Explorative Networks Based on Author Keywords and Hashtags." *Journal of Informetrics* 13, no. 2 (2019): 695–707.

Herrera, Mauricio, Cristian Candia, Diego Rivera, Douglas Aitken, Daniel Brieba, Camila Boettiger, Guillermo Donoso, and Alex Godoy-Faúndez. "Understanding Water Disputes in Chile with Text and Data Mining Tools." *Water International* 44, no. 3 (2019): 302–20, https://doi.org/10.1080/02508060.2019.1599774.

Houser, Heather. "Climate Visualizations as Cultural Objects." *Teaching Climate Change in the Humanities,* edited by Stephen Siperstein, Shane Hall, and Stephanie LeMenager. London: Routledge, 2015, https://www.taylorfrancis.com/books/e/9781317423232.

Houser, Heather. *Infowhelm: Environmental Art and Literature in an Age of Data.* New York: Columbia University Press, 2020.

James, William. *Pragmatism: A New Name for Some Old Philosophy, Old Ways of Thinking: Popular Lectures on Philosophy.* New York: Longmans, Green, 1907.

Kentikelenis, Alexander, and Erik Voeten. "Legitimacy Challenges to the Liberal World Order: Evidence from United Nations Speeches, 1970–2018." *Review of International Organizations* 16 (2020): 721–54, https://doi.org/10.1007/s11558-020-09404-y.

Kraicer, Eve, and Andrew Piper. "Social Characters: The Hierarchy of Gender in Contemporary English-Language Fiction." *Journal of Cultural Analytics* 3, no. 2 (2018), https://doi.org/10.22148/16.032.

Lee, Crystal, Tanya Yang, Gabrielle Inchoco, Graham M. Jones, and Arvind Satyanarayan. "Viral Visualizations: How Coronavirus Skeptics Use Orthodox Data Practices to Promote Unorthodox Science Online." *ACM Human Factors in Computing Systems (CHI).* 2021.

Lerner, Steve. *Sacrifice Zones: The Front Lines of Toxic Chemical Exposure in the United States.* Cambridge, Mass.: MIT Press, 2012.

Lethbridge, Emily, and Steven Hartman. "Inscribing Environmental Memory in the Icelandic Sagas and the *Icelandic Saga Map*." *PMLA* 131, no. 2 (2016): 381–91, https://doi.org/10.1632/pmla.2016.131.2.381.

Linley, Margaret. "Ecological Entanglements of DH." In *Debates in the Digital Humanities 2016*, edited by Matthew K. Gold and Lauren F. Klein, 410–37. Minneapolis: University of Minnesota Press, 2016.

Liu, Alan. "Toward Critical Infrastructure Studies." Paper presented at the North American Society for the Study of Romanticism, April 21, 2018, https://cistudies.org/wp-content/uploads/Toward-Critical-Infrastructure-Studies.pdf.

Maharawal, Manissa M., and Erin McElroy. "The Anti-Eviction Mapping Project: Counter Mapping and Oral History toward Bay Area Housing Justice." *Annals of the American Association of Geographers* 108, no. 2 (2018): 380–89, https://doi.org/10.1080/24694452.2017.1365583.

Majdik, Zoltan P. "A Computational Approach to Assessing Rhetorical Effectiveness: Agentic Framing of Climate Change in the Congressional Record, 1994–2016." *Technical Communication Quarterly* 28, no. 3 (2019): 207–22, https://doi.org/10.1080/10572252.2019.1601774.

McElroy, Erin. "Countermapping Displacement and Resistance in Alameda County with the Anti-Eviction Mapping Project." *American Quarterly* 70, no. 3 (2018): 601–4, https:/doi.org/10.1353/aq.2018.0039.

Mills, Tom. "What the BBC Can Learn from Its Journalists' Use of Twitter." *The Guardian*. 2020, https://www.theguardian.com/commentisfree/2020/dec/02/bbc-journalists-twitter-study-reporters.

Moretti, Franco, and Dominique Pestre. "Bankspeak: The Language of World Bank Reports." *New Left Review* 92, no. 2 (2015): 75–99.

Narayanasamy, N. *Participatory Rural Appraisal: Principles, Methods and Application*. Los Angeles: SAGE Publications, 2009.

Nowviskie, Bethany. "Digital Humanities in the Anthropocene." *Bethany Nowviskie* (blog) July 10, 2014, http://nowviskie.org/2014/anthropocene/.

Pellow, David N. *Garbage Wars: The Struggle for Environmental Justice in Chicago*. Cambridge, Mass.: MIT Press, 2004.

Peterson, Beth. *Dispatches from the End of Ice: Essays*. San Antonio: Trinity University Press, 2019.

Posthumus, Stephanie, Stéfan Sinclair, and Veronica Poplawski. "Digital and Environmental Humanities: Strong Networks, Innovative Tools, Interactive Objects." *Resilience: A Journal of the Environmental Humanities* 5, no. 2 (2018): 156–71.

Richter, Amy, Kelvin Tsun Wai Ng, and Bahareh Fallah. "Bibliometric and Text Mining Approaches to Evaluate Landfill Design Standards." *Scientometrics* 118, no. 3 (2019): 1027–49, https://doi.org/10.1007/s11192-019-03011-4.

Risam, Roopika. *New Digital Worlds: Postcolonial Digital Humanities in Theory, Praxis, and Pedagogy*. Evanston, Ill.: Northwestern University Press, 2019, http://www.jstor.org/stable/10.2307/j.ctv7tq4hg.

Schreibman, Susan, Stefan Gradmann, Steffen Hennicke, Tobias Blanke, Sally Chambers, Alastair Dunning, Jonathan Gray, Gerhard Lauer, Alois Pichler, and Jürgen Renn. "Beyond Infrastructure–Modelling Scholarly Research and Collaboration." Conference paper hal-00801439. Digital Humanities 2013, University of Nebraska-Lincoln, July 2013, https://hal.inria.fr/hal-00801439.

Senier, Siobhan. "Dawnland Voices 2.0: Sovereignty and Sustainability Online." *PMLA* 131, no. 2 (2016): 392–400, https://doi.org/10.1632/pmla.2016.131.2.392.

So, Richard Jean, Hoyt Long, and Yuancheng Zhuet. "Race, Writing, and Computation: Racial Difference and the U.S. Novel, 1880–2000." *Journal of Cultural Analytics* 3, no. 2 (2019), https://doi.org/10.22148/16.031.

Starosielski, Nicole. "Resource Operations of the Ecological Digital Humanities." *PMLA* 131, no. 2 (2016): 401–9, https://doi.org/10.1632/pmla.2016.131.2.401.

Taylor, Dorceta. *Toxic Communities: Environmental Racism, Industrial Pollution, and Residential Mobility.* New York: NYU Press, 2014.

Waldron, Ingrid R. G. *There's Something in the Water: Environmental Racism in Indigenous and Black Communities.* Halifax, Nova Scotia: Fernwood Publishing, 2018.

Warren, Christopher N. "Historiography's Two Voices: Data Infrastructure and History at Scale in the Oxford Dictionary of National Biography (ODNB)." *Journal of Cultural Analytics* 3, no. 1 (2018), https:/doi.org/10.22148/16.028.

Washington, Harriet A. *A Terrible Thing to Waste: Environmental Racism and Its Assault on the American Mind.* Boston: Little, Brown, 2019.

PART III][*Chapter 14*

Digital Art History as Disciplinary Practice

EMILY PUGH

The relationship between digital humanities and individual humanities disciplines, both structurally and intellectually, is an uneven one. In the case of art history—the subject of this chapter—two parallel worlds seem to exist. In one part of the discipline, digital humanities and digital art history are accepted and even embraced, while in another (which is also the mainstream of art history) they are at best ignored, at worst rejected entirely. The existence of these two parallel worlds is evidenced by, and to some extent a product of, the discourse around digital art history. On one side of the debate are articles, journal issues, and reports, authored by art historians and information professionals such as Diane M. Zorich, Murtha Baca, Johanna Drucker, Pamela Fletcher, and Anne Helmreich, that argue for the adoption of "digital tools and methods" in the mainstream of art history.[1] On the other side are the criticisms of the use of technology for art-historical research, as articulated most explicitly by art historian Claire Bishop in her article "Against Digital Art History," published first in 2017 on the website of the Franklin Humanities Institute and again in 2018 in the *International Journal of Digital Art History*.[2] The two sides of this discourse largely unfold within separate spheres, and on the rare occasions when these critics engage directly with one another, they do not seem to have a shared understanding of the terms of the debate. For example, in the exchange between Drucker and Bishop published in the 2019 edition of *Debates in the Digital Humanities* as "A Conversation on Digital Art History," the two scholars at times talk past one another, as if engaged in two separate conversations.

Moreover, both proponents and skeptics alike often conflate digital art history with digital technology broadly conceived, discussing the use of computing as a phenomenon that is external to disciplinary practice. This perception, however, belies the fact that all kinds of digital technologies, from email to digital cameras, from online library catalogs to PowerPoint, are integral to almost every aspect of contemporary practice in art history and indeed all humanities disciplines. Any lingering doubts regarding scholars' reliance on digitized information or online repository access have likely been dispelled in recent years, as measures enacted as a result of

Covid-19 made in-person visits to libraries, archives, and museums impossible. As should now be clear to us all, no one can opt out of technology in the contemporary moment, regardless of their attitudes toward it or toward the digital humanities. At the same time, no one would argue that the use of something like PowerPoint itself constitutes digital humanities practice. This begs the question: What *does* constitute such a practice? Where do the borders between the mere use of technology and digital humanities practice lie? How much of current disciplinary practice is already embedded in, for example, the logics of computation and digitally encoded information?

To address these questions, this chapter proposes to initiate a discourse that considers not only questions of technology but questions of disciplinary practice that technological development has made more apparent or more pressing. Such a discourse might address, for example, the post-processing methods used to create digital images of artworks in imaging studios of museums, how the use of computer vision for processing archival materials influences how such archives are searched or how scholars interpret the results, or the influence that digital reformatting of materials like Betamax videos or an architect's 1980s-era computer-aided design (CAD) drawings can have on the interpretation and analysis of such sources. As issues that influence how art-historical knowledge is produced and disseminated, these are of interest to all art historians, whether or not they are specialists in digital art history. Addressing such issues entails critiques of technological tools and processes but also engagement with questions related to evidence, certainty, and argumentation that phenomena like computer vision or digital imaging raise.

Strengthening the connections between the practices and concerns of the mainstream of art history and those of digital art history is key to facilitating a more robust, incisive, and productive discourse, one that provides a clearer picture of the challenges, dangers, and potential of the use of computational approaches to the research and study of art history and the humanities more broadly. Three strategies in particular will help strengthen those connections: (1) use of more precise terminology and a general avoidance of the word *digital*; (2) the embrace of conceptual frameworks that are based not on all-or-nothing binaries but on ranges of possibility; (3) the establishment and development of areas of inquiry that historicize tools and methods associated with the digital humanities and connect them with disciplinary concerns.

Strategy 1. Use Precise Terms to Facilitate Incisive Discourse

The field of digital humanities in large part resulted from the recognition, by librarians, archivists, scholars, and others, of technology as a force that implicates the humanities as a whole, cutting across disciplinary and institutional boundaries and across multiple stages of practice, from research to publishing. The establishment of digital humanities as a field over the past twenty or so years—the creation of digital humanities institutions, positions at universities, publishing outlets, and funding mechanisms—is one result of this widespread realization. However, the emergence of digital humanities as a field has arguably also had the effect of reinforcing the impression among some that the digital humanities, including subfields like digital art history, exist apart from normative disciplinary activities. For example, although she does not explicitly define the term in her 2012 report, "Transitioning to a Digital World: Art History, Its Research Centers, and Digital Scholarship," Diane M. Zorich discusses digital art history as a discrete entity that exists apart from the discipline itself. Writing of art history's "ambivalence about digital art history," she maintains that "those who believe in the potential of digital art history feel it will open up new avenues of inquiry and scholarship, allow greater access to art historical information, provide broader dissemination of scholarly research, and enhance undergraduate and graduate teaching" (6). Similarly, Claire Bishop comments in "Against Digital Art History" that "practitioners of digital art history have a limited awareness of critical debates within art history," a statement that implies such practitioners are non-art historians (125).

Statements like Zorich's and Bishop's help create the impression of two art histories: one digital and one nondigital. Framed in this way, any use of technology is external to art history, brought into the discipline only *via* digital art history. Furthermore, all things related to digital technologies—hardware, software, data, methodologies like social network analysis, digitization of library and archival materials—are conflated within a single, undifferentiated category. As art historian Pamela Fletcher notes, these diverse things and activities have been collapsed in art-historical discourse, at least, into the concept of "the digital."[3] Thus, the word *digital* is deployed as a catchall term used to refer to any project, tool, or method that involves the use of computers. Projects are often titled "Digital X."[4] Critics and practitioners discuss "digital projects" when referring to a wide range of initiatives that involve different aspects of the scholarly process (e.g., research, scholarly communication), formats (e.g., websites, epubs), methods (e.g., social network analysis, topic modeling), computing applications (e.g., databases, programming, computer vision), and outcome types (e.g., publications, teaching tools, research platforms).[5]

As a result of this leveling, critiques of digital art history muddle together concepts and issues that are at best loosely related. In their "Conversation on Digital Art History," for example, Drucker and Bishop address an astounding range and variety of topics, from labor practices and graduate student training to the use of data and databases to support research, methods of computational analysis, neoliberalism, funding sources for digital humanities, and the materiality of objects. Indeed, Drucker points out to Bishop that "dismissing 'digital art history' as if it is singular or monolithic does not do justice to the complex variety of work being done and its proven and potential value." As Drucker suggests, a debate that treats such disparate phenomena as equivalents is a blunted one, limited to high-level, unspecific, or scattershot critiques that obfuscate rather than clarify what is at stake in the encounter between digital technologies and art-historical research and scholarship.

Furthermore, within this unfocused discourse, projects and publications are often defined by (or confined to) their "digital-ness"—that is, their computerized format or means of production—rather than on the extent to which an author or project team has engaged critically with a particular method or taken advantage of some affordance specific to the digital environment. In "Against Digital Art History," for example, Bishop takes issue with the network diagram presented as part of the 2012–2013 exhibition *Inventing Abstraction* at the Museum of Modern Art (MoMA), arguing that with the diagram, "carefully reasoned historical narrative is replaced by social network (the avant-garde equivalent of LinkedIn) and has no room for non-human agents that elude quantification" (125). Bishop points to this diagram as a failure of "digital art history," yet her analysis does not distinguish between a critique of the use of social network theory as a methodology and the related but separate critique of the digital means through which the social network diagram was created—for example, of the software application or dataset used to produce it. It remains unclear if what Bishop finds problematic is the digital components of the diagram, its underlying methodology, or both.

Compare Bishop's assessment with a similar one authored by art historians Nicole E. Reiner and Jonathan Patkowski. In their critique of the *Inventing Abstraction* diagram, Reiner and Patkowski agree with Bishop that the diagram problematically injects into the exhibition a set of neoliberal attitudes toward labor and art-making and moreover, in doing so, excludes non-European objects (8). However, the two scholars level their critique specifically at social network theory rather than at "the digital" overall. In articulating their position, they provide a thorough analysis both of social network theory as a method and how it was applied in this case, contextualizing their argument within art-historical discourse by referencing, for example, critical appraisals of contemporary museum practice authored by sociologist Tony Bennett and art historian Carol Duncan (Reiner and Patkowski, 12). Of course, Reiner and Patkowski's article is devoted entirely to the *Inventing Abstraction* diagram, as opposed to Bishop's article, which mentions the diagram only briefly. However, this reflects another issue that results from defining something like the MoMA diagram in vague terms as a "digital art history approach." When a variety of disparate initiatives, methods, and tools are collapsed into the same broad category of "the digital," discourse remains stuck at an abstract level. The specificity of Reiner and Patkowski's analysis exemplifies the kind of critical engagement that would facilitate a more robust and productive discourse on digital art history.

Like the use of the phrase "digital art history approach" to characterize the MoMA diagram, the use of terms like "digital method" can, directly and indirectly, often encourage rhetorical conflation. In fact there is no such thing as a digital method, although there are methodologies that rely more heavily than others on technological tools. Social network analysis, for example, is a method that is particularly well served by computer-based tools like AllegroGraph or Gephi, but the approach is not a wholly digital one. Social network theory has roots in the nineteenth and early twentieth centuries, having emerged from the discipline of sociology as a way to model and research the way humans interact and behave in groups.[6] Like any established methodology, social network theory is associated with a specialized bibliography and a specific critical discourse, both of which stand apart from, although they are linked to, the digital humanities.

Of course, it is important and necessary to investigate the mutual influence between a research methodology and the various tools used to apply it. The key in doing so is to distinguish between the two and not to confuse one with the other. It is entirely appropriate to critique the MoMA's specific application of social network theory, as Reiner and Patkowski do, or to debate whether the methodology is appropriate for use in art history. However, it is important to recognize this kind of methodological critique is not necessarily the same thing as a critique of digital art history. Indeed, a critique of "digital art history" is akin to disciplinary shadowboxing: an argument with a convenient but insubstantial phantom. Rather than engage in a critique of "digital art history," what is needed is a discourse around technology that investigates the precise ways in which particular software platforms or computational techniques intersect with concerns that are specific to our discipline.

In her article "Keeping Our Eyes Open: Visualizing Networks and Art History," art historian Stephanie Porras provides an example of the kind of critique I mean. Porras presents a cogent analysis of the use of network diagrams and data visualization in her field of early modern Flemish art. Similar to Reiner and Patkowski, Porras does not suggest that either visualizations of datasets or network analyses are inherently problematic. Rather, she presents a critique of several different research initiatives, examining the data used for each, how that data was visualized, and the relationship of both to the underlying research questions the individual scholars were using their networks and visualizations to explore.

Porras's article explores the positives and negatives of these projects, citing the specific kinds of research questions that these approaches can be used to investigate. Even as she points to the potential of data visualization for "exposing creative, social and economic collaborations that may have previously been marginalized," Porras cautions against the thoughtless or uncritical use of data-driven analyses (42). She furthermore argues that scholars who engage in these practices need to ground their approach in a thorough understanding of where their data came from and what it represents, as well as being "transparent about the limitations and biases of their datasets" (48). Moreover, she connects her critique to concerns specific to the field of Flemish art history and to her own research, noting, for example, the differences between the sources and datasets she has found in European institutions versus those she has found in Peru or the Philippines.

Porras's critique is less an examination of digital technology per se and more an exploration of the questions related to evidence, argumentation, veracity, and standards (or lack thereof) that are raised by the practices and tools associated with data visualizations. What results from her critique is a clear picture of the kinds of interventions that would be necessary to realize the potential of data-driven research in art history. For example, Porras's article illustrates the importance of educating art historians in data literacy, since art historians need to know how to collect, edit, normalize, analyze, and share data in order to understand the potentials and biases contained in their datasets. Her article also demonstrates the need for shared standards and infrastructures for the use of research data in art history, which together would create a disciplinary framework in which art historians could expose the processes by which they have collected and analyzed their datasets in ways that could be understood by their colleagues. Porras, like Reiner and Patkowski, asks not so much *whether* technology was used but explores *how* and *why* it was used. More of this kind of precise analysis of the intersection between discipline-specific concerns and practices and the use of digital technologies would counteract the current fuzzy state of discourse.

The adjective "digital" is a useful term when it is signaling issues that concern multiple aspects related to the use of technology in humanities research and scholarship at a high conceptual level. Including the term "digital" or "digital humanities" in a project title or description can also be a means of attracting resources or attention to that project, as in grant applications. In addition, the term "digital art history" is a useful and necessary one, referring to a subfield of digital humanities whose practitioners—a group that includes art historians, information specialists, and computer scientists, among other experts—focus on the development and refinement of computational tools, practices, and systems designed to facilitate art-historical research and scholarship in the discipline as a whole. This work includes building tools and platforms, using them to conduct as well as publish research; crucially, it also includes establishing and sharing effective practices and standards so that these tools and platforms can be critically appraised, not only by those using them, but also by those working in the mainstream of art history.

To date, those involved in digital art history have understandably focused more on developing and using tools, practices, and systems, and far less on the kinds of activities that would integrate these with existing standards and infrastructures of art history. Yet activities related to such integration are crucial if we are to both leverage the potential and avoid the pitfalls of using computing technologies in our scholarly work. Digital art history, that is, cannot exist hived off from art history as it currently is, to a large extent. To achieve a deeper integration of art history with digital humanities, we must understand digital technologies as the result of ongoing historical processes and within their cultural, social, and political contexts. Rather than thinking only in terms of "the digital," we must think of technological change in a more historical and socially and culturally inflected sense, to encompass, for example, both analog photography and digital imaging, or the physical printing of books as well as the production of online publications using static site generators.

Critical engagement with technologies of image production and knowledge production and dissemination is something many art historians already do. Our discipline has long been concerned with the relationships among materials, practices, tools, and techniques of artistic production and how they each (and together) inform the appearance and meaning of the artworks that result. As the next section will demonstrate, we should apply the methods of our own field to develop a nuanced discourse on digital art history that avoids conceptualizations centered on either/or, yes/no propositions. In other words, we should think in analog terms about the digital.

Strategy 2. Employ Frameworks Based on "Both/And" Instead of "Either/Or"

The notion that the use of technology exists apart from disciplinary practice fuels the perception that humanistic disciplines like art history and "the digital" are fundamentally incompatible, with the former defined by notions like subjectivity, open-ended inquiry, human intuition and invention and the latter linked to objectivity, the end of ambiguity and nuance, the replacement of humans by machines, and the dominance of corporations like Google.[7] For example, critics writing about digital art history, or digital humanities more generally, often dismiss computational approaches as overly reductive and flattening in comparison with traditional approaches and portray those engaged in projects associated with digital humanities as naively fascinated by technology.[8] Those praising digital art history, such as Zorich and Helmreich, traffic in similar dichotomies, characterizing the mainstream of art history as overly conservative and "slow" to embrace the technology, for example, in comparison with digital art history, which is treated as inherently more innovative and collaborative.[9] The Manichaean terms of this debate leave little room for ambiguity. Furthermore, they create a scenario wherein the daily use of technology is invisible while other, more specialized applications are defined only in terms of the presence of technology.

"Both/and" formulations would help foster a discourse that resists polarizing binaries and focuses our attention instead on the ways that categories such as digital/analog, science/humanities, machine/human, and materiality/immateriality might not be mutually exclusive but in fact may shape one another in fundamental ways. Considering where, for example, exactitude becomes nuance, where and how data is transformed into knowledge, or where the virtual shades into the material (or vice versa) can create a more robust discourse that foregrounds the interconnectedness of these apparent dualities. Finally, conceptualizing digital humanities debates in terms of "both/and" creates a discourse around technology and humanities practice that can address a broader range of activities, from our daily use of digital technologies, like PowerPoint for slide lectures, to the more computationally or expertise-intensive practices commonly associated with the digital humanities.[10]

Art history already brings together the open-ended, subjective, and qualitative practices associated with the humanities with the precise, objective, and quantitative practices thought of as the purview of the sciences. Elizabeth Mansfield makes this point in her essay "Art History and Modernism" in the edited volume *Art History and Its Institutions: Foundations of a Discipline.* She argues that art-historical practice "combines the authenticating and valuating mission of the connoisseur, the hagiographic indulgences of the biographer, the cataloguing impulse of the botanist, the alternately reflective and reflexive tendencies of the historian, and the philosopher's willingness to calibrate aesthetic transcendence" (11). This fusion of the scientific and humanistic that characterizes art history is perhaps most apparent in the field's engagement with the art object through conservation science.

Conservators working in museums, archives, and libraries employ scientific analysis to date artworks and determine what they are made of or how they were made, with the goal of maintaining and preserving them. Analyses of paints or pigments, types of paper, and the weave patterns of canvas not only inform strategies for repairing damaged paintings or manuscripts or mitigating their physical deterioration, they can also become the basis for broader, more interpretive arguments about these objects. Conservator and art historian E. Melanie Gifford, for example, used x-radiography, false color infrared reflectography (IRR), and pigment analysis through light microscopy and scanning electron microscopy to analyze Peter Paul Rubens's *The Fall of Phaeton* (begun ca. 1604–1605, completed ca. 1610–1612) for a 2019 essay in the *Journal of Historians of Netherlandish Art.* Gifford's scientific analysis helped her develop a more precise understanding of how the painting's composition evolved; moreover, it supported her conclusion that in reworking the painting, Rubens had sought "not to update *The Fall of Phaeton* for sale but to use it for research as he sought a solution to a specific compositional problem raised by other works" (para. 8).

Gifford uses material evidence, scientifically derived, to draw subjective conclusions about Rubens's practice and the significance of *The Fall of Phaeton* within his oeuvre. Her examination of "the painting sequence and the handling of paint revealed in IRR and x-radiography" allows her to determine the order in which the various parts of the painting's composition were executed, information that forms the basis of her interpretation of Rubens's "individual working habits" (para. 25). Pigment analysis, combined with direct, visual inspection, supports Gifford's conclusion that particular passages (a figure's cloak, another's hand) convey a subjective "sense of brilliant, painterly immediacy" (para. 16).

The example of Gifford's analysis of *The Fall of Phaeton* reminds us that the divisions between the objective and subjective or scientific and humanistic are not always so neat; moreover, such categories are not inherently oppositional nor are they mutually exclusive. A particular observable characteristic, such as color, can have multiple dimensions. Color can be represented in a word like *yellow,* through a chemical notation like CdS (cadmium sulfide), as a hexadecimal notation (#FFF600), as a standardized descriptor ("vivid greenish yellow"), or a refractive index (2.529). None of these appellations are better than any other; rather, the appropriateness of one versus another depends on the argument a scholar is trying to make. Thus, in one part of her essay, Gifford cites "vermilion" as part of making a particular point, while elsewhere she mentions "red-orange strokes" (para. 20, 11). Conservation reports on *The Fall of Phaeton,* meanwhile, likely documented colors by wavelengths or chemical notations. Each of these formats exists within specific systems of analysis and interpretation, and part of our training as art historians and humanists is learning how to navigate these systems in ways that are often inflected by the practices and standards of particular disciplines.

The nuances of how such systems operate is worth remembering in the context of digital art history debate, in which information and evidence are often discussed in terms that are totalizing and that do not necessarily reference these systems. Data is (much like "the digital") treated as a monolithic entity, at once abstract and generalized, real and specific. For example, Bishop complains that in digital art history, as she defines it, "theoretical problems are steamrollered flat by the weight of data," while in a 2012 critique of the digital humanities, writer Stephen Marche defines data in a similar way as "information" that is always complete and can be "processed," in contrast to literature, which is "incomplete," "messy," and therefore data's "opposite" (Bishop, 125; Marche). Through such language, all data is characterized as overly neat and tidy and lacking in nuance. Its compilation is "mindless" rote work and thus nonintellectual.[11] This characterization of data, however, assumes that it exists in a vacuum, outside particular information systems, which it virtually never does. A data element like "CdS" is interpretable within the system of chemical notation, and the phrase "vivid greenish yellow" means something precise within the standardized vocabulary created by Inter-Society Color Council and the National Bureau of Standards. Are either of these terms overly precise or "flattening"? The question does not make sense in the abstract.

In fact, data is neither inherently neat and precise nor ambiguous and messy, but it can be characterized as either or both, depending on factors like its context, the specific research questions of the scholar using it, and the specific systems for which it was formatted.[12] The variety of systems that process data, along with the numerous standards for formatting and entering it, mean that in daily practice, data can absolutely be messy, ambiguous, or incomplete. Data can contain and express inexactness and subtlety, as in modifiers like "circa" for dates or "school of" for creators' names. Moreover, such concepts are contingent, and what is precise in one context may be ambiguous in another. The data element "school of Rembrandt" could be regarded by a researcher as very precise, and indeed the term "school of" is defined very specifically in the Getty Vocabulary Program's *Categories for the Description of Works of Art* (*CDWA*).[13] If one knew nothing else about the artwork it referred to, the designation "school of Rembrandt" would at least place the work in a particular place and time. If one's research question required knowing more about the work's author, however, this term could be considered too vague to be helpful; while "school of Rembrandt" creates a meaningful association, the nature of that association, such as how the artist came to know and be influenced by Rembrandt, is open and subjective.

Data is not inherently messy or neat, and likewise the amassing of data, in databases for example, cannot be considered either wholly rote or entirely subjective. Rather, different forms of data compilation require different degrees of objectivity and standardization versus interpretation. In art history, the catalogue raisonné is essentially a work of data compilation, yet no art historian would characterize such a project as purely mechanistic or entirely objective. At the same time, catalogues raisonnés are considered the definitive testament of an artist's oeuvre, used to help determine whether a particular artwork is authentic or a forgery. They document facts about artists and artworks but at the same time require interpretative acts. Scholars use a variety of means to ascertain authorship, for example, but such determinations are not always conclusive.[14] Thus, a single artist can be the subject of multiple catalogues raisonnés, and the debate about how many drawings are considered the work of Michelangelo can remain open, even one hundred plus years after it began. The catalogue raisonné can exist at once as a definitive and authoritative document, establishing the oeuvre of an artist, and as work of art-historical scholarship.

The either/or framing of questions related to digital art history has obscured those areas of art-historical research and scholarship that lie between the digital, objective, and definitive and the analog, subjective, and open-ended. This framing has also fueled a preponderance of what historian Gabrielle Hecht calls "rupture-talk," a term describing a discourse that unfolds in totalizing and binary terms. Hecht's use of the term is part of her analysis of the debate around nuclear weapons, which during the Cold War were discussed either as guarantors of peace or agents of annihilation but, in any case, as having "changed the world forever" (Hecht, 691). In the context of art history, rupture-talk is evident in debates that present technology as a force that that will either kill the discipline or save it from its inflexibility and irrelevance, but which regardless will wholly transform it.[15] This kind of rupture-talk is problematic, according to Hecht, not only because it creates a discourse in which complex issues are distilled into black-and-white polarities but also because it "produce[s] vacuums between the poles" (Hecht, 693). Critics focus on extremes and effectively cannot see what lies between them.

With regard to digital art history, rupture-talk has been filtered most often through a conceptualization of "digitized" versus "digital" art history suggested by Johanna Drucker in her 2013 article "Is There a 'Digital' Art History?" In it, she argues that "a clear distinction has to be made between the use of online repositories and images, which is *digitized* art history, and the use of analytic techniques enabled by computational technology that is the proper domain of *digital* art history" (7). Drucker's distinction is cited frequently in texts authored both by those who embrace the use of computational technologies for art-historical practice, such as the introduction of the *Routledge Companion to Digital Humanities and Art History,* and by those who are skeptical of it, including Bishop in "Against Digital Art

History" (Brown, 2; Bishop, 123). Regardless, those who reference it generally characterize "digitized art history" as a convenience that has only an "incidental impact" on the field, in the words of a 2014 Ithaka S+R report on "Preparing for the Future of Research Services for Art History" (Long and Schonfeld, 200). In contrast, digital art history, as Drucker defines it, is interpreted as "affecting the evolution and fundamental approaches of the discipline as a whole" (Drucker et al., 13, n1), and thus as having a greater potential to transform art history.

Filtered through Drucker's conception, rupture-talk around "the digital" and art history creates a framework in which technology is understood either to be wholly transformative or entirely incidental. As result, the continuum between these two poles and, moreover, the ways in which technology is already embedded in our art-historical practice are obscured. For example, the use of digital images and PowerPoint has been absorbed into the daily practice of art history to the extent that most art historians would not understand the use of digital images as related in any way to digital art history. Yet, this kind of daily use, especially when one considers that it takes place at the scale of the entire discipline, has a potential to be as transformative as any "analytic techniques enabled by computational technology." It is significant, for example, that art historians regularly treat these images uncritically as digitized equivalents to the 35-millimeter slide. Images of paintings, for example, are pasted into PowerPoint "slides," usually as two-dimensional, frontal-view representations, often stripped of their frames.

Around the time the use of digital images was becoming common in art history, art historian Robert S. Nelson pointed out the "profound impact" the traditional slide lecture had had on the discipline in an essay that considered questions such as "How do art historians make arguments with slides? Why do audiences accept speaker and reproduction and the conclusions they offer? And, above all, what is a slide, and how does its presence condition the entire presentation?" ("The Slide Lecture," 415). Certainly, the same kinds of questions could be asked of digital images and PowerPoint slideshows and related phenomena, such as repositories like ArtStor and, with Covid-19, the rise of Zoom-based presentations. Drucker herself argues in "Is There a 'Digital' Art History?" that "*digitization is not representation but interpretation*" (italics in original), noting that "every choice made about transforming an analog image into a digital file or, in the case of born-digital materials, creating the original format, is part of a chain of decisions." Moreover, she maintains that "these decisions carry interpretative inflection; they are not neutral or value-free, and each privileges one aspect of a digital artifact at the expense of others" (12).

I would argue that the distinction Drucker made between digitized and digital art history has been mischaracterized as a *difference.* While it is certainly true that the digitization of photographs is not the same thing as, for example, the use of a computer vision algorithm to detect similarities across a corpus of images, critics have overemphasized the difference between these two phenomena. At the very least, they are discussed as if they are wholly disconnected. However, as I have argued thus far, and as Drucker's own essay demonstrates, digitized and digital art history are deeply interconnected aspects of the same technological evolution. For one thing, the application of computationally enabled techniques like computer vision is built on and facilitated by what she calls digitized art history.

Ultimately, the set of practices and tools associated with both digitization and computational analysis are manifestations of the changed and changing interactions between the domains and systems that process and provide access to art-historical information—namely, libraries, archives, and museums—and the domains and systems in which art-historical knowledge is produced by curators, professors, critics, and other practitioners of art history. As Drucker argues, and as I have argued elsewhere, this is an ecosystem in which changes in one domain can create ripple effects across the entire system.[16] Thus, while art historians certainly do not need to theorize their use of digital images in every PowerPoint slide they create, they should neither forget that a digital image is not a direct equivalent of an analog photograph nor dismiss their reliance on such images as wholly inconsequential.

If we exclude activities like digitization from our understanding of digital art history or even digital humanities, we obscure the cultural, social, and economic circumstances that precede and are produced by processes like technical imaging or the preservation of digital data.[17] Furthermore, we exclude critical issues that fundamentally shape how or to what extent the computational tools, practices, and systems being developed in digital art history are integrated into the mainstream of art history. An example of one such issue is the labor of digitization, which is explored by digitization specialist Astrid J. Smith and English professor Bridget Whearty in Chapter 2 of this book. Smith and Whearty explicate the complex and arduous but largely unseen work that is required to transform documents, artworks, video and audio media, and other analog materials into digital formats that can be processed, cataloged, and accessed using contemporary information systems, arguing that "terms that are conventionally used in humanities scholarship obfuscate digitization and what it produces." The authors present a critical analysis of the labor of digitization in specific terms, highlighting the dependence of computational analyses on digitized materials and exposing the implications of ignoring the logistic processes and economic concerns that digitization entails.

It is understandable that critics have tended to dismiss routine uses of technology, such as the creation of a PowerPoint slide deck or the digitization of an archival document, as largely insignificant vis-à-vis scholarship. The nature and extent of technological changes can be difficult to detect in the time in which the changes are unfolding. A development that might seem transformative at the time can later appear less noteworthy; alternatively, what might seem like a minor development can in hindsight be regarded as a watershed moment. Gaining perspective can be difficult, which is one reason why grounding debates about technological change in historical contexts can be very helpful in revealing the true effects and extents of such changes. Once again, the discipline of art history already provides models for analyzing technological change and innovation within social, historical contexts. Photo historians and other scholars, for example, have explored the notion that photography existed as an idea before the invention of the camera.[18] Similarly, as I will explain in the next section, projects that are framed in such a way as to situate contemporary technologies within longer historical time frames and broader social, economic, and cultural contexts can provide insight into which aspects of modern technology's use or implementation may be more fleeting versus which might be more lasting.

Strategy 3. Situate Inquiry in Historical, Social, Economic, Cultural, and Disciplinary Contexts

In *The Railway Journey,* historian Wolfgang Schivelbusch describes nineteenth-century travelers as overwhelmed by the train, which seemed to them to have "interjected itself between the traveler and the landscape" (24). Perceived as an incursion, the train "did not appear embedded in the space of the landscape the way coach and highway [were], but seemed to strike its way through it" (37). In contrast, older travel technologies were regarded as more authentic and organic, even as "having more 'soul'" in comparison with the train, which with its "tremendous technical discipline" was thought of as "more derived, more unnatural, even more restrictive" (24, 13). The train and its related infrastructure were so physically imposing and so different from previous modes of transportation that for some travelers in the nineteenth century, their presence threw into stark relief what was being lost versus gained through technological innovation. In responding to this technological change, travelers focused their attention on its physical manifestation, what Schivelbusch terms "the machine ensemble," yet what he demonstrates with his study is that one of the most transformative and lasting effects of the train's invention was also one of its most ineffable: the "industrialization of space and time."

Similarly, those skeptical of the relevance of technology for humanities practice often view technology as an external force invading the discipline and as restrictive and soulless.[19] Moreover, they focus their critique on the computer itself and its related infrastructure—the internet, data systems, software, algorithms, or corporations like Google or Amazon. However, in directing attention on the "digital ensemble," to paraphrase Schivelbusch, there is a danger that the larger social, cultural, and economic changes that precipitated and that follow the computer's invention are not considered thoroughly enough. If projects and initiatives proceed instead from a broader historical view, modern digital technologies can be situated within a longer evolution of innovation and change that includes, for example, the invention of photography as well as the train. This kind of approach seems particularly relevant for art history, a discipline that was not only shaped by this evolution but in many ways was born of it.

While the invention of photography made distanced viewing of art objects easier and more accessible, train travel allowed more people to view art objects in situ. These two technologies not only facilitated more widespread engagement with art, they also made art history as a *discipline* possible, allowing for its development on a scale beyond that of small groups of connoisseurs and collectors. The fundamental connection between art history and technological innovation has been documented by scholars.[20] Even so, there are fewer examples of projects or scholarship that explore the mutual influence of technology and art history in more detail. Among these are the initiatives associated with Pharos, a consortium of art-historical photo archives, including the PhotoTech project of the Getty Research Institute (GRI), and Mapping Senufo, a collaborative project led by art historians Susan Elizabeth Gagliardi and Constantine Petridis that examines the artistic production of the region and people commonly designated by the term *Senufo.*

The consortium of art-historical photo archives called Pharos was formed in 2011 with the goal of bringing renewed attention to the research value of historic photo archives.[21] Photo archives contain photographic reproductions of works of art and for decades were one of the most important tools for the study of art history.[22] Within Pharos are represented some of the field's oldest and most influential photo archives, including the collections of key figures in the development of the discipline such as Bernard Berenson (Villa I Tatti, Florence), Aby Warburg (The Warburg Institute, London), and Erwin Panofsky (GRI, Los Angeles). The fourteen institutions represented in Pharos seek to digitize a significant portion of their holdings and make the resulting corpus freely available for study and research. In working together in a consortium, these institutions also collaborate and share best practices for the digitization of photo archives and for the research on the resulting digital image corpora.

I am involved in the GRI's effort to digitize and make its own photo archive available, in part through the Pharos platform. This project, called PhotoTech, includes a research initiative designed to explore a series of questions: What roles have technologies of reproduction played in, for example, the formation of the art-historical canon or biases toward Renaissance art and more specifically painting? How might digital technologies of image production but also distribution be shaping the field in fundamental ways?[23] We are interested in ways to explore the historical and historiographic influence of photo archives on the practice of art history and formation of the discipline. We are equally interested in how contemporary technologies of image analysis, such as computer vision, may be leveraged to shape current and future art-historical practices. By exploring the potentials and the limitations of computer vision in the context of the art-historical photo archive, we are able to situate our examination of this approach in the longer history of reproductive imaging technologies. As a result, our project constitutes an investigation less of technology than of visual analysis, a category that includes direct observation as well as the kinds of facilitated viewing enabled by cameras and computers.

Mapping Senufo is similar in that it both uses and interrogates the use of a particular practice: mapping. With their research, Gagliardi and Petridis seek to interrogate the appellation "Senufo," a term coined by Europeans that is used to refer to a set of West African places, people, and objects but which they argue is problematic in its evocation of a singular, ahistorical, and "timeless" cultural or ethnic group ("Mapping Senufo," 136). The scholars frame their project through mapping as a literal and conceptual practice, attempting to expose the impossibility of truly locating so-called Senufo objects and people in ways that both acknowledge colonial paradigms while resisting them. Instead of traditional, positivist maps, for example, Gagliardi and Petridis have instead focused on creating spatial representations of individual data elements to create visualizations that would challenge the notion of a single, discrete "Senufo." "Through its emphasis on specific details," argues Gagliardi, "Mapping Senufo aims to fill an intellectual void, unsettle colonial assumptions, and assess African arts with a rigor and attention to detail that parallels the rigor and attention to detail that scholars have used to study arts of Europe" ("Mapping Senufo," 136).

Mapping Senufo is an art-historical project focused on an examination of the power structures of art history—the system of galleries and museums, curators, collectors, auction houses, universities—as well as the structures of European economic and cultural power, including the art market and the act of mapping itself. It is a project that moreover provides a reminder of how entwined these structures are, as evidenced by the activities of particular collectors, colonialists, gallerists, and museum curators who created the concept of "Senufo" for particular reasons. Mapping Senufo thus provides a model for the engagement with data—museum collections data, for example, or linguistic data—that does not ignore the power structures that produced that data, that created the systems used to manage and express it, and that instrumentalized it. Gagliardi and Petridis's search for collections that contained objects labeled "Senufo," for example, led to a reflection on museum cataloguing practices, the slippery nature of data and description, and how something like cataloguing can both derive from and perpetuate colonial agendas ("Mapping Senufo," 144). Mapping Senufo is thus not only a project that employs particular technology tools, but one that examines the larger cultural, social, and economic forces that have driven technological innovation, both before and since the arrival of personal computing and the internet. As Gagliardi and Petridis's project demonstrates, exposing the larger forces that shape technological innovation and are influenced by it is a critical part of developing a more inclusive, more globally oriented art history.

In a 2016 interview on the digital humanities for the *Los Angeles Review of Books*, media critic Alexander Galloway argues that "there is one approach, which investigates the *nature* of letters and numbers, and there is another approach, which focuses on the *use* of letters and numbers for other ends" (italics in original), concluding, "I think most of [digital humanities] has been the latter" (Dinsman). Projects like Mapping Senufo and PhotoTech seek both to *use* technology and to investigate its *nature.* Art historians should initiate more of the kinds of projects that examine the power structures on which the discipline was built and has been maintained for decades. They must acknowledge computing technology as part of the daily practice of art history rather than a mere utility that individual scholars can either embrace or safely disregard. Indeed, one may think that by eschewing the use of computational analysis or engagement with digital humanities, one has shielded oneself from the harmful effects of, for example, neoliberalism, positivism, or the undue influence of corporations. In reality, however, these are phenomena with long histories that have shaped and are shaping all aspects of contemporary academia, including digital humanities but also individual humanities disciplines—art history perhaps more acutely than others.

In her exchange with Drucker, Bishop expresses her interest in "thinking through how the dominance of networked technology, especially Google Images, is exerting its own pressures on the study of art history," an interest she characterizes as outside the purview of digital humanities or digital art history, as she understands them. In fact, an exploration of the influence of Google Images has the potential to be a meaningful exploration of interest to all art historians, including those who work in the subfield of digital art history, because it addresses both the use digital technologies to conduct research and the standards of practice by which art historians find images more broadly. I could imagine one iteration of such an inquiry in which a scholar investigates the algorithms that drive a Google Image search, how they operate, and the kinds of image corpora that do, or do not, populate the results of such searches. Another scholar might approach the same question by exploring such searches within the longer history of image repositories, exploring the holdings of art-historical photo archives and comparing what a search for Johannes Vermeer's *Lacemaker* (ca. 1669) might yield when conducted on Google Images as opposed to one conducted on site in the photo archive of the Netherlands Institute for Art History or RKD.

There is a need for all art historians to engage critically with issues related to technological change and innovation in ways that are rooted in broad disciplinary concerns. The study of the role of technologies and their historical formation, and their influence on the development and practice of art history; the development of methods and best practices that leverage digital technologies to improve existing and establish emerging art-historical practices and outcomes to make them more critically relevant, efficient, and sustainable; and the investigation of how and when the management of art-historical information intersects with or influences the production of art-historical knowledge—these are all areas of concern for the entirety of art history, even if they might be associated with the scholars who identify themselves with digital art history in particular. As Ulrich Pfisterer has noted, "the need for critical self-reflection on forms of representation and the conditions of visual knowledge production in the digital domain [is] a bridge that art history could and should help build" (136).

Engaging in a critical discourse that strengthens the connections between art history and digital art history, in part by identifying areas of shared concern, would create a discipline of scholars who are prepared to conduct research and produce scholarship in the already-digital world of the twenty-first century. Such a discourse would produce a broad-based critical engagement with technologies and technological change that would productively advance both digital humanities and art history alike.

NOTES

The ideas in this text were shaped in direct and indirect ways through conversations and collaborations with colleagues over the past several years at the Getty Research Institute and beyond. In particular, Elizabeth Mansfield and Tracy Stuber have served as thoughtful and generous interlocutors around the issues I present here and also offered comments on various drafts. My thanks and appreciation go also to my fellow authors Kate Elswit, Anastasia Salter, and Abraham Gibson, who provided feedback on an earlier version of this chapter. Finally, I am grateful to Matthew K. Gold and Lauren F. Klein for their incredibly helpful attentive and insightful critiques on the text, as well as their guidance throughout the editorial process.

1. Baca and Helmreich; Baca, Helmreich, and Gill, "Digital Art History," 1–5; Drucker; Fletcher; Zorich. Fletcher's 2015 article marked the inauguration of the review of projects and publications related to digital art history in the *caa.reviews*, a publication of the discipline's professional organization, the College Art Association.

2. I cite the *International Journal for Digital Art History* version of Bishop's essay throughout.

3. See also Cordell; Sayers. Both are accessible at https://dhdebates.gc.cuny.edu/projects/debates-in-the-digital-humanities-2016.

4. Some examples are "Digital Karnak" (UCLA, https://humtech.ucla.edu/project/digital-karnak/), "Digital Mellini" (see Baca, "Digital Mellini"), "Digital Serlio" (Columbia University, https://library.columbia.edu/libraries/avery/digitalserlio.html), "Digital Silk Road" (National Institute of Informatics Tokyo, http://dsr.nii.ac.jp/), and "Digital Thoreau" (SUNY Geneseo, https://digitalthoreau.org/).

5. Bishop repeatedly uses the ambiguous term "DH projects" in her exchange with Drucker (see Drucker and Bishop).

6. For example, an early influential article in this field looked at class and committees in a small community in Bremnes, Norway. See Barnes; see also Mitchell.

7. This binary understanding is undoubtedly the legacy, at least in part, of C. P. Snow's "two cultures" thesis.

8. Claire Bishop's "Against Digital Art History" is one example of such a critique, as are articles like Stephen Marche's "Literature Is Not Data." In addition, in her conversation with Johanna Drucker, Bishop maintains that "DH projects" are "driven by technophilic rather than intellectual questions" (Drucker and Bishop).

9. Zorich's 2012 report introduced the notion that "there is a pervasive sense that the discipline is too cautious, moves too slowly, and has to 'catch up' in the digital arena" (20).

This idea has since become accepted as fact, repeated, for example, in the 2014 Ithaka S+R report (and in a related article in the journal *Art Documentation*), the 2015 introductory text authored by David Raskin for Fletcher's "Reflections on Digital Art History," and the editors' introduction to the 2019 special issue of *Visual Resources* on digital art history. See Long and Schonfeld, "Supporting the Changing Research Practices of Art Historians," 6; Long and Schonfeld, "Preparing for the Future of Research Services for Art History"; Raskin; Baca, Helmreich, and Gill, 2.

10. Other scholars have made similar arguments in connection with digital humanities. For example, in their introduction to *Bodies of Information,* Jacqueline Wernimont and Elizabeth Losh write that "the digital humanities should also advocate attention to technosocial environments, the interfaces and platforms of mediation, and the procedures, protocols, and platforms of playable systems." See also Berens and Sanders.

11. Bishop remarks, "I feel bad about paying students to do mindless data entry rather than more exploratory intellectual work" (Drucker and Bishop).

12. See also Loukissas; Rawson and Muñoz.

13. See "school of" as described in the section "4.1 Creator Description" in Baca and Harpring.

14. See, for example, Cohen.

15. See Baca, "Getty Voices: Rethinking Art History."

16. See Pugh.

17. For an excellent overview of the kinds of issues that are excluded when one removes topics like digitization from a conception of digital art history or digital humanities, see Chapter 2, "All the Work You Do Not See," by Smith and Whearty.

18. See Batchen; Daston and Galison; or Galassi.

19. See Bishop; Drimmer; and Pollock.

20. In addition to Schivelbusch's book on train travel and Nelson's essay on the slide lecture, see Bohrer. See also Berenson. Many proponents of digital art history argue that the use of technology in art-historical research is "not really a new phenomenon," citing the work of Father Roberto Busa or Jules Prown's use of a computer in support of his study of John Singleton Copley's patrons. Baca, Helmreich, and Gill, "Digital Art History," 1. See also Baca and Helmreich; Drucker et al., 7; and Zweig.

21. A description of Pharos and a full listing of its members, which includes my own institution, is on the consortium's website at http://pharosartresearch.org/.

22. For an in-depth account of photo archives and their history, see Caraffa.

23. For a longer description of the research aims and methodologies associated with Pharos, see Caraffa et al.

BIBLIOGRAPHY

Baca, Murtha. "Digital Mellini: Project Update and Observations on Translating Historical Texts." *Getty Research Journal* 4 (2012): 153–60.

Baca, Murtha. "Getty Voices: Rethinking Art History." *The Getty Iris.* March 4, 2013, http://blogs.getty.edu/iris/getty-voices-rethinking-art-history/.

Baca, Murtha. "Introduction." *Visual Resources* 35, no. 1–2 (April 2019): 1–5, https://doi.org/10.1080/01973762.2019.1556887.

Baca, Murtha, and Patricia Harpring. "4. Creation." *Categories for the Description of Works of Art.* Los Angeles: J. Paul Getty Trust, 2016, https://www.getty.edu/research/publications/electronic_publications/cdwa/14creation.html#Creation-Creator.

Baca, Murtha, and Anne Helmreich. "Introduction." *Visual Resources: An International Journal of Documentation* 29, no. 1–2 (June 2013): 1–4, https://doi.org/10.1080/01973762.2013.761105.

Baca, Murtha, Anne Helmreich, and Melissa Gill. "Digital Art History," *Visual Resources* 35, nos. 1–2 (March–June 2019): 1–5, https://doi.org/10.1080/01973762.2019.1556887.

Barnes, J. A. "Class and Committees in a Norwegian Island Parish." *Human Relations* 7, no. 1 (February 1954): 39–58, https://doi.org/10.1177/001872675400700102.

Batchen, Geoffrey. *Burning with Desire: The Conception of Photography.* Cambridge, Mass.: MIT Press, 1999.

Berens, Kathi Inman, and Laura Sanders. "DH and Adjuncts: Putting the Human Back into the Humanities." In *Disrupting the Digital Humanities,* edited by Dorothy Kim and Jesse Stommel, 249–66. Santa Barbara, Calif.: Punctum Books, 2018, https://doi.org//10.2307/j.ctv19cwdqv.18.

Berenson, Bernard. "Isochromatic Photography and Venetian Pictures." *The Nation* 57, no. 1480 (November 1893): 346–47.

Bishop, Claire. "Against Digital Art History." *International Journal for Digital Art History* 3 (July 2018): 122–31, https://doi.org/10.11588/dah.2018.3.49915.

Bohrer, Frederick N. "Photographic Perspectives: Photography and the Institutional Formation of Art History." *Art History and Its Institutions: Foundations of a Discipline,* edited by Elizabeth Mansfield, 246–59. London: Routledge, 2002.

Brown, Kathryn. "Introduction." *The Routledge Companion to Digital Humanities and Art History,* edited by Kathryn Brown, 1–6. London: Routledge, 2020.

Caraffa, Costanza. *Photo Archives and the Photographic Memory of Art History.* Berlin: Deutscher Kunstverlag, 2011.

Caraffa, Costanza, Emily Pugh, Tracy Stuber, and Louisa Wood Ruby. "PHAROS: A Digital Research Space for Photo Archives." *Art Libraries Journal* 45, no. 1 (January 2020): 2–11, https://doi.org/10.1017/alj.2019.34.

Cohen, Patricia. "A Modigliani? Who Says So?" *New York Times.* February 2, 2014, https://www.nytimes.com/2014/02/03/arts/design/a-modigliani-who-says-so.html.

Cordell, Ryan. "How Not to Teach Digital Humanities." In *Debates in the Digital Humanities 2016,* edited by Matthew K. Gold and Lauren F. Klein. Minneapolis: University of Minnesota Press, 2016.

Daston, Lorraine, and Peter Galison. "The Image of Objectivity." *Representations* 40 (October 1992): 81–128, https://doi.org/10.2307/2928741.

Dinsman, Melissa. "The Digital in the Humanities: An Interview with Alexander Galloway." *Los Angeles Review of Books*. March 27, 2016, https://lareviewofbooks.org/article/the-digital-in-the-humanities-an-interview-with-alexander-galloway/.

Drimmer, Sonja. "How AI is Hijacking Art History." *Salon*. November 11, 2021, https://www.salon.com/2021/11/11/how-ai-is-hijacking-art-history_partner/.

Drucker, Johanna. "Is There a 'Digital' Art History?" *Visual Resources* 29, no. 1–2 (June 2013): 5–13, https://doi.org/10.1080/01973762.2013.761106.

Drucker, Johanna, and Claire Bishop. "A Conversation on Digital Art History." In *Debates in the Digital Humanities 2019,* edited by Matthew K. Gold and Lauren F. Klein. Minneapolis: University of Minnesota Press, 2019.

Drucker, Johanna, Anne Helmreich, Matthew Lincoln, and Francesca Rose (interview of authors by Rose), "Digital Art History: The American Scene." *Perspective* 2 (December 2015): 1–16, https://doi.org/10.4000/p.6021.

Fletcher, Pamela. "Reflections on Digital Art History." *caa.reviews*. June 2015, https://doi.org/10.3202/caa.reviews.2015.73.

Gagliardi, Susan Elizabeth. "Mapping Senufo: Mapping as a Method to Transcend Colonial Assumptions." In *The Routledge Companion to Digital Humanities and Art History*, edited by Kathryn Brown, 135–54. London: Routledge, 2020.

Galassi, Peter. *Before Photography: Painting and the Invention of Photography.* New York: Museum of Modern Art, 1981.

Gifford, E. Melanie. "Rubens's Invention and Evolution: Material Evidence in *The Fall of Phaeton.*" *Journal of Historians of Netherlandish Art* 11, no. 2 (September 2019), https://doi.org/10.5092/jhna.2019.11.2.1.

Hecht, Gabrielle. "Rupture-Talk in the Nuclear Age: Conjugating Colonial Power in Africa." *Social Studies of Science* 32, no. 5–6 (2002): 691–727, https://doi.org/10.1177/030631270203200504.

Long, Matthew P., and Roger C. Schonfeld. "Preparing for the Future of Research Services for Art History: Recommendations from the Ithaka S+R Report." *Art Documentation: Journal of the Art Libraries Society of North America* 33, no. 2 (September 2014): 192–205, https://doi.org/10.1086/678316.

Long, Matthew P., and Roger C. Schonfeld. "Supporting the Changing Research Practices of Art Historians." *Ithaka S+R*. April 30, 2014, 192–205.

Loukissas, Yanni Alexander. *All Data Are Local: Thinking Critically in a Data-Driven Society.* Cambridge, Mass.: MIT Press, 2019.

Mansfield, Elizabeth. "Art History and Modernism." In *Art History and Its Institutions: Foundations of a Discipline,* 11–27. London: Routledge, 2002.

Marche, Stephen. "Literature Is Not Data: Against Digital Humanities." *Los Angeles Review of Books*. October 28, 2012, https://lareviewofbooks.org/article/literature-is-not-data-against-digital-humanities/.

Mitchell, J. Clyde. "Social Networks." *Annual Review of Anthropology* 3 (October 1974): 279–99.

Nelson, "The Slide Lecture, or the Work of Art 'History' in the Age of Mechanical Reproduction." *Critical Inquiry* 26, no. 3 (Spring 2000): 414–34, http://www.jstor.org/stable/1344289.

Pfisterer, Ulrich. "Big Bang Art History." *International Journal for Digital Art History* 3 (July 2018): 134–38, https://doi.org/10.11588/dah.2018.3.49916.

Pollock, Griselda. "Computers Can Find Similarities between Paintings—but Art History Is about So Much More." *The Conversation*. August 22, 2014, https://theconversation.com/computers-can-find-similarities-between-paintings-but-art-history-is-about-so-much-more-30752.

Porras, Stephanie. "Keeping Our Eyes Open: Visualizing Networks and Art History." *Artl@s Bulletin* 6, no. 3 (2017): 41–49.

Pugh, Emily. "Art History Now: Technology, Information, and Practice." *International Journal for Digital Art History* 4 (November 2019): 3.47–3.59, https://doi.org/10.11588/dah.2019.4.63448.

Raskin, David. "Introduction to 'Reflections on Digital Art History.'" *caa.reviews*. June 2015, https://doi.org/10.3202/caa.reviews.2015.73.

Rawson, Katie, and Trevor Muñoz. "Against Cleaning." In *Debates in the Digital Humanities 2019,* edited by Matthew K. Gold and Lauren F. Klein. Minneapolis: University of Minnesota Press, 2019.

Reiner, Nicole E., and Jonathan Patkowski. "Inventing Abstraction, Reinventing Our Selves: The Museum of Modern Art's Artist Network Diagram and the Culture of Capitalism." *Rutgers Art Review* 32 (2013): 8–18.

Sayers, Jentery. "Dropping the Digital." In *Debates in the Digital Humanities 2016,* edited by Matthew K. Gold and Lauren F. Klein. Minneapolis: University of Minnesota Press, 2016.

Schivelbusch, Wolfgang. *The Railway Journey: The Industrialization of Time and Space in the Nineteenth Century*. Oakland: University of California Press, 2014.

Wernimont, Jacqueline, and Elizabeth Losh. "Introduction." In *Bodies of Information: Intersectional Feminism and Digital Humanities*, edited by Elizabeth Losh and Jacqueline Wernimont. Minneapolis: University of Minnesota Press, 2018, https://dhdebates.gc.cuny.edu/read/untitled-4e08b137-aec5-49a4-83c0-38258425f145/section/466311ae-d3dc-4d50-b616-8b5d1555d231#intro.

Zorich, Diane. *Transitioning to a Digital World: Art History, Its Research Centers, and Digital Scholarship*. New York: Samuel H. Kress Foundation. May 2012, https://www.kressfoundation.org/Resources/Sponsored-Research/Research-Items/Transitioning-to-a-Digital-World.

Zweig, Benjamin. "Forgotten Genealogies: Brief Reflections on the History of Digital Art History." *International Journal for Digital Art History* 1 (June 2015): 36–49, https://doi.org/10.11588/dah.2015.1.21633.

Building and Sustaining Africana Digital Humanities at HBCUs

RICO DEVARA CHAPMAN

Building and Sustaining Africana Digital Humanities at Historically Black Colleges and Universities (HBCUs) is a relatively new terrain when we think of current digital humanities (DH) spaces in the academy. But as an interdisciplinary field, Black digital humanities, or what I call Africana digital humanities, has also been practiced for decades, though not under the moniker of DH. Africana DH can be traced back to the late nineteenth century with the publication in 1899 of *The Philadelphia Negro,* in which W. E. B. Du Bois meticulously mapped neighborhood demographics of Philadelphia's Black Seventh Ward. And it continues into the present with projects that seek to preserve and digitize stories of neighborhoods, such as the Cascade Community Oral History Project in Southwest Atlanta and the Digitizing the Black Experience in Waller County, Texas. This chapter provides a brief history of the interdisciplinary field of Africana studies while highlighting research initiatives at HBCUs that center Black storytelling by lifting local voices and exploring Africana DH as distinct from traditional DH. Since the majority of DH labs and centers are located at predominantly white institutions (PWIs), Africana DH is often underrepresented in the discipline. But Africana DH in its various forms, as it is currently being practiced at HBCUs, can have an enriching impact on the digital humanities. It can bring a new perspective on the recovery and honoring of local history through community collaboration and storytelling using available digital tools and resources. HBCUs are often located in predominantly Black neighborhoods, offering the opportunity for graduate students and research faculty to conduct meaningful work that could potentially impact these neighborhoods in positive ways. Moreover, establishing DH programs as part of Africana studies is a natural fit because of the interdisciplinarity of both. Taking its cues from Du Bois's work conducted at the Atlanta University Center in the 1900s, Africana DH charts a new course for Africana studies programs and departments, particularly at HBCUs. Africana DH claims Atlanta University as its institutional origin, thus HBCUs, which to some degree are absent the white gaze, are priority spaces for Africana DH.

An early exemplar of Africana DH is found in the late nineteenth century in the work of Du Bois, who spent twenty-three years at Atlanta University from 1897–1910, serving on the faculty of the history and economics departments, and, later, from 1934–1944 as chair of the sociology department. Atlanta University, founded in 1865, was the first HBCU to award graduate degrees.[1] In 1900, at Atlanta University, Du Bois created a series of data portraits, "a collection of graphs, charts, maps, and tables" with a team of students, faculty, and scientists that "reflect a moment just before the disciplines had hardened into the academic specializations and structures of knowledge that we are familiar with today" (Battle-Baptiste, 13). This interdisciplinary collaborative approach to research has become a hallmark of digital humanities in the twenty-first century, as DH projects often require a team of experts ranging from city planners and computer scientists to historians and visual artists, depending on the desired outcome. Du Bois's comprehensive study of the Black experience through imagery ranged from local Georgia population diagrams to graphs charting Black businessmen in the United States and bar charts examining African American religious affiliations. This work completed over one hundred years ago is not only foundational to current practices in Africana DH, where data visualization is critical in making research findings accessible to a broader audience, but to the field of Africana studies, whose development was also closely tied to the community.

Africana studies is an outgrowth of the Black Studies Movement of the late 1960s, a student-led movement that demanded courses, programs, and departments that focused on the African and African diasporic experience. While the creation of Africana studies is also part of a longer history of mobilization and organization by people of African descent, the student efforts that culminated in the field's creation can be traced directly to the civil rights and Black Power movements of the 1960s. That decade was one of the most turbulent eras in U.S. history.[2] There were a number of court cases that led to the eventual desegregation of America's white colleges and universities, such as *Sweat v. Painter* (1950), *McLaurin v. Oklahoma* (1950), and *Brown v. Board of Education* (1954), all of which challenged segregation at educational institutions (Chapman, 44). Students across the American South challenged racist Jim Crow laws using nonviolent direct action to desegregate whites-only lunch counters, libraries, restrooms, and department stores. The tactic of nonviolence began to wane as white racism continued to reveal its cruelty, particularly in education as white students violently resisted integration of public schools and colleges in the South. The Black Power Movement partially grew out of the need for self-defense in opposition to white terror, and college campuses were often sites of contestation and confrontations with police, some of which were protests and demonstrations to establish Black studies.

In the late 1960s and 1970s partly due to the affirmative action policies that resulted from the student protests, there was an influx of Black students to predominantly white colleges and universities. This increase in Black student enrollment, in turn, allowed for the collective organization necessary to mobilize for the canvassing, demonstrations, and takeovers that would lead to the establishment of Black studies departments and programs (Chapman, 44). Unsurprisingly, Black college campuses were also sites of contestation and assertiveness through which ideas of Black self-empowerment began to take root. Students at HBCUs throughout the nation, particularly the South where most HBCUs are located, joined civil rights organizations such as the Student Nonviolent Coordinating Committee, the National Association for the Advancement of Colored People, the Congress of Racial Equality, among others, in order to ally themselves with larger collective actions.[3] Oftentimes, the conservative administration of these campuses discouraged involvement in such actions. However, many faculty members were supportive of the student demands for more courses that related to the Black experience and introduced courses in the various humanities disciplines such as African art, Black political thought, and African history. Entire academic programs also began to emerge. Howard University offered one of the first African studies programs at an HBCU, and Black studies programs and institutes were established at Jackson State College and Clark College in 1968. Through these student efforts and those of their allies, between 1968 and 1971, over 500 Black studies programs, institutes, and departments were established at dozens of colleges and universities throughout the United States (Chapman, 44). Africana studies, one outgrowth of Black studies, coalesced as an interdisciplinary academic field of study that centered on the research, interpretation, and presentation of the history, culture, and life of people of African descent throughout the world.

Africana Digital Humanities

Africana DH grows out of Africana studies, as well as the Du Boisian legacy of interdisciplinary collaborative research. Africana DH studies the Black experience through the lens of various disciplines using digital and computational tools. Though many of the tools originate in the Global North, Africana DH claims African ancestral communicative technology as its true early beginnings, where healing, recovery, and fulfillment of purpose was its primary role as opposed to industrial, commercial, and military technology uses as found in the West (Somé, 61). African ancestral communicative technology recognizes the role of spirit as a technological concept while also informing technology. Some of these technologies were embedded within the people themselves as griots, healers, and conduits of information from early lineages meant to serve the individual and community. Malidoma Patrice Somé notes that "technologies in the indigenous world are developed in order to fulfill basic human needs, such as community, health, harmony, and a sense of meaning and purpose in life" (71). This point of view is in direct conflict with many Western technologies that surveil Blackness. Ruha Benjamin, in her book *Race After Technology,* opines that "the plight of Black people has consistently been a harbinger of wider processes—bankers using financial technologies to prey on Black homeowners, law enforcement using surveillance technologies to control Black neighborhoods, or politicians using legislative techniques to disenfranchise Black voters" (32). André Brock links spirit to Black interiority and reflexivity in *Distributed Blackness,* "demanding full engagement with a world structured to displace Blackness" (80). Likewise, Africana DH centers Blackness and is less about the computational tools and more so the epistemology that connects an African identity with technology.

Africana digital humanities recognizes that the African continent has a long and ancient history of technological innovations that have spread throughout the diaspora. Africana DH also acknowledges that enslaved Africans were the technology used to build modern white supremacist colonial empires. Jessica Marie Johnson, in her essay "Markup Bodies: Black [Life] Studies and Slavery [Death] Studies at the Digital Crossroads," notes that these ancestors continue to aid in the Black freedom struggle and "have themselves taken up science, data, and coding, in other words, have commodified themselves and digitized and mediated their own black freedom dreams, in order to hack their way into the system." Africana DH, though global, starts locally and extends throughout the diaspora, respecting the process of recovery with the use of tools and processes that incorporate material and immaterial indigenous technologies. Africana DH aligns with postcolonial DH as asserted in Roopika Risam's book *New Digital Worlds* by having a basis in tools and methodologies designed with local practices in mind. "These practices," Risam asserts, "favor the particular over the universal [and] offer the promise of a more expansive humanities that takes advantage of the technological means of digital knowledge production to create space for underrepresented communities to populate the digital cultural record with their own stories" (Risam, 9). Africana DH goes further by acknowledging that the process of knowledge recovery and production happens before digitization and computation, allowing communities to be empowered regardless of technological prowess.

Africana DH is the study and exploration of history, literature, sociology, politics, and the arts using technology as a means of recovery, healing, and knowledge production. "Recovery rests at the heart of Black Studies," as Kim Gallon suggests, and Black digital humanities "troubles the very core of what we have come to know as the humanities by recovering alternate constructions of humanity that have been historically excluded from that concept" (44). Africana DH can function as a tool to reclaim the histories in danger of being lost. Collaborating with communities to gather stories of past and present that have shaped their lived experiences can potentially have a healing effect, whereby residents find new meaning and a sense of purpose in preserving local history. Working-class and elder members of longstanding Black communities face imminent displacement because of gentrification, which brings with it increased taxes and rent, making it near impossible to live in the communities that are now becoming safer, more pedestrian friendly, with more food options and amenities that cater to a younger and oftentimes whiter clientele. I am not suggesting that white is wrong and Black is right, but rather that Black residents have lived through and sustained their neighborhoods through what can be considered one of the most devastating epidemics of the late twentieth century: crack cocaine (McIlwain, 150–51). Now that inner cities are becoming attractive to millennials and Gen Zers, who detest suburban life and commuting, Black residents who held on to property in what were once considered slums are finding it difficult to maintain their homes and may be forced to abandon their beloved neighborhoods at a time when they should now enjoy its newfound conveniences. Atlanta, Georgia, where Du Bois conducted over two decades of interdisciplinary research in the Atlanta University Center, is facing such challenges and can benefit from Africana DH with its emphasis on recovery, healing, and community collaboration, with technology being a means not an end.

Taking a cue from Du Bois, who "pioneered the nation's most sophisticated quantitative research on race and the black population," (Battle-Baptiste and Rusert, 32) Africana DH can be vital in sustaining the history and integrity of communities whose residents and stories are rapidly being displaced. Some of these communities, such as those in Atlanta, Washington, D.C., Houston, and Nashville, are now changing because of gentrification. Moreover, many HBCUs reside in historic districts, and their campuses are often sites of memory and conscience. Their stories are important to preserve and tell through DH tools such as mapping, data visualization, digital exhibitions, and virtual reality experiences. These tools can help capture the rich oral tradition passed down through family tales while also adding layers of context, allowing the user to engage in historical and contemporary moments virtually. Africana DH challenges traditional DH by affirming the role of spirit as a necessary indigenous technology that moves through time and space, allowing the user to experience narration in new meaningful ways.

Africana digital humanities centers the local, recognizes the power of interdisciplinary collaborative approaches that are community-oriented, and values ancestral communicative technology demonstrated through storytelling. Projects exemplary of Africana DH have been conducted at two different HBCUs—one public, one private; one located in urban Atlanta, Georgia, at Clark Atlanta University (CAU) and the other located in rural Texas at Prairie View Agricultural and Mechanical University (PVAMU). These two institutions by no means represents all HBCUs, but they do give one a sense of the work that is important as it relates to digital humanities and place. Both projects sought to preserve local stories using DH tools, community involvement, and partnerships. Both projects align with Risam's assertion that "digital humanities, as a field, can only be inclusive and its diversity can only thrive in an environment in which local specificity—the unique concerns that influence and define digital humanities at regional and national levels—is positioned at its center and its global dimensions are outlined through an assemblage of the local" (Risam, 359).

CAU is located in the historic Atlanta University Center (AUC), which is also home to Morehouse College, Spelman College, Morris Brown College, the

Interdenominational Theological Center, and the Robert W. Woodruff Library. CAU was founded in 1988 after the consolidation of Atlanta University (1865), the nation's first institution to award graduate degrees to African Americans, and Clark College (1869), the nation's first four-year liberal arts college to serve a primarily African American student population.[4] PVAMU is located roughly forty-five miles outside Houston, Texas. It is the first state-supported college in Texas for African Americans and the second oldest public institution of higher education in Texas, established during the Reconstruction Period after the Civil War in 1876.[5]

At CAU, an oral history project that sought to preserve local history using digital tools was conducted in collaboration with the City of Atlanta's Historic Preservation Division, the Atlanta branch of the Association for the Study of African American Life and History (ASALH), and the AUC Robert W. Woodruff Library. The project, titled the Cascade Community Tour, demonstrates how partnerships between municipalities, nonprofit organizations, and higher education institutions can foster cooperation and promote intergenerational dialogue within communities that experience rapid demographic changes. The Cascade Community of southwest Atlanta is well known for being a bastion for African American leadership and consists of a treasure trove of historic sites and living history. As the city changes, it is important that the history of this vibrant community be recorded, shared, and celebrated. The Cascade Oral History project reflects the aims and approaches of Africana DH by centering Black storytelling, ensuring local participation through community collaboration, and making accessible the digital record to a broader audience. Merging oral history and digital humanities, the project employed graduate students to conduct interviews and offered a digital humanities course the following fall semester with the focus being the Cascade Community. It was important that students connect with the community in a way that allowed for an appreciation of local stories while incorporating DH tools. The more than forty interviews conducted of community residents are archived and available to the public from the AUC library so that "data might be made more accessible to the populations and people from whom such data is collected" (Battle-Baptiste and Rusert, 13).

At PVAMU, the Digitizing the Black Experience in Waller County, Texas, project resulted in an interactive online map with an app portal that preserved and made more accessible the history of that county. The project's aim was not simply historic preservation; rather, the goal was to recover the historical impact and cultural contributions of the Black residents of the county: Waller County, Texas, has a long storied history going back to the antebellum period that includes the experiences of enslaved Africans, freed people, and second-class citizens during the Jim Crow era. An equally important part of Waller County's historical narrative and the Black experience in the area is the story of Prairie View A&M University. (In more recent times, Waller County is where Sandra Bland was stopped by police, taken to jail, and found dead in her cell on July 13, 2015.) The project centered Black storytelling, a pillar of Africana digital humanities, as well as acknowledged the process of recovery that is essential to preserving and constructing new narratives that incorporate local voices, which is in line with Roopika Risam's observation that "local practices are good practices" (Risam, 143). The project incorporated topographies of local history into an interactive online map that functions as a voice-narrated three-dimensional virtual tour of historical markers and sites around Waller County and the campus of Prairie View A&M University.

Both the CAU and PVAMU projects are in keeping with Kim Gallon's claim that "recovery rests at the heart of Black studies, as a scholarly tradition that seeks to restore the humanity of Black people lost and stolen through systematic global racialization" (44). The examples of DH work at these two HBCUs symbolically represent the past, present, and future work of digital humanities in predominantly Black spaces where recovery is vital to survival.

Africana studies and digital humanities combining into Africana digital humanities identifies the presence of a global African world with a shared historical experience that stems from slavery and colonialism that make up the African diaspora. This unique historical and cultural experience can be seen in foodways, architecture, spirituality, language, and technology that undergird the significance of Africana DH in a local context. Africana DH takes on a scholar-activist posture as did its Du Boisian forebears. It resists racism and seeks also to challenge traditional DH by acknowledging the communicative power of spirit as a technology. Africana DH seeks to offer insight into marginalization and displacement by addressing the issues of race, class, gender, and place in predominantly Black communities. Safiya Noble correctly states that "this turn or institutional shift away from the interrogation of exploitation often leads us to focus primarily on cultural production, such as collecting and curating artifacts of culture among those communities underrepresented in traditional DH work; it leads us to digitize Black culture, but not use it in service of dismantling racist systems that contain and constrain freedom for Black bodies" (Noble, 29). Africana DH takes up the challenge to "interrogate colonialist and neocolonialist politics through project design to intervene in the epistemologies of digital knowledge production," (19) making it possible to center the local and acknowledge the global African diaspora as seen in shared African retentions that exists in communities. Africana DH exists as a continuum of the Black freedom struggle and not only digitizes the Black experience, which is significant and necessary, but also challenges traditional thinking around digital humanities by centering Black voices and prioritizing accessibility.

NOTES

1. Atlanta University founded in 1865 and Clark College founded in 1869 merged in 1986 to form Clark Atlanta University.

2. See Chapman, 42. In the early stages of the discipline's growth, the term "Black studies" was widely used until the 1980s when the designation of "African American

studies" became more commonplace, although most programs and departments would have used African American studies to broadly mean the study of African-descended peoples in the United States and abroad. As more programs, centers, institutes, and departments emerged, some being called "Black studies," "African and African American studies," "Africana studies," and "Pan-African studies," there arose the need to be more specific in scope.

3. HBCUs are institutions established before 1964 for the expressed purpose of educating African-descended peoples. There are 102 HBCUs that exist today.

4. The institutional history of Clark Atlanta University is detailed at https://www.cau.edu/presidents/institutional-history.html.

5. For the college history of Prairie View A&M University, see https://www.pvamu.edu/about_pvamu/college-history/.

BIBLIOGRAPHY

Azevedo, Mario, ed. *Africana Studies: A Survey of Africa and the African Diaspora.* 4th ed. Durham, N.C.: Carolina Academic Press, 2019.

Battle-Baptiste, Whitney, and Britt Rusert. eds. *W. E. B. Du Bois's Data Portraits Visualizing Black America: The Color Line at the Turn of the Twentieth Century.* New York: Princeton Architectural Press, 2018.

Benjamin, Ruha. *Captivating Technology: Race, Carceral Technoscience, and Liberatory Imagination in Everyday Life.* Durham, N.C.: Duke University Press, 2019.

Benjamin, Ruha. *Race After Technology: Abolitionist Tools for the New Jim Code.* Cambridge: Polity Press, 2019.

Biondi, Martha. *The Black Revolution on Campus.* Berkeley: University of California Press, 2012.

Boyd, Douglas A., and Mary A. Larson, eds. *Oral History and Digital Humanities: Voice, Access, and Engagement.* New York: Palgrave McMillan, 2014.

Brock, André. *Distributed Blackness: African American Cyber Cultures.* New York: NYU Press, 2020.

Chapman, Rico D. "African American Studies and the State of the Art." In *Africana Studies: A Survey of Africa and the African Diaspora.* 4th ed., edited by Mario Azevedo. Durham, N.C.: Carolina Academic Press, 2019.

Du Bois, W. E. B. *The Philadelphia Negro: A Social Study.* Philadelphia: University of Pennsylvania Press, 1899.

Favors, Jelani M. *Shelter in a Time of Storm: How Black Colleges Fostered Generations of Leadership and Activism.* Chapel Hill: University of North Carolina Press, 2019.

Gallon, Kim. "Making a Case for the Black Digital Humanities." In *Debates in the Digital Humanities 2016*, edited by Matthew K. Gold and Lauren F. Klein. Minneapolis: University of Minnesota Press, 2016.

Gold, Matthew, and Lauren Klein, eds. *Debates in the Digital Humanities 2016.* Minneapolis: University of Minnesota Press, 2016.

Gold, Matthew, and Lauren Klein, eds. *Debates in the Digital Humanities 2019.* Minneapolis: University of Minnesota Press, 2019.

Johnson, Jessica Marie. "Markup Bodies: Black [Life] Studies and Slavery [Death] Studies at the Digital Crossroads." *Social Text* 36, no. 4 (137) (December 1, 2018): 57–79, https://doi.org/10.1215/01642472-7145658.

McIlwain, Charlton D. *Black Software: The Internet and Racial Justice, from the AfroNet to Black Lives Matter.* New York: Oxford University Press, 2020.

Myers, Joshua M. *We Are Worth Fighting For: A History of the Howard University Student Protest of 1989.* New York: NYU Press, 2019.

Noble, Safiya. "Toward a Critical Black Digital Humanities." In *Debates in the Digital Humanities 2019,* edited by Matthew K. Gold and Lauren F. Klein. Minneapolis: University of Minnesota Press, 2019.

Risam, Roopika. "Navigating the Global Digital Humanities: Insights from Black Feminism." In *Debates in the Digital Humanities 2016,* edited by Matthew K. Gold and Lauren F. Klein. Minneapolis: University of Minnesota Press, 2016.

Risam, Roopika. *New Digital Worlds: Postcolonial Digital Humanities in Theory, Praxis, and Pedagogy.* Evanston, Ill.: Northwestern University Press, 2019.

Rogers, Ibram H. *The Black Campus Movement: Black Students and the Racial Reconstitution of Higher Education, 1965–1972.* New York: Palgrave MacMillan, 2012.

Somé, Patrice Malidoma. *The Healing Wisdom of Africa: Finding Life Purpose through Nature, Rituals, and Community.* New York: Penguin Putnam, 1999.

Williamson, Joy Ann. *Radicalizing the Ebony Tower: Black Colleges and the Black Freedom Struggle in Mississippi.* New York: Teachers College Press, 2008.

A Call to Research Action: Transnational Solidarity for Digital Humanists

OLIVIA QUINTANILLA AND JEANELLE HORCASITAS

Remember back when people used to go to the U.S. in pursuit of "The American Dream?" Well, that's all it was and ever will be: a pipe dream. No matter how they try to spin it, they never really wanted outsiders in their country. And once the right person got in power, he built that wall. Yeah, the one nobody took seriously. Just like those people who said climate change wasn't real, and look here, we are: on the brink of extinction. Barely making it with the resources we have left. Living out our lives in the VR.

—Maria, the *transfronteriza* from Front|eras

Imagine the world thirty years from now. A world where Mexican immigrants such as Maria are forced into a type of technological oppression that compels them to provide physical and intellectual labor. A world so uninhabitable that you must wear a mask to avoid the toxic air. A world where, if you have enough wealth or privilege, you never have to leave the house. Instead, you have the luxury of escaping the dystopian realities surrounding you through virtual reality technology that transports you to other worlds, places, and even timelines. But for those who cannot access virtual reality: What is left in the world for them to live for? More importantly, *who* is left in the world, and how will they survive?

This is the premise of our choose-your-own-adventure game, Front|eras.[1] In retrospect, we could have never predicted how stories like Maria's could resonate so strongly with our current moment amid a pandemic, social unrest, and political uncertainty. As in the game, we too worry that the air is too dangerous to breathe, and a nation that requires "essential workers," who are predominantly people of color and poor, risk their lives outside (and inside) while wealthier and more privileged members of society wait out the pandemic at home. We face hate crimes and gun violence, with memories of the vitriol brought about by the Trump administration never far from our minds. Even in the administration of President Joseph Biden, large-scale movements across borders remain controlled and exploited for profit by governments and corporations. We need more urgent conversations and collaborations grounded in transnational solidarities, relations of mutual support, and recognition that connects communities beyond borders to alter our future course.

Solidarity can take many forms among individuals, groups, and organizations and is typically constituted through shared values that elicit unity and support. Practices focusing on justice and mutual care, and manifesting through advocacy and action commitments, lie at the core of solidarity. In May 2021, the Black Lives Matter movement issued a statement of solidarity with Palestinians, affirming the movement's commitment to end all forms of settler colonialism and pledging to "continue to advocate for Palestinian liberation."[2] Since oppression and systems of exploitation, dispossession, and violence are (re)produced through transnational processes, resistance and solidarity must, together, take transnational form.

Our call to action is to cultivate transnational solidarities as a collective care-driven response to the everyday experiences of those living under colonialism and struggling with intersecting forms of violence and oppression. Especially in the era of Covid-19, where national borders are more visible and restrictive than ever, nation-states should not be defining elements that shape the legitimacy or resilience of transnational solidarity relationship building. But what might this look like for a digital humanities (DH) project, and how might we use it in our pedagogical practices?

We have been working to establish a fertile foundation where ideas can be seeded and grown to evolve into a DH toolkit grounded in transnational solidarity. The toolkit contains questions to help practitioners get started with their projects and provides an access point for students (especially historically underrepresented ones) to draw from their everyday lived experiences and visualize how they can create meaningful connections and collaborations among their networks. As a result, students build a solid footing in their own communities, histories, and stories so that they can begin to share them with others and develop relationships that seek to capture the spirit of transnational solidarity. The following sections will preview these questions and provide examples of how we envision transnational solidarity in practice.

The purpose of creating our DH project Front|eras was not to simply represent "transnationalism" but rather to illuminate the conditions that inspire transnational solidarity, when people form relationships and networks of care that exceed the logic of national boundaries. The game's storyline emphasizes decision making that is not solely focused on transnational solidarity as a form of resistance and survival but as a method of community building and "home-making" across borders.[3] By emphasizing future transnational possibilities of resistance and solidarity in Front|eras, we call attention to how fraught the concept of transnationalism can be when forming meaningful connections among communities. Often, transnationalism is seen as purely transactional, tied to social, political, and economic advantages possible when relationships are developed across borders, typically only to serve the powerful and privileged. However, in creating Front|eras and characters such as Maria, we sought to reimagine how transnationalism can be based on reciprocity and care. We created characters who have been marginalized by technology and social and economic "benefits" in the future and their response through transnational connections in virtual reality. Our game focuses on storytelling from the perspective of immigrants, refugees, and Indigenous communities and, as a result, can position players to foster future transnational solidarities that are premised on a community of support and care in a real-world and digital space.

Our doctoral training in ethnic studies and literature influenced our approach to game design and DH more generally through a transnational lens. As educators and community college professors, we approach digital humanities from a framework that centers *everyday ways of knowing* and begins with the understanding that categories of identity are always intersecting, in flux, and transforming together across time and space. We encourage our historically underrepresented students to position themselves in a starting place of transnational solidarity from which they can reimagine their realities through the Front|eras game. We have encountered the cross-border commuter student who relies on technology primarily as a source of survival by way of transportation to and from school, work, and home. In this case, technology, DH included, is not perceived as a welcoming place or tool for creative contributions on the surface; rather, it is a means to an end. With our call to action, we insist on changing the narrative that students can only engage with technology when necessary for survival to one where they engage with technology for resistance, innovation, and community building. A network immersed in transnational solidarity will recognize the intersectional identities our students bring and encourage them to participate in changing larger structural issues. For example, suppose students can shift their perspective to understand their networks as a larger community ripe for transnational solidarity. In that case, we hope that they can reimagine the futures they want together—especially their relationship with technology as a tool for their empowerment.

We specifically work with community college students, and this demographic is already in a transitory state. Often, they are faced with a short window of time and a long list of required courses they must complete before transferring to a university or returning to the workforce. This means there are hardly any opportunities for students to engage in creative and critical work related to DH that could help them develop these essential life skills we know are vital for building inclusive and equitable futures. This is why, as community college professors, we intentionally modify our syllabi to provide time and space for this critical and creative teaching and practice to happen. Although we have not been assigned to teach formal digital humanities classes, we insist on modifying our syllabi when teaching literature and history to include digital humanities projects and approaches. Our engagement with Latinx community college students and our own experiences as women of color community college alumnae in the San Diego/Tijuana border region inspired the Front|eras characters we created. It was important for us to create characters that represented people we see every day and to critique the intersecting issues of border crossing, technology, labor exploitation, immigration, and displacement that we learned from our students' personal stories. Our students' stories inspired the game's creation, and by making them visible and accessible with Twine,[4] we hope to inspire other students to share their lived experiences.

Our approach to DH and pedagogy, as shown by how we used Front|eras in the classroom and with our DH toolkit, builds from the strategy of a collective of scholars associated with the Center for Interdisciplinary Environmental Justice. They align their efforts with Indigenous land and water protectors to develop practices for decolonization grounded in anti-racism and feminism. They follow a framework of "decolonial feminist science" and explain:

> Building on decades of community-based organizing, grassroots activism, and slow intimate relationship-building practices, we leverage Western science and laboratories in support of Indigenous knowledge as science in its own historical and cosmological right. We call this emergent practice *decolonial feminist science*: a science for land, life, and radical liberation. When we say "decolonial," we mean that our work is in service of Indigenous communities working to keep or regain agency over their land and livelihood. When we say "feminist," we take as a starting point the argument that feminist science must aim to eliminate research that leads to the exploitation and destruction of nature, the destruction of the human race and other species, and that justifies the oppression of people on the basis of race, gender, class, sexuality, or nationality.

We argue that the same choices to center Indigenous community priorities and relationships based on respect for nature and reciprocity are necessary to show transnational solidarity in DH and lay the groundwork for decolonial and sustainable futures. Digital humanists can create DH projects that work in service of underrepresented and underresourced communities internationally and within national borders as a method of (transnational) solidarity and decolonial DH. While we do not have a clear blueprint for what decolonial futures should look like, a decolonial analysis of DH can gesture away from the violent and unsustainable modes of existence underwritten by settler colonialism and move toward reinvestments in different options for the future. Preventing the destruction of nature and actively working to care for our global environments is a necessary component of all research endeavors because our work will not serve much good if we collectively do not have a livable and healthy planet to call home. The responsibility DH scholars have to serve the environment cannot be overstated. DH scholars can build from decolonial feminist science to hold their projects accountable and prevent exploitative research practices and the destruction of nature while also ensuring that the processes and outcomes of their work build toward Indigenous resurgence and challenge relationships with land, people, and states. Emphasizing a decolonial feminist science consciousness brings us to critical starting points to begin DH projects.

Digital humanists must address the legacies of science that have enacted diverse forms of oppression against cross-border or Indigenous communities and their data, knowledge, stories, health, and priorities.[5] Decolonial DH projects and methods "that foreground intersectional engagement with race, gender, class, nation and other axes of identity that shape knowledge production"[6] can play a critical role in not only preventing further and future violence against these communities but also in breaking away from such frameworks entirely. Ahistorical and diversity-driven trends to "decolonize" DH risk becoming empty metaphors without the specificity required to transform colonial dynamics. In *The Routledge Companion to Media Studies and Digital Humanities*, Roopika Risam notes that Eve Tuck and K. Wayne Yang have argued that "invoking decolonization solely as a metaphor undermines the real possibility of decolonization for those whose lives are, in fact, determined by colonialism" (3). Decolonial DH moves away from reproducing colonial discourse and practice through digital tools and projects that create opportunities for reimagining communities, relationships, infrastructure, and power dynamics not dependent on Indigenous displacement, erasure, exploitation, occupation, and militarized violence. In response to Tuck and Yang's warnings of misplaced decolonial aspirations that inevitably "rescue settler futurity," our call for research action asks how scholars can create DH projects and teaching exercises rooted in decolonial critical awareness to prevent resettlement and reoccupation practices that further settler colonialism. To be sure, our DH toolkit and call to action do not alone decolonize DH; rather, they begin the process for the necessary thinking, teaching, conversations, relationship building, and storytelling to happen for real decolonization to transpire.

We employ storytelling using DH tools as a tactic for (re)imagining and (re)investing our time, energy, teaching, and DH practice in transnational solidarities. Because colonialism and decolonial DH is a process rather than one event, we look for opportunities in our pedagogy to plant decolonial seed-starters in as many creative forms as possible. The narrative tools of Twine and story maps can bridge decolonial DH theory with practice. We also use this approach with our DH toolkit as a starting point for readers to consider the communities they are speaking with, who they may be designing their projects for, and understanding the issues and values of the communities they plan to work with. By offering "everyday" starting points, DH storytelling that leads with perspectives and knowledge from those not in power can spark reflective conversations that transform into investigations, discoveries, and actions that build communities grounded in care, respect, reciprocity, and solidarity.

Our work builds on several existing models of DH projects approached from decolonial frameworks, such as Torn Apart/Separados and the Critical Refugee Studies Collective (CRSC) story map project.[7] Torn Apart is part of a mobilized and responsive humanities intervention in global humanitarian and migration crises. In it, scholars, librarians, students, community members, artists, and activists came together to map locations of federal detention facilities across the country to track where immigrant children separated from their parents were possibly being held. This volunteer collaboration enacted transnational solidarity through data mapping and grassroots DH community action to help alleviate the crisis and foster collective knowledge production and sharing that transcends borders. The CRSC story maps, created by scholars from across California, invested in facilitating new forms of knowledge and narratives about refugee life with those displaced instead of studying refugees as objects of inquiry without agency. The interactive multimedia maps were crowdsourced from refugee communities. The CRSC story maps revise history to reflect creative and holistic forms of transnational solidarity not represented in the dominant narratives of refugee life.

As seen in these examples, DH can be a strategic tool to support transnational struggles when it is mobilized to reframe oppressive versions of storytelling and respond to community needs and desires to share alternative histories and futures. We provide an example of this mobilization and resistance in the next section with the character Maria and the group ContraVR, who organize together to dismantle the technological systems meant to exploit and oppress them. By honoring their connection to the community and partaking in transnational solidarity, they successfully recode their virtual reality (and actual reality) to provide a more equitable future for marginalized communities.

Front|eras: Capturing Transnational Solidarity and Collaboration across Borders

Our Front|eras project critiques the technologies we use while asking how we can provide more access to those without it and create more inclusive spaces in the academy and beyond for others to make contributions. This is where our DH toolkit and prompting questions are integral to our call to research action, primarily because they provide the framework for fostering transnational solidarity and collaboration. We explain that designing a DH project must be an intentional and thoughtful process that always centers on the communities involved. In *Intersectionality in Digital Humanities*, Barbara Bordalejo and Roopika Risam refer to Moya Bailey's arguments that DH work is not about simply diversifying voices but rather making DH "open to the inevitable transformation of scholarly practices that an intersectional approach to digital humanities provides." Yes, including more voices, histories, and stories is always important for inclusivity and diversity, but are we ethical about how they are represented? One of the questions from our DH toolkit directly asks: What and who gets represented in your project, and why? And as a follow-up: What gets elided and glossed over? More importantly, we ask: What community-specific ethical concerns are there for your project? We recognize that qualitative research, especially with oral histories, can sometimes misinterpret or misrepresent what is said, how it is said, and what the intended message may have been. When it comes to representation in a digital space, this becomes even more complex because of the various ways in which data can be altered and compromised through hacking, image and video alteration, and surveillance. As a result, we want researchers and students to develop DH projects that center questions of ethics, knowledge sharing, transparency, and proper acknowledgments. These efforts are already being tackled with grassroots groups that bring together students, scholars, and practitioners across the United States and beyond, in response to the vulnerability of corporate trends of hyper-surveillance and education outsourcing. One example is Ethical EdTech.[8] Starting a DH project without this framework—that is, without reflecting on these questions based on trust, care, and mutual support—risks forming one-sided and exploitative relationships in favor of the researcher's project. One of the most important questions we ask students as part of our DH toolkit is: What are the anticipated outcomes (of their DH research), and who do those outcomes benefit in the short and long term? This question is key for a framework of transnational solidarity because researchers and students should create and sustain community relationships beyond transactional project purposes. In doing so, their DH projects are not simply detached and empty deliverables. Rather, they can be collaborative works-in-progress that encourage community involvement and directly contribute to ongoing community priorities.

Many of these DH toolkit questions guided our creation of Front|eras, a choose-your-own-adventure game that would be accessible, understandable, and invite players to contribute their own narratives. For this project, we chose to use Twine, an open-source interactive platform for creating nonlinear digital narratives. Twine is premised on collaboration and features multimodal design with story maps (in the shape of networks that follow the various storylines) that show the interconnected stories or "choices" people can be led to as they navigate the game. The platform gives users the agency to design a narrative structure, such as a fixed or nonlinear path. Creating a Twine story does not require high-level coding skills beyond HTML to change fonts, colors, and backgrounds; as a result, it provides an opportunity for various disciplines to be involved in the project and reduces the hierarchies between those more tech-savvy and those who are not. We wanted to create a DH project that highlighted transnational solidarities in the future while fostering collaboration beyond any technological or discipline-specific barriers that often prevent those from the humanities, social sciences, visual arts, and STEM (science, technology, engineering, and mathematics) from working together.

This collaborative and interdisciplinary project was made possible through the University of California San Diego (UCSD) Arthur C. Clarke Center for Human Imagination, which worked with three groups to develop speculative design projects that imagined San Diego in 2049. Our group consisted of a computer scientist, a visual artist, literary writers, and social scientists; Twine served as the collaborative platform to share our expertise and stories. Front|eras was not just a DH project; it was also an example of public scholarship that we shared with our colleagues, students, and domestic and international communities.

Our game provided six different narratives from protagonists and antagonists: a federal agent, a refugee, a *transfronteriza*, a university student, and two queer U.S. citizens trying to navigate love and intimacy in a future where virtual reality is preferable to real connections. As a player, you could choose to follow the path of one character, or you could traverse back and forth across the U.S.–Mexico border without a border checkpoint, move forward, then move backward, or switch characters in seconds. This reproduced the border as a space always in flux, constantly shifting rather than fixed; it was integral to our goal of representing transnational solidarity where marginalized communities have the power to shift narratives as well as the physical and abstract borders that exploit and dehumanize them as laborers. There were a few core characters and aspects of the game that embody our call to action for transnational solidarity:

- Maria: A *transfronteriza* who crosses the border each day from Mexico to the United States for work. She is a virtual reality (VR) laborer who provides hospice-like care to her employer, who is hooked into his VR technology all day to escape the real world. She is also a member of the resistant group ContraVR and plays a large role in hacking the VR system in hopes of overthrowing it.
- Benny: A Haitian refugee working as a ride-share driver for a company called SWYFT in Mexico. He was displaced from his home in Haiti as a result of climate change, which made his home island uninhabitable. As a driver, he takes clients to a VR vacation of their choosing, but he often goes to visit the VR version of his home in Haiti since the memory is all he has left of it.
- ContraVR: This radical group is arguably one of the most important aspects of the game. The name translates to "against" VR in Spanish and is representative of the transnational solidarity that exists between the communities of immigrants, refugees, and U.S. citizens to organize together against the oppressive technological systems in place. Various characters in the game refer to ContraVR or see the graffiti tag with cryptic details about the next meeting time and place. ContraVR is a group that reimagines new futures and worlds and illuminates what collaboration and social change could look like among our diverse and transnational communities.

Our characters and ideas were not simply a result of thought experiments but were influenced by our graduate research and, more importantly, by the students we work with at our community college and refugee-led community centers. For example, in creating Front|eras, we developed a DH project that told stories we knew were invisible in a predominantly white and heteronormative narrative. As a result, this inspired the way we approached our pedagogy and expanded what we know can be possible for future DH research and pedagogy.

As educators, we argue that using DH to tell stories—to think beyond just how digital tools might be used in our classroom by students and beyond the parameters of the classroom and toward the possibilities of the future—will generate new DH projects that challenge the technologies we use and the power and privilege of those who do (or do not) have access to them. Projects designed with a goal of transnational solidarity in mind will center the stories of immigrants, refugees, and Black, Indigenous, and people of color. Scholars such as Roopika Risam, Barbara Bordalejo, and Kathryn Wymer have argued for more intersectionality in DH, where there is an "openness to the transformation of practices that the inclusion of practitioners from a broader range of scholarly backgrounds particularly in African diaspora, feminist, ethnic, and postcolonial thought, might bring" (2). Our Front|eras project represents an intersectional DH that speaks to the transnational communities we are personally a part of and those we learned about in the classroom, primarily through working with students from historically underrepresented backgrounds. Although the characters in Front|eras are fictional, the ideas they represent are rooted in real-world social justice, organizing, and world-building practices.

Fostering Ethical, Collaborative, and Transnational Solidarity DH in Pedagogy

Front|eras seeks to highlight the transnational solidarity possible among intersectional and diverse communities and leads us to an important question: How can we teach our students to adopt a transnational solidarity framework for their DH projects and encourage collaboration with their communities to build better worlds and futures? How can we do so in a way that incorporates the knowledge and experience that they already bring to the classroom? How can we acknowledge the realities of our students' lives and the strength and commitment they demonstrate by being present in the classroom each day? How can we spark interdisciplinary reflections on transnational solidarity and decolonial DH?

We teach at Hispanic-Serving Institutions (HSI) in San Diego and are immersed in Latinx students' realities every day. For example, students have shared their difficulties getting to class on time because of border-crossing delays or the need to leave class early so they do not return too late at night when it might be dangerous. We have also heard stories from our students who may not have access to computers at home and rely on using the public library or their mobile phones. These are just a few examples of the inequities that exist on many college campuses and the struggles certain students face getting to class, let alone having the tools they need to be successful. We need to rehumanize our educational institutions to support our students through their struggles, validating them for showing up and doing the work and empowering them to pursue the futures they aspire to have.

We also want our historically underrepresented students to be critical of the current political, sociological, and environmental conditions so that they can help prevent a dystopian future like Front|eras from happening while actively creating the future they desire. Therefore, we introduce the history of technology and science from Indigenous and Latinx perspectives.[9] Further, we use digital humanities tools to create space for students to reimagine different trajectories for themselves and their communities using speculation and worldmaking as methodologies. Teaching DH through underrepresented histories is critical to counter the colonial logics that framed Indigenous peoples as barbaric and backward and that underpinned the use of technology and science as methods for human and environmental control, violence, and occupation. Learning such history empowers students to craft critical and often regenerative DH projects. We urge students to envision and write themselves into alternative decolonial futures to challenge existing relationships with people, land, and the state and to open up new possibilities for transnational solidarity and equitable futures. Using DH to examine decolonial theory, Indigenous futurism, and technology, we can deepen the awareness of place-based struggles, overlapping oppression, and the interconnected nature of decolonial DH and transnational solidarity as tools of cooperation and worldmaking.

We argue in our teaching that visualizing transnational partnerships, connections, and care through a storytelling and world-building platform such as Twine can play an important role in offering possibilities of solidarity. The process of collaboratively designing our game and coordinating the moments where our characters' realities crossed paths in our imagined world allowed us to apply the practice of collective worldmaking. Prototyping the San Diego border region in 2049 allowed us to test out ideas and concerns we had in the present for ourselves and our communities by playing out the thread of thought to the point of completion, where our character was interacting and living the life of our imagination and experiencing the implications of decision making from 2019 and beyond.

Portraying solidarity and resistance among our characters as they would appear in 2049 required reconceptualizing solidarity practices in a game world where the tech-transportation and tourism industry had taken advantage of solidified borders by capitalizing on future ride-share drivers' labor and experiences without the consumer ever having actually to speak to the driver. For example, Benny's story is a Haitian refugee living in Mexico and working as a ride-share driver. Communication between the passenger and driver transpires only through the company's app. The passenger could access stories, recommendations, and conversations from the driver by the touch of a button. This story was inspired by the rush for driverless cars and the option for "silent" ride-sharing experiences. Simultaneously, major ride-share companies exploit driver labor for profit, classifying them as "independent contractors" and not employees in order to skirt paying real benefits and sharing profit with their employees. Twine gave us the ability to extrapolate the concerns of the present and reveal how the consequences of current policies might take shape in a dystopian future.

ContraVR, the radical resistance group in our game, provides another example of how we envision the possibilities for cross-border transnational solidarity. With limited or no access to VR technologies in this future, the people comprising this group (primarily low-income immigrants and people of color) seek to hack the system and recode their own prototyped VR technology so that they too may have access. Again, this exemplifies one of our DH project's purposes—bringing visibility to open-access and technology issues, especially for those from marginalized communities. Similar to how we represent transcending physical borders, Maria's character overcomes abstract borders through her various identities and roles. She holds an intersectional identity as a VR worker, a transfronteriza, an immigrant, and social activist. Players get a glimpse of some of the struggles that characters such as Maria and Benny experience. Depending on the storyline one follows, players may be exposed to moments of transnational solidarity and community/world-building through the ContraVR group. Consider this scene from Front|eras:

> Everyone's eyes shift from one to the other. Capturing a true moment of hope and solidarity among them. So many years have gone by without any progress, without any sort of belief in the future. Time seems to stand still while everyone is suspended in silence, waiting for Matador's orders.
>
> Matador whispers, "Get ready for a new beginning."

Ultimately, we argue DH has the power and capacity for helping imagine and build sustained transnational solidarity and mobilization. Solidarity, expanded and reconceptualized from its original localized forms, can now mean more transnational supportive interrelationships connecting people worldwide.

Working toward Change and Transnational Solidarity in DH

Our experiences as educators, researchers, and first-generation women of color from low-income and immigrant families have shaped our own visions of the positive impact we hope to make, especially to foster transnational solidarity in the digital humanities. We want to inspire a generation of future projects and conversations, both inside and outside the academy, told by these communities themselves. In our efforts to expand transnational solidarity through projects like Front|eras, we implemented world-building activities inspired from the game's characters into our own classes—a practice that offers a final example of how future researchers and educators might work toward similar goals.

"No one's ever asked me about what I think about these things before. I've never had to think about designing the future. I just always thought it was too hard to change, but now I see how we can actually start making changes." This testimonial comes from a student in our Chicana/o studies history class at a San Diego community college. This student reflects on their experience with this activity, specifically, how they chose to design a future San Diego border region in response to their assigned character's needs and life trajectory.

Students were also asked to take stock of the systems necessary to build a future that took into account the history and current developments of the region. For example, what do food, social services, waste management, technology, air quality, and politics look like in 2049? What does a day in their character's life look like, and what systems and issues do they encounter? What are their character's priorities, and what kind of community-building/action makes sense for their reality? Students represent their character by working in small groups to collectively draw out their vision of the San Diego border region in 2049 on a large poster board throughout three class sessions.

The next step in this activity is the moment of transnational solidarity and collaboration we hope to initiate. Once the groups present their collectively created drawing and storyline, the poster boards are then displayed around the classroom, and students take turns going on a tour of the future. After engaging with the other groups' renderings, students revisit their story and find ways to connect with each other's characters and modify their original version to support the visions of others. For example, one group described a pollution problem in the Tijuana region. Another group based in San Diego created a cross-border clean-up system using new technology that provided jobs, clean water, and a cross-border community garden to address food insecurity.

Using Front|eras and prompting questions helped our students get started. From there, our students analyzed transnational challenges and opportunities to rethink connections across the border region. Most strikingly, students expressed feelings of inspiration and responsibility to create equitable relationships in their imagined future because they felt empowered to think beyond the constraints they experience in real life. One student remarked, "I never thought of myself as a designer before," and now she feels more optimistic about the future. After completing this activity, many students expressed an interest in pursuing a path in urban planning, policy making, and digital humanities.

Whether it is thought experiments manifested in the form of a game like Front|eras, classroom activities such as the one above, or a resource like our DH toolkit, our call to research action urges scholars to consider the role of digital humanities as a transnational vehicle for solidarity and decolonial knowledge. Starting with everyday realities for people of color and prioritizing spaces for marginalized communities to collaborate and implement recommendations can improve our research methods and strengthen our relationships as social justice–driven digital humanists.

NOTES

1. Run the Front|eras game at https://ucsd-fronteras.itch.io/fronteras.

2. See Diwakar.

3. We define "home-making" in the context of displaced people, especially refugees, who are driven out of their home country by political, social, or economic strife or degraded environments and, as a result, must remake their home in a different country while simultaneously attempting to (re)learn aspects of their original homeland such as culture, language, and history.

4. Twine is an "open-source tool for telling interactive, nonlinear stories." We will discuss the benefits of using this platform at length in a later section.

5. For historical context and discussion of Indigenous communities' history and engagement with science, technology, environmental racism, and communication technologies, see Duarte and also Voyles.

6. See Risam, "Decolonizing the Digital Humanities."

7. For Torn Apart, see http://xpmethod.columbia.edu/torn-apart/volume/1/. For CRSC, see www.criticalrefugeestudies.com.

8. See the Ethical EdTech Wiki at https://ethicaledtech.info/wiki/Meta:Welcome_to_Ethical_EdTech.

9. See Dalton; Tu and Nelson; and Benjamin.

BIBLIOGRAPHY

Benjamin, Ruha. *Race after Technology: Abolitionist Tools for the New Jim Code.* Medford, Mass.: Polity Press, 2019.

Brito-Millán, M., A. Cheng, E. Harrison, M. Mendoza Martinez, R. Sugla, M. Belmonte, A. Salomón, L. Quintanilla, J. Guzman-Morales, and A. Martinez. "*No Comemos Baterías:* Solidarity Science against False Climate Change Solutions." *Science for the People* 22, no. 1, The Return of Radical (2019), https://magazine.scienceforthepeople.org/vol22-1/agua-es-vida-solidarity-science-against-false-climate-change-solutions/.

Dalton, David. *Mestizo Modernity: Race, Technology and the Body in Post Revolutionary Mexico.* Gainesville: University of Florida Press, 2018.

Diwakar, Amar. "Kindred Struggles: Black America Enduring Solidarity with Palestine." *TRTWorld.* May 21, 2021, https://www.trtworld.com/magazine/kindred-struggles-black-america-s-enduring-solidarity-with-palestine-46897.

Duarte, Marisa. *Network Sovereignty: Building the Internet across Indian Country.* Seattle: University of Washington Press, 2017.

Risam, Roopika. "Decolonizing the Digital Humanities in Theory and Practice." English Faculty Scholarship, Salem State Digital Repository. May 2018, https://digitalrepository.salemstate.edu/handle/20.500.13013/421.

Risam, Roopika, and Barbara Bordalejo, eds. *Intersectionality in Digital Humanities.* Yorkshire: ARC Humanities Press, 2019.

Tu, Thuy Linh H., and Alondra Nelson. *Technicolor: Race, Technology and Everyday Life.* New York: NYU Press, 2001.

Tuck, Eve, and K. Wayne Yang. "Decolonization Is Not a Metaphor." *Decolonization: Indigeneity, Education & Society* 1, no. 1 (2012): 1–40.

UCSD-Fronteras. Front|eras interactive fiction game. Accessed August 13, 2022, https://ucsd-fronteras.itch.io/fronteras.

Voyles, Traci. *Wastelanding: Legacies of Uranium Mining in Navajo Country.* Minneapolis: University of Minnesota Press, 2015.

Wymer, Kathryn. *Introduction to Digital Humanities: Enhancing Scholarship with the Use of Technology*. United Kingdom: Taylor & Francis, 2021.

Game Studies, Endgame?

ANASTASIA SALTER AND MEL STANFILL

In 2001, video game scholar and hypertext theorist Espen Aarseth named computer game studies as an emerging field. Yet even as he asserted the importance of coming together to understand computer games, he suggested that other forms of "digital" theorists would eventually return to their disciplinary homes, as "every sector of the humanities and social science must see the digital as part of their own territory" (Aarseth). Twenty years later, his prediction that other "digital" associations would be reclaimed into their home disciplines has proved wrong: the Association of Internet Researchers is alive and well; the Office of Digital Humanities still remains its own division of the National Endowment for the Humanities (NEH); and the Association for Computers and the Humanities, far from becoming irrelevant, has been revitalized with a biannual conference. In a 2015 response to Aarseth, scholar and game designer Ian Bogost observed that the predicted future had not come to pass, contending that game studies "is an improbable, fledgling discipline whose future is hardly secure," and he further asserted that drawing such a sharp boundary around game studies might not be for the best: "It's possible we've all made an error in isolating any media form from its kindred, particularly in the post-2008 era of austerity, where perhaps the only way for media studies to flourish is by teaming up, Voltron-style" (Bogost, "Game Studies, Year Fifteen").[1] We are drawn to reconsider Aarseth and Bogost's words during a moment of even greater precarity and argue that digital game studies, far from remaining separate, has become—and must continue to be—vital to driving the discourse of digital studies more broadly.

In this chapter we look back at key crises in the games industry and game studies in order to look forward, arguing that game studies has become the canary in the coal mine for the digital everything. From the toxic masculinity exemplified by GamerGate to increased scrutiny over labor practices (including the abusive model of "crunch" and the lack of unionization), and the growing concern over the environmental impact of the industry, the debates most pressing in game studies are the same debates that will soon characterize the "digital" writ large, if they do not already. Just as it has presaged problems that have become intensely visible in the games industry, so too can game studies offer guidance to digital humanities (DH) on essential interventions. Feminist and queer approaches to game studies challenge that field's epistemological foundations—particularly as the discipline reflects on its very existence—and can help chart the path through our digital future. In our manifesto for digital game studies twenty years on, we argue that the DH community must learn from game studies as it confronts these same issues of racist and misogynist toxicity, precarious and exploitative labor, and environmental impact.

It's a GamerGate World: Toxicity in Digital Spaces

While intersectional feminist and queer game scholars (Kishonna Gray, Elizabeth Losh, Bo Ruberg, Adrienne Shaw, and T. L. Taylor, to name only a few) have pushed against the homogeny of the discipline in some cases even before Aarseth's declared "year one," the failure of both the games industry and the field of game studies to confront its own misogyny and racism reached a visible peak in 2014, with the start of GamerGate. This multiplatform harassment campaign started with personal attacks on game designer Zoe Quinn and escalated rapidly to include attacks on both designers and scholars seen as threatening the centrality of white, straight, cisgender men in the industry. The fallout of this culture war has given rise to questions in game studies that are existential in nature and overwhelming in scale: How do we address the misogyny, racism, and other exclusionary practices present not only in our objects of study, but also in our academic communities? How do we talk about something, or push for reasoned discourse, when—much like the villain Voldemort of *Harry Potter*—even naming GamerGate draws the attention of trolls to conference hashtags or encourages mobs to attack scholars on Twitter? These problems are not unique to game studies, as there have been flare-ups around other cultural products such as films and comics. DH writ large relies on the same platforms that power fan communities and thus cannot avoid similar confrontations.

After all, GamerGate not only prompted soul searching about what academia had missed in gaming culture, but it also provided an example of the world outside academia taking note of digital scholarship. One illustrative flashpoint was a session at the Digital Games Research Association (DiGRA) conference in 2014. GamerGaters found a set of notes from this session in which feminist game scholars discussed their work and approaches—made public in a spirit of openness and collaboration—and started investigating the participants. Because the frameworks of academia were opaque to them, they concocted a conspiracy theory about the government controlling and destroying video games out of the combination of the fact that some scholars had received funding from the Defense Advanced Research Projects Agency (DARPA), perceived parallels between calls for inclusion in academia and industry, and the unfamiliar scholarly language in which the ideas were presented. As Shira Chess and Adrienne Shaw, the organizers of the session, wrote in their piece reflecting on this incident: "It has become apparent how quickly academia can be misunderstood, and more specifically how feminist academic research can be misappropriated for non-feminist purposes" (217). Notably, this event changed some academics' practices: Warnings against live tweeting became common before controversial subjects were discussed at conference panels in the field, and some scholars removed themselves from public platforms entirely. These events raise a broader issue about how we communicate—or don't—outside our scholarly audiences. Digital scholars must continually confront this challenge, as the work of social media scholar Whitney Phillips reminds us that "until the conversation is directed toward those who engage in behaviors similar or identical to those of trolls, until sensationalist, exploitative media practices are no longer rewarded with page views and ad revenue—in short, until the mainstream is willing to step in front of the funhouse mirror and consider the contours of its own distorted reflection—the most aggressive forms of trolling will always have an outlet, and an audience" (159). The expertise of digital games studies scholars in topics such as the role of affective ties in online communities, the ways platforms affect how information travels and changes, and the semiotic analysis of memes is increasingly vital to understanding contemporary culture writ large.

Moreover, game studies has served as a warning because it has needed to clean its own house. For example, a keynote at the Foundations of Digital Games conference in 2017 both equated marginalized populations to nonhumans and included troubling images of physical devices designed for transference of physical affection such as kissing, demonstrated on student participants. When audience members challenged the speaker on the misogyny, racism, and homophobia expressed in his talk, he dismissed their concerns, as feminist games scholar T. L. Taylor noted.[2] When another feminist scholar offered a concerned critique on Twitter, she became the target of a mob incited by the speaker. The conference organization team and the organization board of directors later issued a half-hearted condemnation of the keynote, focusing not on its dehumanizing content but instead condemning the "ad hominem" attacks on the tenure-track faculty member targeted for her critique. In 2018, the same keynote speaker would go on to chair the Advances in Computer Entertainment Technology (ACE) conference and invite white supremacist leader Stephen K. Bannon as a keynote speaker, demonstrating that visible misogyny and racism is still embraced in parts of the game studies community. As the work of games scholar Kishonna Gray reminds us, this centering of whiteness and masculinity continues to threaten the essential work that marginalized members of gaming culture, and particularly Black gamers, are doing to push back against toxicity.

Nevertheless, post-GamerGate, there have been some productive moves both in theory and in praxis. The coalitions formed in response to the GamerGate attacks have brought increased intensity to intersectional feminist and queer critiques in the field. These in turn have brought critical attention to pedagogy in the field as well as to the issue of gatekeeping, with a corresponding push for more inclusionary practices and active responses to toxicity. Bo Ruberg and Adrienne Shaw's landmark volume *Queer Game Studies* offers a transformative vision of the field while other scholars directly challenge the centering of gamer masculinity (Condis) and the illusion of "meritocracy" in gaming culture (Paul). Conference themes, such as the Foundations of Digital Games 2021 conference on Inclusivity, reflect the field's continual reckoning with the challenges of public games scholarship (Salter and Blodgett) and the need to support marginalized scholars. As conflicts of this type continue to play out beyond the field, the interpretive apparatus built to make sense of GamerGate has become useful across a variety of online environments. For example, Adrienne Massanari coined the term "toxic technoculture" to articulate the combination of platform affordances and culture on GamerGate's hub, Reddit, and in doing so provided a way of understanding a wider range of social media spaces that shape popular discourse. Examples of this toxicity are increasingly urgent: Conspiracy forums drive QAnon, which alleges that Donald Trump is fighting Satan-worshipping pedophiles, and assisted in the election of two members of Congress in 2020. Similarly, the "red pill" sites of the misogynist manosphere unite men in hatred of women, with affiliated groups often claiming credit for doxing (releasing private information such as real names and addresses) and revenge porn. As DH scholars study and in turn confront the consequences of these movements, the lessons of GamerGate about toxic online behavior, though acquired at a steep cost, have helped move all of digital studies forward.

Playbour and the Portfolio Self: Taking Labor Seriously

Additionally, confronting exploitative practices in game development work, and the pleasures of the work that supports that exploitation, sheds light on many kinds of contemporary digital labor. Both games studies and the games industry benefit from popular narratives that center work as "fun," a model that industry activists have pointed out enables intense and exploitative working conditions in game production. These "crunch" working conditions have been exposed thanks to the work of games journalists such as Jason Schreier. His 2018 exposé on Rockstar Games and the making of *Red Dead Redemption 2* featured accounts of unpaid overtime, evening and weekend work, and imbalance that came at the cost of "friendships, family time, and mental health." However, there are even contradictions in the accounts of employees, with some noting the satisfaction they took in their work despite a lack of compensation. This is consistent with what digital labor scholar Melissa Gregg has observed about white-collar work more generally. As work can be a source of enjoyment, "these pleasures and intimacies underwrite professional workers' willingness to engage in work outside paid hours" (Gregg, 5–6). The underlying rhetoric of playful labor, or what games scholar Julian Kücklich has termed "playbour," encourages not only outside observers but also those embedded in the culture of the games industry to dismiss these working conditions.

These patterns of industry exploitation of unpaid or undercompensated yet apparently willing labor extend beyond games to adjacent creative spaces—including games journalism and digital culture more broadly. Labor scholar Eran Fisher argues that this potential for exploitation is inherent to non-alienated work—that is, work that does not prevent the "possibility to express oneself, to control one's production process, to objectify one's essence and connect and communicate with others" (173). When we ourselves do not perceive our labor as work, it is easier to dismiss that it has economic value. Studies of modders echo this trend: the participants only acknowledged their labor when the work of making at-home game modifications *became* drudgery (Banks and Humphreys).

Games are also a key site of what communication scholars Kathleen Kuehn and Thomas Corrigan call "hope labor." Game programmers are expected to train themselves—paying for undergraduate and graduate degrees, paying for expensive software, or even just learning on their own by making unwaged modifications for commercial games until they have a sufficient portfolio. The historical model of companies taking on the responsibility of training their workers on the job has disappeared from all industries, but its absence is particularly visible in game development. Would-be employees willingly take on significant unpaid tasks like game modding, with the belief that it will inaugurate or further their careers as professional, paid workers. Asking questions about labor, and in particular about the enormous costs that must be taken on to have even an opportunity for a paid job, encourages us to take a hard look at the poverty imposed by graduate school, adjuncting, and other insecure contract work. Importantly, these kinds of hope labor are unevenly possible—those with generational wealth and without student loans (disproportionately white) and those without caregiving responsibilities (disproportionately men) are much more able to take such risks, perpetuating such people's overrepresentation in DH. Though games labor is particularly spectacular in its exploitation, the same broader issues of precarity and extreme work conditions can be found in academia and across the platforms of our digital work.

The recognition that people who love their jobs are especially susceptible to accepting excessive and escalating demands should give us pause in an era of adjunctification, exploding class sizes, and other austerities. In the DH, this trend is often experienced through the labor model of DH projects, which frequently rely on unequally credited and underpaid collaborators. As Rachel Mann's work reminds us, such labor often falls to graduate students, who in turn are often left out of the "thinking" and publishing aspects of a project. The increasingly urgent conversations in the games industry echo the calls to action from labor scholars examining internet culture more broadly. As Tiziana Terranova notes in an examination of invisible internet labor, such work is "pleasurably embraced and at the same time shamelessly exploited," and it fundamentally cannot be understood without acknowledging both of these facts (37). This framework has been documented among game workers and particularly noted for creating cultural norms where it is "difficult for workers to resist their own extreme working conditions" (Peticca-Harris, Weststar, and McKenna, 570). It should also sound familiar from things like scholarly publishing's entire free labor edifice, which relies on the framework of service to the field in spite of the increasing precarity of the field's workers and the diminishing numbers of tenured and tenure-track faculty.

The project-based, hire-and-fire cycles of games work also tell us much about other digital media labor. Looking at the whole of capitalism across space and time, Fordism and its stable, career-long employment is the exception rather than the rule (de Peuter). Yet formerly it was mostly marginalized people like the working poor, (disproportionately) people of color, and people in the Global South who needed to cobble together enough work to live on from various sources. After World War II, skilled, white, primarily male middle-class workers had decades of relative security that has only recently eroded—perhaps predictably producing white male resentment (Rodino-Colocino). This trend is echoed in the gig economy, which business scholar Jeremias Prassl says works to "make labor less visible" while rebranding people as a service (6). The digital economy's invisible labor is unevenly distributed, and, as anthropologist Mary L. Gray and computer scientist Siddharth Suri warn us, has already begun to create a new "global underclass" of unacknowledged workers. This broader labor context puts the decline of tenure-line jobs into a new perspective, emphasizing our kinship to those who design and code the technologies we use and research and asking us to reflect on whose invisible labor we in turn take for granted in the systems we rely on for our work. In particular, scholars using digital methods that employ humans as service (e.g., researchers using Amazon's "Mechanical Turks" or indeed DH scholars employing students for the tedious work of text coding) must consider our role in these cycles of exploitation. Turning a labor framework on game development and game studies makes possible key questions about the distribution of benefits and costs that we should ask about all of our work, within and outside the academy, as well as the work we ask of others.

Instead of stable, permanent jobs, temporary and contract work without benefits has progressively become the new norm for workers in almost all industries and only threatens to grow as a consequence of the economic disruptions resulting since 2020 and the Covid-19 pandemic. These disruptions disproportionately affect people of color and women, which provides an important reminder of the interrelatedness of racism, misogyny, and labor precarity. Framing a temporary and precarious job not as a radical weakening of the position of the worker but as an opportunity to grow one's portfolio and increase mobility, such that workers are increasingly understood as entrepreneurs of the self, has diminished resistance to such shifts. In addition to interrogating other costs of precarity, we must acknowledge how the ability to be flexible is unevenly distributed—particularly since the global pandemic has drawn attention to the continued inequities in parental labor expectations. It is useful to attend to how "always on" connectivity colonizes leisure hours with work and with play that is hard to distinguish from work, adds a second shift of playbour to ever-expanding groups of people, and either adds a third shift for the women already doing what sociologist Arlie Hochschild has termed a "second shift" as caretakers or excludes them from participation altogether in the rapidly developing new norm. These labor inequities (and their costs to people of color and white women) must be centered not only in games but in every field, particularly in the wake of the ongoing Covid-19 crisis.

Playing (for) the Planet: Interrogating Environmental Impact

Finally, as climate change draws worldwide attention but seems only to spur local inaction, we turn to games for insights into our collective environmental challenges. In 2019, a number of game companies (including Sony, Ubisoft, and Microsoft) gained positive press coverage for their announcement of the "Playing for the Planet" initiative, which included "pledges ranging from reducing supply chain emissions by 30 percent by 2030 to, a little less impressively, 'putting green nudges' into games' plots" (D'Anastasio). The pledge, unsurprisingly, does not hold up to scrutiny and does not address the reliance of the industry on conflict minerals and other materials sourced with no concern for human rights violations or environmental impact. Cloud gaming and cloud and server-based services more widely amplify power usage thanks to demands on both data centers and networks, as well as using large amounts of water for cooling in the arid U.S. Southwest, where many data centers are located.

Games studies coexists in many academic spaces with game design programs and thus is not only complicit in but fundamentally dependent on these games industry practices. It is therefore incumbent on us to recognize that educational and "serious" game design that might seek to intervene in climate change also contributes to the same system. These serious games are in dialogue with industry representations of climate change and impending environmental disaster.

Acknowledging these growing concerns, game studies has taken a much-needed environmentally conscious turn. Games scholar Alenda Y. Chang's *Playing Nature* suggests that an ecocritical approach to games and game design can be a valuable part of rethinking our relationships with the world, inviting players to rethink their agency within the complex chains of environmental impact in which they participate. Importantly, Chang's work points us toward a move in game studies that is emerging across digital spaces, and in reflections on the infrastructural usage of "big data" projects in DH, but must eventually become pervasive: the need to reconcile games design intentions with environmental impact realities.

An ecocritical turn in DH has been raised by Posthumus and Sinclair's work on "digital environmental humanities," which suggests the value of DH methods to bring "the non-human world into the foreground where it was before in the background" (269). However, the need to foreground this critical turn itself is long overdue. Safiya Noble notes that centering Black studies can remind us of environmental challenges and the role they play in inequality: "The extraction of minerals needed for digital computing technologies, the impact of conflicts over rare minerals, and the exploitive nature of the flow of global capital in and out of the regions where they are sourced have a serious impact on human rights and the environment" (31). Such an approach is needed because institutional interventions, such as NEH Infrastructure Grants, encourage overhauling computer labs and creating power-consuming, energy-inefficient, single-purpose devices, from virtual reality headsets to makerspaces. DH workshops and practices encourage the integration of more such technology throughout the university, with the demands of a constant cycle of upgrade and discard. While professors argue over whether smartphones belong in the classroom, the discussion of how these same smartphones contribute to global emissions is far less frequent. Similarly, critics such as Jonathan Wolff have drawn attention to the hypocrisy of academics perpetuating existing models of conference travel while participating in ecocritical discourse. While such commentary frequently ignores the realities of disciplinary isolation and academics' need for communal discourse and support, Covid-related shifts to digital conferences suggest that mediated modalities are more feasible than has previously been acknowledged for sustaining some types of interaction. Thus, even as we critique the data center, the networks that sustain our fields are also suspect and must be confronted.

Digital humanist Bethany Nowviskie's keynote address on "Digital Humanities in the Anthropocene" offers a powerful reminder of the costs of inaction and the need for more attention to this area: "We must attend to the environmental and human costs of DH—from our complicity with device manufacturers and social media manipulators, to the carbon footprint and price tag of conferences like this—and ask ourselves seriously what we might change, or grow to be" (Nowviskie, i13). Other exemplars, such as the fully online and free-of-charge Electronic Literature Organization conference and the Foundations of Digital Games conference and other virtual events in 2020, suggest what some of these compromises might look like at the intersection of games and DH communities. However, these too demand computing power and cloud services. Jentery Sayers advocates for a DH reflection that rejects this bulk, noting that minimal computing might offer a solution by reducing reliance on scale and thus "also a reliance on middleware, databases, peripherals, and substantial pieces of hardware." Through this lens, we are reminded that the "must-haves" of today's world of online education and conferences, such as Zoom, were unnecessary to online community and exchange in the past—and can perhaps be eliminated again in favor of sustainable approaches to DH computing.

Play It Forward

Academia is in crisis as Covid-19 brings with it closures of departments and universities, the halting of PhD program admissions, and the loss of staff and faculty jobs. This trend compounds the existing crisis in the humanities, where the decline in tenure-track job listings and external threats targeting critical race theory and gender studies point toward increasing precarity. If DH is to rise to the occasion as a meta-discipline, we must confront the fact that many of the challenges facing academia as a whole—an increasing atmosphere of divisiveness and outright hostility to intellectualism and even attacks on faculty, the mounting inequities of academic labor, and the need to rethink our practices and limit our impact on a rapidly changing climate—are amplified, not minimized, by the digital technologies that power our practice. The tense relationships of games studies and industry, and the ongoing conflicts examined here, illustrate the important role games discourse can play in foreshadowing our collective challenges.

Pandemic education is the latest in a series of existential threats to humanist education, which has declined in the face of tech-driven initiatives that reduce education to passive consumerism and witnessed the shuttering of humanist departments in the face of college "rightsizing" initiatives. The ranks of humanist academics with dedicated time for research are shrinking. The Modern Language Association conference, once attended by over 10,000 members in 2002, has dwindled to fewer than half as many participants. Even those who are still able to convene at such meetings are confronted by the reality of a changing profession. The conference's 2020 Presidential Theme, "Being Human," asked participants to consider questions of technology and labor, including these pressing questions: "How can we imagine more humane spaces of working and teaching? Is a pedagogy of care possible in late industrial society?" (Gikandi). No answer is easily forthcoming, but when tweets from the conference appeared at the same time as tweets from graduate students at the University of California Santa Cruz protesting unlivable wages, the collective challenges remained clear. These questions still resonate alongside the escalating challenges of Covid, where labor practices in universities have been particularly dehumanizing, as Ian Bogost observed in his essay "College Leaders Have the Wrong Incentives," calling out poor leadership in a time of crisis. If, among digital studies, games studies has been early to see these struggles, the renewed commitment to doing better, as exemplified by the labor-organizing actions of Game Workers Unite, suggests paths forward. In the present moment, the problems that beset us are many, but so too are people with deep awareness of these problems and the dedication to work toward solutions.

NOTES

1. Voltron is a giant robot composed of smaller robots working together to protect the universe. It is part of the franchise of the same name (1983 to present).

2. The comment was in a since-deleted Facebook post, summarized in Lawley's blog post.

BIBLIOGRAPHY

Aarseth, Espen. *Computer Game Studies, Year One.* July 2001, http://www.gamestudies.org/0101/editorial.html.

Banks, John, and Sal Humphreys. "The Labour of User Co-Creators: Emergent Social Network Markets?" *Convergence: The International Journal of Research into New Media Technologies* 14, no. 4 (2008): 401–18, https://doi.org/10.1177/1354856508094660.

Bogost, Ian. "College Leaders Have the Wrong Incentives." *The Atlantic.* June 30, 2020, https://www.theatlantic.com/ideas/archive/2020/06/leadership-crisis-campus/613678/.

Bogost, Ian. "Game Studies, Year Fifteen." *Bogost.Com.* February 2, 2015, http://bogost.com/writing/blog/game-studies-year-fifteen/.

Chang, Alenda Y. *Playing Nature: Ecology in Video Games.* Minneapolis: University of Minnesota Press, 2019.

Chess, Shira, and Adrienne Shaw. "A Conspiracy of Fishes, or, How We Learned to Stop Worrying about GamerGate and Embrace Hegemonic Masculinity." *Journal of Broadcasting & Electronic Media* 59, no. 1 (2015): 208–20, https://doi.org/10.1080/08838151.2014.999917.

Condis, Megan. *Gaming Masculinity: Trolls, Fake Geeks, and the Gendered Battle for Online Culture.* Iowa City: University of Iowa Press, 2018.

D'Anastasio, Cecilia. "Video Game Companies Vow Action on Climate Change, but Critics Say They Need to Do More." *Kotaku.* September 24, 2019, https://kotaku.com/video-game-companies-vow-action-on-climate-change-but-1838420425.

de Peuter, Greig. "Creative Economy and Labor Precarity: A Contested Convergence." *Journal of Communication Inquiry* 35, no. 4 (2011): 417–25, https://doi.org/10.1177/0196859911416362.

Fisher, Eran. "How Less Alienation Creates More Exploitation? Audience Labour on Social Network Sites." *TripleC: Communication, Capitalism & Critique—Open Access Journal for a Global Sustainable Information Society* 10, no. 2 (2012): 171–83, https://doi.org/10.31269/triplec.v10i2.392.

Gikandi, Simon E. "2020 Presidential Theme: Being Human." *Modern Language Association.* Accessed August 9, 2022, https://www.mla.org/Convention/Convention-History/Past-Conventions/2020-Convention/2020-Presidential-Theme.

Gray, Kishonna L. *Intersectional Tech: Black Users in Digital Gaming.* Baton Rouge: Louisiana State University Press, 2020.

Gray, Mary L., and Siddharth Suri. *Ghost Work: How to Stop Silicon Valley from Building a New Global Underclass.* New York: Harper Business, 2019.

Gregg, Melissa. *Work's Intimacy.* New York: John Wiley & Sons, 2013.

Hochschild, Arlie Russell. *The Second Shift.* New York: Avon Books, 1989.

Kücklich, Julian. "Precarious Playbour: Modders and the Digital Games Industry." *Fibreculture* 5. Accessed November 3, 2022, https://five.fibreculturejournal.org/fcj-025-precarious-playbour-modders-and-the-digital-games-industry/.

Kuehn, Kathleen, and Thomas F. Corrigan. "Hope Labor: The Role of Employment Prospects in Online Social Production." *The Political Economy of Communication* 1, no. 1 (2013), https://www.polecom.org/index.php/polecom/article/view/9.

Lawley, Liz. "Thoughts on the FDG '17 Keynote Controversy." *Medium*, October 28, 2018, https://medium.com/@mamamusings/thoughts-on-the-fdg-17-keynote-controversy-d9ede0b83b.

Mann, Rachel. "Paid to Do but Not to Think: Reevaluating the Role of Graduate Student Collaborators." In *Debates in the Digital Humanities 2019,* edited by Matthew K. Gold and Lauren F. Klein. Minneapolis: University of Minnesota Press, 2019, https://dhdebates.gc.cuny.edu/read/untitled-f2acf72c-a469-49d8-be35-67f9ac1e3a60/section/ea501a60-dd3c-4c22-a942-3d890c3a1e72.

Massanari, Adrienne. "#Gamergate and the Fappening: How Reddit's Algorithm, Governance, and Culture Support Toxic Technocultures." *New Media & Society* 19, no. 3 (2017): 329–46, https://doi.org/10.1177/1461444815608807.

Noble, Safiya Umoja. "Toward a Critical Black Digital Humanities." In *Debates in the Digital Humanities 2019,* edited by Matthew K. Gold and Lauren F. Klein, 27–35. Minneapolis: University of Minnesota Press, 2019, https://doi.org/10.5749/j.ctvg251hk.5.

Nowviskie, Bethany. "Digital Humanities in the Anthropocene." *Digital Scholarship in the Humanities* 30, no. 1 (December 2015): i4–i15, https://doi.org/10.1093/llc/fqv015.

Paul, Christopher A. *The Toxic Meritocracy of Video Games: Why Gaming Culture Is the Worst.* Minneapolis: University of Minnesota Press, 2018.

Peticca-Harris, Amanda, Johanna Weststar, and Steve McKenna. "The Perils of Project-Based Work: Attempting Resistance to Extreme Work Practices in Video Game Development." *Organization* 22, no. 4 (2015): 570–87, https://doi.org/10.1177/1350508415572509.

Phillips, Whitney. *This Is Why We Can't Have Nice Things: Mapping the Relationship between Online Trolling and Mainstream Culture.* Cambridge, Mass.: MIT Press, 2015.

Posthumus, Stephanie, and Stéfan Sinclair. "Reading Environment(s): Digital Humanities Meets Ecocriticism." *Green Letters* 18, no. 3 (September 2014): 254–73, https://doi.org/10.1080/14688417.2014.966737.

Prassl, Jeremias. *Humans as a Service: The Promise and Perils of Work in the Gig Economy.* Oxford: Oxford University Press, 2018.

Rodino-Colocino, Michelle. "Geek Jeremiads: Speaking the Crisis of Job Loss by Opposing Offshored and H-1B Labor." *Communication and Critical/Cultural Studies* 9, no. 1 (2012):. 22–46, https://doi.org/10.1080/14791420.2011.645490.

Ruberg, Bonnie, and Adrienne Shaw. *Queer Game Studies.* Minneapolis: University of Minnesota Press, 2017.

Salter, Anastasia, and Bridget Blodgett. "Playing the Humanities: Feminist Game Studies and Public Discourse." In *Bodies of Information: Intersectional Feminism and Digital Humanities,* edited by Elizabeth Losh and Jacqueline Wernimont. Minneapolis: University of Minnesota Press, 2018, https://dhdebates.gc.cuny.edu/read/untitled-4e08b137-aec5-49a4-83c0-38258425f145/section/7920a6ee-baa9-4d31-a115-c962131dfcd6.

Sayers, Jentery. "Minimal Definitions." *Minimal Computing*. October 2, 2016, https://go-dh.github.io/mincomp/thoughts/2016/10/02/minimal-definitions/.

Schreier, Jason. "Inside Rockstar Games' Culture of Crunch." *Kotaku*. October 23, 2018, https://kotaku.com/inside-rockstar-games-culture-of-crunch-1829936466.

Terranova, Tiziana. "Free Labor: Producing Culture for the Digital Economy." *Social Text* 18, no. 2 (63) (Summer 2000): 33–58.

Wolff, Jonathan. "What Hypocrisy, I Think Guiltily, as I Jet Off to Academic Conferences Far and Wide." *The Guardian*. October 29, 2019, http://www.theguardian.com/education/2019/oct/29/hypocrisy--guilt-jet-off-to-academic-conferences-plane-travel.

PART IV

PEDAGOGIES AND PRACTICES

The Challenges and Possibilities of Social Media Data: New Directions in Literary Studies and the Digital Humanities

MELANIE WALSH

During the Q&A after my 2017 talk at Michigan State University's Global Digital Humanities conference, a faculty member raised his hand and asked a series of questions that challenged me—even scared me—because I wasn't confident about the answers. "How would you describe your ethical approach to this data?" he asked. "Did you get IRB approval for this research?" At the time, I was a graduate student in English literature, and I had just presented a paper about my nascent digital humanities project—an analysis of #BlackLivesMatter tweets that cited the American novelist and civil rights activist James Baldwin. Then, as now, I argued that social media data can provide a rich archive of reading, literary reception, and textual circulation, that it can help us understand how people feel about books and authors and how they use them in the world. This social media data might include tweeted quotations, like the ones I referenced in my paper, but it might also include Goodreads ratings, TikTok (or "BookTok") videos, fanfiction stories, Tumblr discussions, Reddit memes, YouTube reviews, or countless other kinds of content from countless other platforms. Because this material is published on the internet, and because it can be collected as data, I believed, and still believe, that it can fuel new, data-rich approaches to literary history, opening up additional understandings of how literature lives in the contemporary world.

Yet the audience member's questions about ethics and obtaining approval from the IRB gave me pause. I understood the Twitter users in my dataset as authors in their own right, people who deserved credit and citation in my paper, and I had planned to inform these users before I formally published any research that cited their tweets. But I had not discussed this approach with many other scholars, nor was I certain about best practices for the field. And I pointedly shied away from the second question. *What's an IRB again?* I thought to myself.

An IRB, or institutional review board, is an administrative body that evaluates and approves the ethical dimensions of research involving human participants, with the goal of protecting the rights and welfare of the people involved. These review boards, a requirement for any U.S. institution or university that receives federal research money, were established in response to heinous human subject research abuses committed in the early- and mid-twentieth century.[1] Though familiar to many scholars in the sciences and social sciences, IRBs were not familiar to me, an English literature graduate student. Working with human subjects is not common in literary studies research—or at least, historically, it has not been. Though I later learned that publicly available data like tweets do not typically require IRB approval, I also learned that IRB approval or exemption is hardly the end of the story when it comes to dealing with social media data.[2] As Moya Bailey argues, "social media users require a level of forethought that extends beyond the purview of the IRB."[3] This perspective is shared by many other scholars as well as by the social media archiving project Documenting the Now, which has specifically grappled with the difficult questions raised by archiving #BlackLivesMatter data.

I begin with the story of this conference Q&A because I think it highlights a basic disconnect between my humanistic training and the more social-scientific research that I was beginning to do, a kind of interdisciplinary research that has come to characterize my scholarship and that has been embraced by other digital humanists and quantitative literary critics, too. Literary studies education does not typically cover how to conduct responsible research about people, or at least not "ordinary" people—in other words, people who are not published authors. Yet research that involves social media data always demands understanding how to treat people and their information with responsibility and care. As social media data becomes a more commonly used source in the digital humanities—and I use "social media data" as a catchall term for any user-generated content published on the internet—the absence of ethical frameworks to guide this type of research will become an even more pressing problem.

To be clear, I believe that social media data holds great promise for the humanities and for literary studies in particular, especially for an emerging subfield that I call *computational reception studies,* which explores questions related to reading, reception, and textual circulation.[4] But social media data is a fundamentally different kind of data than the digitized text collections that are familiar to most digital humanists and quantitative literary scholars. Most consequentially, social media data is tethered to living people who, unlike traditionally published authors, may not be expecting to be featured in scholarship and may even by harmed it. This difference demands that humanists who use social media data in their research must engage with the people behind the data being studied and with the ethical questions that their data invites.

The many challenges involved with collecting and analyzing data produced by communities has already been a central focus of digital humanities scholarship, and this body of thought serves as an essential resource. But there is additional work that needs to be done to connect this scholarship to the specific practices associated with computationally assisted social media research, and there are other gaps that remain. In the first half of this chapter, I sketch out the subfield of computational reception studies, showing how social media data resembles earlier forms of reception data featured in existing digital humanities work (e.g., nineteenth-century library records or twentieth-century book reviews) and how it also figures in emerging research on contemporary literature, readership, and politics. In the second half, I highlight the approaches to social media data being used and recommended by leading researchers at the border of the social sciences and digital humanities. These scholars—including Sarah J. Jackson, Moya Bailey, and Brooke Foucault Welles; Deen Freelon, Charlton D. McIlwain, and Meredith D. Clark; Dorothy Kim and Eunsong Kim; Brianna Dym and Casey Fiesler; and members of the Documenting the Now project—are currently pursuing the complex questions animated by the scholarly use of social media data. By drawing on these scholars as well as my own research experience, I outline three unresolved questions for humanists who plan to study social media data with the help of computational tools: (1) How should scholars engage with the online communities whose data they computationally collect and analyze? (2) How should scholars cite social media users in published research? (3) How, if at all, should scholars share users' data? These three issues—community engagement, citation, and data sharing—do not have easy or universal solutions, but I suggest some best practices for addressing them.

Though this chapter mostly focuses on the reception turn in quantitative literary studies, social media data is already being used in other parts of literary studies and the humanities, and the best practices that I offer also apply to those areas. Matt Kirschenbaum, for example, has argued that scholars "cannot write seriously about contemporary literature without taking into account myriad channels and venues for online exchange." Proving Kirschenbaum's point, Laura McGrath has studied how aspiring authors pitch their work to literary agents on Twitter by using both qualitative and quantitative methods plus an archive of computationally collected tweets. Advocating for the broad potential of social media data in digital humanities research, Michael L. Black has suggested that it might help build a more interdisciplinary and global digital humanities community, drawing in "fields like new media studies, software studies, science and technology studies, and Internet history" while also offering an alternative to "major print data repositories, which continue to rely on cultural categories defined around national identities" (96). Whether or not this exciting vision is fulfilled, an increasing number of scholars and students will inevitably apply the technical methods of the digital humanities (e.g., computational text analysis, data mining, machine learning) to the social media sphere. The issues of community engagement, citation, and data sharing will thus become essential considerations not only for scholars who are interested in reception, or scholars who plan to use social media data in their own research, but for many more. We must shift the way we teach and do research with computational methods in the humanities so that we can more responsibly engage with communities and the social data they create, and so that we can build a lasting framework for the research to come.

The Reception Turn in Quantitative Literary Studies

At the 2020 Modern Language Association (MLA) annual convention, Ted Underwood heralded a shift in quantitative literary studies, or "distant reading," when he announced a turn away from the field's primary focus on the text of books and toward evidence about the life of books. "The collections distant readers built ten or twenty years ago informed us about literary production, not circulation or reception," Underwood said. "But if we want to learn about the other half of a book's life cycle, we're going to need other kinds of evidence." This shift has partly been driven, as Underwood acknowledged, by scholars like Katherine Bode and Lauren Klein, who argue that quantitative approaches to literary history are reductive if scholars only apply them to a single copy of a literary work and do not account for the work's publication or circulation history (Bode, 79), or if they frame their analyses only along the axis of "close" and "distant" reading and do not consider additional dimensions of scale (Klein, 25). In their own research, both Bode and Klein offer promising ways to enrich quantitative approaches to literary history. But using more and better evidence about reception is another clear way that scholars can produce deeper, more complex cultural histories.

Many digital humanities scholars have in fact already begun to produce these multidimensional cultural histories by incorporating a wide variety of reception evidence in their work. Bode, for example, has pointed out that many of Franco Moretti's claims about readers are tenuously based on the "publication [date] and/or formal features of literary works," not on actual evidence about readers (Bode, 92).[5] Anne DeWitt, rather than relying on formal textual features alone, explores reader responses to nineteenth-century theological novels through their discussion in newspapers. Lynne Tatlock, Matt Erlin, Doug Knox, and Steve Pentecost similarly study late-nineteenth-century readership by examining library book checkout records digitized by the What Middletown Read project. Underwood, Wenyi Shang, and their team at the University of Illinois Urbana-Champaign are parsing twentieth-century book reviews from volumes like *Book Review Digest,* hoping to understand how reviews influence literary prestige, popularity, and style. There are other leading digital humanities projects that rely on reception and circulation data as well.[6] Projects like Viral Texts and America's Public Bible use newspaper archives to track the reprinting of texts and the popularity of biblical quotations; the Reading Chicago Reading project relies on library records from the Chicago Public Library to understand how people across the city engage with the same books; and the Open Syllabus Project uses crowdsourced syllabi to understand the contours of college curriculum and the most frequently taught texts and authors. By shifting attention away from primary textual evidence and toward these other forms of evidence, this emerging subfield seeks to answer questions that have long been central to critical traditions like reader-response criticism, reception studies, book history, audience theory, and the history of reading.

These reception-oriented approaches, which first took shape in the 1970s and 1980s, emerged, much like their digital humanities descendants, from a dissatisfaction with the narrow scope of then-dominant critical methods and with scholars' excessive focus on the text. "Although theorists of reader-oriented criticism disagree on many issues," as Jane Tompkins once put it, "they are united in one thing: their opposition to the belief that meaning inheres completely and exclusively in the literary text" (201). The same could be said of computational reception studies, which, while varied in its approaches, seems united around the belief that "other kinds of evidence" are required to understand literary and cultural texts.

The kinds of evidence discussed thus far—historical book reviews, newspaper articles, library circulation records—are largely familiar to scholars who use computational methods in the digital humanities because they come from familiar databases (e.g., the HathiTrust Digital Library, the Library of Congress's *Chronicling America* newspaper archive) or entail familiar processes of digitization (e.g., scanning and optical character recognition). But data about reading and reception is also being curated from a source far less familiar to the field: the internet, where book reviews, fanfiction stories, tweeted quotations, and other forms of reception evidence are routinely and copiously published by readers, writers, and amateur critics. Compared to more traditional digitized text collections, this born-digital data offers new affordances. Its abundance, its relative ease of collection, and its unique, often intimate documentation of reader responses open new possibilities for literary research.[7] For example, Goodreads, the social networking site for readers, currently has more than 120 million users who have published, since the site's founding in 2006, more than 90 million reviews of books. While bigger data is not always better data, bigger data, in this case, represents an expanded archive of reception. Goodreads reviews and other social media data also represent readers' responses in their own words, a kind of evidence that has been historically difficult, if not impossible, for literary critics to find, especially in large quantities.[8] Further, because these reviews are published on the internet, they can be "scraped" or otherwise computationally collected as structured data, and scraping data from the web is generally easier and faster than digitizing print materials.[9]

Social media data's abundance, availability, and richness have made it a growing focus in humanistic research. For example, literary scholars have used Goodreads reviews and ratings to empirically investigate various differences between reception communities: the readers of best-selling novels versus the readers of critically acclaimed novels (English et al.), the language of amateur reviewers versus the language of professional reviewers (Hegel), the tastes of conservative readers versus the tastes of liberal readers (Piper and So), and the books rated by Goodreads users versus the books cited by literary scholars (Manshel, McGrath, and Porter).

Additionally, teams at the Stanford Literary Lab have explored how genres of fanfiction, in which amateur authors write and share stories based on existing fiction, evolve over time and how *Harry Potter* fanfiction compares across different languages. A team at the University of Pennsylvania's Price Lab for Digital Humanities, meanwhile, has studied how quotations get recycled from movies to *Archive of Our Own* fanfiction stories. They have also published an interactive tool, The Fan Engagement Meter (fanengagement.org), which can be used to explore these trends. In my own research, I have drawn on an archive of #BlackLivesMatter tweets to explore quotations of the writer James Baldwin, showing that Twitter users overwhelmingly cited Baldwin's 1960s mass media material as well as circulated various misquotations of his words (Walsh).[10] And while Twitter has received outsized scholarly attention because it makes data more available to researchers, many other platforms—such as YouTube, TikTok, and Reddit—can also give us enlightening perspectives on how people discuss, deploy, and use literature in everyday life.

Though social media data clearly offers new opportunities when compared to traditional digitized texts, it also poses new challenges. The most serious challenges stem from the fact that social media data is published by people who, unlike traditionally published authors, may not be expecting or may not want to be the subjects of research. These are people who may, consequently, be at special risk of doxxing, trolling, harassment, or of otherwise experiencing negative, undesired outcomes from the mishandling of their data. Scholars who study fanfiction communities, are intimately familiar with such risks and with the difficulties of separating online texts from the people who authored them. One of the most complicated questions for fanfiction scholars, as Kristina Busse puts it, is "whether online evidence ought to be viewed as a textual document or as an utterance by the person who wrote it" (11). Scholars of computational reception studies must face the same question. Is a Goodreads dataset, for example, a collection of *texts* or a collection of utterances made by *people*? It is both, of course. But I believe that we can take a cue from fanfiction scholarship in more clearly recognizing the people in the data and the living quality of the data. "Unlike traditional texts," as Brianna Dym and Casey Fiesler write, "fan works are personal and tied to the people and communities they are created in as *living data,* so they carry consequences with their use and analysis" (emphasis added). For scholars who use fanfiction stories or similar "living data" in their work, these consequences are necessary to address.

This is not, of course, the first time that humanists or literary critics have engaged with living data. Perhaps the most influential work of reception scholarship, Janice Radway's *Reading the Romance*, is centered around a community of real Midwestern women romance readers. Interestingly enough, Underwood has previously pointed to Radway as a proto-quantitative literary critic because she uses, in this study, social-scientific methods like experimental design, samples, and hypotheses. This genealogy, as Underwood tells it, is meant to highlight quantitative literary studies' investment in social-scientific approaches rather than in digital technology or the digital humanities. But Radway's decision to engage with actual readers—"to move beyond the various concepts of the inscribed, ideal, or model reader and to work with actual subjects in history" (5)—demanded not only that she formulate hypotheses and create samples, but also that she incorporate ethnographic approaches such as interviews, surveys, participant observation, and collaboration. This aspect of Radway's social-scientific approach is, in my view, not what disconnects quantitative literary studies from the rest of the digital humanities but perhaps one of the things that most meaningfully connects them.

As many of the chapters in this 2023 edition of *Debates in the Digital Humanities* testify, digital humanities scholars have been leaders in conversations around data ethics and at the forefront of developing guidelines for data-driven research with and for communities. In Chapter 8 (The Feminist Data Manifest-NO), Tonia Sutherland, Marika Cifor, T. L. Cowan, Jasmine Rault, and Patricia Garcia propose distinct principles for feminist approaches to data that center minoritized communities. These principles—informed by humanistic thinking about data and ethics, people and lives—can be carried over, and indeed have been carried over, into social-scientific work. In the sections that follow, I show how current computational research with social media data must continue to bridge digital humanities and social science perspectives, particularly with regard to three key challenges: community engagement, citation, and data sharing. To think through these challenges, I draw on models and recommendations from the Documenting the Now project; from research about social media activism by Moya Bailey, Sarah J. Jackson, Brooke Foucault Welles, Deen Freelon, Charlton D. McIlwain, and Meredith D. Clark; and from research about ethical approaches to fanfiction data by Brianna Dym and Casey Fiesler. These researchers and their projects are especially helpful because they focus on the data of marginalized or otherwise vulnerable communities, such as Black activists and LBGTQ fanfiction writers. Centering research on these communities can help scholars develop best practices that consider the most vulnerable as a baseline and adjust from this baseline based on context.

Community Engagement

Because of the technical affordances of social media data, it is not only possible but common for researchers to collect users' personal data without their permission and even without their knowledge. Fiesler and Nicholas Proferes have shown that many Twitter users are not aware that researchers can and do collect their data. Perhaps equally worrisome is that researchers often lack knowledge about the users and communities whose data they collect. As Bergis Jules, Ed Summers, and Vernon Mitchell of Documenting the Now assert, "the internet affords the luxury of a certain amount of distance to be able to observe people, consume information generated by and about them, and collect their data without having to participate in equitable engagement as a way to understand their lives, communities, or concerns" (3).

For these reasons, they and other scholars argue that researchers should engage with and be knowledgeable about the communities whom they are studying and collecting data from—whether through conversation, collaboration, interviews, or ethnographic approaches. This insistence on community engagement aligns with one of the principles of the Feminist Data Manifest-NO (see Chapter 8), in which the authors refuse "work *about* minoritized people" and commit instead to "working *with* and *for* minoritized people in ways that are consensual and reciprocal and that understand data as always co-constituted" (emphasis added). Here, I argue that humanities scholars who work with social media data must meaningfully and deliberately engage with the communities they study, as well.

The significance of community engagement for humanistic social media research has already been demonstrated in some of the public discourse surrounding the Fan Engagement Meter, the fanfiction project out of Penn's Price Lab for Digital Humanities. Led by Peter Decherney, James Fiumara, and Scott Enderle, the Fan Engagement Meter is an interactive tool that displays lines of film dialogue commonly reused in *Archive of Our Own* fanfiction stories—stories that were computationally collected and analyzed for the purposes of the project. After the Fan Engagement Meter was spotlighted by the university's news publication, *Penn Today,* some fanfiction writers and scholars, who were previously unaware of the project, began to voice concerns about it (Shepard). In a piece for the online publication *Mary Sue,* fanfiction writer Jessica Mason referred to the project's methods as "creepy data mining," and she amplified similar criticism from fanfiction scholar and literary critic Alexandra Edwards, who tweeted: "And I have to wonder . . . did they go through IRB for this? How do we know these researchers won't sell the aggregated data (especially the bullshit predictive model stuff)? Are works on AO3 protected from this kind of exploitation in any way?"[11] These comments and questions register some people's discomfort, confusion, and apprehension about researchers collecting their data and the subsequent uses or potential misuses of that data. Such apprehension is especially heightened for fanfiction communities, as Dym and Fiesler address, because they often represent vulnerable populations and privacy-sensitive contexts "due to not only the large number of LGBTQ participants . . . but also different stigmas associated with fandom." For computational reception studies, and for broader digital humanities research, these concerns underscore the importance of addressing ethical questions head on and clearly explaining approaches to data collection, data analysis, and data sharing in all published results.

But the central criticism voiced in Mason's piece is not ultimately about data mining or even quantification, but rather it is about a lack of engagement with the fanfiction community on the part of the researchers and, more specifically, about a lack of dialogue with relevant work by women, queer people, and people of color:

> The use of quantitative, data-based research isn't new in fan studies. In fact, there are many academics and non-academics out there doing amazing work,

> such as DestinationToast on tumblr. The problem here is these men approaching fanfic like they're the first people to analyze it. . . . I hope this tool can somehow be useful, but I also hope these researchers take the time to listen to the female, queer and POC voices in fan studies that are doing great work and see what they can learn. (Mason)

This hope, the conclusion of Mason's piece, underlines that working with, understanding, and listening to communities—as well as to scholars already researching in these spaces, even if they do not use the same methods—is one of the most important considerations for computational research with social media data, and indeed for all academic research.

By directly engaging with the users and online communities whom they hope to study, scholars can also make better, more informed, and more context-dependent decisions about other parts of the research process, such as whether to cite a specific user in published research. For example, in Dym and Fiesler's extremely useful best practices for studying online fandom data, they recommend that researchers who are unfamiliar with fan communities "spend time [in online fandom spaces] and take the time to talk to fans and to understand and learn their norms," not only to learn more about the community but also to become more "mindful of each user's reasonable expectations of privacy, which may be dependent on the community or platform."[12] They further underscore that making connections with individual users is possible even for large-scale, data-driven research: "Even for public data sets in which individual participants might number in the tens of thousands to the millions, it might be possible to talk to some members of the target population in order to better understand what values and concerns people might hold that would deter them from consenting to their data being used" (Dym and Fiesler). Likewise, for digital humanities scholars, even those working with large datasets, talking to actual internet users can be an essential step toward producing more ethical research.

Mixed-methods approaches to social media data have already proved successful in leading research at the border of the social sciences and digital humanities. For example, in her research on the #GirlsLikeUs hashtag, created by trans advocate Janet Mock, Moya Bailey sought Mock's permission to work on the project before it began, and she collaborated with Mock to develop her research questions and determine the project's direction. Though Bailey's research included data collection and quantitative analyses, it was also shaped by a consenting collaborator who was part of the community being studied. In their 2020 book *#HashtagActivism: Networks of Race and Gender*, Bailey and her colleagues Sarah Jackson and Brooke Foucault Welles similarly frame the social media users whom they study as collaborators, and they intentionally make space for "hashtag users to speak for themselves" (Jackson, Bailey, and Foucault Welles).[13] To this end, they pair each chapter of their book with "an essay written by an influential member of a particular hashtag activism network" (Jackson, Bailey, and Foucault Welles). Along similar lines, Deen Freelon, Charlton

McIlwain, and Meredith Clark used large-scale network analysis techniques to study 40 million #BlackLivesMatter (BLM) tweets, but they also interviewed dozens of BLM activists and allies "to better understand their thoughts about how social media was and was not useful in their work." Such mixed-methods approaches, shaped by the social sciences, offer a productive model for computational reception studies and broader digital humanities research.

Yet, as we have seen, mixed-methods approaches are also not without precedent in the humanities, as Radway's study of romance readers clearly demonstrates. After all, in *Reading the Romance*, Radway does not argue that ethnographic approaches should "*replace* textual interpretation" but rather that they might be "fruitfully employed as an essential component of a multifocused approach that attempts to do justice to . . . historical subjects" (6). In a similar vein, I argue that direct interactions with online users and ethnographic approaches need not *replace* computational text analysis, but rather that they might be integrated as one part of a multifaceted approach that can more richly and responsibly consider what readers, writers, and amateur critics actually care about, what texts mean to them, and why they share texts in the contemporary world.

Citation

Researchers often face another difficult question when dealing with social media data: how, if at all, to quote or cite specific social media posts in published research. While some researchers attempt to avoid this issue by sticking with aggregated representations of data, more humanistic research often demands engagement with specific examples. In my research on Baldwin and the BLM movement, for instance, I found that one of the most popular tweeted quotations was a misquotation of Baldwin's words, one that had many subtle mutations in the dataset, and I wanted to attend to these differences by closely reading some of the individual tweets (Walsh). But I then faced the difficult decision of how to cite the authors of those tweets, how to balance protecting users' privacy and safety with honoring their creativity and agency. I ultimately decided to contact each user, inform them of the citation, and give them the option of not being included in the article. Most people replied and actively voiced interest in being included. Some of these users asked for more details about the research, some expressed surprise that one of their tweets had been deemed research-worthy, and some conveyed mild shock that they had even authored the tweet I was referring to, forgetting about the 140 characters they had released into the ether years earlier. While this approach to citation worked for me at the time, I have continued to reflect on my choices, and today I would make slightly different ones. In alignment with arguments by Dorothy Kim and Eunsong Kim, I would now follow a stronger consent-centered approach, one that recommends that researchers who wish to cite specific social media posts should make their best effort to contact the authors (especially if they are nonpublic figures) and that they should seek *explicit* permission to use posts, in addition to asking for a desired authorial attribution, such as a username, real name, or pseudonym. Even when researchers make their best efforts, however, gaining direct permission from users is not always possible—a challenge that fanfiction scholars have noted and that my own research experience affirms as well.[14] In these cases, it can be helpful to turn to other citation strategies, which I will discuss in more detail below.

First, however, it is important to establish why both citation *and* anonymization are potentially harmful for users.[15] Citation can be detrimental to users because it can expose their material to a new, unexpected, and/or larger audience, which can lead to unwanted attention, harassment, doxxing, physical harm, adverse professional consequences, personal complications, and other negative outcomes. For example, the Documenting the Now project discusses how "activists of color . . . face a disproportionate level of harm from surveillance and data collection by law enforcement," and thus amplifying their words or actions (as documented through social media) might put them in danger, even more so than the average social media user (Jules, Summers, and Mitchell). In a similar vein, when fanfiction writers were asked how they felt about researchers or journalists citing their stories, many fanfiction writers, "whether identifying as LGBTQ themselves or simply thinking about their friends, worried that exposing fandom content to a broader audience could lead to fans being accidentally outed" (Dym and Fiesler). Because of such risks and other privacy concerns, some scholars choose to anonymize social media posts. This would seem to be an easy way to protect the privacy of individual social media users while also including direct textual evidence in published research.

Yet anonymity is not a sufficient strategy both because it is not actually effective for protecting users' privacy and because it robs users of authorship. "Even when anonymized by not including usernames, content from social media collected and shared in research articles can be easily traced back to its creator," as Dym and Fiesler assert, drawing on a study by John W. Ayers and colleagues. Furthermore, anonymity does not give users proper intellectual credit, as Amy Bruckman argues. For these reasons, seeking explicit permission from users is usually the best approach to citation, and it can even lead to more meaningful and substantive forms of community engagement. For example, in my research with Maria Antoniak on Goodreads reviews, we sought permission from each Goodreads user whom we directly quoted in our published work. We messaged these users on the Goodreads platform, described our research, asked for permission to quote from a specific review, and offered different attribution options, such as their real name, username, or the anonymous pseudonym "Goodreads user." While some users simply replied with a quick "yes" or "no," many users responded with follow-up questions about the research, how exactly we planned to cite them, and where they could find the article when it was published. Some users even offered helpful contextualization and further explanation of their reviews. Asking for consent thus opened the door to a more reciprocal, collaborative, and informed relationship with the users whom we were studying.

Though seeking explicit permission from these Goodreads users was a rewarding experience in many ways, it also highlighted some of the drawbacks of this approach, including the fact that many Goodreads users did not respond to our inquiries at all.[16] When it is not possible to gain permission from users, Dym and Fiesler recommend paraphrasing posts in such a way that they are not traceable back to the original post or ethically "fabricating" material in ways that Annette Markham has advocated and described, such as by creating a composite account of a person, interaction, or dialogue. Paraphrasing strategies were effectively used by Antoniak, David Mimno, and Karen Levy in their computational analysis of the Reddit community r/BabyBumps, a community for sharing birth stories. The authors chose to paraphrase Reddit posts included in the article in order to "minimize the possible identification of and harm to the authors" (23). Taking a different tack, Freelon, McIlwain, and Clark decided to include links to tweets rather than the full texts of tweets in their study, which allowed Twitter users to delete their tweets and to effectively remove themselves from the research. Additionally, they only linked to tweets that were already reasonably exposed to the public, such as tweets with more than 100 retweets, tweets published by officially verified Twitter accounts, or tweets published by Twitter accounts with more than 3,000 followers.[17] Such thresholds—metrics that can be used to assess whether republishing a post will unduly increase exposure or risk to the author—can be devised for other platforms and contexts as well. All of these strategies—paraphrasing posts, linking to posts rather than quoting text, and establishing "reasonably public" thresholds—can be effective approaches to citation in humanistic research with social media data.

Yet it is important to acknowledge that many of these approaches disrupt comfortable and commonly used methodologies in humanistic scholarship, such as close reading. I feel the discomfort, too. As a literary critic with a reverence for texts, it is slightly painful for me to think about paraphrasing an especially colorful tweet or a hilarious Goodreads review. Yet I also recognize that the evolving nature of humanistic research demands that we expand beyond our comfort zones and disciplinary trainings. If embracing new approaches means better protecting people, isn't it worth the discomfort?

Sharing Data

Sharing data and code has become an important practice in quantitative literary studies and in the broader digital humanities. As the *Journal of Cultural Analytics,* one of the field's leading research journals, contends: "Shared data helps foster a community of critical analysis and widens the circle of who can participate."[18] In keeping with this conviction, the *Journal of Cultural Analytics* requires that "all data and code relevant to articles published in [the journal] will be made publicly available," including "underlying text, audio, or image files; derived data used in the analysis; and code used to acquire, clean, and analyze collections." But social media data troubles this policy, as the journal acknowledges, because "user-generated content should not be recirculated without permission." The risks previously discussed with regard to social media citation are amplified many times over when sharing full datasets, because full datasets include more potentially identifiable data about more users.

Testifying to such risks, the authors of a white paper on the Documenting the Now project discuss how their technical lead, Ed Summers, was once asked to share some of the Twitter data that he had collected about the 2014 #Ferguson protests—data that documented both virtual and on-the-ground protests sparked by the unjust murder of Michael Brown, who was shot and killed by a police officer in Ferguson, Missouri. The person asking for this #Ferguson data, Summers discovered, was an employee of a social media data mining company that was collaborating with law enforcement and security services. Though Summers refused the request, the Documenting the Now team members realized "how easy it could be for the collections we build to be used against marginalized communities" (Jules, Summers, and Mitchell). On the other hand, Jackson, Bailey, and Foucault Welles have also stressed how essential social media data access is for research and knowledge production: "The threats to privacy and security that are introduced through unwanted use of social media data are real, but so too are the threats to social-scientific insight if we are unable to create pathways for researchers to access data within and across social media platforms" (206). The question of how to safely share social media data is an extremely challenging one, and there is no universal solution to the issues that are raised.

While the conversation around the sharing of social media data is still evolving, I will briefly point to two potential paths for ethically sharing social media data: sharing data in ways that allow for users' right to be forgotten, and sharing data in repositories that offer varying levels of restriction and access. The first path is perhaps best exemplified by Twitter's policies for sharing data. Twitter's terms of service do not allow users to share full datasets of tweets, but they do allow the sharing of tweet IDs—unique identifiers assigned to every tweet that can be used to retroactively access tweets from Twitter's application programming interface (API). If an ID is connected to a tweet that has been deleted, however, the tweet can no longer be accessed. "If you squint right," Ed Summers has argued of this policy, "Twitter is taking an ethical position for their publishers to be able to remove their data: to exercise their right to be forgotten."[19] This system allows researchers to share Twitter data while also allowing individual users to remove themselves from future versions of the data if they wish. Many researchers, such as Freelon, McIlwain, and Clark, have shared their data in this format, and the Documenting the Now project even hosts a crowdsourced repository of tweet IDs that currently contains more than 6 billion of them (catalog.docnow.io). Though this policy is specific to Twitter, the same principles can be applied to other platforms and domains. If a researcher collected millions of photos from Instagram, as the *Journal of Cultural Analytics* describes in one of its data-sharing scenarios, that researcher would be discouraged from sharing the actual photo data, but they would be encouraged to share the code used to collect the photo data. This would allow other researchers to collect similar data while also affording Instagram users more time to remove their posts. Admittedly, this prioritization of users' privacy comes at the cost of replicability. These data-sharing strategies do not allow for the *exact* replicability of data or the *exact* reproducibility of results. But they can still come close to replicating data and reproducing results, and they can do so, importantly, in ways that honors users' right to be forgotten.

The second possible path for safely sharing social media data is to use data repositories that offer varying levels of restriction and access. For example, when Ryan Gallagher and his colleagues collected tweets for a study about the #MeToo movement and online disclosures of sexual violence, they chose to share tweet IDs for the underlying data through the Inter-University Consortium for Political and Social Research (ICPSR), housed at the University of Michigan (Gallagher et al.). ICPSR is a data repository commonly used in the social sciences and affiliated with more than 780 universities and research organizations around the world. To download any data from this repository, interested parties must agree to terms of responsible use, which include pledges to protect users' privacy and commitments not to redistribute or sell data. ICPSR also allows researchers to place restrictions on who can access their data—only affiliated ICPSR members, for example, or, more restrictively, only affiliated ICPSR members who fill out an extensive application and gain IRB approval. Because of the sensitive nature of #MeToo tweets, Gallagher et al. chose to place strict restrictions on their data.[20] To access it, a researcher must submit an application package that includes, among other things, IRB approval, an approved security plan, and a confidentiality pledge. I believe that data repositories like ICPSR may also be useful for humanistic research with social media data. In fact, ICPSR is developing a repository specifically designed for social media data, the Social Media Archive (SOMAR), which will make it particularly useful (Hemphill, Leonard, and Hedstrom; Hemphill). More important than the specific data repository, however, is the larger principle of controlling who data can be shared with, and by what means it can be shared. For scholars who wish to share full social media datasets, especially if the data involves sensitive information, I recommend placing restrictions on who can access it.

Living Data

Computational reception studies is not just a future chapter of quantitative literary studies—it is one that is already being written. This exciting work, as I have shown, is already taking place. But the living data that computational reception studies often relies on (and will increasingly rely on)—Goodreads reviews, fanfiction stories, Tumblr comments, and more—requires a rethinking of how we cite texts, how we share data, and how we engage with the communities who produce these texts and data. Moving forward, we must listen to and participate more fully in data ethics conversations happening in other areas of the digital humanities and in the social sciences, and we must recognize our deep connections to both of these fields. The ethical complexities involved with studying social media data can be overwhelming, especially for scholars who have not worked with social media data before. But if we take the time to understand current best practices and ethical guidelines, we can continue to author this exhilarating new chapter of quantitative literary studies and the digital humanities.

This type of research can also help advance a goal that has long been associated with the digital humanities: connecting our work back to the communities that initially inspired it. Among Dym and Fiesler's findings on fanfiction data was that, "despite some risk—many of [their] participants were excited about the idea of research shining a light on the practices and communities of fandom." I have witnessed similar excitement when interacting with Twitter and Goodreads users. Some of them have sent me long direct messages explaining why they love books and publishing reviews online, and some have been unexpectedly eager to learn about my research. It has been a surprise and joy to meet the people behind my data, and it has made me ever more aware that this data is, in the words of Dym and Fiesler, living data. Recognizing and being responsible to the people behind social media data may be one of the most difficult and challenging aspects of future research in this area, but as I have found in my own work, it may also be one of the most rewarding.

NOTES

1. For more on the history of institutional review boards and the egregious abuses that motivated them, see Won Oak Kim, "Institutional Review Board (IRB) and Ethical Issues in Clinical Research," *Korean Journal of Anesthesiology* 62, no. 1 (January 2012): 3–12, https://doi.org/10.4097/kjae.2012.62.1.3; Todd W. Rice, "The Historical, Ethical, and Legal Background of Human-Subjects Research," *Respiratory Care* 53, no. 10 (2008): 5; Patricia Cohen, "As Ethics Panels Expand Grip, No Field Is Off Limits (2007)," *New York Times*, February 28, 2007, Arts, https://www.nytimes.com/2007/02/28/arts/28board.html.

2. Some IRB offices still recommend caution with publicly available data, however. For example, as of 2013, Cornell University's Office of Research Integrity and Assurance recommended that researchers who use publicly available social media data seek "formal confirmation of non-human participant research status for the study . . . because of the emerging ethical sensitivities in this area" (see https://researchservices.cornell.edu/sites/default/files/2019-05/IRB%20Policy%2020.pdf).

3. See Bailey.

4. Though the subfield that encompasses this work does not yet have a coherent or widely recognized name, I offer *computational reception studies* as one potentially unifying term. I use the term *reception studies* because it capaciously captures the diversity of data relevant to the subfield, and I use the term *computational* rather than quantitative

because computation holds special consequences in this area (e.g., the computational collection of users' data).

5. See also DeWitt, who points out that readers are often "central" to Franco Moretti's arguments yet completely "absent from his evidence" (162). Similarly, Tatlock and colleagues claim that quantitative approaches in literary studies tend "to downplay reader agency and heighten attention to 'objective' textual features." However, they emphasize that the same methods can also be used to analyze reading behavior and "enhance our understanding of how meaning is co-constructed" (Tatlock et al.).

6. See Ryan Cordell and David Smith's 2017 "Viral Texts Project: Mapping Networks of Reprinting in 19th-Century Newspapers and Magazines," http://viraltexts.org; Lincoln Mullen, "America's Public Bible: Biblical Quotations in U.S. Newspapers," http://americaspublicbible.org/; "Reading Chicago Reading," https://dh.depaul.press/reading-chicago/; and "Open Syllabus," https://opensyllabus.org/.

7. See Black, who similarly argues that "using the Internet as a data source would afford access to text written by both professionals and amateurs, a distinction that is often not available when working with more formal archives" (103).

8. Emphasizing the usual absence of firsthand evidence from readers, Richard D. Altick once said of Victorian readers that "the great majority of the boys and girls and men and women into whose hands fell copies of cheap classic reprints did not leave any printed record of their pleasure. Only occasionally did the mute, inglorious common reader take pen in hand." Altick, "From Aldine to Everyman: Cheap Reprint Series of the English Classics 1830–1906," *Studies in Bibliography* 11 (1958): 3–24, https://www.jstor.org/stable/40371227.

9. Scraping data from the web is by no means free of complication. As my work with Maria Antoniak shows, Goodreads and its parent company Amazon purposely limit the amount of review data that can be accessed from the website (Walsh and Antoniak).

10. Similarly, Micah Bateman traces references to poets such as Maya Angelou and Audre Lorde in the tweets of Democratic politicians, arguing that the citation of these Black poets is strategically intended to mark the politicians as progressive. Micah Bateman, *Lyric Publics: The Uses of Poetry in American Social Media Campaigns* (PhD diss., University of Texas at Austin, 2021). He also traces quotations of Bertolt Brecht in Trump-era tweets; Micah Bateman, "Tweeting (in) 'Dark Times': Brecht's Second Svendborg 'Motto' Post-Trump," *Ecibs: Communications of the International Brecht Society,* no. 2020:1 (April 6, 2020), https://e-cibs.org/issue-2020-1/#bateman.

11. Alexandra Edwards, PhD (@nonmodernist), "And I have to wonder . . . did they go through IRB for this?" Twitter, December 19, 2020, https://twitter.com/nonmodernist/status/1207804598414647296.

12. This emphasis on the contextual nature of privacy echoes another principle of the Feminist Data Manifest-NO, which asserts that "risk and harm associated with data practices can[not] be bounded to mean the same thing for everyone, everywhere, at every time" and that "historical and systemic patterns of violence and exploitation produce differential vulnerabilities for communities" (see Chapter 8, The Feminist Data Manifest-NO.)

13. "We view hashtag users and creators as researchers themselves, and we see part of our charge as practicing a more egalitarian model of research whereby our 'subjects' are understood to be collaborators, particularly in light of the way some researches have exploited prominent Twitter and hashtag users. We shift this practice of potential harm by working collaboratively, ensuring that creative voices are front and center" (Jackson, Bailey, and Foucault Welles, xl).

14. See especially Busse (12–13) for an insightful reflection on why hard permission policies are not always tenable.

15. As Moya Bailey puts it, "Digital Humanists interested in conducting research that is ethical and feminist must go beyond the simple politics of citation, as citation itself may be the thing that creates the harm to the community."

16. Busse (12–13) discusses encountering similar issues with regard to permission.

17. Freelon, McIlwain, and Clark note that 3,000 followers placed a user in the top one percent of the most followed Twitter accounts at that time.

18. On its About web page, the *Journal of Cultural Analytics* explains various policies, including its Data Sharing Policy.

19. Ed Summers, "On Forgetting," *Medium,* May 19, 2017, https://medium.com/on-archivy/on-forgetting-e01a2b95272.

20. See also Ryan J. Gallagher, Elizabeth Stowell, Andrea G. Parker, and Brooke Foucault Welles, "#MeToo Tweet IDs, October 15–28, 2017," Inter-University Consortium for Political and Social Research, November 11, 2019, https://doi.org/10.3886/ICPSR37447.V1.

BIBLIOGRAPHY

Antoniak, Maria, David Mimno, and Karen Levy. "Narrative Paths and Negotiation of Power in Birth Stories." *Proceedings of the ACM on Human-Computer Interaction* 3, CSCW (November 2019): 1–27, https://doi.org/10.1145/3359190.

Ayers, John W., Theodore L. Caputi, Camille Nebeker, and Mark Dredze. "Don't Quote Me: Reverse Identification of Research Participants in Social Media Studies." *Npj Digital Medicine* 1, no. 1 (2018): 1–2, https://doi.org/10.1038/s41746-018-0036-2.

Bailey, Moya. "#transform(ing)DH Writing and Research: An Autoethnography of Digital Humanities and Feminist Ethics." *DHQ: Digital Humanities Quarterly* 9, no. 2 (2015), http://www.digitalhumanities.org/dhq/vol/9/2/000209/000209.html.

Black, Michael L. "The World Wide Web as Complex Data Set: Expanding the Digital Humanities into the Twentieth Century and Beyond through Internet Research." *International Journal of Humanities and Arts Computing* 10, no. 1 (2016): 95–109, https://doi.org/10.3366/ijhac.2016.0162.

Bode, Katherine. "The Equivalence of 'Close' and 'Distant' Reading; or, Toward a New Object for Data-Rich Literary History." *Modern Language Quarterly* 78, no. 1 (2017): 77–106, https://doi.org/10.1215/00267929-3699787.

Bourrier, Karen, and Mike Thelwall. "The Social Lives of Books: Reading Victorian Literature on Goodreads." *Journal of Cultural Analytics* 5, no. 1 (February 2020), https://doi.org/10.22148/001c.12049.

Bruckman, Amy. "Studying the Amateur Artist: A Perspective on Disguising Data Collected in Human Subjects Research on the Internet." *Ethics and Information Technology* 4, no. 3 (2002): 217–31, https://doi.org/10.1023/A:1021316409277.

Busse, Kristina. "The Ethics of Studying Online Fandom." In *The Routledge Companion to Media Fandom,* edited by Melissa A. Click and Suzanne Scott, 9–17. New York: Routledge, 2017, https://doi.org/10.4324/9781315637518-3.

Dewitt, Anne. "Advances in the Visualization of Data: The Network of Genre in the Victorian Periodical Press." *Victorian Periodicals Review* 48, no. 2 (2015): 161–82, https://doi.org/10.1353/vpr.2015.0030.

Dombrowski, Quinn, Steele Douris, and Masha Gorshkova. 2020. "Harry Potter and the Global Phenomenon of Fanfic." Presentation at the Center for Spatial and Textual Analysis (CESTA) Seminar, January 21, 2020, https://cesta.stanford.edu/events/cesta-seminar-harry-potter-and-global-phenomenon-fanfic.

Douris, Steele, Mark Algee-Hewitt, and David McClure. "Fanfiction: Generic Genesis and Evolution." Accessed August 24, 2022, https://litlab.stanford.edu/projects/.

Dym, Brianna, and Casey Fiesler. "Ethical and Privacy Considerations for Research Using Online Fandom Data." *Transformative Works and Cultures* 33 (June 2020), https://doi.org/10.3983/twc.2020.1733.

English, Jim, Lyle Ungar, Rahul Dhakecha, and Scott Enderle. "Mining Goodreads: Literary Reception Studies at Scale." Price Lab for Digital Humanities. Accessed August 24, 2022, https://pricelab.sas.upenn.edu/projects/goodreads-project.

Fiesler, Casey, and Nicholas Proferes. "'Participant' Perceptions of Twitter Research Ethics." *Social Media + Society* 4, no. 1 (2018), https://doi.org/10.1177/2056305118763366.

Freelon, Deen, Charlton D. McIlwain, and Meredith Clark. "Beyond the Hashtags: #Ferguson, #Blacklivesmatter, and the Online Struggle for Offline Justice." Center for Media & Social Impact, American University. 2016, https://doi.org/10.2139/ssrn.2747066.

Gallagher, Ryan J., Elizabeth Stowell, Andrea G. Parker, and Brooke Foucault Welles. "Reclaiming Stigmatized Narratives: The Networked Disclosure Landscape of #MeToo." *Proceedings of the ACM on Human-Computer Interaction* 3, CSCW (November 2019): 1–30, https://doi.org/10.1145/3359198.

Hegel, Allison. "Social Reading in the Digital Age." PhD diss. University of California, Los Angeles, 2018, https://search.proquest.com/pqdtglobal/docview/2061506661/3AEADF32C9E44C24PQ/1.

Hemphill, Libby. "Updates on ICPSR's Social Media Archive (SOMAR)." Presentation, May 30, 2019, https://doi.org/10.5281/zenodo.3612677.

Hemphill, Libby, Susan H. Leonard, and Margaret Hedstrom. "Developing a Social Media Archive at ICPSR." In *Proceedings of Web Archiving and Digital Libraries (WADL'18).*

New York: Association for Computing Machinery, 2018, https://pdfs.semanticscholar.org/3006/94cfbcb169c55bd14331a493d983aaa352ed.pdf.

Jackson, Sarah J., Moya Bailey, and Brooke Foucault Welles. *#HashtagActivism: Networks of Race and Gender Justice*. Cambridge, Mass.: MIT Press, 2020.

Journal of Cultural Analytics. "About the Journal: Data Sharing Policy." Accessed December 1, 2020, https://culturalanalytics.org/about.

Jules, Bergis, Ed Summers, and Vernon Mitchell. "Ethical Considerations for Archiving Social Media Content Generated by Contemporary Social Movements: Challenges, Opportunities, and Recommendations." Documenting the Now White Paper. April 2018, https://www.docnow.io/docs/docnow-whitepaper-2018.pdf.

Kim, Dorothy, and Eunsong Kim. "The #TwitterEthics Manifesto." *Model View Culture* (blog). April 7, 2014, https://modelviewculture.com/pieces/the-twitterethics-manifesto.

Kirschenbaum, Matthew. "What Is an @uthor?" *Los Angeles Review of Books*. February 6, 2015, https://lareviewofbooks.org/article/uthor/.

Klein, Lauren F. "Dimensions of Scale: Invisible Labor, Editorial Work, and the Future of Quantitative Literary Studies." *PMLA* 135, no. 1 (January 1, 2020): 23–39, https://doi.org/10.1632/pmla.2020.135.1.23.

Manshel, Alexander, Laura B. McGrath, and J. D. Porter. "Who Cares about Literary Prizes?" *Public Books*. September 3, 2019, https://www.publicbooks.org/who-cares-about-literary-prizes/.

Markham, Annette. "Fabrication as Ethical Practice." *Information, Communication & Society* 15, no. 3 (April 2012): 334–53, https://doi.org/10.1080/1369118X.2011.641993.

Mason, Jessica. "Researchers Use Algorithm to Mansplain Fanfiction and Miss the Whole Point." *The Mary Sue*. December 20, 2019, https://www.themarysue.com/researchers-use-algorithm-fanfiction/.

McGrath, Laura B. "America's Next Top Novel." *Post45*. April 8, 2020, https://post45.org/2020/04/americas-next-top-novel/.

Piper, Andrew, and Richard Jean So. "Study Shows Books Can Bring Republicans and Democrats Together." *The Guardian*. October 12, 2016, https://www.theguardian.com/books/2016/oct/12/goodreads-study-books-bridge-political-divide-america.

Porter, J. D. "Popularity/Prestige." *Stanford Literary Lab*, pamphlet 17 (September 2018), https://litlab.stanford.edu/LiteraryLabPamphlet17.pdf.

Radway, Janice A. *Reading the Romance: Women, Patriarchy, and Popular Literature*. Chapel Hill: University of North Carolina Press, 1991.

Shepard, Louisa. "'May the Force Be with You' and Other Fan Fiction Favorites." *Penn Today*. December 18, 2019, https://penntoday.upenn.edu/news/penn-digital-humanities-fan-fiction-meter-star-wars.

Tatlock, Lynne, Matt Erlin, Douglas Knox, and Stephen Pentecost. "Crossing Over: Gendered Reading Formations at the Muncie Public Library, 1891–1902." *Journal of Cultural Analytics* 3, no. 3 (March 2018), https://culturalanalytics.org/article/11038.

Tompkins, Jane P. *Reader-Response Criticism: From Formalism to Post-Structuralism*. Baltimore: Johns Hopkins University Press, 1980.

Underwood, Ted. "No Such Thing as Bad Publicity: Toward a Distant Reading of Reception." Presentation at the Modern Language Association Annual Convention, Seattle, Washington, January 10, 2020, https://tedunderwood.github.io/badpublicity/.

Walsh, Melanie. "Tweets of a Native Son: The Quotation and Recirculation of James Baldwin from Black Power To# BlackLivesMatter." *American Quarterly* 70, no. 3 (2018): 531–59.

Walsh, Melanie, and Maria Antoniak. "The Goodreads 'Classics': A Computational Study of Readers, Amazon, and Crowdsourced Amateur Criticism." *Post45* 1, no. 7 and *Journal of Cultural Analytics* 6, no. 2 (April 2021).

Language Is Not a Default Setting: Countering DH's English Problem

QUINN DOMBROWSKI AND PATRICK J. BURNS

Language should be everyone's concern in the humanities, although it is often rendered invisible for scholars who work on Anglophone materials and live in Anglophone countries. In such a context, it is easy to not ever think about language beyond fleeting hints and shadows evoked by an accent mark in a text or a grammatical imperfection. The English language becomes simply "language"; English literature becomes, sweepingly, "literature." In "Distant Reading after Moretti," Lauren Klein calls for "more corpora—more accessible corpora—that perform the work of recovery or resistance" as a step toward addressing structural problems of sexism and racism in computational literary studies.[1] We would like to echo the urgency of this call and amplify it with a twist: that language is another important axis of diversity that has received too little consideration, particularly in North American digital humanities (DH). In developing corpora and models—and, perhaps just as importantly, in developing the tools and tutorials needed to create, transform, or analyze these corpora and models—it is essential that we also challenge the role of English as a default setting in DH research.

Structural power may be held disproportionately in the Anglophone world, including but not limited to DH.[2] English itself, however, has an impact beyond its role as a lingua franca of scholarly communication. Many marginalized voices are "hidden" in plain sight. They are inaccessible for enriching our collective understanding of concepts such as gender, race, and ability simply because they are written in languages without, for example, high-quality optical character recognition (OCR) options or natural language processing (NLP) tools, while funding and attention from both the academy and industry continue to be directed toward further refining tools for English. Without high-quality OCR, scholars are limited to creating images of text. Yet OCR alone is only the first step toward having a text that is usable for text analysis (Smith and Cordell). Digitized text without language-specific preprocessing tools may not even be usable with "language-neutral" methods such as topic modeling because of the variety of word forms present in the text. Digital humanities scholars are well placed to work toward developing more robust tools for non-English languages, particularly when that development takes the form of international collaboration. We argue that such tool development should be viewed as part of a broader agenda for diversifying DH.

The development of user-friendly tools that are accessible to scholars without a coding background is an expensive proposition, and it is reasonable to question whether the development of such tools in a language-specific manner is desirable or feasible. Tool-based methods are particularly common in pedagogical contexts, where it may be impractical to teach humanities students without previous technical backgrounds the fundamentals of code and the basics of implementing text analysis methods before they can see the potential value of those methods for answering disciplinary questions.[3] Tools reduce the number of decisions that have to be made before a scholar can run an analysis, in part by providing default settings (e.g., tokenization, stopword removal) that should work in most cases—however, these default settings are often premised on the characteristics of the English language, such as a convention of separating words with spaces, a left-to-right reading order, and a relatively fixed word order. These characteristics of English are partly shared by other Indo-European languages, but they are not necessarily generalizable to other languages. User interface–based (UI) text analysis tools with English-oriented preprocessing rules give Anglophone scholars who are new to DH an easier on-ramp; if they continue with computational text analysis, they may move toward code-based workflows that provide more control, though at the cost of more complexity. But for students working in many other languages, there is no meaningful on-ramp: DH methods—including anything connected to counting words—simply "don't work" when applied to a text that has not been preprocessed using algorithms that are not included in the easy-to-use DH tool.

Counting words is the simplest kind of text analysis, and the concept of word frequencies underpins more complex methods commonly used in DH, such as topic modeling and word vectors. But surely the definition of "word" is open to debate if one space-delimited "word" in an agglutinative language like Turkish translates roughly to fifteen English "words."[4] For character-based languages like Chinese and Japanese that do not separate words with whitespace, different segmentation algorithms (that artificially insert white space) disagree about how many words are in a text or where to place those boundaries. If students working with languages other than English simply substitute their own texts for English-language examples used in class, they are likely to find themselves frustrated or facing results that are misleading or erroneous.[5]

Code-based workflows that require scholars to specify the entire workflow avoid the constraints of UI-based text analysis tools with defaults that are hard to change. However, similar challenges arise for scholars who work with languages other than English. Pedagogical materials designed to teach students how to write code for implementing DH text analysis methods are often based on English-language examples and choose dependency libraries accordingly. Major libraries—Natural Language Toolkit, SpaCy, Stanford CoreNLP and Stanza, Stylo—support different sets of languages to varying degrees.[6] If the library described in a tutorial supports the language that a scholar needs, adapting the tutorial to work with that language may simply be a matter of downloading different model data and substituting the name of the new model. This may still take a fair bit of guesswork, particularly for less technically proficient scholars, as tutorials rarely make explicit which steps are generic and which steps are language-specific. But if the library does *not* support the language a scholar needs, the tutorial is essentially useless. Some of the most effective libraries for less widely spoken languages are developed by researchers who are themselves native speakers of those languages.[7] While the existence of these libraries is a tremendous help for scholars, the libraries often lack the kind of detailed, beginner-friendly documentation—let alone tutorials—that tend to accompany larger libraries, with a result of making them more difficult for beginners to use.

And yet, these conundrums—how to find an effective code library or adapt tools to meet the language-specific demands of a particular project—still assume a best-case scenario where work has already been done on developing NLP resources for the language. This is not the case for the vast majority of the world's languages, particularly Indigenous languages and languages of the Global South (Risam, 44–46). While tremendous progress has been made in improving support for working with non-English languages in the last fifteen years, this progress has largely been concentrated in areas where there is perceived commercial value (like machine translation or audio recognition for languages with a large, affluent speaker base) or where grants and dedicated researchers have worked to close a gap after initial commercial investment (as, for example, with the expansion of Unicode to cover more African scripts; see Osborn, Anderson, and Kodama).[8] New algorithms and approaches, including neural networks, have led to significant technical advancements in fields that digital humanists often borrow from, including computer science, computational linguistics, and information science. At the same time, Anglophone-centric tendencies in those fields take root in Anglophone digital humanities in indirect and subtle ways—for example, working toward hyper-optimized NLP algorithms as applied to a widely used English *Wall Street Journal* news corpus rather than improving the poor or mediocre accuracy of those algorithms for other languages and genres.[9] Furthermore, when work is done on low-resource languages within computational linguistics or computer science, there are no structural incentives for scholars to advance their prototype to a point of usability, so there is a great deal of research that never results in tool development.[10] This is another manifestation of the structural power held by Anglophone academia to the detriment of broader global communities: Prestige comes from publishing academic papers, not from developing something that people can use. A new prototype can lead to a new publication, but the labor required for a usable tool is not publishable, visible, or rewarded.

There have been notable steps forward within the DH community to improve the support landscape through more language-aware tutorials and the development of tools that are either linguistically flexible or designed specifically to support under-resourced languages. Stéfan Sinclair and Geoffrey Rockwell's Voyant Tools is one example of a project engaging with requests for supporting linguistic diversity, from building in features to handle segmented Tibetan to working through the details of stopword lists for ancient Greek and Latin.[11] Other digital humanities scholars whose work aligns closely with tool building, such as David Bamman, have directed attention toward supporting communities of scholars who work with the "long tail" of languages in developing NLP tools that meet their research needs. Within and beyond DH, groups of committed individuals with the relevant linguistic expertise are collaborating through events like the African Language Dataset Challenge and the Masakhane Project for developing machine-translation models for African languages.[12]

We also see a clear bright spot in mitigating the lack of pedagogical materials for languages where NLP resources do exist from the *Programming Historian,* which introduced a Spanish version of the site in 2017, a French version in 2019, and a Portuguese version in 2021 (Afanador-Llach; Papastamkou; Alves and Isasi; Walsh).[13] These projects—at the time of writing there were fifty-seven Spanish, twenty-two French, and twenty-six Portuguese tutorials—started largely with translations of existing tutorials, but it is clear from a recent call for submissions that there is interest in developing language-specific content. That is, there is an interest in avoiding an English-as-default approach to the site's workflow.[14] Fourteen original Spanish lessons have been published since the call. While we wait for more Spanish-, French-, and Portuguese-originating tutorials, it is worth calling attention to the subtle ways that *Programming Historian* decenters English through its "internationalization strategy."[15] One tutorial adds a section called "Notas sobre las palabras en español" ("Notes about the Spanish words"), effectively drawing attention to the ways in which Spanish words need to be handled differently than English words in text analysis (Turkel and Crymble). Another tutorial adds a supplementary French bibliography so that readers can pursue further reading in the same language (Froehlich). In the tutorials, comments referring to external documentation like "disponibles solamente en inglés" ("only available in English") and "en anglais seulement" ("only in English") expose the Anglocentricity latent in the tools and gesture toward an alternative future of linguistically complete support that *Programming Historian* aims to provide in time (Dewar; Laramée). More work, however, remains to be done, particularly in the development of tutorials building on the needs, interests, and opportunities emerging from other languages (e.g., the analysis of salient grammatical structures like politeness markers in Japanese) that have no easy analogue in English.

In their 2017 article on defining a critical approach to interdisciplinary work in modern languages and digital humanities, Thea Pitman and Claire Taylor write: "As DH continues to mature and see itself less as providing tools, and more as enabling critical ways of thinking, [the field of Modern Languages] can contribute . . . a contestation of assumptions regarding (unstated) Anglophone models of the digital." We agree that research at the intersection of modern languages and DH is essential to contesting linguistic assumptions. At the same time, we note that "providing tools" *is* a way of "enabling critical ways of thinking." This is in keeping with Roopika Risam's reminder that "digital humanities tools, methods, and projects must be used and built with the understanding that biases and values are built into these essential elements of practice" (40). And as James Dobson writes, "Any humanities method using computation must apply reflexive thought to all stages of computation, iteratively applying an interpretative frame to those filters, functions, tools, and transformations that would otherwise obscure the interpretative work embedded within these building blocks of computation" (131). Assumptions latent within the tool can have massive implications on interpretation and as such must be subject to critique.

At the same time, before these assumptions can be subject to critique, they need to be acknowledged. Luckily for digital humanists, we have an example that we can follow in the adjacent field of natural language processing. Emily Bender has advocated for NLP researchers to be more explicit about naming the languages they are working on, a formulation now referred to as the "Bender Rule."[16] Bender argues that for NLP to move toward being "language independent"—that is, to become more generalizable across more languages—the field must incorporate specific linguistic knowledge.[17] For this to happen, the first step is for researchers to be more transparent and more explicit about which languages they are working on.[18] As we have argued above, a failure to make use of specific linguistic knowledge and a tendency to assume English as a kind of default for text analysis work raises similar issues in DH. It is in this spirit that we suggest the following: digital humanities needs a Bender Rule.

Explicitly acknowledging English as the language of the texts we study (when what we are studying is, in fact, English-language text), as the basis of the corpora we draw from and train our models on (when we build on computer science and NLP methods developed using English), and as the reason for the default parameters of the tools we use (when they are developed by or for the Anglophone world) promotes a critical digital humanities at a fundamental level and from the outset of the research process. Challenging the "unearned advantage" afforded to native English speakers in learning to code, Gretchen McCulloch writes that "when we name the English default, it becomes more obvious that we can question it." For digital humanities, it is not precisely a matter of advantage or disadvantage (although that does manifest itself). Rather, we have a humanistic responsibility to recognize, challenge, and overcome our assumptions, including those linguistic assumptions discussed above that too often pass without notice or debate. Only then can we avoid reinforcing structures of power and begin to take steps to undermine these structures by surfacing and centering hidden voices, regardless of whether they are obscured on account of race, gender, ability, or language.[19]

NOTES

1. See Klein, citing and building on previous scholarship from Moya Bailey, Miriam Posner, Lisa Rhody, Tanya Clement and Jessica Marie Johnson, and Laura Mandell.

2. See numerous critiques of the structural power of English within digital humanities over the last decade, including Cohen (236–37); Fiormonte; Clavert; Galina; Grandjean; Ortega ("Local and International Scalability" and "Multilingualism"); Spence; Dacos; Gil and Ortega; Mahony; Risam.

3. We have in mind here what Rockwell and Sinclair (*Hermeneutica*) refer to as "tools-as-methods"—that is, computer-assisted text-analysis environments, interfaces, toolboxes, and so on that do not require programming skills of their users.

4. On Turkish grammar, see the "Longest Word in Turkish," *Wikipedia,* https://en.wikipedia.org/wiki/Longest_word_in_Turkish. Knowles and Don (80) ask similar questions about "lemmas," or dictionary headwords, and whether it is possible to apply this concept in a meaningful way across languages as different as English, Latin, Arabic, and Malay, concluding that a failure to acknowledge features specific to individual languages could unhelpfully lead to "the practice of looking at all languages as though they were varieties of English."

5. See Galina: "Methods that have worked effectively in one cultural setting may fail spectacularly in another (and vice versa) and certain reasoning of how things should work does not apply similarly to other frameworks."

6. There are also projects like Universal Dependencies (Zeman et al.), a collection of linguistic treebanks developed to enable cross-linguistic comparability of syntactic structures, that run the risk of flattening the more nuanced features of individual languages—features that may be among the more interesting things to track, particularly in a literary context. While projects of this sort provide value for some research questions, they can also suggest a kind of "specious universalism" (Risam, 40).

7. See, for instance, the work of the Ixa group on Basque at http://ixa.si.ehu.es/.

8. While much progress has been made in the last decade, a call in bold, red letters at the top of the Script Encoding Initiative's website (http://www.linguistics.berkeley.edu/sei/index.html) reminds us that "over 100 scripts remain to be encoded."

9. It must be noted that the particular prevalence of the *Wall Street Journal, Wikipedia,* and other modern web-based text corpora privilege modernity as much as English. Scholars of premodern English face the same scarcity of NLP resources as scholars of non-English languages.

10. Note, for example, the ratio of software to scientific papers in the list of NLP research and engineering for American Native/Indigenous Languages maintained by Manuel Mager, Ximena Gutierrez-Vasques, Gerardo Sierra, and Ivan Meza-Ruiz at https://github.com/pywirrarika/naki.

11. The tools are available at https://voyant-tools.org/. The focal point for discussion of improving language support in Voyant is the Issues section of their GitHub repository; for Tibetan segmentation, see https://github.com/sgsinclair/Voyant/issues/342 and

for ancient Greek and Latin stopwords, see https://github.com/sgsinclair/Voyant/issues/382. See also Chapter 3 in this book for a longer discussion of how the Arabic version of Voyant was developed.

12. For the African Language Dataset, led by Kathleen Siminyu, see https://ai4d.ai/african-language-dataset-challenge/; for the Masakhane Project, see https://www.masakhane.io/.

13. It should be expressly stated that *Programming Historian en español, Programming Historian en français, and Programming Historian em português* as is made clear from the index page at https://programminghistorian.org, are not sections of the "initial English version" but online journals in their own right, each with a unique ISSN. See also Sichani: "These new full-language initiatives stand as huge milestones in our linguistic diversity strategy."

14. See Isasi and Motilla: "Nos han motivado a abrir un convocatoria para la recepción de propuestas de tutoriales de contenidos originales en español, los cuales, una vez aprobados y publicados, pueden ser traducidos al inglés para su amplia difusión en el mundo no hispanohablante." ("[Various factors in Spanish-language DH] have motivated us to open up a call for original-content proposals written in Spanish, which once accepted and published, can be translated into English for better distribution outside of the Spanish-speaking world.")

15. According to Sichani: "As part of our internationalization strategy, we encourage authors to write for a Global Audience by making choices (methods, tools, primary sources, bibliography, standards) with multi-lingual readers in mind while also being aware of cultural differences." *Programming Historian*'s "Author Guidelines" (https://programminghistorian.org/en/author-guidelines) include a section that similarly advises authors to take care in choosing methods and tools as they "may not support other character sets or may only provide intellectually robust results when used on English texts."

16. The rule is best seen in action as the hashtag #BenderRule; see https://twitter.com/search?q=%23BenderRule.

17. Bender ("Linguistically Naïve") notes here that at the 2008 Annual Meeting of the Association of Computational Linguistics, the most common language studied was English with eighty-one papers; the second most common languages were Chinese and German with five papers each.

18. The first formulation of the rule comes in a section on "prescriptions for typologically-informed NLP," a ten-point list of best practices for computational language research (Bender, "On Achieving and Evaluating Language-Independence in NLP," 18–19). The "prescription" reads: "Do state the name of the language that is being studied, even if it's English. Acknowledging that we are working on a particular language foregrounds the possibility that the techniques may in fact be language-specific. Conversely, neglecting to state that the particular data used were in, say, English, gives false veneer of language-independence to the work."

19. See Gorman: "We must not confuse the act of perceiving and naming the hegemon with the far more challenging act of actually combating it."

BIBLIOGRAPHY

Afanador-Llach, M. J. "¡Bienvenidos a The Programming Historian en español!" *Programming Historian.* March 5, 2017, https://programminghistorian.org/posts/lanzamiento-PH-espanol.

Alves, D., and Isasi, J. "Publicação do Programming Historian em português." *Programming Historian.* January 29, 2021, https://programminghistorian.org/posts/launch-portuguese.

Bamman, D. "Natural Language Processing for the Long Tail." Presentation at DH2017, Montreal, Quebec, Canada, 2017, http://people.ischool.berkeley.edu/~dbamman/pubs/pdf/dh2017.pdf.

Bender, E. M. "Linguistically Naïve != Language Independent: Why NLP Needs Linguistic Typology." In *Proceedings of the EACL 2009 Workshop on the Interaction between Linguistics and Computational Linguistics: Virtuous, Vicious or Vacuous?* edited by Timothy Baldwin and Valia Kordoni, 26–32. Stroudsburg, Pa.: Association for Computational Linguistics, 2009.

Bender, E. M. "On Achieving and Evaluating Language-Independence in NLP." *Linguistic Issues in Language Technology* 6, no. 3 (2011): 1–26.

Bender, E. M. "The #BenderRule: On Naming the Languages We Study and Why It Matters." *The Gradient.* September 14, 2019, https://thegradient.pub/the-benderrule-on-naming-the-languages-we-study-and-why-it-matters/.

Clavert, F. "The Digital Humanities Multicultural Revolution Did Not Happen Yet." *L'histoire contemporaine à l'ère numérique.* 2013, https://histnum.hypotheses.org/1546.

Cohen, M. "Design and Politics in Electronic American Literary Archives." In *The American Literature Scholar in the Digital Age,* edited by A. E. Earhart and A. W. Jewell, 228–49. Ann Arbor: University of Michigan Press, 2011.

Dacos, M. "La stratégie du sauna finlandais: Les frontières des Digital Humanities." *Digital Studies/Le Champ Numérique* 6, no. 2 (2016), https://www.digitalstudies.org/articles/10.16995/dscn.41/.

Dewar, T. "Datos tabulares en R." Translated by Jennifer Isasi, Joseba Moreno, and Antonio Rojas Castro. *Programming Historian.* September 5, 2016, https://programminghistorian.org/es/lecciones/datos-tabulares-en-r.

Dobson, J. E. *Critical Digital Humanities: The Search for a Methodology.* Champaign, Ill.: University of Illinois Press, 2019.

Fiormonte, D. "Towards a Cultural Critique of the Digital Humanities." *Historical Social Research/Historische Sozialforschung* 37, no. 3 (2012): 59–76.

Froehlich, H. "Analyse de corpus avec AntConc." Translated by Hugo Bonin and Sofia Papastamkou. *Programming Historian.* June 19, 2015, https://programminghistorian.org/fr/lecons/analyse-corpus-antconc.

Galina, I. "Is There Anybody Out There? Building a Global Digital Humanities Community." *Humanidades Digitales.* July 19, 2013, http://humanidadesdigitales.net/blog/2013/07/19/is-there-anybody-out-there-building-a-global-digital-humanities-community.

Gil, A., and Ortega, É. "Global Outlooks in Digital Humanities." In *Doing Digital Humanities: Practice, Training, Research,* edited by C. Crompton, R. J. Lane, and R. Siemens, 22–34, London: Routledge, 2016.

Gorman, K. "Action, Not Ritual." *Wellformedness.* 2019, http://www.wellformedness.com/blog/action-not-ritual/.

Grandjean, M. "Le rêve du multilinguisme dans la science : l'exemple (malheureux) du colloque #DH2014." *Martin Grandjean.* June 27, 2014, http://www.martingrandjean.ch/multilinguisme-dans-la-science-dh2014/.

Isasi, J., and Motilla, J. A. 2018. "Convocatoria para lecciones en español en The Programming Historian." *Programming Historian.* April 6, 2018, https://programminghistorian.org/posts/convocatoria-de-tutoriales.

Klein, L. F. "Distant Reading after Moretti." *Arcade.* 2018, https://arcade.stanford.edu/blogs/distant-reading-after-moretti.

Knowles, G., and Don, Z. M. "The Notion of a 'Lemma': Headwords, Roots and Lexical Sets." *International Journal of Corpus Linguistics* 9, no. 1 (2004): 69–81.

Laramée, F. D. "Introduction à la stylométrie en Python." Translated by François Dominic Laramée and Sofia Papastamkou. *Programming Historian.* April 21, 2018, https://programminghistorian.org/fr/lecons/introduction-a-la-stylometrie-avec-python.

Mahony, S. "Cultural Diversity and the Digital Humanities." *Fudan Journal of the Humanities and Social Sciences* 11, no. 3 (2018): 371–88, https://doi.org/10.1007/s40647-018-0216-0.

McCulloch, G. "Coding Is for Everyone—as Long as You Speak English." *Wired.com.* April 8, 2019, https://www.wired.com/story/coding-is-for-everyoneas-long-as-you-speak-english/.

Ortega, É. "Local and International Scalability in DH." *Readers of Fiction (in Internet Archive Wayback Machine).* July 14, 2014, https://web.archive.org/web/20140714103841/http://lectoresdeficcion.blogs.cultureplex.ca/2014/07/02/scalability/.

Ortega, É. "Multilingualism in DH." *Disrupting the Digital Humanities: 2015 MLA Position Papers (in Internet Archive Wayback Machine).* December 31, 2014, https://web.archive.org/web/20210424073656/https://www.disruptingdh.com/multilingualism-in-dh/.

Osborn, D. Z., D. W. Anderson, and S. Kodama. "Support for Modern African Languages and Scripts in Unicode/ISO 10646: Where Are We Today?" Presentation at the 32nd Internationalization and Unicode Conference, San Jose, California, September 2008.

Papastamkou, S. "Bienvenue au Programming Historian en français!" *Programming Historian.* April 8, 2019, https://programminghistorian.org/posts/bienvenue-ph-fr.

Pitman, T., and Taylor, C. "Where's the ML in DH? And Where's the DH in ML? The Relationship between Modern Languages and Digital Humanities, and an Argument for a Critical DHML." *DHQ: Digital Humanities Quarterly* 11, no. 1 (2017).

Risam, R. *New Digital Worlds: Postcolonial Digital Humanities in Theory, Praxis, and Pedagogy.* Evanston, Ill.: Northwestern University Press, 2019.

Rockwell, G., and Sinclair, S. *Hermeneutica: Computer-Assisted Interpretation in the Humanities.* Cambridge, Mass.: MIT Press, 2016.

Sichani, A.-M. "Linguistic Diversity and Ad-Hoc Translation of the Programming Historian's Lessons." *Programming Historian.* November 30, 2018, https://programminghistorian.org/posts/ad-hoc-translation.

Smith, D. A., and R. Cordell. "A Research Agenda for Historical and Multilingual Optical Character Recognition." 2018, https://ocr.northeastern.edu/report/.

Spence, P. "Centros y fronteras: el panorama internacional." *Janus*, Anexo 1, April 11, 2014, https://www.janusdigital.es/anexos/contribucion.htm?id=6.

Turkel, W. J., and A. Crymble. "Contar frecuencias de palabras con Python." Translated by Victor Gayol, Jairo A. Melo, Maria José Afanador-Llach, and Antonio Rojas Castro. *Programming Historian.* July 17, 2012, https://programminghistorian.org/es/lecciones/contar-frecuencias.

Walsh, Brandon. "The Programming Historian and Editorial Process in Digital Publishing." *Brandon Walsh* (blog). January 15, 2021, http://walshbr.com/blog/the-programming-historian-and-editorial-process-in-digital-publishing/.

Zeman, D., J. Nivre, M. Abrams, E. Ackermann, N. Aepli, Ž. Agić, L. Ahrenberg, et al. "Universal Dependencies 2.6." LINDAT/CLARIAH-CZ Digital Library. Institute of Formal and Applied Linguistics (ÚFAL), Faculty of Mathematics and Physics, Charles University. 2020, http://hdl.handle.net/11234/1-3226.

Librarians' Illegible Labor: Toward a Documentary Practice of Digital Humanities

SPENCER D. C. KERALIS, RAFIA MIRZA, AND MAURA SEALE

Digital humanities projects often require significant labor from various types of workers from within different institutional locations and disparate academic hierarchies. Within academic libraries, for example, the mass digitization efforts that underlie many digital humanities projects require the labor of librarians, academic staff, and armies of graduate and undergraduate students. The mechanized tasks required of digitization—like scanning documents, entering metadata, cleaning optical character recognition (OCR) documents, and other data processing—involve the work of both staff and students, each with varying degrees of technical and domain specialization. Platform-based web hosting for such projects additionally requires IT professionals with server-side expertise, and potentially designers and developers with the skills to create and customize the project site. Because the people contributing to these highly collaborative projects represent many scholarly and technical disciplines, accounting for and crediting this labor can be challenging. Digitization, for example, is often perceived as an "on demand" service by scholars, who are unaware of the institutional priorities, including preservation, funding, and staff time as well as existing projects in the queue for finite technical infrastructure, that may already be in play. Digital humanities (DH) projects have the potential to make these conflicting priorities, the contingencies of labor and money on which they depend, and the differentials of power that erase or elide these contingencies more visible to stakeholders and decision makers alike. In this chapter, we argue that academic librarians can better represent how their labor contributes to the complex ecosystem of digital scholarship in the humanities through what we describe as a *documentary practice of digital humanities,* one that reveals librarians' positionality within and among other DH stakeholders. This documentary practice can provide a model of self-advocacy for others in the DH ecosystem whose labor is similarly elided or assumed and can help make DH more sustainable, equitable, and just for all of its practitioners.

DH research is not often easily recognized by leadership and policy makers in the academy because the projects that result do not often conform to the outputs of scholarly communication that are expected by those tasked with evaluating scholarly work, such as the peer-reviewed article, the monograph, the edited collection, and the critical edition. The continued prioritization of traditional modes of scholarly communication has led to a perception on the part of senior research faculty in the humanities that DH research lacks the rigor of more familiar scholarly outputs. A 2020 joint Modern Language Association (MLA) and Ithaka S+R report reveals the attitudes of research faculty in languages and literature. "Confusion about how to define [DH] still abounds," according to the respondents (78 percent of whom were tenured faculty; teaching faculty were explicitly excluded). Indeed, one "interviewee even expressed reservations about the rigor of their own digital project" (Cooper et al., 27). While this observation undoubtedly says more about this individual's project than about DH writ large, the deep misunderstandings described in the report, and the resulting prejudice against recognizing the wide range of scholarly works in DH, represent significant obstacles for DH being taken seriously in the fields of languages and literature.

Elsewhere in the Ithaka report, it is made explicit that the respondents continue to imagine themselves as "a solo act." But scholarship is never truly solitary. All humanities scholarship depends on the labor of librarians, archivists, and other contributors, including students, to help conduct and disseminate their research, even as most scholars do not perceive these contributions as collaboration (Cooper et al., 20). Indeed, many humanities scholars see themselves as entitled to the labor of others. Such attitudes exacerbate the challenges faced by contributors to DH projects who are not tenure-track research faculty, as they struggle to have their work properly credited and recognized for their own career advancement. This lack of recognition masks a deeper misunderstanding—or even an intentional disregard—of the disciplinary differences within and among academic hierarchies outside the tenure track. While tenure-track members of a project team require credit akin to authorship in order to advance their careers, librarians, whether classified as faculty or staff, require evidence of having contributed to faculty scholarship for their own career advancement. Unfortunately, because of the attitudes documented in the Ithaka report, the actual work invested in a digital project is not always reflected in the way that credit, including authorship, is bestowed.

As described by Matt Kirschenbaum, digital humanities, perceived as a "culture that values collaboration, openness, nonhierarchical relations, and agility, might be an instrument for real resistance or reform" of wider systemic problems in the academy. However, the failure to properly credit the labor of librarians and archivists points to larger tensions about labor in the digital humanities as well as the academy as a whole. Indeed, there have been recent interventions arguing for recognition of the labor of students (Di Pressi et al.; Keralis), graduate student workers (Mann), and postdoctoral laborers (Alpert-Abrams et al.) in digital projects. Manifestos, bills of rights, and polemics decrying labor exploitation are not necessary when things are good. There is a there, there. The challenge faced by advocates is that structural inequities, a lack of accountability for tenured faculty, and indeed, a lack of documentation defining roles, responsibilities, and boundaries serve to hide unjust practices and the real costs—financial and human—of DH projects and programs.

In what follows, we frame the relationship of the academic librarian to other laborers in the digital humanities ecosystem, including research faculty, in terms of positionality—which we take to mean a description of an individual's situatedness within a hierarchical system in relationship to other individuals in that hierarchy. We consider how documenting this positionality can render explicit what is too often assumed. Such documentation can empower librarians to better advocate for themselves as collaborators and make the relationship between librarians' labor and the research mission of the university more clearly legible to administrators and other stakeholders. But its generative potential can be complicated by the hierarchical slipperiness of librarians and others whose labor DH relies on: Is a librarian a service provider or a partner? Is a grad student a grad student or a university employee? The concept of positionality thus also helps to expose the structures of power that influence discussions, perceptions, and practices around the labor of digital scholarship and the ways in which vocational awe, scope creep, emotional labor, and false meritocracy are deployed in the academy.

Other scholars and practitioners of digital humanities have proposed documentary practice in DH to address other challenges we face as a community. Rebecca Sutton Koeser observes that at the 2019 Association for Computers and the Humanities (ACH) conference, interest was expressed "both in how we charter and plan our projects, and in how we maintain them," with a particular emphasis on project management (PM) and process documentation, including a "living will" or "Long Term Service Agreement" for a project. Zach Coble, Sarah Potvin, and Roxanne Shirazi go further to advocate for an understanding of digital humanities that "emphasize(s) the back-and-forth, give-and-take process of scholarship over a polished product," in which the process itself becomes an outcome, as in innovations in scholarly communication like open peer review, and iterative, multimodal publications (7). We acknowledge that project and process management are key to sustainable projects, but we share Lynne Siemens's perspective that humanists view project management as "a rather-dubious application of management tools from the other side of campus (i.e., business schools)," and these elements are frequently and regrettably absent from the planning of DH projects. As a result of this transdisciplinary disdain, responsibility for PM, and thus responsibility for the sustainability of a project, often devolves to center managers, librarians, or archivists, who are compelled to make decisions regarding a project's viability and sustainability after the fact.

And while we know (and will undoubtedly hear on Twitter) that #NotAllFaculty choose to compel others to manage their projects for them, we must acknowledge that the "knowledge and skills related to this topic are typically not a formal part of training in the humanities" (Siemens) and not allow the "sleight of hand" of the #NotAll hashtag to efface the structural imbalance that makes this discussion necessary (Keralis, 275). Training in project management skills within universities tends to be ad hoc, relying again on centers and libraries to provide this professional development to humanities scholars and, more frequently, students. Project documentation can help identify needs for training and could lead to a more programmatic approach to filling this gap on the part of humanities departments. It is also important to acknowledge that project management as a discipline also encodes certain ethical challenges. From years in project management at a national telecom and in the nonprofit sector, Keralis (one of the authors of this chapter) recognizes that PM documentation typically renders contributors as assets rather than as individuals. This is helpful in making transparent the financial and, to a degree, time costs of project activities—the Gantt chart familiar to project managers visualizes the cost of a contributor's activities over time—but it can make the individual performing the actions invisible to higher-level stakeholders reading the document. This in turn can exacerbate structural barriers that prevent proper recognition for an individual's contribution.

The problem of crediting the labor of digital scholarship is indeed structural. We propose that the range of labor contributing to DH projects can be conceptualized and made visible through documentation that makes explicit the inherent and implicit power dynamics and expectations around labor. We advocate for documentation that directly connects to a focus on process rather than on outputs or project completion, and for using documentation as a tool to make both the amounts and types of work that are being done visible and legible to those with institutional authority. Documentation in and of itself is not the end goal but rather a tool deployed intentionally to promote transparency and accountability in DH projects. Without transparency around labor and accountability between project members, digital humanities projects can and often will default to academic hierarchies that privilege research faculty at the cost of student workers, early career, non-tenure-line and contingent faculty, and staff. Documentation has the potential to create space for more equitable collaboration across academic hierarchies, reveals exploitative practices that might otherwise be invisible, and distributes authority and credit more evenly. We propose a documentary practice of digital humanities that focuses on process and also allows emphasis on issues such as sustainability and preservation—issues that are often neglected when credit and recognition for research faculty are prioritized. The labor of librarians is central to establishing this practice, as well as a continuation of Bobby L. Smiley's 2019 work on "naming the legacy of marginalization" around library labor in DH projects.

Power in the Academy

Structural imbalances in the academy are frequently baked into the culture of institutions. While the divides between and among faculty and staff are perhaps most visible, divisions between research and teaching faculty, or between faculty and students, are also frequently inequitable. Further, the increasing "adjunctification" of teaching throughout colleges and universities and reliance on short-term and contingent labor in academic libraries have created a growing underclass of laborers whose security is tenuous at best. Some academic hierarchies rely more on tradition than policy to be perpetuated. For example, the processes of infantilization and hazing that are part and parcel of both graduate education and tenure and promotion resist documentation, since documenting these practices could both expose disparities in the organizational hierarchy and require that the individuals within the organization perpetrating these actions be held accountable. Maintaining the inscrutability of traditional inequities by leaving no paper trail helps naturalize them, giving them a cultural power that is difficult to challenge. Other inequities are encoded in job classification charts and salary bands. When expectations of service, not collaboration, are enshrined in library mission statements and are literally written into librarians' job descriptions, asymmetry between librarians and research faculty is written into the culture of the library and the institution.

Brian Greenspan argues that digital humanities makes "all too visible the dirty gears that drive the scholarly machine, along with the mechanic's maintenance bill" and recognizes that student labor is an underfunded element in the DH machine. Greenspan's argument focuses on "the materiality of archival practices, bibliography, and publishing across media, as well as the platforms and networks we all use to read and write texts in the twenty-first century" and the real costs associated with making this work possible. Here we wish to focus on the people engaged in making Greenspan's dirty gears turn. For even as digital humanities "scandalously reveal the system's components," structural inequities are rendered invisible to those at the top through the language of interdisciplinarity and of the network. Organizing to change the architectures of power within the academy is challenging, since without a proper understanding of the relationships that rely on and reinforce these power relations, the underclass of the academy—staff members, librarians, IT professionals, and indeed, students—can feel powerless to effect change. As Jane McAlevey describes it, "People participate to the degree they understand—but they also understand to the degree they participate" (6). Absent doing the work of power-structure analysis, which McAlevey claims "is the mechanism that enables ordinary people to understand their potential power and participate meaningfully in making strategy," marginalized laborers within the academy will remain unable to fully participate in effective organization. Documentary practice focusing on revealing the labor of librarians and other collaborators will necessarily require a similar level of analysis and cannot reflect on the positionality of librarians without considering that of others within the DH ecosystem and the efforts of others to gain recognition for their labor.

There have been a variety of efforts over the past decade to help provide language for, and to frame the debate around, the rights of those whose labor is necessary for digital projects. Early considerations of DH labor focused almost exclusively on recognition for tenure and promotion for teaching and research faculty (Modern Language Association; Rockwell). This continues to be important since much DH labor is additive and still not universally recognized for tenure and promotion. Though this is slowly changing, resistance still remains, as we saw in the MLA/Ithaka S+R report. The "Collaborators' Bill of Rights" (CBR), which will be a decade old by the time this chapter appears in print, emerged from a workshop on professionalization in digital humanities centers, "Off the Tracks: Laying New Lines for Digital Humanities Scholars," funded by a 2010 National Endowment for the Humanities DH Level 1 Start-Up Grant. The CBR is part of the discourse of alt-ac, "alternative academic careers," in this case "hybrid scholar-programmers . . . staffing many DH centers." The CBR is driven by the acknowledgment that "such staff members are not well accounted for by the normative division between the 'research' usually associated with faculty positions and the 'service' usually associated with staff." The report that frames the CBR includes recommendations on collaboration; career paths, assessment, and promotion; institutional support; and "paths for transformation."

"Library Faculty" is one of the recommended career paths for digital humanists, though the CBR authors acknowledge that " 'library faculty' is a slippery term. About a third of library faculty are tenure-track faculty (as recommended by the Association of College and Research Libraries); others are on faculty equivalency continuous appointments based on a step system for promotion; others are not considered faculty at all." Libraries, along with universities, museums, and archives, are acknowledged as "locations of creativity and innovation" (point 3 of the CBR), and as such, "intellectual property policies should be equally applied to all employees regardless of employment status. Credit for collaborative work should be portable and legible." While the report has been widely discussed, its impact is unclear largely because the principles it describes are aspirational and unenforceable and largely do not engage with the systemic issues that created the need for this advocacy in the first place. The same problem confronts other efforts to advocate for undergraduate students (Di Pressi et al.; Keralis), graduate student workers (Mann), and postdoctoral workers (Alpert-Abrams et al.). These efforts, while sometimes polemical, are generally what Keralis describes as "soft solutions" that have no teeth in terms of enforcing just and ethical division or recognition of labor for these vulnerable populations or holding faculty abusers accountable. These efforts are also further complicated by the ways in which contributors, including library staff as well as students and postdoctoral workers, are expected to engage in the reproductive labor of the academy (Shirazi). This labor is necessary for a successful DH project, and indeed for the perpetuation of the academy, but it is often illegible within academic hierarchies. When it is seen, it is perceived to be service rather than more prestigious research (Alpert-Abrams et al.; Di Pressi et al.; Shirazi). As Jen Guiliano points out about some senior faculty, "These are people looking for labor to get them to where they want to go; not collaborators who are seeking true partnerships where all members of the team are elevated to be better researchers, teachers, and scholars." What we hope to do here is to demonstrate how incorporating documentation into the development of digital projects can render the invisible visible and provide clear, enforceable boundaries that protect the interests of all parties involved, whether researcher, collaborator, or service provider. If work is not recognized as scholarship when it is perceived as service, it should at least be recognized as labor. As Shirazi points out, "perhaps the problem isn't service itself, but exploitation."

DH Labor in the Library

We now move to considering the positionality of librarians within both DH projects as well as within the broader academic hierarchies in which those projects are carried out. In a 2016 Digital Library Federation (DLF) presentation, "The Expansion and Development of DH/DS Librarian Roles: A Preliminary Look at the Data," Paige Morgan and Helene Williams analyzed digital humanities/scholarship job postings in libraries. They found that postings had increased from 2010 to 2016 and noted that while the most heavily sought-after skills changed from year to year, postings overall focused on specific technologies (e.g., DSpace), specific abilities (e.g., visualization), specific knowledge (e.g., copyright), and project management. Morgan and Williams did not find "soft skills" specifically in their analysis, perhaps because they are associated with less identifiable language or encapsulated in the term "project management." DH positions in libraries generally are described in terms of managing projects or technology rather than people (Posner 2014). The tension between requiring highly specific technical skills and broad domain knowledge of fields such as scholarly communication reflects uncertainty around what forms of labor constitute DH labor as well as an acknowledgment that myriad forms of labor are necessary and critical for sustainable DH projects. The growth and shape of DH positions within libraries during this time period is, in our experience, as much connected to what the libraries of aspirational peer institutions are doing in regard to hiring and academic libraries' tendencies to create "messianic unicorn" positions as to anything else (Smiley).

DH projects, then, often entail very specific demands on the labor, time, and skills of library workers, but it is not always clear what the payoff is for those workers. As DH scholars and practitioners Miriam Posner and Trevor Muñoz have argued, the biggest obstacles to DH, whether within or outside the library, are often connected to working with people of varying positions and statuses across institutional boundaries. DH projects also often rely on multiple technological infrastructures, created and maintained by a variety of units and divisions, both within the library and across the broader institution. In "What Are the Challenges to Doing DH in the Library?," Posner identifies the lack of authority and overcautiousness that often result from working across institutional boundaries and suggests they can be solved with more time dedicated to DH tasks and a higher status for DH workers. In contrast, Trevor Muñoz, in "Digital Humanities in the Library Isn't a Service," seeks to solve the problem of institutional and administrative barriers by working outside of those barriers, in a "space outside existing commitments." Within this space, outside of existing academic hierarchies that primarily position library workers as service providers rather than scholars, library workers and other non-research faculty collaborators on DH projects could become legible as scholars within those same academic hierarchies (Sample). As Bobby Smiley points out, although the dominant discourse around DH emphasizes collaboration and flat, networked structures, both academic libraries and DH are "arenas overly concerned with monitoring boundaries for who is in or who is out." This observation resonates with the experiences of the authors, who would extend Smiley's observation to academia writ large and would indeed identify academic hierarchies (and, as always, limited resources) as the source of much boundary policing within both fields.

While Muñoz's assertion that DH in libraries is not a service is well intentioned and may reflect the reality at his institution, "DH-as-a-service" is fundamentally the reality for many, perhaps most, librarians working in academic libraries. Even when librarians are themselves tenure-track faculty, in some cases 50 percent or more of their duties must conform to some definition of "librarianship." As Roxanne Shirazi exhorts us, "when we call for librarians to approach collaborative digital work as partners and not service providers," we must acknowledge "the fact that there are different power relations at play in these collaborative relationships. Power relations that are embedded in the hierarchies that make up academia, in both the social stratification of varying job ranks and the hierarchical classification of service and scholarship." Smiley echoes her analysis, pointing out that by beginning to "discern those power relations and structural inequities in greater relief," DH librarians can "reposition themselves as collaborators and intellectual peers." There are, however, structural obstacles to this repositioning. At the University of Illinois at Urbana-Champaign (UIUC), as just one example, librarians are tenure-track faculty and generally governed by the same provost-level policies as other faculty (UIUC Office of the Provost). However, librarians have a separate section in their promotional dossiers that defines librarianship explicitly in terms of services provided to students and research/teaching faculty, along with collection development, outreach, and "educating library users" (UIUC Illinois Library). More tellingly, reviewers in the tenure process "are drawn from among a pool of people the candidate *serves*" (emphasis added), making service, not collaboration, central to the professional identity of these faculty. This creates an asymmetric relationship between research faculty and faculty librarians that is not merely perceptual but structural and that can be exploited by those faculty who demand service as described in these policy documents. This effectively disempowers librarians from asserting their rights as faculty. Despite their rank on paper, librarians can be compelled to participate in projects that may be exploitative if their faculty "peers" deem such participation to be necessary. No protections, boundaries, or expectations for credit are implied in the model expressed in these documents. And in a library and university culture in which librarians have to fight to be believed in order to receive disability accommodations that are *federally mandated* (Pionke), no untenured librarian wants to be the test case for what the real cost is for standing up for themselves on the basis of things as nebulous as ethics, or boundaries, or equity. This dramatically underscores Shirazi's point "that some of us might need to embrace the label of service—or, perhaps, might not be able to escape it."

Negotiating these hierarchies, and effectively coordinating, collaborating, and working across these myriad administrative and institutional inequities, is a significant element of DH labor in the library, one that goes unnamed in job postings. This work is fundamentally interpersonal and emotional in orientation—consider having to anticipate, manage, and respond to the work, feelings, and expectations of everyone working on a DH project—and as such, it is often not recognized or compensated as work. It is care work that contributes to the reproduction of the academy (Shirazi). DH labor in the library is also often accountable to multiple stakeholders with varying expectations: more grant money, more favorable comparisons to aspirational peers, new positions, but also fear of losing positions or resources. DH labor is susceptible to coordinator syndrome: Coordinators lack authority, resources, and infrastructure to actually implement a service but at the same time are responsible to multiple institutional stakeholders for the success or failure of that service (Library Loon; Douglas and Gadsby). Moreover, coordinators occupy an unstable position within both academic and library hierarchies as they might lack an organizational home and their work occurs across institutional structures. Dorothea Salo astutely satirizes these conflicting demands in relation to scholarly communication initiatives, which are similar in that they require multidirectional coordination. In her article, "How to Scuttle a Scholarly Communication Initiative," Salo indicts administrators' magical thinking in "calling staff 'change agents' while insisting that they 'not rock the boat.'" Gabriele Griffin and Matt Hayler point to broader systems that produce instability—namely, workplace hierarchies, interpersonal relationships, and the "neoliberal research landscape."

The interpersonal care and coordination of library DH work relies on the creation and, perhaps more importantly, the maintenance of relationships. The organizational home of DH plays a crucial role in creating and cultivating relationships across campus. If, as in one author's experience, the library is perceived to be incompetent by tenure-line faculty, those faculty will be reluctant to collaborate with those who work in and for the library. In this way, DH labor in the library, even if performed by recently hired library workers, often relies on already existing relationships with faculty, staff, and students and is inflected by the library's existing credibility or lack thereof. These relationships and perceptions may be connected to non-DH library labor—purchasing decisions, library instruction, work on faculty committees—but it is up to the DH librarian to negotiate this interpersonal infrastructure. Technical infrastructures matter as well; DH projects are contiguous with and directly engage earlier forms of scholarship. The maintenance and reproduction of the scholarly knowledge production and communication system, the more traditional work of academic libraries, and the information technology and labor infrastructures that make these systems possible might therefore also be understood as a crucial element of DH library labor. These forms of labor are often invisible to those with institutional power. Interpersonal and emotional work is invisible; the need for maintenance only becomes apparent when infrastructures break. Library services are ideally frictionless, and it is generally difficult to account for the diverse forms of labor and knowledge that contribute to DH projects (Douglas and Gadsby; Mirza and Seale; Ettarh). Dominant understandings of DH library labor are very different from what we perceive as actual DH library labor. This lack of understanding or silence around collaboration as a learned skill allows magical thinking around the process of DH projects to grow; they are perceived as inadvertent, minor, and unimportant, rather than critical processes that we have agency over (Griffin and Hayler). To paraphrase Bethany Nowviskie, this results in the eternal September for collaborative knowledge production.

Rafia Mirza and Maura Seale (two of this chapter's authors) have argued elsewhere (see "Who Killed the World?"; "Empty Presence") that the interpersonal and maintenance work performed within libraries is gendered and racialized, both within the library and within academia, and consequently it is devalued (see also Douglas and Gadsby; Leon; Shirazi; Harris). Within academic libraries, these forms of labor are more likely to be performed by staff rather than librarians, and those staff members are more likely to be people of color than librarians (Seale and Mirza, "Empty Presence"). As Smiley notes, academic library workers are invested in specific notions of prestige, which are often connected to questions of which library workers are "professionals" and which are not. The investment in hierarchy within the library is, we suggest, a result of the status of the library as a service provider within academia, a feminized, low-status role. Library workers (both librarians and staff) are often subject to exploitation by those with more status within academia: namely, tenure-line faculty and university administrators.

The low status of the library within academia is reinforced by a pervasive incomprehension around the work of the library, by both faculty and university administrators, and by library administrators' commitment to always be doing more with less in the name of service rather than pushing back against increased demands and decreased resources (Seale and Mirza; Ettarh). At the same time, academic library administrators continually seek out external markers of prestige in order to improve the status of the library within academic hierarchies, continually attempting to do something university administrators might value and looking toward aspirational peers to decide what to do next. Mirza and Seale argue that these external markers of prestige have recently taken the form of various sorts of technological innovation within the library. DH, as a recent and innovative form of scholarship that uses information technology, arguably functions as a marker of external prestige for academic libraries both within academia and in comparison to other academic libraries. It appeals to administrators of the neoliberal university in its development of technological "products" and "marketable skills." But because DH is valued for its prestige, academic library administrators at libraries of all sizes tend to look toward well-funded and well-staffed institutions, often libraries that belong to the Association of Research Libraries, and expect the same results with fewer staff and resources. DH work that takes place in less prestigious libraries or at a smaller scale is, at the same time, ignored.

Regardless of institutional context, the library workers who support DH are thereby seen as valuable within these hierarchies, but that labor is narrowly defined, as Morgan and Williams observed in their analysis of DH librarian job postings. DH library labor is understood to be primarily technological rather than interpersonal or maintenance work. Interpersonal work and maintenance, Mirza and Seale argue, are devalued not because they are not valuable but because they tend to be performed by white women and people of color; it is the positionality of these workers within a series of hierarchies—academia, libraries, and broader society—that leads to their devaluation and erasure. Technological innovation, by contrast, is associated with Silicon Valley, a site of economic and political power, and is performed in the popular imagination by individual white men. DH projects that incorporate library labor can similarly become the property of a single faculty author, who, to be fair, is also negotiating academic hierarchies and likely attempting to demonstrate their productivity for promotion, but in the process can erase library labor that is already in a fraught position because of those same academic and social hierarchies (Leon). As Griffin and Hayler argue, the "neoliberal imperatives which govern contemporary academe" have resulted in "the simultaneous rise of collective work and individualized accountability in a context of heightened competition." Predictably, this is "partly supported by the hierarchies within academe which construe certain staff as subsidiary and which continue to instrumentalize both tools and people rather than recognizing them as co-producers of knowledge." Those tasks perceived as prestigious will go to those higher in the hierarchy; other "service" tasks will belong to care workers, "the feminized servants of the collaboration process who simply facilitate the 'real' academic work" (Griffin and Hayler). DH projects that rely on library labor must contend with not just academic hierarchies but also academic library hierarchies that rely on and reproduce in miniature broader social hierarchies in order to accurately account for library labor.

Praxis: Making Labor Legible

If the labor of librarians in digital humanities projects is frequently rendered invisible or is regularly misrecognized and devalued by faculty who do not see librarians as collaborators, we suggest that making that labor legible might lead to more sustainable and ethical practices in the field. We argue for a more intentional DH that focuses on making implicit expectations explicit. One possibility is a formal memorandum of understanding (MOU) between the members of the project team. Other forms of documentation can communicate expectations for librarians' roles in projects to help preempt assumptions about their potential contributions. Transparent policies, decision trees to help researchers identify contingencies and potential points of collaboration, and even email messages documenting conversations can all contribute to rendering librarians' labor as collaborators more legible to research faculty. If librarians cannot convince their colleagues to document, or do not have administrative support to do so, we argue it is useful for them to document their own collaborative DH experiences themselves, to see how the choice to do so shapes what is created. Even the simplest forms of documentation can provide clarity to help avoid conflicts and potential exploitation before they begin or, failing that, at the very least can provide a paper trail to determine where a project diverged from otherwise ad hoc agreements.

One of the most critical steps in avoiding exploitative labor practices is to have a discussion about expectations and goals before the project starts and *then write down or otherwise document those expectations.* It is incumbent on administrators, tenure-line faculty, and others with institutional power to support collaboration that allows for both discussion and documentation. Documentation helps assess shifting responsibilities and allows for tracking how much labor, and whose labor it is, for each project (Currier, Mirza, and Downing). Documentation can be a useful tool and process to ensure transparency, and a culture that consistently engages in debriefing around DH projects also brings in accountability. These debriefings could work through questions around success—whether the project was successful and also how we define success—and around credit, blame, and the positionality of project members. The sharing of documentation and debriefings is key to a culture that values all forms of DH library labor; as Currier and colleagues note, "Without documentation and reference to past projects, an institution runs the risk of burnout or fatigue, since every project is essentially reinventing the (DH) wheel" (Currier, Mirza, and Downing). If the project is unstructured, or if the structure is informal, the rules of the project will only be known to a few, and power is limited to those who know the rules. In order for everyone to be involved and to participate equitably, the structure and rules of the project must be explicit and available to all participants. Collaboration is an active process. Too frequently we want to believe that good intentions and institutional goodwill can "organically" produce ethical collaboration and enable us to do "good work." But without intentionality, we will merely reproduce the hierarchies of the systems we live in. Process is not just a means to an end but inextricably bound up in what we produce. DH projects will reproduce the inequities of the system they are created within; they will suffer from scope and feature creep, as well as the "tyranny of structurelessness" (Freeman). Or in Sara Ahmed's framing, "You have to record what you do not want to reproduce" ("Why Complain?"). However, accountability cannot exist from the bottom up without administrative support; all the documents and debriefings in the world will not change an exploitative culture.

Individuals without institutional power or authority (or the backing of unions) can introduce friction by pushing back on accelerated timelines, pointing out labor or technical challenges, or even just asking questions about the process. However, the danger is that systemic labor issues become individualized and situated ahistorically in the questioner rather than in the sociotechnical system itself. Sara Ahmed argues that institutional processes can frame complaints as negative factors, as slowing things down unnecessarily, but that complaints also function as diversity work because by slowing down and introducing friction, they allow for time to consider and interrogate normative practices that cause harm. Ahmed discusses how complaint can be a feminist queer model to transform an institution and how complaint can open up an institution for those for whom it was not intended. In Chapter 8, "The Feminist Data Manifest-NO," the authors discuss centering refusal as a "generative praxis of Indigenous survivance," as a way to avoid "reproduc[ing] systemic patterns of exploitation," to center consent (actual consent, not the colonial "ruse of consent," where there is no actual way to refuse participation), and to value and credit all contributors to a project. Our argument (previously made by others) is for a documentation praxis in which "participants are self-reflexive about their positionality in power structures/hierarchy relative to other people, acknowledge historical events that led to current power structures, and then avoid reproducing inequity as much as possible and mitigating inequity" (Currier and Mirza). Transparency doesn't mean anything if you cannot say no.

We argue for documentation as process and praxis: Documentation manages expectations and makes labor visible. It is a means unto itself and not just a means to an end (Currier and Mirza; DLF 2016). The tools used for documentation, and the end product, whether an MOU or project management product board, are not as important as the process, which begins with reflection and discussion that draws on critical approaches to management, higher education, librarianship, and DH in which normative, often invisible, practices and mindsets are interrogated and their power structures and ideologies are made visible. We follow the authors of "The Feminist Data Manifest-NO" in acknowledging a genealogy of praxis as a term of art grounded in Black and Indigenous feminisms. By recognizing this origin, we hope to restore a discourse of liberation to the term, similar to the work Audrey Watters and Meg Worley did around the co-opted term "disruption" in their contributions to *Disrupting the Digital Humanities.* In this spirit, Sareeta Amrute discusses how "postcolonial and decolonising feminist theory, moves the discussion of ethics from establishing decontextualised rules to developing practices to train sociotechnical systems . . . to begin with the material and embodied situations in which these systems are entangled, *which include from the start histories of race, gender and dehumanisation*" (58, emphasis added).

To conclude, we offer a series of assertions in the form of a manifesto. While these assertions are nonprescriptive, we have attempted to frame them as provocations that get at the structural problems other aspirational documents do not. These principles undergird our praxis of documentation, and if applied and taken seriously by all project stakeholders, they have the potential to provide a practical means to make digital scholarship a more just and equitable place for all of its citizens. It is our hope that you can use these principles as tools to refuse, to complain, and to transform praxis within your DH ecosystem.

Librarians' Labor: A Documentation Manifesto

Before committing to any project, librarians may ask:

- **Why?**
  Why are we doing this project?
  Why is my personal involvement necessary?
- **How?**
  How are resources allocated?
  How will I be compensated?
  How will I receive credit for my work?
- **When?**
  When does the project begin?
  When will I be allotted time to work on it?
  When will my role end?
  When will the project end? (And *all* projects should end.)
- **For Whom?**
  Who is the audience for the project?
  Who is the project about?
  Do these communities have a voice in the project?
- **By Whom?**
  Who gets credit?
  Is credit (Principal Investigator status, authorship, etc.) really just going to one person?
  Who gets paid and by whom?

Librarians have a right to document the answers to these questions (and others). These answers should have the weight of a contract for the duration of a project.

- What is written down may change with the consent of all parties, but any changes must be written down.
- Revisions that amount to "scope creep" may require new agreements.
- Project communication should be in writing. Conversations should be followed up in writing.
- Meeting notes should be shared with everyone on a project team, whether or not they were present in the meeting.
- No assumptions, no hidden curricula. All contingencies must be made explicit and written down in language that is clear to all parties.

In the absence of documentation, librarians have a right to say "No" to projects in these situations:

- When expectations are unclear
- When the project appears to be exploitative
- When credit is not equitably assigned
- When there is a conflict with their ethical positions regarding research, student and other labor, and academic integrity

Such a refusal should be without personal or professional consequences and should also be the beginning of a conversation to address these concerns.

Neither library leadership nor individual librarians should make commitments of labor or resources in the absence of documentation.

BIBLIOGRAPHY

Ahmed, Sara. "Complaint as Diversity Work." *Feministkilljoys.* November 10, 2017, https://feministkilljoys.com/2017/11/10/complaint-as-diversity-work/

Ahmed, Sara. "Why Complain?" *Feministkilljoys.* July 22, 2019, https://feministkilljoys.com/2019/07/22/why-complain/.

Alpert-Abrams, Hannah, Heather Froehlich, Amanda Henrichs, Jim McGrath, and Kim Martin. "Postdoctoral Laborers Bill of Rights." *Humanities Commons.* April 2019, https://hcommons.org/deposits/item/hc:26741/.

Amrute, Sareeta. "Of Techno-Ethics and Techno-Affects." *Feminist Review* 123, no. 1 (November 2019): 56–73, https://doi.org/10.1177/0141778919879744.

Clement, Tanya. *Professionalization in Digital Humanities Centers.* National Endowment for the Humanities Digital Humanities Start-Up Grant HD-51161-10. March 2010 to September 2013, https://securegrants.neh.gov/publicquery/main.aspx?f=1&gn=HD-51161-10.

Clement, Tanya, Brian Croxall, Julia Flanders, Neil Fraistat, Steve Jones, Matt Kirschenbaum, Suzanne Lodato, Laura Mandell, et al. "Collaborators' Bill of Rights." *Off the Tracks: Laying New Lines for Digital Humanities Scholars* (blog). 2011, http://mcpress.media-commons.org/offthetracks/.

Coble, Zach, Sarah Potvin, and Roxanne Shirazi. "Process as Product: Scholarly Communication Experiments in the Digital Humanities." *Journal of Librarianship and Scholarly Communication* 2, no. 3 (2014): 1–11 https://doi.org/10.7710/2162-3309.1137.

Cooper, Danielle, Cate Mahoney, Rebecca Springer, Robert Behra, Ian G. Beilin, Guy Burak, Margaret Burri, et al. "Supporting Research in Languages and Literature." *Ithaka S+R.* Last modified September 9, 2020, https://doi.org/10.18665/sr.313810.

Currier, Brett, and Rafia Mirza. "Towards a Praxis of Library Documentation." Presentation, Digital Library Federation (DLF) Annual Forum, Las Vegas, Nevada, October 17, 2018, https://osf.io/tuvcw/.

Currier, Brett D., Rafia Mirza, and Jeff Downing. "They Think All of This Is New: Leveraging Librarians' Project Management Skills for the Digital Humanities." *College & Undergraduate Libraries* 24, no. 2–4 (October 2017): 270–89, https://doi.org/10.1080/10691316.2017.1347541.

Di Pressi, Haley, Stephanie Gorman, Miriam Posner, Raphael Sasayama, and Tori Schmitt, with contributions from Roderic Crooks, Megan Driscoll, Amy Earhart, Spencer Keralis, Tiffany Naiman, and Todd Presner. "A Student Collaborators' Bill of Rights." *UCLA HumTech.* June 8, 2015, https://humtech.ucla.edu/news/a-student-collaborators-bill-of-rights/.

Dombrowski, Quinn. "Towards a Taxonomy of Failure." January 30, 2019, http://quinndombrowski.com/?q=blog/2019/01/30/towards-taxonomy-failure.

Douglas, Veronica Arellano, and Jo Gadsby. "All Carrots, No Sticks: Relational Practice and Library Instruction Coordination." *In the Library with the Lead Pipe.* July 10, 2019, http://www.inthelibrarywiththeleadpipe.org/2019/all-carrots-no-sticks-relational-practice-and-library-instruction-coordination/.

Ettarh, Fobazi. "Vocational Awe and Librarianship: The Lies We Tell Ourselves." *In the Library with the Lead Pipe.* January 10, 2018, http://www.inthelibrarywiththeleadpipe.org/2018/vocational-awe/.

Freeman, Jo. "The Tyranny of Structurelessness." Accessed January 30, 2020, https://www.jofreeman.com/joreen/tyranny.htm.

Greenspan, Brian. "The Scandal of the Digital Humanities." In *Debates in the Digital Humanities 2019,* edited by Matthew K. Gold and Lauren F. Klein. Minneapolis: University of Minnesota Press, 2019, https://dhdebates.gc.cuny.edu/.

Gregg, Melissa. *Counterproductive: Time Management in the Knowledge Economy.* Durham, N.C.: Duke University Press, 2018.

Griffin, Gabriele, and Matt Steven Hayler. "Collaboration in Digital Humanities Research—Persisting Silences." *DHQ: Digital Humanities Quarterly* 12, no. 1 (April 2018).

Guiliano, Jen. "Don't Call Me." February 8, 2013, http://jguiliano.com/blog/2013/02/08/dont-call-me/.

Hamilton, Jennifer. "Critical Perspectives on Whiteness and Technoscience: An Introduction." *Catalyst: Feminism, Theory, Technoscience* 4, no. 1 (May 2018): 1–12, https://doi.org/10.28968/cftt.v4i1.29634.

Harris, Roma M. *Librarianship: The Erosion of a Woman's Profession.* Norwood, N.J.: Ablex, 1992.

Hochschild, Arlie Russell. *The Managed Heart: Commercialization of Human Feeling.* Berkeley: University of California Press, 2003.

Irani, Lilly. "'Design Thinking': Defending Silicon Valley at the Apex of Global Labor Hierarchies." *Catalyst: Feminism, Theory, Technoscience* 4, no. 1 (May 2018): 1–19, https://doi.org/10.28968/cftt.v4i1.29638.

Keralis, Spencer D. C. "Disrupting Labor in Digital Humanities; or, The Classroom Is Not Your Crowd." In *Disrupting the Digital Humanities,* edited by Dorothy Kim and Jesse Stommel, 273–91. Santa Barbara, Calif.: Punctum Books, 2018.

Kirschenbaum, Matthew. "What Is Digital Humanities and What's It Doing in English Departments?" In *Debates in the Digital Humanities 2012,* edited by Matthew K. Gold. Minneapolis: University of Minnesota Press, 2012, https://dhdebates.gc.cuny.edu/.

Koeser, Rebecca Sutton. "Document ALL the Things!" The Center for Digital Humanities at Princeton, August 12, 2019. https://cdh.princeton.edu/updates/2019/08/12/document-all-things/.

Leebaw, Danya. "Participatory and Ethical Strategic Planning: What Academic Libraries Can Learn from Critical Management Studies." *Library Trends* 68, no. 2 (2019): 110–29, https://doi.org/10.1353/lib.2019.0033.

Leon, Sharon. 2016. "Returning Women to the History of Digital History." *[bracket].* March 7, 2016, https://www.6floors.org/bracket/2016/03/07/returning-women-to-the-history-of-digital-history/.

Library Loon. "The C-Word." *Gavia Libraria* (blog). Internet Archive version. December 15, 2011, https://web.archive.org/web/20150224221922/https://gavialib.com/2011/12/the-c-word/.

Mann, Rachel. "Paid to Do but Not to Think: Reevaluating the Role of Graduate Student Collaborators." In *Debates in the Digital Humanities 2019,* edited by Matthew K. Gold and Lauren F. Klein. Minneapolis: University of Minnesota Press, 2019, https://dhdebates.gc.cuny.edu/.

McAlevey, Jane F. *No Shortcuts: Organizing for Power in the New Gilded Age.* Oxford: Oxford University Press, 2016.

Miller, Claire Cain. "Tech's Damaging Myth of the Loner Genius Nerd." *New York Times.* August 12, 2017, https://www.nytimes.com/2017/08/12/upshot/techs-damaging-myth-of-the-loner-genius-nerd.html.

Mirza, Rafia, and Maura Seale. "Who Killed the World? White Masculinity and the Technocratic Library of the Future." In *Topographies of Whiteness: Mapping Whiteness in Library and Information Science,* edited by Gina Schlesselman-Tarango, 175–201. Sacramento, Calif.: Library Juice Press, 2017.

Modern Language Association. "Guidelines for Evaluating Work in Digital Humanities and Digital Media." 2000, rev. 2012, https://www.mla.org/About-Us/Governance/Committees/Committee-Listings/Professional-Issues/Committee-on-Information-Technology/Guidelines-for-Evaluating-Work-in-Digital-Humanities-and-Digital-Media.

Morgan, Paige. "Getting Started: Strategies for DH Professional Development." In *Doing More Digital Humanities: Open Approaches to Creation, Growth, and Development*, edited by Constance Crompton, Richard J. Lane, and Ray Siemens, 25–37. London: Routledge, 2019, http://blog.paigemorgan.net/assets/pdfs/Morgan_DMDH_Getting_Started.pdf.

Morgan, Paige C., and Helene Williams. "DLF: The Expansion and Development of DH/DS Librarian Roles: A Preliminary Look at the Data." November 2016, https://osf.io/vu22f/.

Morozov, Evgeny. *To Save Everything, Click Here: The Folly of Technological Solutionism.* New York: Public Affairs, 2013.

Muñoz, Trevor. "Digital Humanities in the Library Isn't a Service." August 19, 2012, https://trevormunoz.com/archive/posts/2012-08-19-doing-dh-in-the-library/.

Nowviskie, Bethany. "Eternal September of the Digital Humanities." *Bethany Nowviskie* (blog). October 15, 2010, http://nowviskie.org/2010/eternal-september-of-the-digital-humanities/.

Pionke, J. J. "The Impact of Disbelief: On Being a Library Employee with a Disability." *Library Trends* 67, no. 3 (December 2019): 423–35, https://doi.org/10.1353/lib.2019.0004.

Posner, Miriam. "Commit to DH People, Not DH Projects." *Miriam Posner's Blog.* March 18, 2014. https://miriamposner.com/blog/commit-to-dh-people-not-dh-projects/.

Posner, Miriam. "Digital Humanities and the Library." *Miriam Posner's Blog.* Last updated April 2013, http://miriamposner.com/blog/digital-humanities-and-the-library/.

Posner, Miriam. "What Are Some Challenges to Doing DH in the Library?" *Miriam Posner's Blog.* August 10, 2012, http://miriamposner.com/blog/what-are-some-challenges-to-doing-dh-in-the-library/.

Rockwell, Geoffrey. "Short Guide to Evaluation of Digital Work." *Journal of Digital Humanities* 1, no. 4 (Fall 2012), http://journalofdigitalhumanities.org/1-4/short-guide-to-evaluation-of-digital-work-by-geoffrey-rockwell/.

Russell, Andrew, and Lee Vinsel. "Innovation Is Overvalued. Maintenance Often Matters More." *Aeon.* April 7, 2016, https://aeon.co/essays/innovation-is-overvalued-maintenance-often-matters-more.

Salo, Dorothea. "How to Scuttle a Scholarly Communication Initiative." *Journal of Librarianship and Scholarly Communication* 1, no. 4 (August 2013): 1075, https://doi.org/10.7710/2162-3309.1075.

Sample, Mark. "When Does Service Become Scholarship?" *@samplereality.* February 8, 2013, https://www.samplereality.com/2013/02/08/when-does-service-become-scholarship/.

Seale, Maura, and Rafia Mirza. "Empty Presence: Library Labor, Prestige, and the MLS." *Library Trends* 68 no. 2 (2019): 252–68, https://doi.org/10.1353/lib.2019.0038.

Shirazi, Roxanne. "Reproducing the Academy: Librarians and the Question of Service in the Digital Humanities." *Roxanne Shirazi* (blog). July 15, 2014, https://roxanneshirazi.com/2014/07/15/reproducing-the-academy-librarians-and-the-question-of-service-in-the-digital-humanities/.

Siemens, Lynne. "Project Management." In *Digital Pedagogy in the Humanities: Concepts, Models, and Experiments,* edited by Rebecca Frost Davis, Matthew K. Gold, Katherine D. Harris, and Jentery Sayers. New York: Modern Language Association, 2020, https://digitalpedagogy.hcommons.org/keyword/Project-Management.

Smiley, Bobby L. "From Humanities to Scholarship: Librarians, Labor, and the Digital." In *Debates in the Digital Humanities 2019*, edited by Matthew K. Gold and Lauren F. Klein. Minneapolis: University of Minnesota Press, 2019, https://dhdebates.gc.cuny.edu/projects/debates-in-the-digital-humanities-2019.

Sutherland, Tonia, Marika Cifor, T. L. Cowan, Jasmine Rault, and Patricia Garcia. "The Feminist Data Manifest-NO: An Introduction and Four Reflections." In *Debates in the Digital Humanities 2023,* edited by Matthew K. Gold and Lauren F. Klein. Minneapolis: University of Minnesota Press, 2023.

University of Illinois at Urbana-Champaign. Illinois Library. "Statement on Promotion and Tenure to the Library Faculty at UIUC." April 21, 2022, https://www.library.illinois.edu/staff/statement-on-promotion-and-tenure-to-the-library-faculty-at-uiuc/.

University of Illinois at Urbana-Champaign. Office of the Provost. "Communication #9: Promotion and Tenure." Last revised March 28, 2022, https://provost.illinois.edu/policies/provosts-communications/communication-9-promotion-and-tenure/.

Watters, Audrey. "The Myth and the Millennialism of 'Disruptive Innovation.'" In *Disrupting the Digital Humanities,* edited by Dorothy Kim and Jesse Stommel, 49–60. Santa Barbara, Calif.: Punctum Books, 2018.

Worley, Meg. "The Rhetoric of Disruption: What Are We Doing Here?" In *Disrupting the Digital Humanities,* edited by Dorothy Kim and Jesse Stommel, 61–78. Santa Barbara, Calif.: Punctum Books, 2018.

PART IV][*Chapter 21*

Reframing the Conversation: Digital Humanists, Disabilities, and Accessibility

MEGAN R. BRETT, JESSICA MARIE OTIS, AND MILLS KELLY

Making software, websites, and other digital products more accessible is a growing consideration in the digital humanities (DH).[1] Whether incorporated into design conversations, tacked on before a project launch, or retrofitted onto projects with long-standing problems, accessibility is slowly becoming part of the DH workflow. But while conversations around design and access are a necessary and welcome development, these conversations often remain limited by two crucial factors: the oversimplification of disability and the perception that people with disabilities are external to DH communities.

For digital humanists to take a proactive approach to addressing accessibility, we must first understand that people with disabilities are not just in our audiences. "They" are *us*, and we have diverse, often competing needs for accommodations that enable us to fully participate in the creation, consumption, and analysis of digital scholarship. Creating accessible work or accommodations for people with disabilities is not a hypothetical need or a requirement imposed by law; rather, it is a moral imperative if the digital humanities are to be the inclusive and welcoming community we publicly aspire to be.[2]

The authors of this chapter have a variety of disabilities—including sensory, motor, and cognitive disabilities—that impact their DH work. One author has astigmatism as well as auditory processing issues and intermittent hearing loss, which can make it difficult to hear or follow conversations in loud spaces like conference halls. Another has migraines and astigmatism that makes it painful to read white text on black backgrounds—ironically, a design choice many make to accommodate forms of visual disability requiring high contrast (Otis). She also has asthma, which has been triggered by DH conference locations, and knee issues that have prevented her from being able to access DH conference spaces. The third author has met the legal definition of deaf/hard of hearing since high school, has worn bifocals for more than two decades, and was diagnosed with severe osteoarthritis a decade ago, a condition that makes sitting for more than thirty minutes painful.

Thus, while our individual practices are variably informed by disability studies, this chapter is grounded largely in the lived experiences of the authors as disabled practitioners of DH.

What Are Disabilities?

In the United States, where the authors are based, disability is legally defined as a physical or mental impairment that substantially limits the ability of an individual to perform a "major life activity" as compared to most people in the general population (Department of Justice, "Final Regulatory Assessment, Final Rule"). The 1990 Americans with Disabilities Act (ADA) made it illegal to discriminate against individuals "on the basis of disability in the full and equal enjoyment of the goods, services, facilities, privileges, advantages, or accommodations of any place of public accommodation" ("Americans with Disabilities Act of 1990, as Amended"). Eight years later, as the importance of computers and the internet became increasingly apparent, the Rehabilitation Act of 1973 was updated to mandate the creation of accessible "electronic and information technology" (Department of Justice, "Workforce Investment Act of 1998"). Together, the ADA and Section 508 of the Rehabilitation Act created an ideal of full inclusion for people with legal disabilities into all aspects of American society, including the digital. Although Canada and the European Union member states take similar approaches, and the United Nations adopted the Convention on the Rights of Persons with Disabilities in 2006, policies and enforcement vary widely around the world.

Reality in the United States often falls far short of the ideals expressed in these laws, in part because disabilities are more complicated than the legal definition. Major life activities, as defined by law, include walking, breathing, and thinking, but not driving, caring for children, or using a computer. Disabilities that do not warrant legal accommodation, such as moderate carpal tunnel syndrome, may still significantly affect a scholar's ability to engage with the digital humanities. Conversely, some people with legally recognized disabilities, such as cancer, may feel their disabilities have little to no impact on their engagement with DH (Forlano).[3] An individual remains legally disabled even if medication or assistive technology gives them the ability to perform those life activities, with the sole exclusion of glasses and contact lenses; this technology has become so normalized that only uncorrectable vision problems (20/200 vision or lower vision acuity) qualify as legal disabilities. An individual may be completely asymptomatic—such as a cancer patient in remission—yet legally disabled. Disabilities are thus complex conditions that may or may not be constant in the experience of an individual (as anyone with depression can attest) and that exist on a spectrum that includes, but is not limited to, conditions with legal recognition.

The social model of disability reframes the understanding of disability not as the individual impairment but rather the societal barriers—physical, cultural, or digital—that cause unequal access for persons with an impairment (Goering). Accessibility is the process of removing barriers, mitigating access, or creating alternate points of entry. The Web Content Accessibility Guidelines (WCAG) are organized around four characteristics for all accessible content: perceivable, through multiple means including assistive technologies; operable, regardless of input device; understandable, both in language and layout; and robust, or broadly compatible with a range of assistive technologies ("WCAG 2.1 at a Glance"). Whereas accessibility is built in to the system, accommodations provide access by modifying an existing structure or system. A physical world example would be the difference between an entrance with stairs and a ramp (accessible) and a folding ramp placed over stairs temporarily (accommodation).

While disabilities and accessibility are universal concerns, they affect digital humanists directly. No one in DH communities lives untouched by disability, whether they have a disability themselves or their relatives, collaborators, or students do. In America, one in four adults is legally considered to have a disability ("Disability Impacts All of Us"). Approximately 75 percent of Americans need vision correction, while around 4.4 billion people worldwide have myopia and other vision impairments (World Health Organization; Vision Council of America). Color blindness affects one in 12 men and one in 200 women worldwide ("Color Vision Deficiency"). Over 31 percent of Americans will experience an anxiety disorder at some point during their lives, and 20 percent of college students were diagnosed with anxiety in 2018 (Kane). Similarly, 13 percent of American adults aged 18 to 25 have at least one major depressive episode, making anxiety and depression the most common mental health concerns among college students ("Any Anxiety Disorder"; "Major Depression"). Difficulty walking or climbing stairs affects 14 percent of American adults, while 11 percent have serious difficulty concentrating, remembering, or making decisions ("Disability Impacts All of Us"). These and other disabilities can be "invisible," making it easy to overlook their prevalence within the DH communities and among our audiences. But given the ubiquity of people with disabilities and an emerging consensus about accessibility best practices, digital humanists must become more attentive to the complexities of disabilities and accessibility as we plan and execute our projects.

How We Fail

Digital humanists are familiar with failure and often embrace it pedagogically, although we are less comfortable with being public about the failure of high-status projects.[4] Yet when it comes to accessibility, digital humanists often fail to notice we are failing. For examples of failures to meet even the most basic web accessibility standards as laid out in WCAG, we the authors did not need to look very far. Though our center, the Roy Rosenzweig Center for History and New Media, was founded in 1994, we did not start consistently adding subtitles or closed captions to videos and screencasts until 2015. Since then, we have endeavored to make new videos more accessible but have not had the resources to completely remediate our older materials. We are not the only ones. A quick scan of recent winners of the Roy Rosenzweig Prize for Innovation in Digital History, completed using the WAVE Web Accessibility Evaluation Tool, flagged accessibility issues in every site's home page.[5] Some issues are easily remediated, such as changing font colors or adding alt-text. But others are baked into the project design. Entire technologies such as the now-deprecated Flash can be inherently inaccessible and only partially modified for accessibility, while other technologies such as JavaScript may have only limited accessibility even if set up correctly, which digital humanists often fail to do.[6]

Digital humanists do not have the resources to plan for accessibility for all disabilities, especially given the wide range of permanent and transitory disabilities people experience. Indeed, there are certain forms of DH projects that may be inherently inaccessible to people with certain types of disabilities; for example, we have yet to figure out a way to make a network "hairball" visualization fully comprehensible to a screen reader. However, we still need to be attentive to accessibility concerns among our colleagues and our audiences and consider creating multiple avenues of access to our scholarly evidence, data, analyses, and arguments. For example, the data driving a network visualization may be presented in a fully accessible manner, even if the visualization of that data cannot be described by a screen reader. In general, we need to budget more time and money for accessibility. We need to coordinate with our primary stakeholders in order to assess our projects for accessibility and revise them if necessary. We need to call on our funders to allocate money to accessibility and make accessibility a priority in proposal evaluation processes. Most importantly, we need to not be afraid of trying and failing to do better.[7] Try-fail cycles are a normal part of the DH workflow; the only permanent failure is in not trying.

How We Can Succeed

We have spent several years thinking critically about how digital humanists can incorporate greater consideration of people with disabilities into our work. There is no straightforward "quick fix" or even a difficult but attainable universal design that can solve all our problems: Disabilities are myriad, complex, and the accommodations needed by one person may cause problems for someone else. For example, a ramp may seem more accessible than stairs, but there are disabilities that render ramps difficult to manage. Instead of a one-size-fits-all approach, a multimodal approach can accommodate a wider range of people.[8] Our conversations have given rise to a series of proposed first steps we can take toward a more proactive approach to accommodation in several areas of intervention relevant to the field. We intend these initial proposals to be just that—a place to start, not a set of standards to be adhered to. We hope these proposals will be a starting point for productive conversations among those working in the digital humanities.

COMMUNITIES OF PRACTICE

Teams and Collaborations

The first and necessary step for digital humanities scholars is to acknowledge the existence of and respect the lived experiences of colleagues with disabilities. Whether DH work is taking place within an informal collaboration or a formally organized center, department, or team, we can start by adopting a set of guiding principles for accessibility. It is incumbent on those in positions of formal or informal authority to press their colleagues to think critically about what such guiding principles might look like and how they might shape future projects. Collaborators and teams should have open, honest conversations about their own accessibility needs and make self-identification of disability something that feels safe and normal, while understanding that team members may still decide not to disclose their disabilities (as discussed later). Holding a conversation about accommodation needs in the first meeting of a new collaboration makes it clear these issues are being taken seriously. Regardless of whether team members have conditions that have been legally recognized as disabilities, identifying and meeting those team members' needs will make the process of creating a DH project more productive, enjoyable, and inclusive for everyone.

Even small accommodations can have a significant impact for ourselves and our colleagues. For example, most people can point to the experience of taking part in an audio-only conference call where they have had difficulty hearing a speaker, but a person with a hearing impairment may have difficulty understanding or tracking *anyone* on the call and become completely unable to contribute. Agreeing to conduct remote meetings by video conversation platforms like Zoom or Google Meet—which many people became familiar with during the Covid-19 pandemic—rather than audio only makes it possible for those with hearing impairment to read visual cues or employ live captioning and better follow the conversation. Alternatively, learning that a team member is color-blind might steer the team away from project planning tools that use color as the only signifier of importance—again, denying that team member access to information necessary for full participation—while at the same time helping the team to identify the team members who might be best able to assess the readability of information on a project web page.[9] Acknowledging the myriad ways we perceive, process, and store information makes it possible to accommodate those team members' accessibility needs within the context of a project and can improve collaboration on multiple levels.

Scheduling is another potential area of accommodation, and one that digital humanists are particularly apt to ignore during periods of intense concentration or in the excitement surrounding the start of a new project. One of the authors of this chapter has a congenital orthopedic issue that makes sitting in a chair for more than thirty minutes increasingly painful and distracting. Other conditions can cause a person to require frequent and longer bathroom breaks. Those with cognitive differences, including attention-deficit/hyperactivity disorder (ADHD) and processing disorders, need periodic short breaks to completely process any given information. There is evidence that even neurotypical people can become more focused and productive after a bathroom or stretch break, so that an accommodation intended for one person can actually benefit the whole team (Weir).

However, it must be emphasized that we cannot assume that all collaborators will initially be comfortable self-disclosing their accommodation needs. They may prefer to do so in a one-on-one conversation or at a later date once they are more comfortable with the team. They may wish to disclose anonymously, through human resources, or they may not wish to disclose at all. No matter how normalized discussions about disability might become within DH communities, our wider cultures continue to stigmatize people with disabilities. One need only skim the stories in the Twitter hashtags #AcademicAbleism and #ChronicallyAcademic to see how people with disabilities are mistreated in academia, which simply indicates that academia is no different from the wider societies where we work. We should remain mindful that people may be hesitant to ask for an accommodation and make it clear that our collaborators can disclose needs when and how they are most comfortable. We must respect our colleagues' right to privacy. It is also important to remember that not all disabilities are lifelong or constant; people may have events in their lives that require new or changing accommodations.

Once an initial accommodation plan for a project team is completed, everyone involved should have time to review the plan to ensure that their current needs, and those of their colleagues, have been clearly understood and met. Optionally, if the project has access to a campus office of disability services or assistive technology, an ADA compliance officer, or a similar accessibility group, these professionals can be asked to review the team's plan, both at the start of the project and as needs change, to see if they have additional suggestions. A caveat is necessary here because the quality of available services can vary greatly from organization to organization. If the services most readily available are not well regarded by members of the local disability community, the team should look elsewhere. Many academic campuses have community groups that discuss accessibility and disability, and some cultural heritage organizations have access to consultants and companies that contract to perform accessibility assessments. Once the team asks for professional assistance, they should invite that person or group to take a holistic approach to their work, assessing their processes as well as their end results.

Social Media

Beyond the project team, digital humanists create communities of practice online through social media platforms. Given the importance of social media and "gray literature" for knowledge sharing in DH, this is a vital space to make inclusive for our colleagues with disabilities, particularly on digital humanists' current platform of choice: Twitter. While not perfect, Twitter currently offers built-in accessibility features that we should learn to use consistently. We should also be alert to new accessibility features as they are introduced, and we should advocate for the creation of such features for all our digital content.

Most notably, Twitter has an option for "alt-text" or textual descriptions to be added to images, to make them describable by screen readers (Twitter Help Center). This is vital given the current trend of creating images from plain text. Twitter's user interface for this is not ideal, as it sometimes leads people to accidentally post tweets as alt-text when tweeting an image taken from within the smartphone app. At the time we wrote this, it also displayed the text (or partial version of longer text) as a caption on top of the image in very small font, rendering it illegible and obscuring the image for anyone not using a screen reader. However, this small blip aside, Twitter makes it easy for users to generate accessible images.

Even when not using images, there are ways to make our presence on Twitter and other social media platforms more accessible. We should always camelCase our hashtags, starting each new word with a capital letter, as this allows screen readers to recognize the tag is made up of multiple words ("Camel Case"). Hashtags written in camelCase are also easier for everyone to read: Consider the difference between #demouser—which could be read as de-mouser—and #DemoUser. "Threading" tweets, using the thread functionality or by replying to oneself, also improves the readability of our content by establishing a linear flow of connected tweets. This reduces the cognitive load of following a conversation on Twitter and speeds up the process of using a screen reader to find and listen to a conversation.

Adding an image description, using camelCase, and threading a conversation requires only a few moments for most users and can vastly improve the accessibility of our professional conversations on social media platforms. For some of us, these techniques may be challenging to implement because of workflow issues when using speech-to-text, additional cognitive load, or additional typing time. However, those of us who are able to take these steps with a minimal investment of time and energy should make it standard practice to use social media in a more accessible manner.

Public Presentations

Another area where we can make significant improvements to the accessibility of our communities of practice is in presentations at conferences, at public talks, and in our classrooms. Beyond the basic ability to access the presentation space—which is not a given, especially when doors are heavy, aisles narrow, chairs tightly packed, and platforms raised—there are a host of physical, sensory, and cognitive accessibility issues at play in these spaces. Event organizers should pay specific attention to the accessibility of their spaces and solicit accommodation requests during preregistration. Attendees should hold organizers accountable for choosing physically accessible spaces, proactively and publicly identifying potential hazards, providing assistive technology, creating spaces such as quiet rooms, and ensuring attendees have easy avenues of communication for on-site difficulties.

While many organizational decisions are ultimately out of the control of event participants, speakers can control the accessibility of their presentations. The most common battles over presentation accessibility have been over auditory accommodations. Many of us have experienced presenters opting to shout rather than use a microphone. While the speaker's volume—and the signal-to-noise ratio between their voice and the ambient room noise—is an important component of being heard by those with and without hearing impairments, it is only one of several factors in intelligibility, even when direct transmission from the microphone to a hearing aid is not involved. Speaking "louder" changes the decibel level and frequency of the sound waves the speaker produces, distorting the voice and paradoxically making it more difficult to understand. Crucially, for those speaking in atonal languages such as English, the most important sounds are those produced by consonants, which are produced at pitches over 500 hertz (Hz) and primarily around 2000 Hz for all genders as compared to vowels at 100 to 120 Hz for men's voices. These higher frequencies do not travel as far as low frequencies and *must* be artificially amplified to be audible, particularly to those with hearing impairments in those ranges ("Facts about Speech Intelligibility"). The sound-dampening properties of most speaking venues, in the form of carpeted floors and fabric-covered walls, further distort and prevent the travel of sound waves to all corners of a room.

For audience members with hearing impairments, speakers who refuse a microphone are often very difficult to hear, forcing listeners to choose between interrupting the speaker, self-identifying as having an auditory disability, or not hearing the speaker at all. As a speaker, choosing not to use the microphone prioritizes one's own convenience over the needs and privacy of the audience members. Similarly, faculty members who ban laptops from their classrooms, except for students with accommodations, single out their students with disabilities for all to see (Rose). If microphones are available at an event, everyone should insist on their use by both speakers and audience members with questions.[10] If microphones are not available—and this is something speakers should ask about in advance—speakers should print out large font (18 point) versions of their notes or speech and make them discreetly available at the room entrance so that attendees can have a written transcript to supplement the spoken word.

Whenever possible, it is vital that event organizers ensure every room has at least one microphone. They should also coordinate with any required American Sign Language (ASL) or transliterated English interpreters. For events or organizations with the resources to go further, there are additional possibilities. In the past decade, real-time video captioning has improved dramatically, to the point where one of the authors recently attended a small conference where all three keynote presentations used closed-captioning in real time. The system used for those presentations managed to correctly capture more than 90 percent of what the speakers were saying.[11] Those of us at cultural heritage institutions could inquire about obtaining access to such technology for our presentation spaces, while faculty, staff, and students at U.S. institutions of higher education should have some sort of office of disability services that can help us obtain access to similar tools to improve the accessibility of our presentations. All of us can independently explore community resources as well.

Another issue that receives far too little attention is the need for presentation materials to be visually accessible. How often have you sat through a presentation where the text on the screen is smaller than 24 points and the presenter says, "I know this is kind of hard to read. . . ." Or a presentation where there is text displayed over an image? Or where the color contrast between the text and the background color makes it difficult to read? Or where the font is difficult to read from the middle or back of the room? All of these same readability issues exist in DH projects, and *all* can be easily avoided.

We might want to choose artful fonts, but readability is more important than aesthetics. Arial (the font the authors used when drafting this chapter) may be boring, but it is also known to be more legible to people with visual impairments or dyslexia than many other fonts (Rello and Baeza-Yates). The Penn State IT Accessibility Group maintains an excellent guide to accessible fonts, and there are many other resources online. Accessibility best practices also argue against placing text across an image or, if doing so seems critical to the design, making sure that the color contrast is so strong that those with visual challenges can read the text despite the background image. The website A11y.com offers a free color contrast accessibility validator that lets you test for readability.[12] Bear in mind that choices that are accessible for some may be inaccessible for others; for example, light text on a dark background can be ideal for viewers with light sensitivity but terrible for those with astigmatism.

The best way to create accessible presentations is to begin with established best practices and then adapt as needed, based on feedback from your audience. It may ultimately be the case that the easiest way to accommodate a particular person is to give them digital copies of your files and let them adjust their copy of the presentation themselves in order to fit their specific circumstances. We need to be flexible to ensure that our colleagues and our audience members have the tools they need to engage with our scholarship. We also need to be willing to listen to the needs expressed by our audience members so that everyone in the room has equal access to the content of our presentations.

WHAT WE BUILD

From Collaborators to Users

While it is vital to consider accessibility within our communities of practice, it is also necessary to extend this consideration to our users and make accessibility a normalized part of design conversations. Just as we make space from the beginning for collaborators to request accommodations, we should invite potential users into our work early on through peer review or user testing. Having people with a variety of abilities attempt to use a research product and record what happens allows us to find and correct potential accessibility problems. Selecting testers and reviewers should be done with the openness and care to ensure that they represent a diverse user base. For larger projects, a local or institutional disability service or ADA compliance officer might even help the team convene a user testing group that includes people with the specific disabilities that are expected to be present in the project's users and audiences. By inviting feedback on our work early in the process, we have a higher chance of a more accessible final project, regardless of what form(s) it takes, and we can avoid problems that are obvious to someone with a particular disability that might otherwise escape our notice until after we no longer have the resources to fix them.

Websites

Many DH projects include the production of a website, often as the home for a tool, argument, or dataset. There are abundant resources regarding the basics of creating an accessible website or page. They range from the formal guidelines of Section 508 and WCAG to online articles and a full suite of accessibility checkers like WAVE. These resources can seem like a blessing to someone just starting to think about accessibility in their work, or they can seem overwhelming. But many of the same basic accessibility improvements that we discussed in the context of communities of practice—from color contrasts to camelCase—can also be deployed to make websites more accessible. Others can be identified through a straightforward process of user testing.

At the most basic level, user testing helps identify issues with navigation and design for physical, sensory, and cognitive disabilities. It can tell us whether the tab order for site navigation makes sense, if the internal navigation links are functional, and whether we have implemented visual navigation (icons and text) in a consistent manner throughout the site. User testing can help ensure that the site's JavaScript is configured properly for visual accessibility, with attention paid to focus management, polite alerts, and dynamic content changes. Project creators can discover if they have built a site that cannot be navigated without reliance on a mouse, or if they have made assumptions about a user's speed in navigating the site, forms, or dynamic content that might prevent people with a variety of disabilities from using the site as intended.[13] While some of these issues might be anticipated by an alert programmer, one thing that can arise in user testing that is harder to predict is clarity: things that make "intuitive" sense to us as creators may create steep learning curves for our potential users.[14]

User testing can also assess the overall cognitive accessibility of our work and whether our project succeeds in the scholarly goals we have set for it. We should ask audience members and peers to engage with our content and summarize what they understand to be the key points of the project. What is the argument, the big idea? Ideally, most testers should be able to articulate at least one goal of the project. If they cannot, we need to evaluate the readability of the text, images, and other graphical elements, as well as the cognitive load imposed by navigating the site's pages.

For academics used to reading dense and specialized jargon, a point of particular concern is making our text "readable" to a web audience (WCAG 2.1,"Understanding Guideline 3.1"; "Cognitive Accessibility"). Accessibility guideline 3.1 suggests including a glossary of specialist terms through a linked page or as hover text. It also recommends providing short summaries of longer selections of text and of nontextual material, written in clear, simple language.

We can also make our writing more readable for the web by using shorter paragraphs, breaking ideas and key points into separate chunks of information ("Writing for the Web"). Shorter paragraphs not only help lessen the cognitive load of reading, they are also easier to view for people who increase text display size to address vision issues or who are attempting to read on the small screen of a smartphone. In general, we should give serious consideration to our word choices and text structure. Lessening the cognitive load of reading a paragraph allows the user's brain more room to understand the overall concepts. If users are struggling to simply parse what we are trying to say, it will take them additional time and effort to understand the larger argument. Many will simply click away before understanding the major concepts or analytical methods.

Tools

In addition to building websites, many digital humanists also build software tools, which have their own accessibility challenges to consider. Is our code accessible to programmers with disabilities, especially if we are using an open-source license? Is our tool accessible to users with disabilities, both in terms of using it to create something and of the products it creates? Is our tool documented, and is that documentation accessible? All of these factors have to be taken into consideration over the life span of a tool, for as long as it is supported. While this approach may take longer to implement and more effort to maintain, the upside is that taking more time to release the tool gives us the opportunity to correct previous failings and incorporate new techniques and technologies along the way. This, in turn, allows us to improve the accessibility of our tools and their attendant resources. It is always our goal to create tools that will be used by the greatest number of people, so being attentive to accessibility at the front end of tool creation will help ensure we have done everything possible to maximize our user base.

Code

While there are not as many resources on making code itself more accessible, some of the same practices that we use for websites can be employed in our coding to similar effect. Programmers with disabilities already know which development environments and settings will maximize their access to code, so the primary thing we must pay attention to is the code itself (Doustdar). Using camelCase or underscores make variables more legible, while using logical and memorable variable names can aid programmers with cognitive disabilities as well as those who cannot easily scroll to see how "foobar" was defined. In languages such as JavaScript, that don't assign meaning to white space, using additional white space might help someone visually process information. At the same time, white space must be used carefully because indentations and repeated spaces are tedious to read through with a screen reader (Stevenson; Radaelli).

Most importantly, we must always *comment our code.* While this is generally best practice for programming, adding explanatory comments to code also accommodates a variety of disabilities, from people who need assistance cognitively processing a complicated subprogram to people who are using screen readers and need to be able to skip through the program to the code of interest. Writing comments with these issues in mind will result in more useful, legible code for everyone.

User Interface and Products

In addition to the code, we must ensure that the user interfaces of our tools and the products which these tools produce are accessible to users with a wide variety of abilities. The processes we use to guide the creation of websites can be helpful here as well. The fact that many DH tools are open-source tools adds a wrinkle to working toward accessibility: We can guarantee the original work we launched onto the internet but not what our community of users creates from it. There is no guarantee that every member of the developer community who contributes to a tool is aware of or abides by standards of accessibility, even to the point of meeting the legal minimum for their home country. However, an open-source project also makes it possible for us to accept the contributions of others to a codebase. Semitechnical users can file issues against projects on GitHub (and they have) to point out, for example, inadequate contrast between text and background or their inability to select and manipulate something with a keyboard.

It is therefore important to make clear to our communities that we strive to create accessible tools. We can provide links to the standards that we use and to existing resources for accessible development, as well as highlight any key code or design requirements that are likely to crop up when developing our tools.[15] This information could be contained in the tool's ReadMe file or wherever the developers feel it is appropriate. The purpose is to include accessibility in our processes and communicate the ways in which diverse abilities can be accommodated in our work.

Documentation

In addition to making the tool itself accessible, we must ensure our documentation is as accessible as possible. There are four main rules that we follow when writing documentation: (1) Always include an image description or alt-text when using images. (2) Add captioning or subtitles to all videos, as well as ensure access to a transcript of the audio. (3) Emphasize clarity of language. (4) Break any process down into small steps.

The first two rules we have already discussed in other contexts above. Image descriptions and alt-text are essential for anyone with vision-related disabilities. We use the Amara service to create subtitles for all of our screencasts, a process that requires someone on the project to transcribe the screencast and assign timings to the subtitles. We now incorporate the estimated time to subtitle into our estimations of producing any screencast.

The key point for accessibility in documentation, however, is the language used. Regardless of how digital humanists choose to write elsewhere, they need to follow standards for cognitive accessibility in their documentation ("Cognitive Accessibility"). Reading documentation should not take effort because the action of working with the tool is already a cognitive activity. Although documentation necessarily includes some jargon, we must strive to write clearly, using common language whenever possible. For example, the documentation guidelines for Omeka S encourage shorter paragraphs and breaking tasks out into lists whenever possible (Omeka Team). Our overall ethos in writing documentation is the model of the "exact instructions challenge," in which adults ask children to write instructions for making a peanut butter sandwich, beginning with a bagged loaf of bread, a jar of peanut butter, and a knife.[16] In general, we find it is better to include steps that might seem obvious to an experienced user; it is easier to skip a step when reading instructions than to try and intuit a step that is not there.

Voluntary Product Assessment Templates and Accessibility Conformance Reports

A clear way to assess and communicate our commitment to creating accessible DH tools is to complete a Voluntary Product Assessment Template (VPAT) for the tool, resulting in an Accessibility Conformance Report (ACR), and to ensure that an up-to-date ACR is always available on the tool's website or documentation.[17] We recognize this process is not without challenges, particularly for scholars working independently, but the effort yields enough downstream results to make it well worthwhile. The VPAT 2.3 International Form uses WCAG guidelines in addition to the United States' (Section 508) and European Union's standards for digital accessibility (EN 301 549). The WCAG section helpfully includes links to explanations of success criteria for each, with examples of techniques and failures. There are free tools to help a team conduct their own assessment, such as the WAVE Web Accessibility Evaluation Tool, Accessibility Insights for the Web, color contrast checkers, color-blindness simulators, and text-to-speech readers, which can be used to complete the VPAT.[18] However, even with these resources, it can be difficult for someone just learning about accessibility to gauge where their tool falls in the possible choices of conformance to accessibility standards.

When completing a VPAT for a team project, we need to involve the entire team, including designers and developers who can make code changes, as necessary. One approach is for one or two members to do a preliminary pass through the VPAT once the tool is close to being released, in order to identify errors and problems. They can then bring this initial report to the entire team, ensuring that issues are resolved before the final release. Because this process can be time-consuming, teams should be sure to schedule adequate time in their work plans to conduct a VPAT evaluation and tweak the tool as needed before every release or update. Although the time and effort required to create an ACR may seem like a burden, there are organizations—including educational institutions—that cannot use a tool unless it comes with an ACR.

Furthermore, having an ACR demonstrates a commitment to accessibility on the part of the project team. It can also serve as a starting point for any cultural heritage organization or university/college that must conduct an accessibility review before using a tool. Our own center only adopted this process in 2015, but the ACRs for all three versions of the content management platform Omeka are linked from the accessibility statements in their documentation.[19] In addition, a dedicated page for your accessibility statement provides an opportunity for translating the legal language and technical requirements of the VPAT into a readable, accessible series of paragraphs or bullet points.

MULTIMODALITY AT THE LIMITS

While there are many areas of intervention where digital humanists can successfully improve the accessibility of our scholarship, we acknowledge there are practical limits. We do not intend to argue that all digital humanists should be expected to provide 100 percent accessibility for *all* possible audiences in *everything* that we make, create, or present—especially given the possibility of people with competing and mutually exclusive accommodation needs. Digital humanists are almost always "making do" with limited resources. Many people engaged in DH work do so as sole practitioners and not as part of a team or center. Even those who do work at such a center are often stretched thin across multiple projects. Despite these limits, we can be mindful and deliberate about designing our scholarship to accommodate the most common disabilities found in our intended audiences. We can also provide multiple routes into our research products to improve the probability that even people who we have not deliberately accommodated—or who our decisions may have accidentally *dis*accommodated—can still access our work.

Similarly, digital humanists are often engaged in pushing the boundaries of the digital and creating products that do not easily fit into established accommodation conventions. But just because it is difficult or, at times, not possible to make an experimental research product accessible to certain audiences does not absolve us, as a field, of the responsibility to make our arguments and sources as accessible as possible. Just as alt-text can be used to label an image, it can be used to label the important features of a network diagram. Information presented on an interactive visualization or layered map can also be provided using tables and text that allow people with disabilities to access it differently. By designing a project with accessibility in mind from the beginning, we can anticipate when our decisions will cause issues for people with disabilities and either find new, creative, and innovative ways to build our project or at least build in alternative routes to our core arguments and ideas when the technology does not—yet—do what we need.

Where Do We Go from Here?

Digital humanists need to become more proactive in our approaches to the many and complex issues surrounding accessibility. One step we can take toward this goal is to identify members of our professional networks who have expertise related to specific disabilities. Many people with disabilities are already working in DH and can contribute their own expertise and experiences to making our work more accessible. Furthermore, we can partner as needed with local disability advocacy groups, offices of disability services, and consultants who specialize in access and disability. No one needs to be an expert in all things; we only need to reach out to experts when we find ourselves encountering unfamiliar challenges. Refusing to seek advice—especially when it is freely offered and costs us only time—actively contributes to the marginalization and exclusion of people with disabilities from DH.

An additional solution that we believe holds some of the greatest promise is the deliberate development of professional capacity networks that will allow digital humanists to share knowledge and expertise. Through these networks, we can share information about accessibility tools, how we use them, and what does and does not work for the kinds of projects we are creating and our disabilities or access needs. If someone has worked with a particular disability community to determine an accessible alternative presentation of the data contained in a D3 visualization, they could present that method to their professional networks, thereby enabling even more accessible visualizations. The more widely these experiences are shared, the more likely they are to become standards of practice in our field.

Sharing our varied experiences, as digital humanists with disabilities and as digital humanists working toward accessibility, and respecting the experiences of others, benefits DH communities as a whole. It furthers the spirit of collaboration that is held up as a standard in DH. An accessibility lens also forces a team to identify what is essential to their project or an element of that project, in order to ensure that these key elements are communicated in every accessible iteration of the project. Yet that is not the reason to create accessible work and include accommodations. These are collateral benefits that come from taking the ethical course of action to ensure that we, disabled members of DH communities, are included in the work of those communities.

Living with a disability is a complicated reality, one that should not be limited by definitions of legal disability or by expectations that a disability be permanent or visible. Either through our own lived experience or through interactions with others, we all encounter disabilities in our lives. As DH communities, we should acknowledge this reality and strive to improve the accessibility of our work. We will fail and we will make mistakes, but we must accept these failures as an opportunity to learn and improve rather than denying them or becoming unproductively defensive. Although there is no "magic bullet" for accessibility, no single solution that makes something universally accessible, we hope that DH communities will use the areas of intervention that we have identified and the suggestions that we have laid out to move forward with making accessibility a consistent and active part of their work, for themselves, their collaborators, and their audiences.

NOTES

1. See, for example, Williams, along with pushback on Williams's ideas about universal design from Godden and Hsy. See also Hill.

2. See, for example, Dacos's 2011 "Manifesto for the Digital Humanities," or Tom Scheinfeldt's "Why Digital Humanities Is 'Nice.'"

3. Different cancers had varying impacts, of course, but one author's experience with cancer had no real impact on her DH work.

4. See, for example, Graham; Croxall and Warnick; Mlynaryk.

5. Some of the links from the American Historical Association's list of Roy Rosenzweig prize winners (https://www.historians.org/awards-and-grants/past-recipients/roy-rosenzweig-prize-recipients) failed to resolve to live sites. WAVE is available at https://wave.webaim.org.

6. For more on Flash and content accessibility, see https://www.washington.edu/doit/flash-content-accessible. For Cascading Style Sheets (CSS) and JavaScript best practices, see https://developer.mozilla.org/en-US/docs/Learn/Accessibility/CSS_and_JavaScript.

7. One caveat is that some people with disabilities need to expend exponentially more effort to complete a try-fail cycle of try, fail, and try again. They may not have such effort available to give for these activities; to use a common disability metaphor, they run out of spoons. It is incumbent on those of us who can implement a try-fail cycle more easily to do so and to be empathetic toward those of us who cannot ("Spoon Theory," *Wikipedia*, December 8, 2019, https://en.wikipedia.org/wiki/Spoon_theory).

8. Confusingly, educational technologists often call this "universal design for learning," which is distinct from the older idea of "universal design" that originated in architecture and interior design.

9. For a good website on designing for color blindness, see https://usabilla.com/blog/how-to-design-for-color-blindness/.

10. A caveat should be made regarding the use of "catch box" microphones, which are a good example of an accommodation causing accessibility issues for people with a

different set of disabilities. Not everyone is physically able to catch such a device; speakers should accommodate their needs by having someone else bring them the microphone or repeating an unamplified question into the microphone before answering it.

11. These systems are not always so accurate. The automatic captions on Google's YouTube are of inconsistent quality, and one software purporting to automatically caption images determined that our university's home page was, in fact, a picture of a dog.

12. The A11y Color Contrast Accessibility Validator is available at https://color.a11y.com/Contrast/; another free contrast evaluation tool can be found at Contrast Ratio (https://contrast-ratio.com/). The WCAG 2.0 statement on contrast ratio for text (https://www.w3.org/TR/WCAG/#contrast-minimum) explains which ratios are acceptable for font sizes and uses.

13. For examples of known issues to look out for when designing websites, see https://www.accessiblemetrics.com/blog/top-8-most-common-accessibility-issues-to-avoid-and-solve/, https://medium.com/@matuzo/writing-javascript-with-accessibility-in-mind-a1f6a5f467b9, and https://alistapart.com/article/standards-for-writing-accessibly/.

14. In an extreme example, one of the coauthors was so baffled by her first iPod that she had to use a computer to search online for how to turn it on. Apple products notoriously come without instructions, and what is intuitive to the person who designed a product is not intuitive to everyone.

15. See, for example, the A11Y Style Guide at https://a11y-style-guide.com/style-guide/.

16. The peanut butter challenge, which is one variation of the "exact instructions" challenge, went viral in 2017 thanks to videos posted by parents doing the challenge with their children, most notably Josh Darnit (https://www.youtube.com/watch?v=cDA3_5982h8).

17. VPAT resources are available from the Information Technology Industry Council (ITI) at https://www.itic.org/policy/accessibility/vpat.

18. See WAVE (https://wave.webaim.org/); Accessibility Insights (https://accessibilityinsights.io/).

19. For an example of an accessibility statement, see https://omeka.org/s/docs/user-manual/accessibility/.

BIBLIOGRAPHY

"Americans with Disabilities Act of 1990, as Amended with ADA Amendments Act of 2008." *ADA.gov.* January 1, 2009, https://www.ada.gov/pubs/adastatute08.htm#12182.

"Any Anxiety Disorder." National Institute of Mental Health. Last updated November 2017, https://www.nimh.nih.gov/health/statistics/any-anxiety-disorder.shtml.

"Attention-Deficit/Hyperactivity Disorder (ADHD)." National Institute of Mental Health. Last updated November 2017, https://www.nimh.nih.gov/health/statistics/attention-deficit-hyperactivity-disorder-adhd.shtml.

"Camel Case." *Wikipedia.* Last edited January 30, 2020, https://en.wikipedia.org/w/index.php?title=Camel_case&oldid=938311603.

"Cognitive Accessibility." *MDN Web Docs.* Accessed June 20, 2021, https://developer.mozilla.org/en-US/docs/Web/Accessibility/Cognitive_accessibility.

Collinge, Robyn. "How to Design for Color Blindness." *Usabilla Blog* (blog). January 17, 2017, https://usabilla.com/blog/how-to-design-for-color-blindness/.

"Color Vision Deficiency." Genetics Home Reference. *MedlinePlus.* Accessed June 20, 2021, https://ghr.nlm.nih.gov/condition/color-vision-deficiency.

Croxall, Brian, and Quinn Warnick. "Failure." In *Digital Pedagogy in the Humanities,* edited by Rebecca Frost Davis, Matthew Gold, Katherine Harris, and Jentery Sayers. New York: Modern Language Association, 2020, https://digitalpedagogy.mla.hcommons.org/keywords/failure/.

Dacos, Marin. "Manifesto for the Digital Humanities." *THATCamp Paris* (blog). Last updated March 26, 2011, https://tcp.hypotheses.org/411.

"Data and Statistics about ADHD." Centers for Disease Control and Prevention. October 15, 2019, https://www.cdc.gov/ncbddd/adhd/data.html.

Department of Justice. "Final Regulatory Assessment, Final Rule—Amendment of ADA Title II and Title III Regulations to Implement ADA Amendments Act of 2008." 2016, https://www.ada.gov/regs2016/final_rule_adaaa.html.

Department of Justice. "Workforce Investment Act of 1998, Section 506. Electronic and Information Technology." August 6, 2015, https://www.access-board.gov/law/ra.html#section-508-federal-electronic-and-information-technology.

"Disability Impacts All of Us." Centers for Disease Control and Prevention infographic. March 8, 2019, https://www.cdc.gov/ncbddd/disabilityandhealth/infographic-disability-impacts-all.html.

Dombrowski, Quinn. "Towards a Taxonomy of Failure." *Quinn Dombrowski* (blog). January 30, 2019, https://quinndombrowski.com/blog/2019/01/30/towards-taxonomy-failure/.

Doustdar, Parham. "The Tools of a Blind Programmer." *Parham Doustdar's Blog.* Accessed June 20, 2021, https://www.parhamdoustdar.com/2016/04/03/tools-of-blind-programmer/.

"Facts about Speech Intelligibility." *DPA Microphones.* March 3, 2021, https://www.dpamicrophones.com/mic-university/facts-about-speech-intelligibility.

Forlano, Laura. "Data Rituals in Intimate Infrastructures: Crip Time and the Disabled Cyborg Body as an Epistemic Site of Feminist Science." *Catalyst* 3, no. 2 (2017): Science Out of Feminist Theory Part 2: Remaking Science(s), https://catalystjournal.org/index.php/catalyst/article/view/28843.

Goering, Sara. "Rethinking Disability: The Social Model of Disability and Chronic Disease." *Current Reviews in Musculoskeletal Medicine* 8, no. 2 (2015): 134–38, https://doi.org/10.1007/s12178-015-9273-z.

Godden, Rick, and Jonathan Hsy. "Universal Design and Its Discontents." In *Disrupting the Digital Humanities,* edited by Dorothy Kim and Jesse Stommel, 91–115. Santa Barbara, Calif.: Punctum Books, 2018, http://www.disruptingdh.com/universal-design-and-its-discontents/.

Graham, Shawn. *Failing Gloriously and Other Essays.* Fargo: University of North Dakota, 2019, https://thedigitalpress.org/failing-gloriously/.

Hill, Heather. "Universal Design: An Accessibility Solution for Digital Humanities?" *IXD@PRATT.* October 4, 2017, http://ixd.prattsi.org/2017/10/universal-design-an-accessibility-solution-for-digital-humanities/.

Kane, Will. "Anxiety 'Epidemic' Brewing on College Campuses." University of California. April 22, 2019, https://www.universityofcalifornia.edu/news/anxiety-epidemic-brewing-college-campuses.

"Major Depression." National Institute of Mental Health. Last updated February 2019, https://www.nimh.nih.gov/health/statistics/major-depression.shtml.

Matuzovic, Manuel. "Writing JavaScript with Accessibility in Mind." *Medium.* September 19, 2018, https://medium.com/@matuzo/writing-javascript-with-accessibility-in-mind-a1f6a5f467b9.

Metts, Michael J., and Andy Welfle. "Standards for Writing Accessibly." *A List Apart* (blog). January 23, 2020, https://alistapart.com/article/standards-for-writing-accessibly/.

Mlynaryk, Jenna. "Working Failures in Traditional and Digital Humanities." *HASTAC* (blog). February 15, 2016, https://www.hastac.org/blogs/jennamly/2016/02/15/working-failures-traditional-and-digital-humanities.

Omeka Team. "Documentation Guidelines, Omeka S Enduser." Last updated January 17, 2018, https://github.com/omeka/omeka-s-enduser/wiki/Documentation-guidelines.

Otis, Jessica. "Never Use White Text on a Black Background: Astigmatism and Conference Slides." *The Dev Log* (blog). November 6, 2017, https://jessicaotis.com/academia/never-use-white-text-on-a-black-background-astygmatism-and-conference-slides/.

Penn State IT Accessibility Group. "Font Face on the Web." December 18, 2013, https://accessibility.psu.edu/fontfacehtml/.

"Quick Statistics about Hearing." National Institute on Deafness and Other Communication Disorders. August 18, 2015, https://www.nidcd.nih.gov/health/statistics/quick-statistics-hearing.

Radaelli, Lucas. "How Do Blind Computer Programmers Code?" *Huffington Post.* April 28, 2015, https://www.huffpost.com/entry/how-do-blind-computer-pro_b_7163674.

Rello, Luz, and Ricardo Baeza-Yates. "Good Fonts for Dyslexia." Presentation at the Fifteenth International ACM SIGACCESS Conference on Computers and Accessibility, Bellevue, Washington, October 2013, http://dyslexiahelp.umich.edu/sites/default/files/good_fonts_for_dyslexia_study.pdf.

Rose, Katie. "When You Talk about Banning Laptops, You Throw Disabled Students under the Bus." *Huffington Post.* November 27, 2017, https://www.huffpost.com/entry/when-you-talk-about-banning-laptops-you-throw-disabled_b_5a1ccb4ee4b07bcab2c6997d.

Scheinfeldt, Tom. "Why Digital Humanities Is 'Nice.'" *Found History* (blog). May 26, 2010, https://foundhistory.org/2010/05/why-digital-humanities-is-nice/.

Stemler, Sam. "Top 8 Most Common Accessibility Issues to Avoid and Solve." *Accessible Metrics* (blog). July 16, 2019, https://www.accessiblemetrics.com/blog/top-8-most-common-accessibility-issues-to-avoid-and-solve/.

Stevenson, Leeann. "Whitespace: Not Just a Waste of Space!" *Callia Web.* October 17, 2018, https://www.calliaweb.co.uk/whitespace-not-just-a-waste-of-space/.

Twitter Help Center. "How to Make Images Accessible for People." Accessed August June 20, 2021, https://help.twitter.com/en/using-twitter/picture-descriptions.

United Nations. "Convention on the Rights of Persons with Disabilities and Optional Protocol." December 13, 2006, https://www.un.org/disabilities/documents/convention/convoptprot-e.pdf.

Vision Council of America. "U.S. Optical Overview and Outlook." December 2015, https://web.archive.org/web/20190501162429/https://www.thevisioncouncil.org/sites/default/files/Q415-Topline-Overview-Presentation-Stats-with-Notes-FINAL.PDF.

WCAG 2.1. "Understanding Guideline 3.1: Readable." Accessed August 24, 2022, https://www.w3.org/WAI/WCAG21/Understanding/readable.

"WCAG 2.1 at a Glance." July 2008, updated June 5, 2018, https://www.w3.org/WAI/standards-guidelines/wcag/glance/.

Weir, Kirsten. "Give Me a Break." *Monitor on Psychology.* January 2019, https://www.apa.org/monitor/2019/01/break.

Williams, George. "Disability, Universal Design, and the Digital Humanities." In *Debates in the Digital Humanities 2012,* edited by Matthew K. Gold. Minneapolis: University of Minnesota Press, 2012, https://dhdebates.gc.cuny.edu/read/untitled-88c11800-9446-469b-a3be-3fdb36bfbd1e/section/2a59a6fe-3e93-43ae-a42f-1b26d1b4becc.

World Health Organization. *World Report on Vision: Executive Summary.* Geneva: WHO, 2019, https://www.visionimpactinstitute.org/research/world-report-on-vision-%7C-world-health-organization.

"Writing for the Web." *Usability.gov.* December 7, 2016, https://www.usability.gov/how-to-and-tools/methods/writing-for-the-web.html.

PART IV][*Chapter 22*

From Precedents to Collective Action: Realities and Recommendations for Digital Dissertations in History

ZOE LEBLANC, CELESTE TƯỜNG VY SHARPE,
AND JERI WIERINGA

What is digital history? As historians and scholarly organizations wrestle with digital sources, tools, and methods, this central question remains. Efforts to address it have involved the development of guidelines for tenure and promotion in the field of digital history, the push to include digital scholarship in established history journals or create new digital history journals outright, and a range of discussions about the role of argumentation in digital history as well as its overall scholarly impact.[1] While these discussions carry profound implications for the entire field, there is a pressing need to consider the ramifications of the digital turn in graduate education and, in particular, in the idea and practice of the digital dissertation.

We are three recent graduates of doctoral programs in history who each authored a digital dissertation: Sharpe and Wieringa in the Department of History and Art History at George Mason University, and LeBlanc in the Department of History at Vanderbilt University. In this piece, we describe our experiences creating our dissertations to show how the challenges that we encountered, and the questions that our projects prompted, expose the significant disconnects between the high-level conversations about the definition of digital history and the practicalities of creating digital scholarship at the doctoral level. As Virginia Kuhn argued in 2013, "While we need precedents [for digital dissertations], no real change will occur without collective action." Thus, we detail our experiences as part of this continued call to action. We further propose two interventions. First, for graduate students undertaking this work, we identify and offer some practical suggestions for navigating the material constraints that limit the current practice of digital history. Second, for faculty advising graduate students and overseeing graduate programs, we offer recommendations for rethinking the curricular and institutional structures required to support digital dissertations.

We acknowledge that implementing some of these recommendations would require changes at the level of the discipline, including within professional organizations and scholarly presses. Even still, we believe that the problems we highlight here have broader relevance, both with respect to other subfields within digital humanities (DH) and to other institutional and national contexts in which questions remain about how best to train, support, and evaluate graduate students who undertake digital dissertations. We offer our experiences, gained mainly through trial and error, as case studies for what is currently possible. By drawing attention to the issues we encountered, we aim to pave the way for the structural changes that are needed for digital scholarship in history to thrive—at the dissertation level and across the whole range of digital scholarly production.

What Is a Digital Dissertation in History?

It is important to clarify what we mean by a "digital dissertation." In some respects, all modern dissertations are "digital" in that the final format is an electronic PDF file. For our argument here, however, we use the phrase "digital dissertation" to refer to dissertation projects that self-reflectively experiment with digital affordances in terms of their format, their modes of analysis, or both. For these projects, digital technologies shape the very questions asked, the possibilities of interpretation, and the resulting form of the scholarship.

We also argue for a distinction between the work of digital records management and the creation of a digital dissertation. Digital records management is increasingly ubiquitous as more sources and data are being digitized and made available online. The work of categorizing, organizing, cleaning, and managing data and digital materials is vital to historical scholarship and should be acknowledged as intellectual work.[2] A digital dissertation, however, is a work of scholarship that goes beyond data management by integrating and interrogating digital theories, methods, and materials in the creation of a sustained research project.

Even within this constrained definition, there exists a multitude of examples of digital dissertations from across the humanities. Some of the most notable include Amanda Visconti's critical digital edition of James Joyce's *Ulysses*; Nick Sousanis's comic book dissertation to study perception; Lisa Rhody's use of topic modeling to explore contemporary ekphrastic poems; and Matthew Lincoln's network analysis of Dutch and Flemish art print productions. Scholarly attention to digital dissertations themselves has been the focus of Virginia Kuhn, herself the author of an early digital dissertation in English. She identifies the earliest example of a digital dissertation as Christine Boese's *The Ballad of the Internet Nutball: Chaining Rhetorical Visions from the Margins of the Margins to the Mainstream in the Xenaverse* from 1998.[3] Within the field of history, Erin Bartram and Lincoln Mullen explore database design in capturing and organizing conversion narratives in the United States;

Jean Bauer uses database construction to model correspondence networks in the early American republic; Micki Kaufman explores the application of topic modeling to Henry Kissinger's "memcons" and "telcons"; and Jason Heppler and Cameron Blevins apply mapping technologies to explore the role of place in the history of Silicon Valley and the U.S. Postal System, respectively.[4]

This range of work represents an abundance of effort and creative thinking on the part of the scholars behind them. However, we caution against the impulse to use these projects as evidence to claim that a digital dissertation is an established option for junior scholars in the humanities. We are particularly concerned that this collection of successful projects might make it seem that there are structures in place to support digital dissertations across the board, when in reality this is not the case.

The Many Paths to a Digital Dissertation in History

Our argument is informed by our successful completion of three digital dissertations in history: Sharpe's *They Need You! Disability, Visual Culture, and the Poster Child, 1945–1980,* uses the multilinear mode of presentation built into the Scalar scholarly publishing platform to present an argument about how the visual rhetoric of poster-child campaigns in the post–World War II United States shaped contemporaneous understandings of physical disability. Wieringa's *A Gospel of Health and Salvation: Modeling the Religious Culture of Seventh-day Adventism, 1843–1920,* uses topic modeling to explore cycles of millennial expectation in the development of Seventh-day Adventism, while concurrently evaluating methods for using computation as part of historical analysis. LeBlanc's *Circulating Anti-Colonial Cairo: Decolonizing Information and Constructing the Third World in Egypt, 1952–1966,* uses a range of digital methods to explore how anti-colonial information circulated in the 1950s and 1960s and, specifically, how local perspectives shaped the internationalism of the Third World.

We each took a different path to our decision to pursue a digital history dissertation. For example, when LeBlanc arrived at Vanderbilt in 2011, there was no established digital humanities center or curriculum on campus. It was only at the 2012 conference of the Humanities, Arts, Science, and Technology Alliance and Collaboratory (HASTAC) that LeBlanc first learned of multimodal and digital dissertations. Through subsequent DH-related fellowships and summer workshops, she began to experiment with digital research and pedagogy. When LeBlanc's in-person research in Egypt became increasingly difficult, especially after the murder of Giulio Regeni, a Cambridge University doctoral student, in Cairo in January 2016, LeBlanc decided to pivot her dissertation toward the history of information and anti-colonialism, fully integrating digital history methods into her scholarship. Thus, LeBlanc's motivation for undertaking a digital history dissertation was in part one of timing and in part a reflection of how her scholarly interests had transformed. Whereas she first saw the contributions of digital history as primarily pedagogical or utilitarian, she later recognized how digital methods could reshape both her archival research practices and how she produced historical knowledge.

By contrast, Sharpe and Wieringa, who both entered the history doctoral program at George Mason in 2011, were required to take a two-course digital history sequence: one in digital theory and methods, and one in digital tools for historical scholarship. The resources of the Roy Rosenzweig Center for History and New Media (RRCHNM) and the general interest in digital scholarship in the department created opportunities that both Sharpe and Wieringa used to pursue fully digital dissertation projects. For instance, Sharpe entered the PhD program curious about the possibilities of digital history, but with few technical skills and little idea how to pursue a digital project. The required digital theory class provided a valuable foundation in digital theory, methods, and practical applications that she used to look for examples of digital work and projects that could inform the shape of her dissertation.

Wieringa, on the other hand, entered the program with the goal of pursuing a digital project, having previously experimented with digitization and website development. As part of a minor field in history and new media, she took a third digital history course on programming that solidified her interest in computational text analysis and the epistemological implications of interweaving computation and historical analysis. The history of Seventh-day Adventism and the centrality of print in the development of the movement, as well as the denomination's investment in the digitization of historical materials, provided a unique opportunity for her to bring together this methodological interest in computation and topical interests in religion, gender, and millenarianism in American culture. As we discuss below, the resources available within our respective programs shaped how we went about gaining the required technical skills and the extent to which our digital scholarship was considered part of the final dissertation.

Learning the Hard Way

While our approaches and paths to our digital dissertations varied, we all experienced similar challenges in the process of pursuing our projects. Now, to some degree, every dissertation is plagued by unexpected complications, such as not finding expected materials in the archives or discovering certain relevant scholarship late into the research process. But graduate students undertaking digital dissertations experience these complications as well as others far beyond the established expectations about the degree of difficulty and uncertainty surrounding dissertation-level research.

Given the limits in available training, each of us had to decide on our own how we would acquire the digital expertise that was required for us to complete our projects. We all had on-campus support for our projects, to varying degrees. At George Mason, formal and informal training was available through coursework and assistantships with RRCHNM. Additionally, because of George Mason's reputation for digital history, the community of graduate students provided a peer support network as well as access to the broader DH community through events such as THATCamp and introductions to the DH community on Twitter. At Vanderbilt, LeBlanc had a similarly loose network of supporters, including other graduate students, digital scholarship librarians, directors of humanities and digital humanities centers, and faculty both within and outside her department. While these networks were essential, there quickly emerged gaps between the generalized knowledge that was available in these spaces and the specific knowledge that each of our dissertation projects required. For example, LeBlanc learned the basics of coding in Ruby and databases in DH summer workshops, but at Vanderbilt she was unable to enroll in additional courses to help build on these introductory courses. And even at George Mason, the specialized technical skills that were required for the digitization of sources, computational text analysis, or advanced website creation were beyond what could be accomplished within the formal coursework of the degree program. Both Sharpe and Wieringa relied on external opportunities, such as coding workshops and online resources, to gain the skills necessary to understand and solve the technical problems that arose while creating their digital projects.

We want to stress that these decisions were ones that we all continually negotiated over the course of our dissertations as we experimented with digital platforms and methods. In each of our cases, we started with common off-the-shelf tools that helped us think about what was possible. But these tools often proved to have limited direct applications for our specific research questions. For example, at the inaugural THATCamp College Art Association (CAA) gathering held in 2013, Sharpe was exposed to ImagePlot, as presented by Lev Manovich, as well as John Resig's early work on ukiyo-e (Software Studies Initiative; Resig). While she spent significant time learning these tools, she eventually came to the conclusion that neither would suit her project: ImagePlot was a dead-end because of the variation in size, color, and reproduction quality of her images; and Resig's work built off a partnership with TinEye, with significant custom coding requirements that would be impossible to emulate. In assessing the benefit of these tools for her project, Sharpe had to decide, with almost no guidance, if either was a good fit—and more generally, how much investment in personal time, energy, and resources was worth spending for her dissertation goals.

LeBlanc also came up against the limitations of off-the-shelf tools as she first tried the then-available tools for text analysis, including Stéfan Sinclair and Geoffrey Rockwell's Voyant Tools, David McClure's textplot, and Andrew McCallum and David Mimno's Mallet. She struggled to interpret the results, however. Drawing from her previous experience of intensive Arabic language study, LeBlanc decided to adopt a similar approach and enrolled in a coding boot camp at the Nashville Software School. While the nine-month part-time course provided technical depth, it was also in many ways a poor fit for what LeBlanc needed to learn; it was focused primarily on web development and professionalization for developers rather than academic research involving computational methods. LeBlanc ultimately used this knowledge in her dissertation when she built a custom web application to transform periodicals from Cairo and other anti-colonial capitals into datasets. But she was still required to teach herself the text analysis methods and foundational statistics that she used to explore how discourses transformed in the pages of these magazines. This self-guided approach also led to several dead-ends—from trying to use unsupervised computer vision algorithms on her sources to attempting to create word embedding models of datasets that were too small. At one point, this frustration led her to turn to Twitter to ask if it was even possible for one person to do "meaningful #dhist [digital history] work" (@Zoe_LeBlanc).

Further compounding the problem of training is the fact that many of the digital dissertations and digital history projects that are often highlighted as exemplars in the field elide the real division of labor in the project and how those involved in the project acquired the requisite knowledge. These omissions, while often unintentional, muddle any future assessment about how much work one person can reasonably undertake in creating a digital project. While more transparency in the acknowledgments sections of these projects would help graduate students who hope to emulate them be more realistic in their expectations, fundamentally there remains a haziness surrounding the expectations for what an individual graduate student can and should realistically produce as a digital dissertation project.

In our case, the lack of transparency, on the one hand, and the lack of relevant training opportunities, on the other hand, left us not only teaching ourselves new skills but also determining how much time and effort would be required to implement this new knowledge in our projects. Because the contributions of digital history are so often framed as methodological, discussions about the digital components of digital dissertations often frame this required knowledge as "skills." But this framing obscures how much concentrated effort is required to actually translate these *skills* into making historical arguments. While this problem exists for all digital humanists, it is particularly acute for graduate students in history because of the small cohort of digital historians available to train students, as well as the disciplinary skepticism toward methodology. While the three of us found ways to teach ourselves what we needed to know, it required a significant amount of work and time to synthesize this knowledge into our historical scholarship. This, in turn, held profound implications for our time to completion as well as the final shape of our dissertations. Ultimately, relying on self-teaching rather than institutional training and support will continue to exacerbate graduate students' frustrations with digital history. What's more, it will remain one of the biggest barriers to diversifying the field.[5]

The Dangers of Digitization

Resolving the issue of training in digital methods requires changes at both the disciplinary and institutional levels. But there are additional issues related to the availability of sources for doing digital history that lack clear solutions. This might seem surprising, given the vast number of digital collections that already exist, from the collections of HathiTrust and the Library of Congress to the digital holdings of small archives and historical societies. But the fact remains that the types of historical research that are encouraged for the dissertation are at odds with the types of content that have been prioritized in most digitization efforts (Milligan).

To be sure, most dissertations rely on sources that the researcher must digitally capture for themselves, and there is substantive intellectual work in digital source and data management as discussed above. However, to capture images of these sources at a quality level suitable for presentation and analysis, rather than merely reference, requires a much more substantial outlay of work. Working with private, partially cataloged archives meant that Sharpe had to digitize all the materials used in her project before she could even begin to analyze them, forcing her to significantly extend her time in the archives. In addition, she had to contend with how to normalize image quality across her materials. Many of her sources were already reproductions, whether photocopies or reprints of originals, which resulted in a variety of resolutions. A lack of access to professional digitizing equipment compounded the challenge of creating a corpus for computational image analysis. In the end, Sharpe chose to forgo computational methods altogether because of the complications posed by the source base.

LeBlanc similarly struggled with transforming her digital photos of archival sources into digitized datasets that could be used in her dissertation. LeBlanc first attempted to scan and digitize her archival sources through ABBYY FineReader, but at the time, the individual-license version was ill suited to processing multiple sources with variable formats and languages—the enterprise version was likely better but far beyond LeBlanc's price range. Instead, LeBlanc undertook what was initially intended to be a small project to build a tool to annotate and extract data from periodicals, newspapers, and diplomatic cables. Yet very quickly, questions about how best to account for metadata from many different archival sources, and how to best implement optical character recognition (OCR) algorithms, presented significant challenges.

Even when digital sources are available, there is significant work required to prepare those texts for different forms of computational analysis. In the example of Wieringa's dissertation, the periodical literature of the Seventh-day Adventist denomination had been digitized, but because of a lack of information about OCR accuracy and errors in both text and layout recognition, Wieringa devoted a large percentage of her time evaluating and correcting the available textual data.[6] Even with those efforts, problems with data remained. Combined with the time and resource constraints of the dissertation, those issues shaped which computational methods could be reliably applied to the data, which in turn shaped the interpretive possibilities of the dissertation itself.[7]

Digital scholarship in history requires machine-readable data, and yet the intellectual work of identifying the appropriate source material, creating and verifying the digital versions of those materials, and then matching the computational methods to both theoretical frameworks and data is often disregarded. This is especially detrimental to dissertation-level research, where time to completion, opportunities for collaboration, and external resources are severely constrained. For scholars who take on digital projects, the creation and management of sources constitutes a significant intellectual and scholarly contribution and should be recognized as part of the dissertation project.

Defending and Submitting Digital Dissertations

Even as we were each able to navigate the challenges associated with the lack of training in digital methods and the lack of access to digitized sources, we faced additional constraints when it came time to defend and submit our dissertation projects. Both legal restrictions on our digitized sources and a lack of familiarity on the part of our departments with the range of intellectual work required of digital scholarship resulted in final submissions that did not fully reflect the work we had put in or that did not fully reach the audiences that we had initially envisioned for our projects.

As Sharpe began to complete her dissertation, for example, she discovered that the private organizations that she studied were largely concerned with reputation management and took restrictive positions on copyright and image permissions. When she turned to her institution for guidance, she found limited support. Both the library and the history department saw issues of copyright, fair use, and intellectual property as the responsibility of the individual researcher.[8] Furthermore, none of Sharpe's committee members had firsthand experience negotiating copyright and image permissions on their own; they relied on their publishers to navigate that process. Thus, when the copyright holders of the images included in Sharpe's dissertation asserted limits on which images she could include, she had no support to effectively negotiate. Ultimately, Sharpe agreed to password-protect the final dissertation project and manage access to the site, which went against her initial vision for making her project public (Sharpe, "Precarity and Promise").[9]

Whereas the final form of Sharpe's dissertation was affected by issues of copyright, LeBlanc and Wieringa were shaped by disciplinary and departmental norms in their work. LeBlanc had ongoing discussions with her committee about how her technical work would be included in the final dissertation, but she was consistently counseled to adhere to traditional dissertation norms. This advice was intended to help LeBlanc avoid timing out of her degree program, but it also resulted in significant aspects of her dissertation work not being included in the final product. The custom web application that she built was seen as equivalent to archival research, and as such, she was advised to move her discussion of that process to an appendix. Her interactive data visualizations became another obstacle when she had to rework them for the print format that her committee and department required. Ultimately, LeBlanc decided not to pursue a publicly accessible web-based version of her dissertation, in part because it would have involved additional unrecognized work and in part because, as Sharpe learned, an online version would raise copyright issues that she had little guidance on how to address.

For Wieringa, her department's commitment to digital scholarship and its guidelines for digital dissertations created the space for her to include her technical work within the dissertation project. The flexibility of the web-based format that she chose let her include an interactive visualization of the project's core topic model as well as the code she created to process, analyze, and interpret the data, even though her committee primarily engaged with that work through the written chapters on methods. The process of negotiating a balance between her desire to focus on methodology and her committee's insistence that she produce a historical narrative strengthened the final result but added to the work required to complete the project. As such, her experience offers a model of how departmental support, coupled with clear guidelines for digital dissertations, can ease many of the conversations and negotiations that are required of innovative digital work.

For Wieringa, although the web-based project was accepted by the department, the formal submission process at George Mason is managed by the university libraries, where the dissertation is expected to be a single PDF document, formatted according to standards set by the university. Rather than attempt to negotiate new standards for digital projects, Wieringa pursued a workaround, albeit one that increased the work required. At George Mason, dissertations could include "supplemental files" that could be anything from media files to the related source code. Wieringa submitted source files and web-archive files of the digital project as "supplemental" materials while creating a stand-alone PDF document for the formal dissertation submission. This document included the abstract, a summary of the dissertation "modules," and a process statement required by the department to provide an overview of the digital project. This additional step let her fulfill the official requirements while maintaining the digital format of the dissertation project, though with the side effect that the official "dissertation" on record is merely a description of the project she defended.

Recommendations for Graduate Students

While our experiences might seem unique, we believe that they allow us to articulate some of the major considerations that face graduate students who might want to pursue a digital dissertation. The first is how both project and time management differ substantially from more traditional dissertations. As we highlighted above, whether or not you are enrolled in a digital history program, you will find that getting relevant training for a digital project is a significant obstacle and one that will likely extend your timeline. One question you should consider as early as possible is whether your program offers digital history courses, and if not, whether you can enroll in courses in other departments or workshops beyond your campus. Another consideration is how much time you will spend on data work—that is, the work of collecting, digitizing, cleaning, and curating your data. We all found that some of the most time-consuming but also crucial work was this "preprocessing" step. Furthermore, applying computational tools to your data is not straightforward. Many tools require data to be organized in particular ways, necessitating significant data manipulation, or the tools have a steep learning curve in order to use them effectively. In addition, technology changes quickly and tools are often abandoned. Carefully reading the documentation and determining whether there is an active community of users can help you choose tools that are compatible with your data and research questions and also have long-term support. Planning for this additional work and communicating regularly with your committee to set and update expectations for the final version are vital. You may also need to prompt your committee for feedback on early prototypes or questions around technical matters, since they may not fully understand the implications for the final shape of your project.

Furthermore, you should also plan for additional work around the formal submission of the dissertation project, as the digital components may not fit within the existing institutional structures for the dissertation. For Wieringa and Sharpe, it was most effective to create a separate PDF document so that it could be submitted to the institutional repository and to ProQuest. But the actual digital projects were archived by the library separately and linked in the metadata records. Even gaining support for this solution, both from the dissertation committees and from the libraries, added time to the process. Until there is university-level support for digital scholarship, particularly in terms of the infrastructure for submitting digital projects as dissertations, it will require more time for students to submit digital dissertations. In general, program funding and time restrictions are critical considerations when deciding whether to embark on a digital dissertation.

Another major recommendation is to identify and build relationships with the people and departments that will support your project at your institution and beyond. While this recommendation can be applied to all dissertators, those pursuing digital dissertations will undertake additional conversations to manage technical details at each stage of the project. We recommend identifying the key figures who will be involved at each stage of the project and initiating conversations early and often about any requirements. They may include (although titles may vary) department administrators, copyright librarians, digital publishing or digital scholarship librarians, thesis and dissertation coordinators, data librarians, archivists, preservation librarians, and research centers with DH experts. If you are unsure where to start, your subject librarian and director of graduate studies can help you begin to identify whom to work with at your institution.

We recommend looking for a balance of committee members who can speak to the various fields and methodologies encompassed by the project. While this advice also holds true for all dissertations, it may be more difficult for a digital dissertation given that DH practitioners are usually spread across different units. Even if you have access to a DH center, the affiliated staff or faculty may not have the skills that are most relevant to your project. DH staff are usually some of the most knowledgeable experts on campus, so if you do decide to ask them to be on your committee, be sure to find out early if you need to get special dispensation for their participation. We also recommend reaching out to experts in cognate fields like media studies, digital studies, science and technology studies, and computational social science, who may not identify as part of DH but whose work is often speaking to similar intellectual questions. Finally, keep in mind that DH remains relatively controversial among humanists, and so we recommend ensuring that your non-DH committee members are willing to engage in this space.[10]

We also recommend selecting committee members who are comfortable with and committed to having conversations about what constitutes "enough" for the dissertation, including its digital components. An openness to a give-and-take approach is critical since you will likely have to assist your committee in navigating the methodological and technical aspects of the project. In addition, all three of us found that committee feedback increased dramatically once we were able to show tangible work-in-progress. Thus, we would encourage working quickly to a proof of concept or prototype that will engage your committee so that you can lay the foundation for how and in what form their feedback will be offered. Lastly, while the dissertation committee is the formal body for advice and feedback on the project, we suggest that you also build your own informal support networks. Fellow graduate students and faculty outside your institution can provide valuable support and mentorship for yourself and also for your committee.

In hindsight, we each made substantial compromises in order to balance innovation, time-to-completion, and institutional sign-off. LeBlanc chose to argue for the inclusion of computational analysis and methods in her finished dissertation; Sharpe chose to argue for an alternate presentation of her historical scholarship; and Wieringa chose to argue for both methods in the creation of the project, but she ended up compromising on what was deposited with the library and ProQuest.[11] Existing guidelines for digital dissertations and digital scholarship from other institutions can also be helpful when explaining the process and components of a project in discussions with committees, departments, and libraries. We hope that by sharing the ups and downs of our dissertation processes, we have underscored our basic takeaways: be strategic in your choice of digital interventions and be mindful of what is possible within existing institutional structures.

Recommendations for Advisers and Institutions

Our experiences demonstrate that while a digital dissertation can be completed in history, additional structural changes are required for digital scholarship at the dissertation level to thrive. In the remainder of this chapter, we identify four key places where curricular and institutional change is needed. We address these recommendations toward prospective digital dissertation committee members, doctoral program directors, department chairs, and university administrators who oversee graduate programs. While we acknowledge that these recommendations might not make sense in all institutional contexts, we propose them to help move campus-specific conversations about supporting graduate students interested in pursuing digital projects toward concrete reforms.

COMMITTEES, PROGRAMS, AND SUPPORT NETWORKS

Generally, dissertation committees are ad hoc groups, with the dynamics between members and students emerging over time. However, even within this nebulous space, the prospect of a digital dissertation can exacerbate tensions over how mentorship should operate, as well as how committee members should communicate and share their expertise. Committee members will likely be confronted with the responsibility of adjudicating what "counts" as historical scholarship, legitimizing the dissertation work and outputs of the project, and navigating department and institutional guidelines. It is important that the committee recognize that this additional labor will be required and that it should not fall on the student alone to argue for the legitimacy of their work or the legibility of their methods. At all three of our defenses, the underlying debate among the committee members centered on the question of what constitutes historical scholarship, suggesting that a committee for a digital dissertation should include at least one member versed in the digital humanities who can support the student in their claims.

Even as each of our committees contained scholars with experience in digital history projects, we discovered that the idea of the digital dissertation as a single-authored sustained work sat in tension with our committee members' understanding and experiences of digital history as collaborative work. Traditional history dissertations are proto-monographs. Professors in history—the people who form the majority of dissertation committees in the field—have cleared the hurdles of the dissertation and the monograph, often before embarking on their digital scholarship. But digital dissertations introduce new pressures on the adviser-advisee relationship. "Develop your voice as an author" or "Just start writing" mean something quite different to someone preparing a manuscript than to someone who is creating interactive data visualizations.

Since digital dissertations in history are still relatively new, guidelines that encompass both faculty effort and student expectations are especially important. Such guidelines should specify what constitutes enough work for a dissertation, what counts as a meaningful scholarly intervention, and how digital scholarship is situated in the discipline at large. These guidelines are needed at both the department and disciplinary levels, and ideally they expand the definition of scholarship to include data creation, analysis, interface design, and so on, as well as help to distinguish the intellectual work that underpins digital records management.[12] Expanding dissertation guidelines to account for the advising and evaluation of digital scholarship by committee members, as well as the responsibilities and processes of institutional units, would also have transformative effects for dissertations and for publishing, career paths, and tenure and promotion.[13]

On a more practical level, committee members, program directors, and department chairs can help establish affinity groups and peer support networks among graduate students and faculty within their departments and across institutional boundaries. To be sure, some of this already happens through conferences and social media, but formalizing these networks can provide needed support and shared information among students and faculty alike. For example, a panel at the American Historical Association (AHA) annual meeting organized by the authors was the first time that Sharpe and Wieringa's committee members discussed the process of advising digital dissertations, even when both were housed within the same department. During the panel, all three advisers expressed their regret that the conversation had not happened sooner and their enthusiasm for more conversations among faculty advisers about how best to support their students' projects. Faculty can also draw on their existing networks to connect graduate students with experts in other fields. For example, Wieringa was connected to a computer science professor at George Mason who helped her think through what was possible with topic models and discouraged her from using a database when flat data files would do, saving her significant amounts of work. Ultimately, there are limits to how much top-down organizing can nurture these support networks, but the burden of helping foster these relationships should not fall solely on the shoulders of graduate students.

EDUCATION AND TRAINING

As discussed above, training in digital methods, analysis, and technical skills largely remains a diffused constellation of formal and informal options that vary widely across disciplines.[14] One option would be to provide more coursework in digital methods; however, we caution that this coursework cannot simply be added on top of existing program requirements. An alternative would be to restructure the comprehensive exam or other program milestones. Allowing a student to declare a field in digital methods, for example, might result in a shorter reading list but the expectation that the student would spend more time synthesizing and experimenting with the methods they are studying.[15] Both of these solutions would require someone to teach or advise about this content, however. For programs that lack faculty versed in digital methods, another option would be to allow more flexibility for students to enroll in courses in other departments. This option also comes with caveats: Courses designed for computer science students, for example, might result in increased computational literacies, but they would still not address the issue of how to apply those literacies to historical research. Furthermore, these courses are often designed to be part of a larger curriculum, so it can be difficult to assess whether any particular course will cover sufficient or even relevant content.[16] Some graduate students may wish to pursue a master's degree in another department concurrently with their doctorate. But for many history departments, the prospect of their students enrolling in more than one course in another department is often not encouraged.

In addition to these curricular options, there is also room for more creative approaches. One example might be to modularize courses and training to mirror the practical ways that digital humanists experiment and explore new methods and tools. A regularly scheduled "boot camp" or micro-course could address technical fundamentals and lower barriers to entry for students who might not have envisioned themselves as pursuing digital work when they entered the program. Such a model would also ensure that all students develop the same foundational knowledge, rather than implicitly privileging the students who have had previous coding experience.[17] More advanced digital courses could use the boot camp as a prerequisite and as a result could move more quickly into the applications for historical inquiry. Smaller courses could also be designated specifically for learning and experimentation, with a goal of building formal spaces for the kind of exploratory work that we each conducted independently. A further benefit of a modular framework would be that the associated faculty could concentrate on their particular areas of expertise rather than being required to teach broad methodological surveys. They could also more easily update courses based on technical developments in the field. Regardless of which solution any particular program decides to implement, the faculty should be committed to scaffolding digital history within the curriculum.

AUTHORSHIP AND COLLABORATION

Our experiences creating digital dissertations also highlight the tensions between the authorship models operative in digital scholarship and those in the humanities generally, and particularly in graduate education. Projects in the digital humanities are often explicitly collaborative, the work of multiple scholars and practitioners, each of whom contributes their own expertise to the overall project. This aspect of DH work is highly transformative for humanities scholarship. Yet this collaborative model has yet to be adopted within the context of dissertation research, where the single-author model remains dominant. As a result, individual graduate students have to engage with the complexities of digital scholarship at every level of their projects, from source collection and preparation through analysis and presentation, something that is rarely required of faculty working on large-scale digital projects. As long as the single-author paradigm persists, graduate students undertaking digital scholarship will remain limited in terms of what they can accomplish.

The idea of historical scholarship as a solitary enterprise is itself a fiction, after all. All historians rely on the expertise of others for the collection and management of historical materials, for theoretical frameworks to apply to those materials, and for feedback on both interpretation and methods. Reading the acknowledgments of any scholarly work underscores this reality, and while the sole-authored model persists, it is increasingly being challenged, whether by archivists who critique the erasure of their labor or by growing recognition of collaboratively authored work in the field (Theimer).[18] In this regard, digital dissertations can be used as a model for how to bring collaboration into the dissertation process across the field.

Collaboration could take many forms, such as peer collaboration between graduate students, projects that build off existing faculty research, or work that takes place within the more formal collaborative research structure of a lab. In many of these areas, graduate students are already leading the way. Projects such as Mapping Gay Guides and Photogrammar began as collaborative work done in parallel with dissertation research. Faculty-led projects such as Viral Texts and the Colored Conventions Project have supported successful dissertation work in both English and history. While more common in Europe, formal DH labs may recruit graduate students to work on specific aspects of broader research projects as their dissertation work.[19] The latter two models have the added benefit of making it possible for graduate students to participate in digital scholarship at an earlier career stage. Within these models, the work of data collection, cleaning, analysis, visualization, and presentation is spread across multiple researchers rather than falling to a single doctoral student. These models also allow researchers to build on each other's scholarship and together create more ambitious projects. This approach has the added benefit of easing some of the infrastructure questions around digital dissertations, since the archiving and preservation of the overall project would not be the sole responsibility of the student.

This is not to say that all digital dissertations should be collaborative. As all three of us have demonstrated, one can successfully complete a digital project as an individual graduate researcher. However, there need to be more realistic expectations about how much work one graduate student can do. For all of us, taking on our projects as individual scholars greatly limited what we could accomplish. Digital humanities is largely collaborative because the work requires it and as such presents an alternative model of knowledge creation. It is important to bring that alternative model to the digital dissertation as well. Departments creating digital history programs and institutions encouraging digital scholarship by students must look to collaborative research models for this scholarship to be sustainable and thrive.

SUBMISSION AND PRESERVATION

With more robust networks, more formalized training, and a greater recognition of the alternatives to single-authored digital projects, the conditions for digital dissertations would be markedly improved. Yet as we have outlined in earlier sections, there remain a number of infrastructural and institutional issues that also need to be addressed—issues that require the coordination of various administrative units on campus. As such, we recommend that departments, schools, libraries, and other stakeholders, rather than graduate students, take the lead in updating the cultural and technical systems surrounding the dissertation process so that they can support the complexities of digital scholarship.

One of the key challenges for stakeholders will be to understand how the digital elements of a dissertation fit within the existing systems for archiving scholarship, as well as how that work fits within the intellectual ecosystem of the university. Digital projects often rely on large collections of digital sources that are owned and maintained by external entities. While such projects require access to these data and sources to run, there are not clear practices around whether these materials should or even can be included within a project's archived version, as Sharpe's dissertation experience revealed.[20] In fact, the need to capture and preserve the sources used in an individual project, as well as the physical constraints of storage for archiving those sources and the legal and financial aspects of working with copyrighted material, are active research questions in their own right. The practical issues of digital projects need to be addressed through collaboration and conversations between institutional stakeholders, including departments, DH centers, and university libraries, both for dissertations and for digital scholarship generally.

Additionally, clearer guidelines and processes are needed around submitting digital dissertations. At both George Mason and Vanderbilt, the process of submitting a dissertation is managed by the university libraries. At both institutions, the dissertation approval process involved conforming to formatting guidelines for a single PDF document. Even as these guidelines were fairly new, given that university libraries have only recently moved from the submission of printed and bound dissertations to handling electronic files, they have not caught up to the realities of digital research.

Resolving the issues related to the submission of digital dissertations will require an investment of both time and leadership at the institutional level. While there are some workarounds for submitting digital dissertations within existing systems, as described above, these workarounds profoundly limit the potential engagement with and impact of the work itself. For example, Sharpe's decision to include a JSON export of her Scalar project site as a supplemental file in her submission, in order to adhere to the submission guidelines, has left her uncertain as to whether future researchers will be able to use this file to re-create the site, which itself is not archived in the library. Haziness on digital dissertation submission guidelines also influenced LeBlanc's decision not to build a digital storytelling interface for her data visualizations, even though the interface would have made them accessible to more people, since she was concerned about having to undertake additional work to translate the interface into the print version required for submission. Wieringa used a combination of web-archive snapshots and zip files of her code and website files as the content she submitted to the library. This content, like Sharpe's, was not the same as the website she created, and the archived version is not "viewable" within the institutional repository. These ad hoc strategies not only limit the preservation of digital scholarship but also create a bifurcation between "traditional" and "digital" work. Institutional resources need to be put in place so that the scholarship associated with digital dissertations can be captured, archived, and preserved. This is necessary both to legitimate the digital artifacts as scholarship and to provide some semblance of stability so that they can be part of an ongoing scholarly conversation.

Redefining Historical Scholarship

Digital dissertations push at the boundaries of what counts as scholarship. Our three projects present a vision of scholarship that includes, but is also more than, the construction of historical narratives and interpretations. In this way, our work is part of a broader discussion about whether digital history should be considered as scholarship in its own right or whether it should be understood as processing work done in the service of an interpretive narrative ultimately published in article or book form.

This debate is acutely difficult for graduate students to navigate. Graduate students are increasingly encouraged to undertake digital work, often with the implicit assumption that it will make them more competitive in the academic job market and somehow simultaneously prepare them for a range of alt-academic positions. At the same time, well-meaning advisers often privately tell their graduate students that digital work should be something that they pursue on the side until they have the safety of tenure, especially since most departments still require a print book for tenure or promotion. This conflicting advice underscores the profound structural problems surrounding digital dissertations in history.

Counseling graduate students to sideline their digital projects or wait until tenure to undertake them highlights the continued precariousness of digital scholarship. Given the constraints of time, money, and resources involved in the dissertation, the risk in not valuing the technical work involved in creating digital projects is that they become unfeasible altogether. Digital scholarship is not just an add-on; it fundamentally reshapes the very questions asked and the possibilities of interpretation. This underscores the fact that digital scholarship is more than preliminary work on the way to the "real" scholarship of interpretation and narrative building. Indeed, elements such as data selection and preparation, computational modeling, and interface design are all part of research and analysis and as such should be valued (and evaluated) as scholarship.

As more digital dissertations are produced, departments and publishers will need to work through what constitutes revision for digital work, as well as how the infrastructure that supports digital dissertations can translate into digital publications. We would like to see publishers provide more transparency around their digital infrastructure for potential submissions, as well as information about how peer reviewers might evaluate the technical aspects of the project, for example. We would also like to see granting agencies and universities begin to offer fellowships to support graduate students as they build the digital infrastructure required for their dissertation projects. Combined, these changes would help make creating digital projects a sustainable part of the larger dissertation process and post-dissertation career.

Digital dissertations highlight the disconnect between the desire to support digital scholarship, as increasingly expressed by programs and departments, and the realities of the profession. Projects such as ours are difficult for traditional history departments to understand, even those looking to hire a tenure-track "digital historian." The dangers for the lone digital historian in such a department are strikingly similar to those we encountered with our digital dissertations, in that much of the digital work remains difficult to evaluate and thus tends to be viewed as secondary, as a basis for teaching digital methods while one continues along the established trajectory of writing historical monographs and journal articles. Those in tenure-track positions, who may have comparatively more resources than graduate students, face similar constraints of infrastructure, authorship expectations, and publishing outlets.

Digital history training is not a seamless fit for alt-academic positions, either. Marketing digital methods as a way of easily transitioning into other professional careers overstates the generalizability of digital history and understates the knowledge needed to work in spaces like DH centers, libraries, museums, or granting agencies. Clear career opportunities for digital historians are currently limited.[21]

The "digital turn" has changed the methods and processes around archival research, historical analysis, and scholarly publishing in fundamental ways. But undertaking work that makes critically informed use of these new methods and processes will require significant changes to current models of scholarship at all levels, including the dissertation. While a generalized enthusiasm for digital history has successfully supported the first few waves of digital dissertations, a deep investment in digital scholarship is now required for it to truly thrive. Each of us has shared the particularities of our digital dissertations because we believe that the commonalities across them help to make visible the larger structural issues that are often elided in debates over digital scholarship. Without addressing these issues, we believe that digital history will remain in the "perpetual future tense," as Cameron Blevins has described it, with graduate students bearing the brunt of the unresolved tensions in the field. The potential for digital scholarship in history is vast. The time for action is now.

NOTES

1. For examples of guidelines, see "Digital Dissertation Guidelines" and "Guidelines for the Professional Evaluation of Digital Scholarship by Historians." For journals geared toward digital scholarship, see "Digital History Reviews"; Robertson, Mullen, and Swain;

and the *Journal of Digital History* (https://journalofdigitalhistory.org/). For discussions about argumentation in digital history, see Arguing with Digital History Working Group.

2. For examples of data management and research methods, see Karl (whose work includes the YouTube series Research/Craft and relevant tweets). Additionally, new tools such as Tropy (https://tropy.org) are being developed to aid in that work. Tropy is jointly developed by RRCHNM, the Luxembourg Centre for Contemporary and Digital History (C^2DH), and Digital Scholar.

3. See Kuhn; also see Kuhn and Finger. In addition, since 2012, there has been an active Humanities, Arts, Science, and Technology Alliance and Collaboratory (HASTAC) group dedicated to digital dissertations maintained by Jade E. Davis.

4. It is important to note that for every successful digital history dissertation, there are many examples of attempted projects that have been abandoned because of the structural and cultural constraints that we discuss in this piece. Often unrecognized because of the ways the academic community relies on successful defenses to mark scholarly work, these projects reveal the work involved in creating digital scholarship in history just as much as, if not more than, the high-profile successful ones.

5. See Hicks, for example; see also Posner.

6. Problems such as this are not uncommon for digitized sources, as is outlined in Cordell and Smith ("A Research Agenda for Historical and Multilingual Optical Character Recognition"), work that was funded by the National Endowment for the Humanities (NEH).

7. One project where the work of text evaluation and preparation is discussed is the Mapping Texts project (Torget et al.).

8. April Hathcock, director of scholarly communications and information policy for NYU Libraries, and Nancy Sims, copyright program librarian at University of Minnesota Libraries, are two leading examples of trained librarians and lawyers whose work on issues of copyright and intellectual property create supportive environments for researchers navigating these areas. With respect to institution-wide initiatives, see the ongoing efforts of the MIT Open Access Task Force, https://open-access.mit.edu/.

9. A key point of consideration raised by issues of copyright and public-facing scholarship is the default in digital humanities work toward openness (i.e., public access) and what this means specifically for the dissertation.

10. See, for example, Fish. For internal criticisms of the origins of digital humanities, see Allington, Brouillette, and Golumbia.

11. Within higher education in the United States, large corporations such as ProQuest serve as both a resource and a gatekeeper for academic work, the dissertation included. Most PhD programs include a requirement for dissertations to be uploaded to ProQuest's Dissertations & Theses service as part of the final submission process.

12. Critical engagement throughout the process of digital records management is necessary and should be explicit, for both digital and nondigital work in history. A strong example of the need to critically engage source bases, especially digital ones, is outlined in Spedding; the general issue is discussed in Underwood.

13. See "Guidelines for the Professional Evaluation of Digital Scholarship by Historians"; "Digital Dissertation Guidelines"; Leon. While guidelines exist for evaluating digital projects in tenure and promotion, as well as guidelines for graduate students undertaking digital dissertations, there are none that currently address committees supervising digital dissertations.

14. The difficulty of teaching both content and methods is well known in DH but remains far from solved. For example, see Goldstone.

15. At George Mason, graduate students can declare history and new media or digital history as a field in their qualifying exams. For Wieringa, her minor field in history and new media had a strong media studies emphasis, which she relied on to theoretically ground her engagement with computational tools and methods.

16. For example, an introductory course in computer science is rarely useful for a digital historian since it is usually focused on teaching students foundational programming knowledge. Conversely, an introductory course in critical geography or computational social science or data science might be a good fit, though again, many of these courses use examples and assumptions from the sciences rather than the humanities.

17. While in the future this may be less of a barrier as students are increasingly introduced to programming in their precollege education, we believe that digital history, and DH generally, could do more to provide opportunities for not only introductory but also intermediary and advanced training in digital methods, specifically for groups that remain underrepresented in computational work.

18. See also the "Collaborators' Bill of Rights" and "A Student Collaborators' Bill of Rights" (Clement et al.; Di Pressi et al.).

19. While DH centers in the United States and Canada offer vital opportunities for graduate students to participate in the work of digital scholarship and to learn technical skills that they can apply to their own work, that scholarly work is generally seen as tangential to, rather than part of, dissertation research.

20. It is important to note that fair use is not in itself a solution to this problem. Fair use can be used as a legal defense, but it may require a lawyer. That is a bar too high to expect of graduate students. Additionally, libraries are not keen to take on this burden; they often require scholars to certify that they are not archiving copyrighted material at the point of submission. Even when the digital sources are published explicitly for use in research, such as JSTOR's Data for Research or materials from ProQuest, the availability or organization of these digital files can change over time. While one solution is to duplicate this data and store it with the final project, this approach presumes infinite storage capacity and also legal permission to redistribute copyrighted or proprietary digitized materials.

21. It is worth noting that while all three of the authors have secured tenure-track jobs, only Sharpe is in a history department, and in her case, because the context is a community college, her path to tenure is primarily defined by her contributions to teaching and the scholarship of teaching and learning. LeBlanc is now housed in the information sciences and Wieringa in religious studies.

BIBLIOGRAPHY

Allington, Daniel, Sarah Brouillette, and David Golumbia. "Neoliberal Tools (and Archives): A Political History of Digital Humanities." *Los Angeles Review of Books.* May 1, 2016, https://lareviewofbooks.org/article/neoliberal-tools-archives-political-history-digital-humanities/.

Arguing with Digital History Working Group. "Digital History and Argument." White paper. Roy Rosenzweig Center for History and New Media. November 13, 2017, https://rrchnm.org/argument-white-paper/.

Bartram, Erin. "Jane Minot Sedgwick and the World of American Catholic Converts, 1820–1890." PhD diss. University of Connecticut, 2015.

Bauer, Jean. "Republicans of Letters: The Early American Foreign Service as Information Network, 1775–1825." PhD diss. University of Virginia, 2015.

Blevins, Cameron. "Digital History's Perpetual Future Tense." In *Debates in the Digital Humanities 2016,* edited by Matthew K. Gold and Lauren F. Klein. Minneapolis: University of Minnesota Press, 2016.

Blevins, Cameron. "The Postal West: Spatial Integration and the American West, 1865–1902." PhD diss. Stanford University, 2015.

Clement, Tanya, Brian Croxall, Julia Flanders, Neil Fraistat, Steve Jones, Matt Kirschenbaum, Suzanne Lodato, et al. "Collaborators' Bill of Rights." *Off the Tracks: Laying New Lines for Digital Humanities Scholars* (blog). 2011, http://mcpress.media-commons.org/offthetracks/part-one-models-for-collaboration-career-paths-acquiring-institutional-support-and-transformation-in-the-field/a-collaboration/collaborators%e2%80%99-bill-of-rights/.

Cordell, Ryan, and David Smith. "A Research Agenda for Historical and Multilingual Optical Character Recognition." White paper. Northeastern University NULab for Texts, Maps, and Networks. 2018, http://hdl.handle.net/2047/D20297452.

Cordell, Ryan, and David A. Smith. *The Viral Texts Project: Mapping Networks of Reprinting in 19th-Century Newspapers and Magazines.* 2019, https://viraltexts.org/.

Di Pressi, Haley, Stephanie Gorman, Miriam Posner, Raphael Sasayama, and Tori Schmitt, with contributions from Roderic Crooks, Megan Driscoll, Amy Earhart, Spencer Keralis, Tiffany Naiman, and Todd Presner. "A Student Collaborators' Bill of Rights." *UCLA HumTech.* June 8, 2015, https://humtech.ucla.edu/news/a-student-collaborators-bill-of-rights/.

"Digital Dissertation Guidelines." Department of History and Art History, George Mason University. 2020, https://historyarthistory.gmu.edu/graduate/phd-history/digital-dissertation-guidelines.

"Digital History Reviews." *American Historical Review* 125, no. 2 (April 2020): 579, https://doi.org/10.1093/ahr/rhaa238.

Fish, Stanley. "Mind Your P's and B's: The Digital Humanities and Interpretation." In *Think Again: Contrarian Reflections on Life, Culture, Politics, Religion, Law, and Education.* Princeton, N.J.: Princeton University Press, 2015.

Foreman, P. Gabrielle, and Jim Casey. *The Colored Conventions Project.* 2020, https://coloredconventions.org/.

Gonzaba, Eric, and Amanda Regan. *Mapping the Gay Guides: Visualizing Queer Space and American Life.* 2020, https://www.mappingthegayguides.org/.

Goldstone, Andrew. "Teaching Quantitative Methods: What Makes It Hard (in Literary Studies)." In *Debates in the Digital Humanities 2019,* edited by Matthew K. Gold and Lauren F. Klein. Minneapolis: University of Minnesota Press, 2019, https://dhdebates.gc.cuny.edu/read/untitled-f2acf72c-a469-49d8-be35-67f9ac1e3a60/section/620caf9f-08a8-485e-a496-51400296ebcd#ch19.

"Guidelines for the Professional Evaluation of Digital Scholarship by Historians." American Historical Association. 2015, https://www.historians.org/teaching-and-learning/digital-history-resources/evaluation-of-digital-scholarship-in-history/guidelines-for-the-professional-evaluation-of-digital-scholarship-by-historians.

Heppler, Jason A. "Machines in the Valley: Community, Urban Change, and Environmental Politics in Silicon Valley, 1945–1990." PhD diss. University of Nebraska-Lincoln, 2016.

Hicks, Mar. *Programmed Inequality: How Britain Discarded Women Technologists and Lost Its Edge in Computing.* Cambridge, Mass.: MIT Press, 2015.

"Guidelines for the Professional Evaluation of Digital Scholarship by Historians." American Historical Association. 2015, https://www.historians.org/teaching-and-learning/digital-history-resources/evaluation-of-digital-scholarship-in-history/guidelines-for-the-professional-evaluation-of-digital-scholarship-by-historians.

Karl, Robert A. "Research Methods." *Robert A. Karl* (blog). Accessed August 24, 2022, http://www.rakarl.com/#researchmethods-section.

Kaufman, Micki. "Everything on Paper Will Be Used Against Me: Quantifying Kissinger." PhD diss. City University New York (CUNY), forthcoming.

Kuhn, Virginia. "The Early Days of the Digital Dissertation." *Academe Blog.* January 29, 2013, https://academeblog.org/2013/01/29/the-early-days-of-the-digital-dissertation/.

Kuhn, Virginia, and Anke Finger, eds. *Shaping the Digital Dissertation: Knowledge Production in the Arts and Humanities.* Cambridge: Open Book Publishers, 2021, https://doi.org/10.11647/OBP.0239.

Lincoln, Matthew D. "Modeling the Network of Dutch and Flemish Print Production, 1550–1750." PhD diss. University of Maryland, 2016.

LeBlanc, Zoe. "Circulating Anti-Colonial Cairo: Decolonizing Information and Constructing the Third World in Egypt, 1952–1966." PhD diss. Vanderbilt University, 2021, http://hdl.handle.net/1803/15498.

LeBlanc, Zoe (@Zoe_LeBlanc). "Don't usually post much but I've been thinking abt this problem a lot lately & need answers: can 1 person do 'meaningful' #dhist work???" Twitter, July 24, 2017, https://twitter.com/Zoe_LeBlanc/status/889668601153761280.

Leon, Sharon. "Guidelines for Digital Dissertations in History." *[bracket].* September 30, 2015, https://www.6floors.org/bracket/2015/09/30/guidelines-for-digital-dissertations-in-history.

Milligan, Ian. "Illusionary Order: Online Databases, Optical Character Recognition, and Canadian History, 1997–2010." *Canadian Historical Review* 94, no. 4 (November 2013): 540–69, https://muse.jhu.edu/article/527016.

Mullen, Lincoln A. "The Varieties of Religious Conversion: The Origins of Religious Choice in the United States." PhD diss. Brandeis University, 2014.

Posner, Miriam. "Some Things to Think about before You Exhort Everyone to Code." *Miriam Posner's Blog.* February 29, 2012, https://miriamposner.com/blog/some-things-to-think-about-before-you-exhort-everyone-to-code/.

Resig, John. "Aggregating and Analyzing Digitized Japanese Woodblock Prints." Presentation at the Japanese Association for Digital Humanities Annual Conference, Ritsumeikan University, Kyoto, Japan, September 19–21, 2013, https://docs.google.com/document/d/12ZKfHMbN8dS9aMHirOLn8IqAZVQ22Uf0tktEpsqu4XQ.

Robertson, Stephen, Lincoln Mullen, and Greta Swain, eds. *Current Research in Digital History* 3. Fairfax, Va.: Roy Rosenzweig Center for History and New Media, 2020, https://crdh.rrchnm.org/.

Sharpe, Celeste Tường Vy. "Precarity and Promise: Negotiating Research Ethics and Copyright in a History Dissertation." In *Shaping the Digital Dissertation: Topics in Knowledge Production,* edited by Virginia Kuhn and Anke Finger. Cambridge: Open Book Publishers, 2021.

Sharpe, Celeste Tường Vy. "They Need You! Disability, Visual Culture, and the Poster Child, 1945–1980." PhD diss. George Mason University, 2016, https://hdl.handle.net/1920/10555.

Software Studies Initiative. *ImagePlot Visualization Software.* Accessed August 26, 2022, http://lab.softwarestudies.com/p/imageplot.html.

Spedding, Patrick. "'The New Machine': Discovering the Limits of ECCO." *Eighteenth-Century Studies* 44, no. 4 (2011): 437–53, http://www.jstor.org/stable/41301590.

Theimer, Kate. "Archives in Context and as Context Journal of Digital Humanities." *Journal of Digital Humanities* 1, no. 2 (Spring 2012), http://journalofdigitalhumanities.org/1-2/archives-in-context-and-as-context-by-kate-theimer/.

Torget, Andrew J., Rada Mihalcea, Jon Christensen, and Geoff McGhee. "Mapping Texts: Combining Text-Mining and Geo-Visualization to Unlock the Research Potential of Historical Newspapers." White paper. National Endowment for the Humanities. Accessed August 24, 2022, http://mappingtexts.org/index17dc.html?page_id=271.

Underwood, Ted. "Theorizing Research Practices We Forgot to Theorize Twenty Years Ago." *Representations* 127, no. 1 (August 2014): 64–72, https://doi.org/10.1525/rep.2014.127.1.64.

Wexler, Laura, Lauren Tilton, and Taylor Arnold. *Photogrammar.* 2020, http://photogrammar.yale.edu/.

Wieringa, Jeri. "A Gospel of Health and Salvation: Modeling the Religious Culture of Seventh-day Adventism, 1843–1920." PhD diss. George Mason University, 2019, http://hdl.handle.net/1920/12281.

Critique Is the Steam: Reorienting Critical Digital Humanities across Disciplines

JAMES MALAZITA

How are the digital humanities oriented? I ask this in Sara Ahmed's spirit. To ask how we are oriented is not only to consider how we are situated in a space and to the objects around us, but also to consider how those spaces and objects produce us (*Queer Phenomenology*). Ahmed is concerned with matters of sexual orientation, bodies, and space. Through her "queer phenomenology," Ahmed argues that "bodies take shape through tending towards objects that are reachable": those objects we can quite literally grasp, embrace, strike, and caress, and those for which we desire, resist, and identify with. As bodies "acquire orientation by repeating some actions over others" (Ahmed, "Orientations," 553), material and social orientations are produced over time; they are not inherent or immutable qualities of an object or body. For Ahmed, queerness is best understood as a constant enactment of the self: a constant positioning of oneself toward objects, persons, and concepts within reach and an ongoing production of the spaces inhabited. As we reach out to and practice connecting with objects and spaces, those objects and spaces reach back into our bodies, reorienting us. Our practices of orientation produce our identities, our ways of knowing, and our worlds. Orienting is not a singular event or a unidirectional one. Rather, it is a collection of multiple ongoing practices, each reaching toward different ends and creating different spaces and bodies.

Though perhaps not a body in the phenomenological context in which Ahmed writes, the "body" of the digital humanities (DH) does orient itself. DH scholars make and remake methodological decisions that define and reach toward our objects and subjects of inquiry. In their introduction to *Debates in the Digital Humanities 2019,* Matthew K. Gold and Lauren F. Klein trace some of the multiple, shifting forms of DH: the transformation of a fundamental divide between technical methods and "traditional" humanistic analysis into a more synthetic approach; rapid mobilizations of scholarly and technical resources in response to natural and policy disasters; and specific and grounded engagements with marginalized communities and those most deeply affected by late-stage capital and the rise of authoritarian politics. These orienting practices center questions of epistemology—what does it mean to produce DH knowledge?—and questions of responsibility and labor—who are we producing knowledge with and for? I wish to highlight two other kinds of orientation in DH: that of "space" and that of "critique," and how those two orientations are produced together.

Space is not pre-constituted. We continually practice spaces—especially disciplinary spaces—into being, even as we orient ourselves and our actions within that space. Consequently, following Ahmed, our orientations of and within spaces "matter," both because they have political and epistemic consequences, and because they shape the material practices and scholarly identities of DH. For example, questions of DH's status as a field or subfield or specialization orient us spatially; through our answers we come to produce where DH belongs, what forms it takes, and what activities it is capable of. We come to know what counts as inside DH (i.e., our own expertise, identities, institutional norms, and disciplinary ways of knowing) and what counts as outside DH (i.e., various arrangements of allies, adversaries, and publics). The political capacities of the digital humanities owe as much to our disciplinary spatial formations as they do our critical commitments.

The calls for critique in DH scholarship too have been continually practiced over time. #TransformDH and Alexis Lothian and Amanda Phillips's calls for DH as transformative critique occurred almost a decade ago, and postcolonial and Black digital humanities (Noble) have long leveraged the flexibility of orientations to produce analysis of the privileged geographic dispersion of DH research and centers (Terras), to call for decolonizing literary and archival preservation (Risam and Koh), and to introduce feminist, queer, and "accented" (Risam) pedagogical models. Todd Presner has called for deeper integrations of cultural-critical frameworks in order to highlight the "cludge" inherent in digital humanities practices, particularly in terms of the messy materiality of code and software, echoing Tara McPherson's examinations of how power and culture become materialized through digital platforms ("Designing for Difference"). Shared across these pushes for critical integration are questions of the shape and orientation of the body of the digital humanities: Who are we? Who are our audiences? What tools extend our body, and in what spaces do we belong? Critical DH is not just about working in spaces outside of libraries and literature classrooms; it is also about examining how different formations of scholarly spaces and orientations produce different kinds of research, politics, institutions, subjects, and objects. Calls for public and political scholarship by nature call into question who our multiple publics and politics are.

Critique's usefulness has also been called into question (Latour, "Why Has Critique Run Out of Steam?"; Felski, *The Limits of Critique*). Though we are beyond the "hacking/yakking" dichotomy that characterized some DH debates in the early 2000s, it is useful to remember the multiple impulses driving that wedge. There was certainly a sort of optimism, even mania, marked by the kind of white masculinist techno-solutionism that characterizes a Silicon Valley venture pitch (McPherson, "Why Are the Digital Humanities So White?"). But the split was also driven by needs to make interventions in a world where university budgets are ever shrinking and where the needs for humanities departments to justify their usefulness and ingenuity are ever growing. The needs for the humanities to assert themselves have only deepened since, given the growing tide of fascism and its attendant attacks on tenure, systems of higher education, and scholars themselves. This tide quite literally seeks to destroy both the disciplinary bodies and the personal bodies of the humanities. In the face of such real and material dangers, critique can feel limp, as if navel-gazing, a self-serving idle practice in a world on fire.

Rita Felski has argued that critique most commonly manifests as a "suspicious reading" practice, and one that is politically ineffective. She invokes a narrative of the English graduate student whose political analysis "uncovers" hidden capitalist, misogynist, and heteropatriarchal values woven in between the lines of classic texts. For the imagined critic, text becomes a shibboleth that embodies counter-progressive ideals that must be torn down. The humanities of the twenty-first century, Felski argues, should be more about entangling ourselves with and tracing out the affective networks that powerful texts and works of art create, in order to solve the "legitimation crisis" of the humanities (*The Limits of Critique*, 5). Felski marks critique as itself a spatial orientation, one that distances and disengages the scholar from our texts and material world.

Given these framings, it is easy to see why critique is ripe for dismissal. Critique can be imagined as an internalist project that prevents scholars from doing the "real work" on the ground. It can also be framed as an intellectual and political vulnerability that leaves the humanities open to attack and delegitimization, as seen by the successful selling of white supremacist ideology through vague attacks on "critical race theory" in educational systems. It is concerning that one of the most common defenses against these bad faith attacks is that "critical theory" only happens in graduate-level classrooms. Ceding critique as internalist or as only relevant to the most upper reaches of the academy risks undermining our capacities to make political and material change, both within humanities networks and beyond. Now is not the time to throw away our tools. Felski is correct, however, in that humanities scholars require shifting bodies, orientations, and spaces in order to attend to our present material and political conditions.

In this chapter, I argue for an Actor-Network Theory (ANT) approach to space and to critique that may help us conceptualize additional orientations of DH—disciplinarily, pedagogically, and institutionally—to navigate and build collective action amid that fire. ANT, associated with Bruno Latour though first developed by Michel Callon, is an analytic recognition that objects, like texts, machines, scientific practices, and works of art, do not exist on their own or even within a social context but instead are produced and stabilized through their relations with and enrollments of various actor-networks. The focus on the "actor-network," rather than on a network of actors, gives ANT an interpretive and analytic flexibility that "complements traditional ethnographic techniques employed in STS (Science and Technology Studies)" (Venturini, Munk, and Jacomy, 511) in order to see how social and material elements exist in relation to one another and how those elements can be read at carrying scales. All actors are themselves made up of networks, which provides the analyst the flexibility to zoom out or dig down into networks of relationships (Latour, "Anti-Zoom"). The result is an analysis that refuses reductive determinism—attributing too much agency to a specific material or technical cause—while also seeking to identify the multiple mechanisms that bring social and material objects and spaces into being (Latour, *Reassembling the Social*).

While Felski herself has leveraged ANT as an alternative to critique, adopting ANT as itself a critical stance highlights actor-networks of affective, political, personal, and embodied practices that produce intellectual stances—including critique. It also highlights how the spaces within which critique is practiced are networked and contingent. Both the form critique takes and the spaces it occupies are reorientable and reconfigurable. DH already benefits from the institutional and cultural legitimacy that its technological veneer provides. Combining the power of this legitimacy with a conceptualization of critique as assembling networks of affective, political, personal, and embodied practices can afford DH scholars additional modes of producing knowledge and working toward transformative scholarship.

To conclude this chapter, I will trace an example of a humanities production of the computer science space to show how our political and material capacities can change as we reimagine our critical and disciplinary orientations. DH scholars have already established many working relationships with computer science faculty and information technology specialists, and many of us are already in hybrid humanities–computer science spaces. Leveraging an ANT-oriented sense of critique allows us to see the patterns and mangles (Presner) that produce DH scholarship across disciplinary fields and further allows us to tug on these mangles to reconfigure our practices and those fields themselves. Figured this way, critique becomes part of an affective and intellectual force that enables digital humanities to permeate broader political and institutional boundaries. Critique need not run out of steam, as Bruno Latour famously pronounced. Rather, critique becomes the steam that powers spatial and disciplinary reconfigurations (Malazita, "Re: Configurations"), allowing for new formations of DH to emerge.

critique as part of affective + intellectual force

Networks of Critique

Following Marianne de Laet and Annemarie Mol, "critique's" fluidity—its capacity to be remade and redeployed across a wide variety of spaces while retaining an epistemic wholeness—may be one of the term's enduring strengths. Critical is a slippery (Law and Lien) term, more so as we see it deployed and redeveloped across a wider array of disciplines. It is now common to find calls, programs, and edited volumes dedicated to critical computing, critical design, and critical methodologies. As Jeffrey and Shaowen Bardzell have noted, across design, the social sciences, and technical disciplines, "critical" can simultaneously stand in for literary criticism, the "capital C" Criticism of the Frankfurt School, and broader movements within social and cultural theory, including intersections of feminism, critical race studies, de/postcolonial literature, queer theory, and disability studies (Bardzell and Bardzell). Across the humanities, too, critique has become fluid terrain, both in terms of its definition and in its perceived usefulness. In *The Limits of Critique,* Rita Felski largely constructs contemporary critique as a broad set of "suspicious reading" practices that aim to uncover hidden capitalist, misogynist, and heteropatriarchal values woven in between the lines of classic texts. This suspicious reading, Felski argues, rewards the capacity for scholars to develop a critical distancing from their texts, both in terms of focusing on context over text and in terms of forming a negative affective relationship with the text in order to identify its—or its author's—political failings. Conversely, Sheila Liming has argued that Felski and her "postcritical" stance represent a longing for an imagined precritical institutional past, where the humanities thrive by aligning with, rather than challenging, institutions of power. Borrowing from Laura Wilder, Liming notes that disciplinary and transdisciplinary discourses about critique are often less about defining critique itself and more often about taking public umbrage with other scholars' definitions or research practices. As such, "critique" and its criticisms become transformed into blunt instruments to be wielded against one's rivals.

Latour—himself a divisive figure among the humanities and STS—consistently emerges as a source of both diagnosis and intervention with regard to critique across the humanities, social sciences, and design. Latour is often encountered through his 2004 article "Why Has Critique Run Out of Steam?" (henceforth "Steam"), itself a statement of public umbrage against Latour's sociological rival Pierre Bourdieu (Nelson). Though in "Steam" Latour is writing for a sociological audience, the piece has been widely cited across multiple fields for its tackling of the "double gesture" of the critical stance. The double gesture, Latour argues, is that the critic moves to undermine those who believe an object to be valuable (be it a scientific fact, cultural narrative, or prominent text), first by revealing that value is only projected onto that object by individuals (the fetishizing moment) and second by *also* revealing the shaping of individual minds by external forces, be it of capitalism, culture, or power. Valuers of an object are thus doubly duped—the objects they value have no intrinsic value, and they only value those objects because they are told by others to value them. "Do you see now why it feels so good to be a critical mind?" Latour pokes. "You can turn all of these attachments into so many fetishes and humiliate all the believers by showing it is nothing but their own projection . . . entirely determined by the action of powerful causalities . . . you alone can see" ("Why Has Critique Run Out of Steam," 238–39). The critic adopts a distanced stance—they articulate their power as the ability to stand above and apart from the fetishizing loop.

None of us, of course, can truly stand away from or above the social, including the social forces that fetishize "critique" itself as a valuable object. Felski leverages Latour to argue that critique's power comes not from intellectual robustness but rather through an alliance of powerful theorists, texts, dissertation committees, and advisers who maintain critique's hegemonic power of orientation in humanities scholarship. Felski thus turns the double gesture back on critics themselves: critique has no value in and of itself, only that which is socially projected, and critical scholars only project that value due to powerful institutional and cultural forces that reward them for doing so.

The way to break critique's stranglehold in the humanities, Felski argues, may lie in the use of Actor-Network Theory. For Felski, ANT's focus on tying together webs of relationships—tracing why important texts are powerful and enduring, why they matter—is a counter to the "ethos of negativity" of critique and its invoking of "historical-political *contexts*" (Felski, "Comparison and Translation," emphasis in the original).

Latour and his contributions to ANT are often posited as ways of flattening the analysis of humans and nonhumans in order to develop a more "realist" account of social and material phenomena. This realism can be used as a way of dismissing critical and contextual scholarship and can become leveraged in support of anti-critical political positions (Lossin), often through the argument that contemporary humanities have placed too much value on "the social" or "the contextual." Latour himself writes that when analyzing phenomena, "the social" is what is to be explained, rather than the explanatory factor (*Reassembling the Social*). But herein lies the issue, especially when relying on Latour's "Steam" and his specific spin on ANT to decenter political and normative analysis. Latour desires to do critique better, not less.

ANT provides a methodological framework that allows STS scholars to speak of the agency of concrete material conditions on the social practices of technical and knowledge workers, while also articulating the contingency and co-determinacy of both those material conditions and social practices. In Latour's words:

> To try to follow an actor-network is a bit like defining a wave corpuscle . . . any entity can be seized either as an actor (a corpuscle) or as a network (a wave). It is in this complete reversibility—an actor is nothing but a network, except that a network is nothing but actors—that resides the main originality of this theory. ("Networks, Societies, Spheres," 5)

As Venturini and colleagues note, the "hyphen" in actor-network is not a relational connector, not a way of understanding actors connected within networks. Rather, it is an equals sign: both an actor and a network, and therefore neither fully an actor nor a network (Venturini, Munk, and Jacomy). This point is, unfortunately, often mischaracterized by both STS and humanities scholars, who imagine actors as "individual entities that assert force while interacting with other entities" (Van

Gorp and Bron, para. 8), a characterization that results from the historical and methodological coupling of ANT with social network analysis (Venturini, Munk, and Jacomy). While such a stance can be descriptively useful, it also assumes prebuilt entities that interact, rather than actors that come to be through their relations.

ANT is not anti-political or anti-contextual; rather, it asserts that what counts as the "context" of an object or a text *comes to be* through relations of actor, network, and analyst. Text and context are not fixed. Rather, they are more like an autostereogram—a "magic eye" puzzle—where background and foreground have as much to do with where we fix our eye as with the printed image itself. As we move our eyes, our heads, our hands, as we reorient our relationship to the page, new shapes, contours, and figures emerge—they reach out to us. The image only becomes fixed when we hold our gazes and bodies stable.

It matters what we hold stable in our critical analyses. Felski, for example, holds stable a certain orientation of the humanities in her writings; it is, as Liming notes, a classical institutional definition of the humanities. We again see Felski's particular stabilization when discussing the challenges to her own desire to bring ANT into literary studies pedagogy:

> And yet, while an occasional course on actor-network theory may sneak its way onto an English syllabus, the chances of most classes on the Victorian novel or contemporary women's fiction being refurbished as classes in the sociology of mediation are close to nil. That is not, after all, what most teachers and students come to literature *for.* (*The Limits of Critique,* 184)

The pragmatic points here are well made: It *is* unlikely that Victorian literature classes will become deeply entangled with sociological theory. However, the argument papers over some of the more conceptual nuances of the very framework Felski is calling for. Again, for ANT, neither space nor context preexist the actor-networks that "inhabit" them. Rather, they are productions of those actor-networks, part and production of particular historical, material, and social arrangements (Dourish). "Space," then, is itself an actor-network, in that it entangles and becomes entangled by other pieces of the network from which it is constituted; it coproduces its own stability.

Similarly, students do not come to literature classes. Rather, those students, classes, theories, and texts produce one another, and narratives of what those classes and students are *for* emerge from the practices and material arrangements of classroom-student-institutional networks. The epistemic stability of literature classes is as much a result of social and material arrangements of power as any other stable network. Similarly, texts or works of art on their own do not produce webs of entanglement. Rather, they come to be—as texts, as sources of political and cultural power, as objects of criticism—through the actor-networks they coproduce.

If we map Latour's "Steam" through Ahmed, we may find that critique as a mode of inquiry is not necessarily defunct but that it allows us to trace the shifting orientations of critique, field, and the digital humanities themselves. Tracing what counts as actor and what counts as network in any given moment—and how those accounts shift from moment to moment and from analyst to analyst—is what provides ANT its analytic and political power. An ANT approach would argue that there is no bringing of critique or the political "into" a space. Rather, critique is the disruption of networked space—the recognition that what counts as spatially stable and what counts as fluid or contested is always in negotiation. Critique may be disruptive, but disruption need not be destructive or negative; disruption in an ANT sense means reorientation. Critique becomes redefined—not as a suspicious reading of a text, nor as a form of public airing of grievances, but as a vector for new spatial and disciplinary production. Critique in an ANT sense is not separate or distant from the objects it analyzes, the authors who wield it, or the students who read it—they are all a part of one another.

To return to spaces of critical DH: The field has long since moved past narratives of existing only in English departments (Kirschenbaum) or as a "big tent" cordoned off from more "traditional" humanities research (Svensson). Gold and Klein ("Introduction: Digital Humanities") illustrate how since its inception, DH has permeated through the fields of book history, Black studies, art history, and archaeology, among others. As noted above, however, even these distinct fields have overlapping disciplinary and institutional networks and share many scholarly commitments. There are possibilities for DH to assemble critical spaces even further afield. As Liming argues, critique and critical scholarship's future "continues to bravely take shape outside of traditional, institutional containers." What can DH be if we assemble it elsewhere and allow it to be reassembled by those elsewheres?

A Critical DH Elsewhere

Here I turn to a critical DH project, "Critical Computer Science," an experimental pedagogical-scholarly reorientation of both digital humanities and computer science (CS). Though institutionally this project was housed between a department of computer science and a department of science and technology studies, it has since its inception been articulated as a DH effort and was supported through the National Endowment for the Humanities (NEH) Office of Digital Humanities and Humanities Connections programs. I want to highlight this project here to show what new networks of critical DH "outside" of the humanities can provide both institutionally and epistemically. Institutionally, Critical Computer Science reoriented the roles of both humanities and science departments, including producing new imaginations of the relations the sciences can have in developing cultures of critique and the role humanities faculty can play in the sciences. Epistemically, the project served to produce ways of analyzing relations of politics and code, the actor-networks that produce the ontological boundaries of programming, and how neoliberalism shapes academic structures and scholarly outcomes. Through DH, computer science spaces became reoriented into vectors for humanistic critique.

I undertook the Critical Computer Science project in collaboration with several graduate and undergraduate CS students who felt marginalized by their computer science classes and curricula. Feelings of marginalization occurred for a variety of reasons among the research collaborators, but many had to do with a perceived lack of space to productively address oppressive algorithmic structures from within their computer science curricula and training. It is no accident that the first stages of this project came into being in the wake of the Cambridge Analytica scandal, the (sometimes enthusiastic) participation of Big Tech in the development of a migrant tracking and detention network in the United States during the Trump administration, and the growing public concern over the use of facial recognition and artificial intelligence (AI) technologies in policing and governance. It is also not an accident that the student researchers who voiced these concerns represented a broader array of genders, races, and (sexual) orientations than typically imagined in computer science classrooms.

These students did have some spaces to talk through these concerns in their humanities and social science electives. It was through these electives, in fact, that I met several of the students who would become the first cohort of Critical Computer Science undergraduate researchers. But, by and large, while these students were thankful for the conversational space in their STS and cultural studies classes to discuss algorithmic injustice, they were disappointed that they had to leave their homes in CS in order to do it. These students viewed computer science as a part of their disciplinary and institutional identity. Contra Felski, the critical impulse at work here was not a desire among these students to distance themselves from their object of critique—computer science as a political institution—but rather a desire to build networks that allowed for a deeper entanglement with it. These students did not want to tear apart their CS education, but they did want to reorient it.

The first output of our project occurred, like many critical DH initiatives do, in the classroom. With permission from the CS department head and support from sympathetic faculty members, the students and I designed Critical Computer Science 1 (CCS1), an alternative section of standard CS1. CCS1 centered critical race theory and feminist technoscience studies in the computer science classroom and developed alternative homework assignments and lectures, incorporated classroom reading discussions of STS and DH articles, and formed outside-of-class marginalized student support groups. In effect, Critical CS1 taught the basics of computer science in a contextualized way: Students still learned "core" programming skills—such as lists, loops, conditionals, dictionaries, and classes—via Python, but they did so through engagements with literature and datasets that outlined the histories and cultural values embedded within computational logics and systems. The course also included interrogations of "pre-digital" computationalism (Golumbia), such as the use of pen-and-paper algorithmic decision-making tools in the nineteenth century to identify and ghettoize Irish migrants (Shrout), in order to give students a "long view" of the digitized present. Many of these conversations were made possible by leveraging prior examples of critically oriented DH work, like the collaboratively produced Torn Apart/Separados site and Anelise Hanson Shrout's "(Re)Humanizing Data" project, as tutorials or starting points of projects and assignments. Perhaps most institutionally important was the fact that students who satisfactorily completed CCS1 received the same administrative credit as students who completed the standard CS1 course. This meant that students did not risk missing their CS requirements or being locked out of upper-level CS classes if they chose to enroll in CCS1. It also meant that CCS1 was required to meet the learning objectives and standards of "rigor" of standard CS1, while also maintaining the critical orientations we demanded of it.

Though I am not a computer science faculty member, I was given permission, through an unpaid teaching overload, to teach the class, under the condition that students had to specifically request being placed in the "critical" section and could choose to leave it at any time. The result was a required core curricular science course, structured through STS and DH readings, supported by the NEH, taught by a humanities faculty member, codesigned and co-taught by CS undergraduate students critical of their own education, and delivered to CS students who self-selected based on their desire for a politically oriented computer science. The actor-network analysis is already useful here: This unconventional network coproduced a DH research project, a critical community space, and an accredited computer science course. It allowed critical humanities work to leverage the institutional capital and epistemic infrastructures (Malazita, "Epistemic Infrastructure") of multiple scholarly spaces, including those more integrated into the resource and funding wells of the university. It also, as I will show, allowed for students who may not necessarily have come to a traditional humanities course to imagine productions of critique beyond networks of textual interpretation, which in turn led to political action.

Changing Capacities

It would be easy enough to characterize the Critical Computer Science project as an effort to bring "ethics" via STS and DH into a CS classroom, rather than itself being a DH project. The former was, for the most part, how CCS1 was interpreted by sympathetic faculty in the computer science department, and it was a narrative that was useful in articulating some of the political and institutional implications of the project to administrative audiences. But CCS1's successes—including students in the first cohort transitioning into project researchers, as well as publications in humanities and social sciences journals coauthored with CS undergrads—stemmed from the project's reorientation of concepts and institutions of computing in ways deeply aligned with humanistic critique. In doing so, CCS1 produced students with critical humanistic capacities who would not otherwise have had the networks to develop them. Moreover, the kinds of critique these students were capable of was distinct from those we may see in a more "traditional" humanities student. It was not just the ability to "suspiciously read" code and software—though there is plenty to be suspicious about in contemporary algorithmic culture. Rather, critique came in the students' capacity to continuously reorient the disciplinary conventions of computer science in ways that enabled more politically engaged work to be done.

I mentioned above that since CCS1 awarded formal CS credit, we were made subject to faculty oversight so that we met standards of CS education. This was quite reasonable, and even welcome, because we did not want graduates of CCS1 to be at a disadvantage in their later CS1 classes compared to students who had passed the standard section. However, what became quickly evident was that what was "counted" by overseers as within the actor-network of CS1 consistently shifted. For example, when Critical CS1 began, the research team was told that Computer Science 1 was not about teaching programming; rather, that course is designed as a foundational introduction to computer science principles, such as abstraction, basic logic gates, basic database parsing, and problem-solving skills. That students learned the Python programming language when exploring these epistemic dimensions was considered almost tangential. This was initially a boon for the project, as defining computer science education epistemically rather than instrumentally—as developing knowledge practices rather than as developing a set of technical skills—dovetailed nicely with the critical race and feminist science studies approaches that we sought to introduce to the course. But after we presented our assignments, which taught these computing fundamentals alongside critical perspectives about their raced and gendered dimensions, the oversight group reconstructed the course as "just about learning Python." Within this revised framework, core computational concepts like abstraction were labeled as too advanced, thus coupled STS or DH readings that critiqued foundational assumptions of computer science were positioned as out of scope for the class.

This is not to complain about the tensions that can arise during interdisciplinary work. Rather, these events reinforced for CCS researchers (including myself) the shifting co-constitutive actor-networks of code and programmer identity. The fluidity of these networks has been well documented in STS literature. As Stéphane Couture illustrates in his ethnographies of open-source developers, what counts as legitimate coding practice, as well as who counts as an expert, is heavily dependent on how one's subject position and technical practice are produced within an actor-network. As Couture shows, however, there is no single definition or quality of code; rather, what becomes constructed as code is both paratextual (Genette and Maclean) and also produced by the identity of the coder. Related documents, such as technical documentation, pseudocode, and graphical "maps" of the program's structure are often included by developers as a part of the actor-network of a piece of code. The developers in Couture's study would often refer to source code as both "text" and "textual." Also contributing to the ever-shifting boundaries of source code were gendered dynamics of expertise—women were less likely to identify their technical practice as source code development than men.

In this project, the nature of code became a contested network, both in terms of "what counts" as code and its role in computer science classrooms, as well as what counts as "core" skills CS students need to develop and internalize. The assignments that CCS students codeveloped would pass in and out of "real CS assignment" status, depending on the reader, the challenge of the assignment, the amount of reading (the more an assignment required reading, the less it was a "real" CS assignment), and the identity of the assignment presenter. It was, for example, easier for a CCS assignment to get approved when a CS student presented it to the oversight group than when I (as a humanities faculty member) did. CCS students, in turn, learned to develop a flexible epistemic orientation to their CS identities throughout the course of the project and their remaining student careers that would allow them to smoothly interact with the institutions of computer science while also challenging them. They had to recognize when it was strategic to wrap themselves in their computer science identities, particularly when participating in student-led CS department committees and organizations, and recognize the cachet it provides when their technical capabilities are called into question by other students (as the story at many engineering schools goes, politically oriented students and technically oriented students are mutually exclusive).

However, CCS researchers also internalized fundamentally humanistic questions: What are the shifting boundaries that determine whether or not one is a programmer or a "legitimate" computer scientist? What were the entanglements of the "text" of the course—Python programming and introductory procedural literacy—and the politics and institutional structures of the course, and how did they come to shape one another? Why did the definitions and discourse of what an introductory computer science course was "supposed to be" change as different people—many of whom represented marginalized identities—attempted to intervene in those courses? Students were able to articulate these questions to other student audiences, leading to the creation of student activist groups, reading groups, and protests of software and engineering firms that contract with the border security military-industrial complex—something almost completely unheard of in the history of our engineering institute.

This, I believe, is exactly the kind of institutional capacity that critical DH can exert if it begins making itself a part of the actor-networks outside of traditional humanistic disciplinary spaces. Such forms of critique are not negative, in that they are not distant or dismissive of texts or technical practice. Nor are the analysts and students who wield such critique distant, as their efforts are oriented toward further entanglement with a broader array of institutional and disciplinary activity. This critique is co-constitutive: It destabilizes our own familiar institutional ground so that we create new understandings of the power of humanities inquiry. This reorientation, in turn, can be transformed into reflexive practice, redefining the boundaries of what it means to be a humanities scholar and creating opportunities for the composition of new and effective critical scholarship and political impact.

NOTE

Activities described in this chapter were sponsored by the National Endowment for the Humanities (grant numbers AK-255350–17 and HD-248450–16). The described Critical Computer Science assignments were developed by Audrey Beard, Korryn Resetar, Brookelyn Parslow, Naya Murdock, Jesse Ellin, Chris Reed, Xavier Marshall, Ohad Nir, Eryn Buhat, Damiel Faxon, and James Malazita. I want to give a special acknowledgment to Lee Nelson for our long conversations about Bruno Latour.

BIBLIOGRAPHY

Ahmed, Sara. "Orientations: Toward a Queer Phenomenology." *GLQ: A Journal of Gay and Lesbian Studies* 12, no. 4 (2006): 543–74.

Ahmed, Sara. *Queer Phenomenology: Objects, Orientations, Others.* Durham, N.C.: Duke University Press, 2006.

Bardzell, Jeffrey, and Shaowen Bardzell. "What Is 'Critical' about Critical Design?" In *CHI '13: Proceedings of the SIGCHI Conference on Human Factors in Computing Systems,* 3297–306. New York: Association for Computing Machinery, 2013.

Callon, Michel. "Some Elements of a Sociology of Translation: Domestication of the Scallops and the Fishermen of St. Brieuc Bay." Supplement, *Sociological Review* 32, no. S1 (1984): 196–233.

Couture, Stéphane. "The Ambiguous Boundaries of Computer Source Code and Some of Its Political Consequences." In *digitalSTS: A Field Guide for Science & Technology Studies,* edited by Janet Vertesi and David Ribes. Princeton, N.J.: Princeton, 2019.

De Laet, Marianne, and Annemarie Mol. "The Zimbabwe Bush Pump: Mechanics of a Fluid Technology." *Social Studies of Science* 30, no. 2 (2000).

Dourish, Paul. "What Do We Talk about when We Talk about Context?" *Personal and Ubiquitous Computing* 8, no. 4 (2004).

Felski, Rita. "Comparison and Translation: A Perspective from Actor-Network Theory." *Comparative Literature Studies* 53, no. 4 (2016).

Felski, Rita. *The Limits of Critique.* Chicago: Chicago University Press, 2015.

Genette, Gérard, and Marie Maclean. "Introduction to the Paratext." Probings: Art, Criticism, Genre, *New Literary History* 22, no. 2 (Spring 1991): 261–72.

Gold, Matthew K., and Lauren F. Klein. "Introduction: A DH That Matters." In *Debates in the Digital Humanities 2019,* edited by Matthew K. Gold and Lauren F. Klein. Minneapolis: University of Minnesota Press, 2019.

Golumbia, David. *The Cultural Logic of Computation.* Cambridge, Mass.: Harvard University Press, 2009.

Kirschenbaum, Matthew. "What Is Digital Humanities and What's It Doing in English Departments?" In *Debates in the Digital Humanities 2012,* edited by Matthew K. Gold. Minneapolis: University of Minnesota Press, 2012.

Klein, Lauren F., and Matthew K. Gold. "Introduction: Digital Humanities: The Expanded Field." In *Debates in the Digital Humanities 2016,* edited by Matthew K. Gold and Lauren F. Klein. Minneapolis: University of Minnesota Press, 2016.

Latour, Bruno. "Anti-Zoom." In *Scale in Literature and Culture,* edited by David Wittenberg and Michael Tavel Clarke. London: Palgrave, 2017.

Latour, Bruno. "Networks, Societies, Spheres: Reflections of an Actor-Network Theorist." In *International Seminar on Network Theory: Network Multidimensionality in the Digital Age.* Los Angeles: Annenberg School for Communication and Journalism, 2010.

Latour, Bruno. *Reassembling the Social: An Introduction to Actor-Network Theory.* Oxford: Oxford University Press, 2005.

Latour, Bruno. "Why Has Critique Run Out of Steam? From Matters of Fact to Matters of Concern." *Critical Inquiry* 30, no. 2 (Winter 2004): 225–48.

Law, John, and Marianne Elisabeth Lien. "Slippery: Field Notes in Empirical Ontology." *Social Studies of Science* 43, no. 3 (2013).

Liming, Sheila. "Fighting Words." *Los Angeles Review of Books.* December 14, 2020, https://lareviewofbooks.org/article/fighting-words/.

Lossin, R. H. "Neoliberalism for Polite Company: Bruno Latour's Pseudo-Materialist Coup." *Salvage # 7: Towards the Proletarocene* (2019).

Lothian, Alexis, and Amanda Phillips. "Can Digital Humanities Mean Transformative Critique?" *e-Media Studies* 3, no. 1 (2013).

Malazita, James W. "Epistemic Infrastructure, the Instrumental Turn, and the Digital Humanities." In *People, Practice, Power: Digital Humanities Outside the Center,* edited by Anne B. McGrail, Angel David Nieves, and Siobhan Senier. Minneapolis: University of Minnesota Press, 2021.

Malazita, James W. "Re: Configurations: A Shared Project for Literature and Science." *Configurations* 25, no. 3 (2018): 269–75.

McPherson, Tara. "Designing for Difference." *differences* 25, no. 1 (2014).

McPherson, Tara. "Why Are the Digital Humanities So White? Or Thinking the Histories of Race and Computation." In *Debates in the Digital Humanities 2012,* edited by Matthew K. Gold. Minneapolis: University of Minnesota Press, 2012.

Nelson, Lee. "Bourdieu and Latour in STS: 'Let's Leave Aside All the Facts for a While.'" Master's thesis. University of British Columbia, 2014.

Noble, Safiya Umoja. "Toward a Critical Black Digital Humanities." In *Debates in the Digital Humanities 2019,* edited by Matthew K. Gold and Lauren F. Klein. Minneapolis: University of Minnesota Press, 2019.

Presner, T. "Critical Theory and the Mangle of Digital Humanities." In *Between Humanities and the Digital,* edited by Patrik Svensson and David Theo Goldberg. Cambridge, Mass.: MIT Press, 2015.

Risam, Roopika. *New Digital Worlds: Postcolonial Digital Humanities in Theory, Praxis, and Pedagogy.* Evanston, Ill.: Northwestern University Press, 2019.

Risam, Roopika, and Adeline Koh. "Postcolonial Digital Humanities Mission Statement." Accessed August 25, 2022, http://dhpoco.org/mission-statement-postcolonial-digital-humanities/.

Shrout, Anelise Hanson. "(Re)Humanizing Data: Digitally Navigating the Bellevue Almshouse." *Current Research in Digital History* 1, no. 1 (2018).

Svensson, Patrik. "Beyond the Big Tent." In *Debates in the Digital Humanities 2012,* edited by Matthew K. Gold. Minneapolis: University of Minnesota Press, 2012.

Terras, Melissa M. "Infographic: Quantifying Digital Humanities." *UCL Centre for Digital Humanities Blog.* 2012, https://blogs.ucl.ac.uk/dh/2012/01/20/infographic-quantifying-digital-humanities/.

Van Gorp, Jasmin, and Marc Bron. "Building Bridges: Collaboration between Computer Sciences and Media Studies in a Television Archive Project." *DHQ: Digital Humanities Quarterly* 13, no. 3 (2019).

Venturini, Tommaso, Anders Kristian Munk, and Mathieu Jacomy. "Actor-Network versus Network Analysis versus Digital Networks: Are We Talking about the Same Networks?" In *digitalSTS: A Field Guide for Science & Technology Studies,* edited by Janet Vertesi and David Ribes, 510–523. Princeton, N.J.: Princeton University Press, 2019.

Wilder, Laura. " 'The Rhetoric of Literary Criticism' Revisited: Mistaken Critics, Complex Contexts, and Social Justice." *Written Communication* 22, no. 1 (2005).

PART V

FORUM

#UnsilencedPast

KAIAMA L. GLOVER

Whenever [Black] women speak, they displease, shock, or disturb.

—Maryse Condé, "Order, Disorder, Freedom, and the West Indian Writer"

At the end of the month of May 2020, a forty-six-year-old Black man named George Floyd was killed by members of the Minneapolis Police Department. In the wake of his killing, the perennial question of whether or not Black lives truly matter in the United States came to the fore with renewed urgency and extraordinary global reach. Over the weeks and months that followed, both mainstream and social media sought to grapple with this tragedy, and scholars and intellectuals in particular seemed to feel intensely the heightened stakes of their public engagement.

As the world turned feverishly to Twitter to try to gain some sort of purchase on a moment that felt at once utterly despairing and somehow full with possibility, two related but contradictory phenomena came into view. On the one hand, a persistent rhetoric of surprise punctuated our media world: "How could this have happened? In 2020? In the United States?" Countless voices lamented as we watched (or could not bear to watch) a uniformed officer of the law kneel on the neck of an unarmed Black man. Then, as videos of local, state, and federal police tear-gassing, kettling, and otherwise brutalizing peaceful protestors surfaced, the bewilderment and righteous outrage intensified measurably: "American citizens treated like enemy combatants as they exercise their First Amendment freedoms of speech and of assembly? How could this be?" wondered the internet across six continents.

On the other hand, and in parallel to these expressions of shocked indignation, an unofficial cohort of Black women scholars—historians in the main, but not exclusively so—had also taken to Twitter, television, and radio, and to the op-ed pages of various print and online publications, to call bullsh*t on this narrative. And they had receipts. This moment, they declared, is nothing new under the sun. We have no right to be surprised. If what is happening feels "unheard of" or "unprecedented" or in any way astounding, then shame on us all for not seeing, not hearing, and not acknowledging our own history.

The #UnsilencedPast project emerged as a direct counter to the disingenuousness of a worldwide "awokening" that in many ways elided the unfettered police violence and equally persistent anti-racist practices of refusal that mark our national and global past. In four weekly conversations, convened and moderated by Kaiama L. Glover, professor of French and Africana studies and faculty director of the Digital Humanities Center at Barnard College, Columbia University, the series sought to highlight the vanguardist work of eight Black women academics: Marlene L. Daut and Annette Joseph-Gabriel, Kim Gallon and Marisa Parham, Mame-Fatou Niang and Maboula Soumahoro, and Jessica Marie Johnson and Martha Jones, women who used the digital humanities and social and other media to intervene in this moment from perspectives rigorously grounded in historical knowledge.

The liberationist imperative that so thoroughly animates each one of these scholars' contributions speaks to the too-often silenced past of knowledge production and struggle on the part of those who have been most marginalized by white supremacy and its constitutive structures of domination. Taking Haitian anthropologist Michel-Rolph Trouillot's foundational 1995 work *Silencing the Past: Power and the Production of History* as their point of departure, the conversations we held in July 2020 were premised on the understanding that silence is a verb. As such, they proceeded from a committed refusal to be quiet or quieted, even at the risk of displeasing, shocking, or disturbing adversaries and would-be allies alike. More precisely, these dialogues make clear how we as Black women in particular have staked claims to unsilenced humanist inquiry within the potentially generative but necessarily perilous space of the digital humanities and the wider online world.

#UnsilencedPast signaled a specific response to this moment's exceptionally muscular call for us all to mobilize whatever platforms we have at our disposal in thoughtful and immediate service to the project of racial and social justice in our local, national, and global communities. Inasmuch as the university has called on us to embrace the digital as a space of pedagogical innovation and enrichment, it felt particularly important to go beyond discursive claims. It felt important to use our resources, both human and capital, to engage decisively with the world beyond our campuses—to put our time and money where our mouths are—and to do so in step with that world, without limiting our interventions to the chronology of the academic calendar or to the brick-and-mortar space of our campuses.

These were the aims we aspired to meet, the call we aspired to answer in convening these conversations among these scholars in the summer of 2020. We know well that the tragic moment in time that inspired us to gather has by no means passed, and so the urgency that runs through each conversation is as deeply resonant now as it was then. We know, too, that while we cannot undo the past of our unconscionable present, we can commit to intervening persistently throughout the networks of our digitally expanded world. We can commit to demanding alternative futures. We can keep choosing to remain disorderly and unsilenced.

Being Undisciplined: Black Womanhood in Digital Spaces

A CONVERSATION WITH MARLENE L. DAUT
AND ANNETTE K. JOSEPH-GABRIEL

KAIAMA L. GLOVER (KLG): I will start by asking you to reflect on the ideas that frame the conversation we are going to have today: Michel-Rolph Trouillot's concept of silencing the past and Maryse Condé's evocation of the particular disorder presented by women, as these two notions relate to your work.

ANNETTE K. JOSEPH-GABRIEL (AKJG): I really appreciate your framing of this series of conversations through the lens of Condé's essay, "Order, Disorder, Freedom, and the West Indian Writer," because I think order, disorder, and freedom, and the West Indian writer are really pertinent intellectual lenses to be thinking through in this moment.

There's a part of that essay that I want to quote because I think it's a really useful way to begin our conversation. Condé, when she's talking about women writers, says, "In a Bambara myth of origin, after the creation of the earth and the organization of everything on its surface, disorder was introduced by a woman. Disorder meant the power to create new objects and to modify existing ones. In a word, disorder meant creativity." And I want to dwell on this word *creativity,* because when we think about the context for our conversation—about how Black women enter digital spaces, how Black women are present in digital spaces, how they use digital tools—we tend to think in terms of newness, in terms of novelty, in terms of departure from order.

But Condé is situating this in the myth of origin. It nudges us not just to think about creativity in terms of creation but also in terms of the ability to bring alternate worlds into being. Worlds that are against order. Because "order" doesn't just say, this is how things are. "Order" says, this is how things should be. Order isn't just descriptive; it's prescriptive. So how do we introduce *disorder* into this sort of order, this prescribed silencing?

Currently, I'm thinking a lot with Shirley Graham Du Bois, who reflects on how we use technological advancements. How do we use tech tools in the work that we seek to do? Graham Du Bois is thinking a lot about the origins, the functioning, and the technical details of the new technologies that she hoped to use in the twentieth century in Black liberation struggles. So alongside Condé's quote, I want to add a quote from Graham Du Bois. I like the idea of a constellation of women thinkers, of Black women thinkers.

This quote is from a moment in history, in 1962–1963, when Graham Du Bois is working as a founding director of the Ghana Broadcasting Corporation. Now, we're talking DH [digital humanities] today, so radio and TV might seem quaint and antiquated in some ways.

KLG: But technology is technology.

AKJG: Technology is technology, right. And in that moment, radio and TV was that newness. So Graham Du Bois travels to Europe to visit the BBC to see how they are working with broadcasting and to think about how to implement a similar system in the newly independent Ghana. She writes to Kwame Nkrumah, who was Ghana's president, and asks, "What line system does Ghana plan to use? Great Britain at present uses 405 lines. Channel Two, however, is being set up to use 625 lines, and as soon as possible, the old channel will switch to 625. All Europe today, including the Soviet Union, excluding France, uses 625 lines for television broadcast. But the United States and Canada have always used 525 lines. Now, most of our technicians are being trained in the United States and Canada, will Ghana therefore use 525 lines for broadcast, which will bind her to the United States and Canada, but separate us from Europe?"

I always pause at this moment when I read this letter because it is entirely gibberish! I have no idea what "lines" are, or how broadcasting works. But I am struck by the fact that the letter is so technical in its detail. Graham Du Bois was attuned to the relationship between function and content. For her, asking how many lines will be used for broadcasting is also about asking to whom her voice, to whom Ghanaian voices, will be bound. So, to return to our conversation about unsilencing, speaking out, articulating ideas, and sharing histories through digital media, I want to ask: To whom do these technologies tether us? And are those bonds or ties ones that we can live with? That's where I am in my thinking right now.

For example, I work a lot with digital maps. My project, *Mapping Marronage,*[1] tries to show how enslaved people in the eighteenth and nineteenth centuries moved through the Atlantic and asks questions about liberation and its connection to mobility. In the beginning, I was seduced by the idea of having Google Maps as the base layer for my map. I liked the idea of "Powered by Google" because it sounded like you could do so much. But knowing that Google Maps was founded on a desire and need for surveillance, it seemed to counter the very things I was trying to show.

Also, Google's linear way of mapping didn't work for this kind of mobility. These people's movement was a lot messier.

Mapping Marronage is my attempt to account for that mess through a network map as opposed to a linear map. When you go to the site, you can choose to see two kinds of maps: flight and networks. You can also select a short biography of someone who's featured on the map. These multiple options trouble the linear map as well as the standard triangular frame for thinking about the geography of the Atlantic. More generally, the project shows how movement can be subversive and how movement can be generative.

So, that's where my thinking is currently in terms of questions about silencing, unsilencing, and the way that Black women introduce disorder into oppressive orders using digital tools.

KLG: Thank you, Annette. Marlene, I am going to ask you to pick up the ball and run with it.

[Editors' note: At this point in the conversation, an anonymous listener directed a racist comment at Joseph-Gabriel in the chat.]

MARLENE L. DAUT (MLD): I'm going to pick up the ball. I'm also going to address what just happened in the chat, because it is about unsilencing. When Annette was talking, I was thinking about another word: discipline. Part of discipline is imposing order, but another part is to discipline when there is disorder. We talk a lot now in the U.S. academy about interdisciplinarity. I work in two interdisciplinary departments, African American studies and American studies, and I've often wondered if it is enough to be interdisciplinary. Maybe we need to be undisciplined instead.

I noticed that the comment in the chat had the word "speaking" in it. That made me think of Tracy Sharpley-Whiting's term, "seen invisibility," the condition for Black women when we are simultaneously seen and not seen. And then reflecting on Mame-Fatou Niang's comments on Twitter the other day, when she was advertising this event, and she said, "It is not that people don't have a voice, it's that people don't listen." It's not even that they're not heard—it's not passive—it's very active that people have willfully sought not to listen.

This idea both complicates and extends Trouillot's concept of silencing. Because we use the word "silencing" a lot, but you really can't silence people unless you actually kill them. This is actually the metaphor that Trouillot uses. He says, "You silence like you silence with a gun." But this is a metaphor. Reflecting on what it means for us, as Black women, to constantly position ourselves or think of ourselves as people without voices when we see very strongly that we are speaking. And when we teach, I feel like it comes to the fore even more strongly. For example, when I am teaching Mary Prince and talking about the mediated voice and Prince's subject position, the students' response is, "Well, she's not silenced, though."

But what sort of voice can be heard? And how can it be heard, and who's listening? I think that's the larger issue for me, especially working in Haitian studies. In Haitian studies, you get these statements like, "No one has studied this!" or "No one has studied that!" I don't want to constantly be that person who says, "Yes, the Haitians have! In the nineteenth century! Louis-Joseph Janvier! Antenor Firmin!" And yet, I think it's so important to say because it's just that people chose not to listen—they chose not to read, they chose not to engage, they chose to say that everyone is a Marxist, they chose to say that people were reading Foucault, and they chose not to look at how Frederick Douglass made statements about power and who has it, and how you can defeat it, many decades before Foucault.

To me, it's the condition of seen invisibility that I constantly think about in relationship to my own work, and in relation to the various issues that I know we are going to get to later—that have recently erupted online and in digital spaces but that have really always been there. This moment of incredible wakefulness, or wokefulness, or whatever you want to call it, is baffling to anyone who's really been paying attention. I grew up in Inglewood, California. I knew about police violence in the eighties. I never thought it was new when Michael Brown happened, or when Ferguson happened. And it was baffling to me that it was new for so many people, that they had forgotten about Rodney King, that they had forgotten about all the women and children throughout the years who were killed by police.

So I want to rest on that idea that silencing is actually an active process. It's not passive. It is something that people do, and it is something that they try to do to others. Again, that Trouillot statement about silence, like when you put a silencer on a gun. It is something that you actively have to do because guns are very, very, very loud, and everyone hears them for miles around when they go off—unless you do this very active thing.

With that said, today what I want to introduce, before we jump to the next topic, is *La Gazette*.[2] It's a website of Haitian newspapers from the nineteenth century. I did not discover them. The vast majority of them were cataloged, although some of them were miscataloged, because cataloging is difficult work. For the website, we collected as many issues of these newspapers as we could from the State of Haiti first and then the Kingdom of Haiti, and we transcribed them. We also made the PDFs available, with the help of many archivists around the world.

The idea was to make it less easy for people to have the excuse of inaccessibility for not consulting these documents. Because these newspapers are collected in libraries and archives all across the world: Ireland, Jamaica, various states in the United States, England, France, Haiti, etcetera. Bringing them together provides a fuller picture of what life was like under Henry Christophe, the ruler of the Kingdom of Haiti, at least from the official perspective. Hopefully, *La Gazette* makes them more accessible.

The last thing I want to say about the project relates to the concept of silencing. There are layers to the silence here. These are state-run newspapers, so they constitute the official record. They contain the stories that the state built, by Henry Christophe and his journalists, that they wanted you to remember. The vast majority of the Haitian people do not appear in these papers. These are papers about world events and the nobles of the kingdom, and, yes, anti-slavery and anti-colonialism and combating Napoleon. But they are not papers about the everyday lives of Haitian people, those who lived in the countryside, those who deliberately put themselves outside of the eye of the state, or what Jean Casimir calls the counter-plantation. To me, this is a silence that is heavy—like the statement in *Silencing the Past,* it's a silence "thrown against a superior silence." I want to bring to the fore that this is one record and one archive, but it's not *the* record or *the* archive of early nineteenth-century Haiti.

KLG: Thank you so much, Marlene. There are some keywords that thread their way through the questions I asked and the answers you all offer. In earlier conversations, I talked about frustration, and you used the word *baffling.* I think we're talking about a similar thing, which is an inability to recognize or to really grapple with the history of the present. That's one of the reasons I wanted to have this opening conversation with the two of you because I know that in your work, both analog and digital, that's what you're up to: the history of the present, refusing the rhetoric of surprise that would have us become somehow suddenly undone by what's happened yesterday, when we have accepted for so long the things that have happened so many yesterdays before.

That's what animates my next question, this question of the history of the present. Can you give me your thoughts on the idea of looking backward in this present moment, past the moment that we are often encouraged to compare it to—the 1960s? We're quite comfortable talking about the echoes of 1967 and 1968 and just before. But what the two of you have done in your work is to show that this is a longer history. Yes, a longer history of anti-Black racism and oppression, but also a long history of anti-racist struggle and achievement and success and a peeling back of these layers of silence, as you put it, Marlene. And as you said, Annette, standing before archives and not understanding everything but knowing that there's something there that deserves attention. I was hoping either of you or both of you could comment on this notion of the longer history of the present.

AKJG: The question of the history of the present is so crucial because Black uprisings and Black refusal of white supremacy—these things have existed for as long as white supremacy has existed. We think about the Haitian Revolution as one of those key moments, and there were also labor movements in the Caribbean throughout the twentieth century that were about wage theft but were also about racialized policing as part of slavery's legacy in the present.

One of the examples that comes to mind is the Affaire des 16 de Basse-Pointe, in Martinique, in 1948, when an agricultural workers' strike ended in the death of a white plantation overseer. The ensuing events were about Black workers' refusal of police violence and of racialized police violence. Most gendarmes in Martinique are white, and at that moment, police violence was used as a tool to protect property and profit for the descendants of the white planter class. Like Marlene said, we are seeing things that are not new. But at the same time, there is also a feeling of uniqueness in this moment because we are looking at the confluence of Black liberation struggle and a pandemic.

One of the ways that we can think about this beyond, or in addition to, the question about the historical moments that give us precedence is the question of how we rethink revolutionary time. What are the qualities of time, as cyclical, as linear, as disrupted, or as repetitive, that allow us to rethink ideas of progress? Because we're all trying to think about this against the backdrop of Covid-19, I've gone back to earlier Black women's writings to look at how they were thinking about the convergence of health crises and time and Black liberation struggle. And when you look specifically for that, you see it everywhere in astounding ways.

I mentioned Shirley Graham Du Bois already, but Suzanne Césaire was thinking similar things. Césaire was thinking about that with real urgency as she was battling a brain tumor. Marie Vieux-Chauvet was also thinking in terms of urgency in the context of the dictatorship and her own illness. You have lots of Black women writers who are thinking about this convergence. And then for others, it's a question of time as direction. Graham Du Bois keeps asking, over and over again, "Progress which way?" Where do we go from here? She sees time as direction. So the question becomes how we rethink revolutionary time in ways that push back against the idea of progress as technological advancement—when we are still in the same moment, and we even see a retrenchment in terms of racism and racist attitudes.

I'm trying to think a lot about how the convergence of these different things asks us to consider not just what are the historical moments that give us precedence, but also how we rethink time entirely to bring that necessary disorder into the order of the notion of progress. What kind of anti-progress narratives are Black women writers working with that allow us to think about the future that we are really trying to build and create?

MLD: I've seen so many people posing the question, "How is it different?" Which is, again, a passive question. I want to turn that around and say, "How are we going to make it different?" Because it isn't going to just be different. It will be exactly the same if we allow it to be exactly the same. In three months, six months, we'll be right back here when the next police killing happens that flashes up. Because the fact of the matter is that it's happening all the time. Almost every day, there is some account of some police brutality somewhere in the United States. So how are we going to make it different?

That's what I see in the Black women writers of the 1960s and beyond, to Toni Morrison, to Maya Angelou. They kept asking, "How is it going to be different? How are we going to make it different?" But no one was listening. Again today, we hear the refrain on Twitter, in op-eds, and online in various media, "When are you going to listen to Black women?" Again, it is up to us to provide the answers. For example, Black women have been decrying the high mortality rates of women of color for years, not just in the United States but in England, in France—but who is actually listening? I think settling on not just what we can do, but if it is other people who are asking that question, ask them how it is going to be different, and what they are going to do as well—put the question back to them.

KLG: I am trying not to get totally depressed by your answer, because it dovetails but then goes in a different direction from the way that Annette was talking about refiguring and refashioning time and our notion of cyclicality. You used the word *answers,* and obviously the three of us aren't going to come up with all of the answers in this conversation, but one thing that seems clear is that there's the listening and then there is the answering, and there needs to be some space for those two things to come together for the people who are the most capable, or have not been allowed to show their capacity to address them. That's part of the frustration as well. We have been using this expression, "the rhetoric of surprise." And this surprise comes from a sort of tunnel vision or a holding of the ears, an active silencing of the voices that are out there saying the things that need to be heard.

I've asked about time, and its partner is space. I want to ask the two of you, who work in spaces beyond the borders of the United States, to think about the importance of thinking about #BlackLivesMatter and anti-racist struggle beyond the geocultural bounds of the United States, and even beyond the geocultural bounds of U.S. Black studies and U.S. Black activism. I know the three of us are attentive to thinking more broadly about the Black diaspora and its expression in other places, but these places are not often brought into the conversation because just as the U.S. is hegemonic, or has been hegemonic, broadly speaking, U.S. Black studies and U.S. Black voices have also been rather hegemonic in diasporic thinking with Blackness globally. Can you talk about the places that you work on, outside the United States?

AKJG: In the same way that Black refusal of white supremacy has existed for as long as white supremacy, Black uprisings have also refused the limited boundaries of what the local means. Police violence in the United States is also local in relation to police violence in France. There's this astounding mural right now in Paris which juxtaposes the faces of George Floyd and Adama Traoré, which makes a powerful statement about how we think and rethink the local, and how we think and rethink space. For example, Suzanne Césaire's archipelagic thinking is one that connects Martinique not just to France as the imperial power but also to Puerto Rico and Haiti as sites of U.S. imperial aggression.

Looking at the Caribbean is one way to rethink how we think about space, how we think about spaces that are contiguous, and how we think about the idea of the local. There's a quote by Ramon Grosfoguel that I really appreciate, which says that a global problem cannot have a national solution. We are talking about policing, police violence, anti-Black violence in the United States, but we need to understand those as manifestations of the global problem of white supremacy.

I always get so frustrated because sometimes in conversations online, you'll have a smug European who jumps in and says, "Well, in Denmark, things are not as bad as the U.S." And I'm like, "Who are you speaking to in Denmark? Who are you speaking to in the Netherlands? Who are you speaking to in France, and do you think their experience resonates with yours? Or are you going to enact that kind of holding the ears and being surprised because you are being forced to confront a reality that you have always hoped was not the case?"

So, the ways that we should think about space as a set of continuous repeating manifestations of a global problem, which is global white supremacy, is something that the Caribbean can point us toward. Especially because of its geographic terrain—of islands that are not closed off—the archipelago is asking us to think about islands that open out in the rest of the world. The way Suzanne Césaire asks us to think about archipelagic concepts of space is one way that really forces us to grapple with the global nature of this problem.

The last thing I'll say is that sometimes when we think about U.S. imperial aggression, we think about it as projected outward. But if we go to *Discourse on Colonialism,* Aimé Césaire reminds us that in Europe, for example, the violence that it had previously turned outward on the colonies eventually came home to roost, as manifested in Nazism. The fascism that we see internally, in the spaces we're in currently, are always continuations of the imperialism that is projected outward. To think about space as neighboring and contiguous spaces as opposed to as separate ones is a really helpful framework.

MLD: As Annette was talking, it made me think about the passage in *The Wretched of the Earth* where Frantz Fanon says the goal cannot be to replace a white police officer with a Black police officer. One of the things that happens when you take a more global perspective is that it becomes clear that the color of the police officer is not the only problem, but policing itself is a problem. We cannot reform policing. We have to reimagine what it means to live communally with other people with a sense of justice while also preserving freedom. When you look at a case like Haiti, and you look at the Tonton Makouts, you can very clearly see that violence and brutality are baked into the concept of policing itself.

For another example, in eighteenth century France with the Police des Noirs, we see the very word *police,* and the policing of Black people, at this very early date. So the Europeans, who want to point the finger—literally had a body called the Police des Noirs and made codes and laws that were specifically targeted at Black people: the Black codes. These laws and policing and surveillance that have been around far before the internet, broadcast television, radio—all of these techniques—are really just ways of shoring up and making it easier to do what the state has always sought to do, which is to police its inhabitants and to lure them into a false sense of security.

Now, when you talk about abolishing the police, people come up with the most absurd scenarios like, "What if you're kidnapped for seven days and thrown into the Grand Canyon?" That's what they imagine will happen if the police are abolished, instead of using their imaginations—the same imaginations that brought us Google, that brought us the iPhone, that brought us people in screens like us now talking—to think of a better way to organize society with a sense of justice and freedom. I think of bell hooks and what she calls "feminist masculinity"—the idea that we can teach ourselves to love justice and freedom while not giving into the patriarchal idea that the way to achieve justice is to discipline bodies, to put people in prison, to throw them in the back of police cars when they don't behave exactly the way that you want them to. To be sure, it's not an easy question, and as Kaiama mentioned, we are not going to come up with the answer here. But I do think the conversation starts by posing the question as legitimate, not as a radical or crazy.

This should be a question that everybody wants to answer, not just people who are the victims, or the biggest victims I should say, because really, policing is dangerous for everyone. That is something that some people learned for the first time during the George Floyd protests. When they saw police shoving an elderly white man down to the ground, when they found themselves tear-gassed, when someone—a white woman—died from being tear-gassed, when Heather Heyer was killed in Charlottesville. They have learned that policing and white supremacy are dangerous for everyone. That was really Frantz Fanon and Aimé Césaire's point, and so many others, that you're not safe from this. You might be safer in numbers, but you as an individual can also fall prey to it. So that's what I would like to see, this sort of imagination, what Edward Brathwaite calls the womb of space. Let's use this and let's think more deeply about it.

KLG: I promise after this we'll get back to DH. But picking up on Annette's really rich encouragement to think of both time and space less teleologically and less linearly and less bordered, and thinking back to the idea of the Black code, and the Police des Noirs, and how these are things from the European past—the inability of, let's say, certain Europeans to recognize the persistence of that past in their present and in our present is part of the inability to see the concentric circles of time. Rather than say, "Oh, that's part of our past. We have progressed to a new place but the U.S. is still stuck in that place," when in fact that same claim of progressiveness is what enables them to do things like take race out of the constitution—you would have thought that we learned our lesson about the impossibility of post-racial societies. But that's still being dangled as the carrot that the U.S. somehow has not managed to get to. It goes back again to what you both stated, which is this inability to see the inextricability of the past in our present.

I also wanted to put out into the world a term that I love so much, from your book, Annette, in the introduction: the "geographies of resistance." I've been thinking a lot about reconceptualizations of space and the offerings that Black women scholars have given us to reconceptualize space. Katherine McKittrick's *Demonic Grounds* is another one, of course. But this we can save for later.

I need to bring us back to the digital, and the digital humanities pedagogical tools that the two of you have put together—Marlene, primarily your curated digital archives, and Annette, the mapping visualizations. They are useful within the classroom and in a research context. And you also recognize that this is knowledge and information that plenty of folks out in the nonacademic world clearly need. So I want to ask you to think from inside the classroom space to the outside, to the possibilities and the perils of public or online scholarship, and we can certainly get into but hopefully not be undone by what happened recently on H-France.

AKJG: The primary utility of doing digital work with students in the classroom is a sense of accountability. Because the students immediately feel accountable to a wider audience. The site I just described, Mapping Marronage, is entirely student-produced, save the profile of one person that I set up as a model. The content was produced in the context of a class, and I structured the entire course around the map. The project is different from a paper, where they have to perform the kind of knowledge they think I want them to have. Instead, they're accountable to a larger audience. But—and this is not something that I quite factored in when I began teaching the course—the students also feel accountable to the people that they are writing about. They feel accountable to the enslaved people whose narratives they are bringing to the fore. I had one student who went up to Montreal, to photograph sites where she thought Marie-Joseph Angelique might have been or might have fled, and brought those back as images to overlay on the map.

Students felt responsible for doing this right. I am still trying to interrogate with them what it means to tell someone's story the right way. But I found that conversation to be really generative. Students always feel a lot more beholden to a larger audience outside the classroom. But to the historical figures that they're writing about as well? The promises and perils are many. Hopefully, the promises outweigh the perils because we are still doing this. To be honest, one of the promises for me is being in constant conversation with the community outside of the privileged and hallowed halls of the academy, because much as my students feel accountable to the people they're writing about, I too feel accountable to the communities that we write about, that we study, that we think with. So, having that opening out into that wider community is, I think, one of the promises of doing DH work.

And then also the ability to escape institutional mandates and accounting. Who matters, what matters, what kind of work matters? A lot of the things that you shared in introducing me, Kaiama, are things that I realized, much to my chagrin, are not on my CV because I don't know how to account for them in institutional language. To hear them be the things that are valuable for this conversation is interesting to me because it suggests the need for a rethinking of what is valued, and that even if an institution will not value those things, then we must ask how we determine and shape value for ourselves. I don't think that I will ever put them on my CV because maybe the idea of marronage—the escape from that institutional accounting—the idea that this kind of work for me will remain outside of that framework of productivity might be helpful. For me, those are the promises.

The perils are many, as we saw in the chat, and as we saw with some of the recent kerfuffles on message boards and such about what kind of history you want to remember, who you want to remember in history, and even what the purpose of history is. I think that what we need more conversation around in DH is how we think about protecting ourselves and our work but thinking about protection outside the framework of gatekeeping and exclusion. I haven't yet found that balance, and doing editorial work online is one of those moments where I ask myself, "At which point are we gatekeeping and excluding? At which point are we doing the necessary work of protecting people who are targeted and victimized by vitriol online?" I think that finding the balance is a potential promise, but right now feels a lot more perilous than promising.

MLD: I really appreciate this discussion about "does this go on the CV or not," because I had that same sort of discussion with myself when I remember going up for tenure—like, "Oh, should I put this website on there?" And then someone said, "Just don't introduce that as a question that your committee might not know how to understand." Now, there's a different question, and I'm not sure if it's a problem or not, but it's interesting to think about. Maybe a CV is a problematic gatekeeping thing in and of itself, and the goal shouldn't be to have more kinds of things eligible to put on the CV. Maybe the goal is to rethink what accountability looks like. Somebody being really valued by the community that they're engaging with can't ever go on a CV, but it is far more important than whatever journal or whatever the outside reviewers think, right? At least I hope.

With the *Gazette* website that I discussed earlier, one of the most surprising ways in which it has been used is by genealogists in Haiti who are going back through the almanacs and the newspapers and finding information about their family members to construct family trees and family histories. It wasn't what I had intended when I thought of putting these papers online. I also wasn't sure if we should transcribe the almanacs because they are over one hundred pages each, and mostly lists and lists and lists of names, but there are also all kinds of symbols and corresponding legends to tell you who each of those people on the lists were, and we need those symbols to be there to understand the full significance of the almanacs. I couldn't just leave them out.

Initially, I thought it might just be enough to put those PDFs there and make them accessible. But it was the searchability of the transcription that really allowed people to use the website for genealogical projects. So then, thanks to the Institute for Advanced Technology in the Humanities at UVA [the University of Virginia] that funded the transcription of the almanacs—because the site was done with essentially no funding before that—which preserved not only the diacritics but all the symbols, it allowed the site to have this life and accountability that is greater and more wonderful than I had ever imagined because it became a kinship project, and it was allowing people to connect.

The last thing I will say is that barriers to entry is one of the reasons I first began to be interested in digital humanities and digital archiving. Because if you are at these really well-funded universities, you're getting grants to go to archives all over the world, and you're collecting all of these documents. The typical scholarly model is that you hold these documents precious and they are yours, and then you write a story about them and you're the only one who has access to them. When you read a lot of historiography from the 1990s and early 2000s, and certainly from before that, it's all about how this one person gained access to this archive, and they're the only person. It's just a way to gatekeep and keep other people out. That's a way to keep independent scholars from having access; it's a way to keep high school teachers who are engaged in a lot of digital humanities projects and a lot of public scholarship from having access. It's a way to keep the communities that are "understudied" from having access, as well as scholars from institutions where they don't have the same kind of access to institutionalized capital. So one of the reasons I wanted to do the project, and was encouraged by a general climate in which others were already doing this type of work, was just to put these documents out there. Let's see what others have to say and what they will do, just like with the *Gazette* newspapers. And they always do something beyond what you could even have imagined yourself.

To the question of pedagogy and teaching, I would say that the digital humanities projects that I have done, and when I taught the Caribbean Digital—which was riffing off the conference with Kaiama and Alex Gil and Kelly Baker Josephs—the students knew that other people inside of UVA who wanted to use this same software would be able to see what they did. And they knew that the class, because they had to do a presentation, would see it. And they knew that the other people in their group were counting on them. So even though collaboration is something that some people are better at it than other people, and some people like it more than other people, it has a way of encouraging a kind of accountability that, when we're the lone sojourner, as Frances Smith Foster says, "Creative collaboration is as African American as sweet potato pie." That's her phrase.

I think that in the digital humanities, collaboration is the only way to get many of these projects done, especially for someone like me, who doesn't have the coding skills to be able to create an apparatus for a website myself. I need help, and that help is just as intellectual and baked into the project. There is so much dialogue happening, and forgetting that obscures the community-based aspect of digital humanities. That's what we are doing in the classroom as well, creating a community and a space for these dialogues to happen.

NOTES

1. http://mapping-marronage.rll.lsa.umich.edu/.
2. http://lagazetteroyale.com/.

BIBLIOGRAPHY

Casimir, Jean. *The Haitians: A Decolonial History*. Translated by Laurent Dubois. Chapel Hill: University of North Carolina Press, 2020.

Césaire, Aimé. *Discourse on Colonialism*. Translated by Joan Pinkham. New York: Monthly Review Press, 2000.

Condé, Maryse. "Order, Disorder, Freedom, and the West Indian Writer." *Yale French Studies*, no. 97 (2000): 151–65, https://doi.org/10.2307/2903218.

Fanon, Frantz. *The Wretched of the Earth*. Translated by Richard Philcox. New York: Grove Press, 2021.

Joseph-Gabriel, Annette K. *Reimagining Liberation: How Black Women Transformed Citizenship in the French Empire*. Urbana: University of Illinois Press, 2020.

McKittrick, Katherine. *Demonic Grounds: Black Women and the Cartographies of Struggle*. Minneapolis: University of Minnesota Press, 2006.

Trouillot, Michel-Rolph. *Silencing the Past: Power and the Production of History*. Translated by Hazel V. Carby. Boston: Beacon Press, 2015.

How This Helps Us Get Free: Telling Black Stories through Technology

A CONVERSATION WITH KIM GALLON AND MARISA PARHAM

KAIAMA L. GLOVER (KLG): I am going to start off the way I did last time, by asking each of you to reflect on the ideas that are framing our conversation—notably Michel-Rolph Trouillot's call to consider silence in relation to history and power, and Maryse Condé's insistence on the creative disorder generated by women. Can you situate yourselves with respect to those two framing ideas?

KIM GALLON (KG): Thank you for inviting me to be a part of this really important conversation. I am so honored to be able to speak a little bit about some of the ideas that I have been working with around technology and Blackness and then more specifically health, and health in the context of Covid-19. Thinking about this notion of silencing and Trouillot's work, as a historian, and as a Black historian and a historian of Black life, this notion of unsilencing is an incredible way to think about digital humanities and Black digital humanities in this particular moment. We can look at how Trouillot talks about the notion of silencing in terms of the making of the sources, the making of archives, the making of narratives, and the making of history. The work that we do at COVID Black, which is at the intersection of health data, information, the humanities, race, and social justice, anticipates silences, quite frankly. To already expect a silencing in this particular moment, what it means to be Black in this particular moment, and what it means to be human in this particular moment.

It can be really challenging to think about anticipating silencing. To think about how to do that work in the humanities, how to act as an early responder to the silencing. It requires a certain level of agility because of the way that power works, because of the way that silencing works. It is a moving target. So if we think most recently about the [Donald] Trump administration's demand that Covid data come to the Trump administration before it goes to the CDC [Centers for Disease Control and Prevention], then what does that mean for the work that we do at COVID

Black, or any other sort of work that's trying to make sure that this present moment isn't constructed as erasure?

I'll share just quickly one of the ways that we are doing that at COVID Black, and it is to think about how to recover already lost data, if you will. We have created a huge spreadsheet that takes the lives of Black people that have succumbed to Covid-19 and tries to convert that to what the assistant director of COVID Black, Faithe Day, calls "Black Living Data"—data for and by Black people that captures the essence of Black life and community.[1] How do we take these numbers and these names and humanize them? How do we move them to the point of actually thinking of them as Black living data? So, we are painstakingly combing through and collecting the information about Black life and death that we can find online in this time of Covid. We're trying to think about how to take this information from a spreadsheet and transform it into what will be a digital memorial, to create narratives that can unsilence the active silencing that's actually going on in the world.

COVID Black is less invested in trying to actually construct the past than it is in thinking about how silencing works. And again, about anticipating that silencing. We are caught up in this multilayered notion of silencing, as Black women who are doing this work—and if we think about Condé's quote about how when Black women speak, or when women speak, they are being disruptive and disordered, or disorderly, if you will. But it's interesting. We are in a moment when Black women's voices, bodies, and presence are hyper-visible in ways that we haven't yet necessarily seen.

If we even think about the possible pick for the Democratic vice president, several Black women's names have been floated. Or if we think about the visibility of Dr. Uché Blackstock and Dr. Nomi Blackstock in terms of Covid-19. But the parallel reality is that we can't get justice for Breonna Taylor's death. Just to call out her murderers, Myles Cosgrove, Brett Hankison, and Jonathan Mattingly—someone reminded me on Twitter that we need to call out these people's names in our call for justice.

KLG: Thank you, Kim. Before we go on to Marisa, can I ask you to give us the two-second description of COVID Black?

KG: Sure. COVID Black started with me raging on a Saturday afternoon when the data came out, raging and tweeting. From there, I quickly joined forces with Faithe Day and Nishani Frazier to think about what an early response to Covid looks like from a Black digital humanities perspective. What this looks like is creating digital tools and technologies that respond to the very real crisis that's being highlighted about the disparities in Black health outcomes. But COVID Black exceeds the notion of Covid-19, if you will, in reflecting more expansive thinking about how the humanities can work in intersectional ways and how to think about Black people's lives and their lived experiences from a Black health perspective.

KLG: Thanks so much, Kim. All right. Marisa, you're up.

MARISA PARHAM (MP): I was thinking about your opening questions and about how we see this question in this moment. If you think back to the earliest days of Covid, combined with the various Black Lives Matter resistance moments around the country, so many Black people and people of color lead with, "This is exhausting." I've been thinking a lot about that, and I've been thinking in my work about the real question about what it means to actually live in a differential time and space. That's just a fancy way of saying that the things that feel really new to some people feel really old to others. Navigating that becomes deeply problematic from the perspective of even the notion of silence or speaking, right? Is one silent because they've been silenced or because speaking is experienced as a repetition of harm?

We know, for instance, that if we are thinking about this from a trauma studies perspective, we are thinking about the difference between a person being "silent" and a person going unheard because they carry a plaint or complaint that is in some way inadmissible, unacceptable, or fundamentally unspeakable in the moment of response. I really like the #UnsilencedPast hashtag because the "silence" in Trouillot's formulation to me feels very active, and pairing it with a hashtag foregrounds silence as something that might thrum below mainstream epistemologies. There's no such thing as silence in most settings. We're all almost always emitting or expressing some kind of transmission, and the forms and possibilities of those transmissions are deeply contingent upon whether or not there is a person in that space who knows how to hear it. Even a person who's actively not speaking might still be saying something, but it's information on a different register, what the poet Bob Kaufman might have recognized as knowledge emerging from the space between beats, or what in *Invisible Man* Ralph Ellison articulates as ultimately transmitted on a lower frequency (Kaufman). It goes unspoken, but it also speaks volumes, if you know how to hear it. In my recent work I foreground unsilencing by using digital methods to demonstrate how the very terms and forms of my speaking are often discursively differential. In expanding what we've inherited from Black art, its attention to this difference, how might we use our digital scholarship to counterbalance hegemonic discursive frames, both by unlocking what feel like self-authorized possibilities for utterance and also by offering improved modalities for listening?

I'm also thinking about the difference between speaking and responding. There's always that moment when you are having a difficult conversation with someone—this happens at institutions all the time—who wants to ask you a question about racism or about misogyny or "your experience" or etcetera, and they frame it immediately as a debate. In that setting, I'm always like, "This is not really me speaking because you are merely using me so that you might summon forth your imagination of me. I'm simply being called to the floor to somehow respond to your needs, not to tell you what I actually think you need to hear."

Of course, there are all kinds of moments when we want to make valuable responses. So I'm thinking also about this and what it means for scholarship to develop digital tools and experimental techniques to "get at a way of telling," to use Simone Brown's distillation of one of the artist Mendi Obadike's use of digital work to reveal painful truths. I am really interested in taking deadly seriously Condé's call to develop representational tools that actually represent our ways of being in the world, even as we also navigate how digital tools, like the colonial languages we nonetheless transform through our use, also potentially echo the roots of various state oppressions. Condé's "creative disorder" isn't only about our presence and its effects; it's also about the often subtle tools we hone in the name of unsilence.

So it is incredibly critical to carefully interrogate how our moments of speaking are enabled, so that they don't end up reproducing the terms through which our silence first came into being. With digital tools, that can be particularly difficult. I'm thinking, Kim, about your team's spreadsheets. The work of accounting, tabulation, carries its own terrifying histories in the Americas. At the same time, in many cases the needs of contemporary communities cannot be addressed without a proper accounting of our presence and how we are impacted by various forces—impacts that otherwise go unnamed, thus leaving us to express symptoms, while the causes are left to a kind of constant misprision. Much as silence is actually rare, the power of unnaming or refusing to name is the more active version of refusing to listen or hear. This is where Trouillot is again so useful. The notion of silence itself is simply about a certain kind of state apparatus. It's a configuration of power, and what constitutes speaking and silence are themselves configurations of power.

If I could summarize, then, what I am interested in is thinking about how we can use digital tools to identify and disaggregate those kinds of workings, and to enable me to self-express, and the people around me—other Black people—to be able to self-express in ways that feel germane to their way of being in the world, rather than being locked constantly into a modality that requires response to questions that we don't actually get to write.

KLG: This is precisely why I was so excited to have the two of you speak to one another. Already, in the course of this conversation, and in the work that you do, you are in dialogue with one another around both tools and technology, and the cost of those tools—both capital cost and the emotional cost. What you both have come to is this question of health and well-being. So let's probe a bit more into this deep concern with the digital humanities, both as methodology and as object of study. Let's look at the ways in which your work is both invested in responsibly and ethically using digital humanities to get to the bottom of things and at the same time invested in querying and refashioning and refusing and inventing the tools and the methods that are available.

With COVID Black, for example, when we see this data, when we see those names, the first thing that comes to mind is: How do we think about sharing and surveillance when those become, as you said, Marisa, surfaced? And maybe Marisa, if you can take this opportunity to talk about your various means of resisting erasure, and also your refusals to work within the bounds of what's offered. I'm thinking of your research pockets, your microsites.[2] This came to mind when I was reading Saidiya Hartman's beautiful essay, in *Artforum,* where she talks about Du Bois's imaginative capacity and commitment to experimentation as "lines of flight," away from something and toward something else, something self-determined.

KG: I want to start where Marisa left off in talking about the state apparatus. I'm going to come back to the spreadsheet in a second because it is related. But it made me think again of the Condé quote about what women's voices mean. She says whenever women speak out, they displease, shock, or disturb. It made me think, yes, that's true, but what are the responses? How do women in general, and Black women specifically—what are the ways that their relationships to institutions and state apparatus bring to bear the responses to their voices?

Again, there have been lots of Black women speaking about, for example, Breonna Taylor and a whole range of things. But these institutions and state [apparatuses] act in bad faith in the sense that they don't hear Black women's voices. There's a willful neglect or dismissal of their voices. So no longer can anyone suggest, if they ever have been able to say, "We can't hear these women's voices. We didn't understand. We didn't know. We were unaware." It makes me think about this notion of surveillance and the ways that that data puts a spotlight on Black life in a way that can create vulnerability.

But starting from the standpoint that this data is not for the consumption of the state, and this data is not for the consumption of the institution that I may work for—that this data, this information, these stories, these narratives, come first and foremost from a deeply personal space. . . . As a Black woman, to think about recovery as a very personal act and a very collective act of Black people—I wouldn't suggest that starting from that standpoint doesn't mean that there will not be mistakes, flaws, or missteps that might create vulnerability, particularly from a privileged position as a Black academic. But thinking about this notion of information or data less as about needing to convince or provide evidence of these disparities, or the way that power works, and more about what this data and this information does for creating narratives and stories for Black communities to memorialize, to grieve, to mourn, to recover what it means to be Black in this moment, is a very, very different position.

I don't have any answers yet to what this actually looks like in digital form or as digital technology. We have to start off in some ways from the dehumanizing part of the spreadsheet to get the list, to get the numbers, to create order out of the information that's very disparate. But then how do we go from dehumanization to the humanity of Black people? That's the beauty, I would argue, of the digital humanities—that it requires that curiosity and both the breaking and using of digital tools and technologies.

MP: I'm thinking, Kim, about what you are saying about that willful neglect thing, the willful neglect of Black women's voices. I would even argue that what we see in the current moment, and previous moments, is actually—and this is in huge quote marks—"real love" for Black women's voices, a real craving for Black women's voices, a real seeking out of Black women's voices. It just doesn't feel that way to me as a Black woman because this love really just emerges out of an imagination of Black women's voices; this desire is not attached to any actual person.

It comes down to the multiple ways we're often asked to be signatories upon some social moment, some kind of social understanding. But the one thing that is not actually being sought is our presence. In the Black intellectual tradition we have generations of rumination on the desire for Blackness without Black people. That's all I'm saying, to be clear. But I'm also thinking about what heuristics we can use to tilt that to the side that might help us most broadly imagine our relationship in digital humanities to data itself, as the desire for Black people's voices or Black women's voices with no Black presence is a desire for data that can be carried immediately to abstraction, ignoring the messy burden of what happens between the extraction of data and the abstraction of its meaning, the "creative disorder" that also generates information. It is the desire to ask Black people to offer themselves up as a data point that can be reconfigured, cut and pasted for purposes positive and negative, but regardless disconnected from its source. I think there's some really interesting stuff to do here around catachresis, when data is understood as useful by virtue of the distance between the spreadsheet and the site of its extraction, between datum as an object and the unruly subjecthood from which is it is derived.

These, I think, are the kinds of challenges clarified by the multiple kinds of discursive and numerical inclusion that interventions like Kim's project require and thus make possible. Kim, I know you have done the deep work of evaluating what it means to scrub (organize, regularize, rectify) data and to think of that in relation to what's lost, and of thinking about data that is processed in the interest of return to its source, its people. So I won't rehearse that anymore because you can say it better than I will. This is all just a way of saying that one place my work in electronic lit and experimental scholarship intersects with yours in data and recovery in digital and health humanities is via this notion of when society wants voices without bodies or bodies without voices, and how we create communities of scholarly intervention and transformation that can dismantle the hegemonic impulses of order and control that enable extractive data practice.

In other words, I am also thinking back to that notion of lines of flight, Kaiama, and the evasion of erasure. How do you create a world in which you are always making new things, breaking what you have, but not also becoming exhausted? How do you find a freedom? These are not just rhetorical questions, of course, and they're not actually negative. At the end of every project, I ask myself, "How does this help us get free?" I am thinking about what it means to instantiate that question earlier in scholarly processes in ways that really influence our use of technology itself.

KLG: I am going to ask you to pick up on something that I am hearing come through both directly and indirectly. Phrases like the desire for data and voices without bodies. You are both demonstrating this incredible fluency in technology, paired with an insistence on the human and the corporeal and the intimate and material. So I'm going to pop in a few keywords, to borrow a term of our times, and ask you to play with them a little bit. Recovery. Sustainability. Speculation. Value. Any one of those four things. I think they are resonant with what you're bringing to us now. Do any of them intrigue you enough to think about them a little bit more out loud?

MP: I was thinking how, in ".break .dance," a digital essay I published with *archipelagos journal,* so much comes down to the various ways that Black writers are picking up the notion of speculation.[3] I love the word *speculation,* even as it also terrifies me because it is also a financial term, and we must insert a pause whenever we are thinking about Black life in the Americas through terms that carry these other simultaneous histories, like data, like speculation.

At the same time, acts of Black speculation are also an assertion of value, of belief in the self and its capacity for both personal and collective transformation; "freedom" is a speculation, a gamble, often of faith without evidence.

Throughout ".break .dance" and many of my other digital "pockets," interventions that step in, out, and across time, I find myself constantly looking for a way to balance the speculative and the evidential, which I find necessary because the drive to evidence can itself violate my rights as an individual, if I can refer back to my comments above about speaking versus responding. We all have much we can prove, but feeling that I "must" or "should" provide proof can sometimes feel like something very different: "I don't want to feel made to tell you this, but I do want you to know it." Thinking about this as a modality in digital spaces has become a different way of thinking about recovery. Sometimes there's some real sleight of hand. I just bury things. I'm not a religious person, but I do have these moments where I'm like, "Well, if God wants my reader to find this otherwise unspeakable thing, they'll find it. If they weren't meant to see it, they won't see it." Working digitally and experimentally can enable and enact modalities of unsilence, modalities through which one can offer up the things that can't necessarily be hyper-articulated, but at the moment of presentation nonetheless resonate with the viewer or the reader or the listener in ways that enable them to make their own speculations about the relationship between their own experiences and the ones I write about. One thing we learn in the balance between digital work, trauma studies, and in the enduring power of Black joy is a kind of possibility for expression and connection that doesn't just rely on denotation and bare, easily fungible, evidence.

When Kim, for instance, is working with COVID Black's spreadsheets, we need those spreadsheets because that data must be organized. But when we think about what that data becomes, that's the place where the special touch of her hand from her own experience produces newly rich opportunities for that data and its impact.

Producing opportunities for that data to actually sing. The difference between a line item and something that sends out an actual call to communities is a thing that we have to always be thinking about.

KG: That's great. I love that. So first, for me, those keywords made me think of grant applications. Sustainability. This notion of value. This idea of exhausting the text or language to demonstrate value for funding, to quantify our work and in many ways, quantify ourselves. Maybe we'll come back to this, but thinking about what Black women's work or Black people's work means in this moment when we see many organizations and institutions funding a variety of projects to intervene, and how Black women's voices particularly, in terms of trying to demonstrate their value, are still not being heard in the ways that other voices are heard.

But I also think about this notion of pleasure and how pleasure is operating at this moment for me in very complicated, very difficult ways to navigate. The pleasure of being in community with other Black women doing this work, the pleasure of working with Black women and hearing their voices—particularly Black women, but Black people in general—through these social media spaces, and creating these really interesting communities that were unbeknownst to me before COVID-19. This notion of pleasure is sitting alongside what it means to be Black in this moment, with the over-policing, the voter suppression, the dying from Covid-19, and am I even allowed, as a Black women, these moments of joy and pleasure while doing this work and meeting with my COVID Black team and working in this sort of space? What does it mean for me to think about my own humanity and to recover what it means to be a Black woman in this moment?

It is an incredibly difficult time for everyone, but being Black and human in this moment—and that is the cornerstone of the humanities as far as I'm concerned, the question of what it means to be human—I think Black people are ground zero for asking that question. So what does it mean for the humanities to be in crisis when we've had—and I'm writing about this now—a discourse from at least the 1940s and 1950s, right after World War II, that the humanities are in crisis. But that crisis of the humanities does not mention Black people, or the lived experience of what it means to be Black. You see that this notion of crisis and the humanities are intricately connected at the moment when Emmett Till was murdered, when you have the dehumanization of Black people in all sorts of ways—we can go on and on and on when we're talking specifically about that moment.

By aligning the corporal and the technological, we can look at how Black digital practice brings those two together and helps to ensure that Black people are not further dehumanized in the moment of a crisis. Blackness and technology and the digital and the humanities all sit at the intersection of those concepts and ideas.

KLG: Thank you, Kim, for bringing pleasure and intimating play into this conversation. I appreciate that enormously. I think that's what was in my mind when I was thinking, Marisa, about your microsites, for example, and running through those and feeling the joy of the flexibility and the unboundedness that's present in the fact of doing that kind of work. I also want to highlight what you said, Kim, [about] this question: What does it mean to be human—and the particularly generative response that can come from the digital humanities and the Black digital humanities? Just to add, perhaps, that to entertain this question not from a position of defensiveness, like to prove oneself human, but rather from a position of creativity, brings me back again then to Condé [and] this notion of disorder as creativity. It's not about proving that we are human but showing how to be human in ways perhaps unexpected or unimagined.

KG: I love that. I still sometimes come from a very defensive posture, of wanting to protect and keep Blackness safe, rather than thinking about Blackness as opening up and expanding. So I really appreciate this notion of the expansiveness of a Black positionality. I've been telling my colleagues, and this is probably impolitic to say, but if there's ever a moment to be unapologetically Black, it is this moment right now. Both in a very pleasurable way, but also in a very necessary way, to foreground the expediency and the value of a Black positionality—not just for Black people, but for everyone.

KLG: Pleasure, pleasure, pleasure. That, too, can be part of our conversations.

MP: Yes. And with that, and thinking about the humanities in general, every moment of crisis is also, Kim, as you point out, concurrent with a moment of opening up.

At my previous institution, every course description seemed to precipitate some sort of crisis. It was never "will this be a good class?" Or "will students take it?" It was always, "Will this destroy our curriculum?" I was like, "I'm glad you've imbued me with so much power to destroy the humanities." It was always framed with those sorts of stakes. I do, for instance, a lot of work in environmental humanities and the intersection between the environmental and digital humanities around race. At some point, I had a course description include the term "deep time." I got a response like, "If you use that term in relation to your work, I'm not sure it would have meaning anymore." I was like, "Damn. I'm very powerful." So, in thinking about this and thinking about pleasure, also in response to that notion of defensiveness, and thinking about that in relationship to the difference between owning that power and transforming it into an actual real power that's not just a precipitate of other people's paranoia—it seems like when you are working with COVID Black, Kim, you feel the pleasure of not just getting the work done but of getting it done on your terms.

KLG: I promised to be more responsible about time when I ended last week. So this is going to be my last question. It's a plea to help with something that, I would imagine, crosses many of our timelines and many of our thoughts. The frame is how pedagogical uses of the digital humanities can, in fact, endanger actual humans. I'm thinking in particular of the story that *ProPublica* broke regarding the fifteen-year-old girl who was sent to a juvenile facility for not having completed her online homework, which was a condition of her parole for another criminal offense. So, as we celebrate the digital—and that's part of what this series is, a query of digital—an opportunity arises to really think about its material impacts and specifically its material impacts on women and girls. There are not two better people I can imagine helping us think through what to make of this.

KG: I don't know if I have a good answer, but I have been thinking about this in terms of institutions. I have been studying a lot about the construction of the humanities and the institutionalization of the humanities after World War II. Then putting this in a conversation with Condé—I want to read this quote. She's asking herself about the West Indian writer and she says, "Although West Indian literature proclaims to be revolutionary and to be able to change the world, on the contrary, writer and reader implicitly agree about respecting a stereotypical portrayal of themselves and their society. In reality, does the writer wish to protect the reader and himself against the ugliness of the past, the hardships of the present, and the uncertainty of the future?"

What does this have to do with this young woman and the horrible punitive actions against her for not doing her homework? It occurred to me that—again, this is thinking about Black women's relationships and Black people's relationships to institutions—part of our job is to protect these institutions, to obscure the ugliness of the past, to obscure even the ugliness of this moment, and certainly to obscure the uncertainty of what the future may hold for our positionalities in the institutions. It takes a lot of effort to start from the position that we are going to place Black people at the center of our work—not the institutional frameworks, not the institutional metrics of what work looks like or what success looks like. When we are thinking about digital humanities and thinking about digital pedagogies, who are we really teaching and who are these pedagogies, and who are these courses or this work for? It can't be for the institution if we want to use this work to actually liberate people. It has to be centered in a Black lived experience and grow out of that.

I'm going to talk about user experience for a second. Thinking about developing personas or developing a particular sort of archetype or user. It can be very dehumanizing, in some sense. But if we think about, again, who we are working for and why we are doing what we are doing, I think it creates—not that there's not going to be harm—but it creates some safeguards, perhaps, to make sure that digital humanities and digital pedagogies are not either unwittingly or explicitly harming the very people that we hope that they're for.

MP: Thinking about the things we make and, in summary, how not to be part of the problem. I have to say also, as a former juvenile delinquent, that we have to remember that the structures through which the *ProPublica* situation emerges are structures that were in place long before the digital. If it hadn't been this, it would have been something else, because she was already under the state's surveillance before the turn to online learning. The *ProPublica* example gives us a frighteningly common story of structural incompetence masked as state concern. No amount of cleverness, no canny perspective, would have saved this girl from incarceration. Thinking about that particular young person's life actually requires us to think about what it means to live in a world where everything is deadly all the time, and about the strategies through which people survive that deadliness. Until they don't.

So more Ellison, "change the joke and slip the yoke," and with a nod to Zora Neale Hurston's attention to strategic implementations of culture: there's a transformative power in constantly being able to find ways around the rules (Ellison; Hurston). I come from a world where everything about survival is about getting through in ways that flip things to your advantage. There's no straight line. There's no right way to do things. It's not on the table for you. Because even if you were to do everything right, they would just change what has to be done. At the same time, there have to be actual structural solutions. I've been thinking more and more about what that means. In the *ProPublica* case the resonance with the digital is most in how her situation results from a carceral logic that is fundamentally algorithmic. Once she was brought into the system, onto that platform, almost every aspect of her physical and psychic life became a possible site of reinscription. There are real pleasures and radical possibilities in digitality, but there are also briars, dead ends, and the terror of automation.

Kim, there was a great conference you organized a few years ago at Purdue, where I made an off-the-cuff argument that I've been playing with a lot in some recent work, about bots and AI [artificial intelligence] in relation to representing Black people. I made the argument that one reason it might prove difficult is because Black people have mastered changing so constantly and so quickly, because we're such a profoundly linguistic culture in every sense of the term. I know it's Pollyanna, intentionally so. It was intended to remind us of the pleasure in resistance against the deadly automation that characterizes so much of Black life in America. Black youth can master TikTok and other forms of social media, but what would it mean for Black youth to bring that pleasure and transformation to other technologies, for instance mesh networking or minimal computing or wearables?

I know it's problematic to make an argument about tools of oppression and surveillance by bringing forth more tools. At the same time, I think there's something at stake in realizing the ways in which the "average person" doesn't have access to very simple tools. Understanding how to use the basic building blocks of web communication, rather than merely the constant overlay of services, actually matters. This goes beyond just imagining that "everyone should code." I'm also thinking, for instance, about when online schooling first started and the kids were intentionally crashing the learning apps by downloading too many things, or the joke we have about the person who figures out that they can just put a picture or a video of themselves up during a Zoom meeting, and it looks like they're there.

We joke about these things, but there's something very radical about thinking about what it would mean for a young person to have access to ways of thinking intentionally about technological oppression. Everyone doesn't need to know how to code, but they should have a sense of what it means to hack digital formations. Because it means that they would actually have access to understanding how the things that they own, the tools they interact with, are problematic but also subject to reinscription, because they also belong to them. They have that understanding about books, about history, about classes, about teachers. What would it mean to pass that over to thinking about digital tools as well? I do wonder what would happen if more people understood all the various ways that resistance could be played out digitally.

NOTES

1. https://fjday.com/projects.
2. https://mp285.com/sections/portfolio/.
3. http://smallaxe.net/sxarchipelagos/issue03/parham/parham.html.

BIBLIOGRAPHY

Condé, Maryse. "Order, Disorder, Freedom, and the West Indian Writer." *Yale French Studies* 97 (2000): 151–65, https://doi.org/10.2307/2903218.

Day, Faithe. *The Black Living Data Booklet.* 2020, https://fjday.com/projects.

Ellison, Ralph. "Change the Joke and Slip the Yoke." *Partisan Review* 25, no. 2 (Spring):1958.

Hurston, Zora Neale. "Characteristics of Negro Expression." In *Negro Anthology: 1931–1933*, edited by Nancy Cunard, 39–46. London: Wishart, 1934.

Kaufman, Bob. *The Ancient Rain: Poems, 1956–1978*. New York: New Directions, 1981.

Parham, Marisa. ".break .dance" *Small Axe Archipelagos* 3 (2020), http://smallaxe.net/sxarchipelagos/issue03/parham/parham.html.

Parham, Marisa. "Sample | Signal | Strobe: Haunting, Social Media, and Black Digitality." *Debates in the Digital Humanities 2019,* edited by Matthew K. Gold and Lauren F. Klein. Minneapolis: University of Minnesota Press, 2019, https://dhdebates.gc.cuny.edu/read/untitled-f2acf72c-a469-49d8-be35-67f9ac1e3a60/section/0fa03a28-d067-40b3-8ab1-b94d46bf00b6.

Trouillot, Michel-Rolph. *Silencing the Past: Power and the Production of History*. Boston: Beacon Press, 2015.

"Blackness" in France: Taking Up Mediatized Space

A CONVERSATION WITH MABOULA SOUMAHORO
AND MAME-FATOU NIANG

KAIAMA L. GLOVER (KLG): In our last two conversations, we talked about digital ventures in pedagogy, as well as about the practice of building a digital world in alignment with the Black feminist ethics of generosity, citation, refusal, and care. Now we'll look in a slightly different but related direction and think about how other media contexts, particularly old media—remember those, like TV and newspapers?—and alternative media, like photography and film, can also provide spaces of public intellectual engagement.

We'll start with the question everyone should know is coming by now, which is your thoughts on this frame: the matter of silence, power, narrative, and historical knowledge, and then, the particularly disordering force of women who refuse those silences that, historically, have been posed by people in power.

MABOULA SOUMAHORO (MS): I have to say that it was refreshing to go back to [Michel-Rolph] Trouillot and *Silencing the Past,* which I hadn't read in years. It was refreshing, but it was also, perhaps, a little disheartening, because it's been twenty-five years. One of the questions could be, "What hasn't the world gotten from this beautiful writing, and these deep, deep analyses that were provided to us twenty-five years ago, and these reflections and analyses that go back to the Second World War, to the nineteenth-century United States, to the Caribbean, and the plantation economy, to slavery, and to all those periods of time, back to ancient Greece?" That's what is disheartening.

But what I do want to reflect on today is the way power operates through silence and invisibility. What I mean, and what we all mean by that, in this Western world—because this is our locale—is that the reflection and the construction of the past, this official reconstruction of the past that becomes the history of all the nations we are grounded in, within the Atlantic world, in particular, they are, of course, constructions and have little to do with truth and reality.

We need to keep in mind the complication of our approach to the past and to what Trouillot calls "pastness." What we need to understand is that, in those narratives that do not have to be fictions, the fundamental question is the purpose of those narratives and the production of those narratives and the circulation of those narratives. Who is in charge of that narration of things past, and what is the current use of the past and of this constructed, even construed, past for the present? How can I say it? This back and forth between the meaning of the present and the past and the relation that ties both. There can only be a past because there is a present, and a present because there is a past, and what we are trying to envision is the future based on our understanding of the present in relation to our understanding of the past. The three tenses are to be taken into account.

How does power unfold in this production, circulation, understanding, and even memory? And all of that meaning in the control of the narration of this past? These questions are of the highest importance. And when it comes to the role to be played by women—and the role played by Black women in particular—we could, in this Western framework, think of men and women beyond gender studies as the ultimate embodiment of difference: difference in the bodies. We could talk about the differences and the hierarchies along ethnic lines, along religious lines, along racial lines, along social lines. But when it comes to this Western configuration of men and women—two bodies that are understood as different, and two shapes of bodies, because they're understood as different—they need to be placed within a hierarchy within which man is on top and woman is at the bottom.

This is an interesting way to organize things, precisely when we remember that this rigid framework is resting only on this men/women dichotomy, that it erases any third gender, any third body. When we pay more attention today to trans identities, and when we pay more attention today to Black women's identities, we are really talking about bodies, racialized bodies, gendered bodies that come to disrupt this attempt to organize, in such a rigid matter, this Western world. So, of course, when thinking about the Black feminist tradition, we are talking about the ultimate possibility of challenge, because the woman's body was understood in this Western world as the opposite of the empowered body that is the male body. And the Black woman's body was constructed in this Western world as the total opposite of the white body, male or female.

We are both lucky and unlucky enough to be at the vanguard. That's the vanguard in action. That's the vanguard anchored in the body. That's the vanguard that has manifested itself intellectually and politically and religiously, all those forms, because that is embodiment. Black women bodies disrupt, and trans women bodies disrupt as well, and they're really the marker of hierarchies. This is where these hierarchies can be located. So when we think about silence, power, and history, we are really talking about these erasures, these moments of not being taken into account, these marginalizations that are systematic in this part of the world that is called the West.

KLG: Merci, Maboula. Thank you. I know you think a lot about embodiment, materiality, and bodies, and when we are in the context of social media and disembodied space, I think these become even more crucial questions. But let me turn to you, Mame-Fatou.

MAME-FATOU NIANG (MFN): I want to start by acknowledging this moment and what it means for me to be in this space to discuss this hashtag, #UnsilencedPast, with my colleague and big sister, Maboula Soumahoro. Maboula is only three years older than I am, but she's one of the reasons that I do what I do. I was engaged in what we call in French the *voie royale* [proper path], in the whitest of studies, and in the mid-2000s—this is around the time of the 2005 fall riots. I didn't know Maboula personally, but in this very white state of French epistemology, her singular voice and her presence became a fixture in national and public debates around race and identity. I was aware of the vitriol being shown toward her, but her relentless engagement, and that evidence that she carried around like, "l'heure de la récré a sonné!" ["playtime is over!"], it was something that really opened something in me. It freed me, liberated the master's student that I was at the time.

And even when I saw Maboula being publicly attacked, I also saw what Saidiya Hartman called "the moment of tenderness"—moments pointing to the fact that a future is possible. For me, that future was in Black studies, a field that I was repeatedly told to not engage with. I address myself to become my subject of study, and I was going to engage with the gazes surrounding my body as a Black woman in the West, engage with the noisy silences that have haunted me, those white noises that would not leave my head from the minute I finally allowed myself to hear them. Maboula has been central to many of my projects, from the documentary *Mariannes Noires* to the photo series coproduced with Pittsburgh visual artist Njaimeh Njie, on Black Islam in Paris. She's a sister. She's a cheerleader, and she has the best laugh, and I just wanted to start with that.

Now, reflecting on the framing of the series through the lens of [Maryse] Condé and the disorder brought by Black woman voices, and through Trouillot's study of history, power, and silence, I will briefly talk about two elements that have been the cornerstone of my work for the past decade now: companionship and pleasure. These are two politics that I actively engage with in my teaching and in each of my projects. First, companionship: To be Black within the European modernist project is to live on the fringe of official narrative. It is to exist in the dead angles and silences. But it also means that we are never alone. Once we realize that silence is our companion, we are never alone. We are constantly surrounded by the silences of history. And my body of work is what I call a "sonarcheology" of sounds and silences, both in writings and in our lived environment. I investigate the means that Black people have developed to domesticate, to harness those silences.

For example, this is what we're doing right now when we push against the rhetoric of surprise around the current climate. While many seem lost or struck by the novelty of the event, we have lived with the silences, and through this companionship we've acquired a deeper sense of the present. And this brings me to my second point, which is about the politics of pleasure. Even when writing from a place of rage, of despair, of mourning, I try as much as possible to ground it, to root it in pleasure. And that contrasts so much with what I see in front of me, in the eyes of my detractors—something that I long thought to be power but that actually revealed itself to be sheer fear: what [James] Baldwin was saying, sheer terror. Once you realize that grounding yourself in pleasure is something that you actually carry with you, the balance of power internally shifts in your head. And that's what has been carrying me for the past ten years.

And it's true, at a global level, that systemic racism is smothering our communities, taking our sisters' lives, crushing our brothers' hopes and lives, but this politics of pleasure is really an affirmation that I carry with me, an affirmation of self, but also a refusal to be erased, to be silenced.

KLG: I knew this conversation would be a good one. And especially, I love where we have gotten words that are resonating: study, and this notion of companionship as being part of the practice of study, as part of the politics of studying in the way that we do. I would have framed it as lineage, finding oneself in the lineage and identifying the door that is Maboula's presence. So, going back to your point, Maboula, about the body, her material, physical, actual visible presence. How did that door open for you, Mame-Fatou, as a scholar?

And from there, I have a lot of questions. I want to think about the continuum between academia and activism, which I know is something that has been a double-edged sword for both of you—the extent to which, by doing activist work, there are ways in which your academic contributions are obscured, or put into question, or undermined even. And yet, and still, you are both persistent in engaging in these other media spaces: newspapers, television, etcetera. I wonder if you can talk to us about how your public interventions are informed by your training as scholars.

MS: I think that what could be interesting today for our U.S.-based or, at least, Atlantic-based or outside-of-France audience is to understand the context of France, in which Black studies, Africana studies, Pan-African studies is not an academic field. And it's important to remember that fact, because even though things are quite difficult in the States as well, at least there is an institutional presence of specific topics. We are not there yet in France.

But even though these departments, programs, and initiatives exist in the United States today, we also need to remember how they came into being and when they came into being. It takes us back to the civil rights movement and the social mobilization of the time period. I am really focusing on the 1950s and 1960s. We're not going to get into the details of the long civil rights movement. We are all aware of the long history of the civil rights movement, but we're really talking about departments and programs that emerged in the late 1960s and on.

I am insisting on these facts because in France, we are in the late 1960s and 1970s. That is to say, academics who perhaps at first really thought of themselves as scholars and professors are perceived and presented as activists. But, to talk about my personal experience, I never thought of myself as an activist, and to this day, I don't present myself as an activist. But what I know and what I have noticed within the public sphere, and also within academia, is that I am systematically presented as an activist. I feel ambivalent about this term because, on the one hand, of course, I understand my activism, but on the other, my activism is really about a general interest in social justice, and social justice involving academia—meaning more topics, a greater diversity of what is taught and what is circulated, what is valued, what is recognized as scientific scholarly knowledge within academia. I understand the stakes. I understand what is silenced, what is erased, what is never passed down—that is to say, what is never taught and what is systematically left out of the general narrative, national, scholarly, political, all those things.

So, I understand that. But I also want to highlight the fact that I don't belong to any organization, that I support many causes, that I can sign petitions, and that I can march a little, but that's not my job. I find it very interesting that people want to place me in the category that is, based on reality, simply not mine. What it reveals is the stakes. What it reveals is what is supposed to be invisible, and what is invisible is power. So everything that is normal, everything that is acceptable, everything that is respectable, everything that is legitimate, is supposed to be invisible. I enter this space and those spaces as highly invisible, so what do I disrupt? What do I make visible, through my body, through this reading of my body, through the reading of my scholarship, and through the reading of my alleged activism? I'm the one who is in the struggle, in the fight. What I think could be more interesting is to look at what remains invisible, and what also reveals the ongoing struggle and fight, even for maintaining the status quo.

There is an active activism. There is an active activism that operates, again—I think we're going to say it a few times within this discussion—through silence and normativity, and that is the embodiment of power. So, how does my body enter those spaces? My body, because it becomes so visible, actually highlights what has been made invisible, and what is more active, and what has much more power than I have—much more, so much more. What I disrupt might cause a certain level, but a minimal level, of discomfort. It becomes uncomfortable for people. But I think my personal discomfort is much greater, and the collective discomfort is much greater.

MFN: Thank you, Maboula, for giving this very specific context for talking about race and racism in France and in French academia. It's always funny to me when we are told to keep militancy or activism out of our world as scholars, and how academia is about scientific objectivity, when academia has been and is still a breeding ground for active militancy aimed at upholding or reproducing hegemonic discourses. Academic discourse is activism. To me, the question is not whether activism is seen with a bad eye in our world. It's more a question of whose activism is seen under a keen light. Understanding that perspective—that holding the mirror up to my interlocutor, whether it's at MLA, NEMLA, at my professional organizations' meetings, or even on TV—has been liberating. I don't have to justify myself.

But as a scholar who straddles France and the United States, I understand the nuance that the word *activist* can have. I still grapple with the translation of "scholar-activist." In the United States, I am a scholar-activist, and I can present myself as such. But in France, because "activist" and "militant" are such loaded words—used as Maboula said, to disqualify a scholar, especially if the scholar is a woman, or God forbid, a Black person—I'm really struggling. Ten years later, I'm still struggling with that term.

As far as my scholarship and my public interventions, whether through films, documentaries, or just being on TV or writing articles, I see them as part of the same project. I had that issue with *Mariannes Noires,* where people were asking me, "Is it scholarship? Is it a fun project with a student?"—I made the film with a nineteen-year-old student. People ask, "Should it count for your tenure dossier? Is it art? Is it scholarship?" I don't see that boundary. For me, my art is scholarship. It's militancy. It's born out of and nourishes what I write. For example, chapter five of my latest book was an analysis of *Mariannes Noires.*

To reflect on that idea—what you talked about, Kaiama—of the media as a space of pedagogical intervention outside the classroom, or outside the university community, I think of our use of the term *intervention* in the clinical sense of actively working, intervening on behalf of a sick relative, in this case, the French body. For my current book project, *Reformulation of Blackness in Twenty-First-Century France,* I am working on actually extracting the diseases in that French body through media installations. There is a chapter titled *Les Trois Grâces de l'anti-noirité française: innocence, ignorance, arrogance*—the three graces of anti-Blackness in France: innocence, ignorance, and arrogance—where I analyze French attitudes toward anti-racism. In the French context of memory, identity, and the writing of history, I define innocence as the state of being left in the dark by institutions. It's the childish state in which the *L'Education Nationale,* the French public system, keeps the children innocent through public education and a plethora of cultural institutions like museums, etcetera, and reinforces that mythical republican narrative of a Frenchness that is one and singular and that cannot be hyphenated. Ignorance, in the French context, is the willful and active process of maintaining that innocence once you realize that the narrative is a myth. And it takes an active, strong, and determined will to remain ignorant. I argue that ignorance is not passive. It is never passed down collectively, nor is it inherited. It is cultivated at an individual level, and it has to be cherished, watered like a plant and groomed in order to bloom. And the last concept is arrogance. Arrogance is defined as the need to not need to know—the arrogance of not needing to know—the being so full of the universalist narrative that you cannot envision that it could be flawed. That's the same arrogance that drives people to constantly question me or Maboula's intelligence or credentials, when we ask them to shut up and listen, and listen not to what is being said, but listen to what is left out, what is forgotten, who is forgotten, why, when, and what do these silences—just like Maboula said—say about inequalities of power?

I often come back to Trouillot's notion of the unthinkable, with this difficulty for France to come to terms with history—not as they wanted it to have happened, but how it actually happened—for example, the impossibility of thinking about the Haitian Revolution. This is what we have to push against, this discourse around, "Oh, race and racism, we're past that. We have that universal magic pill that places us light-years ahead of the United States." And Black French women's voices complicate those ultra-localized—and this is at the heart of Maboula's book—those very linear, hexagonalized understandings of how time and space intersect.[1] I am thinking here about Audrey Célestine's *Une Famille Française,* or *A French Family,* an autobiographical account of how her own family's circulation between Martinique, Algeria, and northern France subverts the simplistic view of how Frenchness is constructed and functions. Also thinking of the French historian Olivette Otele's book *Afro-Europeans: An Untold History.* When it was promoted on Twitter, somebody smartly commented that the book looked really nice, but it was not about the story being untold—it's more that it was a nonevent. There was no story of Afro-Europeans. So, that arrogance of not even wanting to listen is astounding.

It is very interesting when we look at the way we minorities in France address this space, and—this is an image that I use a lot, holding the mirror—we've always been thought of as this sick abnormal body, and now we allow ourselves to be the doctors being *au chevet de la France* [at France's bedside]. It's like, these are the three diseases that I was able to see in my patient today, my beautiful France.

KLG: This is about taking seriously the idea of a socio-diagnostic to address what is in fact a pathology—one that can, with certain efforts, be routed out. It goes back to Maboula's ambivalence between despair and optimism, which, one might argue, is the perspective of any doctor faced with a critically ill patient to some extent.

I had the opportunity, with my colleague Tami Navarro at Barnard College, to interview the poet and the performance artist Staceyann Chin. At one point in our conversation, we were talking about various media platforms, and she said, with an equal measure of weariness and resolution, "I'm not quite sure what the answer is. I just know that for as long as I can speak, for as long as I can talk to an audience, that I will be present in the conversation, and the way I can be present right now is by staying on social media."

There was something she was communicating in her tone, and in her body language, about the resignation of who and where she had to be online to do the necessary work, and that this was a source of frustration for her. So I want to ask the two of you your thoughts on the obligation and the desire to do your work—to do your work that is intellectual, that is scholarly, that is in community in conversations like this—and yet your equally great compulsion to push back against existing media representations of Blackness with your own contestatory representations. How much do you have to speak to a crowd that is not your crowd? How much of that feels more burdensome than empowered?

I thought about this a lot, seeing you in these spaces on French television and realizing the extent to which oftentimes, even when you are offered space, how the silences work within that space. That is, how often you are cut short by presenters, or asked questions that are either non sequiturs or inappropriate, and how much negotiation and navigation of those forms of silencing you do. It's a big question, but I am asking about the labor, and how that labor might interfere with some of the intellectual work that you're doing.

MS: I think this labor is both burdensome and necessary. The scholarship that we want, the comfortable scholarship—like right now, we are having a comfortable conversation, and we are trying to think collectively—this other scholarship might be less comfortable, but it is still necessary, and still doable in practice, and the practice includes those media interventions. When we go to the mainstream media, we know exactly where we are going, and we know that this is a war—a symbolic war—because in our presence, our bodies, and not only our discourse, we become the impossible. We become the disqualified teacher or professor or PhD only when we teach certain things, or when we write our PhDs on certain topics, or when we publish articles on certain topics. If we were in agreement with the national narrative, we wouldn't be. As Black women, we could be disqualified as teachers, but that disqualification would not unfold in the same manner.

This is what I mean: If we keep in mind that the PhD is simply the highest degree ever, that there's nothing more than a PhD—there's nothing people can say, in theory, in terms of the training Mame received and that I received. We are at the same level. So what is happening when, twelve years later, people are still calling on Twitter for people to read my PhD dissertation and perhaps reveal the truth and say, "She's a fake doctor." Or why, when I appear in *The New York Times,* which they read three times a day, which they love, which they revere, then all of the sudden, *The New York Times* is not what it used to be. This is what they say. So, when we go to the media, that space is not the only space. It works hand in hand with my teaching and my more scholarly, more traditional activities. But I don't have the luxury. I don't have the leisure to restrict myself to academia, because academia is too much of an ivory tower.

Right now, with what is happening in hexagonal France, it's very important to make visible the connections within and without academia. When we are more comfortable, I will be more than happy to just teach, write, and simply do my work. But we're not there yet. And so, I think that my media intervention, to a certain extent, might also be understood and approached as just as valuable as what I teach. It is a form of scholarship in practice. The theory is desirable, the loftiness, the abstraction, but we're not there yet. I do not have the means, and I don't understand how people think they have the means. We can't. Our bodies still talk, and they speak very loudly, and it's still something to be a Black woman in an amphitheater in a university in hexagonal France. It's just a fact.

For me, the first step was for students, and staff, and colleagues to understand that I can be their colleague, and then through the media, to make all of France understand that I am somebody's professor. I am somebody's advisor. I am somebody's colleague, and you're going to deal with it. The paradox is that our training as scholars is also the training required for speaking in public, for articulating an argument, for mastering all these social codes, which makes us valuable media guests. So, to a certain extent, these audiences find themselves trapped, because we are products of France. We are the fruits of their education. We are like them. We simply, totally, deeply disagree on everything, but we speak the same language. We speak multiple languages, but one of them is common to theirs, and we are going to use that particular language to not simply converse but have them hear, and then they'll listen, and then they'll obey.

KLG: That's an ambitious program, Maboula, that you have just outlined. I want to ask you, Mame-Fatou, to respond.

MFN: I second everything that Maboula has said, and I have to add that I've centered my work around the politics of companionship and pleasure because I have matured. I'm in my fourth decade on earth, but I used to work with a third force, which was the politics of trolling. I realized that we were being trolled in this project, like Maboula said—that we are the product of an extremely rigorous mold of the French society and French educational system. And even with all that, and even with all the hurdles—like my mom used to say, "If they ask you for fifteen points, go get twenty-five, because they will still find a way to steal five. But you know what, you'll still have twenty and be on top"—we always had to do more than everybody else. And then with all that, our bodies will always talk before we even open our mouths. So, once I realized that we were being trolled, it was liberating for me, because I ended up trolling the system. And one of the ways I trolled the system was by not caring about the politics of representation, not anymore.

I have centered my work around one question, which is: How is it possible to be Black, a woman, and a human when the Western national fictions were not written with me and my body in mind? Actually, let me rephrase it: How is it possible to be Black, a woman, and a human when Western symphonies were composed with me as the counter model? In my work, I develop this idea of the close listen, which shows that silences can be just as eloquent as the noises of the *roman national*, the French national narrative. For example, in my movie, I asked the women this question around representation, "What do you think of the representation of Black women in French public spaces?" Seven women, all of them, had this moment of silence before they could come up with an answer. I remember being shocked the first time—it was with Maboula—and then the second day being the same, the third day the same, and I found myself chasing that moment of silence, and it came back the fourth, the fifth, the sixth, the seventh day.

And I put it all together. It's a minute and thirty-two of silence, and that silence is deafening. It's the silence of numbers. It's the silence of ethnic statistics, of still being a subject of contention. It's the silence of our absence. But the way I turned around that obligation of always having to be present while being absent is that I just decided to shy away from the concept of representation—of thinking about how am I seen, how people perceive me, what they think of me—in order to frame my inquiry, my scholarship, and my project around questions of dignity, life, and death. To that end, I have been chasing and capturing silences and sounds in nation and landscape.

To illustrate that, I will talk just briefly about one of my newest projects called "From the Most Beautiful City in the World to the Most Livable City in America: Black Invisibilities in Paris and Pittsburgh." The project analyzes the impact of rapid urban changes in the Black communities of Paris and Pittsburgh, as well as the ways in which co-creation practices involving artists, researchers, and residents address these changes. The project has multiple components: one short movie of about three minutes that builds on Ayo Coly's *Postcolonial Hauntology,* and the notion of postcolonial hauntology.

The protagonist is a little girl who visits *la maison de France,* the house of France, and she's warmly welcomed; everybody shows her around. She's given a tour of the place, and she's introduced to the great lineage of Napoleon, of Charles de Gaulle. But every time she approaches the basement, the attic, or any of the closets in the house, she hears muffled sounds, like hums and sounds of daily activities—people cooking, laughing, crying, police sirens—and she sets out to investigate what lies behind those beautiful French artisan-made closets. What are literally the skeletons in France's closet?

Another component is a sound installation called the Sounds of Silence, where I've juxtaposed digital sound archives of selected heavily gentrified areas in Paris and Pittsburgh with recent sound recordings of the same places, in 2019, 2020—church bells, Sunday markets, kids playing at a water park, and the hushed ambience of a newly installed yoga studio—and I analyze what the new sound instead of the silence says about the city.

By working with media of my choice—by choosing to publish an article in a peer-reviewed journal, or to write for *Slate* or for *Elle* magazine—I also liberate myself from the knowledge that it doesn't matter. I could publish with Harvard University Press every day, and the vision of my body will not change. I will not allow that external burden to weigh me down so much that I can live an extra sixty years and not enjoy what I'm doing. I allow myself to follow my imagination, my creativity, and wander around, play with tools that are part of the mosaic that helps me tell the same story.

KLG: Yes. I framed the question around resignation, being resigned to inhabiting a body that constantly speaks before you have a chance to open your mouth. You've both flipped that on its head and proposed it as resolution, saying, "That's the fact, but I have the choice to not care." So many things are coming together. This reminds me of what Marlene Daut said in our first conversation, "There are options where you can simply walk out of the room and decide not to integrate this space." And it makes me think about what Marisa Parham was saying: "Where can we find the pleasure and play in the work that we're doing, even if on the other side of that is indignity and death." You make that very plain.

NOTE

1. Hexagonalized means limited to the mental and geographical boundaries of metropolitan France.

BIBLIOGRAPHY

Célestine, Audrey. *Une famille française : des Antilles à Dunkerque en passant par l'Algérie.* Paris: Textuel. 2018.

Coly, Ayo A. *Postcolonial Hauntologies: African Women's Discourses of the Female Body.* Expanding Frontiers: Interdisciplinary Approaches to Studies of Women, Gender, and Sexuality. Lincoln: University of Nebraska Press, 2019.

Condé, Maryse. "Order, Disorder, Freedom, and the West Indian Writer." *Yale French Studies* 82, no. 3 (1993): 121–35.

Hartman, Saidiya. *Wayward Lives, Beautiful Experiments: Intimate Histories of Riotous Black Girls, Troublesome Women, and Queer Radicals.* New York: Norton, 2020.

Niang, Mame-Fatou, and Kaytie Nielsen, directors. *Mariannes Noires.* Mariannes Noires LLC. 2021, https://www.mariannesnoires.com/.

Otele, Olivette. *African Europeans: An Untold History.* London: Hurst, 2020.

Soumahoro, Maboula. *Black Is the Journey, Africana the Name.* Translated by Kaiama L. Glover. Cambridge: Polity Press, 2022.

Trouillot, Michel-Rolph. *Silencing the Past: Power and the Production of History.* Boston: Beacon Press, 2015.

PART V][*Chapter 27*

The Power to Create: Building Alternative (Digital) Worlds

A CONVERSATION WITH MARTHA S. JONES
AND JESSICA MARIE JOHNSON

KAIAMA L. GLOVER (KLG): I always ask the same first question, which is about narrative, silence, history, and power, as related to the specific purchase of women's interventions in public discourse. I'd love to hear your thoughts on that. We are going to start with you, Martha.

MARTHA S. JONES (MSJ): I thought I would tell you what came to my mind as I have reflected these weeks on this question, and it comes from a different place, but I hope you'll let me make the intervention.

Many years ago, legal scholar Jerome Culp plumbed the question of silence in the academy in his 1991 article, "Autobiography and Legal Scholarship and Teaching: Finding the Me in the Legal Academy." Plumb is a polite word. Culp was terribly vexed about the degree to which white supremacy—my words, not his—continued to determine not only what and who was in the legal academy, but what was scholarship. What was worthy of the imprimatur of the law journal?

His experience, as a Black man standing at the podium in a law school like Duke, where he taught for many years, was the extraordinary degree to which students demanded that he break a kind of silence. In the first class, the question would come, "Where did you go to law school? How did you get here? Who are you?" Culp was a brilliant and pretty cheeky guy, and he had a provocative answer, which was a truth: He was the son of a poor coal miner. That was part of his biography, but the lesson that he wanted to teach us in that story was about the power of silence, and not the perniciousness of silence, but the power. What Culp understood well was the ways in which silence, in our world of academia, meant that some members of the faculty enjoyed the assumption of merit, the assumption of excellence, the assumption of belonging, and that others of us were never permitted silence. Because students, remarkably, along with colleagues, will query us about our bodies, about our persons, about our very beings, about our biographies, about our genealogies, openly and notoriously, and we, then, are drawn into a kind of unsilencing that only furthers the distance between us and the colleagues who maintain the silence.

Culp's project was not successful, but I think what he wanted to do was provoke those who were hiding behind their own silence and benefiting from the kinds of assumptions that came to them as a consequence of that—he wanted to goad them into putting their own stories on the table, breaking the silence that is essential to white supremacy in the academy. And I have wrestled with that ever since—what to disclose, how to disclose. For a long time in my professional life, I thought it was important to keep all that wrapped up. I thought that was where my power lay. And maybe that was true. But today, I do a kind of teaching and a kind of writing and a kind of speaking that attempts to open some of that up to scrutiny and to discover what kind of power there is when I, as a Black woman in the academy, actually tell my own story. It doesn't do the work that Culp hoped it would do, which is to say, I don't think it shifts the balance of power in places like hiring committees. But it has permitted the construction of another kind of power and another kind of community that, for me, this series really embodies.

KLG: Thank you so much, Martha. We are going to come back to this question of the power of alternative communities. It's been brought up before, about when to speak and for whom—the question of audience. Who do we care to speak to? But Jessica, please, if you would offer some initial thoughts.

JESSICA MARIE JOHNSON (JMJ): I really love this question. I love how different people have answered it. I love, Martha, your answer, and I find that I am stuck between two kinds of responses. I'm thinking back to Maboula [Soumahoro]'s response, about what it means to be called an activist in the academy. What does it mean to walk into a room and be overrepresented in your Black woman figure, and to know that it's doing a particular kind of work in the room that it is not doing for your colleagues who are presenting as male, who are presenting as white, whatever it might be.

#WhatDoesAProfessorLookLike is a hashtag that has been going around since maybe 2015, 2017, and it still comes back around because it is needed, and that's a very real reality—that there is something that speaks before we appear. There's something that speaks in our names when they appear on paper. There's something that speaks in the work that we do.

I am really privileged and blessed to have ended up in a department where, in the junior cohort, we are obviously not all Black, and we are not all necessarily non-Black either, but we are all doing work that, even within our respective fields of empire or Europe or whatever it might be, are pushing the boundaries of the field. There has been something very important about speaking to our experiences and speaking to communities that have not always had the space in scholarship, in the public sphere, and in the media.

There's that impulse, and then there's the other impulse, which is to question this idea that there has ever been silence. I say this as someone who is very new to the academy, who is first generation in all the things, but it strikes me that the ways that academic privilege—elite privilege—replicates itself is in very intimate ways, by asking, "Who are you? Where did you go to school? Who else do you know?" Those are things that need to be asked because those are relations that, among a certain academic elite class, they already have. You already know who went to the Ivies. Your adviser's adviser is part of your genealogy of your doctorate or your master's degree or your law degree, whatever it might be.

These are the ways these relations already existed. They were already heavily intimate. It's one of the reasons that smokers at AHA [American Historical Association] were such an issue, because they were these spaces for masculine—white masculine, in particular—socialization. Then, out of contestation with that, you have the Berkshire Conference of Women Historians. Out of contestation with white scholars closing out Black historians and Black scholars, you have things like ASALH [the Association for the Study of African American Life and History].

So there's something to me about not just the privilege of silence—though I think it's very, very real—but also the privilege not to have to ask that question, not to have to ask about my white male colleagues' intimate practices, not to have to ask who they are having drinks with, who else is on their committee, who is also an adviser, how many generations of PhDs are created in any given department that then come back to that same department to be employed. These are the kinds of things that are so assumed and so ingrained; they don't need to be outed as silence. But they also are very loud. These are the actual intimate practices that maintain difference and privilege in the academy.

There's something interesting there. On the one hand, yes, there is a reality to stepping out and, literally, my body being a spoken word. Then, the other side of it is that we just don't assume that that same spoken word operates on X white male colleague. We take it for granted that it does not. That's the piece that is both challenging for even the most well-meaning white colleagues who want to do the work, particularly in this Black Lives Matter moment, and also it is the piece that we need to continue to confront—that all of our intimacies are always on the table. Whether they should be or not is probably the better question than whether they actually are, because they always have been.

KLG: I am struck by the persistent ambivalence that both of you seem to be touching on. Even the terms that I have used to frame this, *power* being one of them, that term is not—the pun is terrible, but it's happening—it's not black and white. There are ways in which this power is out there in a way that can be approached differently, depending on the context. This brings me back to what Marlene [Daut] was saying about when we can walk out of the room or, again, what Maboula was saying about her body doing all of the talking. Is it more powerful for her to speak against whatever that body is saying, or should she just turn around and say, "I don't have time for this"?

So this is a question that I wanted to ask the two of you, in particular, because I don't know if it feels like this for you at Johns Hopkins University, but there is a little nugget of power that comes from your intimacy as colleagues, as friend-colleagues, as collaborators, as like-minded in your approach to pedagogy, in relation to what happens within the walls of campus and also regarding what your responsibilities are to the outside world. I'm wondering if you can talk about that, about what that position feels like in terms of power, and how, if at all, that thing I'm calling some sort of power can be marshaled to create alternative communities, to create alternative genealogies. That was a beautiful word you have introduced into this conversation, Jessica.

MSJ: I'm not going to speak for Dr. Johnson, but I suspect that I might be more interested in power than she is—or at least, I feel that way oftentimes when we are working. That is to say that I now recognize, and perhaps it is the beauty of hindsight, that part of my style and part of my way of working and being in the academy has been always to approach power—to learn, as best I can, how it works, to experience what it's like when I can garner a little bit of it. That has meant, at some moments, I am able to go places and to be things, to contribute to what I think of as the disruption or the dismantling of the academy in ways that are meaningful to me. But it has also meant that I have confronted the stark limits of whatever bit of power I imagine that I exercise.

The thing I want to say, and the conversation that I confess I do crave, is one in which, more directly, Black women who occupy or possess a bit of conventional power in the academy, that we talk about that. That is to say, it took a very long time for me to work for a woman in the academy, and I have still never worked for a Black woman. But I know y'all are out there, and you're doing things and building things and dismantling things and making things happen and making decisions.

That, to me, seems almost generationally distinct from where I began my career. Where we saw Black women was, perhaps, on our faculties. There was one in my graduate program as I was coming up at Columbia. But we are in a distinct place now. I don't want to name-check, but when an Alondra Nelson is running first the college at Columbia, and then the SSRC [Social Science Research Council], and on and on; when Elizabeth Alexander goes to the Mellon Foundation . . . I do think that there are concrete lessons that come from that. But more importantly, I want to know how our critical Black feminist capacities—robust, creative, transformative, even—are informing that kind of work. Is it possible, right? Is it even possible to maintain, to persist, to bring all you have learned, all that you are, to those kinds of spaces, those kinds of roles? Or are we inevitably changed when we get too close to power and when we even wield a little bit of it?

KLG: Talking about infiltration here, to some extent, and what the cost could be as you do that work in those spaces, Jessica, do you have some thoughts?

JMJ: I'm not uninterested in power. I'm actually very interested in power. I want to pick up on what you were saying about possibilities. Power is certainly the keyword, but I think *possibility* is also a keyword here. We are both concerned about what possibilities are available. I'm interested in what are the possibilities of Black freedom, in particular, whether it's in the academy or well beyond.

What are the possibilities available to people in different positions, I think, is an important question—like for someone like Alondra Nelson, who is magnificent and brilliant, or someone like Elizabeth Alexander, who's also magnificent and brilliant, and like yourself. What are the possibilities of the university as a structure, and what are the possibilities that are beyond and that are also about dismantling all the things that make the university an industrial complex in the way that it has increasingly become?

Some of those possibilities mean direct confrontations with power. I think of the Johns Hopkins students doing the Gilman sit-in.[1] I think of the students who are organizing around Lorgia García-Peña's tenure case at Harvard, the students at University of Chicago who are organizing to unionize, who are fighting for the right to be able to do that. All around the country, there are movements happening among faculty, tenure track and non-tenure track, among staff, trying to create space and possibility out of a structure—the university as a structure—that has replicated itself by foreclosing possibility and foreclosing opportunities and foreclosing demographics or exploiting demographics that have come to seek knowledge or seek space from their own situations.

So, I am really interested in that, and I think that possibility can happen. I hope that it can happen as people occupy certain positions of power. I am also skeptical of positions that are created within the academy itself as the sole mechanism for activism and agitation, because again, the university exists to replicate a kind of truncation of freedom and space and air to breathe. What are the ways that those spaces and those positions, either through challenges from other sectors of the university, the town, town-gown situation, the city, the 'hood, the maroon swamps, wherever they might be—how can those positions be pushed?

But in the end, are those the positions that we want? I'm thinking of what Dylan Rodriguez said in the Ethnic Studies Rise roundtable.[2] I'm paraphrasing: Maybe the point is to make the university unrecognizable to itself. Afterward, do those positions still exist? Do different versions of them exist?

In 2015 or 2016, at the Allied Media Conference, I had the privilege and the honor of cohosting a network gathering called "Dismantling the Ivory Tower" with Kai Green, Moya Bailey, and Van Bailey, who are some of the smartest organizer/activist/scholars that I have ever encountered. One of the things that came out of that was the realization that the best parts of the academy, the best pieces that we wanted to take with us, the pieces that we actually wanted to reproduce, were labor issues: space to write, space to think with archives or documents or texts, space to create, resources to create so that people didn't feel like they were starving, health care, summers "off"—off, quote unquote—because we've seen what this summer has been.

These are things that are part of and pockets of the institution, that I think are some of the best things to carry out of it. But they are also the things that the university kind of holds over our heads—that a university holds over its workers' heads as ways to police, to self-discipline, to say, "Don't speak too loudly because we'll take this from you, or we'll cut your benefits." Those are the kinds of grapplings that, well, if we think of really dismantling the university, it's going to look nothing like what it did. But, as with all abolitionist tracks, nothing in society will look the same.

KLG: You just ended with the word *abolition,* abolitionist, but what you were talking about all the way along, obviously, is more like marronage, right? So maybe we could talk about marronage in its widest sense, not only petit/grand—that is, small acts of refusal versus full-throated attempts at escape from the material reality of literal enslavement—but also as a metaphor. So, when I am thinking about marronage, I also am not just thinking about escape, but the workarounds, the ways of doing with what one has in the space one is granted, or within the constraints one is granted.

MSJ: Maybe I should go first before Jessica tells us what the word really means. I want to use the idea in a more capacious sense to say that, for me, reflecting on marronage was really a way to understand my own strategy and my own trajectory in the academy. There have been many moments, maybe too many moments, when I have encountered resistance and more. I was remembering today that the first time I did an exhibition, a brick-and-mortar exhibition—it couldn't have been more conventional—and I shared it with the colleagues in my department. Someone sort of tossed the postcard on the table and said, "We just don't do this." And I thought, "Wow." And there are lots of moments like that—the "We just don't do this."

So, what to do? For me, it has been to fugue. It has been to flee. It has been to find and to construct another kind of community within the vastness that is many of our universities. My best compatriots, my allies, my fellow travelers have been librarians and curators and artists. I have gone places I've never imagined in part because of the need to change, to fugue, to remake my own space and my own community. I think that's the way I have survived, and maybe even the way I have thrived—to the extent that I have thrived—because I've followed that old venerable and essential instinct, which is to recognize that this is a space that is not only not productive but that can't see me, that this is a space that is sort of toxic, that this is a space that tells me, "We don't do what you do." And it turns out there always are folks who see it otherwise. I think that if I have been successful, it's because I have been willing to, in a sense, make myself a fugitive and build someplace else, through the kind of visions, through the sense of possibility that I carry, even as within the conventional space of a department or a school, I have been perceived as out of bounds.

I think the thing to say, and then I'll hand it over to Jessica, is that this has brought me into some curious places. It is partly how I got curious about power, because there are moments in which the people with less power are less hospitable to my vision or my possibility, and I can find at least a temporary haven with folks who turn out to have a great deal more influence than those who have been my adversaries in the academy.

KLG: I like that point that it has brought you to some curious places. It's a beautiful idea—out of the resistance and the hostility can come spaces where you can indulge a curiosity and find something that you didn't expect. Jessica, maybe you'll pick up on this as well. Just your mention of the ways in which this marronage doesn't necessarily have to be in the lines of the work that you are doing specifically, but that there are alternative artifacts and practices that can contribute to getting you to these curious spaces. You mentioned art. We're talking about the digital. We're talking about multimedia. What are these alternative artifacts and conversations you can have around the work you thought you were going to do that can land you in a curious place?

JMJ: I think you are a maroon, Martha, perhaps more than you think you are, because there's another thing that maroons had to know, that fugitive enslaved Africans had to know—they had to know about power. They had to know where power was more than slave owners did. They needed to know where slave catching raids might come from or patrols might be. They needed to know who might catch them, and they needed to know who, even within the enslaved community, would be able to have their back.

That's what I hear you articulating, the ways that we need to be exquisitely knowledgeable about how things work in places. We don't have to agree with them, and we don't have to be prepared to take everything down immediately, but we do have to know how it works because that is the kind of knowledge that lets us find the path through the swamp, as opposed to the road where the paddy rollers are rolling. That is something that I also increasingly learned, working alongside Martha.

I do want to talk a little bit about Electric.Marronage.[3] It fits into this conversation in some really unanticipated ways. The project started more years ago than I quite remember, a collaboration between me and Dr. Yomaira C. Figueroa-Vàsquez, who is at Michigan State University (MSU). What we were trying to think through were some of the ideas and concerns that Martha is articulating, like, in this space that feels like it wants to kind of crunch and condense all the things that have made us—me and Dr. Figueroa, in particular—made our experience possible. The kinds of flagrant feminisms and rabid commitment to the Kitchen Table, to Black women, to Black womanhood, to community, that has sustained us in so many ways through our journey in life, not just into the academy—that those things were not only not seen in the academy, speaking of silence, but were denigrated—"acting a certain way" denigrated: being too much, too Black, too flagrant, too ratchet, too this, too that, too hoodrat—don't be that, don't be all the things that have made us survive. . . .

So, how, in that space of the university, if those were the rules that had to be danced to for a certain part of the day, what were the other spaces that we could create? We were both very interested in the digital humanities, and so we conceived of Taller Electric Marronage as an online space that could exist otherwise. Since then, it has become this beautiful project, more than we could even have expected. It's both a site and an event series. The first event series was hosted at MSU last spring. It was cut short, unfortunately, because of Covid, but we did host Drs. Randi Gill-Sadler and Savannah Shange. Then we did podcasts with them. Those podcasts are on the website.[4]

We also were able to work with some amazing graduate students who are trying to forge their own kind of escape and their own fugitivity. We have the pleasure of working with Christina Thomas, who is the lead editor and based at Johns Hopkins University (JHU), Halle-Mackenzie Ashby, Kelsey Moore, Ayah Nuriddin. All of them are on the JHU side, and on the MSU side, we have Jada Similton and Stephany Bravo. Sarah Bruno, a graduate student at Northwestern University, has also joined us. Together, they are called "the Electricians."

There are other people who have been involved and who will be supporting the work, particularly as it moves to Johns Hopkins in the fall. People like Margaret Burri at the Sheridan Libraries at Hopkins have been extremely supportive. Jennifer Kingsley in Museums and Society has been very supportive. The podcast gurus, especially Donte Smith at MSU, because you give your tech support props for doing things that you can't possibly do!

We have populated the Electric Marronage site and space on social media, and we meet in person with each other. We have a Slack channel that goes all day, all the time, for alternative knowledge that gets created: knowledge that appreciates the ways that our families are part of how we create scholarship, that appreciates the ways that thinking about fugitivity and enclosure go hand in hand and the ways that they diverge. We are interested in Black and Brown life, in particular, and with Indigenous life and humanity. The Electricians move across borders. They move across archipelagos.

We have made this space that is our swamp to abscond away to when things are too tough. It's a three-year project, so we will be continuing it into next year. But Taller Electric Marronage is one of those things that *can* be created when the power that we have as faculty—me and Dr. Figueroa—can be shared, can be spliced, redistributed, stolen—in the kind of Harney and Moten sense—and used in a different direction. Maybe these are seeds for a different kind of academy, a different kind of university, and maybe they are too small to be seeds. I'm a big fan of ephemerality, so I think that that's fine. Maybe instead of seeds we are just marking a moment to be here and to rest and to have a dance and have a drink, but that is still something. That is also an important part of the story that we're telling, that we're unsilencing.

KLG: Thank you, Jessica. My final question is something of a departure, but you invited us, Jessica—and so did you, Martha—to step outside the academy and think about these other spaces, whether through marronage or through wielding power in other institutions, as it were. I want to talk about both of your work in the more public sphere, so your roles as public scholars or educators of the public—like the incredible Black Womanhood Syllabus, for example, or the fact, Jessica, that you give history lessons on Twitter.[5]

The underlying question that I want to ask about that work—when you take on the responsibility of educating the public, beyond the space of campus —is how do you get to complexity? How do you do justice to the things that you have distilled and deciphered in your teaching over weeks and months and years and writing prizewinning books about? How do you get that on Twitter, in the *Atlantic,* in the *Post,* in a form that does honor to the depth and complexity of the subjects that you are grappling with?

MSJ: It would be fair to say, on some level, I have to let other people be the judge of whether I actually get to what you describe, Kaiama. But I would say, for me, there came a time when the public work was many things, including part of my own process, which is to say that I needed to be more out of the academy with my ideas and more in the roiling, fraught, not always safe but I think important public space that we step into when we write for news outlets or we spend time on Twitter.

I'm somebody who makes sense of it because I'm interested in staying around for the long haul. So, I don't think any one tweet or any one op-ed is the project at all. It is about being a sustained presence, a sustained set of ideas, about coming back again and again. It's a conversation in those spaces, isn't it? It's not simply a one-off for me. So, I think that my sense of integrity and my sense of the value of that work is an outgrowth of my willingness to stay in for the long game and be part of sustained exchanges with people, whether it's many, many tweets over many, many days or a series of writings on a related subject. They are our body of work. None of them is the entirety of what I hope to say, what I need to say. I see it as a body of work.

Maybe only I see it that way because I am the only one who sees the whole. But I hope people glimpse parts of it and stay with me over time, and I hope people ask me questions. One of the things that is very important to me about that space, that is different than the classroom, different than the workshop or the seminar, is that people are more inclined to ask the things they really need to know. I'm interested in that, and I'm here for that, even when those are hard questions for me. I'm here for them, and it takes me and my work to new places by encountering questions and grappling with them in real time or taking them away and thinking about them for days and weeks and years before I learn how to engage with them well.

KLG: Thank you. That was incredibly, beautifully put. Jessica?

JMJ: I feel very similarly. I have been on Twitter for almost a decade now and have been somewhere on the internet for as long or longer. The long haul is absolutely true and has to be part of this work. But the arc of my public engagement has moved so much. Once upon a time, the internet was smaller. There were fewer of us on it. It was definitely a space where I found community and craved community and created community, and those are people I talked to. Now those are people I talk to in real life. I have group chats with them. I see them in person when I can, or on screens when I can. So, there's ways that the internet is not the same—for me, at least—although I do think there's a kind of circular motion to the internet. As people get on it, they begin in smaller communities and enclaves and then branch out.

I think that the internet has changed, and so, my relationship to what I am doing and what kind of engagement is needed, and what that complexity looks like, has also changed. There are things that I don't explain on the internet, necessarily, because I'm not sure that they can be laid out clearly. But then there are moments—for example, the Viola Davis cover in juxtaposition with "The Scourged Back" image.[6] There are moments where the work that I'm engaged in, the length of time I've been able of speak to the people I feel I'm accountable to online, and the luck I have had in being able to piece together thoughts in 140 or, well, now it's 280 characters, come together in a fruitful way. But I don't think that is always the case.

Martha, I remember that you had some tweets when the news was circulating about children being separated from families and children in the concentration camps because of ICE [Immigration and Customs Enforcement], and how that went viral. There are moments when—often unfortunately—the stars align, and we, who have the knowledge and have done the deep work, and who have had the privilege and the space to do the deep work, can speak back to current events. I don't think that's an academic thing. It's those who have been in the discipline of Black study, whether you are in the academy, whether you are an organizer, whether you are an activist, whether you are in policy work, whatever it might be. These moments come, and you have to get into the nitty-gritty.

But I also think there are some complex things that are just hard to piece out, and so, that's where the long haul becomes very, very important. Because both the commitment that you have made to being accountable online, and to whom you're accountable, shows through in how you are able to hold and witness for yourself and for those communities and for those complex issues. If we are always challenging ourselves to see the complications, to see the messy, to see the things that don't have easy resolutions, then we are doing the best work that we can be doing. The challenge is to always curve the line a little bit, or a lot, and find ways to see the complications even online.

KLG: I can see the ways in which your scholarship in your traditional mode, as educators in research, informs your public persona and your public scholarship. But do you find—and this is very specific, because I'm thinking of your students—that those public pieces of who you are, as scholars, come into the classroom in any kind of way?

MSJ: We taught together a few years ago a course called Black Womanhood, and we were very intentional about taking down the walls around that course with our students by creating a digital syllabus and inviting folks to read along and comment along with us. We both taught on Twitter. So, I'm someone who, again—I think my students, they don't need to know about me. They're not that interested in me—and that's okay. I don't need that. But I do want them to come with me into some of these spaces to experience them, to know them, to see them, with my guidance, if you will, because they are optional spaces for someone of my age, but they are not optional for our students.

I have been eager to take students into these public spaces with me. Sometimes that means putting them in the car or on the plane or the train and coming to a conference. Sometimes that means getting them to sit in an audience, these days on Zoom. And some days it means having a conversation, a very public one, with them on Twitter about course material. Here, the metaphor is the lifting of the veil, right? Of how we work and how we produce ideas and who our communities of accountability are—and who the communities that are concerned about us are also. I try and take students with me.

JMJ: I try and do the opposite. I'm thinking of Maboula's answer about a similar question, where she said, "I don't play in the classroom. We don't need to be that close." I try and do the same thing. It's a personality issue—Capricorn, box boundaries. I also recognize, though, that is not necessarily successful, that in the twenty-first century—and I agree completely with Martha—our students do need to have some skills for engaging with the public, and in particular ways, increasingly, as we don't know what the post-Covid university will look like or academy will look like.

I do think they need to get the skills. I fear running into the same thing as Maboula. "Oh, you're the fun, cool, chill, digital, smart professor." That seems like a compliment. The #WhatDoesAProfessorLookLike. I tweeted at one point, "I'm always the grad student, even when I'm giving the keynote." It's interesting. You take your grace and your compliments where you can. But I think there are some ways of working with the tensions of the hierarchies of our positions that I am still trying to figure out and work out and that I think our students are also trying to figure out and work out and find guidance.

And so it may not be the best strategy to try and have a boundary. I don't follow my graduate students on social media. Because I also don't want them to think, "I have a thing that's due for my professor. They're looking over my shoulder," and I want them to have the space to do that. We've talked about seminars—especially as Hopkins moves to this hybrid format. Should they be on Zoom or should they not be? We have seen amazing versions of events on Zoom—like this one. We have also seen less amazing versions like the SHEAR [Society for Historians of the Early American Republic] 2020 virtual keynote. So, what are the ways that our grad students, even as they are learning to be public scholars and they are learning the skills of public scholarship, also have the space to cloister—and not in the weird, nonsexual nun way, but in a way that's like, "Hey, where can I have a safe space to think through my thoughts and do it with the guidance of somebody who has had these thoughts for years? Even if that somebody doesn't know better, at least they have been doing this academy thing a little bit longer?" Those kinds of safe spaces can be really, really important.

I also find that there are graduate students, and our department is full of them, who are able to juggle and balance the weirdness of the hierarchy and the intimacy of the mentor/mentee relationship in really productive ways. And there are graduate students who just can't, who can't not transgress an intimacy. They are like, "You look young and Black and female. Why can't we be friends? Why can't we be sisters? Why can't you be my electric Mammy?" Whatever it is, that's the kind of interaction that I am trying to . . . not avoid but preempt, for the student's sake. (*Laughs.*) It's less for my sake because at this point I'm used to that kind of interaction.

It's a weird balancing act. I'm sure they follow me. I know the Electricians of Electric.Marronage do, and I'm sure that they see all kinds of things. But when we get in the classroom, and we are in fields and we are in our meetings and we are in seminar, we're here to work. They can bring in things that maybe they saw me tweet out, as in works and readings. But I have never had them bring in a conversation that was not related to the actual work. That is both a testament to the students that I have been blessed to work with and also probably has something to do with my weird proclivity for boundaries.

KLG: Boundaries are good and safe. We're over time, so I am going to say thank you both so much for bringing this to such a beautiful conclusion, for being in dialogue with those who have been speaking over the course of these conversations. This is the end, technically, of #UnsilencedPast. But as I've said to you both, and to everyone who has been an interlocutor in this series, I see it as a robust beginning, a door opened for future collaborations and conversations. I hope you'll take me up on it because it's sincerely meant.

NOTES

1. On the Gilman sit-in, see https://therealnews.com/john-hopkins-university-occupation-ends-with-heavy-police-presence-and-seven-arrests.
2. See Foreman, Rodriguez, and Johnson.
3. http://electricmarronage.com.
4. https://www.electricmarronage.com/podcasts.
5. https://jmjafrx.tumblr.com/post/170195209405/black-womanhood-the-syllabus.
6. https://twitter.com/jmjafrx/status/1283154628784381955?s=20.

BIBLIOGRAPHY

Culp, Jerome. "Autobiography and Legal Scholarship and Teaching: Finding the Me in the Legal Academy." *Virginia Law Review* 77 (1991): 539–59.

Foreman, Gabrielle, Dylan Rodriguez, and Jessica Marie Johnson. "War on Ethnic Studies: Ethnic Studies Rising." January 7, 2020, https://ethnicrise.github.io/roundtable/war-ethnic-studies/.

Harney, Stefano, and Fred Moten. *The Undercommons: Fugitive Planning & Black Study.* New York: Autonomedia, 2013.

Johnson, Jessica Marie, and Martha S. Jones. "Black Womanhood: The Syllabus." 2017, https://jmjafrx.tumblr.com/post/170195209405/black-womanhood-the-syllabus.

Acknowledgments

Debates in the Digital Humanities 2023 is a book that took shape over the course of more years than we had anticipated in the midst of a global pandemic. Our debts are many, and we are grateful to everyone who helped bring this volume into the world. First and foremost, we thank our contributors for their incredible patience, for their generous and rigorous peer-review readings of each other's work, and for bearing with us through three intense rounds of revision over multiple years. We are grateful to you for sticking with us, and with this book, through so much.

We want to thank the incredible research assistants who did so much work on this project: Nicole Cote, Janelle Poe, Tuka Al-Sahlani, and Ian Anderson at the CUNY Graduate Center; and Victor Ultra Omni and Kaelyn McAdams at Emory University. We appreciate your time, your attention to detail, your camaraderie, and your professionalism as we worked with you on this volume. Thank you for all of your contributions.

We extend our thanks to our editors and colleagues at the University of Minnesota Press: Leah Pennywark, our fantastic editor, who has approached this book and the Debates in the Digital Humanities series as a whole with care, patience, and wisdom; Doug Armato, whose vision continues to inspire us; Anne Carter, who does so much to steward these volumes into existence; Terence Smyre, whose expertise with Manifold helps us make these volumes available online; and the staff of the University of Minnesota Press, including Susan Doerr, Eric Lundgren, Daniel Ochsner, Emily Hamilton, Heather Skinner, Maggie Sattler, Anne K. Wrenn, Jeff Moen, Rachel Moeller, and Michael Stoffel. Thank you for your work and your partnership.

Matt would like to thank his valued colleagues at the City University of New York (CUNY) Graduate Center: Steve Brier, Luke Waltzer, Lisa Rhody, Louise Lennihan, George Otte, Joan Richardson, Bill Kelly, Maura Smale, David Olan, Josh Brumberg, Jason Nielsen, Elizabeth Macaulay, Kandice Chuh, Jeff Allred, Duncan Faherty, Kelly Josephs, Andie Silva, Robin Miller, Laurie Hurson, Boone Gorges, Krystyna Michael, Jojo Karlin, Stefano Morello, Patrick Smyth, Wendy Barrales, Miryam Nacimento, Filipa Calado, Rafa Davis Portela, Stephen Zweibel, Roxanne Shirazi, Andrew Dunn, Ann Fiddler, Andrew McKinney, and Kristin Hart. Thank you to my family—Danny, Jeanne, and Heather Gold—whose support grounds everything else. Deepest love and thanks to Liza, Felix, and Oliver for bearing with me and for bringing so much happiness into my life.

Lauren would like to thank the members of the departments of English and quantitative theory and methods for welcoming her to Emory University, especially her department chairs Ben Reiss (English) and Cliff Carrubba (QTM) and her colleagues in the digital humanities, Dan Sinykin and Ben Miller. She thanks Wayne Morse, Allen Tullos, Chase Lovellette, and Alexander Cors at the Emory Center for Digital Scholarship, and Sarah McKee, at the Fox Center for Humanistic Inquiry, for supporting the DDH series. She would also like to recognize Dean Michael Elliott for his steadfast support of the digital humanities at Emory. To Greg, Loie, and Aurora on the family front: thank you for keeping me grounded during this long writing and editing process. Thank you to my parents, Diane and Francis Klein, and to my sister Amy Klein, who exhibit tireless support for my work. And to Kate McCandless, thank you for your love and care for our children, which is truly what allowed this book to come to be.

Contributors

GABRIELA BAEZA VENTURA is associate professor of Spanish at the University of Houston, executive editor at Arte Público Press, and co-director of the U.S. Latino Digital Humanities Center (USLDH).

HARMONY BENCH is associate professor in the Department of Dance at The Ohio State University. She is author of *Perpetual Motion: Dance, Digital Cultures, and the Common* (Minnesota, 2020) and collaborator with Kate Elswit on *Dunham's Data: Katherine Dunham and Digital Methods for Dance Historical Inquiry.*

CHRISTINA BOYLES is assistant professor of culturally engaged digital humanities at Michigan State University. She is the director of the Archivo de Respuestas Emergencias de Puerto Rico and cofounder of SurvDH.

MEGAN R. BRETT is a digital and public historian. She was the digital history associate at the Roy Rosenzweig Center for History and New Media at George Mason University from 2014 to 2022.

MICHELLE LEE BROWN is assistant professor of Indigenous knowledge, data sovereignty, and decolonization at Washington State University.

PATRICK J. BURNS is associate research scholar for digital projects at New York University's Institute for the Study of the Ancient World Library.

KENT K. CHANG is a PhD student in the School of Information and Berkeley Artificial Intelligence Research (BAIR) at the University of California, Berkeley.

RICO DEVARA CHAPMAN is professor of history, assistant dean of the School of Arts and Sciences, and director of the humanities PhD program at Clark Atlanta University. He is author of *Student Resistance to Apartheid at the University of Fort Hare: Freedom Now, a Degree Tomorrow.*

MARIKA CIFOR is assistant professor in the Information School and adjunct faculty member in the Department of Gender, Women & Sexuality Studies at the University of Washington. She is author of *Viral Cultures: Activist Archiving in the Age of AIDS* (Minnesota, 2022).

MARÍA EUGENIA COTERA is associate professor in the Mexican American and Latino Studies department at the University of Texas. She is author of *Native Speakers: Ella Cara Deloria, Zora Neale Hurston, Jovita González and the Poetics of Culture.*

T. L. COWAN is assistant professor of media studies (digital media cultures) in the Department of Arts, Culture, and Media (UTSC) and the Faculty of Information (iSchool) at the University of Toronto. With Jas Rault, T.L. is co-director of the Cabaret Commons and the Digital Research Ethics Collaboratory (DREC) and coauthor of *Heavy Processing.*

MARLENE L. DAUT is professor of French and African American studies at Yale University. She is author of *Baron de Vastey and the Origins of Black Atlantic Humanism* and *Tropics of Haiti: Race and the Literary History of the Haitian Revolution in the Atlantic World, 1789–1865.*

QUINN DOMBROWSKI is academic technology specialist in the Division of Literatures, Cultures, and Languages and in the library at Stanford University. They are author of *Drupal for Humanists* and *Crescat Graffiti, Vita Excolatur: Confessions of the University of Chicago.*

KATE ELSWIT is professor of performance and technology and head of digital research at the Royal Central School of Speech and Drama, University of London. She is author of *Watching Weimar Dance* and *Theatre & Dance,* and collaborates with Harmony Bench on *Dunham's Data: Katherine Dunham and Digital Methods for Dance Historical Inquiry* and *Visceral Histories, Visual Arguments: Dance-Based Approaches to Data.*

NISHANI FRAZIER is associate professor of American studies and history at University of Kansas. She is author of *Harambee City: The Congress of Racial Equality in Cleveland and the Rise of Black Power Populism.*

KIM GALLON is associate professor of Africana studies at Brown University. She is author of *Pleasure in the News: African American Readership and Sexuality in the Black Press.*

PATRICIA GARCIA is assistant professor in the School of Information at the University of Michigan.

LINDA GARCÍA MERCHANT is public humanities data librarian at the University of Houston Libraries.

LORENA GAUTHEREAU is digital programs manager for the U.S. Latino Digital Humanities Center (USLDH)/Recovering the U.S. Hispanic Literary Heritage at the University of Houston.

MASOUD GHORBANINEJAD works at a software company and is a digital humanities consultant at several universities.

ABRAHAM GIBSON is assistant professor of history at the University of Texas at San Antonio. He is author of *Feral Animals in the American South: An Evolutionary History.*

NATHAN P. GIBSON is a researcher in Jewish–Christian–Muslim relations and Middle Eastern studies at the Ludwig-Maximilians-Universität, Munich.

KAIAMA L. GLOVER is Ann Whitney Olin Professor of French and Africana Studies and faculty director of the Digital Humanities Center at Barnard College, Columbia University. She is author of *A Regarded Self: Caribbean Womanhood and the Ethics of Disorderly Being* and *Haiti Unbound: A Spiralist Challenge to the Postcolonial Canon.*

MATTHEW K. GOLD is associate professor of English and digital humanities at the Graduate Center of the City University of New York (CUNY), where he serves as advisor to the provost for Digital Initiatives and director of the GC Digital Scholarship Lab. He is coeditor of the Debates in Digital Humanities series at the University of Minnesota Press.

HILARY N. GREEN is the James B. Duke Professor of Africana Studies at Davidson College. She is author of *Educational Reconstruction: African American Schools in the Urban South, 1865–1890.*

JO GULDI is associate professor of history at Southern Methodist University. She is author of *The Long Land War: The Global Struggle for Occupancy Rights* and *Roads to Power: Britain Invents the Infrastructure State* and coauthor of *The History Manifesto.*

MATTHEW N. HANNAH is assistant professor of digital humanities in the School of Information Studies at Purdue University Libraries.

JEANELLE HORCASITAS is a technical writer at DigitalOcean.

CHRISTY HYMAN is assistant professor of human geography and African American studies at Mississippi State University.

ARUN JACOB is a doctoral candidate at the Faculty of Information, University of Toronto.

JESSICA MARIE JOHNSON is assistant professor in the Department of History at Johns Hopkins University and a fellow at the Hutchins Center for African and African American Studies at Harvard University. She is author of *Wicked Flesh: Black Women, Intimacy, and Freedom in the Atlantic World.*

MARTHA S. JONES is the Society of Black Alumni Presidential Professor, professor of history, and a professor at the SNF Agora Institute at Johns Hopkins University. She is author of *Vanguard,*

Birthright Citizens: A History of Race and Rights in Antebellum America; Toward an Intellectual History of Black Women; and *All Bound Up Together: The Woman Question in African American Public Culture, 1830–1900.*

ANNETTE K. JOSEPH-GABRIEL is associate professor of romance studies at Duke University. She is author of *Reimagining Liberation: How Black Women Transformed Citizenship in the French Empire.*

MILLS KELLY is professor of history at George Mason University and director of the Roy Rosenzweig Center for History and New Media at George Mason University. He is author of *Teaching History in the Digital Age* and *Without Remorse: Czech National Socialism in Late Habsburg Austria.*

SPENCER D. C. KERALIS is an independent scholar.

LAUREN F. KLEIN is Winship Distinguished Research Professor and associate professor in the departments of English and quantitative theory and methods and director of the Digital Humanities Lab at Emory University. She is author of *An Archive of Taste: Race and Eating in the Early United States* (Minnesota, 2020), coauthor of *Data Feminism,* and coeditor of the Debates in Digital Humanities series at the University of Minnesota Press.

ZOE LEBLANC is assistant professor in the School of Information Sciences at the University of Illinois Urbana-Champaign.

JASON EDWARD LEWIS is University Research Chair in Computational Media and the Indigenous Future Imaginary and professor of computation arts at Concordia University. He is coauthor of *Against Reduction: Designing a Human Future with Machines* and coeditor of *Educational, Psychological, and Behavioral Considerations in Niche Online Communities.*

JAMES MALAZITA is assistant professor of science and technology studies at Rensselaer Polytechnic Institute.

ALISON MARTIN is assistant professor at Dartmouth College.

RAFIA MIRZA is digital scholarship librarian at Southern Methodist University.

MAME-FATOU NIANG is associate professor of French and Francophone studies at Carnegie Mellon University. She is author of *Identités Françaises.*

JESSICA MARIE OTIS is assistant professor of history and director of public projects at the Roy Rosenzweig Center for History and New Media at George Mason University.

MARISA PARHAM is professor of English and digital studies, and the director of African-American Digital and Experimental Humanities (AADHum) at the University of Maryland. She is author of *Haunting and Displacement in African American Literature and Culture* and coeditor of *Theorizing Glissant: Sites and Citations.*

ANDREW BOYLES PETERSEN is a digital asset librarian at Esri.

EMILY PUGH is principal research specialist for digital art history at the Getty Research Institute. She is author of *Architecture, Politics, and Identity in Divided Berlin.*

OLIVIA QUINTANILLA is professor of ethnic studies at MiraCosta Community College.

JAS RAULT is assistant professor of media studies in the Department of Arts, Culture, and Media at the University of Toronto Scarborough and the Faculty of Information at the University of Toronto. They are the author of *Eileen Gray and the Design of Sapphic Modernity: Staying In* and, with T. L. Cowan, *Heavy Processing.*

ANASTASIA SALTER is director of graduate programs and Texts and Technology for the College of Arts and Humanities at the University of Central Florida and coauthor of *A Portrait of the Auteur as Fanboy* and *Adventure Games: Playing the Outsider.*

MAURA SEALE is history librarian at the University of Michigan. She is coeditor of *Creating Space for All Learners: Exploring Equitable and Inclusive Pedagogies* and *The Politics of Theory in the Practice of Critical Librarianship.*

CELESTE TƯỜNG VY SHARPE is assistant professor of history at Normandale Community College in Bloomington, Minnesota.

ASTRID J. SMITH is a rare book and special collections digitization specialist with Stanford University Libraries' digital production group.

MABOULA SOUMAHORO is associate professor in the English department of the University of Tours. She is author of *Le Triangle et l'Hexagone, réflexions sur une identité noire,* translated by Kaiama L. Glover as *Black Is the Journey, Africana the Name.*

MEL STANFILL is associate professor in the Texts and Technology Program and the Department of English at the University of Central Florida. Stanfill is author of *Exploiting Fandom: How the Media Industry Seeks to Manipulate Fans* and coauthor of *A Portrait of the Auteur as Fanboy* (with Anastasia Salter).

TONIA SUTHERLAND is assistant professor in the Department of Information Studies at the University of California Los Angeles.

CAROLINA VILLARROEL is Brown Foundation Director of Research of the Recovering the U.S. Hispanic Literary Heritage Program and co-director of the U.S. Latino Digital Humanities Center (USLDH) at the University of Houston.

MELANIE WALSH is assistant teaching professor in the Information School at the University of Washington. She is author of *Introduction to Cultural Analytics & Python,* a free online programming textbook for humanities scholars and students.

HĒMI WHAANGA is professor and head of school for Te Pūtahi-a-Toi (School of Māori Art, Knowledge and Education) at Massey University.

BRIDGET WHEARTY is assistant professor of English at Binghamton University.

JERI WIERINGA is assistant professor and director of the REL Digital Lab in the Department of Religious Studies at the University of Alabama.

DAVID JOSEPH WRISLEY is professor of digital humanities at NYU Abu Dhabi.